Two Hundred Years of Accounting Research

This book offers a rich survey of the efforts that accounting academics, and often enough theoretically inclined practitioners, have invested in accounting research during a 200-year period. Although there are several prominent historical books and encyclopaedias on accounting history, an integrated work concentrating on accounting research from an international point of view has long been overdue.

Mattessich's book is the first and only one to offer a comprehensive survey of accounting research on a broad international scale for the last two centuries. Its main emphasis is on accounting research in the English, German, Italian, French and Spanish language areas; it also contains chapters dealing with research in Finland, the Netherlands, Scandinavia, Russia, Poland and the Ukraine as well as Argentina and Japan. A separate chapter summarizes research activity in the rest of the globe from Eastern Europe to Israel, the Arab and African countries as well as India, China and other countries of the Far East.

In a time of financial globalization, familiarity with accounting research in countries beyond the English language boundary is no less important than familiarity with the recent, comprehensive research activity in the English language area. This book fulfils both of those needs; it may serve practitioners and auditors all over the world, no less than students of accounting interested in the evolution of its research efforts. It also offers a survey of the present state of the art (from empirical to analytical accounting and from such esoteric subjects as gender issues to the archaeology of accounting); finally, it casts a glance into the future.

Richard Mattessich is Professor Emeritus of Accounting at the Sauder School of Business, University of British Columbia, Canada. He has received many awards and is profiled in such works as Edward's *Twentieth Century Accounting Thinkers*, Chatfield and Vangermeersch's *A History of Accounting – An International Encyclopedia* and Colasse's *Les Grands Auteurs en Comptabilité*.

Routledge new works in accounting history
Edited by
Garry Carnegie
Melbourne University Private, Australia

John Richard Edwards
Cardiff University, UK

Salvador Carmona
Instituto de Empresa, Spain

Dick Fleischman
John Carroll University, USA

8   Two Hundred Years of Accounting Research
An international survey of personalities, ideas and publications (from the
beginning of the nineteenth century to the beginning of the twenty-first
century)
Richard Mattessich

Two Hundred Years of Accounting Research

An international survey of personalities, ideas and publications (from the beginning of the nineteenth century to the beginning of the twenty-first century)

Richard Mattessich
University of British Columbia, Vancouver, B.C., Canada
in collaboration with (in alphabetical order): Svetlana M. Bychkova (St Petersburg State Agricultural University), Daniel Carrasco Díaz (University of Málaga, Spain), Jean-Guy Degos (University Montesquieu of Bordeaux, France), Belén Fernández-Feijóo Souto (University of Vigo, Spain), Giuseppe Galassi (University of Parma, Italy), M. Frendzel (University of Łodż), Esteban Hernández Esteve (University Autónoma of Madrid), Alicja Jaruga (University of Łodż), Yoshiaki Koguchi (Chuo University, Tokyo), Hans-Ulrich Küpper (Maximilian University of Munich), Konstantin Redchenko (Academy of Commerce, Lvóv, Ukraine), Yaroslav V. Sokolov (St Petersburg Institute of Commerce and Economics), Anna Szychta (University of Łodż), Enrico Viganò (University of Naples), Cristina Wirth (University of San Andrés, Buenos Aires)

Routledge
Taylor & Francis Group

LONDON AND NEW YORK

First published 2008
by Routledge
2 Park Square, Milton Park, Abingdon, Oxon, OX14 4RN

Simultaneously published in the USA and Canada
by Routledge
270 Madison Ave, New York NY 10016

Routledge is an imprint of the Taylor & Francis Group, an informa business

First issued in paperback 2011

© 2008 Richard Mattessich

Typeset in Times by Wearset Ltd, Boldon, Tyne and Wear

British Library Cataloguing in Publication Data
A catalogue record for this book is available from the British Library

Library of Congress Cataloging in Publication Data
A catalog record for this book has been requested

ISBN10: 0-415-77256-7 (hbk)
ISBN10: 0-415-62042-2 (pbk)
ISBN10: 0-203-93985-9 (ebk)

ISBN13: 978-0-415-77256-3 (hbk)
ISBN13: 978-0-415-62042-0 (pbk)
ISBN13: 978-0-203-93985-7 (ebk)

To Hermi

Contents

Preface

This book is based on a series of papers and other material that the author (occasionally in co-authorship with others – see Acknowledgements) has written during the last decade or more. Several of these papers were from the very outset intended to be integrated in this book, but no chapter is identical to any previously published material. Other chapters are new and exclusive to this book. We hope that this is more than a collection of incidental articles but a systematic survey of the efforts that academics and theoretically oriented accounting practitioners made over a period of some 200 years.

Although we tried to put special emphasis on countries where most of the *original* accounting research occurred, we wanted to cover the academic accounting community of many countries and language areas. This made it necessary to include occasionally even textbooks and similar publications from authors that became prominent not so much through their originality but due to their prolific writing, charisma or other qualities. We believe that the publication efforts of no language area ought to be disregarded and we tried, wherever possible, to pay attention to valiant efforts of promoting the creation and spreading of accounting knowledge in a variety of countries or language areas. Such an attitude seems to be particularly important at a time of economic globalization.

Despite the availability of several excellent historical books and encyclopaedias on accounting history (see the Introduction), an integrated work concentrating on the *history of accounting research* from a *general* and *international* point of view has, so far, been lacking. In a time of intensive and international academic exchange, the need to be informed about past and present accounting research in other countries is greater than ever.

Thus, our focus is not on the history of accounting, but on the *history of its research* and the publications underlying it (though, wherever necessary, accounting facts beyond research were taken into consideration). Nor is the book merely based on accounting literature of the English tongue. A major goal was to offer a broad overview, covering the pertinent publications of an international spectrum, as wide as possible, under the given limitations. Indeed, the book has its origin in our personal curiosity about accounting research in the past, and not only in the English tongue but in other languages as well.

One of the most difficult tasks in organizing the material was the selection of publications to be discussed or listed. Obviously, the choice of what to include or exclude depended, at least to some degree, on a personal point of view. We endeavoured to include material significant enough to withstand the test of time – even if we may not always have succeeded in this effort from the point of an international perspective. Occasionally, we had to take *local* preferences into account; we also had to rely on many secondary sources and their value judgements, as the material that presented itself to us was enormous.

We hope that this book will guide the reader and inspire her or him to turn occasionally to the more specialized literature here listed. The book may also serve accounting historians as a reference work for many years to come, and be an impetus to scholars for delving deeper into historical aspects not yet revealed.

R.M.

Acknowledgements
(including copyrights)

First of all, I should like to express my thanks to the Social Sciences and Humanities Research Council of Canada for its financial support over several decades (in particular for the grant from the year 2002 onwards, pertaining, among others, to this special project). Further thanks go to the Sauder School of Business (formerly, Faculty of Commerce) of the University of British Columbia in Vancouver, its Dean, colleagues, and staff for their unrelenting personal support and the use of research facilities. This also refers to my occasional research assistants, Ms Pattarin Adithipyang, Mr Huasheng Gua, Mr Hamed Mahmudi and Ms Kim Trottier, to all of whom I am much obliged for comprehensive proof reading.

Second, I extend my sincere gratitude to all the friends and colleagues who contributed to this book with great enthusiasm and much competence. Indeed, the vast correspondence – counting hundreds of e-mail letters in the effort to correct and improve the individual chapters – is witness to this cooperative enterprise.

Related to this are my thanks to various editors and publishers (of the *Accounting, Business and Financial History*/Routledge; the *Review of Accounting and Finance*/Barmarik Publications, East Yorkshire, UK; *De Computis*/Asociación Española de Contabilidad, Madrid; the *Asia-Pacific Journal of Accounting*/City University of Hong Kong; and *Canadian Accounting Perspectives*/Canadian Academic Accounting Association) for granting copyrights wherever material from previous publications was used in this book. This refers to the following publications (in order of Chapters):

Mattessich, R. (2003) 'Accounting research and researchers of the nineteenth century and the beginning of the twentieth century', *Accounting, Business and Financial History* 13 (2, July): 125–79 (as basis for Chapter 2).

Küpper, H.-U. and Mattessich, R. (2005) 'Twentieth-century accounting research in the German language area' *Accounting, Business and Financial History* (Special issue on *German Accounting*) 15 (3): 345–410 (as basis for Chapters 3 and 4).

Galassi, G. and Mattessich, R. (2004) 'Italian accounting research in the first half of the twentieth century', *Review of Accounting and Finance* 3 (2): 61–82 (as basis for Chapter 5).

Viganò, E. and Mattessich, R. (2007) 'Accounting research in Italy: second half of the twentieth century', *Review of Accounting and Finance* 6 (1): 24–41 (as basis for Chapter 6).

Degos, J.-G. and Mattessich, R. (2003) 'Accounting research in the French language area: the first half of the twentieth century,' *Review of Accounting and Finance* 2 (4): 110–28 (as basis for Chapter 7).

Degos, J.-G. and Mattessich, R. (2006) 'Accounting research in the French language area: second half of the twentieth century', *Review of Accounting and Finance* 5 (4): 423–42 (as basis for Chapter 8).

Carrasco Díaz, D., Hernández Esteve, E. and Mattessich, R. (2004) 'Accounting publications and research in Spain: first half of the twentieth century', *Review of Accounting and Finance* 3 (2): 40–58 (as basis for Chapter 9).

Fernández-Feijóo Souto, B. and Mattessich, R. (2006) 'Accounting research in Spain: second half of the twentieth century and beyond', *De Computis* 5: 7–38 (as basis for Chapter 10).

Mattessich (previously unpublished) 'Accounting research in the English language area: first half of the twentieth century' (as Chapter 11).

Mattessich (1996a, 1996b) 'Academic research in accounting: the last 50 years'; and 'Accounting research: response to commentators', both *Asia-Pacific Journal of Accounting* 3 (1, June): 3–81, 109–35 (as a partial basis for Chapter 12).

Mattessich (previously unpublished) 'Accounting research in Finland, the Netherlands and the Scandinavian countries' (as Chapter 13).

Koguchi and Mattessich (previously unpublished) 'Japanese accounting publications and research in the twentieth century' (as Chapter 14).

Bychkova, Mattessich and Sokolov (previously unpublished) 'Accounting publications and research of twentieth-century Russia' (as basis for Chapter 15)

Jaruga, Szychta, Frenzel and Mattessich (Part I: Poland) and Redchenko and Mattessich (Part II: Ukraine). Both parts of 'Accounting publications and research in Poland and the Ukraine: mainly twentieth century' (as basis for Chapter 16) were previously unpublished.

Wirth, C. and Mattessich, R. (2006) 'Accounting books of Argentina: publications, research and institutional background', *De Computis* 11 (4, June): 137–67 (as basis for Chapter 17).

Mattessich (previously unpublished) 'Accounting in other countries: publications and research reports' (as Chapter 18).

Mattessich, R. (2006) 'The information economic perspective of accounting: its coming of age', *Canadian Accounting Perspectives* 5 (2): 209–36 (as basis for Chapter 19).

1 Introduction

> The history of accounting is similar to that of philosophy.
> It is a history of doctrines. It also is a history of methods.
> At best, it is one of representing financial realities –
> though in a pragmatic way.
>
> R.M.

1.1 The need for a broad international survey

This book offers a survey of the efforts that accounting academics, and often enough theoretically inclined practitioners, have invested in accounting publications and research during a period of about 200 years. Some of these efforts have been previously exposed in such works as, for example, Gaffikin and Aitken's (1982) *The development of accounting theory: significant contributors to accounting thought in the twentieth century*, Edwards's (1994) *Twentieth-century accounting thinkers*, Chatfield and Vangermeersch's (1996) *The history of accounting: an international encyclopedia*, and, finally, Colasse's (2005) *Les grands auteurs en comptabilité* (covering some 23 scholars from Pacioli to our time). All these are excellent historical works (and I personally owe their editors and authors much for recognition of my own contributions to accounting research), but those books pursue a different goal. Their approach, in discussing a relatively small group of distinguished publications and scholars, is more 'aristocratic' than ours.[1] We, in contrast, have endeavoured to offer a very broad perspective of publications and authors on a more international scale, and thus have chosen a more 'democratic' approach. This enabled us to present a large number of pundits and their contributions, even where they attained only 'local recognition'. For this reason, some experts might view this book as 'a catalogue of names and publications'. Indeed, the book is designed to serve, among other things, as such a catalogue – but, hopefully, it is much more than that. On the other hand, we fully realize the limitations of this book, particularly the difference in quality between different chapters. As much as we tried to overcome this weakness, it was too deeply rooted, not only in the time and space limitations, but above all, in the immense difficulties to access sufficient material from some countries or language areas. This book, as so much of human endeavour, is an attempt to do the best under adverse circumstances.

Nevertheless, we believe that such an *integrated* work, concentrating on academic accounting publications and research from a truly *international* point of view, has long been overdue. Yet, our focus is *not* on the history of accounting *practice*, rather it is limited to *research* and the publication activity underlying it. As pointed out in the Preface, a major goal was to offer a broad view, covering the pertinent literature in many languages and countries. The major language areas taken into consideration here are those of English, French, German, Italian, Japanese, Spanish and Russian. We also included a separate chapter on Argentina and on accounting contributions from the Netherlands and Northern Europe (the Scandinavian countries). Another chapter offers representative examples of accounting publications and research efforts referring to other countries (from Eastern Europe to Africa and Asia, including India and China). On rare occasions we have referred to publications on 'business economics' (*Betriebswirtschaftslehre, economia aziendale, bedrijfseconomie*, etc.), particularly wherever accounting subjects are included or implied. But in general, we have limited this book to the theory and research of *accounting*.

1.2   Accounting research as an intellectual endeavour

Although by no means independent of accounting practice or other disciplines, the literature of accounting has become an important cultural manifestation in its own right. Indeed, the big challenge ahead is to reconcile the ever-increasing sophistication of theoretical accounting with the need of practice for relatively simple or, at least, transparent accounting systems that are comprehensible to the working accountant as well as the reader of financial statements. The 'quasi-legislation' on current value accounting of the FASB (USA) in the late 1970s and early 1980s showed that even the relatively simple models of replacement value and inflation adjustments were too complicated for most practitioners and financial analysts. How then, will the much more complex models of the information economic perspective relate to accounting practice? For a better understanding of these difficulties, we have tried to make a more emphatic distinction between accounting practice, on one side, and the cultural manifestation of academic accounting, on the other side. This does not imply that accounting theory is independent of accounting practice or is even a positive science. On the contrary, we firmly believe that ours is an *applied* discipline in the service of a practical goal.

However, the quest for a study of the *evolution* of different research efforts, directions and trends (as well as their contributors), might not be so much different from the need for museums, galleries and historical collections in other intellectual pursuits. We believe that the ideas and publications of prominent accounting scholars deserve no less respect from accountants than the attention given to major painters by art scholars, to literary figures by experts of literature, to composers by musicians, etc. Yet, at present, such interest or knowledge still leaves much to be desired.

For decades we have heard the call for greater breadth and deeper introspection in accounting. Admittedly, our discipline has meanwhile reached a much higher mathematical and empirical-scientific sophistication. But 'breadth and depth' ought to have a broader meaning. When probing the *philosophical* and *historical* knowledge of most accountants, even academic ones, we still have some way to go.

Although both philosophy and history have become stepchildren in the second half of the twentieth century, there are indications that the new century may turn the trend; indeed, the recent interest in accounting history is a positive sign. As to philosophy, an unexpected but exciting trend emerged in Great Britain in the final two decades of the twentieth century. In reaction to the 'American' Positive Accounting Theory, the Europeans, drawing upon their traditional interest in philosophy and the social sciences, formed the so-called 'critical-interpretive' (or critical-interpretative) camp. From the very outset, it was based on sociology, the behavioural sciences and philosophy, occasionally with a socialist slant and often hostile to neo-economics and its modern variants. Whatever the political emphasis, the studying and understanding of the forces behind such historical and intellectual trends deserve high recognition.

Apart from those tendencies, accounting branched off into a myriad of new directions, some of them hardly imaginable to former generations. These include not only new techniques and experiments in auditing, financial and managerial accounting, but also in taxation accounting, international accounting, information aspects, agency theory, control systems, accounting education, and even in such esoteric topics as archaeology of accounting, petroleum accounting, social and environmental accounting, human resource accounting, gender issues of accounting, accounting of intellectual capital, and other new areas.

Taking this great variety into account, we may return to the analogy invoked above. That means, comparing our readers to visitors of an art gallery who leisurely walk from one room or period or country to another, studying the different characteristics of the many 'pictures' confronting them by observing some of them more carefully, others only fleetingly. And in such a 'place', where history becomes truly alive, it is important to reserve one's attention not merely to a few of the most important personalities, but pay homage to the lesser known figures and their creations. For without a rich pool of supporting talents and their ideas, the peak achievements are difficult to imagine. Just as the Leonardo da Vincis, the Michelangelos and Raffaels are unimaginable without the Verrochios, Donatellos or Peruginos, so the Schmalenbachs and Schmidts must not be seen in isolation and without awareness of such important forerunners as the Wilmowskis or Sganzinis, Koveros and others hardly known to most contemporary accountants.

However, such neglect refers not merely to prominent scholars of the distant past, it also concerns some authors of recent times. A typical example is Lawrence L. Vance [1911–78] and his *Scientific methods for auditing* (Vance 1950). This author pioneered not merely statistical testing methods in auditing (and accounting in general), but created the launching point for one of the most widely used scientific tools of the last half-century for auditing practice. Yet, though having been editor of *The Accounting Review* [1962–64] and President of the American Accounting Association [1966–67], he is hardly ever mentioned today. Larry Vance is neither discussed in any of the above-cited books, nor even mentioned in Tucker's (1996) article on 'statistical sampling' in Chatfield and Vangermeersch's (1996) encyclopaedia. Nor does he have a separate profile in this work, as other prominent accountants have (he is only mentioned once in its Index in reference to a paper on 'inventory valuation').

Another fascinating aspect of our study are various *disputes of priority*. For details on one of those notorious cases, we refer the reader to subsections 3.4.3, 13.1.1 and 13.2.1 that deal with the 'competition' between Theodore Limperg and Fritz Schmidt in the dispute over the replacement value theory. Not only is Limperg's precise view on this topic still clouded in mystery (in contrast to the numerous and transparent publications of Schmidt 1921, etc.) but the theory of either was preceded in a once well-known German book by the renowned Finnish scholar Ilmari Kovero (1911). And yet, Limperg's theory has received even more attention in the Anglophone as well as Francophone accounting literature than has Schmidt's theory, while Kovero's outstanding pioneering work and his many other publications are virtually forgotten (save in his own country, Finland).[2]

A further phenomenon that lends spice and flavour to the history of accounting research is the kind of 'hero worship' occasionally encountered in our discipline. It always has deep nationalistic roots and is usually limited to a single country or language area. We find it in Germany with Eugen Schmalenbach, in Italy with Gino Zappa, in the Netherlands with Theodore Limperg, in Australia with Raymond Chambers, and perhaps less pronounced in other countries (for detail, see the pertinent chapters). No doubt, in all these cases we are dealing with charismatic personalities. Their contributions to accounting theory is internationally known, and deservedly so, but in their own countries they have attained an image that seems to be so sacrosanct that, for many of their disciples, exposing the weakness of some of these 'heroic' ideas has become heresy. Yet, occasionally – particularly at a time when the charisma has evaporated or when those ideas may no longer be convincing – such an attitude might be prone to retard rather than boost the progress of local research efforts.

As to the precarious word 'famous' (whether in reference to persons or publications), it obviously is relative and depends on the underlying criterion. Some accounting authors are famous because of their originality or profound insights; others because of their powerful analyses or logical-mathematical acumen; others because of their empirical skills in testing hypotheses; others because of their charisma or acumen in writing best-selling texts; and others again because of notoriety (e.g. promoting the adoption of *Marxist accounting or valuation principles* or advancing the opposite, but hardly less realistic, proposition that accounting is a *positive* science). Furthermore, the significance of a particular research contribution may differ over time – a phenomenon even more pronounced in our discipline than in the hard sciences.

Another interesting historical aspect is the pattern of influence exercised by accounting research of some countries upon accounting publications in others.

Why, for example, did German accounting research, during the first half of the twentieth century, have such a profound influence upon Northern and Eastern Europe as well as Japan (and to some extent upon France and the USA)? And why did it have so little influence in Italy, Spain and most Latin American countries, and hardly any effect in Great Britain and most Commonwealth countries? This phenomenon contrasts markedly when compared with other applied sciences where new and valuable insights spread rapidly. This distinction is a hallmark of our discipline, the understanding of which necessitates familiarity with the importance of the *local* legalistic, linguistic and cultural dimensions.

The major impetus to accounting occurred in the second half of the twentieth century. Previously, middle-sized enterprises dominated the industrial scene, and most of the 'stocks' of large corporations where held by banks. Accounting was primarily oriented towards stewardship (with a strong ethical emphasis), inventory and cost control, wealth and income determination, as well as debt and liquidity management. But later, the changing needs of industry and a growing number of individual investors pushed accounting in the direction of investor information, a different kind of stewardship (that emphasized the efficiency aspect), and occasionally, deceptive short-term profitability. The latter was the root-cause of a host of financial scandals (particularly at the beginning of the twenty-first century). It was then, that such names of Enron, WorldCom, Parmalat, and many others became indelibly impressed upon the annals of fraudulent management. Regrettably, the prestigious public accounting firm of Arthur Andersen & Co. perished as a consequence of the Enron scandal. Apparently this happened because Arthur Andersen's *auditing partners* (trained in ethical aspects) were over-ruled by the growing influence of its *consulting partners* (who lacked such training – cf. Wyatt 2004).

In accounting theory too, the most enduring aspect of our discipline is likely to be its transformation during the twentieth century. From the foundations laid during the nineteenth century (see subsection 2.1.8), accounting explored and clarified in a titanic struggle – where a myriad of different views clashed with each other – a variety of fundamental notions and created many novel ones. The two most important insights seem to be that (1) accounting offers a picture of reality merely from a very *specific point of view* that requires sufficient clarification to become relevant and practically useful; and (2) only a *pluralistic* approach (e.g. in valuation) and a *well-integrated* one (incorporating analytical, empirical, technical and philosophic-historical aspects) will enable accounting research to satisfy the demands of the future.

1.3 The methodology pursued

To achieve a broader goal, we have tried in this book to balance two different requirements: First, we draw attention to the large number of the *nationally* important (but often internationally unknown) literature of many countries, some entries of which could be covered only fleetingly. Second, we deal in greater detail with the more prominent authors and major pioneering works though;

even this research could merely be sketched. There, we concentrated on those contributions for which the authors will be best remembered.

In our view, only such a dichotomous approach can lead to a satisfactory compromise, considering, on one side, the limited space available and, on the other side, the enormous material to be mastered. Specialized and nationally oriented historical publications, as excellent as they may be, are rarely designed to cope with such problems and the dilemma of competing needs for breadth and simultaneously some depth. Even such an encyclopaedic work as Chatfield and Vangermeersch (1996), on which this paper has occasionally drawn, is neither intended nor organized to convey a *coherent* synthesis of that crucial and pregnant period that spans from about 1800 to the beginning years of the twenty-first century. This was a period where immense scientific, cultural, religious, technical, economic, industrial and, above all, social changes occurred. These changes had their undeniable impact on accounting research; and some readers may well accuse us for not having emphasized these forces more explicitly. Indeed, we truly regret this fact and have no better answer than this: look at the size of this work, and you will know why we left this task to other authors or a future generation.

For many decades academic accountants have tried to make our discipline more 'scientific'. Yet, to achieve this goal we also have to overcome the parochialism that dominated accounting and its history during the twentieth century – though some efforts towards a more international presentation of accounting history have undoubtedly been made.

Furthermore, the reader may well ask: Why a history of accounting research from the beginning of the nineteenth century to the twenty-first? Why not an entire history of accounting publications, or one of the last 100 years only? And why not include accounting practice as well? Certainly, the decision is an arbitrary one; but we may justify our particular choice with a few arguments. First, accounting *research*, as a systematic or academic effort, hardly began before 1800 – despite some important earlier publications. Second, accounting research of the nineteenth century is sufficiently close in relation to that of the twentieth century that at least one lengthy chapter ought to be devoted to the former. Third, there exist many excellent and often comprehensive histories of accounting in general. The present book is not intended to compete with those works, it rather wanted to fill the gap that had been open for too long a time.

Finally, some technical notes: to facilitate reference to various sections and subsections, we have chosen to identify them by a frequently used decimal notation (e.g. 14.3.1). Here the first one or two digits stand for the chapter number (e.g. 14), while the other numbers refers to section and subsection, respectively. As to the translation of foreign titles in the References, we have tried to include their English translations in parentheses wherever this was possible. However, in some instances this was not feasible, and we apologise for this.

As to the Index of Names, we have tried – within the limitations set to us – to list there the year of birth or entire lifespan of specific scholars (e.g. as [born in 1935] or [1873–1955]). Such dates are occasionally also listed in the text for renowned persons of the past. Where dates of birth etc. could not be given, we substituted (in this Index) in many cases the dates of 'terminal academic degrees' (usually acquired between the age of 25 and 30). This Index of Names also offers first names (wherever available), but avoids names of institutions. We relegated the latter to a concise Subject Index.

1.4 Overview of the book

1.4.1 Summary of Chapter 2: 'An international survey of the nineteenth century'

This chapter deals with major accounting publications of the nineteenth century. However, for this period, no separate chapters are devoted to the contributions from individual countries or language areas. Instead, we summarized all the pertinent material in a single chapter. This stands in contrast to the subsequent chapters, devoted mainly to the twentieth century. Most of these chapters deal with a specific country or language area (occasionally one chapter covers the first half and the next chapter the second half of the twentieth century). There are some exceptions; for example, Chapter 12 combines the Netherlands and the Scandinavian countries; or Chapter 17 that offers some glimpses into accounting literature of some countries that could not be accommodated separately in any of the previous chapters.

As to the content of Chapter 2, we first note that at the beginning of the nineteenth century the former glory of Italian accounting was overshadowed by its decline during the eighteenth century, when the literature from France, England, Germany, America and other countries took centre stage. 'Theories of accounts' (rather than 'accounting theories') dominated not merely the early but also the later part of this century when Italian accounting had regained a prominent position beside other countries. The relation of those theories to the *'charts of accounts'* – that later became so prominent in Continental Europe – is historically important. The controversies over personalistic versus materialistic accounts and that between entity theories versus proprietary theories, as well as the emergence of other theories are discussed with reference to individual authors. Diverse topics from railroad accounting and auditing to various aspects of cost accounting are investigated. Of particular importance are the *pioneering* efforts of this period. These efforts anticipated further developments, manifested in the following ideas: flow of funds statement, matrix accounting, different aspects of valuation, problems of allocation and depreciation, price-level adjustments and indexation, current values, exit values, residual income valuation, managerial control, the emergence of competing accounting (or *Bilanz*) theories, the separation of fixed from variable costs, fixed and flexible budgeting, zero-based budgeting, PERT, transfer prices, break-even charts, variance analysis, job-order costing, labour and machine hour rates, standard costing, price determination, integrating financial and cost accounting, clean surplus theory, agricultural accounting, holding gains, and other topics.

Among the galaxy of prominent accountants discussed in this chapter, the following deserve special attention: Degrange Sr, Leauté and Guilbault (France); Cerboni, Rossi and Besta (Italy); Cronhelm, Battersby, Pixley, Metcalfe, Garke and Fells, Norton, Dicksee and Mann (Great Britain); Leuchs, Augspurg, H.V. Simon and Wilmoowski (Germany); Sonnenfels, Puteani and Schrott (Austria); Church, Arnold and Dickinson (America, the latter originally from the UK); Hügli and Schär (Switzerland, the latter later in Germany); Brost and Christantes y Cañedo (Spain); Synnerberg and Pohlmann (Sweden); Berciuskiego (Poland). Appendix A offers an overview of nineteenth-century scholars concerned with accounting history (together with one representative work of each author).

1.4.2 Summary of Chapter 3: 'German language area: first half of the twentieth century'

This chapter begins with the pre-eminence of some German scholars during this period. First of all, are Schmalenbach (with his 'dynamic' accounting, his chart of accounts and many contributions to cost accounting) and Fritz Schmidt (with his replacement cost theory). Then, the following names ought to be born in mind (listed alphabetically): Beste, Calmes, le Coutre, Geldmacher, Grossmann, Karl Hax, Isaac, Kalveram, Karl Lehmann, Max R. Lehmann, Leitner, Lion, Mahlberg, Mellerowicz, Nicklisch, Osbahr, Passow, Penndorf, Prion, Rieger, Erich Schneider and Walb (all from Germany); Gomberg, Sganzini and Schär (all having taught in Switzerland, though Gomberg hailed from Russia and Schär later left for Germany); Meithner, Bouffier and Illetschko (Austria).

The chapter offers a survey of the most important theories of accounts classes that prevailed during the first two decades or so. Following the First World War, the issue of hyperinflation in Austria and Germany stimulated a considerable amount of original accounting research. Afterwards, a series of competing *Bilanztheorien* (accounting or balance sheet theories) dominated the scene. Separate sections or subsections are devoted to charts and master charts of accounts in German accounting theory, as well as to cost accounting and the writing of accounting history.

1.4.3 Summary of Chapter 4: 'German language area: second half of the twentieth century'

This chapter continues this survey (occasionally with a comparison between the German and English language accounting literature). 'Dynamic' accounting, developed during the first half of the twentieth century, became the basis of a pagatoric (cash-based) accounting theory (Kosiol). In the 1970s and early 1980s relatively little attention was paid to inflation accounting, apart from research on capital maintenance. Accounting theories shifted towards the present value approach and empirical studies began in the early 1960, gathering momentum in the last two decades of the century. *Codified law* dominated German accounting legislation and, later, by standardization attempts within the European Economic Community. Consolidated statement presentation and auditing research also became prominent, while cost and managerial accounting continued to be major research areas. Competing costing approaches dominated the field, often based on concepts from production theory. Marginal costing (occasionally together with mathematical programming) was further developed, and a closer connection between cost accounting and investment theory was established. The introduction of information theory (and the closely related agency theory) into the German literature greatly influenced recent German accounting research. Some of the prominent names (listed alphabetically) are: Peter Holzer, Seicht and Wagenhofer (Austria); Albach, Baetge, Ballwieser, Busse von Colbe, Chmielewicz, Coenenberg, Ewert, the business economist Gutenberg, Herbert Hax, Kilger, Kloock, Kosiol, Küpper, Moxter, Seicht, Dieter Schneider and Schweitzer (Germany); Fickert, Käfer and Pfaff (Switzerland, though the latter is originally from Germany). Historical accounting research was, in contrast to the first half of the century, of lesser importance in Germany (with the exception of some books by Schneider, Seicht and others).

1.4.4 Summary of Chapter 5: 'Accounting research in Italy: first half of the twentieth century'

This period was decisive for academic accounting research in Italy, no less than in the German, English, French or other language areas. Yet, seen from abroad, it seems that in Italy (more than in other countries), only a single figure dominated the scene, that of Gino Zappa. However, at a closer look, one may discover that the situation in Italy was not so different. There, Zappa overshadowed many other scholars; but for this very reason, their names and major publications deserve to be brought to the attention of a wider audience. Above all, it must be borne in mind that other giants of accounting, like Giuseppe Cerboni and his disciple Giovanni Rossi, and particularly Fabio Besta (Zappa's teacher), were still prominent during the early twentieth century. Other important names to be mentioned are: Alfieri, Amaduzzi, Clitofonte Bellini, Caprara, Ceccherelli, D'Alvise, De Gobbis, Della Penna, De Minico, D'Ippolito, Lorusso, Masi, Melis, Mondini, Onida and Pisani.

Thus, we pursue two goals: first, we summarize Gino Zappa's contributions to accounting research, together with some remarks about the twentieth-century publications of Rossi and Besta. Second, we offer a flavour of Italian accounting studies of other scholars worth mentioning. However, we concentrate primarily on accounting publications, and rarely mention those of *economia aziendale* in general.

Apart from Zappa's contributions, four features seem to be characteristic for Italian accounting of the first half of the twentieth century, particularly in comparison with France, or even Germany. First, an enormous interest in historical accounting studies deeply rooted in Italian tradition. Second, there was a predominant interest in financial accounting theory; some interest in cost accounting, though by no means as much as in Germany. Third, relatively little interest was shown in charts and master charts of accounts. Fourth, an equally limited interest in inflation accounting (compared with Germany and France) – though inflation issues may have influenced Italian accounting more indirectly.

1.4.5 Summary of Chapter 6: 'Accounting research in Italy: second half of the twentieth century'

This chapter starts with the changing international position of Italian accounting research. The chapter shortly discusses the special relation between Zappa's *economia aziendale* (economics of business and non-profit, as well as governmental entities) and *ragioneria* (accounting) in Italy. The subsequent discussion on 'financial accounting' includes subsections on income orientation (versus capital orientation) that proved to be particularly important in Italy during this period, and, finally, the present crisis of *economia aziendale* in relation to *ragioneria* (accounting). Then, we discuss contributions by major Italian accountants of the period (above all, by Onida and Amaduzzi, both continuing Zappa's tradition). After a section on 'cost and managerial accounting' (continuing to be in Italy less significant than financial accounting), and a look at 'novel accounting trends', the chapter closes with a discussion of some representative historical studies of the period.

Further names to be mentioned are: Agazzi, Amodeo, Azzini, Canziani, Catturi, Chianale, Cilloni, Coda, Colombo, D'Ippolito, Fanni, Ferraris Franceschi, Ferrero, Galassi, Guatri, Masi, Masini, Melis, Viganò, Zambon and Zan.

1.4.6 Summary of Chapter 7: 'Accounting research in the French language area: first half of the twentieth century'

It reminds the reader that Francophone authors assumed an eminent position in accounting between the seventeenth and the nineteenth century. Such historical figures as Savary, Mathieu de la Porte, Degrange Sr, Payen, Léautey and Guilbault are indelibly engraved in the annals of accounting. This tradition continued during the first half of the twentieth century (the 'Belle Époque' of the inter-war period), though less prominently, despite a greater volume of publications. The five major topics occupying accounting research during this period in the French language area were: (i) accounting history; (ii) financial accounting theory, including commercial and industrial applications, taxation issues and education; (iii) the assimilation and adaptation of cost accounting and managerial control as developed in Germany, the United Kingdom and the United States; (iv) the need for price-level adjustments during the post-war inflation of the late 1920s; and (v) the construction of charts of accounts, legislations for uniform master charts, as well as creating associations of public accounting (including auditing).

Prominent names to be mentioned are Batardon, Bournisien, Brunet, Calmès, Caujolle, Chezleprêtre, de Fages de Latour, R. Delaport, Delavelle, R. de Roover,

Dumarchey, Dupont, Faure, Fourastié, Gabriel, Garnier, Gomberg, Léautey, Penglaou, Reymondin and Rimailho.

1.4.7 Summary of Chapter 8: 'Accounting research in the French language area: second half of the twentieth century'

French accounting research during this period invested considerable effort in the *Plan Comptable General* (the master chart of accounts) and the related activity of standardization and international harmonization. This may have been at the disadvantage of other aspects of financial and managerial accounting. However, since the 1970s there has been increasing interest in a broader range of academic accounting research. Apart from publications promoted by governmental and public, as well as scientific accounting institutions, research has been advanced by academics among whom the most prominent names were André Cibert in managerial accounting, Pierre Lassègue in financial accounting and Claude Pérochon in exploring the connections between macro- and micro-accounting. Indeed, the growing interest in social accounting (on the micro- and macro-level) may be considered a hallmark of French accounting (similar to Japan) during this period.

Since the 1980s or so, the leading figures have been Colasse and other prominent researchers such as Burleau, Degos, Scheid, Teller and Mévellec. In addition to this, there was considerable publication activity in historical accounting research where such *Belgian* scholars as Vleaminck, Stevelinck and R. de Roover stood in the forefront. To these we add such *French* accounting historians as Jouanique, Le Marchand, J. Richard, Nikitin and, again, Colasse and Degos.

1.4.8 Summary of Chapter 9: 'Accounting publications and research in Spain: first half of the twentieth century'

It offers a guide to major doctrinal trends of Spanish accounting of this period. The categories thereby used are: different viewpoints of the scientific nature of accounting; dominant theories and objectives of accounting; special areas; views on classification and on the recording of transactions; views on valuation and depreciation; cost accounting; inflationary issues; auditing; accounting terminology; historical concerns; and the practical orientation of publications.

A separate section offers further details about prominent Spanish scholars, followed by the conclusion. The latter indicates that during the period under investigation, Spanish accountants contributed little to novel accounting thought, but strongly relied on French and Italian doctrines, though neglecting German ideas. Despite this, Spanish accountants were aware of many theoretical and instrumental novelties of the day, and applied them without substantial delay to their own environment.

Prominent names (i.e. double-family names) to be mentioned are: Ballesteros Marín-Baldo, Boter Mauri, Cañizares Zurdo, Fernández Casas, Gardó Sanjuán,

Goxens Duch, Martínez Pérez, Piqué Batlle, Rodríguez Pita, Ruiz Soler, Sacristán y Zavala and Torrents y Monner.

1.4.9 Summary of Chapter 10: 'Accounting publications and research in Spain: second half of the twentieth century'

An introductory section discusses the fundamental changes that Spanish accounting literature has undergone during this period and offers a concise survey of general studies in accounting theory. The next section discusses more specialized issues – from consolidated financial statements and option pricing to the treatment of leases and social accounting, charts of accounts as well as government accounting. This is followed by a section dealing with various aspects of auditing; subsequently, by one on methodological issues that range from the axiomatization of accounting to positive accounting theory. The next section covers the wide spectrum of cost and managerial accounting issues, including behavioural and environmental ones, as well as the use of artificial intelligence. The following two sections deal with accounting history (a favoured topic of Spanish accountants) and institutional issues, respectively, covering major academic accounting institutions and journals in Spain. As 'representative samples' of particular research directions, we discuss only major works.

Prominent names (i.e. double-family names) to be specially mentioned are: Calafell Castelló, Cañibano Calvo, Carmona Moreno, Carrasco Díaz, Casanovas Parella, Castelló Taliani, Cea García, A. Donoso Anes and R. Donoso Anés, Fernández Peña, Fernández Pirla, Gabás Trigo, García Benau, García García, García Martín, García-Ayuso Corvasí, Giner Inchausti, González Ferrando, Gonzalo Angulo, Goxens Duch, Hernández Esteve, Martínez García, Montesinos Julve, Ortigueira Bouzada, Requena Rodríguez, Rodríguez Flores de Quiñones, Rodríguez Pita, Ruiz Barbadillo, Sáez Torrecilla, Tua Pereda and Vela Bargues.

1.4.10 Summary of Chapter 11: 'Accounting research in the English language area: first half of the twentieth century'

This chapter covers the United States, Great Britain and some Commonwealth countries (e.g. Australia, Canada and New Zealand). Here, the emphasis is on the personalities that dominated various phases of this period. In the early years such eminent British scholars as Dickinson, Dicksee (who later moved to the USA) and De Paula contributed mainly in financial accounting and auditing. Among the renowned Americans, we discuss the contributions of scholars like Sprague, Cole, Hatfield, Sterret, Montgomery, G.O. May, Bentley and Wildman.

Important contributions in cost accounting were made by Fells, Nicholson, Strachan, Longmuir, Arnold, Garry, Harrison, Church, Sir John Mann, Knoeppel, Rautenstrauch, Whitmore, Bentley, Hess, McKinsey and the economists J.M. Clark and Irving Fisher. The research of these scholars anticipated aspects of standard costing and direct costing, as well as the conception and improvement of break-even charts, and budgeting and other issues.

During the next phase, the publications of such scholars and practitioners as Sprague, Hatfield, Paton, Kester, Canning, Sanders, Littleton, Gilman, Scott, Bonbright, MacNeal, Kohler, Preinreich and Sweeney, became crucial in making the USA a major player in accounting research. Their contributions reached from the examination of fundamental problems and accounting standards (including inflation issues) to the pioneering of the present value approach in accounting, and other economic and financial aspects of our discipline.

The last phase includes such prominent British scholars as Baxter, Solomons (foremost active in the USA), Edey and the economist Coase (also active in the USA). Among the great American scholars of this period were Moonitz, Devine, Vatter and Vance. Although these scholars contributed already to the first half of the twentieth century, their major contributions were in the second half (see Chapter 12).

In the area of accounting history, we mention contributions of the following scholars: R. Brown, A.H. Wolf, van Diem, Yamey, F. de Roover, Geijsbeek, Chiera, Hatfield, Littleton, Peragallo, Garner, R.S. Edwards, Rogers, Theiss, Haynes and Jackson, Montgomery and Webster (some of them also mentioned in the Chapter 12).

1.4.11 Summary of Chapter 12: 'Accounting research in the English language area: second half of the twentieth century'

This chapter deals with the explosive growth of research in the Anglophone accounting literature during this period. This not only provided international leadership but many genuine innovations from the USA as well as from Australia, Canada and, last but not least, Great Britain.

This chapter is organized chronologically. It begins with the emergence of a 'new spirit' during the 1950s that manifested itself in the application of such mathematical techniques as statistical sampling in accounting and auditing (Vance, Cooper, Cyert, Rappaport and Trueblood), postulational and axiomatization attempts to improve the foundations of accounting theory (e.g. Chambers, Ijiri, Mattessich, Moonitz, Sprouse and Wells), the application of matrix and linear algebra to financial and, particularly, cost accounting (Corcoran and Demski), budget simulation (Mattessich), the construction of computerized spreadsheets, and related experiments. Cost accounting was transformed to managerial accounting and became a tool of decision making (Anthony, Devine, Horngren, Solomons and Vatter), and exploiting such ideas as marginal (direct) costing, transfer pricing, etc. There were also attempts to create a common basis of macro- and micro-accounting (William Cooper, Ijiri, Mattessich and Powelson in the USA – though with more enduring results in Japan by Harada and Nosse, and in France by Lamson and Pérochon).

Apart from an increasing interest by practitioners in flow of funds statements (promoted by Vatter, Anton and Horngren) and the application of statistical techniques to auditing, the early 1960s were characterized by valuation issues (Chambers, Edwards and Bell, Ijiri and Sterling), allocation problems (Arthur

Thomas and Daniel Jensen), as well as the decision-usefulness approach for investors (Staubus). However, the late 1960s showed a reaction to *a priori* research, marked by the emergence of statistical-empirical studies that began to relate earning reports and capital market events to accounting (Benston, Ball and Brown, and Beaver). Furthermore, this period saw the birth of the analytical information perspective of accounting (Feltham, Demski, Lev and others), as well as such new trends as 'international accounting' (Enthoven, Holzer, Mueller, Schoenfeld and others). This period also saw the introduction of 'events accounting' (Sorter) and a revived interest in auditing and its philosophy (Mautz and Sharaff).

In the 1970s, empirical research continued to refine its tools and conceptual bases (e.g. Bernard, Gonedes and Dopuch, and Verrechia), while vain attempts were made to ostracize descriptive and 'normative' accounting. During the increasing inflationary trends, replacement value accounting (and other inflation accounting schemes) received growing attention. They created a host of publications (Baxter, Bedford, Chambers, Dyckman, Edey, Gynther, Mathews, Peasnell, Revsine, Whittington, etc.) and ultimately resulted in temporary quasi-legislative pronouncements in the USA (FASB) and similar attempts in several Commonwealth countries.

Towards the end of the 1970s, but mainly during the 1980s, behavioural accounting (Ashton, Briloff, Birnberg, Gibbins, Libby, Swieringa and others) established itself, possibly re-enforced by the related, yet very different British direction of 'critical-interpretive' accounting (Hopwood, Tinker, Chua, David Cooper, Lowe, Macintosh, Merino, Hopper, Scapens, etc.). This latter direction emphasized organization theory and sociological research in accounting rather than economics; it may be regarded as a reaction to the more radical empirical and economic trend that meanwhile emerged in America under the term of 'positive accounting theory' (Watts and Jerold Zimmerman). The advent of agency theory in business administration (Jensen and Meckling) gave a boost to accounting through the development of an *analytical* agency theory (Baiman, Demski, Feltham, etc.) and its incorporation into the information economic perspective.

The 1980s and 1990s saw a revival and refinement of Preinreich's 'clean surplus theory' (Brief and Peasnell and Ohlson) and its incorporation into the information perspective. The latter was further consolidated, and so was empirical and market-based accounting research (Bernard, Burgstahler, Lev, Sloan, Palepu, etc.), and the critical-interpretive approach as well as other novel directions. There also was a slow recovery of managerial accounting from the stagnation experienced in the 1970s. New ideas, partly home-grown, partly from abroad (e.g. 'strategic cost management', 'activity based accounting', the 'balanced score-card' and 'target costing' from Japan) began to revitalize this important branch of accounting (Atkinson, Bromwich, Horngren, Kaplan and Sunder). Research in auditing and its standards also widened its horizon (Antle, Kinney, Dopuch, Holthausen, Mock, Moonitz, William Scott, Simunic, Stamp, Vasarhelyi, etc.). Questions about accounting standard-setting and regulation continued to be raised (Abdel-khalik, Basu and Milburn, Kohler, Leftwich, Schipper, Skinner, Stamp, Trueblood Report, Wyatt, etc.). And even more foundational questions about the nature of accounting (scientific versus pragmatic) and its ability to represent reality were explored (Lukka, Mattessich, Macintosh, Thornton and others).

Furthermore, historical accounting research expanded considerably during these decades (Brief, Chatfield, Frank Clarke, Graeme Dean, J. Richard Edwards, Fleischman, Thomas Lee, Lee Parker, Robert Parker, Previts, Vangermeersch, Yamey, Zeff and many others). This also holds for such well-established areas as 'governmental and non-profit accounting' (e.g. Anthony and Berry and Wallace), tax accounting and tax planning (e.g. Davidson and Wolfson and Scholes), and 'accounting education' (see Sundem, and the AAA list of Innovation in Accounting Education Award Winners), no less than for new areas, such as petroleum accounting (e.g. Butterworth and Falk and Wolfson), gender issues (see Gender Issues in Accounting Newsletter of the AAA), segment statements (e.g. Barefield and Holstrum and Ijiri), environmental and socio-economic accounting (Belkaoui, Epstein), and others that emerged as legitimate sub-areas of our discipline.

As to prominent persons (beyond those mentioned above), the list of creative scholars in the English language area during this fertile period is enormous. Only the best known names can here be mentioned: Abdel-khalik, Antle, Bedford, Baxter, Bernard, Belkaoui, Benston, Brief, Briloff, the economist and Nobel laureate R.H. Coase, Davidson, Falk, Hendriksen, Kohler, T.A. Lee, Libby, Rappaport, Schipper, William Scott, Skinner, Sorter, the economist and Nobel laureate R. Stone, Sundem, Thornton, Wells and Wyatt.

1.4.12 Summary of Chapter 13: 'Accounting research in Finland, the Netherlands and the Scandinavian countries during the entire twentieth century'

All these countries had a well-established history in accounting, but the names of Ilmari Kovero from Finland and Theo Limperg from the Netherlands are best known. Kovero (who anticipated essential features of Limperg and Fritz Schmidt's theory, and thus also of that by Edwards and Bell) and other early Finnish accounting pioneers, like I.V. Kaitilia, H. Brommels and V.P. Nurmilhati, were strongly influenced by German scholars.

In the second generation of Finnish accounting scholar, Martti Saario establishes (from 1945 onwards) a 'Finnish' direction of accounting by reacting to some features of Schmalenbach's notions. This new trend continued in E. Artto and J. Lethovouri. At the same time, various publications of Martti Saario, Esa Kaitilia, Unto Virtanen and Henry Virkkunen became well known in the area of managerial and behavioural accounting, ethics and other fields. A further prominent Finnish accountant and financial expert is Jaakko Honko (with his investment orientation and promotion of the present value approach).

The currently active generation includes such notable names (in alphabetical order) as: Laitinen, Lehtonen, Kari Lukka, Majala, Mäkinen, Juha Näsi, Salmi Näsi, Neilimo, Philanto, Reponen, Riistama, Salmi, Tamminen, Vehmanen, Wallenius, Wallin and others. Their work spans a wide range of topics and approaches (from the analytical-philosophic and empirical-positive methodologies, to the decision-oriented and action oriented approaches). The chapter continues with reference to some historical accounting publications and a section on managerial accounting. Apart from some prominent cost accountants, mentioned above, the following names are to be added: Riistama and Jyrkkiö (with a well-known textbook), Alaluusua, and Lukka (with some studies on budgeting), a cost study by Kasanan, Lukka and Siitonen (also translated into English), and other interesting work in this area by such authors as Lumijärvi, Kasanen and Malmi and Granlund, and above all, by Lukka and Granlund.

The subsection devoted to the Netherlands, begins with Theodore Limperg (of the University of Amsterdam), the father of the Dutch version of business economics (*bedrijfseconomie*) and one of the pioneers of the replacement value theory. Limperg (despite a limited publication record, and most of it in Dutch) dominated accounting of the Netherlands during the first half of the twentieth century (despite some opposition from the Rotterdam School of Accounting). Limperg also expressed some new and, at this time radical views about auditing. Yet, his dogmatic stance on replacement cost accounting may have impeded the full development of modern cost accounting in the Netherlands.

In the second half of the twentieth century, Limperg continued to be highly revered in his country and the tradition he established is still flourishing. Major authors are: De Waal, Meij, ten Have, Kraayenhofen, and some Dutch-American scholars such as Hendriksen, Enthoven, Vangermeersch and van Seventer. During the last few decades of the century, the following Dutch accounting authors have, among others, become prominent: Bouma, Camfferman, Hoogendoorn, Feenstra, Klaassen and Schreuder. Accounting research of the Netherlands has certainly broadened beyond the traditional foci, and the literature has expanded to most of the fashionable topics.

As to historical accounting research in or of the Netherlands, many pertinent publications deal with Limperg's contributions or other aspects of Dutch accounting. Nevertheless, this literature (predominantly in Dutch) has great breadth, as can be seen from Camfferman's (1997) survey, covering close to 200 publications.

Accounting research in the Scandinavian countries begins with Oskar Sillén a prominent Swedish author (and former student of Eugen Schmalenbach) who is best known for a German paper on the history of valuation theory in Sweden. The other early prominent Swedish scholar was Albert ter Vehn (a former student of Fritz Schmidt) whose main interest ultimately became cost accounting. For further names of the many prominent accounting scholars from the Scandinavian countries, see last section of the References for Chapter 13.

1.4.13 Summary of Chapter 14: 'Accounting publications and research in twentieth-century Japan'

After some remarks on nineteenth-century accounting in Japan and its English influence, the chapter refers to the German influence that held sway until the end of the Second World War – afterwards, the American influence became predominant. The major early scholars of twentieth-century Japanese accounting were Tetsuzo Ohta (with his *dynamic* theoretical point of view), Kiyoshi Kurosawa (Japan's most prolific and eminent accounting scholar), Wasaburo Kimura (with his interests reaching from financial and cost accounting to bank bookkeeping) and Iwao Iwata (concerned with the scientific advancement of accounting). Among the next generation were such prominent accounting scholars as Kenji Aizaki, Nobuko Nosse and Fujio Harada (all of whom were as much concerned with macro-accounting as micro-accounting). Furthermore, the chapter takes into consideration the internationally known contributions of the Japanese-American scholar Yuji Ijiri. After shortly discussing the contributions of those academics, the special interest of Japanese accountants in ecological problems (e.g. by Kawano, Koguchi and Kokubu) as well as Japan's pioneering achievements in managerial accounting (e.g. *kaizen* costing, target costing) are emphasized. The chapter closes with some historical accounting studies by Japanese scholars, and a short Epilogue.

1.4.14 Summary of Chapter 15: 'Accounting publications and research of twentieth-century Russia'

This chapter deals with accounting publications and research under the Tsar, the Soviet Regime and the Russian Federation. During the beginning of the twentieth century, three important 'schools' dominated accounting in Imperial Russia: The thoroughly 'nationalistic' *Artel* school and its leader Ezersky; the more internationally oriented St Petersburg school and its leader A.M. Wolf and such internationally renowned members as Gomberg; and the Moscow school with a galaxy of more locally renowned members. The section on 'Accounting publications and research of Soviet Russia before 1930', begins with the utopian attempt to abandon 'money', and the endeavours of 'restoration' in the 1920s, when Veitsman emerged as an important leader in accounting. Other important names of this and the subsequent period were: Blatov, Sivers, Galagan, Losinsky, Lounsky, Popov, Stumilin, Struve, Leontieve and, of course, the Nobel laureate Leontief. Soviet Russia under Stalin saw new scholars emerge, but even those became discredited as 'bourgeois' until a new set of politically more acceptable persons came to the fore. Zhebrak became prominent by introducing a kind of Russian standard costing system. Financial accounting declined, and most of the discussions centred on costing issues. Some historical reflections close this section. The last section (with several subsections on financial accounting, auditing and management accounting) deals with 'Cost and management accounting in the Russian Federation' when the influence of Western accounting research became effective. Many Russian translations of Anglophone accounting textbooks emerged and Russian academics began to publish occasionally in English. For prominent names of recent Russian accounting scholars, see References to Chapter 15.

1.4.15 Summary of Chapter 16: 'Accounting publications and research in Poland and the Ukraine: mainly twentieth century'

The two countries discussed here are related by political history (both were divided for lengthy periods) no less than by Pawel Ciompa, a renowned accountant that both countries may legitimately claim. The chapter begins with Poland. Despite Ciompa's important contribution in the first decade of the century, the other accounting or bookkeeping texts published in the first two decades of the century were mainly practical manuals. Possible exceptions were the works by Gora, and some reflections on inflationary accounting issues by Lulek, as well as the books by Byszewski and by Skalski. In the 1930s, the situation did improve thanks to a series of publications by Scheffs and additional ones by Aseńko, Skalski, Lulek and Góra. These works reflected recent achievements of European accounting thought.

During the Cold War and afterwards some academics, like Jaruga, Krzywda, Szychta, Vellam and others, tried to remain in close contact with the West by publishing in English on Polish accounting issues, or in Polish about recent issues of the Anglophone accounting literature. In the new millennium a series of international accounting research conferences were organized in various cities of Poland (by Dobija and others). The proceedings of these also contain many papers (in English) some on Poland but all of interest to an international audience.

The second part of this chapter deals with the Ukraine. After a concise introduction, there is a discussion of the 'Western' Ukraine from about 1850 to 1939 that, up to the First World War, belonged to Austro-Hungary. At the early phase, this was the most progressive and prosperous part of today's Ukraine where Ciompa was active. The 1920s also manifested (in comparison with the rest of the USSR) vigorous development. The 'Eastern' Ukraine was more backward, but towards the end of the nineteenth century it developed a series of new industries. Around the turn of the century the first professional accounting associations appeared. In the 1950s the leading accountant was Nimchynov, founder of the Ukrainian school of accounting and an expert in agricultural accounting. Later, Chumachenko, an industrial and cost expert, became prominent – and not only during the Soviet era, but also today and in the West. Of special importance is the next section, dealing with the formation of modern accounting and auditing in the independent Ukraine. The subsection dealing with accounting theory and auditing mentions a series of pertinent publications; it also emphasizes the initiative of Kuzminsky in creating (in 1992) the first modern Ukrainian accounting journal, and the founding of several influential accounting associations. The subsection on management and cost accounting devotes merely a short paragraph to the Soviet era but offers greater insight into the development and publications during the new, independent phase of the Ukraine. Although the majority of those accountants have embraced the lead of the West (based on the Russian translation of several Anglophone textbooks) there are still Ukrainian experts questioning the usefulness of managerial accounting. The last subsection deals with auditing that obtained official and legal status in this country as recently as 1993. Nevertheless, a series of texts in auditing theory and practice have already emerged.

1.4.16 Summary of Chapter 17: 'On the development of academic and professional accounting in Argentina, its publications and research'

This chapter discusses twentieth-century accounting publications and research in Argentina (as one of the South American countries most active in accounting publications and research). The English accounting literature offers relatively little insight into past and current research and publication efforts in Latin America. In trying to fill this gap, we investigated this issue from the viewpoint of Argentina. After some explanations about the special methodology employed here, we review the evolution of Argentine accounting institutions and its close relationship to academia as well as its accounting journals.

Then we discuss the major foreign influence (from Spain, France, Italy, America, England and Germany) on Argentine accounting publications during the earlier part of the twentieth century. Later we offer a survey of Argentine accounting publications during the first half of the twentieth century, and its major authors (above all, Alberto Arévalo). The rest deals mainly with authors and publications of the second half of the twentieth century (and its Anglo-American influence) from the point of view of such sub-areas as general accounting theory, financial accounting, auditing, cost and managerial accounting, social accounting and governmental accounting.

Alberto Arévalo is undoubtedly the best known among Argentine's accounting scholars. Other prominent names from the first half of the twentieth century are: J. Bayetto, A. Cassagne Serres, H. Floriani, S.U. Pagano, L. Ruiz Soler and F.P. Zipitria. More recently, the following names have become prominent: E. Fowler Newton, C.L. García Casella, M.C. Rodríguez de Ramírez, M. Wainstein and the Brazilian scholar Lopes de Sá. Other well-known Argentine accounting authors are: M. Biondi, W.L. Chapman, F. Cholvis, L.N. Fernández Lorenzo, L. Fronti de García, L. González Bravo, A. Lavolpe, S.C. Lazzati, H. López Santiso, E.R. Scarano and R.J. Pahlen Acuña.

1.4.17 Summary of Chapter 18: 'Accounting in other countries: publications and research reports'

This chapter tries to offer some representative examples of Anglophone accounting publications (and in a few cases of 'local' publications) and research about areas not covered in previous chapters (from some Eastern European countries to areas of Africa and Asia). The chapter begins with 'accounting in some Eastern European countries (Rumania, Lithuania, Hungary, former Yugoslavia, Greece and Cyprus) and Israel'. A separate subsection is devoted to Portugal and Brazil. A subsequent subsection deals with 'other Latin American countries (beyond Brazil and Argentina)'. The next two subsections refer to accounting literature on 'Arab and other Moslem countries, as well as some African countries' (e.g. Tunisia, Egypt, Jordan, Saudi Arabia, Kuwait, Turkey, Pakistan, Nigeria, Ghana and Ethiopia) and 'some countries of the Far East' (India, China and Hong Kong, Thailand and South Korea), respectively. The chapter closes with a subsection dealing with 'Publications on developing countries in general'.

1.4.18 Summary of Chapter 19: 'The information economic perspective of accounting: its coming of age'

This chapter closes the book with a discussion of the latest and most rigorous twentieth-century accounting development (referring inevitably also to some works published already in the twenty-first century). It discusses several recent publications in the area of information economics as applied to accounting. The paper emphasizes the contrast between the traditional 'value approach' and the more recent 'information perspective' as well as the major methodological and theoretical tenets of the latter. Additional sections are devoted to 'issues beyond the competence of the information perspective', 'opposition and criticism' (with such subsections as 'resistance to the mathematical-analytical approach', the 'neglect of traditional accounting terminology' and 'other objections'), an inquiring section on 'towards a general theory of accounting?' and, finally, there is a 'conclusion from a wider angle'.

Prominent names of accountants in this area – apart from the two major pioneers, Gerald (Jerry) A. Feltham and Joel A. Demski – are, among many others: Amin H. Amershi, Rick Antle, Stanley Baiman, Victor L. Bernard, John A. Christensen, Peter O. Christensen, Ronald A. Dye, Ralf Ewert, Froystein Gjesdale, Nils H. Hakansson, Raffi J. Injejikian, Richard A. Lambert, Baruch Lev, James A. Ohlson, Steven H. Penman, Robert E. Verrechia, Alfred Wagenhofer and Xiao-Jun Zhang.

1.5 General remark to the reference sections of all chapters

Many of the references could not be accessed directly and were taken from secondary sources. Therefore, names of publishers or page numbers were not always available. Frequently several editions of the same book exist; also wherever possible we tried to list early or later editions in parentheses.

2 The nineteenth century

An international survey[1]

2.1 The pioneers of early accounting research

This chapter reflects the need for a *concise* overview of nineteenth-century accounting research. The *national* nineteenth-century accounting literature of many countries, though by no means unimportant, has been relatively neglected in the *international* literature (dominated by English publications). Furthermore, many professionals seem to be unaware of how many (and often which) 'modern' accounting ideas were conceived or hatched during the nineteenth century. Finally, some scholars who might be aware of all this, may not realize that the primacy of a certain idea, long attributed to one person or country, may actually belong to another.[2]

Italian accounting dominated the fifteenth and sixteenth centuries but lost its leadership afterwards. During the eighteenth century it was in sharp decline. This was still the case during the first third of the 1800s despite the high repute of a few Italian authors like D'Anastasio (1803), Scandellari (1803) and Bornaccini (1818). The 'foreign theoretical invasion', as Melis (1950: 718) called it, continued; and foremost among the 'invaders' was the Frenchman Edmond Degrange Sr (1795, 1801),[3] who himself belonged partly to the eighteenth century, though his work was most influential during the nineteenth. Degrange was an original and innovative author who simplified the fairly complex eighteenth-century accounting by reducing the number of accounts to merely 'five' (Cash, Goods, Receivables, Payables, Profit and Loss, which he later extended by a sixth, Miscellaneous). His particular merit was the invention of the so-called 'American bookkeeping system', employing a synoptic form that combined the journal with the ledger in a single table. This system was still used in the twentieth century in many firms that could get along with relatively few accounts. The misleading name 'American' seems to have been due to a Belgian accountant.

Similarly, the book by the English eighteenth century author Robert Hamilton [1743–1829] (1777–79), with its famous chapter on *farm accounting*, continued to be influential in the nineteenth century. Another economist and accountant born in the eighteenth century, pioneering agricultural economics, was Albrecht D. Thaer [1752–1828] with a well-known book in German, see Thaer (1809). A further expert from the eighteenth century, exercising influence in the next, was Edward (Thomas) Jones [1767–1833] from Bristol. His book *The English System of Bookkeeping by Single or Double entry* (Jones 1796/1816) attempted to combine the simplicity of single-entry with the checks available in double-entry (later he wrote *The Science of Bookkeeping* 1832). This hybrid system consisted of a three-column daybook, a ledger, an alphabetical chart of accounts and, if so desired, a journal. According to Chatfield (1996b: 356), this system did not show current balances of sales and purchases; thus income determination seems to have required separate side calculations. Nevertheless, Jones was regarded as an important critique of the double-entry system and, according to Melis (1950: 725), his publications were translated into several languages and became popular in Continental Europe. In later publications he employed tabular account books and some devices which adapted Luca Pacioli's system to the needs of the nineteenth century (see also Yamey 1956).

Other authors and publications of the *first half of the nineteenth century* – some of them rarely mentioned, though of considerable national and sometimes international importance – ought to be mentioned: From *Germany and Austria*: Fredersdorff (1802), who already differentiated between financial and factory accounting; von Sonnenfels [1733–1817] (1804 – with regard to cameralistic accounting), Leuchs (1806), who used 'cost or market value, whichever is lower' and divided acquisition cost into sales-related and independent (or fixed) cost; von Puteani's [1782–1847] (1818) foundations of accounting, Rau (1822 – also with regard to cameralism) and Maisner's (1828) introduction for beginners. From the *French language area*: Battaille (1804), Delorme (1808), Isler (1809) and, above all, Payen (1817) – and later Bruinier (1908) and Bournesien (1917). Payen anticipated job order and process costing, transfer pricing, overhead allocation to each product (though without specifying a particular basis) and other 'modern' costing features by bringing cost accounting under the control of double-entry. Another even more radical pioneer was de Cazaux (1824, 1825); he not only aimed at 'true' profit determination but also analysed the profit sources, conceived of the notion of *idle time*, made the distinction between profits from regular operations versus *holding gains*. He also concerned himself with budgeting and financial accounting, paid special attention to agricultural enterprises, and was (according to Solomons 1968b: 42) the 'first writer ... to show interest in *accounting for the future*' (emphasis added). Further authors of the French tongue were Feigneaux (1827) and Godard (1827). The latter not only traced the flow of costs through industrial enterprises but also dealt with average costing, deferred and opportunity costs, as well as raw material accounting, alluded to 'work in process' and determined the cost of goods sold of inventory. Upon this followed the publications of Jeannin (1829) who employed a specific *work in process account* as well as a *finished goods account*. And F.N. Simon's (1832) two-volume work pleaded for allocating such items as rent, administrative salaries and taxes to overhead costs. Other authors of this 'golden age of French cost accounting' were: Ouvrat (1835), Coffy (1832), Queulin[4] (1840) with his idea of perpetual inventory. Furthermore, Malot (1841), a professor, interested in farm accounting, wrote an accounting text that won a prize for its highly educational value. He also warned against under- as well as over-valuation. Further notable French authors and publications of this period were Deplanque (1842) and Willame (1842).

In *Great Britain* – where, according to Fleischman (1996: 125): 'business leaders did cost accounting by the seats of their pants and frequently got it right' – James Fulton (1800) and Cronhelm (1818) pioneered cost accounting at an even earlier time.[5] He also used algebra to explain double-entry and discusses perpetual inventory. From America the works of W. Jackson (1801) and Gerisher (1817), Bennet (1820), Thomas Jones (1841),[6] as well as John Fleming (1854), in cost accounting, have to be mentioned. From *Sweden* came Synnerberg (1813) and Pholmann (1838); from *Spain* Brost (1825) and Christantes y Cañedo (1838); and from *Poland* Barciński (1833).[7] But no contributions seem to have been more important than those of the French tongue, as Forrester (1998: 160) confirmed by emphasizing the technical ingenuity of this literature (the most prominent of the French authors are profiled, together with scholars from other countries, in Colasse 2005).

However, in the second third of the nineteenth century, beginning with Francesco Villa [1801–84] and his *magnum opus* (Villa 1840–41), the Italians regained some of the territory of accounting literature, though authors from other countries were hardly idle. Although the main concern of many of these authors was bookkeeping theory and its pedagogy, their contributions had far-reaching influence. The major pedagogical goal was to replace, by more rational means, the widespread rote learning of bookkeeping rules (often supported by such mnemonic devices as limericks) that hardly afforded any deeper comprehension of the underlying reason. To achieve this, a logical and often algebraic way of explaining bookkeeping was sought. Before this could be done, the predominant position of the 'journal' had to be abandoned, and the ledger and balance sheet moved into the centre of attention.

2.2 Theories of 'accounts'

The numerous theories of 'accounts' aimed at finding the basic rules of keeping books, sought to disentangle the 'mystery' of double-entry. For example, they tried to explain the puzzles and confusions arising from the fact that some debit entries represent increases, but others are decreases. Or the analogous confusion with credit entries; and the difference between a debit (or credit) in a *nominal* account versus one in a *real* account, etc. Though reasoning and explanation did replace mere description, the bewildering number of theories, based on different classification schemes, were all *theories of 'accounts'* (i.e. bookkeeping theories)[8] rather than 'accounting theories' in the modern sense.

Although those theories were greatly at variance with each other, one can recognise two main issues. First, how to interpret an account? Is an 'account' a pure fiction, or does it stand for a person or for something material beyond persons? And second, which *account classes* are basic? In other words, how many classes are required for a proper understanding of the 'science of bookkeeping'?

Some scholars pleaded for one-series theories (considering all accounts as basically the same); others for two-series theories (asserting, for example, a basic difference between *asset accounts* and *equity accounts*); and again others for multi-series theories (e.g. with subdivisions of asset and/or equity accounts as basic). Often a particular series could be identified with a specific element in the basic equations which varied from author to author (e.g. 'Assets = Equities' vs. 'Assets = Debts + Owner's Equities' vs. 'Receivables + Other Assets = Debts + Owners Equities', etc.).

Among the most frequently mentioned authors dealing with *two- and four-series theories* were several Italian scholars.[9] Skipping a discussion of some of their precursors (like d'Anastasio), the first prominent name to be mentioned is Giuseppe Cerboni [1827–1917/Tuscan School] who, ultimately, became Accountant General of the then newly formed State of Italy. In his book on '*logismografi*' (from the Greek for 'logical recording' or 'tabular recording', as some claim), Cerboni (1873, 1877, 1878, 1886–94) not only aimed at a 'logical' double-entry approach, but also at one *applicable to government* no less than to private business. His system consisted of two summary accounts, one for the proprietor, the other for the 'agents and correspondents', and used a peculiar tabular form (*giornale logismografico* – with the potential of creating many sub- and sub-sub-accounts in separate ledgers). This system, intended to reveal the wealth structure of an entity not merely at year-end, but on a *daily* basis. It influenced not only many Italian authors, like Antonio Tonzig [1804–94] (1879), Michele Riva [1830–1903] (1875), Capparozzo (1880 – see below), Achille Sanguinetti [1855–1915] (1880), Clitofonte Bellini (1883), but also foreigners like López Toral (1878), Schrott (1882) and, in America, Hardcastle (1897) and Sprague (1898).

The next major scholar was Giovanni Rossi [1845–1921], Cerboni's renowned student and associate at the government office, who occasionally has been called the 'philosopher of logismography' (e.g. Rossi 1880, 1901). Though he continued in the effort of his master, he was even more inclined towards a juridical, as well as mathematical, interpretation of bookkeeping (see Rossi 1889). In this book he took up a suggestion by Gneist (1882) concerning the Anglo-Norman Exchequer of the twelfth century, which used a table covered with a cloth divided into squares (like a chess or chequer table on which counters were moved). According to Gneist, those motions may have represented two-dimensional accounting entries. Based on this idea, Rossi developed a fairly sophisticated chessboard theory of accounting (today we would say a '*matrix theory*'), offering a great number of matrix illustrations. Although he did not seem to have been aware of matrix algebra, he used similar algebraic notations and even applied the expression of 'determinants' (though again without their modern mathematical properties). Rossi (1889: 64) even suggested that 'the accounting matrix [*lo scacchiere a schede*] could be transformed into a mechanical computing matrix' (translated). Thus, one may argue, that Rossi made a step, though one forgotten for a long time, towards the advent of the *computerized spreadsheets* that began in the early 1960s – even though he had a mechanical computation in mind (like Babbage's 'analytical engine') and not an electronic one. Thus, it is no surprise that this book by Rossi (1889) soon fell into oblivion – it just was too much ahead of its time (for further details, see Mattessich and Galassi 2000).[10] But it was actually De Morgan (1846) who *first* used a *matrix framework* for accounting (see fifth section – including the Introduction – last paragraph), though he did not apply it to the large extent as did Rossi.

The third eminent Italian was Fabio Besta [1845–1922, Venetian School]. His four-volume work (Besta 1891–1916) was particularly important for the newer trend, partly anticipated by Villa (1840–41) of the Lombard school. The goal was the economic and *management control* for all kinds of enterprises, including those publicly owned. Cerboni's as well as Rossi's theories were still 'personalistic' (clearly distinguishing accounts of the proprietor who provides the capital, from accounts of the administrators of assets). But Besta shifted from a *personalistic* to a *materialistic* (or non-personalistic) theory of accounts (these notions of materialistic vs. personalistic theories are explained in the next section, while those of proprietary vs. entity theories are dealt with later). Schneider highly praises Besta and points out that:

> He is the first to relate accounting to economic theory, e.g. he uses replacement values by appealing to Ricardo's value theory (reproduction costs) and concerns himself thoroughly with present value (*Ertragswert*) calculations of real estate and leases.
>
> (Schneider 2001: 98, translated from German)

However, Besta went farther by daring to oppose logismography (English spelling) and its peculiarities, though he was by no means the only one to do so. It may be no coincidence that soon after Cerboni retired as Accountant General of Italy, the logismographic system (see also Checcerelli 1910), that had dominated the Italian state administration, was abandoned (cf. Melis 1950: 764). Yet Besta's is still a *proprietary* theory (in contrast to the subsequent *entity theory*). These and other theories – e.g. those by Tonzig (1857–59) and Giovanni Massa [1850–1904] (1896) as well as the ones by two Frenchmen, Godfroid (1864) and Courcelles-Seneuil (1870) – were important, as they became sources of influence and contention among the late nineteenth-century and early twentieth-century theorists. One may add that Emmanuele Pisani [1845–1915], with his 'statmografia' (Pisani 1880), developed a kind of synoptic synthesis of Cerboni's and Rossi's accounting theory.

2.3 Personalistic versus materialistic theories of 'accounts'

Considering that Luca Pacioli [c.1445–1517] (1494) himself used pedagogic devices in which stores or accounts were compared to persons, it may be understandable that the so-called 'personalistic theories' enjoyed popularity in the nineteenth century. After all, the 'personalization' made the accounts more plausible by identifying them with people, usually with those administering the accounts. This facilitated the teaching of bookkeeping to beginners, but at a more advanced level it resulted in pedagogic difficulties and explanatory complications (particularly in the case of *nominal* accounts). Prominent representatives of the personalistic theories were (apart from Cerboni and Rossi) some Frenchmen, like Degrange Sr (1795, 1801) and Quiney (1817/39); the Italian D'Anastasio (1803); the Swiss government accountant Hügli (1887, 1900), and others. But, as time went by, the 'materialistic theories' (abandoning the fiction of identifying non-personalistic accounts with persons) became more convincing.[11] Francesco Villa, whom Melis (1950: 745) called the 'father of Italian ragioneria [modern accounting]', even presented a '*mixed*' theory of accounts (Villa 1840–41, see above).

Today, some experts may smile about the immense effort that nineteenth-century accountants invested in those predominantly classificational and definitional devices, as well as in the attempt to prove that one classification was superior to the others. Yet to apply the scientific criteria of one generation as standards of an earlier one would be naive, indeed. Apart from this, with the progress of time, accountants tried to make classification more 'scientific' (for a modern view of how important proper classification can be in cost accounting, see Christensen and Demski 1995). Referring to various nineteenth-century American authors, McMillan points out:

> The 'science of accounts' [was] ... rooted fundamentally in the rational process of account classification [p. 3] .... This basic classification appears to make no ontological claim to explain the reality of the bookkeeping system or to demonstrate the aesthetic symmetry .... It served primarily as a pedagogic tool to aid the novice in grasping the bookkeeping art .... Attacking this rule-setting method, Foster demonstrated the scientific irrationality of the classification by focusing on the economic reality revealed in the bookkeeping system .... Foster [1837] presented one of the earliest classifications that appear to make an ontological claim. His division was not for pedagogical purposes. Rather, he believed his classification had been derived from the immutable essence of bookkeeping, through the application of scientific thought [pp. 5–6].
>
> (McMillan 1998: 3, 5–6)

Indeed, the influence of those theories of accounts continued to linger on, long into the twentieth century. One influence was their impact on various *Bilanztheorien* (German accounting theories). Another legacy was the intensive concern with *charts of accounts* in many Continental European countries (cf. Scherpf 1955). Such a theory of accounts was still pursued in the second half of the twentieth century by Käfer [1897–2000] (1966: 39–72), though the historical part of this book (pp. 1–38) attracted greater attention.

It seems that theories of accounts and their controversies were a predominantly Continental European phenomenon, though American authors, like Foster (1837), Sprague (1898), Hardcastle (1891–92, 1897), Kittredge (1896) and others were also interested in it, and had their own pertinent disputes (for details, see McMillan 1998). In Great Britain, scholars took little part in those controversies, just as they showed little interest in the modern successors of these particular theories, the various charts and *master charts of accounts*, so prominent during a good deal of the twentieth century (from France and Germany to Scandinavia and Russia). But these charts did not catch on in England (which, in compensation, pioneered auditing and the chartered accounting profession)[12] or on the North American continent. Although the '*uniform costing*' scheme – first encountered in the USA with the National Association of Stove Manufacturers after 1872 and the trend towards a '*uniform accounting*' in American accounting at the turn of the century (see Previts and Merino 1979: 185–91) – might have been steps in this direction. In Australia, according to Scherpf (1955: 170–3), there did emerge charts of accounts (at least temporarily) for certain business branches, and supposedly also a 'Basic Chart of Accounts for Australian Industry' (see Australian Institute of Management 1950).

Scholarly controversies encompassed the whole gamut of nineteenth-century research. They were not merely fought out between scholars and groups of them; they even reflected the jealousy between countries. In studying the details, one is surprised not only by the stubborn conviction of every scholar (or group) that his (or their) classification scheme is the only correct one, but also by the national pride involved. For example, Melis (1950: 718–27) not only talked about the theoretical invasion of Italy by foreign accounting thoughts but even of the re-conquest – almost like the Spaniards speak of the 'reconquista' of their country from the Moors. Melis also derided those Italians (for example, the '*cinque contisti*') who followed the ideas of Degrange and other foreigners by using the 'five accounts in journal form' (see above) – a rebuttal against the '*cinque contisti*' can be found in Francesco Marchi [1822–71] (1867). Melis also described the fight of the rest of the Italian scholars among themselves (especially that between the Tuscan school and the Venetian school).[13] But in the end he believed that:

> Whatever the undeniable merit of having generated so many debates and publications – the famous 'battle', full of ardor but always serene, between the logismographists and the partiduplisti [i.e. their opponents] – they were of immense benefit to the advancement of the discipline.
>
> (Melis 1950: 764, translated from the Italian)

2.4 The proprietary theory

Parallel with the various theories of accounts, the proprietary theory, and later the slowly emerging entity theory, have been interpreted as attempts 'to define a conceptual framework based upon logic to replace "rationalization" as used in personification of accounts' (Previts and Merino 1979: 165). The central feature of the *proprietary theory* was its emphasis on the capital account and capital preservation, and later, on the balance sheet, which grew to assume a more dominant position. In this theory the *capital account* was no longer considered to be a residual account but became firmly identified with the owner – just as the entire firm was considered his possession, not something apart from him.[14] Hence, attention shifted from mere transactions (concentrating on the exchange of values) to making profit for the owner – a crucial step in the direction towards twentieth-century accounting theory.

Major representatives of the proprietary theory were: James W. Fulton (1800) and Cronhelm (1818) from Great Britain; two Austrians, Hautschl (1840) and Kurzbauer (1850); two Germans, Augspurg (1852–55), who even concerned himself with *inflation accounting*, and Löw (1860), who offered a survey of accounting development; the Americans Thomas Jones (1841) and, later, Sprague (see below) as well as Hatfield (1909 – see below) and others – apart from the Italian publications mentioned above. In Switzerland, Hügli (1887, 1900), elaborating the work of earlier German authors, became a leading exponent of the *proprietary point of view*, and demonstrated the accounting equilibrium by means of algebraic equations; though Schneider (2001: 98) characterized Hügli's and Schär's contributions as of 'pale one-sidedness' compared to those of Besta's. Johann F. Schär [1846–1924], also from Switzerland, later became especially prominent as professor in Leipzig, and then at the University of Berlin. He too approached the proprietary theory by means of mathematical symbols (see Schär 1890, 1911, 1914) and, more significantly, pioneered *ethics* in accounting and business economics.[15]

In the early twentieth century the Swiss scholar Sganzini (1908) presented what he called a 'realistic theory of accounts', which anticipated not only Schmalenbach's dynamic accounting (see the sections below) but even some of its improvements by others.[16]

> With this [theory] *Sganzini* completely developed dynamic accounting in its formal aspect. *Schmalenbach, Walb, and Rieger* presented his ideas more thoroughly in some details and expressed them differently, but added nothing of essence. Under these circumstances, it is strange that *Sganzini* received so little attention. The time was ripe for his ideas, as attested by the success of *Fischer* [1909] and the subsequently arising dynamic accounting theory of *Schmalenbach*. They [*Sganzini's* ideas] were published in a learned journal. Despite of it, his name is hardly mentioned.
>
> (Borkowsky 1946: 67, translated – see also Seicht 1970: 59, 146)

In England, one of the greatest logicians and mathematicians of his time, August de Morgan [1806–71] – in his famous bookkeeping appendix to a mathematical work (de Morgan 1846) – led the personalistic theory of accounts to its logical conclusion. Jackson (1956: 298) referred to de Morgan's accounting contribution (mainly his formulation of the proprietary theory) as 'probably the most influential piece of writing to be found during the nineteenth century'. As pointed out, de Morgan also 'introduced a matrix framework for accounting, namely in an appendix to the fifth edition of his *Elements of Arithmetic*, containing ... the "Main Principle of Book-keeping"' (Mepham 1988: 375). De Morgan used a rectangular table in which every pair of rows and corresponding columns stood for an account, such that the rows represented the credit sides and the columns the debit sides.

2.5 The entity theory

A crucial step was the slow but steady acceptance of the 'entity theory' by a series of scholars. Its main characteristics were the conceptual and often legal separation of the firm from its owners (e.g. in corporations), as well as a clear distinction between *capital* and annual *income*, and the emphasis of the latter. Assets were occasionally regarded to be future expenses, and the previous distinction between ownership claims and debt claims may become blurred, as both were now accepted as equities (though with different legal implications). A further characteristic of this theory, as later formulated by Paton, required that interest on debt be considered a distribution of income (cf. Cooper and Ijiri 1983: 195). This is still a point of controversy, as in some European countries not only *interest on debt but also on owners' capital*, as well as the *owners' salaries* (sometimes even corporate taxes), are considered expenses and not distributions of income. This may, indeed, make sense from an economic and management point of view.

The entity theory – though traced back by Littleton [1886–1974] (1933) to the sixteenth century – definitely emerged before the mid-1800s, but gained popularity only after the turn of the twentieth century through Nicklisch [1876–1946] (1903, 1912) and other authors. Sykora (1949: 48–58) regarded this as a materialistic 'one accounts series'. But it fully replaced the proprietary theory only during the *second half* of the twentieth century. Its early representatives were: the Italian Crippa (1838); the Frenchmen J.G. Courcelles-Seneuil [1813–92] (1870) and Jean Dumarchey [1884–1946] (1914); according to Sykora (1949: 52), also the Englishman P. Child (1891); the Americans Folsom (1873) and later William A. Paton [1889–1991] (1922); the Dutchmen Brenkman (1882), van Zanten (1890), Bes (1894) and Kreukniet (1896); the Germans Manfred Berliner (1887, 1893) and, as mentioned above, Nicklisch. Berliner claimed to have pioneered and taught an entity theory as early as 1870 (cf. Littleton 1933: 200). This led to a priority dispute with Brenkman, who actually published five years earlier. Yet unbeknown to both, the entity theory had already a considerable pedigree at this time. Some of its features can be traced to medieval *agency (venture) accounting*, as Littleton (1933: 193–4) pointed out. But the actual pioneering work seems to have been done by Crippa (1838) or even earlier (cf. as indicated by Gomberg 1912: 68–71). Töndury [1883–1937] saw (in its emphasis on '*control*') an intention towards '*generalizing*' accounting (beyond business into *government*, etc.). Hence, he would here include authors usually not regarded to be entity theorists, as the following quote reveals:

> The novelty of this view lies not so much in the fact that beside bookkeeping other branches are called upon, but rather in the meta-notion (*Oberbegriff*)

of accounting and its systematic analysis in accord with the purpose that accounting has to fulfil within the firm .... The formation of this meta-notion, as the totality of accounting control in government and business, has its beginnings in Austrian cameralism [*Staatsverrechnungslehre*] of the 1840s, and from there it found its way into the Italian literature, where it was further developed. We find it already in Villa ... and, above all, in a scientifically profounder form, with Fabio Besta, the founder of the so-called Venetian School, just to name only the two. In the German and French language areas the honour falls upon Gomberg to have been the first to systematically elaborate this view in his *Grundlegung der Verrechnungswissenschaft* (Foundation of Accounting). According to him, accounting falls into six parts: taxation or appraisal (*Schätzungstheorie*), inventory taking, budgeting and planning, bookkeeping, statement presentation, and managerial control.

(Töndury 1933: 97–8, translated from German)

The trend towards generalization may have had even farther implications; it acted as an impetus to the subordination of accounting within the more comprehensive discipline of business economics (*economia aziendale* in Italy, and *Betriebswirtschaftslehre* in the countries of German language; both terms are more comprehensive and, possibly, more appropriate). Finally, one may point out that the controversy between proprietary theory versus entity theory continued until the middle of the twentieth century. The importance of this controversy may have been exaggerated, as Zeff (1978, in his book on the '*orientation postulate*') believed. But few would deny that the needs of modern corporations (with their numerous stockowners, limited liability, transferability of interests and, above all, separation between ownership and management) are better met by the entity theory than its 'proprietary' competitor.

2.6 Other accounting theories

There also existed a series of further theories. For example, several versions of the *value cycle theory* (an extension of transaction analysis), emphasizing the constant transformation of values within the firm as reflected in the various accounts. Käfer (1966: 12–18) listed among its representatives Léon Gomberg [1866–1936] with his main works (Gomberg 1897, 1908, 1912), Harry C. Bentley (1911, see below), and later René Delaporte (1926) as well as Wilhelm Rieger [1878–1971] (1928). Among these, Léon Gomberg – a Russian-Swiss scholar who taught in Geneva, and later became professor in St Gallen – published original and significant theoretical, as well as historical, accounting books in Russian, French and German. Indeed, some scholars consider Gomberg (as confirmed in the above quotation from Töndury) as one of the most important accounting academics of his generation (see also Melis 1950: 791). Schneider (2001: 194) praises the planning and control features as well as the use of benchmark figures in Gomberg's *Verrechnungswissenschaft*, but points out that 'his teaching was not appreciated by the first generation of business economists' (translated). In Germany, the controversy between a series of different *Bilanztheorien* (accounting theories) – often based on different views about the valuation of assets and the realisation of income items, as well as the priority of one financial statement over the other (with an interpretation of the balance sheet as either a collection of stocks or flow residuals) – slowly began in the nineteenth century, but came into full bloom after 1920. Veit Simon [1856–1914], writing the first systematic treaties on limited companies (Simon 1899), was a crucial pioneer in this development. Moxter (1984) praises him highly; Schneider (2001: 941) finds Veit Simon's theory even more advanced than Besta's; and Richard (2005: 75–90) ranks and discusses him in a common chapter together with Schmalenbach and F. Schmidt.

In the beginning the juridical *Bilanztheorien*, that regarded income determination as the major or even exclusive purpose of accounting, were juxtaposed to the non-juridical or *static Bilanztheorien*; the latter were particularly concerned with the valuation of assets and ownership as the central purpose of accounting (cf. Sykora 1949: 184–93). Later, *dynamic* accounting theories, in contrast, emphasized again the *income statement* and income determination. Each of these theories was elaborated during succeeding generations by increasingly sophisticated devices and arguments. The competition between numerous *Bilanztheorien* dominated the scene in Continental Europe (particularly in Germany) for a long time, even beyond the Second World War.

The American Silas S. Packard [1826–98], an educator and a proprietor of a commerce school, was one of the first to promote in the USA a scientific and philosophic approach to accounting (see Packard 1881). Of special significance is the aforementioned Ezra Sprague [1842–1912], a banker, who published on *investment and philosophic issues* of accounting (see Sprague, 1880, 1898, 1904, 1907–08, etc.) and became, together with Charles W. Haskins [1852–1903], a driving force in the promotion of American university accounting *education* (see Haskins 1904). He too became a pioneer of the accounting *profession* in America. Meanwhile, George Soulé [1834–1926], the founder of a private school in New Orleans, concerned himself with the scientific and philosophical foundations of accounting, auditing and business education (e.g. Soulé 1881, 1905). In England it was Pixley (1881) who wrote the first important text on *auditing* (cf. Parker 1969: 145).

2.7 Developments in budgeting, valuation, depreciation and costing

Another prominent accounting scholar to be mentioned is Josef Schrott (1871, 1882), a professor in Vienna, who worked on the scientific foundation of accounting, even taking up the Italian notion of logismography. Above all, he explored the relation between traditional *government accounting* (with its *cameralistic* allocations and the practice of juxtaposing budgeted standards and actual results) with the *double-entry* system of business accounting – considering a possible extension of the former to the latter (Schrott 1852).[17] Regrettably, his important idea of using such an Is–Ought comparison as a *control feature* in business accounting has been neglected until the twentieth century. Schneider, therefore, made the following appropriate remarks:

> Today it is self-evident that a purposeful efficiency control and the improvement of decisions by means of accounting is preconditioned upon an Is–Ought comparison. But to gain this insight, business economics took a roundabout-way: *Schmalenbach* envisages the best possible economic control through income comparison with the past or with similar firms respectively. The notion to introduce an intra-temporal or intra-firm comparison remains far behind of what was already known a quarter century before … . How could it be that such a useful idea, derived from cameralistic accounting, was forgotten and that an unforgivable roundabout-way was chosen?
>
> (Schneider 1981: 124, translated from German)

In the rest of the German language area, it was Richard Lambert [1846–1926] of the University of Leipzig, who became one of the first German professors of accounting and business economics, influencing many prominent scholars of the next generation. Among his students were Heinrich Nicklisch, Balduin Penndorf [1873–1933], Willy Prion [1879–1939], Eugen Schmalenbach [1873–1955], Fritz Schmidt [1882–1950] and others.

Depreciation and valuation problems arose during the nineteenth century in connection with railroads and factories – not only in Germany, but also in England (e.g. Matheson 1884) and America (see below). In referring to the German railway statutes, Seicht (1970: 513–14) pointed out that 'with the successful and frequently cited judgement of the [German] *Reichsoberhandelsgericht* (Supreme Court of Commercial Law) from December 3rd 1873, the *future orientation* of the balance sheet was confirmed, and simultaneously a *capital-theoretic valuation* facilitated' (translated, footnote omitted).[18] Von Wilmowski (1895) also concerned himself with depreciation issues and, in a commentary on the Prussian Income Tax Law (von Wilmowski 1896), anticipated, as admitted by Schmalenbach himself, important aspects of the latter's dynamic accounting.

And Schmalenbach began in several articles (Schmalenbach 1899, 1908–09, 1911–12) to develop his theory of cost-output variability and some basic thoughts that led to his much discussed 'dynamic accounting' (Schmalenbach 1919), and to the later development of his influential *Kontenrahmen* (chart or master chart of accounts – for further details, see Chapter 3).

As to Schmalenbach's costing and pricing theory, it *separated* fixed from variable costs (as Babbage 1827, did before him – see below) and allocated only the *variable costs* to product costs for the purpose of pricing competitively.[19] Contrary to this, German engineers, particularly A. Messerschmitt, promoted the allocation of most cost items on the basis of labour costs. Other notable pioneers of German cost accounting were Ballewski (1877) who considered cost behaviour at different output levels and presented a comprehensive description of a price determination system (cf. Coenenberg and Schoenfeld 1990: 96), and Tolkmitt (1894) who analysed the role of costing for management decision making, and later Lilienthal (1907) who analysed various aspects of cost accounting.

As to the use of 'present values' (i.e. *discounted future* net revenues or cash flows) for commercial-legalistic purposes, it seems to go back to Gottfried W. von Leibniz [1646–1716] or even to Simon Stevin [1548–1620] – cf. Schneider (1981: 279). As for balance sheet presentation, Seicht (1970: 341–8, 511–47) traced the present value (and ultimately the *kapitaltheoretische Bilanz*) back to the Railway Statutes of 1863 and various subsequent commercial legislations in Germany (see above); later to Kempin (1910a) and, in the post-war period, to Heina (1925) and the systematic theory of Rieger (1928).

The concern with valuation and depreciation problems was greatly stimulated through the financial practices of *American* railroad companies. As Chatfield (1996a: 96) pointed out:

> after 1850 a tendency to understate profits began to replace the deliberate overstatement that had characterized the speculative inception of the railroads … [and] by 1880 English auditors had made the write-down of obsolete or damaged goods to 'lower of cost or market' prices a standard procedure.[20]

Such instances indicate concern with *accounting problems of fluctuating prices*, as far as 'modern times' are concerned. Systematic price-level accounting was rarely mentioned before the waning nineteenth century, not even during the *inflationary trend* of the American Civil War. Such concern appeared only in the subsequent post-war deflationary period (of the USA); namely, when the controversy between historical versus *replacement costing* arose from the dispute about '*rate setting*' for railroads. While the railroads argued in favour of the historical cost basis, the Interstate Commerce Commission insisted (during those deflationary times) on '*reproduction cost*' to protect the consumer. Finally, in 1898 the Supreme Court ruled in favour of basing the railroad rates on 'a *fair value* of the property' (cf. Boer 1966: 92–3).

In England too, railroads and other large companies created much interest in valuation and depreciation issues (cf. Lardner 1850 – see below). But even earlier, advances and original thoughts derived in the UK from unexpected quarters. The first idea came from the mathematician and visionary Charles Babbage [1792–1871] who, in his work *On the Economy of Machinery and Manufactures* (1827), showed the need for *distinguishing fixed from variable costs*, and other costing requirements in industrial accounting (cf. Solomons 1968b: 9–10). A second surprise came from the idea of *indexation* for measuring *price-level changes*, which, according to Lee (1996), manifested itself as early as 1836.

Jacques Savary's famous (1675) commentary (to the French *Ordonnance de Commerce* of 1673) introduced the *lower of cost or market principle* (see also Parker 1965; Chatfield 1996c), but afterwards valuation problems were neglected for a long time throughout Europe. An exception was (apart from the indexation just mentioned) Leuchs (1806) who used Savary's principle. Another author was the German Augspurg (1852–55, 1873) who concerned himself with the decline of purchasing power almost half a century before the inflation after the First World War.

Furthermore, Lawrence R. Dicksee [1864–1932], a professor at the University of Birmingham, became famous for criticizing *inadequate depreciation procedures* (see Dicksee 1903) and, even more so, for his books on auditing (Dicksee 1892, 1905). This proved to be a successful bestseller and was the model for Robert H. Montgomery's [1872–1953] even more enduring American auditing text (Montgomery 1912 – another even earlier prominent auditing text was that by Pixley (1881)).

As to zero-based budgeting (i.e. budgeting using a new basis that avoids old preconceptions), Burrows and Syme (2000) point out that the

> origins of the zero-based budgeting (ZBB) concept are traced to [C.F.] Bastable [1855–1945, from Great Britain] (Bastable 1892); that is more than 20 years earlier than extant sources indicate. Then the record shows a proliferation of ZBB thought and practice during the period from 1902 to 1917.

2.8 Further advances, particularly in cost and factory accounting

Henry Metcalfe [1847–1927], an ordinance officer of the American army, wrote one of the first books on *modern cost accounting*, pleading for proper cost assignments through *shop order* and *labour cards* – see Metcalfe (1885). This effort was further extended by Arnold (1899) and Diemer (1900). Metcalfe introduced a *job-order costing* system ('shop order cards'), and tied cost accounting to financial accounting (cf. Vangermeersch 1996). Another American, Frederick W. Taylor [1856–1915], the renowned engineer, yet often maligned father of 'scientific management', made decisive contributions to cost accounting by introducing the setting of systematic work standards and exploiting time studies (see Taylor 1895, 1911). This opened the way to *standard costing*. More concrete ideas for this were presented and elaborated by various cost experts such as G.P. Norton [1858–1939] (1889), who developed a *process costing system, promoting transfer pricing and separate profit centres*. The latter were further refined in the UK by Dicksee (1911). As regards process costing, another Englishman, MacNaughton (1899), and the American Arnold (1899) produced the earliest work, while the contrast to process costing was articulated by Hall (1904) and two Englishmen, Nicholson (1909) and Strachan (1909). Longmuir (1902) also concerned himself with *controlling the cost function* but rejected job costing. Garry (1903) dealt with (what nowadays is called) *volume variances* and *price variances*. Whitmore (1908) proposed that *idle capacity costs* should be charged to a separate account (to be written off); he further developed and clarified the ideas on *standard costing* founded by A. Hamilton Church [1866–1936] (1901–02) who also seems to have first recommended 'production centres'. And Harrington Emerson (1908–09), the American efficiency engineer, wrote his classic on standard costing, which used the *standard hour* as the '*real standard unit cost*', though limiting himself to a single *overall variance* between actual and standard costs.

In the 1880s and 1890s cost and manufacturing accounting received a further boost (particularly in the English-language literature) due to the expansion of railroads (see Pollins 1956; Miranti and Goodman 1996) and other industries with large investments and rising problems with *depreciation, cost allocation, price determination* and *budgeting*. For example, Sir John Mann [1863–1955] (1891, 1904) was arguing in favour of separating overhead costs into selling overheads and production overheads, and advanced a proposal for the use of machine hour rates for cost allocation, already previously suggested by Battersby (1878) who described contemporary cost accounting.

Shortly after the turn of the century, Church (1901–02, see also Vangermeersch 1988) published a series of articles that became 'a standard reference work on one of the most difficult questions of cost-finding' (cf. Solomons 1968b: 25). This work, which developed such ideas as *production centres* and *idle capacity* (and its 'supplementary rate'), ultimately drew attention to the difference between 'normal' vs. 'abnormal' costs, and to the '*scientific' machine-hour rate*. It also influenced Whitmore (1908), another contributor to standard costing, and Harry C. Bentley [1877–1967] (1911) with his sharp observations of contemporary cost accounting practice. The latter was the founder and proprietor of a business college, and is best known for his co-authored bibliographic work (see Bentley and Leonard 1934–35). J. Lee Nicholson [1863–1924], see above, contributed importantly to cost accounting by emphasizing *cost centres* and the *measuring of profits for individual departments* on the basis of machine hours (see Nicholson 1909). He also organized the National Organization of Cost Accountants (later called Institute of Management Accountants).

In the UK, further important contributions to cost accounting were made – quite apart from distinguishing between '*prime*' and '*supplementary*' costs, as well as between short-run and long-run processes made by the renowned economist Alfred Marshall [1842–1924], see Marshall (1890). But, long before this happened, Cronhelm (1818) presented his system, which enabled the determination of '*costs of goods sold*' – though Littleton (1933: 334) as well as Solomons (1968b: 8) were sceptical of some of Cronhelm's claims. Later, the Irishman Dionysius Lardner [1793–1859] (1850) formulated the *cost-output variation* clearer than anyone before him and worked out an elaborate scheme of *cost allocation*. And Goddard (1872–73) exercised a stimulus upon Garcke and Fells (1887), the engineer-accounting team who wrote the well-known book on *Factory Accounts*. This work not only traced the flow of costs through the enterprise but integrated cost accounting with double-entry financial accounting.[21] It also pointed at the futility of overhead cost allocation, and, according to Solomons (1968b: 34), has to be counted among the pioneering achievements of the *marginal cost* school of thought. And Garner asserts that:

> This book by [Garcke and Fells] ... probably had more to do with the advancement of cost accounting practice than any single book ever published ... . Another practising English accountant, G.P. Norton [1889], was one of the first to treat comprehensively the cost problems of a firm using the process cost method.
>
> (Garner 1968: 217–18)

Nevertheless, when it came to such economic concepts as 'opportunity cost and differential cost [they] had remarkably little influence on early cost accounting thought and practice' (Parker 1969: 20). E.J. Smith (1899) pioneered *uniform* cost accounting in the UK. And as to *break-even-charts*, Solomons (1968b: 35) pointed out that 'Sir John Mann knew about it in 1904'. But Ferrara (1996) credits Hess [1864–1922] (1903) with 'the earliest published example' of a break-even-chart. Hess also made decisive steps in budgeting (see also Parker 1969: 62–5). Apart from the early efforts on farm budgeting by de Cazaux (1825), the germ of *flexible budgeting* can be found in the remarkable article by Hess (1903), which contained an interesting graphical treatment for comparison of actual cost with budgeted cost. Here is Solomon's pertinent comment:

> By having a line instead of a point for his budgeted expense, he [Hess] expresses clearly the variability of certain expenses as output varies. His lines are straight lines and represent, therefore, an over-simplified relationship between output and expense. But the harnessing for control purposes of the distinction between fixed and variable expenses which he had earlier discussed in relation to questions of output policy shows Hess to have been well in advance of most of his contemporaries.
>
> (Solomons 1968b: 45–6)

Apart from an earlier article on budgeting by the American engineer H.M. Lane (1897), *fixed budgeting* was presented by Sterling H. Bunnell (1911).

For the French language area during the second half of the nineteenth century (and not only confined to cost accounting) were of particular importance the contributions that Eugène Léautey [1845–?] (1897, 1903) and Adolphe Guilbault [1819–96] (1865) made individually as well as jointly (see Léautey and Guilbault 1889, 1895 – see the review by Colasse 1982; and the biographical study by Degos 2005). The excellent and systematic effort of Léautey and Guilbault (1889, 1895) was designed to represent accounting as a mathematical and scientific discipline. Guilbault (1865) also pointed at the crucial distinction between fixed and variable costs. These two authors revived the French efforts of seventeenth- and early eighteenth-century accountants, such as Mathieu de la Porte,[22] Edmond Degrange Sr and others. Other French authors were Reymondin (1909) with his accounting bibliography as well as Monginot (1854), Mézière (1862) and Courcelles-Seneuil (1867, 1870) who, according to Hernández Esteve (1996: 548), considerably influenced Spanish accounting.

From Spain several authors are notable, for example, Brost (1825) with his book on double-entry bookkeeping, Castaño Dieguez (1863), Salvador y Aznar (1846), Oliver Castañer (1885) and López Toral (1878) who, as previously mentioned, followed the 'logismographic direction' (for other Spanish authors of the nineteenth century, see Hernández Esteve 1999). From Portugal, one may list Magelhães Peixoto (1910) and Ricardo de Sá (1912). In the Netherlands two authors, the above-mentioned Kreukniet (1896, 1898), and also Heykoop (1897) are known to have dealt with accounting and commercial knowledge in general. Meanwhile, in Japan Alexander Shand [1844–1930] produced a Japanese translation of his work (Shand 1873). Another book-translation was presented by Yukichi Fukuzawa's [1834 or 1835–1901], the founder of Keio University and one of the most influential persons in Japanese commercial education, see Fukuzawa (1873 – translated from a book by H.B. Bryant and H.D. Stratton). And Naotaro Shimono [1865 or 1866–1939] introduced his *boki seiri* (Shimono 1895), a typical Japanese version of double-entry (see also Chapter 14). And in China, according to Guo (1996: 123), Cai Xiyong seems to have published in 1905 the first Western style double-entry primer. As to industrial applications of early double-entry accounting and cost accounting in Japan and China, see Kimizuka (1991) and Guo (1982–89, 1996), respectively.

In Russia, apart from some of Léon Gomberg's [1866–1936] early publications, the following authors were prominent in the nineteenth century and most of them also contributed to twentieth-century accounting literature (for details, see Chapter 15): Venediktovich Ezersky [1836–1916], Evstaphiy Evstaphievich Sivers [1852–1917], Adolf Markovich Wolf [1854–1920], Alexander Pavlovich Rudanovsky [1863–1931], Nikolay Sevast'janovich Lounsky [1867–1956], R.Y. Veitsman [1870–1936], N.A. Kiparisov [1875–1956], Nikolay Aleksandrovich Blatov [1875–1942] and Alexander Mikhailovich Galagan [1879–1938] (1912). The article by Sokolov and Kovalev (1996: 508) refers to some of those authors born in the nineteenth century with the following words:

> At first, the writings of the Italian, French and German accountants guided practice in Russia. However, an indigenous crop of accounting writers soon developed. F. Ezersky stressed the importance of a perpetual-inventory system, which allowed for profit determination at various time intervals during the year. S. Ivanov focused on prime costs for 'Cost of Basic Production'. I. Valitsky designed the methodology of both a national and a firm's balance sheet along the lines of current and noncurrent classifications. E. Feldhausen introduced standard costs. L. Gomberg created his own original theory of 'economology', which placed theoretical accounting concepts into the system.
>
> (Sokolov and Kovalev 1996: 508)

2.9 Concluding remarks

In concluding this concise survey of nineteenth-century accounting research and its major authors, I may invoke the view of Amaduzzi (1946: 35), apparently shared by Melis (1950: 790). Amaduzzi mentions that the Italian accounting scholars of the nineteenth century seem to have been more systematic, and their expositions were less fragmentary than those of other countries. But as impressive, scholarly and occasionally highly original the nineteenth-century Italian books on the theory of accounts were, one must not overlook other accounting theories of this period. Apart from this, the many accounting ideas (outside of Italy) cannot be judged on the basis of 'systematic exposition' alone. It is the fruitfulness of new ideas and the pioneering effort (as to valuation, income determination, depreciation, cost accounting, etc.) that ought to be taken into consideration. As to possible limitations of this era, such as the claimed failure to clearly distinguish between capital and income or between capital and revenue expenditures, misconceptions about depreciation and asset accounting, the reader is referred to the discussions in Brief (1965, 1966, 1967).

On the practical side, one may point out that railroad companies and other large enterprises were not the only impetus that accelerated the development of accounting. The second phase of the Industrial Revolution (from 1860 to 1890), with the beginning of mass production, *industrial* capitalism, and the increasing numbers of *joint stock companies* in search of cost control, etc., was the other big impetus.[23]

And in the third phase (after 1890, with the growth of *financial* capitalism), the demand for new commercial legislation as well as higher business education increased even more. Thus, many countries not only had to revise various commercial and industrial *legislations* but were impelled to create, particularly during the 1890s, commerce academies with university status. Many of these institutions were later converted into fully-fledged universities. This in turn promoted research, particularly of accounting, as the main pillar of the new twin disciplines of business economics and business administration.[24]

Above all, the nineteenth century established the major directions of future accounting research. Apart from the struggle for the academic recognition of accounting, the following major tasks became central to the first two or three generations of twentieth-century accounting academics world wide:

  i Theory of 'accounts' and particularly 'accounting theory'.
  ii Ethical problems in accounting and management.
 iii General accounting valuation and the presentation of accounting statements.
 iv Inflation problems and different approaches of solving them.
  v Depreciation and other allocation issues.
 vi Costing, pricing and efficiency tasks.
vii Auditing, standard setting and tax issues.

These were, and still are, among the most basic accounting problems for which solutions are still sought or refined today. Even if the fourth generation (particularly active from the 1950s to the 1970s or 1980s) and the fifth generation (presently active) have had at their disposal more refined mathematical and empirical tools, the foundations to most of the scientific accounting issues were created in the first half of this century and before.

2.10　Appendix

2.10.1　Nineteenth-century accounting scholars with publications on accounting history

Hernández Esteve (1997: 620) points out that:

> The history of accounting is a question which [in the nineteenth century] primarily interests Italian scholars and those of German tongue; the first, possibly because the Italian authors were the ones writing the original texts on this subject; and the second, because Germans always manifested special interest in history.
>
> (translated from Spanish)

But towards the end of the nineteenth century, and particularly in the twentieth century such historical interests spread to England, America and many other countries. As to the topics, Luca Pacioli and his treatise have exercised, and still exercise, particular (perhaps even excessive) attraction upon many authors. But one may wonder whether the more exciting and probably profounder work of Kautilya's *Arthaśāstra* (*c.*300 BC) would have attracted the same attention, had it been unearthed before the twentieth century (see Mattessich 2000: 7–8, 130–49). Yet, apart from Pacioli's work, accounting history has been covering a wide range of topics from highly specialized factual studies about accounting practices in specific institutions (monasteries, governments, private enterprises, etc.) in the Middle Ages, the Renaissance and Modern Times to more *interpretive studies* about the consequences of accounting changes, or even (more recently) about the very beginnings (i.e. in the era BC) of the practice and theory of our discipline.

One important figure here to be mentioned is Werner Sombart [1863–1941], the economist and economic historian. Though not having been an accountant himself, he played a special role in accounting history (Sombart 1902 – see Most 1996: 541–2). The high praise he bestowed upon the double-entry system was rooted in his belief that accounting fulfils a crucial measurement function. He asserted that without it, capitalism could not have achieved its full potential – a controversial claim, which has frequently been challenged (e.g. Yamey 1964). It may be noted that Sombart did not regard accounting as passive; he saw it as an actively participating instrument in bringing about economic change. This particular point has been considerably developed during the late twentieth century by what is known as the British *critical-interpretative school* (the major organ of which is the journal *Accounting, Organizations and Society*). Several of its pundits emphasized that accounting is not (or not only) reflecting reality but, above all, is a tool for bringing about changes in economic and social reality (cf. Tomkins and Groves 1983; Mattessich 1995: 203; and Mattessich 2003b).

The fact is that in the twentieth century, accounting history has become an important academic branch that cannot be neglected. Thus, separate attention ought to be paid to a number of accounting historians (by countries), each with one representative of nineteenth- or early twentieth-century publications (even though some of them may have produced several historical theses). For further bibliographies (though not limited to the nineteenth and early twentieth centuries), the reader is referred to Melis (1950), Klein-Blenkers (1992) and Hernández Esteve (1997). For further historical accounting authors and publications, the reader is referred to the publication by the *Ministero per i Beni Culturale e Ambientali* (1984, Italy).

French language area: Victor de Swarte (1885), Gustave Humbert (1886).

German language area: Jäger (1874), Nirmheim (1895), Lehmann (1895), Schiller (1895), Kheil (1896), Sieveking (1898), Beigel (1904), Strieder (1905), Leyerer (1907), Kempin (1910b), Penndorf (1913).

Hungary: Berényi (1894).

Italy: Bonalumi (1873), Cerboni (1878), Mondini (1882), Gitti (1878), Campi (1879), Barduzzi (1880), Capparozzo (1880), Alfieri (1891), Lanfranchi (1891), Ghidiglia (1895), Vianello (1895), Rigobon (1892), Bachi (1896), Brambilla (1896), Rossi (1896), Vitale (1896), Bariola (1897), Tofani (1910), Massa (1911), Bossi (1917).

Netherlands: Volmer and van Rijnberk (1896), Hagers (1903).

English language area: B.F. Foster (1852), W.H. Fox (1887), Worthington (1895), Brown (1905), A.H. Woolf (1910), Geijsbeek [1872–?] (1914).

Russia: Boiko (1898).

Sweden: Sillén [1885–1965] (1929).

3 German language area

First half of the twentieth century[1]

3.1 Introduction

At various times, the leadership in accounting thought fell to different countries or language areas. During the first half of the twentieth century this leadership was claimed by Germany (for evidence, see section 3.8), just as it was transferred in its second half to the English language area. At a first glance one might have expected Great Britain with its advanced industrial, commercial and financial status, and an unmatched tradition of great economists (Adam Smith, David Ricardo, William S. Jevons, John Stewart Mill and Alfred Marshall) – to take the accounting lead in the early twentieth century. Yet, perhaps the British tradition of training lawyers and accountants in actual practice (rather than at universities) prevented this. Add to this the disdain of many economists and other scholars for commerce and accounting, and you obtain an explanation (cf. Napier 1996).[2]

In Germany, industrialization took place during the second half of the nineteenth century (more than a century behind Great Britain) and was accompanied by developments in original accounting thought. Towards the end of the nineteenth century a series of outstanding personalities arose in Germany, Switzerland and Austria. They combined a sound and practical sense of business with the gift to apply this intuition and knowledge in a logical and scientific fashion to the needs of an ever-increasing industrialization and commerce. Many of these thinkers (including Nicklisch, Schär, Töndury and Penndorf)[3] are hardly known in the English language area. All of these were born in the nineteenth century, but still carry high prestige in continental Europe. Yet, these were just the cream of the crop, and many other names could be added. This array of talents was accompanied and greatly enhanced by the emergence of a series of institutions of higher business education, of university rank. From 1898 to 1910 no less than nine such *Wirtschaftshochschulen* or *Handelshochschulen* were newly founded in the German language area: in Aachen, Leipzig, St Gallen and Vienna (all in 1898), in Cologne and Frankfurt a.M. (1901), in Berlin (1906), in Mannheim (1908) and Munich (1910).

For this period, it is difficult to separate the concern for accounting from that for business studies in general. And it is no coincidence that up to the end of the twentieth century, German accounting was treated as a major and integral part of business economics. Generally, this term is translated as *Betriebswirtschaftslehre*, but *Betrieb* usually means 'plant' or any other place where 'operations' (*betreiben* = to operate) are going on. Thus *Betriebswirtschaftslehre* is not necessarily confined to the study of business activities but may refer equally to non-profit and governmental institutions (cf. Murphy and Most 1959: 5). Furthermore, the German literature distinguishes between *allgemeiner* (general) *Betriebswirtschaftslehre* and various specializations (for banks and financial institutions, transportation, small business, etc.). Schneider, in reference to the birth of *Betriebswirtschaftslehre*, stated:

> The first 'general' Betriebswirtschaftslehre, transcending the framework of commercial techniques, was written by ... *Heinrich Nicklisch* [1876–1946] .... A first useful basis for dispersing this knowledge was created in the text by *Nicklisch* (1912) and to a lesser extent by *Schär* (1911) .... The climax, from a decision logical point of view, was achieved by *Eugen Schmalenbach* within the new scientific community.
>
> (Schneider 1981a: 130–1, translated)

This integration of accounting stands in contrast to the treatment in the English language area, where it assumed a more independent role, and where 'there was no substantive emergence of a body of economic theory relating specifically to business' (Napier 1996: 449). The relative isolation of accounting and law from other business subjects in Great Britain during the first half of the century may originally have created an academic tunnel vision about business subjects, and may have temporarily impeded creative accounting research. But during the second half of the twentieth century, when the need for increasing specialization arose, the more independent status of accounting in the English language area proved to be a boon – a possible factor why German accounting research lost its lead to North America. Despite the German endeavour of integrating all business subjects in a single discipline, 'it was not possible to construct a common theoretical foundation covering all aspects of business economics' (Busse von Colbe 1996: 413). This confirms that the pursuit of such an ambitious goal as that of *Betriebswirtschaftslehre* may have been misconceived, at least in the long run.

A further German feature, shared with other continental European countries, was the strong interest in 'theories of accounts' (*Kontentheorien*) which ultimately led to an intensive occupation with charts and master-charts of accounts (*Kontenpläne* and *Kontenrahmen*). While a third feature, particularly of German accounting, was the emphasis on the balance sheet under the term *Bilanztheorie* (*BT*). The term *Bilanz* may occasionally refer to the *entire* accounting system, to the balance sheet *and* income statement, or to the balance sheet *alone*.[4] It is notable that the German accounting literature of this period included a series of significant publications by foreign authors; for example Gomberg (1908) from Russia, Kovero (1912) from Finland, and Ciompa (1910) from Poland. Similarly, many 'foreign' authors published in the English accounting literature during the second half of the twentieth century for the sake of broader exposure.

In both situations, this is also a manifestation of the prestige of the accounting literature of a specific language.

Fourth and finally, the relationship of accounting to German *codified* law is fundamentally different from that of accounting to the *common* law in America or the Commonwealth countries. Closely connected with such legal aspects is the status of private sector accounting bodies. Thus, in the German language area, professional accounting standards cannot (at least not to the same extent) function as quasi-legal regulation, as they do in countries adhering to the British and American tradition.

3.2 'Accounts' as the centre of theories

The cradle of modern accounting research, in Germany and elsewhere, lies in the nineteenth century (for details, see Mattessich 2003). At the beginning of the twentieth century, German accounting was dominated by a series of competing *theories of accounts*, most of which had their roots in bookkeeping theories of previous centuries. In the German language area of the late eighteenth and early nineteenth centuries the pioneers of the personalistic one-account class theory (see below) were Büsch and Buse, and in the late nineteenth century Scherber, Odenthal and others (see Sykora 1949). In the long run, the most successful theory seems to have been Hügli's materialistic theory of two accounts classes. This was further developed by another Swiss, Schär (1890, 1911, 1914), whose 'closed accounts system' was regarded by Scherpf (1955: 8) as the 'first' chart of accounts in the proper sense.[5] However, in general, accounting practice before the First World War was too liberally oriented to show much enthusiasm for uniform or even semi-obligatory charts of accounts, and many practitioners, as well as academics, held such an undertaking (either in certain industrial sectors or in general) to be unrealistic (cf. Meyerberg 1913). Nevertheless, individual theories of accounts and the rivalry between them flourished, and Holzer (1936) even attempted the axiomatization of theories of accounts classes – though this was hardly an anticipation of the more rigorous axiomatization attempts of accounting theory from the late 1950s onwards. From the point of view of accounting theory, Holzer (1936) seems to have leaned in the direction of Schmidt's organic theory, and against Walb's *finanzwirtschaftliche* theory (see below).

In this maze of competing classification schemes, a major criterion was the distinction between personalistic theories and materialistic (or better, 'non-personalistic') ones. The former tried to identify every account with a person responsible for it, while the materialistic theories derided such an attempt. Another criterion was how many classes of accounts were used. Their numbers originally ranged from one to about five.[6] Many combinations of these two criteria existed. But there were also theories beyond those of mere accounts classification. These, and the classification theories, were variously interpreted by different historians. All are formalistic-classificational, and thus can hardly solve factual problems. Just as there are many equivalent theories of standard logic, so there exist many equivalent systems of accounts classification. However, classification schemes may not be arbitrary when it comes to reflecting the structure and objective of a *specific* firm or part of it. Below we concentrate on the more prominent German names and publications of this period:

1   *Personalistic theories with 'one class of accounts'*: These were based on the shorthand equation $(A - L - OE) = 0$. This was supposed to indicate that all accounts, be they of assets, liabilities or owners' equity, were regarded to be identical counting devices. This theory belonged mainly to the nineteenth century, although von Ullmann (1904) and Kohlmann (1902/05) still propagated it in the twentieth.

2   *Materialistic theories with 'one class of accounts'*: The term 'materialistic' did not imply any empirical-theoretical basis but mainly served to distinguish it from the 'personalistic' theories, indicating that every account represented a real counting device independent of a person. This category, too, was a remnant from previous times, but Novak (1902), Berliner (1909, 1911) and, in a somewhat different form, Seidler (1901) continued to promote it.

3   *Materialistic theories with 'two classes of accounts'*: This was undoubtedly the most successful category, and it had many variations. In one version the basic equation is $(A - L) = OE$, which was to indicate that the accounts of assets and liabilities form one single category, and those of owners' equity form the other. This theory was advanced by Hügli (1900, 1923), Ziegler (1904), Calmes[7] (1906, 1910) and, above all, Schär (1911) who classified transactions into those referring to (1) exchanges of stocks and similar items (*Bestände*), (2) changes affecting the profit and (3) mixed transactions affecting either. He employed a more refined and comprehensive algebraic representation of those transactions.

    Another version, where the equation $A = (L + OE)$ indicated that the asset accounts form one class but the equity accounts (external and internal equities) form the other, was typical of the theories of Ciompa (1910), Nicklisch (1912a, 1912b, 1929–32) and Isaac (1929). A similar and particularly popular version emphasized the capital as a whole (be it 'foreign' or 'owners' capital: value of assets = value of capital). Yet, such an interpretation overlooks that legal claims (whether they are capital from outsiders or owners) are a social *reality*, and not something *abstract* (i.e. unreal or merely conceptual).[8] At any rate, the distinction between liabilities and owners' equity was somewhat diminished. Such a view was advanced by Nicklisch (1912a, 1912b) and further propagated by Osbahr (1913), Becker (1914–15), Geldmacher (1914) and Großmann (1921, 1922), as well as Seidel's (1933) *Bewegungstheorie* (movement theory).[9]

4   *Materialistic theories with 'three classes of accounts'*: Their basic formula was $A = L + OE$, indicating that asset accounts, liability accounts and owners' equity accounts were considered completely separate categories. The representatives of this theory were K. Lehmann (1898–1904), Skokan (1914, 1918), Leitner (1922a) and le Coutre (1924).

There were *further theories* independent of accounts classification: The *historically founded accounts theory* of Buhl (1929a; see also 1929b and 1929c) was, at this time, an interesting attempt to explain contemporary accounting and bookkeeping from an historical point of view. However, in the light of modern archaeological knowledge (cf. Schmandt-Besserat 1992; Nissen *et al.* 1993; Mattessich 2000) such explanations are no longer acceptable.

The *juridical bookkeeping theory* of Kempin (1910a, 1910b) not only emphasized the legal dimension, as its name suggests, but also the oppositional relation between manager and owner. This may have foreshadowed aspects of agency theory which became popular in the 1980s. Another prominent legalistically oriented scholar was Passow (1910), who opposed some legal conventions that promoted exit (sales) values. Enderlen (1936), one of the female authors (rare at the time), put special emphasis on the juxtaposition between the *nominal* versus the *real* balance sheet.

The '*realistic*' theory of Sganzini (1906, 1908) attributed the '*objective* aspect' to the conversion process of money into goods and again into money; while the '*subjective* aspect' became the firm's goal to make a profit through performance of useful services. The distinction between 'calculation [*Rechnungs-*] accounts' (cash, receivables, etc.), on the one side, and 'control accounts' (goods, machinery, plant, etc.), on the other side, played a significant role in this theory. But more importantly, Sganzini's theory anticipated Schmalenbach's *dynamic accounting*, as well as some of its improvements by other authors (see below).[10]

The theory of Gomberg (1908) pivoted on the firm's economic cycle. It emphasized its cause and effect relations in such a way that budgeting, cost accounting and financial accounting worked together. Gomberg (1927) later developed another theory that used a geometric matrix form with separate classes for statistical, juridical and economic events. A Russian-Swiss scholar, he taught first in Geneva and later became a professor in St Gallen; he thus published not only in Russian and French (e.g. Gomberg 1897), but also in German. His major works were in theoretical accounting and accounting history. Gomberg is regarded as one of the most original accounting scholars of his generation (cf. Töndury 1933: 97–8, and Melis 1950: 791). Schneider points out that 'his [Gomberg's] teaching, which could have led directly to the modern approach of business economics, finds no response with the first generation of business economists' (Schneider 2001: 194, translated).

Another scholar from a Slavic country, Ciompa (1910), presented his 'econometric' accounting, based on economic theory which, however, has no affinity with the modern notion of econometrics. It used current replacement costs or, alternatively, (discounted) sales values that enabled a separation of realized from non-realized gains. But unlike Kovero (1912), he did not separate corresponding losses in the same fashion.

As to the so-called *Kreislauftheorie* (cycle theory) of Pape (1920) and the *Zahlungsleistungstheorie* (payments and performance theory) of Walb (1926), both belonged to the two-accounts series: capital goods vs. capital sources in the case of Pape; payments vs. performance in the case of Walb. The former theory was of a static nature and looked at the accounts as 'measurement instruments', while the latter was more dynamically oriented, such that the profit and loss account summarized the performance, and the balance sheet summarized the payments. The double determination of income (in the profit and loss account as well as in the balance sheet) received particular emphasis by Walb.

3.3 Inflation after the First World War and accounting theories

Whereas the theories of accounts classes were derived from the nineteenth century, and were a major concern of pre-war bookkeeping theory, the time between the two World Wars created an entirely different economic situation. In consequence of this, the interests of academic accountants turned to other problems, though the attempt to construct new or defend old theories of accounts continued even into the 1960s and 1970s (e.g. Käfer 1966: 39–68; Seicht 1970a: 66–9). Following the First World War, a major concern in Germany and Austria was hyperinflation and its accounting treatment. Of even greater theoretical interest were the competing *Bilanztheorien* that had slowly developed since the late nineteenth century, and became particularly prominent during the second decade of the twentieth century.

3.3.1 The impact of hyperinflation

The German post-war inflation, including the devastating but relatively short-lived hyperinflation (from about June 1921 to November 1923) and the inflation in Austria (with its hyperinflation phase from about 1918 to 1922), stimulated a host of accounting literature. Thus the works by Prion, Schmalenbach, Schmidt, Mahlberg, Isaac and Haar, among others, attained special recognition.[11] These publications influenced other writers, even beyond the German language boundary, particularly in France and later in America. French accounting experts[12] took up this topic and made further original contributions during and after the subsequent French post-war inflation (from 1925 to 1927) (for details, see Degos and Mattessich 2003). The American Henry W. Sweeney (1927, 1928) also became interested in this literature, while another American, Livingston Middleditch, anticipated by a few years some aspects of that particular German accounting literature. Schneider (1981b: col. 624, translated) characterized the success of inflation accounting as follows: 'The detailed analysis of accounting under conditions of inflation and value-fluctuation, is one of the few achievements in which German business economics attained originality on a world scale'. Later, Schneider (2001: 202) added to these 'original' German contributions another one: cost considerations for minimal pricing (*Überlegungen zu Preisuntergrenzen*).

Mahlberg (1921) initially presented an inflation adjustment procedure based on the medium price of gold (cf. Schneider 2001: 985), but later followed

Schmalenbach (1921), who used what Graves *et al.* (1989) called 'forward indexation'. Schmalenbach's concern with inflation adjustments did not arise from his dynamic accounting (with its bent for *nominal* capital maintenance), but was made reluctantly, and only under the pressure of dangerous inflationary conditions. The concept of forward indexation was designed to adjust income and balance sheet data at year's end to rectify the distortions introduced by an accelerating inflationary process. These distortions referred not only to deceptively high income figures but also to investment, costing and pricing policies of individual firms, as well as a taxation policy that contributed to the further erosion of proper capital maintenance.

As the hyperinflation accelerated, this model had to be improved, be it because of too great a volatility of the purchasing power of money, or too little homogeneity of accounting data, or because of the need for a more generally acceptable solution. Hence, Schmalenbach (1922a, 1925), as well as Mahlberg (1923), considerably extended their models (cf. Graves 1989).

A common confusion to be dispelled about gold-mark accounting is the belief that it had to be based on gold and its price. Schmalenbach (1922a: Section IV) suggested three possible bases: some foreign exchange index (e.g. US$): the price of gold, or some German price index (e.g. the wholesale index). His subsequent discussion did not favour the relatively volatile price of gold, but rather some kind of commodity index or an exchange rate with a stable currency. Schmalenbach (1925) compared the different approaches as follows:

> One compares the value of money as of two different dates, and if those values differ, one places them on an equal footing. Either all values at the end of the period are stated in terms of the value of money at the beginning of the period, or all values are stated in terms of the value of money at the end of the period, or all values are stated in terms of a gold mark . . . .
>
> The method of restating successive period-end values in terms of the same base value has a number of important advantages. It produces comparable results from period to period in regard to details as well as in general. In addition, and this is of utmost importance, it records for future reference the values of certain prices and returns that otherwise are lost in the inflationary spiral . . . .
>
> The method of restating beginning values in terms of period-end values is useful when restatement need not occur regularly, but is required for a particular year. It allows integration of the restatement into the ordinary accounting process, while restatement in terms of gold requires a special calculation of its own.
>
> (Schmalenbach 1925; as translated by Graves *et al.* 1989: 106)

In the same publication, Schmalenbach offered a comprehensive illustration of a gold-mark adjusted accounting system in three different versions: (1) through monthly restatement on the basis of the official wholesale index,

(2) through annual restatement based on the same index and (3) through annual restatement on the basis of the gold index of the *Frankfurter Zeitung*. Although a comparison of the actual results of those alternative approaches showed marked differences, Schmalenbach concluded that those differences had relatively little effect upon income determination.

In contrast to all this stands Schmidt's (1921) work with its current market (replacement value) basis. Despite the fact that it grew out of the need for some kind of inflation adjustment, its basic thrust was towards the shift of individual (instead of general) prices. Such shifts occurred constantly, even under normal operating conditions. Schmidt emphasized this point in the Preface to the third edition:

> Organic accounting emerged in times of devaluation through inflation. But already in the first edition it was stressed, that the position is a fundamental attitude to the problem of value change of any kind as affecting the enterprise.
>
> (Schmidt 1929: ii; third edition of Schmidt 1921, translated)

For Schmidt the information purpose of accounting determined the type of adjustment. Since for him the major purpose was to maintain the production potential of the firm, general price-level adjustments (and other 'index adjustments', reflecting average values) were insufficient (Schmidt 1922a). In a further publication (Schmidt 1922b) he still preferred individual current cost values (*Tageswerte*) for statement presentation, but admitted that price indices proved indispensable in some situations; he opted for specific indices to reflect price variations between different assets to assure correct managerial decisions. Specific indices were still averages (though different for each asset category), and thus did not precisely reflect the productivity shifts within an inflationary economy. Hence, for Schmidt the use of specific indices was merely a preliminary and ultimately unsatisfactory solution. Thus he did not attempt to separate the effect of general inflation from the shift in specific prices (as did Edwards and Bell 1961 – see subsections 3.4.3 and 11.3.1).

3.4 Competing *Bilanztheorien*

Nowhere did the controversy between different accounting theories rage more fiercely than in Germany. There, numerous competing *Bilanztheorien* emerged, and the battle lasted for over half a century, into the 1970s and beyond. The original contestants were the 'static', the 'dynamic' and the 'organic' theories (see below). A series of further theories either constituted new developments or sub-categories of those just mentioned. For example: the *rechtswissenschaftliche Bilanztheorie* (Fischer 1905–08; Rehm 1914); the *Bilanztheorie* of Nicklisch (1903, 1929–32); the *geldlich-wirtschaftliche Bilanztheorie der Unternehmung* (Osbahr 1913); the *finanzwirtschaftliche Bilanztheorie* (Walb 1926, 1948); the *Einheits-Bilanztheorie* (Sewering 1925); the *eudynamische Bilanztheorie*

(Sommerfeld 1926); the *Riegersche Bilanztheorie* (Rieger 1928); the *pagatorische Bilanztheorie* (Kosiol 1944a, 1944b, 1956); the *totale Bilanztheorie* (le Coutre 1924) (for translations, see References).

The differences between all those theories are many, but usually pivot on the issues of valuation and realization; they also depend on the definition of income, as well as on the conception of what is to be the prime function of accounting. Since Schmalenbach's time this also involved the question of which of the two financial statements, the balance sheet or the income statement, should be given priority. In other words, which of the two *functions* should be given primary attention, income measurement or asset and capital measurement? The gaps in the various viewpoints were magnified through increasingly sophisticated arguments by each succeeding generation. Hence the competition between different *Bilanztheorien* also had an impact on other Continental European countries and enhanced the prestige of German accounting theory.

Leitner (1905, 1922a 1923, 1929) stood in high repute for his realistic-empirical approach to accounting, particularly to cost accounting, though today he is less frequently mentioned than other German accounting scholars. Similarly, Hax's (1926, 1948) analysis of the notion of profit and the valuation of the enterprise as a whole, as well as some later publications, have become classics. Another study concerning the value of the entire enterprise was the one by Käfer (1946).

Nicklisch's (1912, 1929–32) '*Multi-Bilanztheorie*' had been called (by Sellien and Sellien 1956: Vol. 2, col. 2073) a closed *universalistic* system. It was based on a comprehensive theory of values. Thus, it was a multi-value approach that, however, may have been more closely related to his notion of business economics in general than to his *Bilanztheorie*. Nicklisch was (with Schär, Osbahr and, to some extent, Schmalenbach) well known for his 'normative-ethical' orientation to business economics and accounting (cf. Mattessich 1995: 173–81). He aimed for a cooperative community within the firm, where not profit or profitability but performance (*Leistung*) and efficiency (*Wirtschaftlichkeit*) were the decisive operational criteria, and where the opposition between 'labour' and 'capital' could be eliminated or minimized. According to Schneider (1981b: col. 625) one can find in Nicklisch's (1921b) early endeavours of combining nominal and physical capital maintenance. Furthermore, he conceived the distinction between the *Bestände Bilanz* (a static point of view) and the *Bewegungsbilanz* (a dynamic viewpoint). This may be why critics may find it difficult to classify Nicklisch's *Bilanztheorie* (for a more detailed discussion of Nicklisch's Bilanztheorie, see le Coutre 1939). Nevertheless, Nicklisch was one of the most prestigious figures of academic accounting and one of the earliest opponents of Schmalenbach's version of the dynamic *Bilanztheorie*.

Although Nicklisch is little known in the English accounting and business literature,[13] Schneider points out that 'until about 1945 *Nicklisch* and *Schmalenbach* assume about equal rank, followed by *Schmidt* and *Walb*, while *Rieger* remains the indignant outsider' (Schneider 2001: 211, translated).[14]

3.4.1 *The* Statische Bilanztheorie

Also traceable to the nineteenth century (e.g. to Hermann Scheffler) is the static or *statische Bilanztheorie* although Walb (1933) found dynamic features in Scheffler's work. The older version of the static theory, presented by such authors as Simon (1910) and Rehm (1914), centred on the *valuation of assets* (as manifested by Hügli 1923, Leitner 1923, and Schär 1911, 1914). The 'newer', more systematic static theories were defended by Pape (1920, 1925, 1933), le Coutre (1921, 1924, 1926, 1939, 1949), Gerstner (1921), Kalveram (1922), Ziegler (1930) and others. Their most prominent representative was found in le Coutre's *totale Bilanztheorie*, which concentrated more on correct *capital valuation* than the valuation of individual assets, emphasizing the use and application of funds. Further emphasis was put on the valuation at acquisition costs, the nominal capital maintenance and the use of a specific as well as detailed classification scheme. More generally, the theory aimed, as its author stated in a later edition, at:

> the question of the practical purpose [*Zweckbestimmung*] of the balance sheet as well as the further development of the theory and form of the balance sheet, which leads us to a total balance sheet, i.e., to a *Bilanztheorie* which represents systematically all relations of the balance sheet to economic life in a formal as well as materially logical accord, i.e., a seamlessly coordinated system.
>
> (le Coutre 1956: col. 1172, translated)

3.4.2 *Schmalenbach's dynamic accounting, and precursors as well as followers*

In sharp contrast to the static conception stands the *dynamische Bilanztheorie*, the major goal of which was profit determination. An early prominent but long-neglected version of it can be found in Sganzini's (1908) *realistische Bilanztheorie* (see above). It not only anticipated the much better known version of Schmalenbach, but also foreshadowed important aspects of the latter's improvements by Walb (1924, 1926, 1948), Geldmacher (1929), Kosiol (1944a, 1944b, 1956) and others.

The basic ideas of dynamic accounting did not originate with Schmalenbach but point to different sources. Schmalenbach himself declared the work of von Wilmowski (e.g. 1895, 1896) as a major inspiration. Seicht (1970a: 100, 146) found other sources, and (apart from a series of nineteenth-century publications by Strombeck, Scheffler, Schüler, Simon, Staub and Wilmowski) pointed at Rehm (1914), Fischer (1905–08), Sganzini (1906, 1908, 1910), Skokan (1914) and Müller (1915). Seicht also emphasized that: 'Although Sganzini's works were published in prominent and for experts easily accessible sources, no author, with the exception of the Swiss Rudolf Borkowsky (1946), mentioned Sganzini and his, seen from a dynamic point of view, sensational theory' (Seicht 1970a: 146, translated).

As to the followers of Schmalenbach's *dynamic accounting* during the *inter-war period*, Sykora (1949: 211) listed Geldmacher, Mahlberg, Haar and Leitner. Further, during the period *after the Second World War*, Seicht (1970a: 137–56) and others regarded Walb's *finanzwirtschaftliche Bilanz* and Kosiol's *pagatorische Bilanz* (see also our Chapter 4) as the major efforts to further develop *dynamic accounting* and to make it formally and materially consistent (though they may not have fully succeeded in doing so).

Schmalenbach's numerous and highly praised contributions to accounting and business, may be classified into the following six areas: (1) His renowned and quite formalistic, yet also controversial *dynamische Bilanztheorie* (which incited numerous counter-proposals by such eminent opponents as Nicklisch, Schmidt and Rieger – and later by Hansen, Honko, Engels, Schneider, Seicht and many others); (2) his various contributions to inflation accounting; (3) his important work in cost accounting and pricing theory; (4) his contributions to the construction and spread of the *Kontenpläne* (charts of accounts) and a general *Kontenrahmen* (master chart of accounts); (5) his work in finance theory; and (6) his endeavours towards the creation of the unifying discipline of *Betriebswirtschaftslehre* (the last two, going beyond accounting, will here not be detailed).

The basic feature of Schmalenbach's *dynamische Bilanztheorie* was a strong emphasis on profit determination, mainly for the purpose of efficiency control. Assets and equities at year-end were for him merely *residuals* (arising from the flow of expenses and revenues) claiming that their values reflected reality in any sense. This has often been misinterpreted, particularly by authors who believed that Schmalenbach preferred the income statement to the balance sheet.[15] But a careful reading of Schmalenbach's *magnum opus* shows that this is not the case. On the contrary, Schmalenbach stated that:

> by analysing the various entries in the cash-book and making up a profit and loss account from them [i.e. in the simplest case from a cash-book], is to making himself a great deal of unnecessary work. He would achieve his goal much quicker if he would forgo his profit and loss account and allow his balance sheet to give him the information he requires.
>
> (Schmalenbach 1959: 42–3, translated by Murphy and Most)

Thus, Schmalenbach assigned to the *Bilanz* a dynamic instead of a static task. To relegate income measurement only to the balance sheet instead of the income statement, and to deny the former the task of measuring stocks at year-end, appears perplexing; and regarding the balance sheet with its stock variables as something 'dynamic' seemed absurd. Even many scholars in the German language area, as for example, Rieger or Seicht, have criticized this particular feature:

> To summarize, one can say that Schmalenbach leaves the proof open for the alleged 'unscientific status' of dualism [i.e. the notion that accounting can

properly determine income as well as capital or asset values], but that he himself was highly 'dualistically' oriented. Apart from that, Schmalenbach ought to have recognized that his 'dynamic' accounting differs from static interpretations only in the valuation, in the definition of the asset concept, and the manner of periodization, and that the determination of a 'comparable' profit can be secured, in the long-run, only through separation of profit [*Gewinnspaltung*] but not by an unnecessary abuse of the balance sheet.

(Seicht 1970a: 325, translated)

This contradiction may be even more puzzling to the British and American reader. Yet only a comparison between both, the German and the English linguistic practice, can explain the ultimate reason behind this potential confusion (see above). Thus, by stressing income determination (rather than stock valuation) at the year-end – particularly, when the term *Bilanz* is seen as referring to financial statements in general – it may be easier to understand why Schmalenbach regarded the *Bilanz* as a 'dynamic' instrument. The more so as both statements are capable of measuring income. However, several authors (Seicht 1970b: 97, 118; Engels 1962: 201) did not regard Schmalenbach's approach as genuinely dynamic.

A related explanatory feature of his theory was Schmalenbach's belief that 'correct' income measurement was irreconcilable with 'correct' stock valuation. This 'monistic' view was criticized and refuted by Schmidt (1921) and other scholars who favoured a 'dualistic' approach. Schmalenbach (1959: 34) admitted that: 'In my experience, when business economists disagree about accounting methods, the difference of opinion arises because the disputants have different objectives in mind'. This crucial insight may offer a hint that Schmalenbach may not have considered the entire range of possible accounting objectives, however, he did consider periodic income measurement (guided by the matching principle), income comparability between different periods, controlling the conduct of business (operating efficiency), accountability and ascertaining profit shares. Could these objectives have been attained only by his brand of dynamic accounting?

An interesting difference between Schmalenbach's dynamic *Bilanztheorie* and British or American accounting theory is the fact that Schmalenbach included (in the earlier editions of *Dynamische Bilanz*) an implied interest on owners' equity as well as implied owners' salaries under expenses (*Aufwand*), thus reducing the income figure. This makes sense from a managerial point of view, though less from one of traditional financial accounting. Later editions omitted these and other features, probably to conform more to pertinent legislations – a reason why Schneider (2001: 203) speaks of a 'dilution' of the dynamic income notion. It is because of such dilutions that, from a practical point of view, Schmalenbach's dynamic accounting has become less controversial as time went on.

As far as valuation is concerned, Schmalenbach, who was a highly pragmatic person, accepted various valuation bases for different asset categories.

This multi-value approach was rooted in historical costs (originally *without* the lower of cost or market value principle), with the possibility of *general* price-level adjustments during inflationary times (see above). Engels pointed out that 'Schmalenbach uses current values, historical values, and fixed values, without any visible principle... Schmalenbach does not succeed in demonstrating the variety of his valuation approaches as a manifestation of a leading principle' (Engels 1962: 200, translated). Schmalenbach himself asserted that 'as a rule, a reliable valuation approach is to be preferred to a theoretically correct one based on uncertainty and arbitrariness' (Schmalenbach 1956: 187, translated). Yet despite this apparently tolerant and pragmatic wisdom, he refused to accept Schmidt's current value basis, and never admitted its ability to generate a relevant valuation of assets concomitantly with correct income determination. He regarded Schmidt's current value accounting as fragmentary and unsystematic (Schmalenbach 1925: 161; cf. Graves *et al.* 1989: xviii) and criticized its lack of *general* inflation adjustment. Indeed, the failure to combine his current value accounting with general price level adjustments may have been the greatest weakness of Schmidt's approach – it seems Edwards and Bell (1961) were the first to achieve this (real-current value model) fully and most elegantly.[16] Schmalenbach also rejected the present value method for financial statement presentation (except for some depreciation purposes), but accepted it outside the double-entry scheme, mainly for the total valuation of the firm (Schmalenbach 1917–18).[17]

Finally, variations and extensions of the *dynamische Bilanztheorie* were developed by Mahlberg (1923), Geldmacher (1923, 1929) and others. The most important of these were Walb's (1924, 1926, 1948) *finanzwirtschaftliche Bilanztheorie* as well as Kosiol's (1944a, 1944b) *pagatorische Bilanztheorie*.[18] Schmalenbach's student Ernst Walb was his first major successor who developed his dynamic theory in a consistent way. He shifted from Schmalenbach's emphasis on the balance sheet (as the major means for determining income) to a better recognition of the profit and loss account as an alternative and equal partner. For example:

> Hence this presentation shows that accounting ... possesses the possibility to represent income in two ways: once through recording the money value or price of the exchange-effective performances [*erfolgswirksamen tauschwirtschaftlichen Leistungen*] per se, and alternatively through recording of the payments that result from them.
>
> (Walb 1926: 45, translated)

Walb no longer concentrated mainly on the performance stream (*Leistungsstrom*), but tended to give greater emphasis to the financial flow (*Einnahmen/Ausgaben*) that went into the opposite direction – cf. the graphic comparison of le Coutre's balance sheet scheme with that of Schmalenbach, as depicted in Seicht (1970a: 143). One is almost inclined to see in Walb's (1926) work an endeavour to turn the balance sheet into a flow of funds statement (something first developed in British and American accounting during the second half of the nineteenth century – though within a separate financial statement), and to which le Coutre might also have aspired. Another interesting aspect of Walb's work is his consideration of the different variations of capital maintenance and their impact on the determination of income (cf. Schneider 2001: 1004).

3.4.3 Fritz Schmidt's organic accounting theory, and followers

The personalities of the two giants of German accounting were no less opposite than were their views. Schmalenbach, a most charismatic person, came from a humbler house than did Schmidt. The former was eminently practical (more problem-oriented, but less a system builder); willing to consider compromise solutions. The latter had a theoretical vision hardly matched by any other accountant of this period in the German language area; he also was less amenable to compromise. While Schmalenbach was lionized during his lifetime, and his influence was felt deeply in continental Europe during several decades, Schmidt received somewhat less regard during his lifetime. He anticipated the theory of Edwards and Bell (1961) and thus obtained great attention in British and American accounting – though decades after his death. Indeed, during the 1970s and 1980s accounting standards and quasi-legislations were proposed or implemented in Great Britain, the United States, Australia, Canada and New Zealand that realized in practice important aspects of Schmidt's basic ideas. This holds particularly for the *current value* approach of the Financial Accounting Standards Board (FASB 1979).

Schmidt tried to develop an accounting and valuation theory that is 'organic' from the viewpoint of connecting the individual firm with the national economy in general. Hence, his theory was intended to mitigate the business cycles instead of reinforcing them through distorted accounting valuations (as, according to his view, historical costs would do). Schmidt's concern with business cycles became more intensive with time. While the first edition of this book (in 1921) does not provide any separate chapter on this topic, the last and third edition (in 1929: 325–53) devotes over 27 pages to the subject of '*Bilanz und Konjunktur*' (see also Schmidt 1927a). Above all, he aimed at a theory that would supply 'correct' balance sheet values as well as 'correct' income values:

> such correctness is only attainable through proper asset valuation. We have to insist on the most rigorous distinction between operating profit, on one side, and capital increase or decrease, on the other side. Schmalenbach acts in his income determination essentially in the same way as we would do; but he deprives himself of the great advantage (for a proper economic measure of the firm) by rejecting a quantitatively clear representation of balance sheet valuation [*Vermögensrechnung*]. Thus he is forced to strongly push into the foreground the notion of comparability, i.e., the

comparison of individual periodic results, and where there are doubts, to prefer comparability over correctness ... we [however] will then be able to compare correct income with correct capital value, and determine the profitability of the pertinent period.

(Schmidt 1921: 55–6, translated)

Another essential merit of Schmidt's theory (1921) lies in his pursuit of physical capital maintenance – though his distinctions between realized vs. unrealized gains, and real vs. fictitious gains cannot match the more precise distinctions of Edwards and Bell (1961) (see subsection 12.3.1 in this book, and Mattessich 1986, 1995: Chapter 7). Schmidt's treatment of such distinctions was inadequate despite the fact that he may have been the first modern scholar to distinguish between business profit (*Umsatzgewinn*) versus some holding gains (his *Spekulationsgewinne*). This is a merit; but apart from an unfortunate terminology, his formulation is insufficient and leads to serious problems. Surprisingly, 'holding' gains are for Schmidt non-existent; though they do arise, they are no 'real' gains (Engels 1962: 204, translated). The situation is hardly better when it comes to the distinction between monetary vs. non-monetary gains. To circumvent a careful analysis of this problem, Schmidt chose a shortcut and recommended keeping accounts receivable and accounts payable in balance, thus avoiding such gains or losses. Had he incorporated into his system the changes in market values (i.e. had he distinguished between monetary vs. non-monetary gains or losses), his conceptual apparatus would have been greatly enriched. This could have created many important insights (e.g. to distinguish better between correct and incorrect investment decisions *ex post*).

Since Schmidt did not explicitly recognize value changes of non-monetary assets as income or losses, these changes were recorded in a *Wertberichtigungskonto* (value adjustment account) as a part of total owners' equity. In contrast to Schmalenbach's monism, Schmidt's dualistic view asserted the possibility of representing 'realistic' values in balance sheet as well as income statement simultaneously (cf. Clarke and Dean 1996: 517).

Schmidt's organic current value theory has also been regarded (by Schwantag 1951) as a sophisticated extension of Ciompa's (1910) theory based on sales prices; or, even more appropriately (by Sykora 1949: 220), as an extension of the replacement cost theory of Kovero (see subsection 13.1.1). The outstanding work of Kovero (1912) promoted the use of current or replacement values (and recognition of unrealized gains as well as losses, though under strict separation from realized gains or losses), thus anticipating crucial aspects of Schmidt's (1921) *organische Bilanztheorie* (as well as of the *Bilanztheorie* of the Dutchman, Theo Limperg, 1917). However, no edition of Schmidt's book on the organic *Bilanztheorie* seems to refer either to Kovero's or to Limperg's work. Yet, Schmidt did defend his theory in a Dutch paper (Schmidt 1923b) – be it because of Limperg's belligerent attitude (see also subsections 13.1.1 and 13.2.1, as well as note 2 of the Introduction) or for other reasons. Limperg's claim that Schmidt neglected the larger picture of the business was refuted repeatedly (e.g. Clarke and Dean 1990). Besides, Schmidt (1927a) even showed that the application of current values in accounting may have a wider and beneficial economic effect on business cycles of the economy as a whole.[19] Clarke and Dean (1996: 518) even suspected here an influence of the early nineteenth century American economist Charles Carey.

Variations of Schmidt's *organische Bilanztheorie* might be those by Großmann (1921, 1922), Isaac (1924, 1929) and others. Sommerfeld's (1926) *eudynamische Bilanztheorie* also emphasized profit determination, though its major goal was maintenance or even increase of the physical productive capital by means of special reserves. Thereby, to keep up with technological innovations; and the overall economic growth became important, no less than precautions taken against sudden shifts in value or other critical events. As this theory arose out of the inflationary experience, it stressed valuation in gold-mark, as well as in real or quantitative, measures (e.g. with debts, etc. to be discounted to the closing date). It did not consider non-realized and windfall gains (*nichtrealisierte Konjunkturgewinne*) as genuine profit. A 'dividend reserve' was supposed to secure an even return on capital (cf. Sykora 1949: 225–30; and Wagenhofer 1986: 34–5), similar to some American attempts of smoothing the income stream over time.

Sewering's (1925) *Einheits-Bilanztheorie* suggested the use of market sales values (*Veräusserungspreise*). It may have anticipated valuations similar to those promoted by Rieger.[20] But, in turn, it may have been anticipated by such scholars as Pantaleoni, Fischer and Pape. Furthermore, in criticizing the *Bilanztheorie* of Schmidt for not going far enough, Sewering proposed not merely price-adjustments of individual items (as Schmidt did), but also a *general* inflation adjustment. His ultimate goal was to reconcile the contrasts of the static and the dynamic aspects in a *unified* theory that adapted the valuation approach to the particular momentary economic situation of the firm (a kind of purpose-oriented or relative valuation, which he recommended particularly for fixed assets). Hence, Sewering's theory emphasized physical capital maintenance and, similar to Edwards and Bell (1961), attempted a proper treatment of different kinds of capital gains (real and fictitious, monetary and non-monetary, etc.) in income or reserve (surplus) accounts. This attempt may even be regarded as having foreshadowed some aspects of the theory of clean surplus that became so prominent during the 1990s in American accounting research.

3.4.4 *Wilhelm Rieger's nominal accounting conception*

Wilhelm Rieger (1928) tried to avoid the expression 'theory' in accounting, preferring in its place the German word '*Versuch*' (attempt).[21] For him bookkeeping transactions reflected a constant process of money transformation in which, by his definition, *Aufwand* (expense) always was in equilibrium with *Ertrag* (revenue). He also regarded the closing balance sheet as reflecting a kind of fictitious liquidation of the firm (as previously asserted by von Ullmann 1904). This *nominale* approach considered the financial statements as a purely monetary calculation (*Geldrechnung*). Rieger was sceptical towards all valuation methods, none of which he considered as being correct, except the case of liquidation into cash at the end of the firm's life cycle. He even declared that 'precise valuation is something that goes beyond human capacity' (Rieger 1928: 234, translated). Schmidt had already come to a similar conclusion in 1921:

> the following investigation proves how impossible it is to solve the value problem if one insists on a viewpoint that illuminates the question exclusively within the framework of a single firm.
>
> (Schmidt 1921: 35, translated)

And yet, Rieger had a preferred value notion, the '*heutige Wert*' (today's value) which, however, did not refer to the current or replacement value but to a discounted future sales value. This was interpreted variously in the German literature. According to Schneider (1981b: col. 623; 2001: 215–16) Rieger might have followed in the tracks of such scholars as Fischer (1905–08, 1909), Pantaleoni (1909) and Pape (1925). According to Sykora (1949: 233), on the other hand, there might have been a relation to Sewering's (1925) theory. But since for Rieger the balance sheet was forward looking (in contrast to book-keeping which looked backward), some might regard him as having foreshadowed the *kapitaltheoretischen* (present value) approach, introduced to accounting particularly by Canning (1929) in the US, and perhaps anticipated by Enderlen (1936) (Schweitzer 1972: 181).[22] It may be surprising that Rieger saw no need for a profit and loss account, although he admitted its usefulness as a statistical summary. The fact that the profit and loss account can be dispensed with (by shifting its functions to the owners' equity account), contradicts the view of such American authors as Littleton and Zimmerman (1962: 47) and others who regard it as an essential ingredient of any double-entry system.[23]

In Rieger (1930) one finds heavy opposition to Schmidt's (1921) organic replacement cost theory, and in his later work (Rieger 1936), an entire book is devoted to the refutation of Schmalenbach's dynamic accounting. Indeed, Rieger's own theory is less well known than his criticism of others. He drew wide attention to the weakness of Schmalenbach's theory (that insisted on the *dynamic* nature of such a *static* tool as the balance sheet) with words like this: 'It still remains a mystery how one should recognize from a point of time [*Augenblick*], a movement which is supposed to have taken place between several such time points. There, even the best of endeavours fails' (Rieger 1936: 21, translated). Rieger was taken to task because his critique of Schmalenbach's theory appeared just at a time when Schmalenbach (whose wife was Jewish) had increasing difficulties with the National Socialist regime. However, the persecution of Schmalenbach (and his hiding) during part of the war, did not extend to his work. The latter remained in high regard among practitioners, scholars and students alike. Either his prestige was so high that the National Socialists did not want any publicity about his official 'disgrace' or, less likely, they did not take accounting theory seriously enough to persecute his work.

3.5 Charts and master charts of accounts and state interference

Schär's (1911) original idea of a chart of accounts may have experienced a set-back due to the First World War, but afterwards the economic climate was all the more receptive to it. Even during the war some trade associations became interested in this idea, and in 1921 the *Ausschuß für wirtschaftliche Fertigung des Vereins Deutscher Ingenieure* (Committee for Economic Production of the Association of German Engineers) published a basic chart for cost determination. Subsequent discussions and further charts can be found in Calmes (1920: 159; 1922: 48) and a series of lesser known authors.

Once inflation was mastered after 1923, renewed interest in the construction of charts of accounts arose, partly out of the legacy of the theories of accounts, partly out of greater receptivity for Government intervention. This interest in charts of accounts was greatly stimulated by the publication of Schmalenbach's (1927, 1938) *Kontenrahmen* (master chart of accounts), partly due to new ideas introduced by its author, partly to his immense prestige. The novelty was mainly found in the introduction of a new class of 'neutral accounts', and the separation between *Ausgaben* (expenditure as cash flow), *Aufwand* (expenses; for financial accounting) and *Kosten* (costs; for managerial accounting). But other features made the master chart an influential tool. For example, short-term profit calculation, permanent inventory, decentralized organization, interconnection between financial and cost accounting, the transgression beyond double-entry into statistics, the separation between time costs and unit costs, and the inter-comparison of plants and enterprises. This interest in charts of accounts was officially promoted after 1933 when the state-regulated economy of the Nationalist Socialist regime took over. As to the events between 1933 and 1945, Schmalenbach made the following remark:

> But then, during the time of Hitler's regime one adopted my somewhat modified master chart of accounts as an obligatory master chart. This was, from an economic point of view, a mistake even in a dual sense ... . First, this method makes only sense if one can expect equal advantages of inter-firm comparison in all economic branches ... . Second, one should interfere ... in a free market economy only where it is urgently required.
>
> (Schmalenbach 1948: 61, translated)

The quest for charts and master charts of accounts (and their improvements) continued in Continental Europe after the Second World War. For example, Kosiol (1944c, 1962) and Mellerowicz (1949) addressed German charts of accounts, Illetschko (1947) the Austrian one, Käfer (1947), Lohmann (1948), as well as Kosiol (1948) discussed those used in Switzerland and Lohmann (1950) dealt with the master chart of France.

3.6 Cost accounting and its contributions

The German tradition of cost accounting goes back to the eighteenth and nineteenth centuries,[24] and was faithfully continued into the twentieth century. Apart from the numerous contributions of Schmalenbach (1899, 1908–09, 1924, 1925, 1948, 1956 – see also Lorentz 1926), other authors contributed greatly. For Germany, Leitner (1905, 1922a, 1922b, 1923, 1929) seems to have offered the first comprehensive and systematic analysis of cost accounting. He stood in high repute for his realistic-empirical approach to accounting, particularly to cost accounting. Lilienthal (1907) described the application of cost accounting to a major firm, and the *Verein Deutscher Maschinenbauer* (Association of Mechanical Engineers) surveyed the entire industry of engine equipment production as to pertinent costing procedures (cf. Coenenberg and Schoenfeld 1990: 97). Although the procedures described were predominantly technical, one attempted to base the overhead allocations (to departments and products) on causal principles. The labour cost basis still seems to have been predominant, but some authors, including Brunier (1908), were sceptical regarding its accuracy and relevance.

Many authors contributed to the literature on cost, factory or industrial accounting.[25] But to comprehend the major developments in German cost accounting, a look at the formal definitional framework of costs, cost theory, system structure and applications seems to be necessary.

3.6.1 Expenditures, expenses and costs

In twentieth-century Germany, more than elsewhere, one discussed intensively basic definitions; and there exists a broad literature on cost notions until the 1970s. At the beginning of the century, one was increasingly concerned with a clear separation between financial and cost accounting – probably more than in Anglo-American countries. Heinen (1959: 97–120; 1965: 19) distinguished four (more or less chronological) important steps in this development: (1) equating expenditures (*Ausgaben*) with costs (*Kosten*); (2) equating expenses (*Aufwand*) with costs; (3) differentiating between expenses and costs; and (4) further differentiation in the treatment of costs. He made the following remarks:

> The development of cost accounting [footnote omitted] finds, first of all, its expression in the change [*Wandel*] of the cost notion. Beside this, the development is characterized by a more refined costing approach. The perfection of the procedures serving the determination and allocation of costs, as well as a change in the goals of cost accounting, are manifestations of this evolution. Particularly in recent times, has cost accounting increasingly

been converted to an instrument for the steering of plants [*Betriebe*] and firms [*Unternehmungen*].

(Heinen 1965: 19, translated)

The first step arose out of the practice in trade, where it seemed appropriate to equate costs with expenditures (cf. Leitner 1922b: 64–75; Nicklisch 1939). In the second step one recognized the necessity to differentiate between cash flows and expenses in periodical accounting, or as was the case with Walb (1926), Geldmacher (1923) and Schmidt (1950: 197), to equated costs with expenses in order to have a single uniform (homogeneous) accounting system within a company.

However, Schmalenbach (1919b and later editions) and M.R. Lehmann (1925: 35–74) emphasised the independence of cost accounting in order to control the internal production processes. Thus, the clear separation between the following three categories (also reflected in his master chart) became crucial for Schmalenbach's costing approach: (1) receipts and expenditures (for cash flows) vs. (2) revenues and expenses (for financial accounting) vs. (3) performance (*Leistung*) and costs (for cost accounting). There were costs (for example, for the activity and the buildings of the owner) without being expenses, on the one side. On the other side, there were expenses (for example, for donations or for interest payments) that were not caused by the production process, and therefore not considered to be costs. This led to an articulate conceptual apparatus with such terms as 'neutral expenses', 'neutral costs', etc., characterizing expenses that were not simultaneously costs, and costs that were not simultaneously expenses. Schmalenbach used in his cost accounting system completely different valuation principles (marginal costing) than in his dynamic balance sheet (acquisition costing). Hence, a reconciliation or adjustment of these notions became necessary; and this he executed in his master chart. Only during the last decade of the twentieth century could one observe a return to simpler and more universal costing notions in the German language area. Then, influenced by globalization and financial concepts with greater cash-flow orientation, the connections between cost accounting, financial accounting and investment theory, moved into the foreground.

3.6.2 *The theory of costing*

In Germany, cost theory was a central issue of research during the entire twentieth century. The objectives were to determine the cost-causing factors and the cost functions. From the very beginning, two different sources fed costing research. The first was based on economic theory (e.g. von Stackelberg's 1932, cost-theoretical research), which derived the cost curve from the production curve, based on the law of diminishing returns (Möller 1941: 10–18). The second direction relied on the traditional cost functions, based on the direct relationship between costs and their causes. For the representatives of this view the major problem of cost accounting consisted in a 'quasi-mechanistic' presentation of the relations between the magnitude of total costs of a business and the degree of capacity utilization (Schmalenbach 1919a). As a yardstick for measuring the capacity, the degree of employment (*Beschäftigungsgrad*) was used (cf. Heinen 1965: 21).

Both the law of 'diminishing returns' approach, as well as the 'direct' approach, worked with an S-shaped total cost function. But some authors were opposed to this assumption (e.g. Rummel 1939; Walther 1947: 225–55) and preferred to work with linear cost functions. Henzel (1939: 120–4; 1941: 29–170) even refused to recognize any direct relationship between costs and capacity utilization, but emphasized other costing bases like idle machine time (see also Henzel 1941 – for the subsequent German development in cost theory and production theory, see Chapter 4).

3.6.3 *Cost systems and applications*

Some of Schmalenbach's ideas are still important; for example, his proposal for a basic data bank (*Grundrechnung* – in Schmalenbach 1948) that could be used for a variety of different objectives. This idea influenced later the design of computer-based accounting systems. According to Schweitzer (1995: 37) the 'basic accounting system would have to be constructed in a way independent of [the] objective, yet in a way that allows its data to be evaluated for all possible purposes'.[26]

To refine cost allocation procedures, Rummel (1934, 1939) presented his *Blockkostenrechnung* (block cost accounting). He worked with linear (proportional) cost functions for different variable costs. By doing so, he expected more relevant product cost allocations. Seicht summarized this approach as follows:

> The principle of 'block cost accounting' hence consists of a strict separation of the '*quantitative-proportional*' from the '*time-proportional costs*', whereby the 'quantitative-proportional' costs are being directly allocated to the cost bearers [products], while the 'time-proportional' costs remain undistributed and are collected in a block. To achieve this, Rummel differentiates between five categories.
>
> (Seicht 1977: 70, translated)

These categories were: (1) purely time-proportional costs; (2) purely quantitative-proportional costs; (3) costs that were originally not proportional but could be converted by certain means (other than 'planning'); (4) costs that were made proportional by 'planning'; (5) costs that were collected and allocated as a fixed cost block.

Seicht (1977: 55–72), who discussed Rummel's approach in some detail, suggested that his work pointed in the direction of 'direct costing' (also called 'variable' or 'marginal costing'). Although this claim has been raised in favour of various authors – who may have contributed individual steps towards it – the strongest evidence points to America (see Green 1960: 218–26; Weber 1966), as confirmed by Schneider:

> The thought to charge exclusively proportional [variable] costs to unfinished and finished products, emerges first in the American accounting literature after the world economic crisis from 1929 onwards, for reasons of a more 'cautious' valuation of inventory. After World War II, it is being discussed in the American literature in different variations as 'direct costing'.
>
> (Schneider 2001: 596, translated)

German cost accounting was primarily based on realized data, and estimated costs were not used for planning and control before the Second World War. In Germany, standard costing was first presented by Michel (1941) – though this development was pre-empted by the British and American literature (see also Weber 1966 and Mattessich 2003).

Schmidt did not contribute to cost accounting to the same extent as did Schmalenbach or other scholars, but in some of his studies Schmidt (1930a, 1930b, 1931a, 1931b) made contributions to costing issues, as for example on multi-step income statements (cf. Weber 1966: 24–8). His major concern was: 'to show the futility and even danger of distributing fixed overheads and expenses; of not separating them from the fluctuating overheads and expenses, and placing them in incorrect positions in a statement of costs and earnings' (Schmidt 1931b: 40).

The structure of cost accounting depends on its objectives and its decision usefulness. In Germany, this manifested itself in two pricing problems, the determination of sales prices and of transfer prices (*Verrechnungspreise*). Although full (or absorption) costing prevailed before the Second World War, some scholars recognized that the selling price of a product could not always be based on full (absorption) costs. Schmalenbach suggested using marginal costs as a pricing basis as long as full capacity was not reached. Under S-shaped cost curves, low prices will improve employment and capacity utilization, while high prices will avoid over-employment (*Überbeschäftigung*). Thus depending on the cost curve, such a pricing policy should lead to an optimal employment policy:

> Hence Schmalenbach proposes in 1899 to open for every customer besides the 'legal account' a 'cost account' [*Kalkulatorisches Konto*], whereby the legal account is to be charged with the agreed price, and the cost account with the actual one [footnote omitted]. In this way Schmalenbach wanted to carry out a cost calculation within the framework of accounting.
>
> (Seicht 1977: 15, translated)

Other proposals by Schär (1914: 263–77), Kosiol (1931), Peters (1927: 117–26), Boßhardt (1948: 78–82) and Müller (1949: 92–9) were based on the separation between fixed and variable costs. Thus their basic idea may even have pointed towards direct costing. But they did not take the decisive step to develop it, perhaps due to their use of non-linear cost curves.

The separation of fixed from variable costs is also important for transfer prices. In his 1908–09 work on transfer pricing, Schmalenbach applied von Wieser's (1884) marginal theory to cost accounting. He thus anticipated the principle of shadow pricing of linear and non-linear programming. Some authors see in this application (apart from such feats as Schmalenbach's dynamic accounting, his interpretation of depreciation, etc.) the first truly theoretical reflections of our discipline (e.g. Schneider 2001: 195–6).

Schmalenbach's cost accounting and his system of *pretiale Wirtschaftslenkung* (i.e. transfer pricing and proportional costing) is regarded as having anticipated direct costing, decentralization and other achievements that were also realized in America. Schmalenbach admitted that:

> In general, one may say the investigation is still at the very beginning as to the extent to which the practice of transfer pricing [*pretiale Lenkung*] has actually been applied and how successful it was … I am expecting an advancement in this direction as soon as some experienced public accounting firms would take American firms as an example and adopt transfer pricing.
>
> (Schmalenbach 1948: 17, translated)

3.7 Publications on accounting history (1900–50)

During the first half of the twentieth century, German scholars used to be ranked second, after the Italians, in *historical* accounting research (cf. Hernández Esteve 1997: 620). Early examples were K. Lehmann's (1895/1968) historical development of the public limited company (*Aktiengesellschaft*), and Sieveking's (1901, 1902, 1905, 1909) research into Italian accounts books of the Renaissance and of the Medici's, from Genoa, Venice and elsewhere. Other German accounting historians of this period were Beigel (1904), dealing with bookkeeping in ancient Rome; Strieder (1905), analysing the inventories kept by the house of Fugger; and Kheil's (1906) treatise on Benedetto Cotrugli from Ragusa (now Dubrovnik) (the first to write, though not to publish, on double-entry bookkeeping, thus anticipating Pacioli by more than three decades). Furthermore, Leyerer (1907) also dealt with the books of the Republic of Ragusa and later wrote on the historical development of bookkeeping; Kheil (1908) discussed the emergence of the 'American Journal' in France; and Penndorf (1913) wrote a history of German accounting.

For the inter-war period, the following names and publications are worth listing: Leyerer's (1919, 1922) historical studies on bookkeeping; Isaac's (1923) development of business economics in Germany; Lion's (1928b) and Walb's (1933) papers, and ter Vehn's (1924) book on accounting theory until the end of the nineteenth century. Buhl (1929a) studied the development of the theory of accounts, as well as cameralism (Buhl 1929b); and Weitenauer (1931) studied Venice and the Fugger's account books. Penndorf (1929, 1933b) wrote on Luca Pacioli, on the history of the balance sheet, and on the origin of cost accounting; and Schulze (1933) traced auditing (*Wirtschaftsprüfung*) in Germany; while Seÿffert (1938) studied, for example, the history of business economics. Important Austrian contributions to the history and theory of accounting are the anthology by Meithner (1933a)[27] and Thoms' work (1936) on the history and development of cameralism, as well as Sykora's (1949) book on the theory of accounts and balance sheets. Furthermore, Löffelholz (1935, 1970) presented histories of business economics and of bookkeeping. Borkowsky (1949) offered a survey on the development of accounting theory in Switzerland, and Sillén (1929) published a German language paper on the history of valuation theory in Sweden.

3.8 The international influence of German accounting

Although German accounting research was leading during the first half of the twentieth century, its international influence was by no means uniform. It undeniably had a strong impact in central and northern Europe – some Finnish and Scandinavian authors even contributed notably to German accounting literature, for example, Kovero (1912) and ter Vehn (1924, 1929). It also influenced accounting practice in Eastern Europe, and the notion of the master chart of accounts even materialized in Soviet Russia. Indeed, charts of accounts spread to many continental European countries. This also was true for France (see Degos and Mattessich 2003), where German cost accounting and particularly inflation accounting exercised considerable academic and practical influence. To a lesser extent this held for Italy (see Galassi and Mattessich 2004), and least for Spain (cf. Carrasco Díaz *et al.* 2004) which was more influenced by French and Italian accounting thoughts. The countries where German accounting had the least impact were the United Kingdom and those of the Commonwealth – although some immigrants may have made vain attempts to introduce German accounting ideas to those areas (e.g. charts of accounts to Australia). Even after the publication of an English translation of Schmalenbach's *Dynamic Accounting* (1959), the influence was restricted to such rare occasions as Baxter's (1949, 1967, 1975) investigations of inflation accounting and his attempt at reviving Schmidt's idea that proper accounting practice might mitigate business cycles. Other English language accounting literature, as, for example, Whittington (1983) and Tweedie and Whittington (1984), also referred to German literature, particularly with regard to inflation accounting.

American and, above all, Japanese scholars received German accounting thought more favourably. The latter had traditional ties to German academia, particularly in economics and management. Indeed, nowhere were translations of German books on these topics more frequent – this was true especially after the Second World War, when German literature of the first half of the century was translated in large amounts into Japanese (e.g. there exist Japanese translations of at least seven books by Schmalenbach, some in several editions). In America the influence was either indirect, or through German inflation accounting literature, expounded and given its own slant by Sweeney (e.g. 1936), or through several *English* publications of Fritz Schmidt (1930a, 1930b, 1931a, 1931b) that exercised some influence, though mainly in the second half of the century, as precursors of Edwards and Bell (1961).

4   German language area

Second half of the twentieth century[1]

4.1 Introduction

In Germany, despite tremendous economic deprivation, the time immediately after the Second World War showed continuing concern with cost accounting as well as with competing versions of *Bilanztheorien*, so characteristic of the first half of the century. During this time, the international lead in research was taken over by the English language (particularly American) accounting literature – first in financial, then in managerial accounting. Thus, it was inevitable that novel accounting ideas and approaches from the New World exercised their influence in the German language area no less than in the rest of the world.

Nevertheless, German accounting research in the second half of the twentieth century was very active and produced innumerable publications, some of them highly original. Although no longer exercising the previous widespread influence, its prestige lingered on, mainly due to scholars of the previous period still active in the second half of the century. Among these the best known were (in chronological order of birth dates): Konrad Mellerowicz [1891–1984], Rudolf Seÿffert [1893–1971], Theodor Beste [1894–1973], the Swiss Karl Käfer [1897–2000], Hans Seischab [1898–1965], Erich Kosiol [1899–1990] and Hans Münstermann [1899–1986].

4.2 Financial accounting theories

A home-grown trend in Germany was the continued competition of revised or newly devised *Bilanztheorien*. The most important concepts of the first half of the century influenced academic accountants for at least two further decades. Schmalenbach's dynamic theory continued to be significant, particularly in the extended versions by Kosiol and by Schweitzer. Others, for example, Moxter, also attempted to combine it with modern concepts. Inflation problems were analysed by few and were rarely applied in practice. Whereas these concepts go back to the two central theories of the first half of the century by Schmalenbach and Schmidt, present value and cash flow approaches had only shallow roots in the earlier German literature (e.g. Rieger 1928), but received intensive attention in the theoretical discussions after the Second World War (see below).

4.2.1 *Extensions of dynamic accounting theory*

In financial accounting theory, Kosiol (1937, 1944a, 1944b, 1956) continued the tradition of Schmalenbach's and Walb's dynamic accounting, extending and developing his own *Bilanztheorie* and eliminating previous inconsistencies. Kosiol named this theory '*pagatoric*' (see above), as it interpreted the elements of the balance sheet and income statements as real or virtual, as past or future, as receipts or expenditures. Thus, the term '*pagatorisch*' emphasized the cash flows of the firm. Initially Kosiol insisted on the exclusive valuation at acquisition costs, though occasionally he used the principle of lower of cost or market value. He *rejected* any kind of silent reserves, as well as assets not founded in direct monetary transactions (e.g. goodwill). He also tried to separate the question of income determination from that of permissible or advisable income distribution, and accepted only nominal (but not physical) capital maintenance. In the case of real-financial capital maintenance, he had to take recourse to an additional reserve account (something hardly consistent with the acquisition cost principle). Engels believed that Kosiol's theory was 'the only one of the great balance sheet theories that is logically closed … nevertheless, to us Kosiol's accounting theory appears to be the weakest one – not only is it completely logical, it also is completely tautological' (Engels 1962: 202, translated). Schweitzer (1972: 174), a former associate of Kosiol, rejected this accusation and believed it to be based on misunderstandings. Nevertheless, he himself attempted to improve or extend Kosiol's system by reinterpreting the pagatoric meaning of acquisition costs and also by incorporating decision-logical value conceptions and other aspects of modern accounting (see Schweitzer 1972: 43–153, 201–4).[2]

These later developments of dynamic accounting by Walb and Kosiol are well summarized in Seicht's words:

> Though Walb's and Kosiol's theories are also often appreciated, it is seldom recognized that they showed dynamic accounting a way out of a blind alley [footnote omitted]. This insight might depend on another insight, namely that dynamic accounting theory is not capable of withstanding a scientific test, and that, after its rectification, it would not be different from any other capital-theoretic explanation of the balance sheet, it be through its conceptual formalism.
>
> (Seicht 1970: 116, translated)

Later Kosiol tried to express dynamic accounting theory as an axiomatic structure. Thus, further clarity and precision were ultimately attained in Kosiol's (1970a, 1978) axiomatization. This is one of the earliest manifestations (of the post-Second World War period) where a prominent German author was influenced by English language accounting literature. It reflected the widespread interest in the axiomatization of the accounting framework, particularly from the late 1950s to the 1970s. Kosiol (1970a, 1978) and his disciple Schweitzer (1970, 1972) (as well as a German book by Mattessich 1970) took up these ideas after the emergence of a series of pertinent publications in Great Britain and America (e.g. Mattessich 1957, 1964; Ijiri 1965, 1967, 1971). These ideas manifested their influence in Germany until the 1990s (e.g. in Herde 1992), as well as in several other countries (cf. Mattessich 1996a: 10–11, 33–4).

Moxter (1974) offered another interpretation of Schmalenbach's accounting theory. The purpose was to estimate periodic income (*einkommensapproximative Gewinnermittlung*) by procuring objective data and conventions (*objektivierte Daten und Regeln*). Providing objective annual profit information was a major concern of Baetge (1970). Another variation presented by Chmielewicz (1972) was, in contrast to Schmalenbach's notion, based on both the income statement *as well as* the balance sheet. Furthermore, Chmielewicz' approach emphasized the importance of the cash flow statement. He thus analysed the interrelations between all three of the major financial statements, thereby developing a mechanism for estimating cash flows and profits, as well as the values of assets and liabilities, in a multi-period planning system.

4.2.2 Theoretical concepts in reaction to inflations after the Second World War

In the 1950s and early 1960s, there was no inflation in Germany. Nevertheless, there was one study *related* to inflationary issues that gained long-term attention, namely Hax's (1957) paper on capital maintenance. Towards the middle of the 1970s, a creeping inflation emerged, also in Germany. Although not as virulent as in North America (not to speak of South America), it did raise practical concerns as well as theoretical interest. Nevertheless, it is surprising that Germany, the country that pioneered inflation accounting after the First World War, made this time no truly original contributions to inflation accounting literature, and virtually no practical attempts of introducing it to industry. Among the relatively few theoretical endeavours were those of Schildbach (1979, 1984, 1990), Bucher (1980), Fickert (1983) and Wagner (1982).

This stood in crass contrast to the attempts of accounting standards introduced in the late 1970s in the USA, the UK, Canada, and other Commonwealth countries – not to speak of the huge amount of theoretical and practical English language literature in this field. The lesser virulence of the German inflation may have been one explanation for this. Another reason may have been that, due to the German experience with the previous inflations and subsequent currency reforms, '[a]lmost any kind of price indexation was strictly forbidden' (Busse von Colbe 1996: 417). This may have been the decisive factor in abstaining from any official introduction of inflation or *current value* accounting schemes. In the twenty-first century, one expects to overcome such legalistic hurdles by means of harmonizing the European Union company law – the Fourth EU Directive (see below) was amended in 2001 and 2003 (it permits the use of 'fair values' in financial statements). Finally, there was great concern in Germany that a general introduction of inflation accounting might institutionalize inflation, thus achieving a negative rather than positive effect.

It is surprising how little attention German scholars paid to the work by Edwards and Bell (1961). Some European experts regarded this book as merely a peripheral extension of Schmidt (1921).[3] Thus it seems that Edwards and Bell's true advances and achievements are still little understood in the German language area and, possibly, in Continental Europe in general. Yet everyone thoroughly familiar with this work and that of Schmidt would readily admit the immense conceptual, analytical and practical advances made by Edwards and Bell (1961).[4]

4.2.3 Present value and cash flow approaches

Despite Kosiol's persistent defence of the basic tenets of dynamic-pagatoric (i.e. cash-flow) accounting, and his attempts to export his idea to America (in Kosiol 1978), the new theoretical trend moved in the opposite direction. The balance sheet was instead seen as future oriented, and the *present value* basis moved into the foreground of the theoretical interest – something that had deep roots in Germany but matured only slowly (cf. Seicht 1970: 513–27).

The present value (economic value) as a valuation basis for accounting relies on the discounting of expected future net cash flows (or net revenues). This results in the 'economic profit' (*ökonomischer Gewinn*), supposed to maintain the firm's earnings power (*Ertragswerterhaltung*). The basic idea of this approach goes back to the nineteenth century as well as to economic theories, but was further developed by Fisher (1906) and applied to accounting by Canning (1929) and Preinreich (1940). It began to re-emerge after the Second World War with publications by the Finnish scholar Jaakko Honko (1959) and the Danish scholar Palle Hansen (1962).

The German literature intensely debated the question of how much of income or periodical cash flow can be *distributed* to owners – particularly how much beyond the 'interest' on the opening (or average) capital. This was deemed to be a crucial question of financial accounting. Apart from the difficulties in determining the relevant interest rate (*Kalkulationszinsfuß*), the future cash flows themselves were uncertain and their estimates were not beyond manipulation. Some scholars argued against the present value basis in accounting and traditional financial statements. Schneider (1968), for example, suggested the rule of '*double minimum*' (which goes back to Nicklisch). According to this rule, a firm should try to maintain its financial, as well as its substantial, capital. Therefore, it should limit the distribution of dividends to *the nominal net income or the economic profit, whichever is less*. The difference between these two values ought to be transferred to non-distributable reserves. However, particularly in the 1990s, the notion of economic profit for accounting purposes gained new importance due to the impact of market-based management.

Albach (1965) and Seicht (1970: 558–619) both offer interesting variations of the present value approach. Albach's (1965) synthetic (*syntthetische*) *Bilanztheorie* – heavily criticized by Seicht – is a *synthesis* between two approaches: (1) the valuation of individual *assets* (past expenditures) *at acquisition cost*; and (2) the valuation of owners' capital as *future (expected) receipts* (extracted from a firm's budget), discounted at a rate identified as *interner Zinsfuß* (internal interest or profit rate). Hence, the balance sheet was considered a control instrument for monitoring the degree to which the firm's plan or budget was fulfilled.

Seicht (1970) claimed that his *capital theoretic (kapitaltheoretische) Bilanztheorie* is even more future-oriented. It abandoned the acquisition cost basis for *asset* valuation, and regarded the firm's discounted future receipts (*Einnahmen*) as its *assets*. The debts then became the discounted future expenditures (*Ausgaben*); and the owners' *capital* (valued on an *acquisition cost* basis) became the discounted future capital repayments. Again, the discount rate was the internal interest or profit rate. This circumvented the use of the concept of 'goodwill', a notion that some Germans seem to regard as artificial. In Seicht's theory, 'the sum total of all periodic profits always amounted to the total profit of all periods' (Seicht 1970: 560, translated). This would make him a defender of the *clean surplus theory*, revised and stochastically extended in America by Ohlson during the late 1980s and the 1990s. However, the American literature usually operates with the '*riskless*' (instead of the 'internal') interest rate and with the concept of goodwill (as the difference between book value and market value). Above all, this literature is not deterministic but stochastic, relying extensively on the notion of *statistical expectation*. No future-oriented balance sheet theories were adopted in German accounting *practice* (which, instead, moved towards a *multi-purpose* accounting approach). Yet, the development of those 'capital theoretic' (or economic) balance sheet theories constituted a significant step that cannot be ignored. There may even be a link to the American information economics approach that found slow but growing response in Germany during the 1990s (see below).

Whereas some German scholars looked for a measure of *distributable* surplus and a balance sheet based on future cash flows, others emphasized the lack of information about realized and future cash flows. Busse von Colbe (1966, 1968) and Käfer (1967), for example, revived the research in funds flow statements. Yet, in contrast to the US (where the publication of such statements was obligatory for most corporations), funds flow statements were and still are not legally required in most German firms. Since 2005 they are legally required in consolidated financial statements. Moxter (1966) suggested a special tool, the *finanzplanorientiertes Tableau*, a matrix of projected cash flows. It showed the estimated receipts and expenditures of several future periods. He even posed the question whether such a cash flow oriented statement should replace the balance sheet. The concern with funds flow statements continued in later decades (cf. Busse von Colbe 1996: 420), as manifested in Dellmann and Kalinski (1986), Chmielewicz and Caspari (1985) and Busse von Colbe (1990, 1993).

4.2.4 Empirical studies in the newer German literature

Systematic *empirical* studies began slowly in the German language area, with some papers collected in Loitlsberger (1963). Over the decades, empirical research dealt with a large array of diverse topics. The most important were: income smoothing (e.g. Halbinger 1980; Coenenberg *et al.* 1984; Coenenberg and Haller 1993a), annual reporting and capital markets (Coenenberg 1974; Coenenberg *et al.* 1983; Möller 1983), group reporting (e.g. von Wysocki 1969, 1976; Jäger and Vogelsang 1973), funds flow statements (Coenenberg and Schmidt 1978; Busse von Colbe 1984; Weilenmann 1981), the quality and relevance of corporate reports (e.g. Brockhoff 1975; von Wysocki 1976; Coenenberg *et al.* 1978; Pellens 1989), and further topics such as decision making and its relevance, bankruptcy, mergers, etc.[5] In general, it seems that empirical research in Germany may have been less statistically oriented than in America. In both countries, as well as internationally, empirical accounting research has increased (e.g. Leuz 1998), though still been fragmentary. And the connection between a solid theoretical basis and supporting empirical evidence is still sparse. Indeed, the question arises whether an applied science, as accounting, can ever achieve such an ideal goal.

4.2.5 German and European standards on financial accounting[6]

German accounting was traditionally strongly rooted in codified law. During the 1960s German accounting scholars were preoccupied with two new laws.[7] The first was the *Aktiengesetz* of 1965 (dealing with public limited companies): for the first time, it required a parent company to include the statements of its subsidiaries in a consolidated financial statement (cf. Busse von Colbe and Ordelheide 1993; Busse von Colbe 1996: 419). The second law, the *Publizitätsgesetz* of 1969 ('Publicity' or Disclosure Act), extended the publication of consolidated statements and other requirements to large *privately held* companies. Its impetus derived from the financial difficulties of the well-known, privately held, Krupp Co.

Since the 1970s, the European Union had aimed to establish homogeneous and harmonised rules of financial accounting. Thus, attempts were made towards a compromise between the Anglo-American and the continental European traditions. This was reflected in different EU directives, especially in the 'Fourth EU Directive' (which deals with financial statement formats, valuation and other rules) of 25 July 1978. After intensive discussion, this and other directives were implemented in Germany – through the new and important law of 19 December 1985, the *Bilanzrichtlinien-Gesetz* (Accounting Directives Law) further amended existing legislation. Among other amendments, this directive caused the introduction of a new section (the 'third book') into the *Handelsgesetzbuch* (HGB, the Commercial Code).

More recently, the development of International Accounting Standards (IAS) has gained increasing importance in Germany (cf. Haller 1995). This was due to the growing influence of stock exchanges (international, as well as domestic) in raising capital for corporations. When shares of large German companies (such as the Daimler Benz AG) were first traded at the New York stock exchange in the 1990s, German legislation had to be adapted to facilitate such international listings. As a result, German 'listed companies' were permitted to use IAS or US-GAAP (cf. Böcking and Orth 1998) in their consolidated financial statements. Therefore, IAS and US-GAAP gained tangible relevance for many of the large German corporations (cf. Ballwieser 1996; Wagenhofer 1999). It is an interesting and open question whether traditional German accounting principles (as reflected in the HGB) will remain valid for most German firms, or whether there will be further accommodations to IAS or even to US-GAAP.

4.2.6 *Postulational approaches:* **Grundsätze ordnungsmäßiger Buchführung** *('principles of orderly accounting')*

Parallel to the axiomatization attempts in accounting (see above) emerged related attempts of postulation. These were analytically less rigorous, and became known in English as the 'postulational approach' (e.g. Chambers 1957, 1966; Moonitz 1961; Sprouse and Moonitz 1962). The goal of all those attempts (whether axiomatic or postulational) was to overcome the traditional 'rule-based' approach (i.e. accounting conventions *not* rooted in an overall system, conceptual framework or theory), and to put the foundations of financial accounting on more permanent 'principles'. The rule-based approach was too vague and dogmatic for a time when mathematical economics and finance, operations research and management science became the beacons for most areas of business studies.

In Germany, general rules of financial accounting, called *Grundsätze ordnungsmäßiger Buchführung* (GoB), were traditionally used by firms.[8] Although law courts referred to these rules, they were not codified until 1985. Leffson (1964) attempted to arrange them as systematic principles. This system was goal-oriented, and clearly distinguished between various categories of principles: those of documentation, of the framework itself (*Rahmengrundsätze*), of classification (*Ansatzgrundsätze*) and of capital maintenance. Since the new accounting law of 1985 of the HGB only enumerates several principles, the subsequent literature tried to improve the 'system of accounting principles' through appropriate interpretation of the pertinent legislation (Baetge 1984; Moxter 1985; Ballwieser 1987a, 1987b; Baetge and Apelt 1992; Baetge 2002). Thus, German literature, during the last quarter of the century, had at least an indirect impact upon accounting legislation (Moxter 1976, 1980). Furthermore, the need for interpretation and theoretical foundation of accounting principles (together with the new laws) generated plenty of research opportunities (cf. Baetge 1987; Schildbach 1987; Siegel 1994; Moxter 1989, 1993) and opportunities to analyse the relationship of these principles to the British tradition of true and fair view (cf. Ordelheide 1993, 1996). In America, similar endeavours had earlier led to the official *Conceptual Framework* of the FASB (1978).[9] However, Schipper (2003: 62) argued that US-GAAP is based on a recognizable set of principles derived from the FASB's *Conceptual Framework*, but nonetheless contains elements that cause some commentators to conclude that US accounting is 'rule-based'.[10] In fact, the FASB is exploring a tightening of its conceptual framework through a 'Proposal for a Principles-Based Approach to US Standard Setting' (http://www.fasb.org). A 'principles-based' (or at least 'hybrid') approach may suggest a more logical and analytical conceptual structure of future accounting regulation, and may well be extended to the broader setting of the European Union.

In the last decade of the twentieth century, the *Deutsches Rechunungslegungs Standards Committee* (German Accounting Standards Committee) was established. It consists of members from the public accounting profession, large corporations, financial institutions and academe (cf. Scheffler 1999: 407–17, 2002: 528–37). The Board's task is to develop and recommend financial accounting principles for consolidated financial statements, to offer advice on accounting legislation, and to represent Germany on international standardization organizations. In this way, the Board will have a tangible influence on the development of national and international accounting principles, their acceptance in Germany and their incorporation into German legislation.

Endeavours in finding generally satisfactory accounting standards dominated not merely the practical but also the academic scene. Wagenhofer and Ewert (2003: Chapters 3–9) discuss this process and the challenge arising from two different directions, both developed in America. The first is the analytically oriented *information content perspective*, based on key notions such as systematic belief revision (based on changing probabilities), information efficiency and decision usefulness. The second is the more empirically oriented *valuation perspective*, based on value relevance as well as the correlation between accounting figures and stock prices.[11] But this second view is rejected by the *information content perspective*. It argues that markets are usually neither perfect nor complete; this, in turn, may lead to meaningless value figures.

Wagenhofer and Ewert point at the difficulties and disagreements between these more sophisticated methods, as well as the need for specific purpose-orientation and the lack of closure of this search as far as a satisfactory solution in standard setting is concerned. Nevertheless, they believe that the information economic approach is still viable for standard setting (see Wagenhofer and Ewert 2003: 79). However, this view is not held by such pioneers of the information economic perspective as Demski. For example:

> The aggregation approach, however leads us to social choice and Arrow's celebrated impossibility theorem ... The problem is that the four conditions [required for aggregating individual preferences, and stated by Arrow] are mutually incompatible ... . At present we see this theme played out in the international arena where the FASB and the IASB offer competing views of a 'global GAAP' ... . Can we unequivocally say which is better?
>
> (Christensen and Demski 2003: 430–1)[12]

4.3 Cost and managerial accounting

After the Second World War the strength of German accounting research in costing issues continued, and its influence increased. Many German ideas for improving the theory and technique of cost or managerial accounting emerged in the second half of the twentieth century, especially in its first and its last decades. Yet management accounting also experienced a period of stagnation (during the 1970s and 1980s), not only in Germany, but internationally (cf. Busse von Colbe 1996: 422), from which it recovered towards the end of the century. While the modern practice of direct costing was, or seemed to have been, imported from America, diehard German accountants might claim that it was rather the *fashion* of direct costing that was imported during the 1960s and 1970s, while its basic idea can be traced to earlier German publications.

Yet cost accounting systems were developed extensively in Germany during the 1950s and 1960s. They achieved a high degree of scientific proficiency and used modern methods of planning and control. By separating full and variable costing, firms acquired sophisticated instruments for estimating profits and facilitating decisions. The basis of cost estimation and the separation between variable and full costs both derived from production theory. This development became crucial to marginal costing in Germany (see below).

During the last two decades of the twentieth century, Germany again generated some interesting studies in cost and management accounting. Some of these studies explained, for example, why German industry still worked predominantly with full costing instead of direct costing (Gümbel 1988; Schneider 1984; Pfaff 1993), others examined the rationale for attempts to merge cost accounting with financial accounting (Pfaff 1994; Coenenberg 1995; Küpper 1995; Männel and Küpper 1999; Hax 2002), as executed by some German firms (Ziegler 1994). Furthermore, the idea of integrating managerial accounting with capital budgeting and finance was advanced by Küpper (1985a); and extended conceptualization of control concepts was done by Horváth (2003) and Küpper (1988b, 2001). Finally, various authors extended management accounting beyond operational planning into strategic decision-making (Coenenberg 1992; Ewert and Wagenhofer 1993; Küpper 1993b; Ossadnik 1998; or Schweitzer and Küpper 1998) – for an oversight of management accounting in the German language area from about 1998 to 2004, see Wagenhofer (2006).

4.3.1 Production theory and cost theory

If the idol of German business economics in the first half of the century was a scholar whose main contributions were in accounting, namely Eugen Schmalenbach, the idol in the second half was a business economist, Erich Gutenberg [1897–1984], who had little regard for accounting. And yet, this scholar 'incorporated microeconomics into the *Betriebswirtschaftslehre*' (cf. Schneider 1981: 152), presented new ideas for formulating cost functions, and emphasized insights gained from the English accounting literature, as well as budgetary planning that ultimately benefited accounting (Gutenberg 1951). In doing so, he was not alone; others, particularly the economist Erich Schneider [1900–70] (1951), contributed to such efforts:

> His [Gutenberg's] cost theory, derived from production theory, served as a basis for standard and marginal cost accounting systems, elaborated for instance by his former research assistant Wolfgang Kilger (1961). Gutenberg's counterpart in terms of economic theory was Erich Schneider,

Professor at Kiel University. Both scholars were receptive to microeconomic theories, partly developed in Anglo-American countries.

(Busse von Colbe 1996: 418)

Gutenberg analysed the influence of machines and their technical characteristics upon the input of material and labour (as is customary in engineering production functions – cf. Chenery 1948). In Gutenberg's system the *rate* of production became an important cost determinant in addition to production *time* and potential *capacity* – these three jointly determined the volume. In this, he regarded linear cost functions (in contrast to S-shaped ones) as representative of industrial production.

His work triggered further German research in production and cost theory (by Kilger 1958; Pack 1966; Lücke 1969; and others), production planning (Dinkelbach 1964; Adam 1969a) and investment theory (Albach 1962; Hax 1964). Heinen (1965) further refined Gutenberg's production and cost function, and Kloock (1969) embedded it in the input–output model (see, Leontief 1966; Schweitzer and Küpper 1974). Küpper (1979, 1980, 1985b) and Troßmann (1983) extended the approach to dynamic relations between such variables as stocks (including semi-finished products) and the duration of various production processes and periods.

These concepts aimed at an *empirical* foundation for determining production and cost functions (Pressmar 1971; Schweitzer 1990). American endeavours, on the other hand – such as Koopman's (1951) activity analysis, or linear and nonlinear programming – developed production and cost theory on a more *analytical* basis (cf. Wittmann 1968; Kistner 1981; Fandel 1987). Activity analysis, as well as Gutenberg's approach, made it even possible to analyse ecological costs (see Dinkelbach and Rosenberg 1994; Steven 1991, 1993, 1994a, 1994b; and Dyckhoff 1992). Such publications formed an important basis for 'ecological cost accounting', which received special attention in the last decades of the century.

The intensive concern with production and cost theory gave much impetus to research in cost accounting; it influenced the development of marginal cost systems in academia no less than in actual practice. Such sound theoretical foundations may be the reason for the prestige of applied cost accounting in Germany. Cost accounting systems, based on production theory, dominate many progressive German companies (cf. Küpper 1983, 1993a). In addition, in the last decade, activity-based costing from the USA, and target costing from Japan also influenced German research and practice. The success of the SAP-software for Integrated Product and Process Engineering (SAP 2000) may have been the basis for such developments.

4.3.2 Investment-based cost accounting

The investment approach to cost accounting goes back to Hotelling (1925), Preinreich (1940) and Schneider (1961), and made the notion of net present value relevant to cost accounting theory (see above: Financial accounting theories). The first pertinent attempts of Mahlert (1976), Swoboda (1979), Luhmer (1980) and Kistner and Luhmer (1981) concentrated on variable depreciation methods (e.g. annuity depreciation method). Yet Küpper (1984, 1988a) showed that this approach need not be restricted to depreciation; it can offer a general basis for decision-oriented cost accounting by means of the present value approach. Küpper combined investment theory with cost accounting, thereby connecting long-term with short-term decisions.

This approach shows how to obtain relevant information for short-term and medium-term decisions, such as the planning of production programmes, the determination of order lot sizes, and of minimum prices (Küpper 1985a, 1991; Rieper 1986; Betz 1995). It reveals the connection between short- and long-term planning, and the underlying goals. Beyond that, it permits an examination of the extent to which cost accounting concepts and cost information are relevant. One may interpret this approach as a special case of control theory (Roski 1987; Küpper 1988b). Finally, Maus (1996) combined the investment approach to cost accounting with strategic planning (Ossadnik 1998). In this way 'investment based accounting' reflected the *short-term* constituents of an *operative* and *strategic* managerial accounting system oriented towards *long-term* value maximization (Schweitzer and Küpper 2003; Breid 1994, respectively).

4.3.3 Information economics, agency theory and related approaches

While German scholars developed production and cost theory as a basis of cost accounting, in America one chose a very different path. There, the information economics approach became a stochastic version of analytical accounting. The book by Demski and Feltham (1976) and basic papers of agency theory (such as Demski and Feltham 1978; Holmström 1979; Baiman and Demski 1980; Magee 1980; Christensen 1981; Grossman and Hart 1983; Antle and Eppen 1985) became known in the German language area during the 1980s. Since then the application of information economics and agency theory became central themes in German accounting research. Applications of agency theory to financial accounting (see Ballwieser 1985a, 1985b; Ewert 1986, 1987, 1990; Ewert and Wagenhofer 2000) and to cost accounting (see, e.g. Wagenhofer 1990, 1992b) became popular.

Towards the end of the twentieth century, agency theory seemed to have become the most important theoretical instrument for analysing German accounting problems. For example, in earlier decades, problems of transfer pricing were studied by means of linear and non-linear programming (Hax 1965a, 1965b; Adam 1969b, 1970; Drumm 1972a, 1972b; Albach 1974), but the use of information economic and agency models led to new insights, and demonstrate the advantages of decentralization (Wagenhofer 1992a, 1994; Neus, 1997; Schiller 1999). Other examples are the increased awareness of asymmetric information and the explicit use of utility functions, offering a possible explanation why many companies could not be enticed to use marginal costing (Pfaff 1993). This became a new and fruitful perspective for solving problems of cost allocations and interdivisional coordination (Pfaff 1993; Laux 1995).

A central research issue of agency theory has been the assessment of managerial performance. Residual income measures (like the notion of 'economic value added' or EVA) were used as instruments for the shareholder value perspective and for value-based management, and an old conjecture was revived. Preinreich (1937) conjectured, and Lücke (1955, 1965) proved, that the net present value can be calculated not merely on the basis of net cash flows (receipts minus expenditures) but, under special conditions (Kloock 1981), also on the basis of net revenues (revenues minus expenses or costs). Today this theorem plays a prominent role in German managerial accounting, as does the related concept of 'clean surplus' in financial accounting.

Thus, agency theory revealed the importance and consequences of various strategies of behavioural control in management accounting (cf. Wagenhofer 1995b, 1997). Wagenhofer (1992a, 1994) also showed the potential of delegation, and the determination of transfer prices under uncertainty and asymmetric information. Finally, he demonstrated that information asymmetry affected optimal cost allocation, and how this depends upon the information structure and the planning objectives (see Wagenhofer 1995a).

Furthermore, Göx (1998, 1999) analysed transfer prices from a strategic point of view. Japanese target costing (*Zielkostenmanagement*) was another intensively explored research object within the orbit of agency theory (Riegler 1996; Ewert 1997; Ewert and Ernst 1999). Its main use lies in the introduction of new products where the central question is 'How much cost does the market allow us for this product?' – replacing the traditional question 'What will be the product cost?'.

The use of agency models is, of course, not limited to analysing accounting problems. Thus, the relationship between managerial accounting, planning and control, organizational structure and the firm's incentive system has become another important topic in German research (Ewert and Wagenhofer 1993; Riegler 2000; Schiller 2000; Hofmann 2001). These problems reach beyond accounting; they constitute the core of the so-called '*Controlling*', a new German discipline that includes managerial accounting, but goes beyond accounting and addresses managerial coordination issues.

4.3.4 *German versions of marginal costing*

After 1950 the concept of direct (marginal) costing was introduced to Germany, although some elements of direct costing were already known prior to the Second World War (see Chapter 3). A series of innovations were introduced: the *Grenzplankostenrechnung* (marginal plan costing) of Plaut (1951, 1953, 1955, 1958, 1987) and Kilger (1961, 1976), the *Abteilungserfolgsrechnung* (departmental costing) of Bredt (1956), the *Standard-Grenzpreisrechnung* (standard marginal pricing) of Böhm (1957, 1959) and Böhm and Wille (1974). These were early and important steps related to direct costing (cf. Börner 1961) and to the application of mathematical programming in cost accounting (for detail, see Seicht 1977). Consulting companies introduced these concepts to industry (e.g. Plaut International Management Consulting). Hans G. Plaut and the academic Wolfgang Kilger, a disciple of Gutenberg, developed the theoretical foundation of *Grenzplankostenrechnung*, and extended its practical methods. Indeed, this tool became the most popular version of marginal costing in German industry – also used in SAP-software.

The *Grenzplankostenrechnung*, like direct costing, is based on the separation of variable and fixed costs, reflecting the dependence of costs on the output volume (used for *short-term* planning as well as control purposes where *linear* cost functions and the principle of *decision relevance* play important roles). The determination of unit costs is non-stochastic, cost standards are fixed, the output volume (as the decisive parameter) is variable, and the standard costs are clearly separable into fixed and variable. Furthermore, one developed sophisticated procedures to *estimate* costs and to *control* them in various control centres.

Another variation of marginal costing was pursued by Riebel (1959, 1964a, 1964b, 1972, 1994). In this system (called by him *Einzelkosten- und Deckungs-beitragsrechnung*) the distinction between direct costs and overhead costs was fundamental, and cost allocations depended on the reference basis (e.g. the product, product type, cost centre or the entire company). Thus, Riebel extended the *Deckungsbeitragsrechnung* (contribution margin costing) from a *single-step* to a *multiple-step* calculation. Riebel emphasized that this is 'no predetermined system that can be applied schematically, it rather is a specific way of thinking. As regards practical application, it is only possible to assert certain principles' (Riebel 1983: 45, translated). Perhaps it was for this reason that industry did not adopt it as widely as the *Grenzplankostenrechnung* (cf. Küpper 1983).

However, one recognized specific aspects of this approach as particularly important in designing data banks for the accounting software of SAP and other systems (cf. Wedekind and Ortner 1977; Scheer 1981; Riebel and Sinzig 1982; Sinzig 1983). We are referring to such features as the separation between basic accounting (*Grundrechnung*) and purpose oriented calculations (*Auswertungsrechnung*), multiple allocation (*Zurechnung und Zurechenbarkeit*) of costs and revenues to different decision variables (*Bezugsgrößen*), as well as the multi-dimensionality of this approach.

4.3.5 Concepts and applications of full and variable cost accounting

Before 1985 most accounting academics were in favour of variable costing. One author who did not emphasize it was Laßmann (1968, 1973, 1980). He and Wartmann (1963) became interested in empirically estimating full costs in a large German iron and steel company (see also Franke 1972; Wittenbrink 1975; Kolb 1978). This notion, based on production functions of that industry, revealed how the input quantities of materials, work, machine hours, etc., depend on output quantities and other determinants such as production time, processing temperature and so on. These functions were empirically based on statistical regression. Inputs and the outputs based on actual prices led to costs (including full and variable costs) and revenues. This approach took into consideration different determinants apart from output, and was called '*Einfluß-größenrechnung*' (accounting based on cost determinants). Its main purpose was estimating the costs, revenues and the profit of the entire firm within a single period (but not per product unit). More importantly, the distinction between variable and full costs becomes irrelevant. Thus cost accounting became an instrument for estimating the effect of different alternatives of production planning on profit. The ultimate goal is to attain the 'optimal plan'.

Although most academics supported the idea of direct costing, many companies accepted the systems of marginal and contribution costing, and used simultaneously full costing. For example, the systems installed in industry by Plaut and other consulting firms usually revealed information on the basis of direct as well as of full costing – particularly because direct costing serves short-run decisions, while full costing serves long-run decisions and control purposes. The dissemination of such multiple costing systems was promoted by the advent of accounting software developed during the last two decades of the twentieth century.

During the 1990s, German companies, as well as academia, adopted the ideas of activity-based costing (ABC) and target costing. Horváth and his disciples (Horváth and Mayer 1989; Horváth *et al.* 1993) refined and converted ABC into a *Prozeßkostenrechnung* (process costing), and introduced it to industry. Coenenberg and Fischer (1991) showed its importance for strategic planning. The full costing aspects of ABC and *Prozeßkostenrechnung* led to intensive discussions about their decision usefulness (Glaser 1992; Kloock 1992; Horváth and Mayer 1993). Target costing, on the other hand, aimed at influencing costs in the early production phases (see Seidenschwarz 1993). Hence, it was the *management* of costs (rather than the *accounting* of costs) that became increasingly important. This led to a series of papers analysing methods of cost management (Fischer 1993, 2000; Dellmann and Franz 1994; Vikas 1996; Franz and Kajüter 1997; Freidank *et al.* 1997).

Towards the end of the century, Germany sported a large array of different concepts and systems dealing with cost accounting and cost management. The disseminations of the *Grenzplankostenrechnung* and *Deckungsbeitragsrechnung* since the 1950s offered German companies efficient instruments for internal accounting purposes. These costing systems were also adapted for banks and other service companies (Vikas 1989; Schierenbeck 2001) as well as to special functions, like logistics (Weber 1987). Furthermore, one installed in public institutions such as hospitals (von Eiff 1985) and universities (Küpper 2000, 2002) cost accounting systems and its software. Today, Germany shows a tendency to change government accounting from the traditional cameralistic system to a more modern economic-oriented one; above all, it introduced cost accounting to the entire public administration.

4.4 Historical accounting research by Germans, Austrians and Swiss (1950–2000)

While historical accounting research has always been prominent in the German language area (see Mattessich and Küpper 2003), it has produced relatively little during the second half of the twentieth century, not only in comparison with the English accounting literature of this period but also compared to the *former* output in German. The most formidable work was Schneider's (1981) *Geschichte betriebswirtschaftlicher Theorie* (History of business-economics theory) and its mammoth extension in Schneider (2001), *Geschichte und Metho-den der Wirtschaftswissenschaft* (History and methods of the economic sciences).[13] This history (of well over 1,000 pages) is, according to its title, not limited to *Betriebswirtschaftslehre* but supposed to cover the economic sciences in general. In this regard it falls short in many important details – even as far as accounting history is concerned (to which it devotes some 200 pages). Neverthe-less, the book is a treasure trove of innumerable facts and opinions, often inter-esting, sometimes surprising, but in many respects incomplete (cf. Mattessich 2003: 152, note 17).

A prominent work by Seicht (1970) dealt to a considerable extent with the development of balance sheet theories, and contained numerous important details as well as lengthy quotations. Seicht (1977) also published a further, less comprehensive historical book that covered certain aspects in the development of cost accounting. Beyond these works, there exists a series of survey articles, frequently found in 'handbooks' or other collections – written by Schneider (1991, 1992, 1996), Busse von Colbe (1994, 1996), Coenenberg *et al.* (1984) and others (e.g. Dörner and Kloock 1984), occasionally even written in English as, for example, an appreciation of Schmalenbach's work by Schweitzer (1995).

To this one may add a series of reference works, not necessarily geared to accounting history by nature of their intent, but dealing with recent historical developments (Wagner 1993). Among these, the best known are the 'hand-books' of accounting, in four editions by Kosiol (1970b), Kosiol *et al.* (1981), Chmielewicz and Schweitzer (1993), as well as Küpper and Wagenhofer (2002); and those of auditing: the first and second edition by Coenenberg and von Wysocki (1983/1992), and the third edition by Ballwieser *et al.* (2002). One may add a biographical study by Klein-Blenkers (1992), offering details about many (though by no means all) German professors of *Betriebswirtschaftslehre* (including accounting).

In addition, there also were historical studies among the many doctoral accounting dissertations. Finally, one might mention the book by Karl (Charles) Weber (1966), on *The Evolution of Direct Costing*. However, in contrast to pre-vious periods, truly prominent historical and archival studies of that genre are hard to find for this period.

Historically valuable English language publications on German accounting aspects by the Austrian-American H. Peter Holzer and the German-American, Hanns-Martin Schoenfeld (such as Holzer 1959; Holzer and Schoenfeld 1963;

Schoenfeld 1972) might be mentioned. English language profiles on three authors from the German language area (Schmalenbach, Schmidt and Mattessich) are in Edwards' (1994) book on *Twentieth-Century Accounting Thinkers*. Surprisingly, these three were also the only twentieth-century German language authors to whom the international encyclopaedic work by Chatfield and Vangermeersch (1996) accorded separate profiles. This work also contains a contribution on 'Germany' (mainly with accounting references to previous centuries) and another one on 'Microeconomics in Germany' (with short references to von Stackelberg, Schär, Schmalenbach, Mellerowicz, Gutenberg and others). These contributions by German and Austrian authors to this particular international-historical work were written by Schneider (1996), Schoenfeld (1996a, 1996b, 1996c) and Mattessich (1996b), respectively.

Perhaps most surprising is the relative scarcity of philosophical considerations in the German accounting literature. Germany, often called the 'land of philosophers' has certainly not lost its philosophical tradition, but this is hardly noticeable in its accounting literature. One of the few authors who occasionally deal with epistemological, methodological and ethical aspects was Schneider (1981, 1990, 2001); others were Chmielewicz (1979) and Fischer-Winkelmann (e.g. 1971, 1980). The work of further authors during the 1990s (like Steinmann and Löhr 1994; Wieland 1994; Küpper 1992; Kreikebaum 1996; Ulrich 1998; Küpper and Picot 1999) was more concerned with business ethics in general and rarely with specific issues in accounting and auditing (cf. Homann *et al.* 2002). In contrast to this, the English language literature (particularly in Great Britain) was thriving with philosophical and sociological issues of accounting during the last two decades of the twentieth century (be they of ontological, epistemological, methodological or ethical nature). Admittedly, a good deal of this literature was due to the efforts of the *critical-interpretive* camp and its major organ, the leading European accounting journal, *Accounting, Organizations and Society*. Even those who may object to some views of this direction may find it difficult to deny its daring originality.

4.5 Accounting academics' attitudes in Germany, Great Britain and North America

The last remarks entice us to make a comparison between accounting academics in North America, Great Britain and Germany. However, at a time of instant communication and increasing uniformity, are those attitudes not pretty much the same? Not necessarily – at the risk of oversimplification, let us juxtapose some typical features of each of those areas.

For North America, it seems that modern analytical research, and particularly the *Economics of Accounting* (Christensen and Feltham 2003, 2005), summarizing the highlights of twentieth century American stochastic-analytical accounting, might be taken as its most characteristic feature. Where else can one find a comprehensive theory relating to accounting, and offering not only a comprehensive set of assumptions and definitions, but above all, some 250 propositions (theorems) with rigorous mathematical proofs? Admittedly, there were other achievements, like the introduction of and experimentation with statistical-empirical accounting research, but its results can hardly match those in the analytical arena – for a discussion of American accounting literature from a German point of view, see Ballwieser (1993).

For Great Britain, the most outstanding feature of the last quarter of a century or so is the advent of a direction that, for lack of a better expression, is known as the critical-interpretive camp.[14] Its accounting adepts span a wide range, with achievements ranging from the application of sociology and the behavioural sciences in general, to ethics and other branches of philosophy. As to the political spectrum, the span is hardly any narrower; it reaches from the centre and moderate left to its radical wing. The common ground seems to be a sceptical attitude towards (or occasionally opposition to) economics and to the traditional scientific approach in general (cf. Mattessich 2002). And the journal of *Accounting, Organizations and Society* is no less a hallmark for British accounting at the turn of the twentieth century, as is the work by Christensen and Feltham (2003, 2005) for American accounting. Again, there are other directions among accounting scholars of Great Britain (e.g. a strong historical research trend), yet it is the critical-interpretive one that gives its research the major impetus and has even influenced other directions in that country as well as overseas.

In the German language area, the research attitude, again, is utterly different – and this despite the adoption of analytical and empirical methods. In many respects German accounting research is more meticulously technical, and praxis-oriented. Its competitiveness is very different from that in America. If German scholars of the first half of the twentieth century competed among themselves with different balance sheet theories, their competition in the second half, with different managerial accounting systems, was perhaps less pronounced, though still existent. The orderly and disciplined attitude of German research finds expression in the Schäffer-Poeschel series of handbook encyclopaedias (*Handwörterbücher*)[15] dealing with accounting and business economics.

This series goes back many decades, and several of its individual issues have experienced new editions. The series has become an institution in its own right. The 'tradition' less than the publishers dominate the structure of these books – that have become items of prestige. They are massive tomes with a wealth of painstakingly arranged facts, carefully selected and classified. No expert may supply more than one contribution, nor do these tomes offer any profiles of prominent personalities.

A further difference, this time in financial accounting, is rooted in the different legal system (i.e. *codified law* – see above), which results in a more legalistic orientation. Only by observing such details, does one become aware of the very different mentality between accounting academics in various regions.

What about the future of academic accounting? Will accounting theory become more uniform across national boundaries? Not necessarily; Germany has a long philosophical tradition, and although its accounting academics have hardly exploited this heritage, there still is the hope that it may claim its place – even in accounting research. Indeed, a thorough analysis of the ontology, epistemology and methodology of accounting might offer German accounting academics an opportunity to gain new wings. But there is still another area where recent German accounting literature seems to have attained a comparative advantage. English-language masterworks of the 'information perspective' (such as Christensen and Demski 2003; and Christensen and Feltham 2003, 2005) care little to accommodate the conceptual and terminological schemes of *traditional* accounting. However, two German books by Ewert and Wagenhofer (1993/2003) and Wagenhofer and Ewert (2003) were more successful in integrating the information perspective with traditional accounting concepts (for details, see Chapter 19). For the future application and dissemination of this 'revolutionary' approach among 'traditional' accountants, such a bridge could prove to be quite significant.

To return to philosophy, why should it be important to accounting? First, because the ultimate reason of doing accounting is accountability; and this requires ethical no less than economic, social and ecological considerations. Second, during the twentieth century, academic accounting became much more than an extension of bookkeeping; it became a cultural manifestation, just as other pure or applied sciences have been for some time. Third, without a profound inquiry into the reality that our discipline tries to represent (though in a pragmatic way), as well as how and to what extent it actually achieves such representation, academic accounting is bound to remain an intellectual fragment.

5 Accounting research in Italy
First half of the twentieth century[1]

5.1 Introduction

The first half of the twentieth century was decisive for academic accounting and management research in Italy, no less than in the German, English, French or other language areas. Yet, seen from abroad, it seems that in Italy (more than in other countries) only a single figure dominated the scene, that of Gino Zappa [1879–1960].[2] In Germany, for example, there was a whole galaxy of prominent names besides the two major rival figures of Eugen Schmalenbach and Fritz Schmidt. And in the USA, William A. Paton [1889–1991] and A.C. Littleton [1886–1974] may have been the best known international names, but they were by no means the only ones of prominence.

However, at a closer look, one may discover that the situation in Italy was not so different. There, Zappa overshadowed many other scholars; but for this very reason, their names and major publications deserve the attention of a wider audience. Above all, it must be borne in mind that other giants of accounting, like Giuseppe Cerboni [1827–1917] and his disciple Giovanni Rossi [1845–1921], as well as Zappa's teacher, Fabio Besta [1845–1922], still published during the early twentieth century.

Thus, we pursue two goals: first, to summarize Gino Zappa's contributions to accounting research, together with some remarks about the twentieth century publications of Rossi and Besta. Second, to offer a flavour of Italian accounting studies of other scholars worth mentioning, particularly of such scholars as Vittorio Alfieri, Aldo Amaduzzi, Clitofonte Bellini, Ugo Caprara, Alberto Ceccherelli, Pietro D'Alvise, Francesco De Gobbis, Francesco Della Penna, Lorenzo De Minico, Teodoro D'Ippolito, Benedetto Lorusso, Vincenzo Masi, Federigo Melis, Ettore Mondini, Pietro Onida, Emanuele Pisani, and others. However, we concentrate primarily on accounting publications, and shall rarely mention those of finance or administrative studies in general.

Apart from Zappa's contributions, four features seem to be characteristic for Italian accounting of the first half of the twentieth century, particularly in comparison with France or even Germany.

First, an enormous interest in historical accounting studies deeply rooted in Italian tradition. Indeed, the sheer volume of this kind of research is so comprehensive that we can list only a few representative examples.

Second, some interest in cost accounting, though not as much as in Germany.

Third, relatively little interest in charts and master charts of accounts – apart from the work by Onida [1902–82] (1947a, 1947b) and by D'Ippolito [1894–1977] (1932, 1945, 1952, 1963). The pertinent government project for Italian accounting standards goes back to 1932. Teodoro D'Ippolito was a member of the pertinent *Central Commission for the Unification of Accounting, Uniconti.* The original description of this project is in D'Ippolito (1932), forming the reference point for the framework of the Commission Uniconti and, apparently, for the subsequent French '*plan contable*'. The explanation of the limited interest of other Italian accountants in master charts of accounts (during this period) might be found in the following statement:

> The tendencies towards charts of accounts in Italy are characterized by the fact that – in contrast to many other European countries, like Germany, France, Holland, Austria and Switzerland – the application of the master chart of accounts was not recommended by any official or semi-official authority or any business circles, and that they were promoted and introduced to actual practice by the universities, (p. 100) ... . The classification scheme [of Onida's and D'Ippolito's master charts] in Italy was tied to the controversy between the accounts classes of Cerboni and Besta in a similar way as this was done in the decade before Schmalenbach's master chart of accounts in Germany, namely by means of the 'criterion of homogeneity and value analysis' (p. 101).
>
> (Scherpf 1955: 100–1, translated; notes omitted)

Fourth, an equally limited interest in inflation accounting (again compared with the German and French language areas) – even if inflation may have influenced Italian accounting more indirectly as Canziani (1994: 147) indicated: 'The reality of income – particularly during inflation and with reference to firms – became a topic of troubled speculation in those very years, 1912–1920'.

5.2 Late publications by Cerboni, Rossi and Besta

Cerboni, Rossi and Besta dominated Italian accounting during the second half of the nineteenth century (see Mattessich 2003), but all three of them continued to publish during the subsequent two decades. In the case of Cerboni, there was mainly one notable publication, namely a 'self-reflective' essay on his creation of logismography.[3] This essay by Cerboni (1902) may have been his swan song; by this time logismography was going out of fashion – not only in governmental accounting (where it was abandoned soon after Cerboni left his high position as Accountant General of Italy), but also in business accounting (see also Cerboni 1901, 1902; Rigobon 1914). As an explanation, Canziani (1994: 144) pointed out that: 'the inner bureaucratic complications of Cerboni's system of double-entry were developing rapidly as a result of the increasing complexities of firms during this period of Italian economic development'.

Rossi (1901a, 1901b, 1907a, 1907b, 1921), who also has been promoting logismography, manifested a similar tendency. Already the title of his book, *Nuovi studi di Ragioneria e battaglie critiche* (1907a), revealed the clash between the traditionalists and some challenging 'modern' thoughts. This referred to the thoughts of Besta rather than Zappa, who at the time, was not yet a major force in accounting theory.

Besta, who had become prominent during the last decade of the nineteenth century, was during the first quarter of the twentieth century still the leading scholar when he completed his three-volume *magnum opus* (Besta 1922 – see also Besta 1880). This new trend (rooted in the older version of Spencer's and Comte's positivism) related accounting to economic theory, put great emphasis on *management control* (be it for private or public enterprises), and emphasized the applied scientific nature of accounting. Besta also represented another 'novel' trend, the shift from a personalistic to a non-personalistic (materialistic) theory of accounts along Villa's interpretation. Finally, and for Italian account-ing most decisively, Besta began to oppose the logismography of his predeces-sors. But Besta's thoughts still moved within the framework of the *proprietary* theory, without much consideration of the *entity theory*; above all, his system still rested on the balance sheet and its valuations (see also Besta 1910). Besta's work has been highly praised, also outside of Italy. Schneider, for example, spoke (with reference to Italy during this period) of 'a development of account-ing theory which reaches its climax in the comprehensive and outstanding (*mustergültigen*) work of Fabio Besta' (Schneider 1981: 124, translated).

The first volume of Besta's *magnum opus* (1922) was published in 1891 and the other two between 1909 and 1916. For Besta the centre of accounting was a 'fund', consisting of *active* (or positive) and *passive* (or negative) components, in other words, assets and liabilities. A first series of accounts was kept for the dif-ferent *real* elements (assets and liabilities), and a second series for the *ideal* parts, 'derived from the variable total sum of the fund'. The changes in assets and lia-bilities (original or elementary changes) determined the corresponding changes in the fund (derivative changes); thus, the entries were necessarily double and only double (cf. Besta 1922: Vol. III, 1–3, 61; *passim*). Besta addressed our 'real accounts' as 'position accounts', whereas his 'derived or ideal accounts' corre-sponded to our 'nominal accounts' (i.e. capital and income accounts).

Besta regarded all transactions as changes of proprietorship, and thus recognized only two kinds of transactional effects: those in a single account that constituted an augmentation of proprietorship ('positive'), and those that indicated its diminution ('negative'). In the awkward language of the time, he then regarded positive variations as augmentations of assets or diminutions of liabilities and derivative augmentations of net fund positive magnitude; and negative variations were diminutions of assets or augmentations of liabilities and derivative diminutions of net fund positive magnitude (cf. Besta 1922: Vol. II, book 6th, Chapter II, art. 3: 304ff.; Vol. III, 5ff.). The double-entry system required that the accounts for the total fund and its variations (propri-etorship accounts) and the accounts for the different elements of the fund (assets and liabilities accounts) were in opposition, so that in the first class positive variations were entered in 'credit' and negative ones in 'debit', whereas in the second class positive variations were 'debit' and negative 'credit' entries (Besta 1922: Vol. III, 3ff., 61ff.).

Besta defined accounting as a *science of economic control*, applicable to every sort of enterprise, or economic entity – family properties, the owners' equities of firms or public utilities and government entities. In this light, periodic income was a specific change of capital. Yet, his notion of economic control included the *antecedent and the concomitant as well as the subsequent.* That meant 'control' included not merely all the calculations, estimates, conjectures and final balance sheets that threw light upon the stewardship of management, but also the 'administrative enforcement' or those acts that compelled managers, employees and workmen to carry out their duties with care and precision (cf. Besta 1922: Vol. I, 30–41; *passim*). He established a general business framework, outlining the *organizational design* as a premise for economic control. This allowed management to make rational decisions and govern the business according to economic laws.

Thus, Besta clearly outlined the *proprietorship theory*. His *magnum opus* was the best treatise on an equity-based accounting system. Schneider characterized Hügli's and Schär's contributions as of 'pale one-sidedness' compared to those of Fabio Besta's and pointed out that: '[Besta] is the first to relate accounting to economic theory, e.g. he uses replacement values by appealing to Ricardo's value theory (reproduction costs) and concerns himself thoroughly with present value (*Ertragswert*) calculations of real estate and leases' (Schneider 2001: 98, translated).

Besta had many faithful disciples who developed and refined his ideas: Vittorio Alfieri [1863–1930] (1912, 1918a, 1918b), Pietro D'Alvise [1860–1943] (1920, 1932b), Vincenzo Vianello [1866–1935] (1924, 1935), Francesco de Gobbis [1863–1942] (1915, 1927), Pietro Rigobon [1868–1955] (1902, 1920), Carlo Ghidiglia [1870–1913] (1906, 1909a), Vincenzo Armuzzi [1861–1919] (1902, 1906, 1940), Benedetto Lorusso [1869–1939] (1911, 1912, 1922) and Alberto Ceccherelli [1885–1958] (1915, 1931, 1947, 1948, 1953). Other scholars, such as Vincenzo Masi [1893–1977] (1945, 1946a, 1946–47), Egidio Giannessi [1908–1982] (1935, 1943) and Alberto Riparbelli [1907–71] (1943, 1951–52), can be considered as having further developed Besta's theories. But the most notable of Besta's disciples was Gino Zappa, who, between 1921 and 1949, held the chair of accounting in the University of Venice, where Besta had previously taught.

5.3 Zappa's contributions

In Zappa's view (1920–29; 1937) the central theme of business accounting was income determination. This basic phenomenon became the foundation of all explanations of the accounting process – particularly of accounting theory and the balance sheet and income statement. Zappa emphasized the relevance of the income statement and the *dynamic aspects* of accounting. Just as in Schmalenbach's dynamic accounting theory, the balance sheet was in Zappa's scheme an instrument of income determination.

Zappa's accounting theory, emphasizing income determination, was a four-series-of-accounts theory. Being different from Besta's theory, it distinguished two series of real accounts (those for assets, on the one hand, and those for liabilities and owner's equities, on the other, translated as 'status accounts' by some Italian authors) and two series of nominal accounts (expense and revenue accounts, translated as 'achievement accounts' by some Italians). Debit entries were seen as initial assets, augmentations of assets, diminutions of equities, and expenses. Credit entries were: initial equities, augmentations of equities, diminutions of assets and revenues. The profit and loss account illuminated the general correlation between positive and negative income components attributable to definite activities. The balance sheet showed a system of stocks (a 'fund of values') for future income determination. Income components were based on monetary exchanges (cf. Zappa 1920–29, 1937: 321; cf. Caprara 1923) and were considered as 'amounts of exchange values'. Income is, in essence, a fact of value and therefore of distribution because it is determined only in the exchange and for the exchange (cf. Zappa 1920–29, 1937: 326).

Income expressed the flow of values, measured and based on a well-defined period connecting two points of time and two funds or stocks of values, namely the beginning and ending capital of the period (cf. Zappa 1920–29, 1937: 278f.; see also Caprara 1923). Although the premise for this so-called income system originated with Fabio Besta, Zappa's school imparted to it a new theoretical basis that differed fundamentally from Besta's original theory.[4]

According to Zappa's 'income system', the pre-eminent object of the financial statement was not to determine the status of capital (as Besta did). Zappa did not believe in determining the value of capital by adding up the value of individual elements, he rather equated the value of a business (and its capital) to the amount that could realize its future earnings capacity. Capital, in the sense of *capital value*, was simply future income discounted or 'capitalized' (cf. Zappa 1937: 306, 307). More precisely, the value of any resource was the discounted value of its future returns. In whatever way resources might be distributed and symbolized, the entire system of resources was merely a means to an end, the creation of *income*. The value of capital must be determined from the value of its estimated future net income, but the value of income was not derived from the value of the capital. The income stream was the joint product of many factors; it resulted from the business activity under utilization of an available capital (cf. Zappa 1937: 277, 283, 296–7, 306–7). Discounting the future income flow was seen as a means of determining the value of capital, but not as the only component. Another, a complementary one, was the 'revaluation' of the balance sheet and its capital, from which one attempted to forecast future net income and, specifically, the distributable future income.

The 'balance sheet capital' was determined through the interdependence of the values of its individual elements. In other words, the value of one item was seen as dependent on all the others and *vice versa*. This stems from the interdependence of the production factors represented by those values (based on a more general interdependence principle of evaluation for all elements of the pertinent 'economic system').[5]

Of course, one did not expect too much from the 'balance sheet capital' when used for purposes foreign to its nature, as in the case of 'liquidation' or 'merger' of the firm. In the latter case, the notion of capital value did not derive so much from the 'system of values', but from an autonomous and unitary assessment that resulted from the '*economic capital*' of the firm.

According to Zappa (1937: 87–90) the 'expected future net income' was the fundamental factor in the estimation of *economic capital value*, because the latter could be considered equal to the sum of the anticipated value of the 'income stream' (discounted at the discount rate, whereby due account had to be made for the 'risk factor'). *Capital gains* and *capital losses* were *not* treated as positive or negative items of income of the pertinent fiscal period.[6] They constituted 'adjustments' of the estimated income realized in preceding fiscal periods – where they were regarded as anticipations of the future, upon which every attempt to measure income had to be based. With the passage of time, such capital gains changed the character of income itself (cf. Zappa 1937: § 140). The problem of income measurement was inseparable from the problem of measuring changes in capital value. According to Zappa, 'business income' consisted, above all, of gains generated beyond mere capital maintenance (in real terms). Capital maintenance was a precondition for the existence of income. Although Zappa opted for multi-purpose valuation and periodic re-valuation, his capital maintenance concept was considered neither a real financial (nor a physical) one but one based on the present value notion and supposed to maintain income capacity.[7] Whenever the 'present value' was considerably below or in excess of acquisition costs, a comprehensive revaluation had to be undertaken. This was particularly important in the case of long-lived items; their capital gains were not recorded as realized income. However, capital losses were viewed as *special* losses, and treated accordingly.[8]

In the process of determining the 'business value', the discounting of future income flow was not the only factor; another complementary one was the revaluation of the balance sheet and its capital. From this Zappa attempted to predict the future income flow and, more specifically, the future periodic income to be distributed. This re-valued capital became the initial balance for the subsequent accounting period. It also was one of the points of reference for comparing the *economic capital* value, calculated by means of discounting the future income. This comparison was Zappa's criterion of rationality for measuring economic capital.[9]

Zappa argued that the distinction between *economic* (real) and *monetary* (nominal) revaluation would not suppress the unifying logic underlying the revaluation process. That is to say, general price-level changes (due to changes in purchasing power during inflationary or deflationary periods) or changes of specific prices, were considered part of the 'environmental turbulence' that could critically affect a firm's future. To harmonize the system of values with such changed economic conditions, a general revaluation process was required – and not merely one limited to individual classes of balance sheet values.

Zappa's proposal (1937: 583–6) for revaluations of the net worth in balance sheets relied on conventional accounting based on historical costs. He linked the revaluations to a general periodic revision of the 'system of values'. Thus, he believed that acquisition costs offered the best starting point, even if requiring adjustments later on. Zappa considered specific price indices or other current price indicators as unsatisfactory.

Zappa searched for a method of maintaining 'real capital' by maintaining the income capacity of the firm, measured by the change of *economic capital* during the period under *ceteris paribus* conditions (i.e. without counting dividends or capital withdrawals). Yet, he regarded a general comprehensive revaluation as justified only under *favourable* economic conditions of the enterprise (i.e. increased earnings capacity). Obviously, a revaluation of fixed assets and other items could convert acquisition costs into current market values. In Zappa's opinion, the cost basis was acceptable, provided one made periodic comprehensive revaluations by means of a general revision of the 'system of values'. These would take into consideration realistic depreciation, price-level adjustments, market value, replacement value, appraisal value and so on. In other words, the new conditions and economic prospects were determined by dynamics of the environment and that of the enterprise.[10]

Zappa (1920–29, 1927) was not merely a formal but also a substantive innovator as far as accounting was concerned. He viewed his 'theory of quantitative determination' as inseparable from the study of the organization and the management of an enterprise (avoiding any pure formalism). Consequently, accounting was seen as investigating the structure and economic life of the '*azienda*' (i.e. the 'enterprise', or an 'institution' or other 'entity', by some Italians addressed as a 'concern'), as based on the foundations of monetary-quantitative determination. Its purpose was the managerial-economic control that would attain the objectives of the enterprise efficiently. Thus, organization theory and management theory became inseparable from accounting theory (cf. Zappa 1927: 20, 1956–57: Vol. I, 106). He also devised a kind of 'system methodology' by employing such concepts as system, sub-system and super-system.[11] *Economia aziendale* (as a system) constituted an overall or meta-theory as far as the enterprise was concerned. Thus, the *economia aziendale* was conceived as consisting of interconnected sub-systems that revealed the entire *azienda* in all its complexity. Zappa expressed his view in the following way:

> if one believes that an organic whole can safely be broken down, and if one believes that the even greater range of phenomena under investigation requires a high degree of specialization, then we can accept the scientific autonomy of the three disciplines of management, organization and information systems. However, we must not forget the many ties, both obvious and hidden, that join those three disciplines. A knowledge system

cannot be developed, or worse, given credence, when being isolated from the knowledge that constitutes its natural substratum and logical complement.

(Zappa 1927: 33, translated)

Zappa's approach to *economia aziendale* was that of an institutionalist, as he emphasized typical institutions such as the family, the business enterprise, a public body or a cultural institution. For him the *azienda* was the economic entity, a concept that covered all kinds of economic units (not only the business entities that served the market); it included areas such as:

1 *Azienda di consumo privata* (institutions of private consumption), typically households.
2 *Azienda di produzione privata o pubblica* (institutions of private or public production), i.e. the business firm such as agricultural enterprises, trading companies, financial institutions (banks, insurance companies, etc.), as well as services entities.
3 *Azienda composta pubblica* (public institutions), typically the governmental bodies (municipal, provincial, regional, state and federal governments), i.e. entities generating goods and services and involved in public consumption (specifically through taxation).
4 *Azienda di vari istituti* (various other institutions), e.g. cultural, scientific, religious and educational entities, as well as political parties.

Zappa also stated that the so-called macro-economic phenomena could not be investigated or understood without a sufficient knowledge of micro-economic behaviour. However, *economia aziendale* required the examining of markets and the environment that gave meaning to the economic decisions relating to the management and the organization of each individual *azienda*. The accounting measurement of income, capital, cost of production and so on, were supposed to clarify relevant aspects of changes in market prices and clarify the movements based on the knowledge of every kind of entity participating in production, consumption and exchange. For further details on Zappa's contributions and revolution, see Bianchi (1984), Biondi (2002) and Canziani (1987).

Zappa not only continued Besta's work but also revolutionized Italian accounting (and management theory to an even higher extent), basing it partly on Mach's [1838–1916] critical-positivism, partly on pragmatism as interpreted by the Italian philosophers Giovanni Vailati [1863–1909] and Federigo Enriques [1871–1946]. Zappa's theory manifested influences from a wide spectrum of economists and philosophers. In Zappa (1910) he still adhered to Besta's views, investigating the accounting valuation criteria for limited companies, and presenting a comparison between historical versus current cost basis. But his accounting *magnum opus, La determinazione del reddito nelle imprese commerciali, I valori di conto in relazione alla formazione dei bilanci* (Zappa 1920–29) was hailed as revolutionary. Its pivot was valuation and the economic notion of *income;*[12] it was influenced by the newer trend of neo-positivistic, pragmatic and economic thought. Canziani asserted in this connection that:

> The conclusion of the Pigou vs. Hayek debate is that Great Britain failed to respond to the need for change, but in two countries namely Germany and Italy – innovative (and somewhat controversial) accounting ideas were developed, which tried to cope with the new theoretical and practical problems which inflation (and renewed epistemologies) had given rise to. The standard authors in the field are Eugen Schmalenbach for Germany (*Dynamische Bilanz*, 1919) and Gino Zappa for Italy (*Il Reddito*, 1920–29), who arrived at similar conclusions along different paths.
>
> (Canziani 1994: 152)

The last sentence may give rise to two important questions. First, to what extent did Schmalenbach and Zappa influence each other? Second, why was each of them silent about the other – be it in general or, at least, in their major works? A partial answer to this may be provided by Scherpf (1955: 104, translated) who pointed out that:

> The modern [i.e. before 1950] direction of *Economia aziendale* in Italy is one which Gomberg's [1908] 'Verrechnungswissenschaft' pursued .... Just like Gomberg, the Italian school refuses the notion of *Betriebswirtschaft-slehre* .... It also attacks the German research methods [in footnote, reference to Onida 1947b: 9].

Such a statement may seem surprising (particularly in the face of the similarities between Zappa's and Schmalenbach's theories) but can easily be misunderstood. Obviously, the Italians had no objection to the mere notion of *Betrieb-swirtschaftslehre*; and if they really attacked the German methodology, it was precisely because the difference was a methodological one.[13] To understand this reaction against the German approach, one ought to examine the similarities as well as differences between the Italian *economia Aziendale* and the German *Betriebswirtschaftslehre* and the accounting aspects of both.

Apart from the quest for a smaller number of accounts, for example, by Zappa (making a master chart of accounts practically superfluous), the distinction between the Italian *economia aziendale* and the German *Betriebswirtschaftslehre* was, according to some Italian scholars, the supposed 'fact' that the former referred to a broader and more universal notion. This is the very reason why some Italians preferred to translate *economia aziendale* with the term 'concern economics' instead of, for example, 'management economics' that would sound less outlandish to the English ear. The argument was that an *azienda* need not necessarily be a business entity but could also be that of a household or government organization.[14] Indeed, the Italian, as well as the German, notions were originally conceived as the foundation stones of a new discipline integrating accounting, production and organization theory, marketing, etc. This made

eminent sense at the early part of the twentieth century when the pertinent literature in many of these sub-areas was relatively small, and when one needed a
'united front' to consolidate a young and struggling discipline. Today, when the
immense amount of management and administrative publications can be contained only through increasing specialization, these advantages may no longer
have the same relevancy. And language areas, like the English one – where the
term 'business administration' referred, even decades ago, to a portmanteau
expression rather than a truly unified and unifying discipline – are nowadays
reaping the advantage of unimpeded specialization in research, be it in accounting or any other related discipline. This is not tantamount to loosing sight that all
the specialized subjects are embedded in the common endeavour of studying
business, governmental and other entities. Yet, in Europe this 'Anglo-American
view' is still not yet generally accepted.

For both Zappa and Schmalenbach the pivotal point was relevant income
measurement. Viganò characterized Zappa's accounting theory in the following
words that would hold no less for that of Schmalenbach:

> The concern is a dynamic entity, so costs and revenues really exist as ele-
> ments of the income itself. A concern exists over time; over time only
> income exists. Net worth (in Italian, *capitale netto contabile*) is thus a
> derived concept, static, and artificial, far removed from the dynamic nature
> of the *azienda*. Except for monetary items, net worth is seen as consisting of
> deferred costs and revenues rather than assets and liabilities. The balance
> sheet is thus derived from the profit and loss account.
>
> (Viganò 1998: 389)

As regards valuation, again the basic thrust was apparently the same for
Zappa as for Schmalenbach. Both seemed to have had a bias in favour of the
acquisition cost basis, but they were realistic enough to accept a multi-value
basis when necessary. Thus, in the theories of both scholars one encountered
values other than acquisition costs (in Zappa's theory even replacement values
and present values). A minor difference may have been Zappa's embracing of
Irving Fisher's notion that capital was determined through income, thus paying
slightly more respect to the balance sheet as a *static* picture, though one less
relying on the past than the future. Some believe that this can be reconciled
with a preference for acquisition costs instead of present values because in
Zappa's system the cost basis was acceptable, provided one made periodic
revaluations of the capital on the basis of discounted future income flows.
However, Zappa did have reservations against Fisher's income notion, mainly
because it was conceived in view of personal consumption and not so much for
business entities.

A major distinction between Zappa and Schmalenbach was the latter's comprehensive treatment and important contributions to cost accounting, while
Zappa's interest in cost accounting is still disputed.

This has been admitted by Viganò (1998: 389), who says that such 'theoretical and practical considerations have led Italian accounting theory to disregard almost completely cost accounting and its evolution'. Canziani reinforced this view with the following words:

> A topic relatively set apart was cost (managerial) accounting, due to the two following reasons: (1) the accent has been on income, that is to say on the external operations: production costs were in this way secondary data and determined outside the double-entry system; (2) Zappa (1955–7) had made the firm statement that costs *per se* were impossible to know due to the fact that too many hypotheses and conventions were involved in their calculation.
>
> (Canziani 1994: 160)

However, Zappa did not deny the usefulness of cost determination or its possibility. He merely emphasized that costs could not be the object of a rigorous scientific measurement (e.g. in the allocation of overhead costs). This was a major argument for not involving himself in cost accounting – though he recognized its usefulness from a practical point of view.

Finally, Zappa as well as Schmalenbach contributed essentially to accounting practice and legislation. In the latter area Zappa's influence was felt when the Civil Code of 1942 (which did not prescribe any compulsory contents of the income statement) was revised in 1974 (act 7.6.1974, no. 216). The company law reform (together with the tax law reform) that passed in the 1970s, improved considerably the quality of information supplied in published financial statements, particularly as regards the earnings capacity of an enterprise. Among the many innovations were: (1) the inclusion of a detailed income account (of definite format and minimal content) and specific information on associated company shareholdings. The income account contained *costi, ricavie. rimanenze* (costs, revenues and inventories), classified by functions of the income components (just as proposed by Zappa's income theory); (2) a register of accounting firms authorized to perform company audits issued by the National Commission for Companies and Stock Exchanges (CONSOB); (3) acceptance of the financial statements for tax purposes, provided they were certified by such a registered audit firm.

In summarizing the comparison made above, it seems that (apart from the greater emphasis on cost accounting and master charts by Schmalenbach), the differences between Zappa's and Schmalenbach's views may have looked more formidable during the first half of the twentieth century than they do nowadays when style and technical details are seen to be less relevant. One may also add that both Zappa and Schmalenbach left a decisive legacy in the form of their students, assistants and disciples.

Among the dozens of volumes, essays and articles by Zappa, the further publications ought to be mentioned: Zappa (between 1915 and 1920, 1924, 1935a, 1935b, 1946, 1956–57, 1962), Zappa *et al.* (1949, 1951), Zappa and Marcantonio (1954).

Zappa had many disciples who distinguished themselves in accounting and *economia aziendale* studies: Aldo Amaduzzi [1904–91] (1936, 1955, 1956, 2001), Lino Azzini [1908–86], Ugo Caprara [1894–1990], Giuseppe Cudini, Teodoro D'Ippolito [1894–1977] (1937, 1946a, 1967), Arnaldo Marcantonio (1942, 1950), Carlo Masini [1914–95] (1947a, 1947b), Pietro Onida, Napoleone Rossi (1949, 1950a, 1950b), Tommaso Zerbi [1908–2001] (1940, 1948). Other experts, such as Lorenzo De Minico [1896–1949] (1927, 1931), Domenico Amodeo [1912–98] (1938, 1950b), Paolo Emilio Cassandro (1950a, 1950b), and Amedeo Salzano [1908–84] (1936, 1942b) were not really Zappa's disciples, but their works were in some ways extensions of his basic teaching.

In addition to those scholars and their studies of accounting and *economia aziendale* (concerning foundations and general theories) many other disciples of Zappa published in specialized applied fields (e.g. trade, industrial, agricultural, financial and services enterprises). Among them were scholars like Riccardo Argenziano, Tancredi Bianchi, Ugo Borroni, Giordano Dell'Amore, Luigi Guatri, Ettore Lorusso, Giorgio Pivato, Pasquale Saraceno, Giulio Zunino and others.

Yet the new trend promoted by Zappa in accounting, management and administrative studies also aroused criticism and objections by scholars such as Vittorio Alfieri, Ubaldo De Dominicis [1913–98] (1937, 1950a, 1950b), Francesco De Gobbis, Francesco della Penna [1886–1976], Vincenzo Masi and Vincenzo Vianello (particularly in the 1930s, continuing up to the late 1950s). Yet, despite most aggressive critics, Zappa remained recognized as a major scholar in the field of accounting and management studies, and his work was never belittled. For further aspects on Zappa's work, his disciples and disputes between them and Zappa's opponents, see Serra (1999: 273–93).

5.4 Studies in cost accounting

Research by such scholars as De Minico (1935, 1946), D'Ippolito (1935a, 1935b, 1946a, 1946b), Amodeo (1941, 1950a) and De Minico and Amodeo (1942), concentrated on the methodology of costing and cost allocations, and the link between costs and prices. These were notable Italian contributions in cost accounting, deserving proper attention. Further important cost accounting studies were those by Jannaccone (1904), Argenziano (1910), Battarra (1911), Tognacci (1925), Onida (1926), Pacces (1934), Giannessi (1935, 1937, 1943, 1944), Ceccherelli (1936), Bodrito (1937–38), Giovannini (1938–39), Ardemani (1940, 1944), Sassi (1940), Amodeo (1945a, 1945b), Marcantonio (1942), Riera (1942, 1949), Guatri (1951), Salzano (1951).

However, Italian cost accounting during this period had to overcome a formidable hurdle, namely the resistance of Zappa, the leading accounting authority of the time. Cinquini and Marelli (2002: 97) pointed in this direction by stating that: 'Under this [i.e. Zappa's] teaching, based on a systematic approach to business, the possibility of getting detailed information about management was substantially denied'. And a passage in Bergamin-Barbato and his co-authors articulated this allegation in the following words:

> For Zappa all operation performed within a company and all decisions taken by management are related to one another, and it is impossible to distinguish the financial consequences of one activity (operations and decisions) from those of another. Only the total income can be computed, and specific margins of individual segments of the whole activity are considered misleading.
>
> (Bergamin-Barbato *et al.* 1996: 142)

Yet, the need of industry, the influence of English and German costing literature, and the acumen of scholars interested in costing issues prevailed. It led to interesting contributions, among which we shall concentrate on those by Lorenzo De Minico and his major disciple, Domenico Amodeo (other followers were Sassi and Salzano). De Minico's views may be summarized in five points:

First, instead of regarding costs merely as negative income, De Minico focused on the potential of the services (and their flows) for which costs were incurred.

Second, increasing industrialization and the concomitant economic complexity of factories were not a deterrent in concerning oneself with the seemingly arbitrary and pragmatic problem of allocating 'common costs' (i.e. overhead costs). On the contrary, this growing complexity was a challenge; it rather proved the necessity of attempting such allocation procedures, and of developing a proper methodology for it.

Third, adequate allocation of overhead costs was a matter *relative* to the particular business situation; it required a keen personal judgement based on competent knowledge of the specific circumstances.

Fourth, a thorough analysis of cause and effect relations between costs and benefits was the basis for proper cost allocation. This applied not only to the identification of (what in modern terminology is called) the 'cost drivers', but also to the costs of 'cost allocation' itself in relation to the benefits it offered.

Fifth, a consideration of the time element in cost allocation – particularly when considering such costs as depreciations that not only required allocation to products but also over various periods.

De Minico also believed that many costs can be treated as 'direct' and presented a series of illustrations to confirm the validity of this view (cf. Cinquini and Marelli 2002: 103–4). Above all, in response to Zappa, he stated 'the scientific problem will not be solved if we merely consider cost data derived from manipulated figures, this only leads, from an empirical point of view, to a dead end' (De Minico 1946: 115, translated).

He also questioned thoughtless aggregation and allocating procedures that fail to consider the individuality of each type of cost. And it was on this basis that Amodeo (1941: 192–217) 'analysed different proportional cost methods for tracing common costs; he confirmed De Minico's theories but, at the same time, he left open the possibility of using these methods, even if only in connection with specific situations' (quoted from Cinquini and Marelli 2002: 105).

5.5 Theoretical accounting studies by other Italian scholars

The concern with government accounting, a particularly favourite topic of Italian scholars, was taken up by Besta (1900), Pisani [1845–1915] (1901b, 1909), Rossi (1901b, 1905, 1906, 1909b, 1910a, 1910b, 1912b, 1917), Ravenna (1903), Ghidiglia (1909b), De Brun (1911), D'Alvise (1912, 1939, 1940), Bruni (1914), Lorusso (1924), Ruffini (1924), Vianello (1925, 1927), Cova (1926), Monetti (1926, 1937), Tognacci (1930), Chianale (1935), Rossi-Passavanti (1935), Riera (1935), Masi (1937, 1947), Pivato (1942, 1946) and Marcantonio (1950). But it has to be emphasized that many of these accounting theories were developed to serve both the public as well as the private sector.

Another frequently encountered concern was of a more philosophical nature; namely the scientific status of accounting. Pertinent studies can be found in Masetti (1901), Virgili (1902), Sanguinetti [1855–1915] (1903), Lorusso (1906), Matteucci (1908), Rossi (1901a, 1908, 1909a, 1912a), Mondini [1849–1917] (1910, 1911, 1912), Ghidiglia (1911, 1912), Zorli (1911a, 1911b, 1919, 1939), Germani (1914), Vianello (1914, 1928), Alfieri (1918a), Ceccherelli (1922), Della Penna (1922), Terranova (1924), Zappa (1927), Zorli (1933), De Gobbis (1934a), D'Alvise (1936), Masi (1943), Onida (1947c) and Colletti (1954). Related to this was the controversy between the 'new' versus the 'old' approach to accounting, as studied by Galagan (1912), Masi (1935, 1939a), Bellini [1852–1935] (1924a, 1924b), Alfieri (1928) and De Gobbis (1939).

Finally, there were theoretical investigations often encountered in textbooks, such as those by Pisani (1901a, 1903), Massa (1905–08), Ghidiglia (1906, 1909a, 1909b, 1913–15), Bellini [1852–1935] (1908), Ravenna (1909–22), Alfieri (1914, 1918b, 1921), Gitti [1856–1945] (1915), Mondini (1916a, 1916b), Onida (1927, 1931, 1935, 1944, 1945, 1947a, 1947b), De Gobbis (1931, 1934b), Giovannini (1935, 1936, 1942), Vianello (1935), Della Penna (1937, 1946–50), Masi (1938, 1939b), D'Ippolito (1940), Saraceno (1941), Verna (1942), Pagnano (1943, 1944), Colletti (1945, 1947), De Minico (1946), Ceccherelli (1947), Masini (1947a), Amaduzzi (1949, 1950), Verna (1950) and, of course, the works mentioned in section 5.2 by Cerboni, Rossi and Besta, and in section 5.3 by Zappa.

5.6 Italian scholars and accounting history

History has, for a long time, been a favourite of Italian accounting scholars.[15] They ploughed this field so extensively that only the best-known names and publications can be mentioned. The major works up to the end of the First World War were: Brambilla's (1901) summary of Italian accounting history; Sanguinetti's (1901, 1902) historical survey of Rossi's works; Pisani's (1903) history of statmography (is a theoretical, as well as historical, study); Brambilla's (1905) essay on government accounting in Athens; Cantoni's (1905) history of accounting with a bibliographical appendix; Palumbo's (1906) historical research of accounting in the Monte di Pietà (pawnbroker's shop) of Palermo; the books by Einaudi (the internationally renowned economist and former president of the Italian Republic) (1907, 1908) with his research on accounting and finance of the Savoy State in the eighteenth century.

Other research was done by Massa's [1850–1918] (1907) who presented an historical survey and development of accounting from Roman times, through the Middle Ages and modern times until the contemporary era. In *Opere antiche di ragioneria* (Massa 1911) he produced a survey of antique accounting works, such as those by Pacioli, Manzoni, Casanova and Pietra. Pellerano's (1909) historical survey and critique of Cerboni's work; Ceccherelli's (1910, 1913, 1914) researches on accounting of the ancient Italian medieval companies, and his study of the economics of the Medici bank and of double-entry accounting in fourteenth-century Florence; Guidetti's (1910) essay on double-entry bookkeeping of a foureenth-century Italian municipality; Tofani's (1910) research on accounting in the Republic of Florence; Marchi's (1911, 1912) historical survey of accounting evolution, and accounting as a social function; Bossi's (1912, 1914, 1917) research on accounting and finance of the Vatican during the centuries; Rigobon's (1912) research on some historical-bibliographical notes on synthetic double-entry bookkeeping; Bellini's (1914a) analysis of the combination of journal and ledger in the 'American' bookkeeping method (which might be included among historical studies), and Bellini's (1914b, 1927) historical survey of Cerboni's work and life; Alfieri's (1915) survey of accounting from antiquity to the twentieth century; Riccardi's (1915) research on accounting in ancient Pompey; Besta's (1922: Vol. III, book 9, Chapter IX: 273–359, Chapter X: 360–420) great historical survey of the origin, the development, the practice and literature of double-entry system; and Corsani's (1917) research on criteria of wealth valuation in fourteenth-century Tuscany.

For the time after the First World War, the following publications might be mentioned: Corsani's (1922) research on administration and accounting of an Italian medieval merchant from unedited letters and documents; Caprara's (1923) cultural analysis of the double-entry system. Furthermore, there were Sapori's (1923, 1928, 1931, 1932, 1934, 1940, 1943, 1944–45, 1947, 1952) description of accounting books and accounting double-entry systems of Italian medieval companies and merchants in domestic and foreign trade. Then, Bellini's (1924a) summary of Italian accounting reviews and his (Bellini 1924b) survey of the accountant profession; Ruffini's (1924) study on French government accounting during the Napoleonic era; Chianale's (1926) study on accounting in the Papal state, and his (Chianale 1928) comparison between the German *Betriebswirtschaftslehre* and the business approach in English literature (that nowadays may already be counted as a historical study).

Other important publications were by Chiaudano's (1927, 1933, 1934, 1937) research on accounting and finance of the Savoy state in the thirteenth century; D'Alvise's (1932a) survey of the Italian logismologic doctrine, and his

(D'Alvise 1932c) historical investigation and tribute to Besta's work, as well as his (D'Alvise 1933) historical treatise on innovations in accounting.

Furthermore, there was Vianello's (1932) commemoration of Fabio Besta and homage to his eminent contributions; similarly Ceccherelli's (1933) tribute to the work of Besta. There were Astuti's (1934) analysis of an account book of a Sienese medieval merchant, and Fanfani's (1935) research on the activity of a merchant of the fourteenth century; Masi's (1935) compilation of works reflecting the struggle between various Italian business and accounting doctrines; Rossi-Passavanti's (1935) historical survey of government accounting; Zerbi's (1935, 1936a, 1936b) historical research on the economics and accounting aspects of the bank in the Visconti state, his description of an accounting ledger in a fourteenth century commercial house, and his historical investigation on economic aspects of the Milan market of the fourteenth century.

Belardinelli's (1936) comparison of the works of Cerboni, Besta and Zappa are also worth mentioning, as well as Ceccherelli's (1938) description, analyses and interpretation of ancient accounts books; Riera's (1938) essay on Pacioli's 'Tractatus de computis et scripturis'; Chianale's (1939) remarks on ancient Egyptian accounting; Salvatore Sassi's (1939) remarks about double-entry accounting in the ledgers of a fraternity.

In the 1940s there were: Adamoli's (1940) study of German accounting; Castagnoli's (1940) research on accounting in the Roman world; Cassandro's (1941) historical survey of Schmalenbach's work; Salzano's (1941a, 1941b) description of the accounting and organization of a bank and mercantile entity in a fifteenth-century Italian town, and his research on accounting, finance and economics of a fifteenth-century municipality, as well as the tribute to the work of Antonio Tonzig in Salzano (1942a); Botarelli's (1945) survey of Italian accounting history; Antoni's [1915–2001] (1946) research of the use of the balance sheet in a fourteenth-century Italian firm; Masi's (1946b) tribute to the historical accounting contribution of Fabio Besta, as well as his (Masi 1997) posthumous *La ragioneria nell' età moderna e contemporanea*.

And the 1950s began with Melis' [1914–73] (1950a) monumental work on accounting history, spanning the time from about the third millennium BC to the early twentieth century (see also Melis 1940, 1946, 1947, 1948, 1950b). Furthermore, there was Onida's (1951) comparison between Italian accounting as part of *Economia aziendale* and the accounting and business theory of foreign countries; and, finally, Zerbi's (1952) contribution on the genesis of systematic double-entry accounting.

Zerbi's (1952) work on the origins of double-entry is particularly relevant. It showed the evolution of accounting of many private and public entities, illuminating particularly the changes in moving from simple debit and credit techniques to more sophisticated transactions that recorded economic and financial results. This evolution took place in the period from the first half of the fourteenth century to the middle of the fifteenth century. The many ledgers and journals investigated by Zerbi all date to a time prior to the 'Tractatus de computis et scripturis' by Luca Pacioli, published in 1494. Totally original was the research of the historical precedents of double-entry, based on ledger transactions (of debtors and creditors) that Zerbi called 'tabular entries'. The first three chapters dealt systematically with the methodological features of the 'liber tabulae' (book of tables) and documented the age, the 'autonomy' and the 'splendour' of the tabular technique, probably handed down from the Roman Empire but still in use during the later part of the fifteenth century (particularly in the practice of the Lombard *rationatores*).

Zerbi examined the reasons for developing the 'liber tabulae' in the main ledger. He showed the use of the 'lista debitorum et creditorum libri' (the books of debits and credits) and the 'balantium' (balance sheet) of various wealth components, as well as the 'lucra et perditae' (i.e. the profit and loss account). This is why Zerbi based his accounting theory on market studies of firms. Accounting entries without an 'organic synthesis' of the dual aspects of all transactions could, obviously, not qualify as a double-entry system in the proper sense.

Finally, there is Amodeo's (1953) analysis and interpretation of an ancient financial statement of Naples' Vice-Royalty (though the last few items belong, strictly speaking, already to the next period and chapter).

6 Accounting research in Italy

Second half of the twentieth century[1]

6.1 Introduction

Italian accounting research has assumed a leading role several times in the course of history. However, in the second half of the twentieth century the Anglo-American accounting literature dominated our discipline to a considerable extent. Thus, it is understandable that Italian accounting research played a less influential role during this period, particularly as it continued to hold on to the dogmas of Zappa's *economia aziendale* (for the latter, see Ferrero 1968; Giannessi 1960). Nevertheless, one occasionally has the impression of a self-proclaimed superiority of Italian accounting research combined with some hesitation to learn from accounting knowledge gained abroad. This tendency may possibly have prevented a faster adaptation to the Anglo-American trend.

However, there were exceptions, and slowly new orientations did establish themselves. Important publications referring to foreign accounting research made their appearance already during the early part of this period, though usually without abandoning their *zapparian* heritage (see subsequent sections). It must be borne in mind that Zappa's (1950) influence and activity continued in Italian accounting well into the second half of the twentieth century (see Zappa 1955–57, 1957, 1962; Zappa *et al.* 1951a, 1951b; Zappa and Marcantonio 1954).

But to comprehend *ragioneria* (Italian accounting) of this period, one must be aware of the unique and potent influence that Zappa's *economia aziendale* exercised (cf. Biondi 2002). Therefore, in contrast to other chapters, where such inclusive super-disciplines as 'business and public administration' (in the English language area) or even *Betriebswirtschaftslehre* (in the German language area) played a less decisive role, one has to pay greater attention in this chapter to *economia aziendale*.

6.2 *Ragioneria* and *economia aziendale*

Economia aziendale was conceived by Zappa as a unifying discipline of all productive and economic activities for business *as well as* government entities. At a first glance, such a conception may resemble what in English literature is known under 'business and public administration', but this resemblance is deceiving.

First of all, the *azienda* is regarded as an autonomous and holistic (*unitaria*) system, and *economia aziendale* is claimed to possess 'laws' of its own, independent of its sub-disciplines or even of microeconomics. Second, *economia aziendale* consists of three sections. The *azienda* is examined in terms of the following related fields: *organizzazione* (organization), *ragioneria* (accounting) and *gestione* (management and operations). However, the last area possesses two aspects of which only one is part of *economia aziendale*.

The first of these aspects is 'subjective'; it concerns managerial activities and the decision-making process. The second is 'objective'; it refers to events occurring within the *azienda*, examining the dynamics of various trends and activities. An English equivalent would be 'operations'. Only this latter aspect was part of the early Italian doctrine of the *economia d'azienda* (cf. Onida 1960).

The reason for this relatively narrow view seems to lie in the average size and the typical proprietary structure of the typical Italian *azienda* – particularly at the time when this doctrine was established. In English-speaking countries, the archetypical enterprise is medium or large, with many shareholders (if it is a public company). There, the fundamental problem relates to the choice of the manager and the assessment of his or her success. In Continental Europe, however, the *azienda* is, or used to be, typically medium or of small size – often being a sole or one-family proprietorship. Widespread shareholding was much rarer, and capital markets did not function as effectively. The owner was the only possible manager, self-elected, self-imposed, self-approved, and often irremovable. The problem of selection and evaluation of his activity rarely arose. Thus, the 'subjective' problem of choosing a manager (so well analysed in modern 'agency theory') rarely played a crucial part and, hence, did not represent the object of much research.

The *azienda* was examined in terms of its actual activity as an integrated set of operations, but not so much from the point of view of its various *functions*, and certainly not from the perspective of the quality of its management. This affected the *ragioneria*, because the nature of the *azienda* was conceived in such a way that its operations and accounting were inseparable. In consequence, accounting for control, as theoretically conceived, was very different in the typical Italian *azienda* from what it is today in a large Anglo-American corporation. It is the profound change, experienced during recent decades in European enterprises, partly due to a widespread internationalization, that makes not only the objective aspect but also the subjective one of management research necessary in accounting (cf. Bergamin-Barbato *et al.*, 1996). The recent popularity of agency theory, even in European accounting, is an excellent evidence for the need of such an 'additional' effort.

There can be no doubt that Zappa and his *economia aziendale* was a crucial achievement for Italian accounting (see Chapter 4), and that his publications as well as those of his disciples exercised great influence even after his death. Yet, one might raise the question whether in the second half of the twentieth century these insufficiently challenged ideas were as valid as half a century before. Did these deeply ingrained notions perhaps handicap Italian accounting during subsequent decades – particularly, as far as the adaptation to new ways of thinking were concerned? Monopolistic domination in academy can be no less precarious than in economics. However, whether such a comparison is valid may still be a controversial issue.

Critics of *economia aziendale* do not deny that in the 1920s and 1930s, when it was developed, it fulfilled an important function by embedding several specialized areas of business and government into one holistic discipline. Yet, one may argue that meanwhile dramatic changes have occurred, not only in industry but also in business and government research. The new situation can be better handled through specialization within a relatively loose super-discipline like 'business and public administration' than through *economia aziendale* that claims to be an 'organic' entity with its own laws.

Fanni and Cossar (1994) pointed out that among some supporters of *economia aziendale* there exists a tendency of extreme abstraction (apparently meant in the 'formalistic' rather than a mathematical sense). And Canziani (1994: 161–2), in referring to *economia aziendale*, speaks of the danger of 'progressive seclusion of theory from practice and in some cases its sterile repetition'.

6.3 Financial accounting

6.3.1 Income-oriented accounting

The 'income-oriented' trend had in the first part of the twentieth century an immediate and widespread success in Italy where it still constitutes the dominant approach. Most Italian researchers consider accounting to be an organic part of *economia aziendale*; indeed, the latter largely grew out of accounting that still represents its very core. The central dogmatic notion is the 'unity' (inseparability) of the *azienda* and, in consequence, of income. Events occurring in the *azienda* give rise to positive and negative changes, as elements of the periodic formation of income. Because events are assumed to be inseparable over the entire life of the *azienda*, income (with its cost and revenue components) is also envisaged as a holistic notion, rooted in the *azienda* as a totality. Only for practical reasons is this 'holistic' feature occasionally or temporarily abandoned – though never for periods of less than a year, and not for determining partial or interim results.

Furthermore, *economia aziendale* rejects the notion of matching specific principle cost with specific revenues. It asserts that only the totality of costs is comparable to the totality of all revenues. A single cost does not generate any particular revenue, but rather contributes to the totality of revenues (in Italian accounting there is no recognizable 'matching' principle). Correspondingly, a single revenue item does not derive from a single cost item, but from the contribution of all the costs.

As the *azienda* is a dynamic entity, costs and revenues are elements of the income stream, and the time dimension of the *azienda* becomes that of income. Net worth (in Italian, *capitale netto contabile*) is assumed to be merely as a *derived* concept, static and artificial – far removed from the dynamic nature of the *azienda*. Except for monetary items, net worth is seen as consisting of deferred costs and revenues rather than assets and liabilities (similar as in Schmalenbach's dynamic accounting)[2] – though, the balance sheet is derived from the profit and loss account.

This interpretation is associated with a specific recording method (the 'income system' – Zappa 1950),[3] characterized by the following constraints:

i   Partial results, operational areas, profit centres, interim or segmental reports are *not* permitted (they are seen as denying the holistic nature of the *azienda*).
ii   Income derives from external events only: internal events are meaningless for recording; hence traditional cost accounting is rejected.
iii   Process costing and cost control are both pretty much disregarded because they lead to unreliable figures (they are based on the assumption that costs can be meaningfully allocated).
iv   Financial statements are centred on the profit and loss account (dynamic account), while the balance sheet appears as a derived (and static) account. What is 'real' is income (with the net worth measured in relation to it).
v   The capital value of the *azienda* is simply the present value of the (discounted) average future income. Assets do not have an independent unique value, but their worth depends upon their contribution to the generation of income.
vi   The fact that every *azienda* is considered unique (i.e. no two are alike) does not allow for uniform accounting and standardized financial statements or related legal constraints.

The income-oriented approach grew out of opposition to the preceding *patrimonialistc* approach, identified with Besta (1922). There, the emphasis was on capital (as the ultimate accounting reality) as reflected in the balance sheet. In the eyes of its opponents (in Italian called '*i zappiani*' with their '*reddidistic*' or income-oriented approach), this 'synthetic' and 'analytic' (atomistic) direction would reduce the *azienda* to nothing but the sum of its parts. Each of these components would have to be considered a separate and independent reality with its own value. If capital constitutes the main focus, income becomes the accounting measurement of the change in capital over time. It is interesting to note that this *patrimonialistic* notion comes closer to the modern approach propagated in North America (see Chapter 17) than does Zappa's approach – though the latter is still fervently defended in Italy.

6.3.2 *The crisis of economia aziendale as reflected in accounting*

Economia aziendale in Italy has had a heterogeneous development. Many scholars of *ragioneria* considered *economia aziendale* as an enlargement of their subject area. Indeed, in many ways, *economia aziendale* is foremost a natural extension of accounting rather than a genuine all-embracing discipline. It almost exclusively relies on economic concepts; it neglects sociological and behavioural ones, even though it contains elements from management, organization, marketing, etc.[4] But those 'enriching' aspects can hardly be compared with the vast specialized literature constituting 'business and public administration'. Consider the innumerable Anglophile journals and publications in such areas as modern marketing and advertising, organization theory (behavioural and economic), operations research and production theory, management science, business policy, labour and public relations theory, and many other specializations.

Thus, it is not surprising that some scholars of the *azienda* not specifically engaged in accounting research were reluctant to accept the leading role of accounting, and often adhered to *economia aziendale* only at a formal level. This may be the reason why various academics, including some outstanding ones, have turned their attention to different fields of research.

The success of Italian accounting scholarship in previous periods may have fostered a notion of superiority or even a cultural arrogance. This may have enhanced the inertia towards adapting to foreign accounting research. And in the absence of clearly stated theoretical goals, Italian accounting scholars may, in the name of *economia aziendale*, have steered away from studying relevant empirical and related problems.

Yet, *economia aziendale* is supposed to deal with 'real' phenomena, and its theories and methods, whether exploited in accounting or any other sub-discipline, should have practical applications. However, an Italian reading an American accounting text might deem it to be not integrated or holistic enough, or too pragmatic and, above all, deviating too much from the accustomed dogmas of *economia aziendale*. An American, on the other hand, reading a text on *ragioneria*, would find little to understand, might consider it too general-formalistic, and of little practical relevance (cf. Chatfield 1982).[5]

6.3.3 Onida and Amaduzzi

Pietro Onida was probably the most competent and internationally best oriented of the accounting scholars of the early part of this period. Canziani (1994: 158) compared the scientific relation between Zappa and Onida (in accounting) with that between Keynes and Hicks (in economics). Canziani also pointed out that:

> Onida's most important contributions are expressed by the twin books on finance (1931a, 1931b), by the two monographs on annual and special accounts (1935, 1944), by a book dealing with the new accounting logic stemming from Zappa's ideas (1947), and an historical reconstruction of the development of business and firm studies in Italy since the nineteenth century, also covering the innovative role of Gino Zappa as well as the discontinuities, with Giuseppe Cerboni (1951) [p. 158] .... The general treatise on annual balance sheets – a classical approach like Paton's – is Onida (1945), where the new

economic logic imprints the general framework and technical solutions, while also referring to most categories of industrial and commercial company. This book puts forward the idea, dishonestly applied by some companies, of smoothing net income through special provisions in (highly) profitable years to be drawn upon in difficult years in order to permit the so-called 'dividend stabilisation'. Onida is widely referenced for specialised forms of balance sheets [e.g. of banks], and this theme was further developed by other disciples of Zappa [p. 160].

> (Canziani 1994: 158–1960 – publications mentioned in this citation are listed in the references of our Chapter 5)

Onida was a profound thinker who extended Zappa's thoughts – indeed, his last work was called the *Economia d'azienda* (Onida 1960) – and yet he was open to new ideas. He actively promoted and analysed the contemporary Anglo-American accounting literature, and was, at this time, one of the few Continental European scholars paying attention to the work of Chambers (lionized in the English and particularly Australian literature). Being highly critical of Chambers' ideas (cf. Onida 1970, 1973a), Onida entered into a debate with Chambers, and even translated and published the latter's response to this criticism (Onida 1973b). Onida's view reflected the more purpose-oriented and, in general, very different mentality of Continental Europeans, compared to the search for a single-value approach as pursued in Chambers' work and in parts of the Anglophile literature. In this controversy Onida seems to deviate from Zappa's doctrine – that despite offering a very different outlook than Chambers' – also aimed at a *pure science* of accounting, and was blind to the fact that the very *raison d'être* of this discipline lies in its pragmatic representation of reality (be it physical, social-economical or social-legalistic – see Mattessich (1995: 41–58)).

Although Onida was perhaps the most important disciple of Zappa, it was Amaduzzi who may have been the one best representing the continuation and partial revision of Zappa's theory. This may explain why Amaduzzi (e.g. 1962) is the only one of those disciples to whom Serra (1999) devoted a separate chapter in his recent history of Italian accounting.

Apart from substituting Zappa's classification of accounts by a somewhat different and simpler one, Amaduzzi's most important revision was – according to Serra (1999: 279) – to abandon the one-sided emphasis on income (Zappa's '*systema del reddito*') in favour of a more balanced view that paid more attention to the notion of capital (Besta's '*sistema del patrimonio*'). It is interesting to note that a very similar reaction occurred in German accounting where Schmalenbach's closest disciple, E. Walb (1948), also deviated from his master's monistic income orientation to a more dualistic one that no less appreciates the importance of the capital notion (see Chapter 3). But the attempts to develop the *zapparian* system by Amaduzzi (1965), did not nearly have the impact that Zappa's original work had in Italy – not to speak of the international echo Zappa's theory had in Spain and France.

6.3.4 Contributions of other Italian accounting scholars

Other scholars interested in Anglo-American accounting research, were, for example: Agazzi (1961), drawing attention to accounting axiomatization; Amodeo (1961a, 1961b) studying the matrix formulation of accounting and other novel trends; Fanni (1971), studying the mathematical-statistical trend; Cavalieri (1974), concerned with models of micro-economics, accounting and those based on mathematics and statistics; and Galassi (1978), analysing the theory and axiomatization attempts of Mattessich (1964). More traditional topics such as bank accounting, were thoroughly investigated by T. Bianchi (1975) and Dell' Amore (1978). And as Canziani (1994: 1960) emphasized, studies of income dynamics (stressing profitability and balance sheet valuation aspects) were of particular importance, and undertaken by most of the *zappiani*, including Azzini (1964).

A special concern of Italian accountants of this period were income measurement, valuation theories and related problems, occasionally prompted by inflationary trends (cf. Azzini 1964, 1976; Ferrero 1966, 1977, 1988; Superti Furga 1976; De Dominicis 1977; Masini 1978; AIDEA 1978; Galassi 1978, 1980; AIL 1980; Coda and Frattini 1980; Guatri 1981; Olivotto 1983; Perotta 1983; Canziani 1987; Colombo 1987).

Masini (1963), for example, concerned himself specifically with inflation accounting. He rejected general indexation as well as the current (i.e. replacement) cost approach. Both of these were too pragmatic and, according to *zapparian* doctrines, full of inconsistencies. Thus, Masini opted for a general restatement of annual values (based on revaluation techniques already suggested by Zappa). Thereby, past values were represented *together* with new values based on changes in profit expectations. He envisaged a general restatement of such fixed assets as inventory, plant and machinery (with appropriate depreciations adjustments, etc.), and an adjusted owners' equity. But Masini's (1963) book can hardly compete in precision and conceptual ingenuity with Edwards and Bell's (1961) classic on inflation and 'current cost' accounting.[6] A comparison between these two works clearly reveals the different scientific outlook of Italian vs. American accounting theory of this period.

Methodological studies of the early part of this period continued in such works as Mazza (1968) on the premises of accounting research, or the reflections in Ferraris-Franceschi (1978), or in Fanni and Cossar (1994) and in Catturi (1989). Furthermore, there were studies by D'Ippolito (1952, 1963) that reach from accounting standardization to charts of accounts, respectively.

A related concern was accounting principles, regulations and the harmonization within the European Union as well as internationally (cf. Coda 1968b; CNDC 1977–83; Russo and Siniscalco 1984; Canziani 1988, 1990), balance sheet and profit and loss theories (Salzano 1951; Superti Furga 1987; Mella 1995), and studies on financial statements for corporations (Colombo 1965), particularly for the consolidation with subsidiaries (Rinaldi 1990; Terzani 1992; Pisoni 1995), and Viganò's (1972, 1993) contributions to the accounting of leasing contracts, and to the requirements of European financial statements, respectively.

Italian accounting literature has, traditionally, had a strong interest in governmental accounting (sometimes even macro-accounting). This, again, has been manifested in Capaldo (1973), Guarini (1977), Marcon (1978), Mulazzani (1978) and others. Interest in flow of funds and cash flow statements are manifested in Cossar (1973) and Coda *et al.* (1974). The literature on auditing was relatively rare in the 1960s and 1970s (e.g. Ardemani 1967; Amodeo *et al.* 1975; Colombo 1977), but in subsequent decades pertinent texts greatly increased in number. Among these were A. Viganò and De Cicco (1983), Marchi (1988), Campedelli (1995), Bruni (1996), Dezzani *et al.* (2000) and others.

A few scholars directly challenged the *zapparian* approach, as, for example, Boscarato (1973) who wrote a book about 'the absurdities of income determination according to Zappa's theory'. Other voices, dissenting from the mainstream can be found in Chianale (1962a, 1962b), Masi (1961, 1997), Bergamin-Barbato *et al.* (1966), De Dominicis (1963–69, five volumes), and more recently Cinquini and Marelli (2002) – see also next section. Among these publications Masi's (1997) posthumous study on modern accounting may deserve special emphasis. This work influenced foreign authors (e.g. Montesions Julve 1998: 375, note 9), and emphasized the scientific autonomy of *ragioneria*, rejecting its supposed dependence on the doctrines of *economia aziendale* – apart from having promoted a *neo-patrimonialistic* approach (vs. an income dominated one) already established during the first half of the twentieth century (see our Chapter 4).

6.4 Cost and managerial accounting

As to cost accounting, Amaduzzi, probably the disciple closest to the ideas of Zappa, did go somewhat beyond him by writing a text on industrial or cost accounting (Amaduzzi 1959). Furthermore, Bergamin-Barbato *et al.* (1996: 140–1) discussed Italian costing literature, its impediments and the attempts of some authors to operate 'within the confines' of *economia aziendale*:

> For Zappa all operations performed within a company and all decisions taken by management are related to one another, and it is impossible to distinguish the financial consequences of one activity (operations and decisions) from those of another. Only the total income can be computed, and specific margins of individual segments of the whole activity are considered misleading. (p. 142) ... some of his [Zappa's] academic followers [e.g. Teodoro D'Ippolito, Egidio Giannessi, Luigi Guatri, Carlo Masini, Pietro Onida, Pasquale Saraceno and so on] conceived the possibility of measuring costs of individual segments of business operations without contradicting Zappa's conceptual position. They stated that ... it is 'logically' feasible to calculate some cost figures in order to achieve specific management goals. In other words, product costs can be calculated only if the

purpose of the specific cost information is stated and considered when designing the measurement system. In addition, these figures make sense only within the boundaries imposed by the specific purpose for which they have been calculated.

(Bergamin-Barbato *et al.* 1996: 144, translated)

It is understandable that some scholars of cost and managerial accounting were the first to emancipate from the *zapparian* tradition (see Chapter 4). On the other hand, theoretical and practical considerations have led many Italian accounting theorists to neglect cost accounting and its evolution. At most, Italian accounting hesitantly presented concepts derived from American literature. In practice and teaching, when not ignored altogether, cost accounting was presented mainly as a set of techniques that may occasionally be useful, if applied cautiously.

In the new millennium, it was Cinquini and Marelli (2002: 97), in further criticism of Zappa, who pointed out that: 'Under this [Zappa's] teaching, based on a systematic approach to business, the possibility of getting detailed information about management was substantially denied'. Nevertheless, some Italian scholars might disagree with such an assessment. Considering the spectacular international success that Italian industry experienced during the second half of the twentieth century, one wonders whether this could have been accomplished without managerial accounting in the American sense. Some sceptics might even suspect that this success may have been due to the absence of such a tradition. After all, management accounting did experience a crisis during the 1970s and 1980s, not only in America but also in other countries (cf. Kaplan 1984).

Typical studies of Italian cost accounting and production issues during this period were the following: N. Rossi's (1950) concern with mechanical industries; Guatri's (1951, 1954) and Azzini's (1954, 1957) research on the efficiency of production; Amaduzzi's (1955) research on production variabilities; the costing studies by D'Ippolito (1962, 1967), Coda (1968a), Amodeo (1976), Brusa (1978), Brusa and Dezzani (1983), AIDEA (1980a), Giannessi (1982), Guglielmi (1997), Quagli (1997); and those in saving banks by T. Bianchi (1975, highly praised by Canziani 1994: 159); as well as a discussion of ecological accounting problems in Miolo Vitali (1978).

6.5 Novel accounting trends

The statistical-empirical methodology and 'positive accounting theory' does not seem to have found strong defenders in Italy. However, there are some indications that the 'information perspective of accounting' has aroused greater interest. Several papers (e.g. Galassi 1987, 1991, 1994; Cilloni 1998, 1999) discussed this approach for the benefit of Italian accounting academics, but the most comprehensive attempt is the book by Cilloni (2004). The inception of this book still lies within the timeframe of our study (even if its publication is already beyond it). Yet apart from this, its unique position, as the first serious Italian effort to tackle this esoteric and highly mathematical field, deserves some discussion.

Cilloni's (2004) book on 'information economics and accounting systems' offers to the Italian audience (endowed with the necessary mathematical pre-requisites) a concise introduction into some fundamental aspects of the American information economic perspective. After an introductory chapter on modern decision theory, the book contains a chapter dealing with the foundations of the information economic approach. A third chapter is devoted to the foundations of mathematical agency theory, now considered part of the information perspective of accounting. The fourth chapter seems to be the most original one, though it might prove to be controversial. There, the author leaves the ground explored by previous authors of this field (mainly in the Anglo-American literature), and attempts to connect it with the Italian tradition, referring to Onida, and even to Cerboni's and Rossi's *logismografia*, with a novel juxtaposition of deterministic vs. probabilistic accounting models. The rest is an appendix and a bibliography.

As a first attempt in Italian accounting literature, this effort must be applauded, particularly as there seems to be no equivalent book in other lan-guages, save English and German.[7] However, despite its merits, Cilloni (2004) cannot be compared in pedagogical skill and comprehensiveness with the text by J.A. Christensen and Demski (2003). Nor can it be compared in richness and mathematical rigor with the two volumes by P.O. Christensen and Feltham (2003, 2005), containing some 250 theorems and rigorous mathematical proofs. Another superior work is the two volumes (in German) by Ewert and Wagen-hofer (1993/2003) on managerial accounting, and Wagenhofer and Ewert (2003) on financial accounting. The strength of these tomes is their rather successful attempt to integrate modern information aspects into traditional accounting in a better way than either Christensen and Demski (2003) or Christensen and Feltham (2003, 2005) – see also Chapter 19.

6.6 Historical studies of the period

Historical accounting research – a specialty of Italian accounting, as previously pointed out (cf. Galassi and Mattessich 2004) – continued to flourish also in the second half of this century. Some of the noteworthy studies are: the monumental international accounting history by Melis (1950), Riparbelli's (1951–52) asser-tion on the historical pre-eminence of Italian accounting, Zerbi's (1952) research on the origin of accounting, Masi's (1963, 1964) studies on pre-historic account-ing as well as Greek and Roman accountants; furthermore, the profiles of accounting history by Pezzoli (1977), and the book on Italian accounting history by Serra (1999) and more recently the one on accounting history in general by Amaduzzi (2001), as well as research on an ancient financial statement in the Vice-royalty of Naples by Amodeo (1953). Or studies about renowned accoun-tants and their theories as, for example, about Fabio Besta by Antoni (1970) or about Gino Zappa by AIDEA (1980b), Galassi (1984, 1996a, 1996b, 1996c),

Canziani (1987, 1994) and Took (1993), or about Luca Pacioli (Galassi 1996b). Furthermore, there are is a study by Guglielmi (1997) on cost accounting of an eighteenth-century Venetian firm, or one on the management of the Venetian Arsenal from 1580 to 1650 by Zan and Hoskin (1996); another one, on the development of Italian accounting theory (Catturi and Riccaboni 1992). Finally, there are general surveys on recent and contemporary accounting, as those by Galassi (1984, 1996a, 1996b, 1996c), Zambon and Saccon (1993), Ferraris-Franceschi (1994) and Zambon (1995); or on the historical analysis of cost accounting by Bergamin-Barbato *et al.* (1996), or Antonelli and Cerbioni (1998); Italian accounting during the 1930s by Di Lazzaro (1998). There was also an historical study by Viganò's (1968) on accounting practices from the fifteenth to the seventeenth century, and Peragallo's (1971) English commentary on this study by Viganò. Finally, there was the interesting suggestion by Zan (1994) on creating a history of accounting histories.

More recently, Serra's (1999) history of Italian accounting appeared. Here was a unique opportunity to close the second millennium with a comprehensive survey of Italian accounting thought. Alas, the author did not quite rise to the challenge. We are not so much referring to the fact that, for example, the first two chapters (dealing with the origin of 'Mesopotamian' accounting), are neither up-to-date nor sufficiently researched. Our criticism pertains more to the treatment of the twentieth century. Although Serra did devote a 'four-page' chapter to Zappa's work, his followers fared worse. Chapter 25 contains merely 'two text-pages' (and a table of accounts classification) exclusively devoted to Amaduzzi, as the only *zappiani* so honoured. A more extensive treatment is found in the more engrossing Chapter 26 (of some ten pages) on 'A century of ideological discussions in Italy'. It refers to the lengthy nineteenth-century controversies between Italian accounting theoreticians: For example, that between Francesco Marchi and the *cinque-contisti* (see our Chapter 2), as well as the dispute between Giuseppe Cerboni and his disciples (of *logismografia*, such as Rossi, Bonalumi and Riva) vs. Fabio Besta and his disciples (the *partiduplisti*). Serra's Chapter 26 also refers to the disputes of the early twentieth century between Zappa and his disciples (the *economisti aziendali*, for example, Catturi and Ceccherelli) vs. Besta and his followers (the *ragioneristi*, for example, Masi and della Penna) – see also Chapter 4 above. Yet, Serra does not convey much about accounting studies of the second half of the twentieth century.

Another recent historical work (published posthumously, as far as its first and main author is concerned) is Masi's (1997) book on accounting in the modern and contemporary age. Yet despite such specific reference to modern times, it does not go beyond the first half of the twentieth century. A chapter, dealing particularly with this period, distinguishes *seven* different Italian schools and their disciples (see Chapter 4). It also contains two chapters (authored by Antonelli, of some 23 pages in total) in memory of Vincenzo Masi, detailing the latter's theory of *patrionialism* (i.e. his emphasis on 'capital' rather than 'income') in opposition to his contemporary rival Gino Zappa (with his *red-itismo*, that emphasized 'income'). In Italy, Masi's theory was attacked by several prominent scholars, and was relatively little appreciated by others. However, it was highly praised in foreign countries, such as Spain and Portugal, and particularly in Latin America. In Belo Horizonte (Brazil) there is even a down-town street named 'Vicenzo Masi' in his honour. Most recently, some studies on the history of matrix accounting and computerized spreadsheets have also been published (e.g. Cilloni and Marinoni 2006).

7 Accounting research in the French language area

First half of the twentieth century[1]

7.1 Introduction

French speaking authors assumed an eminent position in accounting between the seventeenth and the nineteenth centuries. Such famous names as Jacques Savary, Mathieu de la Porte, Edmond Degrange Sr, Anselm Payen, Eugène Léautey and Adolphe Guilbault (1889), and many others are engraved in the annals of accounting history (cf. Colasse 2005). This tradition continued during the first half of the twentieth century (the 'Belle Époque' of the inter-war period), though less prominently, and despite a greater volume of publications. The five major topics occupying accounting research during this period in the French language were: (i) accounting history; (ii) financial accounting theory, including commercial and industrial applications, taxation issues and education; (iii) the assimilation and adaptation of cost accounting and managerial control as developed in Germany, the United Kingdom and the United States; (iv) the need for price-level adjustments during the post-war inflation of the late 1920s; and (v) the construction of charts of accounts and legislations for uniform master charts, as well as creating associations of public accounting (including auditing).

7.2 Studies in accounting history

The period's best-known accounting historian of French tongue was Albert Dupont. His works were specialized studies that reached from ancient times (Dupont 1928) to the Middle Ages and Pacioli (Dupont 1925, 1926) and to accounting in subsequent centuries (Dupont 1927, 1928, 1930). Another well-known accounting historian was Raymond de Roover (from Belgium), who became renowned in the Commonwealth countries as well as America through a series of publications in English. His best-known French publications dealt with Jan Ympyn (cf. de Roover 1928a, 1928b) and in English a treatise on the origin of double-entry bookkeeping (de Roover 1937). A particularly prestigious book was Gomberg's (1929) *Histoire critique de la théorie des comptes* (and its precursor, Gomberg 1912). Léon Gomberg was a renowned Russian accounting theoretician who taught in Switzerland (Geneva and St Gallen), but also published important theoretical accounting studies in Russian and German. Furthermore, there was a historical paper, worth mentioning, by S.E. Howard (1932) – and a much later one by Fortin (1996). The best-known history of French accounting, namely Vlaemminck's *Histoire et doctrines de la comptabilité* (1956), also falls outside of our period of investigation. A much earlier publication was the somewhat controversial historical accounting bibliography by Reymondin (1909) – the only one in France covering the period between 1494 and 1909. Surprisingly, there also exist some French historical studies on Soviet accounting, as those by de Sigalas (1936), Gachkel (1946) and Boukovetzki (1947). One might add some publications on the history of the *plan comptable général* (the master chart of accounts), as, for example, the study by Cauvin (1949) – also referred to in section 7.6 – or to Batardon (1950).[2] Most recently, the 500 years' survey with 25 profiles of *Les grand auteurs en comptabilité* by Colasse (2005) has received particular attention.

7.3 Theory and practice of financial accounting

Gabriel Faure was a public accountant and occupied the position of Professor at the School of Higher Commercial Studies of Paris. Although he was a prolific author (e.g. Faure 1905, 1917, 1919, 1921), his publications were fairly technical. Faure's *Traité de compatabilité générale* (1905) was a popular work, widely used as a text until 1939, and exerted considerable influence on French accounting. The author regarded accounting to be a 'true language', which may have been intriguing but created considerable ambiguities. He also continued or revived the personalistic theory of accounts that was particularly popular during the nineteenth century. This theory identified each account with a person – a practice that facilitated the teaching of bookkeeping at lower grades, but introduced pedagogic difficulties at higher levels. For Faure, accounting was a technique in the service of the firm (1905: 142–3) and the economy; he also considered it a basis for intellectual investigations.[3] Colasse and Durand (1994: 44) considered neither Faure nor Bournisien (to be discussed next) as genuine theorists.

Jean Bournisien, tried to integrate legal theory with accounting and was possibly influenced by the entity theory, promulgated in the English literature. He also was a persistent critique of prevailing accounting practices, particularly in the area of costing. Bournisien's *Précis de comptabilité industrielle appliquée à la Métallurgie* (1917) is not merely a textbook but an interesting application of cost accounting to the metallurgical industry – a work that ultimately became an accounting classic.

Jean Dumarchey (1914, 1925, 1926) had been praised by Fourastié (1944) as well as Vlaemminck (1956), and was called by Colasse and Durand (1994: 45) 'the most important, if not the only, French theorist from the first half of the century'. Dumarchey fought the 'personalistic theory' and tried to elevate the scientific status of our discipline on a broad basis (cf. Michaïlesco 2005).

The first of these books bears the title 'the positive theory of accounting', which, however, should not be identified with the American statistical-empirical Positive Accounting Theory of the 1980s and later. He regarded accounting not merely as a technique but a 'social science', and tried to integrate it with philosophy, mathematics and micro- as well as macroeconomics. He anticipated a future trend by trying to establish a link between micro- and macroeconomics through accounting, thus adapting related notions from the socialist Pierre-Paul Prudhon.

Dumarchey was well read in the works of Jean-Baptiste Say, Leon Say and Jean-Gustave Courcelle-Seneuil, taking from each of them ideas to develop his own theory. The first of these writers offered him the notion that accounting reflects the fluctuations of individual wealth; the second one suggested to him that accounting is an information system (an idea by no means as modern as generally thought), while the third enabled him to improve his insight into the objective of accounting. Dumarchey saw the essence of our discipline in describing concretely a complex reality by means of accounts. For him the account is *'une classe d'unités de valeurs'* – i.e. values that varied through space and time. On this basis he constructed such concepts as assets, equity and the balance sheet. His influence on the subsequent generation of French accounting scholars was considerable, though some accountants called him an 'abstracter of quintessence'. According to Colasse and Durand (1994: 46), the editor of the well-known journal *La Comptabilité et les Affaires*, Alfred Berran, even rejected one of Dumarchey's publications, with the argument that 'his studies are far too erudite for the majority of our readers'.

Delaporte (1926, 1930, 1931, 1936) improved accounting techniques during the 1930s, and put considerable emphasis on the need for planning and budgetary control as well as on forecasting within accounting. He too pleaded for a scientific-empirical basis of our discipline. In Delaporte (1930) he defined accounting as a science the task of which is to describe the economic process to calculate costs, and to evaluate the financial status resulting from the transactions and the value of the assets. In Delaporte (1936) he incorporated important ideas of Dumarchey, stressed legalistic and taxation aspects, and made early references to the master chart of accounts.

Penglaou (1929, 1933, 1947) criticized existing accounting practices and joined in the chorus that demanded a better factual and scientific understanding of our discipline. The son of a banker and executive of several banks, Penglaou clearly recognized the weakness of accounting measurements. He originally had in mind to write an encyclopaedia, but wrote instead *Introduction à la technique comptable* (Penglaou 1929). This book was followed by more than 130 publications that dealt with various topics relating accounting to law, taxation, economics, etc. He explored foundational and speculative problems of accounting, and maintained all his remaining life a special interest in statistical techniques, and not least in the writings of young scholars. His own publications fuse ordinary aspects with profound thoughts, particularly on the epistemology of accounting – they still merit to be read (cf. Degos 1998: 97).

Furthermore, one might mention Lucas (1931). He showed interest in charts of accounts at a time when few French accountants were interested in them, and attempted to connect practice and theory by extending the latter to the study of administration and organization. According to Colasse and Durand (1994: 47), Lucas even anticipated the 'conceptual framework' (established in several countries in the last third of the twentieth century). Other contributors to accounting theory were: Leford (1926); Fain (1927) and Ratier (1927), both as regards depreciation issues; furthermore, Garnier (1942, 1947) and Lamson (1950); and earlier, Léautey (1903 – see Degos 2005: 70, where this publication bears the year 1904); writing on the accounting of limited companies was Reymondin (1928), as well as Gomberg (1929). All of these were interesting and original studies by eminent nineteenth-century accounting scholars.

7.4 Cost accounting and managerial control

During nineteenth-century France, engineers were the primary contributors to cost accounting, and this process continued to some extent in the early twentieth century. Among those contributors were Fayol (1916), Julhiet (1920), Calmès (1922, 1925), de Fages de Latour (1924), Fain (1927) and Detoeuf (1941), all of who realized the importance of budgeting, cost control and the need for administrative as well as organizational improvement in factories. Detoeuf (1941) also published a paper on the master chart of accounts (see below). He was one of the authors of the report by the *Commission générale d'organisation scientifique* (CEGOS 1937) on 'cost calculation'.

As to the executive Henri Fayol [1841–1925] (1916) though not having been an accountant, he had, similar to Frederick Taylor, a great impact on scientific management and cost accounting. Furthermore, Alfred Croizé and Henri Croizé (1907) emphasized the distinction between period costs vs. product costs, distinguished selling overheads (excluded from inventory) vs. manufacturing overheads (allocated to product costs), and used *direct labour costs* as an allocation basis. Léon Batardon (1911) anticipated the decimal-classification of Schmalenbach's *Kontenrahmen* by more than a quarter of a century; he also became a pioneer of *loose-leaf accounting*. There also was a comprehensive work on industrial accounting by Louis Deaubresse (1908), dealing with a wide range of topics, including the need for the *smoothing of costs* due to great periodic fluctuations. Bournisien (1919) published his 'philosophy of accounting' which promoted a legalistic balance sheet theory. The latter work reached centuries back to ideas conceived by Mathieu de la Porte.

Eugene Rimailho, a lieutenant colonel, who served 'thirty years in the army and thirty years in industry', assumed a particularly important role in the pioneering of French cost accounting. He became a public accountant, specialized in manufacturing and industrial bookkeeping, and concentrated on problems of time studies to increase the efficiency of French factories. Furthermore, Rimailho (1935) generalized the concept of '*sections homogènes*', that was based on full costing and was later revived and generalized under the name of 'activity-based costing' (ABC). Thus Rimailho could be considered a precursor of this method, and may be remembered as such. That method was even incorporated into the charts of accounts of 1947 and 1957. Rimailho studied the nature of costs and their relation to the sales price. He was one of the first to investigate the connection between expenditures, acquisition costs and the determination of unit costs. He also clearly distinguished between direct and indirect labour costs, and discussed problems of material, labour and overhead costs, particularly as to their allocations to work orders – an area where he may have been most original. As a first-rate expert on industrial organizations, he examined all kinds of manufacturing processes, their installation and control. But other aspects concerned him no less, as has been pointed out:

> For Rimailho the role of accounting is closely tied to his political and social convictions. The management accounting of Rimailho seems to be a strategic tool of social policy for a specific organizational structure, a strategy for protecting those working in a particular technological and competitive environment.
>
> (Bouquin 1995: 5, translated)

Other authors, interested in cost and management accounting and budgetary control before or during the Second World War, were: Satet (1936) who published two works on budgetary control (1936, 1942); Detoeuf (1941), an engineer who began his career in industry, concerned himself intensely with costing issues and management philosophy. He later published an '*exposé*' on the chart of accounts, since he was a member of the commission in charge of implementing such a chart; Bournisien (1917) who studied industrial accounting as applied to metallurgy; Dumarchey (1926) who promulgated a valuation theory based on sales prices. Charles Brunet (1940), who may be regarded as a precursor in integrating industrial accounting with the chart of accounts, strengthened the continuing interest in industrial accounting, even without being followed by a host of disciples; and finally Blairon's text (1926) on industrial accounting.

All those concerns must be seen in the light of two world wars, a harsh industrial competition, the urge to produce more efficiently, and the hope to achieve the latter through appropriate means of accounting. Even if financial accounting literature dominated the scene, publications in management accounting then began to assert their importance and continued to do so at an accelerating pace. Nevertheless, critics in favour of a more theoretical foundation of accounting, like Sauvegrai (1937), continued to raise their voices, but without much avail. Colasse and Durand have characterized the situation as it was before the Second World War:

> At the end of the 1930s, French accounting literature was relatively rich and consistent. It is remarkable that most of this thinking was inspired by the concepts of value, account and classification of accounts in a clear and

comprehensive way. This is the basis of 'process accounting' that would soon expand towards accounting plans and nomenclature.

Yet this richness was not fertile. Theorists, teachers, authors, critics and propagandists were isolated and often divided. They could not gain support from public or private users. The business world, made up primarily of small companies, was not convinced of the supposed advantages of the *science des comptes* which seemed too theoretical and abstract.

(Colasse and Durand 1994: 48)

7.5 Inflation and price-level adjustments

The French inflation of the first half of the twentieth century lasted from about 1914 to 1928. But during the war years various means were available to curb inflationary trends. Often these forces reared their head afterwards, even if the particular country belonged to the victors. It was only during the last and most virulent phase of this inflation that French accountants and businessmen became seriously concerned. Admittedly, the French post-war inflation was much less severe than that of Germany or Austria, but it was graver than the one Great Britain experienced. Yet, it may be surprising that this phase occurred relatively late. The most dramatic end-phase of the French inflation occurred from 1925 to 1927, while the hyper-inflation of Germany happened between 1921 and 1923, and that of Austria between 1920 and 1922.

Undoubtedly, French accountants benefited from the preceding German experience in making inflation adjustments to their accounts or balance sheets. But this is not to say that French accountants lacked originality. Indeed, new solutions and variations to this problem did originate in France. Inflation, whether creeping or rampant, always creates major distortions in the accounting systems and the balance sheets of a country affected by it. If not properly adjusted the following happens:

1   Depreciations (and similar cost allocations) are usually too low, since they are based on (devalued) historical costs.
2   The values of fixed and often current non-monetary assets are evaluated too low in comparison with current prices.
3   The holding of fixed and current non-monetary assets creates unrealized (but realizable) holding gains that remain undisclosed.
4   Accounts payable and long-term debts (e.g. mortgages) create undisclosed real monetary holding gains, while accounts receivables and other monetary claims (cash, bonds, etc.) create real monetary holding losses that have to be balanced against the monetary holding gains that are not necessarily in equilibrium with them.
5   Incorrect valuations from previous years constitute an additional source of distortion.
6   Revenues (stated at inflated prices) containing fictitious gains are deceptively high and lead to dangerously overstated profits.

7   The latter leads to distorted owners' equity values which, in addition, would also have to be adjusted for various real monetary and non-monetary holding gains or losses.

There are innumerable variations to adjust accounts, income statements and balance sheets in order to reveal a more or less realistic financial picture of an enterprise under inflationary conditions. But these variations can be reduced to less than a handful of basic methods. Some are more accurate, though usually more expensive and complicated than others, and none are perfect. One of the basic methods uses specific *current costs* as a valuation basis (or, as a simplifying alternative, specific cost indices for various asset categories). This approach, first proposed by Kovero in 1912, was elaborated and made popular by Fritz Schmidt (1921).[4] The other basic method is *general* inflation adjustment (by some kind of general index, like one of cost of living, of wholesale, of foreign currency, of gold, etc., as suggested by Mahlberg 1921, Schmalenbach 1921, 1922, 1925 and others).[5] Further methods – such as the use of current sales or exit values, present values, or even the combination of general and specific price-level indices – came in vogue much later and played no practical role in any of the inflations before 1950.

A series of books and papers dealt with inflation accounting during and after the peak of the French post-war inflation. But to what extent these or some of the more theoretical suggestions were applied in French accounting practice is uncertain. Wasserman offered the following clue:

> Although French inflation was of long duration and fairly severe, the only inflation system used to any extent in France was the establishment of gold franc balance sheets without any changes made to the entries in, or to the balances of the ordinary paper franc accounts. The reason why no more complicated plan was followed is to be found in part in the fact that many French businessmen were not well aware of the nature and effects of monetary inflation. Others failed to understand the principles underlying the more complicated systems of accounting and failed to appreciate their utility or feared that the use of any of these methods would falsify the standard accounting results.
>
> (Wasserman 1931: 31–2)

Nevertheless, the author continued by asserting, with considerable insight as well as foresight, that:

> The elaboration of these systems by French and German accounting theorists constitutes a definite contribution to general accounting theory ... . It further shows that the economist has much to learn from the results of accounting. Analysis of accounting results will do much towards lending precision to, to say nothing of correcting the errors of, the classical economist's theory of inflation ... . It may be possible that sometime in the future we will again pass through such a period.
>
> (Wasserman 1931: 32)

In the following, we present a concise survey of the most prominent authors and publications in this area, though without any attempt to enter into the many technical details. For the latter, see the survey of various French inflation accounting methods contained in the book by Thomas (1927) and the paper by Wasserman (1931).[6]

Delavelle (1924) was one of the earliest of the French authors concerned with inflation accounting. Based on the US$ exchange rate, he adjusted the accounts at the end of each month. A new account, *depreciation du capital-or*, took care of inflation adjustments to owners' equity. This approach may have influenced Raffegeau and Lacout (1926 – see below), and anticipated certain aspects found in Bayard (1926) that supplemented the regular, unadjusted paper-franc accounts by means of a balance sheet restated in terms of gold-francs. Without any changes of the ledger accounts, the resulting balance sheet account contained two debit and two credit columns. The first columns (on the debit and credit sides) contained items in depreciated paper-francs, while the second columns were restated in gold-francs. Some items (e.g. plant, land, capital stock, etc.) were identical in both columns (cf. table on p. 11 of Wasserman 1931). On the debit side of this balance sheet account appeared an item 'Gold Depreciation', as an adjustment to Capital Stock on the credit side. It expressed the firm's 'deficit' and thus showed up only in the gold-franc column (not in the paper-franc column). On the credit side, the item 'Paper-Franc Profits' appeared only in the paper-franc column.

A related, more elaborate and elegant system, was presented by Raffegeau and Lacout (1926), who spoke of a '*correction en monnaie-or par la méthode retrograde avec rectification du bilan d'entrée*'. Thereby the individual accounts were adjusted at period-end (either on the basis of foreign exchange-rates or price indices). An account *dépreciation du capital et reserves* collected these adjustments, and was closed off to the gold-franc balance sheet. As an alternative to this 'retrograde method', Raffegeau and Lacout (1926) developed the so-called 'progressive method'. It relied on the opening balances as a basis of comparison. At first, the opening balance of each account was scrutinized whether it required any adjustment in terms of paper-francs at the beginning of the fiscal period. Monetary accounts (cash, receivables, payables, bonds) usually needed no such adjustments, while most fixed asset accounts (inventory, machinery, plant and equipment, etc.) might have required them. The counter-entries were made in a correction account to the opening balance sheet. The balance of this account was closed to the account *plus-value du capital et des reserves* (increment to capital and reserves). A further step required the opening balances to be adjusted a second time, now at their *year-end* paper-franc values. This adjustment was not limited to the non-monetary accounts but extended to the monetary ones as well. Though the declining value of the paper-franc did not cause a *nominal* loss, it did result in a *real* monetary loss to be taken into consideration.

Léger (1926) used a simpler but related system of paper-francs with 'correcting accounts', adjusting the fixed asset accounts for inflation to secure their proper replacement. Yet this author was not only concerned with making provisions in reserve accounts for adjusting profit and capital, as well as for individual asset and working capital items. To maintain the latter, he recommended investments not affected by inflation. This reminds us of Schmidt's (1921) related suggestion, to finance accounts payables as much as possible by accounts receivables, so both might be equal.

The method of 'heterogeneous accounts' was presented by Fain (in an undated pamphlet: middle of the 1920s) where every account was presented three times over: once in terms of original (i.e. unadjusted) paper-francs; then restated in year-end paper-francs; and finally, cast into gold-francs (an illustration was offered in a table by Wasserman 1931: 26). The counter-entries were (apart from the profit and loss and balance sheet accounts) to be found in an account *redressement du capital*.

Faure (1926) used a hybrid system, combining balance sheet adjustments with aspects of gold-franc accounting. It ultimately led to a gold-franc balance sheet through the adjustments of individual entries to paper-franc accounts adjusted by the exchange rates on dates of specific transactions. Entries took place in paper-francs and gold-francs simultaneously, and counter-entries were either in the profit and loss account or a separate 'inflation loss' account. Obviously, this is a more accurate but also more cumbersome and expensive way of inflation adjustment than through mere adjustments of balance sheets to gold-francs. To reduce those accounting expenses, one could opt for monthly or weekly adjustments instead of daily ones. A major advantage of this system was its use in cost accounting and price setting instead of merely adjusting profit and owner's equity.

Lucien Thomas (1927) not only provided a survey about various French inflation accounting methods, but also presented his own approach. He employed paper-franc accounts (based on an average exchange rate with the US$) as well as gold-franc accounts (based on the gold-franc itself, as being equivalent to 0.290325 grams of fine gold, officially in force until 1929), and used a 'regulating and compensating account' for making the necessary counter-entries. Its balance was derived from adjustments due to real monetary gains or losses (from holding cash, receivables, payables, mortgages, etc.), shortage or excesses in depreciation, or cost of goods sold, or those from previous periods. This method had the advantage of serving financial accounting as well as cost and managerial purposes, as it enabled its extension to a *cost accounting* system based on gold-francs. This system was highly praised by Wasserman (1931: 9) who concluded that it took 'into consideration many elements which have escaped other authors cited'. But here, as in other sophisticated systems, the advantages had to be weighted against additional costs. Experience during this inflation period, no less than in subsequent ones (including the creeping inflation, for example, in America, Australia and Great Britain during the late 1970s and early 1980s) demonstrated that simplicity and inexpensive operation are primary preconditions for such a system to be acceptable to practitioners. Other French authors writing on inflation accounting were: Bisson (1926), Dumarchey (1926), Durand (1926), Beaupère (1927) and Ratier (1927).

For those familiar with the preceding German inflation accounting literature, this list suggests similarity with or inspiration from the works of Mahlberg (1921, 1923) and Schmalenbach (1921, 1922, 1925), all based on general inflation adjustment by means of some index. However, Wasserman (1931: 9, note 26) mentioned the famous 'replacement price theory' (*théorie du prix de remplacement*) that received much attention in France during the inflation years. This offers a hint that the replacement cost theories of Kovero (1912), Limperg (1917) and Schmidt (1921) may also have been an important inspiration to French authors. This supposition is reinforced by Wasserman's (1931: 9, note 26) subsequent remark that 'Even during stable money times, many enterprises, especially those dealing in imported materials or products for which there was an international market, applied the replacement price theory'. This makes eminent sense. The application of current (i.e. replacement) costs in accounting are an excellent remedy not only in inflationary times, but also during non-inflationary periods when the inevitable shift of prices between commodities occurs (see also Fain's undated pamphlet: 4–9, and Beaupère 1927: 70–80). However, Wasserman hinted at a failure of the French industry to take this idea seriously enough.[7] Furthermore, the title of Dumarchey's (1926) book suggests that in France *le prix de revient* (expenses on purchases + manufacturing expenses + profit margin (later on called '*coût de revient*')) was seriously promoted as a valuation basis, at least from a theoretical point of view.[8] At any rate, French accounting literature reveals that there must have been a lively rivalry between different ideas; and not only as to techniques of inflation adjustments, but also as to the more substantial issue of a proper valuation basis.

7.6 Charts of accounts and public supervision

Interest in master charts of accounts goes a long way back, and has its roots in the competing theories of classes of accounts of the nineteenth century. In the French language area it was Batardon (1911) – simultaneously with Schär (1911) in Germany – who first presented thoughts for a chart of accounts. According to Gomberg (1929) another such proposal appears to have been submitted already in the 1890s by the *Société Académique de Comptabilité* in Brussels, through Scherpf (1955: 78), pointed out that this assertion could not be verified in the literature). Nevertheless, the on-going enthusiasm of the French for the *plan comptable* received its strongest impetus during the German wartime occupation. Then, the Vichy government tried to introduce – under the influence of German accounting literature and the pressure by the Nazi regime[9] – its first master chart of accounts, though Chezlepêtre proposed a tentative master chart as early as 1940. Further underlying theoretical work seems to have been done by Alfred Sauvin and other bureaucrats – partly on the basis of the preparatory work by the *Commission générale d'organisation scientifique* (CEGOS 1937), partly with the help of authors who offered a retroactive evaluation of this project, like Detoeuf (1941), Caujolle (1942, 1943, 1949), Chezlepêtre (1940, 1943) and Fourastié (1943, 1944).[10] The result was *le Plan de 1942*, the objectives of which, according to the vice-president of the pertinent committee, were:

1　to allow the determination of assets, capital, profits and product costs at both the company and the industry level;
2　to make it possible to calculate industry-wide average costs for certain product types for government price control purposes;
3　to decrease the possibilities of deceiving tax authorities by increasing the clarity of accounts;
4　to help the government avoid making mistakes in its tax and economic policies by normalizing accounting for each industry (Detoeuf 1941: 9–12; as translated in Fortin 1991: 5).[11]

However, as Colasse and Durand (1994: 50) pointed out: 'In the entire history of accounting, it is difficult to imagine such a massive effort to present and explain a plan, which was, in fact, never used'.[12] The reason for this 'failure' has been attributed to opposition from industry, insufficient know-how in application, controversial criteria of alignment, political opposition, fear of additional constraints and tighter control, etc.

Yet, the notions of order and rationality were too deeply ingrained in the French psyche, and it did not take long before a counter-plan was developed by Pierre Garnier (1942) in the last chapter of his book. In contrast to some German tendencies that tried to unify financial and cost accounting, Garnier and other scholars, like Brunet (1951), believed that financial accounting and cost accounting required a clearer separation (with stronger emphasis on the latter), as well as a basis that is more logical, yet less complex. A new version issued by the CNOF (1944/46) took such separation into consideration, but committee work for a final and truly official master chart continued. A. Brunet (1947, 1951) chaired this committee. In the second of these two books, the somewhat over-ambitious objectives of such a master chart were described as follows: 'price control, competition control, control of the validity of government subsidies, transport policy, customs, social policy, efficiency improvement, actions against the social evils expected from a theocratic civilization' (cf. Colasse and Durand 1994: 52).

Finally, the official master chart (*Plan National*) of 1947 came into being, bringing in its wake numerous changes from individual bookkeeping and taxation to industrial and macro-economic coordination. Its inspiration derived from the aborted 1942 French master chart and the one submitted by the *Comité National de l'Organisation Française* (CNOF 1944/46). Renowned scholars, some already mentioned, contributed to this effort; for example, Anthonioz, Brunet, Garnier, Demonet, Fourastié, and others. Incidentally, the same day the interdepartmental commission of the chart of accounts was created another decree laid the foundation for creating *l'Order des experts-comptables* (Institute of Public Accountants – see Cordoliani 1947). This institution came into being on 3 April 1942, and lasted until the end of the Second Word War.

In September 1945, it operated under new statutes, the major features of which are still in existence.

Furthermore, a decree of 4 April 1946 created the '*Commission de normalisation des comptabilité*, (a kind of Accounting Standards Board), charged to produce a master chart of accounts, to specify its methods of applications, and to consider the possibility of a system of national income accounting. But this board was soon replaced (on 16 January 1947) by another one, the '*Conseil supérieur de la comptabilité*' (Supreme Accounting Board) to which even wider tasks were assigned. The master chart that arose out of it was – in contrast to the previous French chart or that of Schmalenbach – not a monistic but a pluralistic chart of accounts, where cost accounting was autonomous from financial accounting. Despite much criticism, the chart was employed by a variety of companies; it gradually found its way into the class room, convincing generations of accountants of the advantages of a 'uniform language' as well as of shared principles of documentation and classification (for further information on the French master chart, see Degos 2000).

7.7 Conclusion

During the first half of the twentieth century, France experienced major upheavals: two world wars, several colonial wars, two 'Republics', and many economic and financial misadventures. It slowly passed from a primarily agricultural economy (limited to the processing of colonial products) to a major industrial economy with giant corporations. France adapted to new forms of energy and the exploitation of new means of communication. Its people learned to manage their factories efficiently on the basis of new methods of scientific management and administration.

At first, the foremost interest of accounting theorists was financial accounting and the practice of basic bookkeeping. Later they tried to apply, with modest success, the techniques of cost accounting and management control. Their theoretical efforts towards price control and price-level adjustments (during the inflationary period), were of little practical effect, mainly because of the limited public resources available.

During the last decade of the period under investigation, the major accounting effort in France (and to some extent in Belgium) went into charts and master charts of accounts. It is this research field that fascinated researchers, theorists, teachers and experts from several areas (e.g. from tax authorities, economic administrators and the senior bureaucrats). The epoch from 1900 to 1950 was not a particularly glorious period for French accounting; yet it was a time when important accounting developments took shape.

8 Accounting research in the French language area

Second half of the twentieth century[1]

8.1 Introduction

Accounting as a university subject developed relatively late in France – and this despite a most distinguished accounting tradition in the past.[2] During the period under discussion, accounting was considered a purely technical subject until about 1970. From this time onwards some changes did occur, though perhaps not as radical as some academics had hoped for. It seems that even in the first half of the twentieth century the prestige of French accounting was higher than in the second half. This has been confirmed and explained by Boussard and Rey (1984: 50) who emphasized that in the second half of the twentieth century French influence in accounting theory decreased, partly because of the rise of the English accounting literature, and partly because of an excessive focus on standard setting and neglect of academic research.

Scheid (1986: 123), in a French paper, pointed out that 'In my view, accounting research in France had been insufficient for a long time … . Until 1960–65 there was practically no genuine accounting research. Accounting was not taught at universities; there was no academic research' (translated). Similar views were heard from other quarters: Nioche and Pesqueux (1997: 231), for instance, emphasized that 'French tradition built on a society in which accountants have been regarded as the "poor relations" of the business community.' At first glance there seems to be a parallel with England where, similarly, accounting as an academic discipline received late recognition, but ultimately burst forth with great vigour and originality in the 1970s and especially since the 1980s. But Colasse and Durant pointed out that:

It is surprising that the post-war area gave rise to so few accounting theorists. Some of those who were well-known prior to this period continued to write and publish their work. But almost no new names emerged. Some experts attribute this phenomenon to the emphasis on standardization itself and to the influence of the *Plan*, which was to absorb the energy and expertise of the most capable specialists. The 1950s and 1960s might be considered years of theoretical stagnation, as if the concern with standardization had a sterilizing effect on accounting theory. The literature of the period was, above all, pedagogical in orientation. The number of accounting manuals produced during this period is considerable, but on the whole, they are of only mediocre quality ... . None the less, three authors are worthy of a more detailed examination: André Cibert, Pierre Lassègue and Claude Pérrochon.

(Colasse and Durant 1994: 52)

The comparison with England indicates also other differences, as, for example, the more 'authoritarian' tradition of public administrators and even engineers who had a surprising influence on French accounting, particularly on its cost accounting and the development of the *Plan Comptable*. The first version of this *Plan*, conceived in 1947, was primarily a general chart of accounts but (in contrast to the German charts) went beyond it by incorporating a series of accounting and costing standards. Indeed, the French *Plan Comptable*, and the bureaucracy entailed by it, seem to have absorbed an excessive amount of time, energy and research potential. England and the rest of the English-speaking hemisphere, on the other hand, never mustered much enthusiasm for pursuing this particular path.

But there exists a more deep-rooted difference between French and British accounting. In France accounting as an independent profession was recognized only in 1943 with the establishment of the *Ordre National des Experts Comptables* (now represented by the *Conseil Superieure de l'Ordre des Experts Comptables* or OECCA). In Great Britain, on the other hand, the first public accounting (i.e. auditing) body was already established in the nineteenth century.

In France government organizations such as the *Conseil National de la Comptabilité* (CNC, a department in the Ministry of Finance) and public accounting organizations, such as the *Association Française de la Comptabilité* (AFC) and the above-mentioned *Ordre des Experts Comptables* promoted a good deal of accounting publications and research. Yet, only towards the end of the twentieth century did university accounting research begin to approach the significance accorded to it in the English language area or in some other European countries.

As we have seen, many French scholars frankly admitted the somewhat limited research activity in French accounting, and the growing dependence on imported ideas during the 1950s and 1960s. But in the 1970s, and particularly in the 1980s and 1990s, there were intensive discussions of these ideas and their applications to various aspects of French accounting and auditing. Important contributions towards such efforts were made by various organizations and conferences. For example, in Canada Yves-Aubert Côté (1986) organized at the École des Haute Étude Commerciales de Montréal a 'colloquium' in which scholars from several countries of the French tongue (Belgium, France, Switzerland, Canada) met to discuss the teaching and research of accounting. Since French is the second language in such countries as Algiers, Morocco and Tunisia, there was even a paper presented on accounting and managerial economics in those countries by a scholar from Tunisia (see Ferchiou 1986). Other Canadian contributions (beyond this conference) came from: Zéghal (1984, 1989), on inflation accounting and auditing, respectively; Tremblay and Cormier (1989), on accounting theories and models from a research point of view; Cormier *et al.* (1990, in English), on the evolution of inflation accounting in France since 1960; and Cormier and Magnan (1995, 2005, both in French), offering a profile of Gerald Feltham.

One of the later attempts of promoting accounting research through institutional efforts was organized by the AFC (see Associacion Française de Comptabilité 1997a). There, several prominent French accounting academics (Hoarau 1997a, 1997b; Bouquin 1997; Evraert 1997; Burlaud 1997; Scheid 1997; Colasse 1997) published their views on the evolution of French research in accounting and managerial economics (*sciences de gestion*).[3] And this concern was not limited to the application of 'imported' ideas by the French, but extended to the search for a genuinely French accounting research (e.g. Teller 1997: 6, 17). We agree – as Scheid (1986: 137) pointed out earlier – that publishing should be encouraged through financial support by various French accounting institutions.

But it has to be considered that a good deal of the success of Anglo-American accounting research (during the second half of this century) may lie in several additional factors. First, a market-driven academic environment (that might be more competitive as well as stimulating, offering greater job mobility and clearer promotion criteria based on original research). Second, the greater opportunity of specialization (allowing researchers to probe deeper). And third, the greater amount of time that these colleagues can devote to research (be it because of a smaller administrative burden or less temptation to accept lucrative consulting jobs, etc.). Such an assertion may seem to run counter to the warning by Colasse (1986: 296) against '*technicism et hyper-specialisation*'. This warning against specialization seems to have been directed to the *education* of accounting practitioners; it was hardly meant to deter academics from focusing on a relatively narrow area in their research activity.

The paper continues with a section on general financial accounting (including social and government accounting), with separate sub-sections on 'the plan comptable' (chart of accounts), 'inflation and price-level accounting', 'international accounting harmonization and related topics', as well as 'matrix methods and event theory'. Further full sections are devoted to 'cost and managerial accounting' and 'French historical accounting studies' (offering some representative samples of such research).

8.2 General financial accounting, social and governmental accounting

As hinted at, a good deal of French financial accounting research during the earlier part of this period concentrated on the *Plan Comptable* (the development and extension of a general chart of accounts – pertinent literature, see below in this section, as well as Chapter 7). Apart from those activities, there exist other original contributions made by French accountants during this period. An example is the development of the 'method of surplus accounts'. Yet, it is hardly a coincidence that this concerned the analysis of accounting data in the *public* sector (a long-standing special concern of French accounting studies). This referred to the measurement of productivity changes at different government levels or even the entire economy (pioneered by Vincent 1968).[4] The second example refers to the problem of macro-economic 'income distribution', for which the work by Marshal and Lecaillon (1958) was considered important.

In the area of general financial accounting Pierre Lassègue [1922–] of the *Université de Paris* (*Panthéon Sorbonne*) has been well known for his introductory textbook on financial accounting and corporate management for students of economics (Lassègue 1959). It illuminated accounting from the viewpoint of economics, with emphasis on valuation, rather from that of traditional accounting. Among his other works is a paper on the epistemology of accounting (Lassègue 1962) that sheds light on his wider and philosophical interests. There, he sees accounting as a discipline 'in search of its subject, its very nature, its methods, its flaws, its affiliations and its future' (Colasse and Durand 1994: 54). Lassègue concluded that accounting is not a science but a technical process based on the 'accounting model' that is highly contingent in its representation of an enterprise – see also Panglaou's (1962) response to this paper. Colasse and Durand (1994: 55) believe that Lassègue's critical attitude was a pre-requisite for the renewal of accounting research during the late 1970s and the 1980s. It even helped attract doctoral students in accounting – something apparently especially important in the 1960s.

André Cibert [1912–] also wrote a well-known text on general accounting (Cibert 1968b) following the more traditional pattern of Jean Dumarchey [1874–1946] (see Degos and Mattessich 2003) with its emphasis on a 'net-worth approach' (i.e. focus on the balance sheet) though paying more attention to valuation issues than did Dumarchey (see also Cibert 1986). Yet, as Cibert is considered to have been the major expert on management accounting of this period (Cibert 1968a), we shall say more about his other output in the next section.

The third of the prominent accounting academics of this period is Claude Pérochon [1933–]. He studied under Lassègue, and submitted a doctoral dissertation dealing with a comparison between national income accounting and business accounting (Pérochon 1971) – but even before this date, Sauvy (1970) published his history of national accounting. Later Pérochon (1974) published a textbook based on this dissertation that became a bestseller (by 1994 he was supposed to have sold in total nearly 3 million copies of his books – cf. Colasse and Durand 1994: 55). An even earlier text in 'economic' accounting was that by Lamson (1950). All this reflects a direction of French accounting very different from the British and American one, whether it concerns research or teaching. The only other country where great and sustained attention has been paid to the common basis of macro and micro accounting was Japan (e.g. Harada 1978). Although such a unifying approach of dealing with national income and business accounting under one roof was introduced much earlier in America (Cooper 1949; Powelson 1955; Mattessich 1957, 1964), these publications were by no means as widely accepted as was Pérochon's work in France or Harada's work in Japan. More recently Suzuki (2003) revived this unifying perspective in an English dissertation and paper (under the tutelage of Professor Anthony Hopwood); and it may be no coincident that its author bears a Japanese name.

This particular all-embracing orientation of some French accountants also led to a well-manifested interest in social and *human resource accounting* on the micro-level (i.e. beyond national income accounting). Such studies were undertaken, among others, by Marques (1973, 1978), Chevalier (1976), SYNTEC (1976), Rey (1978), Lequin (1977), Blind (1977), Danziger (1983), Capron (1995) and Capron and Grey (2000), all dealing with social balance sheets and/or social resource accounting of firms in general or more special aspects of it. This peculiar feature seems to have strengthened the bond between business accounting and *governmental accounting* – a subject dealt with by Marshal and Lecaillon (1958), Montagnier (1981) and Prada and Sonrier (1985). This interest in a special kind of government accounting reflects a tradition that manifested itself already in the 1950s (see second paragraph of this section).

Perhaps the most important sub-area of general accounting in France was *le Plan Comptable* together with its revisions and the legislative process of standardization and harmonization, particularly with other European countries. French accounting authors seem to have devoted more time and energy to this subject than to any other. Hence, the pertinent literature is comprehensive and we can afford merely a short glimpse at it. Among the early publications were: Batardon (1950a), Quétard (1950), Veyrenc (1950), Lauzel and Cibert (1959b, as editors of a five-volume work), Lauzel (1965) and Conseil National de la Comptabilité (1986). All these publications were comments on various versions of *le Plan* itself, while Momen's (1957–58) two volume work dealt with the *Plan international*, and Percival *et al.* (1993) focused on the European chart of accounts (in several languages, including English). Standish (1990), Fortin (1991) and Richard (1992, 1993) were all dealing with historical aspects of the *1947 Plan* and further developments, Degos (2000) and Navarro (2000) concentrated on a recent revision of *le Plan*, while Richard (2000) wrote an article on *le Plan* for an encyclopaedic work. In contrast, Brunet (1951), the OECD (1986) and Scheid and Standish (1989) were more concerned with various aspects of the standardization and harmonization process as well as its benefits for France.

The area of price-level adjustment, valuation and inflation accounting has a long-standing tradition in France. Among the many studies during this period, the following may be pointed out: Delmas-Marsalet (1976) who concerned himself with the re-valuation in the balance sheet (mainly on a 'purchasing power' basis), while Lecointre (1977), Panglaou (1978), Burlaud (1979), Boussard (1983) and Zéghal (1984, from Canada), were all dealing with inflation accounting and its methodology. In addition there were numerous studies by various organizations on the topic of inflation, particularly during the late 1970s up to 1980 (cf. Boussard and Rey 1984: 53–4). During the 1977–78 revaluation, the Ministry of Finance leaned towards a kind of 'current value' accounting (cf. Boussard and Rey 1984: 54).

Other publications covered specific topics of financial accounting. For example, the work by Batardon (1950b) dealt with the significance of inventory in the balance sheet and that by Petit (1963) with advanced accounting techniques. Later works were those by Corre (1969) and Dupuis (1969) – both dealing with the consolidation of financial statements. Furthermore, there were publications by Mangenot (1976) on accounting in the service of capital (with a strong Marxist bias); by Blind (1967) on the balance sheets of corporations; by Akoka and Augustin (1983) on 'multi-dimensional' accounting models; by Augustin (1990) on the relation of time and value; by Nioche (1992) on the dangers of 'institutionalizing' evaluation. Of special importance were two comprehensive works on cash and fund-flow statements by Stolowy (1989) and Hoarau (1991).

8.3 International accounting harmonization and related topics

Probably the most frequently discussed accounting topic during recent decades in France (no less than in other European countries) has been that of 'harmonization' of accounting standards with other European countries as well as with America (or the rest of the world) due to the exigencies of financial globalization. A good deal of pertinent publications can be found in the *European Accounting Review*, and are therefore in English. Let us mention a few of them: Zeff (1972), Choi (1974), Barrett (1976), Raffournier (1995, based on Swiss data), Gajewski and Quéré (2001); or in the *Journal of International Management and Accounting*, as the paper by Dumontier and Raffournier (1998), dealing with voluntary compliance and based on Swiss data; or in the *Accounting, Auditing and Accountability Journal*, a paper by Stolowy and Jeny (2001) on 'International accounting disharmony'; or two more recent papers on French group accounting: one in *The International Journal of Accounting*, by Stolowy and Ding (2003), the other in *Abacus* by Ding et al. (2003). Topics like 'harmonization', 'standardization' and related ones abound in the Francophone accounting literature. The best known of these contributions are those by Archer et al. (1995), Hoarau (1995), Lönning (1995), Bernheim (1997) and Evraert (1997).

Furthermore, the *Ordre des Expert Comptable* produced a series of publications among which OEC (1993) – dealing with the accounting profession – received particular attention in the literature. A description of OEC and its activities can be found in Windsor (1982). Other publications by French scholars appeared in English; for example, the papers by Dumontier and Labelle (1998) on earnings and valuation in French accounting, that by Mikol and Standish (1998) on comparing audit independence as related to non-audit services in France and Great Britain, that by Capron and Grey (2000) on an experiment in evaluating corporate social responsibility in France, or the empirical cost–benefit study on voluntary disclosure by listed French companies in Depoers (2000).

Finally, one must emphasize some publications of the rising star of French accounting, Bernard Colasse of the Université de Paris-Dauphine. He is well known (apart from many French journal articles) through several of his historical publications in English (see last section), a series of editions of his text on general accounting (Colasse 1988). He also authored other textbooks on business eco-nomics, finance, etc. and (in English) a paper on 'State versus market: contending interests in the struggle to control French accounting standardisation' (Colasse and Standish 2001). Furthermore, he edited an accounting encyclopaedia (Colasse 2000), and is the editor of the academic journal *Comptabilité – Contrôle – Audit* (cf. Colasse 1997).

Of particular interest are some remarks by Colasse (1992) about French research on statements of flow of funds and cash-flow. Colasse hypothesized that this fertile research area might not have developed in France had the requirement for a fund-flow statement been incorporated in the *Plan Comptable* of 1957 (it was ultimately expressed in its 1982 version). He also points out that:

> Rather than merely reflecting the dictates of the regulatory authorities, the conceptual and methodological development of the fund statement ... resulted from a change in the needs of managers, the emergence and applica-tion of financial theory in the French academic community and from changes in the substantive economic context underlying such development .... Ini-tially conceived and used by bankers to assess the financial health of their clients, the funds statement developed to meet the needs of corporate man-agement in the late 1970s and early 1980s. What had been a retrospective document was changed into a prospective one, increasingly designed and prepared inside the firm, rather than by external agencies.
>
> (Colasse 1992: 246)

8.4 Matrix methods and event theory

Several French authors showed considerable interest in two 'novel' trends. The first was the application of matrix algebra to our discipline as well as matrix accounting in the more narrow sense. The latter was actually conceived in nineteenth-century England (by August De Morgan and in Italy by Giovanni Rossi – see Mattessich 2003: 130, 132), but was later more fully developed in the Anglophone literature by Mattessich (1957) and others – for a survey, see Mattes-sich and Galassi (2000) – as well as in France. The second trend was the 'events theory of accounting', originally conceived by Sorter (1969) in the USA and further developed by others, including some French authors.

In France the following authors and publications contributed to matrix accounting: Cossu (1975) in a doctoral dissertation, Degos and Leclère (1990) with a book on matrix methods as applied to advanced accounting, and Degos (1991) with another book on the history of matrix accounting, as well as Leclère and Degos (2000) with a paper on matrix accounting. These works took as a starting point Mattessich (1957), Shank (1972) and Leech (1986). Several of these and other authors related matrix accounting to computers; this not only advanced the scientific but also practical aspects of this novel direction.

Degos and Leclère (1990) also considered the possibility of introducing further dimensions to matrix accounting (for example, time). But in recent years there was a moving away from matrix-based orthodoxy due to the fact that the 'computerized spreadsheet' (first conceived and developed by Mattessich in the early 1960s – see McHaney 2000) took over most of the tasks that the more traditional accounting matrix was expected to fulfil.

As far as 'events theory' is concerned, the events recorded in the 'data bank' are fairly independent of their possible future use. This enables the user to extract only the kind of information required momentarily for a specific purpose. Although the basic idea is simple, difficulties can arise on various levels – particularly since the system can become extremely complex in large enterprises. There, each user might operate his own retrieval system, geared to his particular needs.

Among French authors interested in 'events theory' were, above all, Gensse (1983) who introduce it in France, and Augustin (1985, 1986) who built a pertinent accounting model of several stages. This helped to arrange the database 'entity-relationship' in such a way that the dissociated data can be re-assembled depending on needs and organizational structure. But in all of these models, whether American or French, the problem of representing managerial facts becomes extremely complex, particularly where there is a large number of multiple users. Such large information systems often have considerable malleability, but at the cost of standardization, simplification and comparability. All these problems have been subjected to scrutiny in the French accounting literature.

8.5 Cost and managerial accounting

The most prominent personality in cost accounting during the early part of this period was André Cibert [1912–], first at the École des Hautes Études Commerciales and ultimately at the *Université de Paris-Dauphine.* Although he wrote a well-known text on general accounting (see above), he is more renowned for his expertise in cost accounting and the pertinent text (Cibert 1968b). This work followed the direction of E. Rimailho, the pioneer of French cost accounting in the earlier part of the century (see Degos and Mattessich 2003: 113). Rimailho developed the so-called '*méthode des sections homogènes*' (a 'responsibility' and full costing approach with overhead allocations from cost centres to products), and Cibert further elaborated this approach by emphasizing its control and responsibility aspect, with additional attention to budgetary control.

An earlier, widely known work on accounting ratios and the so-called '*tableau de bord*' was co-authored with another prominent French accountant (Lauzel and Cibert 1959a). The *tableau de bord* is a device for management reporting, based on ratios and graphs. It is more a statistical or engineering tool than one of traditional accounting, but it has become quite popular in French managerial accounting (for the history of the *tableau de bord*, see Gray and Pesqueux 1993; and for its modern version see the 'balanced score-card', discussed by Kaplan and Norton (1992).

Examples of other authors and works in this field were: Cossu (1975), dealing with costing issues in a multi-product enterprise, Houery (1977), concentrating on measures of productivity and the 'surplus accounts', and Burlaud and Simon (1981), dealing with cost analysis and managerial control. And by Colasse (1973) a book on the analysis of profitability, forecast and control. As to developments since the 1990s, Teller states that:

> As far as management accounting is concerned, all the meetings [of the *Association Nationale des IAE* or Institute of Business Administration] are in agreement that the abandoning of the classical methods of management accounting after 1987, and the new methods of industrial performance evaluation, constitute the actual novelties of management accounting .... A second novelty resides in the development of accounting information systems. The emergence of activity costing goes hand in hand with creating links to accounting information systems.
>
> (Teller 1997: 8–9, translated)

However, by '*systèmes d'information comptable*' the author does not seem to refer to the 'information perspective of accounting' (e.g. in the sense of Christensen and Demski 2003). Indeed, one finds little reference to this *trend* in the Francophone literature (with rare exceptions, as, for example, some bibliographic references in Tremblay 1986: 117). On the other hand, the modern French accounting literature manifests intense interest in more practical questions, such as the 'phenomenon of discontinuities' (*rupture*) and the management strategies to master such managerial and market discontinuities.

Another focus of this literature is the transition (*arbitrage*) between different facets of value creation (from such *internal* aspects of cost value to the *external* and financial aspects of the value of the firm from the shareholders' point of view) – see Teller (1997: 7–10 – also for further references). Indeed, management accounting is no longer an internal matter but an important link between internal and external aspects of the firm.[5]

Bouquin (1997) presented some studies on aspects of ABM (activity-based management), of the above-mentioned '*méthode des sections homogènes*', of ABC (activity based costing) as well as of quality-based management (cf. Atkinson *et al.* 1994). Thereby Bouquin introduced his notion of '*tranversalité*' ('comprehensiveness' might be a possible translation) as a novel approach to (or aspect of) management accounting. This approach aims at going beyond the mere determination of cost and the 'simplistic' separation between fixed and variable costs in the traditional sense. Bouquin offers the following explanation:

> The production cost must not remain the principle objective, one must rather allow management accounting to expand into areas that enable the firm to be competitive ... to organize its pricing around such objectives as 'cost–deadline–quality'; management accounting must be organized to model all aspects of pricing: How much does a delay cost? How much does

the pertinent remedy cost? How best to measure these costs? What are the alternative organizational possibilities?

(Bouquin 1997: 31, translated)

Such ideas are brought up to date and further expanded in the award-winning paper by Pierre Mévellec (1993). This author presented his vision of extending the American ABC (based on an 'instrumental' point of view) to a French ABC method (based on a more comprehensive viewpoint). He concentrated less on production and 'exact' unit costs, more on identifying the many causes of 'resource consumption' – particularly, since many enterprises are no longer dominated by production costs but by *marketing costs*. He also pointed out that:

> The French method of cost calculation (*méthode des sections homogènes* or homogenous cost pool method) is without any doubt a form of activity analysis ... . Therefore, when reading certain American publications [footnote omitted] we can justifiably feel that the Americans are merely re-inventing, 60 years later, the costing method developed in France by Colonel Rimailho [footnote omitted] and the Commission générale d'organisation scientifique (CEGOS) in the late 1920s and 1930s [p. 6] ... .
> In spite of major developments in the economic management culture, since the early 1970s, the use of economic information by senior managers and those at the top of the organizational structure remains limited almost exclusively to budget preparation ... . However, it is to be noted that new production management techniques have recently revived these information systems. Whether it is Just-in-Time or Total Quality, these new approaches require collection and analysis of non-monetary data all the way down to the smallest organizational units. The needs created by these new techniques, as well as the requirements of personnel empowerment and the impact of greater decentralization have contributed in recent years to make the shop floor *tableau de bord* a key managerial tool [p. 7–8, footnote omitted]

(Mévellec 1993: 6, 7–8 – quoted from the English version)

Mévellec produced a series of further challenging cost accounting studies. For example, in Mévellec (2001) he considers, apart from the ABC system, other costing techniques (Cost Management System, Target Costing and Strategic Cost Management), concisely indicating which is suited to which task. But the thrust of the paper is his suggestion to shift from 'Product Life Cycle Costs' (centring on dominant sectors seeking to maximize the value they produce) to 'Whole Life Cycle Costs' (that change from 'Value Chain' to 'Value Constellation' in the sense of Norman and Ramirez 1993). The basic idea behind this approach is to replace the '*production* life cycle' by the 'entire life cycle of the *product*'. This changes the 'perspective' of management accounting; for example, from 'current costs' to 'near future costs', from 'company' to the 'objective', from 'production site' to the 'entire company', from the 'company' to the 'network of its activities' and its various 'participants'. This viewpoint draws partly on ideas such as 'cost inductors', as presented by Shank and Govinderajan (1993).

An important topic of Mévellec (2001) and related publications is the search for further challenging cost accounting studies. He considers, for example, apart from the ABC system, other costing techniques (Cost Management System, Target Costing and Strategic Cost Management) and indicates which of them is suited to which task. Furthermore, this author tried to relate cost and value (something that reminds us of the famous paper by von Wieser 1876, 'On the relation of cost to value'), concentrating on value in a wider sense than traditionally done in accounting. It is 'value for the stakeholders' (including customers), instead of 'value for the shareholders' in which this author is interested. But in all those reflections one no longer finds any trace of such traditional cost accounting topics as, for example, 'full costing vs. direct costing' (and the advantages of each under different degrees of capacity utilization, etc.).

As to agency theory (usually discussed in relation to management accounting), in the French literature it seems to be often dealt more cursorily. There, it is even tied in with 'positive accounting theory' (PAT) or discussed in finance theory (i.e. apart from accounting). Therefore, we add, perhaps surprisingly, in this section some remarks on the reaction to PAT in French accounting. There exist several such publications in the Francophone literature reviewing and discussing PAT (occasionally from a critical point of view). The best known of these are the papers by Chalayer (1995) on explanations for income smoothing, Chalayer and Dumontier (1996), Raffournier (1990), Casta (2000) and Jeanjean (2004). Further publications (e.g. Cormier and Magnan 1995) make references to PAT – though one wonders whether sufficient differentiation is made between empirical accounting in general and the radical wing of PAT.

8.6 French historical studies in accounting

This period also brought forth an impressive amount of historical research. Among several formidable accounting historians, one may first mention some prominent *Belgian* authors and their publications: Vlaemminck (1955) with a treatise on the development of accounting thoughts, and then Vlaemminck (1956) with a general history of accounting dogmas that was very well received and also translated into Spanish. Another well-known Belgian accounting historian, Stevelinck (1970), presented a survey of our discipline 'through the ages', and in Stevelinck (1994) he offered some reflections on the relation between accounting and literature. Furthermore, he produced in co-authorship some historical and theoretical studies of accounting in Stevelink and Haulotte (1958). A third Belgian author of no lesser international stature, de Roover (1990), reflected on some problems that accountants of the nineteenth century had to face. A very particular kind of accounting history, namely accounting archaeology, was pursued with spectacular success by the French-American archaeologist Denis

Schmandt-Besserat (e.g. 1977, 1978, 1992). She showed that Sumerian token accounting gave birth to both pre-cuneiform (and cuneiform) writing as well as to abstract counting (cf. Mattessich 2000).

Among the *French* accounting historians, Rey (1979) concentrated more on *recent* accounting developments, while Richard (1982) focused on the *international* aspects of accounting history. During the 1990s, Richard (1992, 1993) wrote on the development of the *Plan Comptable Français* and the impetus it received (involuntarily) from German occupation forces during the Second World War. Standish (1990) further examined the origins of the Plan and further illuminated this cultural import or even 'intrusion'. Colasse (1989) analysed what he called the 'three ages of accounting'. Durand (1992) concerned himself with the origin and the consequences of separating accounting into sub-disciplines. Lemarchand (1992, 1993, 1995), another well-known French accounting historian, dealt (in succession) with such diverse topics as a profile of the German economist and historian Werner Sombart, and 'an analysis of past armament expenses'.

Nikitin (1992) wrote an acclaimed doctoral dissertation on the birth of industrial accounting in France. Gray and Pesqueux (1993) described the evolution of the French *tableaux de bord* (see above). And Pinceloup (1993) created a comprehensive history of accounting and accountants of two volumes, while Jouanique (1995, 1996) dealt with two major accounting works, namely the treatise of Luca Pacioli, and the classic work of Matthieu de la Porte, respectively. And the work by Burlaud *et al.* (1996) reviews the evolution of depreciation practices in Europe. In a more sweeping vain, the *Association Française de Comptabilité* (1997b) presented a book on accounting personalities, their thoughts and activities. Bouquin (1995) wrote a treatise on E. Rimailho, the father of modern French cost accounting and one of the most eminent engineering-accounting figures of the first half of the twentieth century. Cossu (1997) concentrated on ancient Mesopotamia, while Degos (1991, 1997, 1998) authored a paper on the history of the accounting matrix, as well as a profile on another eminent accountant of this period, Jean Fourastié and, in addition, he wrote a history of accounting (based on his previous historical work on the French ancestors of accounting – Degos 1985). Apart from those, and many other French works concerned with historical aspects of accounting (for example, those contained in the *Cahier d'Histoire de la Comptabilité* and the *Revue d'Histoire Moderne et Contemporaine*), there exists a series of related works, but in English. For example: Parker's (1966) note on Savary's famous book; the paper by Boussard and Rey (1984) on accounting institutions and accounting research in France; Fortin's (1991) analysis of the 1947 French Accounting Plan; the contribution by Colasse and Durand (1994), dealing with French accounting theorists of the twentieth century; Fortin's (1996) contribution on 'France' in the encyclopaedic accounting history by Chatfield and Vangermeersch (1996); Holzer and Schoenfeld's (1983) paper on the French approach to the post-war price-level problem; furthermore, there is Lemarchand and Parker's (1996) bilingual collection of important papers on French accounting history; and finally, Boussard and Rey's (1984) paper on French accounting institutions and research, as well as Nioche and Pesqueux's (1997) paper on accounting, economics and management in France (*Association Française de Comptabilité* 1997). More recently – though this goes beyond the time frame of this book – Colasse (2005) edited a book on *Les grand auteurs de la comptabilité*, discussing 17 accounting authors (from Pacioli to present) and their contributions.

9 Accounting publications and research in Spain

First half of the twentieth century[1]

9.1 Introduction

For Spain, there have previously been no publications summarizing accounting research during the *first half* of the twentieth century, though a survey, mainly concerned with the *second half* of the twentieth century, was presented by Montesinos Julves (1998), followed by a more general study of Spanish accounting (ranging from 1522 to 1943) by Hernández Esteve (1999). The number of accounting publications between 1900 and 1950 was considerable, and in doing this research we encountered nearly 700 items (including those of the nineteenth century).

The early twentieth-century publications continued to reflect the growing interest in accounting, manifested in the last third of the nineteenth century. For this concise survey, we were guided by the following criteria of presentation:

1 A chronological overview of the most prominent authors, their work and theoretical positions.
2 An evaluation of Spanish accounting thought, tracing the influence of major authors on other scholars and, in turn, the influence others exercised on their work.
3 An overview of the general doctrinal trends, disclosing not only topics of major interest to Spanish scholars but also of the various directions and orientations of Spanish accounting due to foreign influence during the first half of the twentieth century.

Our original paper, discussing more publications, also offered a series of Spanish authors and books of the nineteenth century, because of their influence on the subsequent century. The limited space of the present survey permitted only inclusion of the most important and interesting results of our original investigation. As to nineteenth-century accounting literature, we refer to Chapter 2 and acknowledge here the three most important authors and works of this prior period:

• Brost (1825) introduced the work of Edmond Degranges to Spain.
• Salvador y Aznar's (1846) major work attained 19 editions, the last of which came to light in 1910.

- Castaño Diéguez (1876) attained 42 editions, the last of which appeared in 1946.

All of them were followers of the classical French personification theory, called the '*cincocontistas*' – i.e. disciples of the five-accounts-theory of Degranges. This personification theory sustained Spanish accounting thought during practically the entire first half of the twentieth century.

9.2 Main doctrinal trends and major topics of Spanish studies

For the sake of conciseness we decided to present in this abbreviated version the subject matter as classified by various topics. In the original version we offered a more comprehensive overview of the general doctrinal trends, as well as of a series of prominent works, disclosing in some detail the various directions, orientations and influences of Spanish accounting in the first half of the twentieth century. All of this manifested the influence of the personalistic theory that attempted to identify accounts with the persons responsible for the assets or liabilities behind those accounts – precisely as derived from French and, to a lesser extent, Italian accounting of the previous century (Degranges, Cerboni and Besta – for details, see Chapter 2). Only towards the end of the period, with Rodríguez Pita (and in the next period with Fernández Pirla and others), there arose some scientific ambitions. These authors not only supplied valuable bibliographical references, occasionally they also criticized preceding authors and their publications.

9.3 Accounting as a science

During the nineteenth and the beginning of the twentieth century, the central concern was still the classification of accounts. Thus, all the Spanish authors acknowledging accounting as an academic discipline defined it as the 'science of accounts'. From 1909 onwards one encountered authors like Bruño (1919: 68) and Sacristán y Zavala (1918: 6–23) who considered it as a branch of mathematics. The most mathematical-minded of them during this period was Junco y Reyes (1943: 4). Another author, Cañizares Zurdo (1905: 3–26), followed Cerboni. The former listed accounting among the administrative studies (as part of entrepreneurial economics), thereby initiating a shift in emphasis represented by two camps. The followers of one camp focused on the study of *accounts* while the others concentrated on owner's capital. This rift continued in Spain until the end of the 1950s.

Meanwhile, there appeared scholars that regarded accounting as a mathematical-economic science (Campo Recio 1928: 7), while others found the essence of accounting in the analysis and examination of economic relations (Aced y Batrina 1916: 21–7). Some authors, following Besta, regarded accounting as the science of entrepreneurial control (Ruiz Soler 1917: 7).

During the 1920s emerged the notion that accounting was an administrative science that aimed at recording facts – with the focus on the investigation of the enterprise and its capital (Fernández Casas 1926: 7–8). Towards the end of this period, accounting became viewed as the science of studying the laws of equilibrium of wealth (though in the accounting sense, not to be confused with the notion of *economic equilibrium*) – Rodríguez Pita (1945: 7). Yet, whatever specific view one held, most authors agreed that accounting was an *applied* science.

9.4 Major accounting theories

The classical French theory of the *'cincocontistas'* completely dominated Spanish thought at the exclusion of other approaches until the end of the nineteenth century. At this time, the theories of the *'personalistas'* and *'hacendalistas'*, as followers of Cerboni, began to be known in Spain. Their views, together with those of the *'contistas'*, prevailed almost to the end of our period, when Besta's 'control theory' belatedly began to take over.

Rodríguez Pita (1945) completed the incorporation of the modern Italian theories (of such scholars as Rossi, Zappa, Massi, etc.) into Spanish accounting thought. Surprisingly, the theories and ideas of German speaking authors were almost completely absent in the Spanish accounting literature during the entire period.

A few years afterwards, in the second half of the twentieth century – mainly thanks to the endeavour of Fernández Pirla (1960) – this integration with southern (and partly northern) European accounting thought was belatedly completed. Later, the influence of North America was strongly felt in Spain and, again, changed the direction of accounting thought. It was due to the past political instability, the turmoil of the civil war, and the years of economic isolation, that Spain passed readily from the French and Italian ideas to the North American approaches without paying much attention to the accounting discussions that dominated central Europe.

9.5 Purpose of accounting, and information for decision making

Traditionally, the ultimate purpose of accounting was the determination of the firm's income and financial status. Later, towards the end of the 1920s, one also expected accounting to inform about the causes leading to this status and result. Furthermore, one expected accounting to help control the business activity. For governmental accounting, one of the basic tasks was the evaluation of administrators.

After 1925, some authors timidly began to consider the importance of accounting as a source of information for decision-making (Fernández Casas 1926: 8; Cavanna Sanz 1929: 8). Later, Casas Gaspar (1944: 7), a practising accountant, also firmly asserted this, and so did Lluch y Capdevila (1950: 31–5) who included this view in his definition of accounting.

Cardús Rosell (1950), another practitioner, dealt specifically with the information aspect of accounting, explaining to entrepreneurs pertinent techniques that would enable them to take full advantage of such information potential.

9.6 Government accounting

Already since Brost (1825), Spanish authors made the distinction between business accounting (*'contabilidad mercantil'* or *'especulativa'*) and government accounting (*'contabilidad administrativa'* or *'pública'*). This received considerable emphasis, as it became obvious that accounting is not a discipline limited to business. The first Spanish books exclusively dealing with government accounting appeared relatively late, namely those by Torrents y Monner (1910) and Aced y Bartrina (1916). The study of government accounting was also included in the curriculum of commercial schools. In addition to this, one also taught estate accounting (*'contabilidad de casas nobles'*) and accounting for non-profit institutions.

9.7 Specialized accounting

Already in the nineteenth century, one paid attention to specialized or applied accounting (Salvador y Aznar 1846, used the expression *'contabilidades especiales'*). This notion referred to accounting for different business branches, like banks, factories, corporations (*compañías mercantiles por acciones*), estates of the nobility and even government units. Later one spoke of accounting as applied to the *object* (i.e. the type of business), versus the *subject* (i.e. to the type or legal status of the enterprise or owner). All this was related to the practical orientation of instruction, though the majority of the many applied texts also dealt with financial accounting in the modern sense.

9.8 Accounting adjustments and the Spanish term of *'balance'*

For Castaño Diéguez (1876: 125–31) the term *'balance'* still referred to the process of making beginning and closing entries in the accounting cycle (*'balance de entrada'* and *'balance de salida'* or 'to balance' in English). But Ballesteros Marín-Baldo (1924: 739–92) already understood the expression in a wider meaning by distinguishing between 'trial balance of sums' and 'trial balance of balances' (in English *the* 'trial balance') and, in addition, the balance sheet that showed the financial situation of the business at the end of the accounting period.

Fernández Casas (1926: 43–6) explained in some detail the process of making accounting adjustments, thereby distinguishing the following types:

1 asset depreciation;
2 recording the interest earned or charged in payable and receivable accounts;

3   adjusting merchandise accounts;
4   transferring balances of the revenues and expense accounts to the 'profit and loss' account;
5   recording depreciations on bad debts (as charges to the 'profit and loss' account);
6   recording corrections of asset values (in case of actual or required changes);
7   recording transitory items or other provisional entries;
8   transferring the balance from the 'profit and loss' account to the balance sheet and constructing the latter.

In general, such terminology and practices were maintained (with minor variations) until the end of the period studied. Following the same practice, Cavanna Sanz (1929: 201–28) further extended the explanations of various steps for making adjustments and the preparation of balance sheets. Similar steps were adopted by Pérez-Pons Jover (1934: 272–94), Lázaro y López (1935: 405–45), and Rodríguez Pita (1945: 226–28). Junco y Reyes (1943: 472–504) further extended the explanations for balance sheet preparations, introducing a complex classification scheme. On his part, Boter Mauri (1941a: 81–9) was the first Spanish author to propose a structure of the balance sheet based on the degree of liquidity of assets and the maturity of liabilities.

9.9 Classification of accounts

Salvador y Aznar (1846) and afterwards Castaño Diéguez (1864/1876) introduced innovative ideas to further improve the classification scheme of the '*cincocontistas*'. The last years of the nineteenth century witnessed (in addition to a general recourse to the personification of the 'impersonal' accounts) the separation of two major classes: on the one side, the capital account (representing the proprietor), on the other side, the remaining accounts (representing the rest of the business). The trend towards greater exactitude and accuracy in the classification of accounts began in Spain already at the end of the nineteenth century and continued during the entire period under discussion.

9.10 Classification of transactions and entries

Castaño Diéguez (1864/1876: 20) distinguished two classes of accounting transactions: *complete* transactions vs. *incomplete* transactions. To the first class belong transactions reflecting only changes in the *structure* of the owner's wealth. The second class contained transactions causing a change (increase or decrease) of the *amount* of his wealth. Castaño Diéguez's transactions theory possibly anticipated Cerboni's theory of administrative facts. Whether this was so or not, it is undeniable that Castaño Diéguez's classification of transactions survived, in one way or another, in most of the subsequent works.

9.11 Principles of asset valuation

Ruiz Soler (1924: 113–15) distinguished different valuation principles depending on the kind of assets: merchandise, notes receivable, securities, furniture and machinery, accounts receivable and other assets. Ballesteros Marín-Baldo (1924: 36–45) tried to explain the subject more broadly and with greater scholarship. He first explained different valuation principles available:

1   historical (acquisition) cost;
2   current market value;
3   present value (capitalized future net revenues or cash flows);
4   occasional value assessments by experts;
5   depreciated value (initial valuation by any of the former methods, reduced by their annual depreciations).

As to the actual choice of a valuation method, the author envisaged two major positions. First, valuation for the purpose of sale or liquidation; and second, valuation for the continuing operation of the business. In the first case, the recommended method was the current market (or liquidation) value. In the second case, he recommended the acquisition cost method. Not surprisingly, followers of those two positions existed throughout the entire period under study. In a subsequent work, Ballesteros Marín-Baldo (1947: 162–4) added a further valuation method, that of 'face value' (e.g. the nominal value in case of bonds, etc.)

Lázaro y López (1935: 157–92, 221–7) also added a new method, that of the current sales price (in English also 'current exit value'). Gardó Sanjuán (1925) asserted that buildings, merchandise, furniture, machinery, etc., had to be valuated at cost initially; in contrast to this, accounts receivable in foreign currency had to be recorded at present value. Cavanna Sanz (1929: 100–42) specified that the notes receivable could be evaluated either at face (nominal) value or at present value, and the same would hold for owners' equities. In contrast to this, notes payable had to be recorded at face value. Buildings, merchandise, furniture, machinery, tools, ships and animals had to be valued at acquisition cost. Pérez-Pons Jover (1934: 103–9) agreed with such statements, but explained that, even though notes receivable and notes payable were usually recorded at face value, if issued 'at term', they ought to be recorded at present value. Fernández Casas (1926: 20–2) took an opposite position. According to him, notes receivable and notes payable had to be recorded at face value. Boter Mauri (1941b: 80) was only concerned with valuation methods for merchandise. For these, he insisted on cost values but neither permitted valuation at sales price nor at 'commercial cost'.

Junco y Reyes (1943: 23–38) is the first Spanish author to devote two specific chapters to valuation methods, though those chapters contained no remarkable novelties. He also favoured a 'faithful image' (in English, one would say a 'true and fair view') to be reflected in the balance sheet, and advocated valuation at present value, provided the cost value was an unrealistic representation of the asset's worth.

9.12 Depreciation

During the period under study, Spanish authors dealt in more or less detail with depreciation as a factor of assets valuation. Ballesteros Marín-Baldo (1924: 219–32) discussed several depreciation methods, as did (in a similar vein) Pérez-Pons Jover (1934: 112–13). Boter Mauri (1935: 145–61) offered the most complete list of such methods:

1　linear depreciation;
2　declining-balance depreciation (based on a percentage of book value);
3　declining depreciation in arithmetic progression;
4　ascending depreciation in arithmetic progression;
5　Cole's method (a variant of declining depreciation);
6　Matheson's depreciation method (another variant of declining depreciation);
7　accumulated depreciation (indirect depreciation);
8　depreciation based on production (in this method the useful life of machines is not computed according to time but to the number of product units they can produce);
9　annuity depreciation method;
10　replacement cost method (used in times of inflation and monetary instability);
11　method based on expert estimations.

Boter Mauri (1935) distinguished two causes of depreciation: physical deterioration, and obsolescence. Depending on the purpose, Lázaro y López (1935: 221–7) offered some indication on annual depreciation rates for various assets groups:

1　Depreciation of furniture increasing from 5 to 10 per cent of cost.
2　Depreciation of machinery increasing from 3 to 5 per cent of cost.
3　Depreciation of buildings increasing from 1 to 3 per cent of cost. If the buildings constituted the plant of the firm, then the depreciation could be from 3 to 10 per cent.

Most of the authors publishing before 1935, with the possible exception of Fernández Casas, preferred *direct* depreciations. Lázaro y López (1935: 284–5), however, recommended *indirect* depreciation by means of an accumulating depreciation account.

9.13 Cost accounting

Only towards the end of the first quarter of the twentieth century did textbooks on industrial accounting appear (later called 'cost accounting') – e.g. Boter Mauri

(1935). One also began to separate this sub-discipline from financial or general accounting (Gardó Sanjuán 1925). Furthermore, Ruiz Soler (1924: 289–91) distinguished between direct costs and indirect costs. Direct costs were raw materials, labour and other direct expenses. Indirect costs consisted of overhead costs. Ruiz pointed out that the allocation of direct costs (to products), as a rule, did not present much difficulty, in contrast to the complex allocation of indirect costs.

Gardó Sanjuán (1925) wrote the first Spanish book specifically devoted to cost accounting, and distinguished a hierarchy of four kinds of costs:

1   production costs: direct costs;
2   industrial costs: production costs plus overhead costs;
3   commercial costs: industrial costs plus administrative overhead costs;
4   sales price: commercial costs plus profit or minus loss.

The cost categories specified by Gardó Sanjuán were those of Fernández Casas (1926: 64–79). They were based on three main accounts: manufacturing, finished goods inventory (stocks) and finished goods sold (in English, the sales account). As customary, the debit entries of the last account came from the finished goods inventory at cost (industrial costs), while the credit entries (sales) were recorded at sales prices. In the case that costs were based on standards, these *a priori* costs had to be estimated prior to the recording process. Fernández Casas used the following cost categories:

1   direct (raw) materials;
2   auxiliary materials;
3   direct labour hours;
4   maintenance and repairs (of machinery and equipment);
5   depreciation of machinery and equipment;
6   other production overhead costs.

Fernádez Casas pointed out that the greatest difficulty in computing industrial costs consisted in determining the overhead allocation coefficients relevant for each product. He explained several systems for determining those coefficients (apparently influenced by some French authors).

Boter Mauri (1935) wrote the most complete book on cost accounting during this period, though the process he presented was more or less the same as that described by Fernández Casas. Boter Mauri emphasized that once the *actual* industrial costs (or *a posteriori* costs) were determined, they had to be compared with the *standard* costs (or *a priori* costs) in order to take advantage of the corresponding feedback. Although the author quoted several American books, he drew most of his inspiration from French authors. As to cost allocation bases, he explained the following possibilities:

1   manpower (direct wages);
2   direct material cost;

3   mixed basis;
4   product units or product value;
5   direct labour hours;
6   power (energy) consumption;
7   prime costs (direct labour and direct material cost);
8   machine hours.

9.14 Inflation issues and gold currency

For dealing with inflationary effects in accounting, Gardó Sanjuán (1929) as well as Fernández Casas (1931: 367–88) presented (at a time of considerable monetary instability) reflections on adjustments based on gold currency. Years later, at another time of remarkable inflation in Spain, Goxens Duch (1948) reintroduced this theme by studying previous publications, and offered new approaches based on German and French accounting literature.

9.15 Auditing

Oliver Castañer (1904) wrote the first Spanish book dealing particularly with the auditing of accounts – though it did not arouse much interest. From 1910 onwards, some accounting texts devoted a chapter or so to auditing, but again, without much response. Interest in this subject arose in Spain only from mid-1930s onwards when authors like Piqué Batlle (1935, 1936, 1939), Boter Mauri (1943) and Goxens Duch (1944) published auditing texts. In the course of the first half of the twentieth century, Spanish accounting terminology as used today was created step by step. Martínez Pérez (1910: 31) already used the distinction between fixed and current assets (*'capital fijo'* and *'capital móvil'*), that he later called *'capital fijo o inmovilizado'* and *'capital móvil o realizable'* (Martínez Pérez 1920: 64).

In 1918, the concept of the chart of accounts (*'cuadro de cuentas'*) appeared in Sacristán y Zavala (1918: 67). Ballesteros y Marín-Baldo (1924: 121–8) also used this concept under the name of *'cuadro de contabilidad'* and offered some examples. Ruiz Soler (1924) used the term 'applied accounting' (*'contabilidad aplicada'*) for what was previously called 'special accounting' (*'contabilidad especial'* – see our subsection 3.5). Fernández Casas (1931) distinguished special purpose-oriented types of applied accounting, such as *'contabilidad aplicada por razón del sujeto'* (i.e. applied accounting to serve the proprietor), and *'contabilidad aplicada por razón del objeto'* (i.e. applied accounting to serve the business or special tasks of it).

9.16 Studies in accounting history

Cañaizares Zurdo (1933/1996) published the first Spanish book on accounting history), though a series of pertinent articles by López y López (1926–27) had previously appeared. Considering the total contribution of Cañizares Zurdo, his fame mainly rested on the *Ensayo histórico sobre contabilidad*, published when the author was already 73 years. It was an interesting, though somewhat limited work. Its limitations manifested themselves most strikingly in the short and incomplete bibliography (*obras consultadas*) at the end of the book. On the credit side, this was compensated by the presence of many literature references either in the text proper or in footnotes, even if not always listed in the bibliography. The latter consisted of 25 references (including a few accounting journals and a catalogue). Among these only two publications referred to 'general accounting history' (in the narrow sense): a 1922 article (a conference presentation) by the well-known French author Gabriel Faure and a widely referred book by Léon Gomberg. It is presumed that the latter work significantly influenced Cañizares Zurdo's own writing. The rest of this bibliography referred either to important French accounting works or to specific historical works – like some publications about Pacioli or those referring to the time before, as well as after, Pacioli; or related to general historical works beyond accounting. On the other hand, German authors, like Eugen Schmalenbach, Fritz Schmidt and others, who, by 1933, were already quite prominent, remained unmentioned, most likely due to the language barrier. Even more surprising is that this bibliography referred, apart from a translation of Luca Pacioli's treatise, only to a single Italian accounting expert, namely a historical work on Roman accounting by Giovanni Rossi – though the text itself did briefly mention other Italian authors, such as Gitti and Brambilla, Zappa's name was conspicuously absent. Daniel Carrasco Díaz and Francisco González Gomila edited in 1996 a fine facsimile reprint, enriched by an introductory commentary of Cañizares Zurdo's (1933/1996) *magnums opus*. One might add Boter Mauri's (1959) book on accounting doctrines, although it transgresses beyond the period under consideration.

9.17 Practical orientation of Spanish texts

All the Spanish texts published in the nineteenth century provided a practical section that integrated an accounting case in order to illustrate journals, ledgers, accounts and the corresponding entries. This custom began slowly to fade during the second half of the twentieth century in the wake of more theoretical tendencies. Then, illustrating cases were relegated to exercise books. The motivation to deal with practical accounting aspects reached far beyond bookkeeping in the narrow sense. The majority of the books we examined had the task to instruct future or present government clerks and business employees. Thus, accounting texts often contained technical subjects such as business arithmetic, interest calculations on current accounts, the discounting of letters of exchange, etc.

At the end of the nineteenth century, Torrents y Monner (1895) even asserted that accounting consisted of four different subjects: business arithmetic, bookkeeping, statistics and the teaching of commercial documents. This view, even if shared by one or the other scholar, was not widely accepted. But familiarization with commercial documents was practised in several books.

9.18 Further details on prominent Spanish accounting scholars

Apart from a few exceptions, Spanish accounting literature did not bother much with quotations and bibliographies. Indeed, due to the need for mere technical expertise, hardly any of the works were based on profound scholarship or a scientific approach. However, during this period there were several scholars deserving special emphasis (in spite of having discussed some of their special contributions above under various topics).

The book by Aced y Bartrina (1916) proved to be a classic of its kind. For many years it was an indispensable reference work until the time when the pertinent administrative and legislative practices lost their validity (though a third edition of this work still appeared in 1941). The author was associated with the '*Cuerpo Pericial de Contabilidad del Estado*' and served as '*Contador del Tribunal de Cuentas del Reino*' (accountant of the Royal Audit Office). The abovementioned work consisted of an introductory part and three 'books'; it closed with an alphabetical glossary of concepts – a novelty at the time.

Of particular interest seems to be the preliminary part of this book. There, the author revealed his notion of accounting, very different from that of other authors of the period. He regarded 'accounting as the science destined to define economic behavioural relations when keeping continuous account of one's wealth and its changes' (Aced y Bartrina 1916: 21, translated). For him accounting was an applied science involving speculative thought, but he sensed the need to supplement it by something that related it to the realm of facts. This he addressed as 'art' or 'bookkeeping'. Today, we rather distinguish between the analytical and the empirical aspect of accounting; nevertheless, he did realize the necessity for separating two fundamentally different aspects of our discipline.

As far as governmental accounting is concerned, Aced y Bartrina rejected the current classification into legislative, administrative and judicial accounting aspects, and replaced it by the three aspects of *preventive*, *executive* and *critical* accounting. He meant, by that, the phases of budgetary planning, of executing the budget and of ex-post analysing and reviewing it. Such a classification into different aspects or phases of governmental accounting was, at this time, generally accepted.

Rodríguez Pita, aware of the above book, greatly admired its author whom he counted to the camp of '*científicos de la trilogía económico-hacendal*', to which he himself belonged (cf. Rodríguez Pita and Rodríguez Flores de Quiñones 1956: 30). These were for him the authors that took the scientific treatment of accounting most seriously. Aced y Bartrina (1916) took into consideration historical aspects as well as contributions of other authors, mainly Italians, known as '*controlistas*' and '*funcionales administrativos*'. Aced y Bartrina was regarded as one of the most intellectual and scientifically oriented Spanish authors of his time.

Another prominent scholar was Boter Mauri, one of the leading Spanish (precisely speaking Catalán) authors of this period. One of his major publications appeared first in 1924 and then in 1934 in Catalán, followed by its Spanish translation (Boter Mauri 1935), mentioned above. There, the author developed broadly the notion of industrial accounting previously introduced in Boter Mauri (1924). Similarly, the book by Boter Mauri (1943), mentioned in our section 9.15 on auditing, was an extension of an earlier work (Boter Mauri 1924). Furthermore, his later historical treatise (Boter Mauri 1959) was a most valuable work that filled important gaps in this particular area. Moreover, the author was a translator of renowned foreign accounting works, such as several editions of the Spanish translation of Batardón's French bestseller, or of Delaporte's classic, published in 1932 as *Organización y contabilidad bancarias.*

Subsequently, Rodriguez Pita's (1945) book initiated a new era in Spanish accounting, one of scientific ambition and achievements. This work summarized his thoughts previously expressed in journal articles and contributions to an encyclopaedic work. His book was a concise and complex treatise, difficult to read, crowded with definitions, classifications and sub-classifications. Its intent was thorough systematization, written in a sophisticated style and a language of long sentences. Possibly, because of such features, and despite its importance and interest, the work did originally not reach a great audience. The author's difficult and ill-tempered nature may also have contributed to this. However, once published, Spanish authors could not ignore it for any length of time, for it explained the changes that had occurred in the approaches of European accounting theory (not least due to the contributions of the Italians). The major novelty of Rodríguez Pita's work was, succinctly expressed, the incorporation of these 'modern' approaches into the warehouse of Spanish accounting doctrines. As pointed out, these doctrines fed routinely on the classical French school, though somewhat enriched by the novelties of Cerboni's theory that was essentially '*contista*'. The new Italian ideas definitely displaced the former accounting approach, particularly as far as the notions of firm, capital, wealth or accounting equilibrium, and control activities were concerned.

This book was a general text; it dealt with business accounting as well as government accounting. Furthermore, it was scholarly and conceptual, and not burdened with examples of inventories, balance sheets, journals and ledgers, or pertinent entries. Even more importantly, the book was not concerned with the teaching of operational routines; these were assumed to be a prerequisite. The author defined accounting as 'the science that studied the laws of wealth equilibrium, resulting from administrative activity' (Rodriguez Pita 1945: 7, translated).

On the other hand, the book contained neither quotations nor any bibliography, though it presented the author's thoughts and ideas in many details and with some complexity. To remedy its shortcomings, he later published a further work in co-authorship with his son (Rodríguez Pita and Rodríguez Flores de Quiñones 1956). This book, richly endowed with a wealth of rigorous and precise bibliographical citations (a hitherto unprecedented practice in Spanish accounting literature), may be considered his *magnum opus.* Apparently, Rodríguez Pita's favourite author was Gino Zappa, though without ignoring or downgrading Besta and the other contemporary '*hacendalistas*', '*patrimonalistas*' and '*reditistas*'. Rodríguez Pita's own outlook was purely '*hacendalista*', i.e. oriented towards 'enterprise economics', provided the term 'enterprise' was taken broadly enough to include the non-profit organizations, government, etc., just as his book, from the very beginning, emphasized the enterprise, its nature, organization, functions, and so on.

Finally, we should like to mention Ballesteros Marín-Baldo (1924), who originally was teaching in Germany. Despite his earnest intentions to be original, his work only unified ideas expressed by previous authors. Nevertheless, his analysis of major account theories (explaining the true significance of accounts, their classes and forms) was interesting and novel to a Spanish audience. In the face of some preceding authors (who integrated in their texts the elements of organization, administration and management of a firm), Ballesteros Marín-Baldo made a clear distinction between administration and accounting, though admitting that both were intimately related to each other.

The work of Ballesteros Marín-Baldo was mentioned in the Spanish translation of Vlaemminck's (1960: 318) history, with the remark that the author was a fervent defender of the purest Cerbonian theory. This seems to be somewhat exaggerated even if Cerboni's influence on the author cannot be denied. His second book, Ballesteros Marín-Baldo (1927), was similarly organized as the first one, but more concise and simpler. It was also enriched by a separate part dealing with 'applied accounting'. As far as we know, this text reached eight editions, the last one in 1947 (though only with minor changes from the first edition) when its author was already Professor of the School for Higher Commercial Studies in Madrid.

9.19 Conclusion

Based on our investigations, we reach the following general conclusions:

1   During this period, accounting was taught in Spain at high-school level, in the Schools of Commerce. Thus, the major objective of Spanish accounting texts was the practical instruction of clerks and employees. For this reason, authors of accounting texts rarely had particular scientific ambitions. Their main intention was to teach their pupils in an adequate way.
2   Probably due to such circumstances, Spanish authors did not aim at developing their own thoughts on accounting. They rather followed foreign theories.
3   The doctrines that dominated Spain in the second half of the nineteenth century and the greater part of the first half of the twentieth, were the French theories of the '*contistas*'. These authors considered the *accounts* (and theories about them) as the nuclear theme of accounting studies. Among the '*contistas*', Degranges' '*cincocontistas*' (adherents of the five-accounts theory) had special weight in Spain during the beginning of the period investigated. Another French theory widely accepted in Spain during this time was that of personification (identifying an account with a person

responsible for the subject matter behind it). Such French doctrines remained a substratum in Spanish accounting, even towards the end of the period when the Italian doctrines had already began to dominate the Spanish accounting panorama.

4   The first of the 'modern' Italian thoughts to enter Spain was that of Cerboni, manifested in the theories of the *'personalistas'* and *'hacendalistas'*. This shifted the centre of gravity from the 'accounts' to the 'firm'. Later on, Besta's ideas were introduced. They emphasized accounting as the science of entrepreneurial control, and introduced a 'materialistic' (i.e. non-personalistic) theory of accounts. Almost at the end of the period Zappa's view on income determination (as the core of accounting) became known in Spanish circles.

5   Ballesteros Marín-Baldo, one of the relevant authors of the period, had been teaching accounting at the Commerce School of Pforzheim. And yet, no direct influence of the German doctrines on Spanish accounting thought can be found in his work (apart from the theoretical discussion at the end of this period, and attempts to minimize the accounting effects of inflation and price instability). This may be further evidence of Spain's intellectual isolation (during this time) from Central Europe and foreign countries in general (save such 'neighbours' as France and Italy).

6   Despite the absence of native accounting innovations, and relative isolation, Spanish accountants knew and applied to their own environment, without substantial delay, many theoretical and instrumental novelties that emerged abroad.

10 Accounting publications and research in Spain

Second half of the twentieth century[1]

10.1 Introduction

The 1950s were still a time when the prominent works of Spanish accounting literature were textbooks that made the students acquainted with the state of the art as well as some of the foreign literature. As such, the book by Rodríguez Pita and Rodríguez Flores de Quiñones (1956) became quite prominent in the Iberian accounting literature, and so did two works by Fernández Pirla (1957, 1960), all three of them as leading texts (apart from the contribution of such an 'elderly statesman' as Boter Mauri, 1959), Fernández Peña pointed out that:

> After the publication of this work [Fernández Pirla 1957], there was a lull of some years, but at the beginning of the sixties, there was renewed activity, resulting in a number of works of particular interest: Bueno Campos (1974), Cañibano Calvo (1975/79), Bueno Campos and Cañibano Calvo (1978), Casanovas Parella (1976), Requena Rodríguez (1977), García García (1980). Mention should also be made of the exceptional academic theses by Vereda Espada (1977), Hernández Diosdado (1976), García Martín (1978), Larriba Díaz-Zorita (1979), Fernández de Caso (1981) and Tua Pereda (1982). In the field of applied accounting research, we may cite: Alvira Martín and García López (1976) and Cuervo García and Rivero Torre (1986).
>
> (Fernández Peña 1984: 192)

A comparison of the texts by Rodríguez Pita and Rodríguez Flores de Quiñones (1956) and Fernández Pirla (1957) with later editions of Fernández Pirla (e.g. its tenth edition, 1986), shows interesting differences as to the development of academic accounting in Spain during this time. While the former editions still look towards the past, citing heavily Italian and French authors (apart from Spanish scholars and an occasional mentioning of German or English works), later editions (e.g. the tenth edition, 1986) of Fernández Pirla's text relied slowly but increasingly on ideas derived from the English (including American) literature. This edition, for example, already makes reference to input–output models and national income accounting, to analytical methods, as well as to those Spanish authors influenced by them (e.g. Fernández Peña 1957/65; Cañibano Calvo 1975). Montesinos Julve confirmed this in the following remark:

> The publications and axiomatic methodology of Mattessich, Devine and Ijiri had a considerable influence. Cañibano (1974: 4) considered mathematical and logical formulations as the main feature of their research programme adopted by academic accountants adopted during this period, who were leaving behind the legal and economic programmes. Some Spanish academics (Bueno, 1974; Montesinos [Julve], 1975, 1978; Cañibano, 1975: 201 *et seq.*) began to be concerned with the objectives of accounting information and the user's decision-making needs, especially after the issue in 1966 of the ASOBAT study by the American Accounting Association. This methodological concern, as well as the deductive methodology used by formal mathematical approach authors (see Calafell, 1967a; García García, 1972) gave rise in Spain to the development of a theoretical system based on deductive reasoning, and a pragmatic approach based on the setting-up of a set of agreed general principles to be fully developed through concrete standards and principles.
>
> (Montesinos Julve 1998: 365)

Indeed, the bibliographies of most of those modern Spanish accounting works refer more to English literature than to any other. As to the link between accounting and *Economia de la Empresa* (similar to the Italian *Economia Aziendale* or to the German *Betriebswirtschaftslehre*), it still played an important role. Yet, as Montesinos points out, in time, this bond got weaker as it also did in other countries:

> However, the close personal bonds between Business Economics and Accounting characterized by Fernández Pirla have tended to dissipate, the scientific and personal links between the subjects are now very much weaker than in the initial period, when *Economía de la Empresa* sprang up as a separate discipline in Spanish universities.
>
> (Montesinos Julve 1998: 362)

At any rate, modern Spanish accounting adapted easily to new trends and developed more freely than the Italian *Ragioneria* (that has been a hostage to the restrictions imposed by Zappa's view of *Economia Aziendale*).[2]

Generally speaking, Spanish accounting has experienced during this period the following changes:

1   Heavier reliance on Anglophone accounting literature, and overcoming the language barrier (particularly among the younger generation).
2   A more significant presence of Spanish authors and publications in international accounting forums (journals, reviews, conferences, etc.).

3   Enlarging the spectrum of Spanish accounting research topics.
4   Greater emphasis on international accounting standards and harmonization (than on tax regulation and other purely local requirements).

Due to these changes, Spanish academic accounting made great strides during the second half of the twentieth century. It showed an astonishing vitality, particularly in comparison to the first half of this century (the highlights of which were mainly best-selling textbooks). The reason for this Spanish 'renaissance' is partly explained by the economic recovery due to joining the European Economic Union, as well as the pent-up energy released when Spain became a free and democratic country. But the academic advances in accounting have to be attributed to a new outlook promoted by the capable leadership of a group of scholars. They were ready to accept 'foreign' ideas, to disperse them in Spain, and to develop them for the local situation. The most prominent among these academics were: Fernández Peña, Fernández Pirla, Cañibano Calvo, Tua Pereda, García García, Cea García, Buenos Campos (particularly in the area of *Economía Empresarial*), Carmona Moreno, Gabas Trigo, García Benau, Gonzalo Angulo, Montesinos Julve, Requena Rodriguez, and in the area of accounting history, Hernández Esteve (founder and editor of the relatively new and 'free' electronic accounting history journal *De Computis*).

As to the question to what extent Spanish accounting research contributed to advances of the second half of the twentieth century, a fairly positive answer can be given. First, Spanish accounting research adapted to many of the new trends, and in a manner that can easily compete with other Southern European countries.[3] Second, this research has greatly contributed to the European discussion on such topics as international standardization and harmonization, as well as issues of auditing, consolidation and new techniques of managerial accounting (primarily at international conferences and in the *European Accounting Review* – though occasionally also in other accounting journals of English tongue). Third, it has absorbed ideas from the British critical-interpretive camp as well as fundamental American methodological thoughts. However, the application of high-powered statistical methods in empirical research is relatively rare[4] – though there are many empirical studies and some discussions of 'positive accounting theory'. Furthermore, little interest has been manifested in the mathematical information perspective of accounting (see note 4), but it would be most unreasonable to apply the highly technical-mathematical standards of American accounting research to some European countries where the conditions (particularly those of capital markets) are very different. Fourth, the new legal reforms for Spanish university instructors put greater stress than previously on research and publication activity as a factor of promotion.

This fairly positive picture may find *rough* confirmation in the paper by Carmona *et al.* (1999: 470) and its Table 1 of 'Country contributions to leading accounting journals ...'). There, Spain ranked (with a mean of 1.79 contributions per year) before Austria (with 1.22167), Norway (with 1.03176) and Ireland, Italy and Switzerland (each with 0.888333). In other words, Spain ranked in *ninth* place (among 26 European nations) in the *number* of accounting publications in 13 Anglophone accounting journals (during the time from 1992 to 1997).[5]

10.2 General theoretical studies

In the early 1950s a belated translation of Schmalenbach's (1954) book on 'dynamic accounting' appeared. This may have opened the new trend in Spanish accounting – one more open to ideas from 'Northern Europe' and, more importantly, soon afterwards, from the 'West'.[6]

Among the more traditional Spanish texts (apart from the books mentioned in the introduction), there were some theoretical studies, foremost by such authors as Goxens Duch (1954, 1974, 1993), Calafell Castello (1960–61, 1967a, 1967b), and Pique Battle (1960). Yet, despite such endeavours, the 1960s and early 1970s were dominated by French authors and the related problem of establishing charts of accounts. This, as Montesinos Julve (1998: 364) pointed out, 'gave rise to much descriptive and analytical literature, it inhibited a critical turn of mind in accounting research'.

From the mid-1970s onwards, studies by a leading group of accounting theorists changed the scene. Above all, the publications by Cañibano Calvo (e.g. 1974, 1975) led to a genuine revolution towards modern Spanish accounting research. Cañibano's research interests are very broad but with basic reference to the theory and methodology of accounting with a clear formal delineation, as well as an emphasis on foundational research that manifested itself in individual publications or in co-authorship with other scholars.

Another leading member of this group was the late García García (1974, 1975), with his analysis of the circulatory system ('cycle theory') of the firm, and the study of double-entry in modern accounting, respectively. Among the above-mentioned publications, his 'cycle theory' with its 'subtle dissection of variables' is the only *Spanish* work that received special emphasis in Tua Pereda's (2004: 100–2) comprehensive paper on the evolution and situation of modern accounting thought. Tua Pereda, a former colleague of the late García García, points at the importance of these 'eminently formal' and graphical presentations that offer great pedagogic advantages. The significance of García García (1974) for economic circulatory systems in general, has also been affirmed in Cañibano Calvo and Gonzalo Angulo (1995: 47). However, the comprehensive and probing investigations of both, Cañibano Calvo (e.g. 1974, 1975, 1991, 1998) and Tua Pereda (e.g. 1982, 1983a, 1983b, 1991, 2004) himself, would hardly deserve less appreciation.

There are, for example, the following publications by Tua Pereda (1982, 1983a, 1983b, 1991). The last of these offered surveys of empirical studies and utilitarian decision theory, market efficiency, content of accounting information, alternative information models, and other 'modern' concepts. However, this paper (Tua Pereda 1991) is rather a review and discussion than an application or extension of pertinent empirical research.

In the course of his studies, Tua Pereda raises questions of the following kind: In which way does decision theory utilize accounting information? What is the most useful information in such cases? What kinds of decision models are used for different purposes or different users? What is the best way to convey accounting information? How are the capital markets and firms affected by the pertinent accounting information? What effects do accounting figures have on the enterprise? Which accounting information promotes, and which impedes the optimization of resources?

Further notable publications were those by Alvira Martín and García López (1976) on how experts see the notion of 'truth' in accounting; Alvarez López and López Caso (1981) on conceptualizing modern accounting; or Crespo Domínguez's (1993) re-opening of the problem of matching costs and revenues. There were also *empirical* studies: for example, those by Gabás Trigo and Apellániz Gómez (1994), an investigation on accrual vs. cash-basis accounting; Apellániz Gómez and Labrador Barrafón (1995), an examination of the impact of the Spanish Chart of Accounts of 1990 on the calculation of social benefits; and a frequently mentioned work by Giner Inchausti (1995), namely a theoretical and empirical study (with statistical samples) on the usefulness of information in controlling management activity (explaining the reasons for the managerial choice of a specific information). Furthermore, García Benau (1997) critically examined the tension between accounting praxis and theory from an international point of view. Cea García (1996) may deserve particular attention for his endeavour towards establishing a solid and scientific basis of Spanish accounting research – other contributions of this author are more appropriately discussed in the next section. Finally, we should mention a series of studies on standards and principles of financial, as well as managerial accounting by AECA (e.g. 1981–2004, 1990, 1990–2004).

10.3 Specialized theoretical studies

Cea Garcia's works (1974, 1980, 1987, 1990, 1995, 1997) manifest a clear orientation towards accounting's role in explaining social reality. He also published on various special issues, such as changing purchasing power, social balance sheets, accounting issues of future contracts and new financial instruments, as well as foreign currencies. However, his rejection of incorporating value judgements in accounting (including its standard-setting) might create difficulties. To overcome this, a systematic approach for relating the means of accounting to specific and well-defined ends (to 'neutralize' the value judgements) might be necessary (cf. Mattessich 1995: 187–222).

To this category also belongs research on consolidated financial statements (often called in the European literature 'group accounts'), as those by Cañibano Calvo and Cea García (1971), Bueno Campos (1972a), Fernández Peña (1977), Alvarez Melcón (1978) and Capella San Agustín (1975). From 1977 onwards the *Instituto de Planificación Contable* (of the Ministry of Economics and Business) promoted pertinent accounting standards (for details, see Fernández Peña 1984: 195–6).

Another area that aroused considerable interest in Spain was social accounting (in the private-welfare sense). To this group belong such publications as Ortigueira Bouzada (1977), Cea García (1980), Arderiu Gras (1980), Fernández Rodríguez (1980), García García (1980), Giménez Cassina (1980), Keller and Serrano (1980) and Montero Perez (1980). During the late 1970s and early 1980s the interest in social balance sheets disappeared, but from 2000 onwards social accounting emerged in the broader area of Corporate Social Responsibility (e.g. Vallverdú Callafel 2003; AECA 2004).

Further topics were those of valuation and inflation, particularly in the face of a Spanish law of 1961 that offered several options of value adjustments (cf. Fernández Peña 1984: 196). Fernández Pirla (1963), Cubillo Valverde (1967), Cea García (1974), Cubillo Valverde and Fernández Peña (1974) and Serra Salvador (1978). Studies on cash flow and flow of funds were also popular, for example by Pinilla Monclús (1975), Casanovas Parella (1976), Bueno Campos and Cañibano Calvo (1978) and Gabás Trigo and Apellániz Gómez (1994). One may further mention the study on balance sheet analysis by Alvarez López (1970), and the one on liquidity issues by Rodríguez Rodríguez (1979).

Another issue was corporate accounting, dealt with, for example, by Fernández Peña (1957/65) and Cañibano Calvo (1998). Two topics that received less attention were accounting for leasing, as in Vidal Blanco (1977), and the optimal level of reserves in Vereda Espada (1977). Apart from these works, the *Instituto de Contabilidad y Auditoría de Cuentas* (ICAC) published works on the accounting treatment of financial derivatives, as those by Alcarria Jaime (1998) and Borrás Pamies (1999). This subject was also dealt with in some publications by Cea García (1987, 1995).

Furthermore, there is the much broader topic of governmental accounting regulations, accounting standards and harmonization issues with the European Community. It was examined by Fernández Pirla (1963), Ramos Díaz (1969), Montesinos Julve (1980), Gonzalo Angulo and Tua Pereda (1981), García Benau (1995) and Lainez and Callao (2000). Publications on Spanish and European accounting comparability were those by Gonzalo Angulo (1992), Cañibano Calvo and Giner Inchausti (1994), Cañibano Calvo and Mora Enguidanos (1997) and Cañibano Calvo and Cea García (1999). A related work on the social-political determinants in establishing Spanish accounting regulations by Ruiz Barbadillo (1997) received the 'Premio *Carlos Cubillo Valverde*' (an award established in memory of the eminent Spanish accountant and auditor).

More distantly related to this area were a series of studies on the chart of accounts. Soler Amaro (1980), Beascoechea Ariceta (1982), Gabás Trigo (1991), Sáez Torrecilla and Corona Romero (1991), as well as Chauveau (1995) discussed the 1973 Chart of Accounts and subsequent developments.[7] Carmona Moreno et al. (1993), as well as Céspedes (1993), both dealt with the environmental or ecological aspects of our discipline. There were even studies on option pricing, as, for example, the one by Fernández Blanco (1989), though they belong rather to the area of finance.

Other studies concerned themselves with problems of foreign currency in relation to the chart of accounts. In this respect, the 1990 Chart Account Reform was highly criticized by Busto Marroquín and Niño Amo (1990), Larriba Díaz-Zorita (1990), Ramos Stolle and Fernández-Feijóo Souto (1994), Pedraja García (1995), Cea García (1997) and AECA (2001: included in 1981–2004).

More recently, accounting for intangibles (including problems of extractive industries and human resource accounting) has become a topic of interest. These include some publications of the European project MERITUM (led by the Cañibano and Sánchez's research group), such as: Cañibano Calvo *et al.* (1999, 2000a, 2000b), Escobar Pérez *et al.* (2000), García-Ayuso Corvasí *et al.* (2000) and Sánchez Muñoz *et al.* (2000).

Finally, in the area of government accounting the following publications might be mentioned: Calleja Meso (1961), Argüello Reguera and Aracil Martín (1974), Morala Gómez (1990), Ferrer Jeremias and Alamán Sales (1992), Muñoz Colomina (1994) and Sánchez-Mayoral García-Calvo (1997). To this may be added a study on local government by Navarro Galera (1998) that received the '*Premio de Investigación Mestre Racional*'.

Since the 1990s, a research group based at the University of Zaragoza (though including also colleagues from other universities) has become a central focus in this particular area. Among other publications, the following might be of special interest: Torres Pradas (1991), Vela Bargues (1991, 1992, 1994), Montesinos Julve (1993, 1994), Pina Martínez (1993, 1994), Pina Martínez and Torres Pradas (1995) and Montesinos Julve *et al.* (1998). Those studies had a considerable impact on accountants trying to improve public management and control. Their main thrust lies in the proposal to control public expenses by exploiting modern administration methods, above all, by applying to the public sector accounting procedures similar to those of the private sector.

10.4 Studies in auditing

In the early decades of this period, separate publications on auditing were relatively rare. One of the earliest seems to have been by Snozzi (1969); later those by Almela Díez (1987), Urías Valiente (1987, 1990) and Nuñez Lozano (1989) appeared. But during the 1990s a host of publications in this area burst forth, including a series of Spanish publications by particular institutions (see below the section on 'Institutional developments and future prospects'). The best known of the books on auditing were by such prestigious authors as Fernández Peña (1993), Martínez García (1996 – dealing mainly with materiality and auditing risks) and García Benau *et al.* (1998) – the last two received the prestigious *Premio José Mª Fernández Pirla* (a research award named in honour of the most revered Spanish accounting academic of the second half of the twentieth century). Other prominent Spanish publications on auditing were by Cañibano Calvo (1991), Sierra Molina and Bonsón Ponte (1992), Gonzalo Angulo and

Tua Pereda (1993), López Aldea (1995), Sierra Molina and Orta Perez (1997) and Verges Mamé (1998). Even Arthur Andersen Co. (1998) issued a Spanish book on accounting and auditing instructions.

Analyses of 'audit expectations' can be found in García Benau and Humphrey (1992) and García Benau *et al.* (1993), while Castrillo Lara *et al.* (1995) dealt with such topics as ethics and the auditor's independence, and Brío González (1998) examined the effect of conditional audit reports on the pertinent stock prices. Other papers worth mentioning were those by García Díez *et al.* (1996), dealing with auditing for banking, and Medina Hernández *et al.* (1997) exposing the point of view of companies as clients of the auditing profession; other aspects of auditing were investigated by Fernández Peña (1993).

Deserved special attention is given to the papers by García Benau *et al.* (1999) and Ruiz Barbadillo *et al.* (2000); they developed competing research agendas for Spanish auditing. Both of these papers analyse Spanish auditing and the possibilities of improving society's confidence in auditing reports.

Finally, special aspects from the auditor's perspective are discussed in several papers – for example: Martínez Arias (1993), on financial scorecards and their use in auditing, Poveda Maestre (1995), on computer control in auditing, Prado Lorenzo (1993), on the application of the 'going concern principle' and Prado Lorenzo *et al.* (1995), discussing the opinions of auditors on a series of important professional issues, and concluding with a 'state of the art' report.

10.5 Methodological studies

The introduction mentioned that from the 1950s onwards, Spanish authors became increasingly interested in North American literature. This manifested itself in a series of methodological studies, such as Alcocer Chillón's (1956) applications of the input–output Leontief model to accounting; Mattessich (1958 – a Spanish translation of a paper published in England in 1957) and Mattessich (1973), both on accounting axiomatization and matrix accounting; and Ballestero Pareja (1975) on the new trend in accounting. Further studies by Aldaz Isanta (1971) and Bueno Campos (1974) dealt with aspects of economic information theory; and two by García García (1972, 1983) with modern trends in accounting.

Other methodological studies focused on auditing, as, for example, by Balagué Doménech (1986); and others again, as those by Requena Rodríguez (1967, 1972, 1977), were first concerned with general methodological questions but later put greater emphasis on 'multi-dimensional' aspects of accounting, its *epistemology*, and its *analytical* methods, respectively. Later, well-known programmatic studies were those by Prieto Moreno and Pérez Arnáiz (1992) and Monterrey Mayoral (1998), both discussing 'positive accounting theory'; and a third study, by López Pérez and Rodríguez Ariza (2002) examining the cognitive value of methodological discussions. Similarly, the book by Cuadrado Ebrero and Valmayor López (1999) was concerned with methodological problems of modern, particularly American, accounting research. Previously, these two authors explained American standard setting to a Spanish audience (Cuadrado Ebrero and Valmayor López 1992).

Another group of papers concentrated on more specific methodological areas: García Martín (1978, 1980), on accounting in financial institutions; Casanova Ramón (1983), on share pricing based on accounting information; Flores Caballero (1992), on periodical accounting reports and financial states; and Banegas Ochovo (1997) on the use of accounting methods for determining the cost of capital.

10.6 Cost and managerial accounting

Surprisingly, in this area there exist three notable Spanish translations from Northern Europe, and one from America on internal industrial or management accounting: the first from Danish by Hansen (1961); the second from German by Erich Schneider (1969); and the third from English by Ijiri (1972). Of course, there also were numerous studies on cost accounting, planning and budgeting by Spanish authors. Here too, the *Instituto de Planificación Contable* was (as early as 1974) concerned with regulations on cost accounting and the promotion of pertinent publications.

Major studies were, for example: Cardús Rosell's (1950) research on management and business control; González Ferrando's (1960) inter-industry comparison of the shoe industry; general studies on cost accounting and control by Calafell Castelló (1967b) and Bueno Campos (1972b); Hernández Diosdado (1976) on planning and budgeting; and Cea García (1979) and Cañibano Calvo and Mallo Rodríguez (1974) on business behaviour as reflected in accounting and in joint production costing, respectively; a paper on internal accounting by Requena Rodríguez (1974); a renowned dissertation by Gonzalo Angulo (1979) with some cost accounting issues and the claim that accounting theory serves only management in its struggle against other stakeholders; as well as a book by Mallo Rodríguez (1979) on cost accounting that became a basic reference work for cost accounting instructors as well as researchers; finally, a book by Rivero Torre (1977) dealing with problems of depreciation and related issues.

Furthermore, there was a more applied study by Bueno Campos *et al.* (1980), and by BeascoecheaAriceta (1980, 1982) on cost accounting for industry, and its relation to the Chart of Accounts, respectively. There was also a study on entrepreneurial control by Soldevilla García (1978), and one on the structure of costing by Sáez Torrecilla (1982); another study by Gutiérrez Ponce (1991) dealt with the tools of cost control.

Larrañeta *et al.* (1991) even studied the application of artificial intelligence to planning, programming and quality control, while Carmona Moreno (1993) dealt with the relation between managerial accounting and technological changes. Martínez Vilches (1990), AECA (1994: included in 1981–2004) and Fernández-Feijóo Souto (1994) focused their research on cost accounting in the banking and financial sector, while other studies dealt with cost accounting and behavioural issues, as, for example, Blanco Dopico *et al.* (1999).

The most prolific author on Activity Based Costing (ABC) in Spain is Castelló Taliani (1992a, 1992b, 1993, 2000 – including: Castelló Taliani and Lizcano Alvarez 1994). Other well-known publications in this area were Fernández Sevillano (1995), Merlo Sánchez (1995) and Camaleón Simón (1997) – the first one with its socio-economic aspects of ABC costing, the second with its relations to cost allocations, and the third one examining the shortcomings of the ABC approach. Mallo Rodríguez and Merlo Bataller (1995) were concerned with managerial control and budgeting, while Iglesias Sánchez (1996) coordinated several proposals of different authors on the advances and practices of management accounting. Carrasco Díaz (1997) offered a study on cost accounting in a hospital setting, and Alvarez López and Carrasco Díaz (2000) a study for the construction industry.

One of the more recent subject matters of Spanish cost accounting is the Balanced Scorecard (BSC or '*Cuadro de Mando Integral*', abbreviated as CMI). Although there exists much literature on this topic, we emphasize the publications by López Viñegla (1998), who created a BSC school with an empirical perspective, as well as Aparisi Caudeli and Ripoll Feliu (2000) that present the BSC as a basic management tool. Other authors, like Banegas Ochovo and Nevado Peña (1999), stressed its management control aspects; Aparisi Caudeli *et al.* (2000) illuminated it from a technological point of view, discussing the potential of the automation of BSC. Fernández-Revuelta Pérez and Ask (2001) focused on problems of implementation; and Fernández-Feijóo Souto *et al.* (2003) on the application of BSC in small- and medium-size companies.

Recent contributions to the international managerial accounting literature by young Spanish scholars (though in English) are such papers as Fernández-Revuelta Pérez and Robson (1999), an empirical study on hypocrisy in a multi-national company; Larrinaga González and Bebbington (2001), as empirical investigation on the implementation difficulties of environmental accounting; and Bisbe Viñas and Otley (2004) on management control systems in relation to product innovation. Some experts may even add such sophisticated studies by Spaniards living abroad, such as Narayanan and Dávila (1998) and Dávila (2005).

10.7 Studies in accounting history

Spain has had for considerable time special strength in accounting history, and can boast to have some of the word's finest experts in this particular area. Foremost among them is the internationally renowned Hernández Esteve (who gained twice the highest award the Academy of Accounting Historians has to grant, the 'Hour Glass Award'). He expressed the following remark about the present interest of Spaniards in accounting history:

> This interest has been both a result of, and a contributing factor to, the creation of the Comisión de la Contabilidad (Commission of Accounting History) within the Asociación Española de Contabilidad y Administración de

Empresas (AECA) ... . To Spanish archivists, account books have always been an undecipherable enigma, a situation which is now beginning to change thanks to the results of accounting historians ... . Hernández Esteve, on the other hand, paid also attention to the great predominance that English speaking countries (United Kingdom, USA, Canada, Australia) have achieved in accounting history research. This he argued, had some regrettable aspects since writers in those countries ... ignore publications in languages other than English, and also concentrate their efforts on contemporary questions which concern their cultural area directly, such as the formation of the accounting profession, the development of management accounting, the power-discipline relationships disclosed by Foucault and so on.

(Hernández Esteve 1995: 250–1)

The publications and papers by this author (dealing not exclusively with accounting history but occasionally with commercial history in general)[8] are too numerous to mentioned here, but among his best known works, the following ought to be mentioned: Hernández Esteve (1981, 1982, 1988, 1993, 1994a, 1994b, 1995, 1996, 2000). They deal with various historical topics of accounting and its legislation from the Middle Ages onwards to Luca Pacioli (and the 500th anniversary of his work) and beyond.

Other well-known names and historical publications on accounting are: Goxens Duch (1974) on the evolution of accounting doctrines in Barcelona; Luna Luque (1974) and later Donoso Anes (1992) on Bartolomeo Salvador de Solórzano, the first exponent of the double-entry system in Spain; Tua Pereda (1983a, 2004) on methodological and historical questions of accounting norms; Busto Marroquín (1992) on specific accounting methods used in the eighteenth century; González Ferrando (1992, 1993) on Luis de Luque y Leyva who re-introduced double-entry to Spain, and on the royal household of prince Don Juan, respectively; Goxens Duch (1993) on the evolution of professional accounting; Donoso Anes and García-Ayuso Covarsí (1993) on academic issues on the history of accounting; Jouanique (1994) on B. Cotrugli (the first author to write, though not to publish, on double-entry).

As to historical publications on more recent accounting literature and research, there is, first of all, Fernández Peña (1984, 1989, 1992), who produced a number of closely related publications (including two English papers) on Spanish accounting research during the twentieth century. Furthermore, Montesinos Julve (1998) wrote his frequently mentioned paper on 'Accounting and business economics in Spain'; and Carmona Moreno *et al.* (1999) a 'Profile of European accounting research'. And in the twenty-first century appeared (in Spanish) a survey of *international* accounting research during the second half of the twentieth century by Mattessich (2000) as well as a survey of *Spanish* accounting publications of the first half of the twentieth century by Carrasco Díaz *et al.* (2004).

A particularly intriguing paper by Carmona Moreno *et al.* (1999) offered a profile (in English) of European accounting research, comparing the contributions of some 26 countries (see last paragraph of second section above). Furthermore, one may mention an interesting doctoral dissertation by Rivero Menéndez (2000) on Mesopotamian accounting. There also exist some facsimile reproductions of notable accounting books from the past together with commentaries: for example, one by Carrasco Díaz and González Gomila (1996) on J.M. Cañizares Zurdo's (1933, see under Carrasco Díaz and González Gomila 1996) accounting history, and another one by Donoso Anes and Donoso Anes (1998) on the bookkeeping work by Sebastián Jócano y Madaria at the end of the eighteenth century. Finally, we might mention the *Encyclopedia de economia en CD-Rom* by EMVI (2006 – available through: www.eumed.net/emvi.htm) that also contains entries on accounting (such as a paper on 'Los programas de investigacíon Lakatosianos aplicados a la contabilidad').

10.8 Institutional developments and future prospects

Several institutions played a crucial role, not only in the modern development of Spanish accounting practice, but also in accounting theory. The oldest association of public accountants, the *Instituto de Censores Jurados de Cuentas de España* (ICJCE, founded in 1945) with its journal, *Revista Técnica* (The Technical Review of the Institute of Chartered Accountants of Spain) and two governmental agencies. First, the *Instituto de Planificación Contable* (IPC), *Ministerio de Economía y Hacienda* (Institute of Accounting Planning) promoted, under the direction of Cubillo Valverde, a series of important publications on a variety of topics (for details, see Fernández Peña 1984: 198–9). Second, the *Instituto de Contabilidad y Auditoría* (ICAC, successor to IPC) of the *Ministerio de Economía* – in addition to fulfilling mainly practical functions – sponsored a series of important research studies.

Other important Spanish accounting institutions are: the *Agencia Española de Administración Tributaria*, the *Asociación Española de Asesores Fiscales*, the *Asociación Profesional de Expertos Contables y Tributarios de España* (AECE), the *Instituto de Estudios Fiscales* and the *Registro de Economistas Auditores* (REA). But the bulk of the theoretical work was initiated by two academic institutions. The pioneering work was done by the *Asociación Española de Contabilidad y Administración de Empresas* (AECA, Spanish Association of Accounting and Business Administration, Madrid) with its journal the *Revista Española de Financiación y Contabilidad* (first issued in 1972). It also publishes, mainly for professionals, the *Boletin AECA* as well as *The International Journal of Digital Accounting Research* (the latter from the year 2000 onwards), apart from a series of monographs, books, pronunciations of accounting norms and other publications.

The other, somewhat younger academic institution is the *Asociación Española de Profesores Universitarios de Contabilidad* (ASEPUC, Spanish Association of University Professors of Accounting), publishing the *Revista de Contabilidad* (Accounting Review), holding meetings (on a biennial basis) and performing a series of consulting functions. Finally, there is the *Real Academia de Ciencias Económicas y Financieras* (Royal Academy of the Economic Sciences, Barcelona) that also sponsored a series of excellent publications in economics, business and accounting, as well as history.

Among important accounting and auditing journals not yet mentioned (apart from numerous journals in Spanish outside of Spain) are the following (listed in alphabetic order):

Actualidad Financiera, published in Alcobendas (Madrid) by Editora General de Derecho, from 1986 to 2001.

Boletín de Estudios Económicos, published by Universidad de Deusto and the Asociación de Licenciados en Ciencias Económicas, since 1946 till now.

Cuadernos de Investigación Contable, from the Universidad de Sevilla, published since 1987 with irregular frequency.

Cuadernos universitarios de planificación empresarial y marketing, from the Universidad Autónoma de Madrid, published between 1975 and 1981.

Hacienda Publica Española, published since 1970 by the Ministerio de Economía y Hacienda.

Partida Doble-Revista de Contabilidad, by Especial Directivos, a private company that has been publishing it since 1990.

Revista Técnica del Instituto de Censores Jurados de Cuentas, by the Instituto de Censores Jurados de Cuentas, chartered accountant institute, since 1967.

Revista Técnica Económica, from the Ilustre Colegio Oficial de Titulados Mercantiles y Empresariales, founded in 1907 under the name of *Revista Científica Mercantil*.

Técnica Contable, a private review, published since 1949.

An important Inter-Hispanic link (with the motherland as well as among countries of the Spanish tongue) was created through the foundation of the Asociación Interamericana de Contabilidad (AIC) with its journals *Revista Iberoamaricana de Contabilidad* and *Revista Iberoamericana de Contabilidad de Gestión*. A private but prominent journal, the *Revista Internacional Legis de Contabilidad & Auditoria*, mainly serves the accounting community of South and Middle America. Perhaps, this journal constitutes more than any other a crucial link to the mother country of Spain that still is regarded as the spiritual leader. Indeed, many papers in this journal have been authored by academics from Spain.

Although scholars, not institutions, are the backbone of a vibrant research community, an efficient institutional and publication framework can contribute essentially to successful future research. Indeed, there are several such institutions supporting accounting research in Spain as well as in the rest of the Spanish-speaking world (that looks to Spain for intellectual inspiration). Beyond this institutional aspect, there is a competent and enthusiastic group of accounting scholars.

10.9 Conclusion

During the 1970s (before the establishment of university accounting education) most of the pertinent research and publications were done at business schools of a lower level, and through the Institute of Chartered Accountant of Spain (guided by Fernández Peña and Fernández Pirla). This established a basis for Spanish accounting research of later decades.

As the country developed politically, culturally and economically, university instructors played a dominant role in creating the proper climate for solid accounting research: Cañibano Calvo, Cea García, Mallo Rodríguez, Montesinos Julve and Tua Pereda are the most significant names. For a later period those of García Benau, Giner Inchausti and Gonzalo Angulo have to be added.

Since the mid-1970s Spanish accounting research has been strongly influenced by the Anglophone accounting literature (e.g. the concern with a conceptual framework, as in Tua Pereda and Bellostas Pérez-Grueso 2000). Also, there has been a shift of emphasis from commercial and tax regulations to accounting standards from a legalistic point of view. With every new accounting regulation (e.g. 1973, 1990), an increasing number of publications dealt with problems of International Accounting Standards and the 'harmonization' with other European countries.

11 Accounting research in the English language area

First half of the twentieth century[1]

11.1 Introduction

The best-known names of British accounting during the early decades of the twentieth century were those of such nineteenth-century accountants as Arthur L. Dickinson [1859–1935], Laurence R. Dicksee [1864–1932] and Frederic R.M. de Paula [1882–1954]. They are well known for their work in the area of financial accounting and auditing. Other Britons, like Alexander H. Church [1866–1936] and J.M. Fells, acquired their reputation in cost accounting. In America, the most prominent figures of the time were (apart from Dickinson and Church, both of whom established themselves in the USA during this time – though Dickinson ultimately retired in the UK) such scholars as Charles E. Sprague [1842–1912], William M. Cole [1866–1960], Henry R. Hatfield [1866–1945], J. Sterret [1870–1934], Robert Montgomery [1872–1953], George O. May [1875–1961], Harry C. Bentley [1877–1967] and John R. Wildman [1878–1938].

Perhaps one should add here the names of two illustrious persons who were not accountants but contributed indirectly to our discipline. The first of them was the renowned industrial engineer Frederick W. Taylor [1856–1915] with his contribution to time studies and managerial accounting, the second was the no less renowned economist Irving Fisher [1867–1947] whose studies on capital and income and fluctuating purchasing power contributed essentially to financial accounting (e.g. Fisher 1925). However, subsequently we shall encounter many more persons (on both sides of the Atlantic) actively publishing in accounting during the first two decades of the twentieth century.

11.2 Financial accounting and auditing

11.2.1 Sprague, Hatfield and Gilman

One of the earliest treatments of professional ethics was by Sterret (1907). As to Sprague's (1907–08) *Philosophy of accounts*, it might be considered a misnomer; but it was one of the first American accounting books to go beyond rote learning, relying instead on reasoning and a deeper understanding of the essence of our discipline, as Hatfield (1908) pointed out, Sprague's *The accountancy of investment* (1904) combined 'scholarly erudition, philosophic insight and practical experience'. In particular, it abandoned the 'personalistic' theory (of identifying every account with a person) and conformed to a considerable extent to the 'materialistic' (or better, 'non-personalistic') theory of accounts as promulgated in Europe by Friedrich Húgli, Johann F. Schär and other authors (cf. Chapter 2). In this regard, it may have influenced Hatfield's (1909) work, though the latter is no longer a theory of accounts but already a fully-fledged accounting theory.

In those early decades, Hatfield and Gilman were considered to be the leading accountants in America, as expressed in the following statement by Moonitz:

> Without desiring to resort to comparisons, the Secretary believes that Gilman, at Wisconsin, and Hatfield, formerly at Chicago but now at California, did more to establish the present standing of commercial education in universities than any others of their early days.
>
> (Moonitz 1986: 10, referring to Hatfield's obituary as presented by the
> Secretary of the American Society of CPA's, and reproduced in the
> *Certified Public Accountant* 1930: 215)

Hatfield was first an instructor at the University of Chicago and later professor and dean of the University of California. Hatfield's (1909) book on modern accounting is claimed to be 'the first intensive and extensive discussion of accounting theory and practice in the United States' (Moonitz 1986: 8). It experienced revisions and several editions under various titles. Yet, Hatfield's fame rests no less on two other publications. First, the often quoted co-authored work by Sanders *et al.* (1938) that dealt with accounting *principles* (based on the idea of clearly separating income from capital). It was written in response to previous (though less successful) attempts by the precursor of the AAA (the American Association of University Instructors in Accounting 1936) and the precursor of the AICPA (the American Institute of Accountants) to search for a 'tentative' statement of accounting principles (see also later publications of the AAA 1941a, 1941b – for a historical overview, see Zeff 1982). Second, there was an earlier, delightful and witty paper, Hatfield (1924), presenting 'An historical defence of accounting', that encouraged future generations of accountants to study history.

Although Hatfield (1909) rejected *present values* for balance sheet presentation (cf. Montgomery's 1927 review), he discussed them together with the notion of *current cost* accounting (cf. Radcliff and Munter 1981: 17). Hatfield (1909) also emphasized the importance of depreciations, and objected to view them as a kind of 'reserve' for replacement. The topic of depreciation was, of course, repeatedly discussed during this period (e.g. Paton 1920a; Schmidt 1930b; Fowler 1934; Hatfield 1936; Mason 1937; Preinreich 1938).

As to the *historical cost* model and the (traditional) *realization principle*, these were generally accepted by Hatfield, Dicksee and other prominent authors as the basis for sound and conservative accounting practice. Then the balance sheet still had priority over the income statement. Hatfield derived his theories inductively from practical experience, and Mills (1994: 297) counted him to the 'pre-classical school' of accounting, together with Cole, Dickinson, Esquerré, Kester, Montgomery, Sprague and Wildman. And Kozub (1996: 294) emphasized that 'Hatfield was a pioneering scholar in accounting. His writings were a potent formative influence in the development of accounting theory, and as a result of his contributions, accounting grew in professional status'.[2]

Gilman's (1939) book, on the other hand, emphasized the notions of profit and the income statement as opposed to the balance sheet (possibly influenced by Schmalenbach or Zappa who pursued similar goals in Germany and Italy, respectively). Bloom pointed out that:

> Gilman provided a legacy of accounting ideas … to discuss the uncertainties of accounting data … the semantic problem of defining accounting postulates, … the problems of formulating generally accepted accounting principles … . Gilman focused on a number of issues in his book that were later discussed in the accounting literature. He evaluated many misconceptions about accounting and focused on the limitations of accounting.
>
> (Bloom 1996: 280)

11.2.2 Dickinson, Dicksee and other accounting pioneers

Dickinson's work deserves no less appreciation, as the following passage by Chatfield confirms:

> His [Dickinson's] writings dramatically raised the level of American accounting discourse. He argued for the exclusion from product costs of rent and interest expenditures, on grounds that these were distributions of profit. He believed that, in addition to normal depreciation charges, a depreciation reserve should be established to provide for asset replacements. Dickinson invented the format of today's income statement … . [His] *Accounting Practice and Procedures* ([1908] 1914) was Dickinson's attempt to sum up 'twenty-five years of practice on both sides of the Atlantic'.
>
> (Chatfield 1996b: 203)

Dicksee, professor at the University of Birmingham (who, in contrast to Dickinson, remained in Great Britain – for a profile of Dicksee, see Kitchen and Parker 1994a), was no less a prolific writer, though among his 17 books the best known was his *Auditing* (Dicksee 1892/1902). It attained some 19 editions in the UK and was adapted in America by Montgomery (1905) where it became a genuine bestseller (another early auditing text in England was by de Paula 1914). Dicksee, a defender of the 'going concern principle', was deeply concerned about valuation issues (for a detailed appreciation of his contributions, see Brief 1980). Dicksee became famous for criticizing *inadequate depreciation procedures* (see Dicksee 1903) and, even more so, for his book on auditing (Dicksee 1892/1902). It not only proved to be a successful bestseller, but became the model for Robert H. Montgomery's [1872–1953] even more enduring American auditing text (Montgomery 1912). In this connection, two American pioneers of auditing must be mentioned, one was George Soulé (1900), the other Francis W. Pixley (1881). Although the first edition of Soulé's book was published in the 1880s, it attained several editions in the twentieth century. As to the development of auditing in America during the first half of the twentieth century, see Staub (1942), and Cochran (1950). Disksee (1910, 1911) also published on government auditing and advanced accounting, respectively.

Of particular interest is the fact that during the last decade of the twentieth century, when the '*earned surplus*' notion came into vogue again, Dicksee received renewed attention, due to the following of his pronouncements:

> an accountant's certificate as to profits, relating as it does to past events, deals with a subject matter that ought to be capable of absolute verification … . To the limited extent already mentioned it may be permissible, and even desirable, to modify the past results so that they may more usefully serve the purpose for which they are primarily intended, provide a reliable index of future profits.

(Dicksee 1905: 307)

Some scholars (cf. Brief and Peasnell 1996) consider such thoughts to be an early manifestation of the dichotomy or even controversy between a '*clean surplus*' theory with its '*comprehensive income statement*' and *residual income valuation*,[3] on one side, and a '*dirty surplus*' theory with its '*operational income statement*', on the other side. While the latter has the advantage of smoothing out long-term income fluctuations for better estimating anticipated profits (possibly over a longer run), the former may offer a more 'realistic' momentary (or past) picture. More articulate formulations of this controversy appeared later, and Brief and Peasnell (1996: x) point out that 'the controversy continues to the present day. For many decades authoritative literature has tried to resolve the issue of whether or not a policy of clean surplus should be adhered to'. Furthermore, Dickinson, concerned himself with related issues (see also Brief and Peasnell 1996: xii), and wrote an influential book on *Accounting principles and procedures* (Dickinson 1908). There he made a *comparison between English and American accounting*.

The American author, William M. Cole, pioneered in several of his publications (e.g. Cole 1908, 1910) the 'where-got, where-gone' statement (a kind of *flow of funds statement*),[4] and concerned himself with the need for an entity theory as well as with *auditing* issues. Even more importantly, he began to use the notion of *physical capital maintenance*, although he accepted the *lower of cost or market value* approach. And Arthur E. Andersen [1885–1947], starting out in academia but leaving it for actual practice, founded in 1913 the international public accounting firm that at the beginning of the new millennium was dissolved under most regrettable circumstances. He and his firm have been fierce promoters of advances in accounting, its research and education. His many 'addresses' (between 1913 and 1941) were collected in a posthumous publication (Arthur Andersen & Co. 1970). One must also mention the contribution of the renowned American economist Irving Fisher who promoted a somewhat modified 'balance sheet and profit and loss model' as the proper tool for analysing the economists' notion of income and wealth (see Fisher 1906). As to *Canadian* accounting texts, they apparently appeared from the 1860s onwards, and were by authors like W.C. Eddis, S.G. Beatty, W.R. Orr, D. Hoskins, J.W. Johnson and R. Miller – for detail, see Richardson (1996: 91).

11.2.3 The next generation of leading accounting academics

In America, a new generation of famous accounting scholars came to the fore. Above all, there was William A. Paton [1889–1991] who became the most prominent among them (for some essays in his honour, see Zeff *et al.* 1979; and for a retrospective, see Previts and Robinson 1994). The rest of the galaxy comprised the following names: Roy B. Kester [1882–1965], John B. Canning [1884–1962], Thomas H. Sanders [1885–1953], A.C. Littleton [1986–1974], Stephen Gilman [1887–1959], D.R. Scott [1887–1954], James C. Bonbright [1891–1985], Eric L. Kohler [1892–1976], Gabriel A.D. Preinreich [1893–1951] (originally from Austria-Hungary), Carman G. Blough [1895–1981], Kenneth MacNeal [1895–1972], Willard J. Graham [1897–1966], the Yale economist Ralph C. Jones [1897–], Henry W. Sweeney [1898–1967], Herbert F. Taggart [1898–1983] and Perry E. Mason [1899–1964].

The encyclopaedic work by Chatfield and Vangermeersch (1996) contains profiles of most of these eminent accountants. Furthermore, there exist several works offering further details about some of them, as, for example, such books as Edwards and Salmonson (1961) on *Contributions of four accounting pioneers* – Kohler, Littleton, May and Paton; or Cooper and Ijiri (1979) and Cooper (1996) on E.L. Kohler; or Burns and Coffman (1991) on *The Accounting Hall of Fame: profiles of fifty members.*

Further names are: the renowned economist Irving Fisher (1911), who occupied himself with the problem of the purchasing power of money; among the accountants were Roy Kester (1916), who expressed dissatisfaction with the historical cost approach, and Livingston Middleditch (1918), who recommended general price-level adjustments. Their compatriot, Seymour Walton (1918), also concerned himself with changing market prices of assets but assumed a more conservative position. Of similar conservative attitude was J.M. Fells (1919, 1922) from Great Britain. One might also mention Rorem (1928) and his study on the method of accounting, as well as some English publications by a renowned German scholar, Schmidt (1930a, 1930b, 1931).

During the subsequent decades up to 1950 (i.e. the 'classical period' as some called it), many of the accountants mentioned above continued to publish while a younger generation of accounting scholars began to be recognized. In the UK three notable scholars emerged at the London School of

Economics: William Baxter [born 1906] (e.g. 1949); David Solomons [1912–95] (e.g. 1948), who ultimately moved to the USA; and Harold C. Edey [born 1913] (e.g. 1950).

This 'LSE Triumvirate' (as Whittington 1994: 252, called the group) produced their first publications during this time. There also was the more independent F. Sewell Bray [1906–1979] who not only founded the journal *Accounting Research* (resurrected as the *Accounting and Business Research* after many years of suspension), but also made his mark as an original author (e.g. Bray 1947, 1949) – for a profile of Bray and his work, see Forrester (1982). Furthermore, there was the British-American economist (and later Nobel laureate) Coase (1937, 1938) whose highly original contributions to the theory of the firm, transaction costs and the function of the accountant, has been re-discovered, though only in the late second half of the twentieth century (see Plant *et al.* 1987, and Chapter 12). Speaking of British Nobel laureates, one must mention J.E. Mead and J. Richard N. Stone (1941), and particularly Stone (1947) for his important contributions to national income accounting (after all, it is also accounting). And apart from the economists Alfred Marshall [1842–1924] (1905a, 1905b, 1919) and John R. Hicks ([1904–89]; another Nobel laureate), both of whom contributed more or less indirectly to business and accounting research (e.g. Hicks 1931, 1938). Other notable British accounting authors of the time and their publications were: J. Stamp (1921), J. Stamp and C. Hewetson Nelson (1924), Fowler (1934), Rowland (1936, 1938) and R.S. Edwards (1937a, 1937b, 1938a, 1938b).

Among the American authors of this or the next generation were Maurice Moonitz [born 1910], Carl T. Devine [1912–98], William J. Vatter [1905–90] and Lawrence L. Vance [1911–78], who, together with two subsequent generations, dominated academic accounting during the second half of the twentieth century (see Chapters 12 and 19).

Ultimately, the leading American accounting theorist of the twentieth century, or at least of its first half, turned out to be William A. Paton Sr, mentioned above. His doctoral dissertation, published later in book form as *Accounting theory: with special reference to the corporate enterprise* (Paton 1922) foreshadowed later efforts of establishing a postulational system for accounting. It was, along with Montgomery's edition of Dicksee (1905), Sprague's *philosophy of accounts* (1907–08) and Cole's *Accounts, their construction and interpretation* (1908), one of the first major US contributions to accounting literature. Before that, Sprague (1904) published his book, *The accountancy of investment*. Another widely read and influential work that Paton produced, this time with another renowned American (some might say 'the second ranking accounting academic' of the time) was *An introduction to corporate accounting standards* (Paton and Littleton 1940). Many books followed; and among the hundred or more articles of his, the most frequently mentioned were Paton (1918, 1920a, 1920b). For an overview of Paton's essential writings, see Taggart (1964), but before closing this short paragraph on Paton, let us add the concise summary by Thompson:

> [Paton] advocated the importance of earning power. Replacement costs, matching, single-step income statements, the entity-theory, and, more generally, capitalism and clear thinking ... . Paton emphasized the importance of taking into account changing prices ... . Paton, however was not in favour of abandoning historical costs. He generally advocated that changing-price data be provided as supplementary information to historical cost financial statements ... . Paton thought that replacement costs were superior to historical costs adjusted for the change in general price level ... . However, Paton was concerned about the difficulty of obtaining reliable replacement costs of plant and equipment and other long-term assets.
>
> (Thompson 1996: 453)

Another early leader of the American accounting profession was John Raymond Wildman; his paper on 'A research program' (Wildman 1926) in the first issue of *The Accounting Review* attracted repeated attention. Yet, apart from the works of the leading accounting academics of the period, there were several remarkable contributions by other well-known accountants who are remembered for a single decisive work. A striking example of such a pioneer was Frederick G. Canning (1929) with his book, *The economics of accounting*. Its author was a disciple of the renowned economist Irving Fisher who used such accounting tools as the balance sheet and income statement for clarifying economic theory (Fisher 1906). Thus, it was hardly farfetched to apply the economist's and, particularly Fisher's, present value theory to accounting. Nevertheless, such an application was then quite revolutionary and ahead of its time by decades. It slowly caught on in academia from the 1950s onwards and in accounting practice reluctantly in the 1980s and 1990s. A related economic application to accounting and finance that was not only more neglected by accountants than Canning's work, but literally fell into oblivion – was the work by Preinreich (e.g. 1938, 1939, 1996) that was many decades ahead of its time.

Henry W. Sweeney (1936) *Stabilized accounting* (based on an award-winning doctoral dissertation of 1927) was the first fully-fledged inflation accounting theory developed in America – though Middleditch (1918) discussed general price-level adjustments almost a decade earlier in the USA. Sweeney's work was inspired by similar theories that arose in Germany during the 1920s, but has its own peculiarities and some innovative features. Although Sweeney's theory is based on general price-level adjustments, it does consider an additional adjustment for replacement values. Unfortunately, its publication experienced a delay of many years, and when it finally appeared, inflation issues were out of vogue. Thus, it took many years before this book and a series of related papers by Sweeney received due recognition. Towards the end of this period, inflation issues slowly aroused interest again (e.g. Baxter 1949; Graham 1949; Jones 1949); but this trend took off only in the second half of the twentieth century (see Chapter 12).

Of special practical, as well as theoretical significance was the work by Sanders *et al.* (1938) on *A Statement of accounting principles*. As one of the first attempts of formulating such principles, it contained important generalizations from accounting practice. The book even exercised influence abroad, but it was criticized for relying too much on extant practice with insufficient distinction between good and bad accounting practices. Yet the most significant work of this genre seems to have been Paton and Littleton (1940), *An introduction to corporate accounting standards*. It reflected both the analytical thinking of Paton as well as the inductive approach of Littleton, and 'was the first codification of accounting principles to be developed deductively rather than as a series of generalizations from practice' (Chatfield 1996a: 43). Its pivot was 'earning power' (but with acquisition costs as a starting point), and the principle task of accounting was seen to be income determination by means of matching costs and revenues. Subsequent valuation problems were neglected as 'value was assumed to equal cost because asset conversion, not asset valuation was the issue' (Chatfield 1996a: 44) – with the exception of Bonbright's (1937) contribution to real estate valuation, called 'value of the owner', later generalized and becoming prominent as the 'deprival value'.

Similar to Schmalenbach's theory (see Chapter 4), Paton and Littleton put income determination into the foreground and regarded the values of assets as residuals (unexpired costs). Despite initially sympathizing with replacement costs, these authors and others ultimately yielded for practical reasons to historical costs and the realization principle. Another eminent scholar was Eric L. Kohler (e.g. 1935, 1938) who through 'his actions and writings, ... enormously impacted not only accounting thought and practice, but also its institutions, during the critically important 1930s and 1940s' (Cooper 1996: 362). A further author who concerned himself for many years with such problems as accounting standards, depreciation and other problems was Blough (e.g. 1937, 1948) – see Shenkir (1978) and Moonitz (1994).

A typical example (of an author's single work becoming a 'landmark') was the highly original but equally controversial book by MacNeal (1939), *Truth in Accounting*, defending and even fighting bitterly for the *market value* approach. Later proponents of different versions of the exit value theory, such as Chambers (1967) and Sterling (1970: 254), adopted MacNeal as their forerunner and Patron-Saint, though Zeff's dramatic profile of this author and his struggle, rejects the notion that MacNeal's book advocated 'exit-price accounting' (cf. Zeff 1994: 346). Above all, MacNeal applied market prices only to marketable securities and raw materials; occasionally he preferred replacement costs and even suggested that realizable cost savings (in Edwards and Bell's 1961, terminology) ought to be included in income. As to the limited recognition of MacNeal's work, Zeff adds the following remarks:

> Yet the citations of his [MacNeal's] work are not nearly so frequent or substantive as are those to the writings of Paton, Hatfield, and Sweeney – most of whose major works have also been republished in recent years ... Seldom is his [MacNeal's] argument treated at any length. Furthermore, MacNeal is not mentioned in quite a few places where one might have

expected to see his name: Vatter (1947), Fitzgerald (1952), Edwards and Bell (1961), Mathews and Grant (1962), Sprouse and Moonitz (1962), Littleton and Zimmerman (1962), Roy (1963), Mattessich (1964), Deinzer (1965), Goldberg (1965), Bedford (1965), Salmonson (1969), Thomas (1969), Skinner (1972), Rosen (1972), Backer (1973), Ijiri (1975), Previts and Merino (1979). These are all substantial works that evidence a commendable awareness of the genre of writings of which MacNeal's are a part, but he is not cited.

(Zeff 1994: 356–7)

Apart from valuation problems, those of accounting rules, principles and standards, were central. The controversy pivoted not only on the definition of these terms but, above all, on the question whether uniformity of accounting standards is necessary or even desirable, or whether this is not the case. The pertinent discussions were lively and went on for years, but less in academic than in *professional* journals such as the *Journal of Accountancy*. For a valuable survey of this literature (ranging from 1937 to 1964, and from such notable authors as Bryne and May to Moonitz and Story) see Rappaport (1965).

A very different kind of author was D.R. Scott. He began with his *Theory of accounts* (Scott 1925), based on the historical evolution of accounting as dependent on the corresponding economic development. Yet, his fame rests more on his *Cultural significance of accounts* (Scott 1931) in which he applied the social ideas and ideals of the famous institutional economist Thorstein Veblen (1899) to accounting. Scott envisioned accounting as helping to reshape institutions, thus facilitating the need for government regulations to overcome the social inadequacies of the free market.

Another important accounting notion was the idea of flow of funds statements. Although it can be traced to the nineteenth century, it was Cole's (1908) book that raised the question of 'Where got, where gone?' and utilized the 'all resources approach' to financial statements. A related method was later pursued by Esquerré (1925), though Finney (1925, 1930) took issue with it (for details, see Vangermeersch 1996). Vatter (1947) developed a different kind of fund theory – in reaction to the proprietary theory as well as the entity theory, both of which he deemed inadequate. He envisioned no less than six kinds of fund statements: a cash and bank fund, a general operating fund, an investment fund, a sinking fund for current items, another sinking fund for investments and a capital fund. For each of these funds he presented a balance sheet. Although these ideas were not practically realized, they may well have given impetus to the acceptance of flow of funds and cash flow statements in actual practice (see Chapter 12).

George O. May [1875–1961] was an influential practitioner with academic interests and some notable publications (e.g. May 1936, 1937, 1949). But his book on *Financial accounting: a distillation of experience* (May 1943) probably expressed best his pragmatic attitude to accounting (Degos and Previts 2005: 146, point out that even such scholars as Littleton and Paton were infused with this typical '*tradition séculair américaíne*') – for details on his work, see Grady (1962).

As regards accounting problems of consolidation, it was Moonitz (1944) with *The entity theory of consolidated statements*, who presented a 'coherent conceptual approach … based on the objective of treating a group of closely allied corporations as a distinct economic and accounting entity' (Staubus 1996: 423). Moonitz (1948) also concerned himself already during this period with problems of price-level changes (for contributions by Moonitz and others in the English language area after 1950, see Chapter 12). Just as Devine, Moonitz and Vatter published already in the first half of the twentieth century, so did Vance (1943 – with a study on the history in the inventory valuation) who later pioneered statistical methods in accounting and auditing (see Vance 1950).

11.3 Advances in cost accounting

The first step towards *job-order costing*, *process costing* and *standard costing*, as well as *transfer pricing* and *separate profit centres* are found in the nineteenth century (cf. Chapter 2). According to Chatfield (1974: 169), the 'earliest known writings on standard costing' were by Longmuir (1902) and Garry (1903), while Vangermeersch (1996: 550) addressed Charter Harrison as 'the father of standard costing', possibly because of his classic writings on this topic (Harrison 1918–19, 1920, and later publications). A later proponent of standard costing was Carman (1930). Years before Elbourne (1914) wrote on factory administration, Castenholz (1918) examined interest on capital as a cost component, and F.D. Brown (1927a, 1927b) wrote on centralized control and pricing policy, respectively.

Some of the above-mentioned ideas were refined in the UK. H.L.C. Hall (1904) and two Englishmen Nicholson (1909 – see Hein 1959) and Strachan (1909) emphasized the contrast to process costing. Percy Longmuir (1902), on the other side, was particularly concerned with *controlling the cost function*, though he rejected job costing, and Stanley Garry (1903) dealt with *variances* of both *volume* and *price*. H.L. Arnold (1903) emphasized that 'the factory manager's real objective in cost finding is the accurate prediction of *future* production costs' (my italics – from Parker 1969: 22). John Whitmore (1908) suggested *idle capacity costs* ought to be charged and written off in a separate account. Furthermore, he contributed to the *standard costing* notions of A. Hamilton Church (1901–02, 1908, 1910, 1917) who himself advocated the use of 'production centres'. The American efficiency engineer Emerson's (1908–09) classic on standard costing employed the *standard hour* as the '*real standard unit cost*', as well as using a *single overall variance* between actual and standard costs.

Furthermore, Sir John Mann [1863–1955] (1904) continued to argue for separating *overhead costs* into those for *selling* and those for *production*. He also advanced the idea of using *machine hour rates* for cost allocation (that may be traced to the nineteenth century), and almost simultaneously with Hess presented the concept of the break-even chart. Later, improvements of this important tool of cost accounting were made by (among others) Knoeppel (1920) and Rautenstrauch (1922) – who christened the 'break-even chart'. A. Hamilton Church (1901–02, see also Vangermeersch 1988) published several papers that became 'a standard reference work on one of the most difficult questions of cost-finding' (cf. Solomons 1968: 25). Church further developed such notions as *production centres* and *idle capacity* (and its 'supplementary rate'), and drew attention to the difference between 'normal' vs. 'abnormal' costs, as well as to the *'scientific' machine-hour rate*. This seems to have influenced the work of John Whitmore (1906–07, 1908). Another contributor to standard costing was Harry C. Bentley [1877–1967] (1911), particularly known for his acute observations of contemporary cost accounting practice, though he may be even better known for his co-authored bibliographic work (see Bentley and Leonard 1934–35). J. Lee Nicholson [1863–1924] (1909) also made important contributions to cost accounting, emphasizing *cost centres* and the *measuring of profits for individual departments* based on machine hour rates. Furthermore, he was instrumental in organizing the National Organization of Cost Accountants (later, the Institute of Management Accountants).

As to *break-even charts*, Solomons (1968: 35) contends that 'Sir John Mann knew about it in 1904', though Ferrara (1996) credits Henry Hess [1864–1922] (1903) with 'the first publication of a break-even chart'. The remarkable paper by Hess (1903) advanced budgeting decisively by offering a graphical treatment for comparing actual cost with budgeted cost.

A system of *fixed budgeting* was presented by Bunnell (1911), and further work on *standard costing* is found in McHenry (1914, 1916) and, above all, in Harrison (1918–19, 1920) to whom this terminology is traced. According to Solomons (1968: 46–7), McHenry established 'in 1911 the first *complete* standard costing system known to exist'. Vangermeersch (1996) regards Harrison as the 'father of standard costing'. Chatfield writes:

> In 1911, the Anglo-American management consultant G. Charter Harrison [born 1881] designed the earliest known complete standard cost system. He elaborated on this system in a series of articles, 'Cost Accounting to Aid Production' (1918–19) ... . In 'Scientific Basis for Cost Accounting' (1920), Harrison published the first set of formulas for the analysis of cost variances.
>
> (Chatfield 1996c: 291)

A further pioneer of budgeting and the forerunner of Program Evaluation and Review Techniques (*PERT*) was Henry L. Gantt [1861–1919] (1915, 1916). An American pioneer work in budgeting was McKinsey's (1922) *Budgetary control*, the first comprehensive book on business budgeting (see also McKinsey's 1924 text on *Managerial accounting*). One might also mention here Gaines' (1905) discussion of factory cost accounting with the aide of *tabulating machines*, the main theoretical significance of which was less the use of such machines rather than his emphasis on cost *analysis*, and the aim towards *higher profits* rather than mere cost reduction and introducing the notion of contribution margin. Almost a decade later, in England, Judd (1914) also asserted the importance of ascertaining cost data relevant for the *future*. An influential British text on cost accounting, particularly during the wartime, was that by Elbourne (1914). As to the pre-First World War and First World War period, Fleischman and Tyson made the following comparison between UK and US cost accounting:

> Some scholars had an essentially negative view about UK cost accounting's developments [in the pre-First World War period], particularly in comparison with advances made in the US during this formative period [p. 192] .... . Notwithstanding these negative pronouncements, there is evidence to suggest that the pre-war costing milieu witnessed important strides forward, certainly in theory but to some degree in practice as well [p. 193] .... . In summary, the emergencies of World War I brought many new cost accountants into the field and introduced many business enterprises to costing methodologies [p. 198] ... . Meanwhile, on the other side of the Atlantic, CPA's were writing with much more frequency on cost topics between 1914 and 1919, ... The accountant viewed the engineer as an 'encroachment on his functions' and the engineer ignored the accountant's effort with 'amused tolerance' ... manufacturers were reluctant to adopt cost accounting methods because of the detail involved and the associated expenses [p. 206].
>
> (Fleischman and Tyson 2000: 192–206)

Among further American contributions to cost accounting, there is, above all, the economist J.M. Clark [1884–1963] (1923) with his famous *Studies in the economics of overhead*. Clark's slogan 'different costs for different purposes' (the title of his Chapter 9) still rings loud and clear – though many accountants seem to have lost their hearing when it comes the call for genuinely *purpose-oriented* accounting systems. This is important not only for costing but also for financial accounting: costs, as well as asset values, have to be assessed quite differently, for example, under 'continuing business' than under 'liquidation'. But as this book was authored by an economist, it was disregarded for all too long by accountants.

Also, there was the paper by Harris (1936) that seems to have been 'the first important article on direct costing' (cf. Parker 1969: 156). But beyond this, few new ideas were forthcoming during the last few years of this period. Parker (1969: 28) even expresses his disappointment with Neuner's (1939) cost accounting text, particularly when compared to the brilliance of Clark's vision. However, Parker praises one feature of some of the earlier editions of Neuner's textbook; namely the inclusion of a chapter on the 're-examination of cost accounting from a managerial point of view'. But, as Parker (1969: 28–9) points out, it was actually written by Vatter. And only in the second half of the twentieth century, starting with Devine's (1950) *Cost accounting and analysis*, and Vatter's (1950) *Managerial accounting*, did the tide turn. Devine (1944) already contributed to the first half of this century's accounting literature in his examination of depreciation in income measurement, and so did Vatter (1947) with his *fund theory.*

11.4 Studies in accounting history

Apart from nineteenth-century contributions in the area of accounting history (see Chapter 2), there was a considerable output of English writings on accounting history. We shall mention only the most significant ones (for more such publications, even 'foreign' ones, see the *annotated* bibliographical Chapter 5 of Parker 1969: 75–122, that reaches close to the end of the 1960s, and offers some 24 major categories of accounting history). The following British authors or compilers contributed to accounting history during this period: R. Brown (1905) edited the *History of accounting and accountants*; Arthur H. Woolf (1912) with his book *A short history of accountants and accountancy*; de Paula (1943, 1948) wrote a paper on the future of the accountancy profession, and a book on the *Developments in accounting*, respectively (for profiles on de Paula, see Zeff 1974; Kitchen and Parker 1994b); and van Diem (1929) wrote on the development of professional accounting in Continental Europe (Austria, Belgium, Czechoslovakia, Denmark, France, Finland, Germany, Italy, the Netherlands, Norway, Poland, Rumania, Russia, Sweden and Switzerland). A prolific historian of accounting and economics, Basil S. Yamey (1940, 1944, 1949), wrote on the functional development of bookkeeping, and then on E. Jones' bookkeeping system, and finally criticized, in the third of these papers, Sombart's view on bookkeeping and the rise of capitalism. F.E. de Roover (1937, 1941) wrote on cost accounting in the sixteenth century, and then on partnership accounts in twelfth-century Genoa. R. de Roover (1938, 1944) investigated accounting before Pacioli, as well as problems on early foreign exchange, respectively. R.S. Edwards (1937a, 1937b) offered a survey of French cost accounting in the nineteenth century, as well as some notes on the early development of cost accounting in Great Britain. And Lane (1945) wrote on venture accounting in mediaeval business management.

Among the American contributions to accounting history, three of the earliest well known are: Geijsbeek (1914) with his *Ancient double entry bookkeeping*, Chiera's (1921) short but illustrated book on temple accounts of the Near-East, Hatfield's (1924) paper mentioned in 10.2.1, and the book by Littleton (1933) on *Accounting evolution to 1900.* He also authored several other historical works. Baxter (1937) wrote his *Income tax for professional students*, and Rogers (1932) conceived a paper on the development of the modern business budget. Theiss (1937) wrote one on the beginnings of business budgeting, while Grier (1934) published a concise book on *Accounting in the Zenon papyri.* Peragallo (1938, 1941), a priest and well-known accounting historian, wrote a book on the origin on the evolution of double-entry accounting, and a paper on the origin of the trial balance, respectively – and later on related topics. Another prominent accounting historian was Paul Garner (1940) with his dissertation on *The evolution of elementary cost accounting theories and techniques.* This doctoral thesis appeared in book form, and became prominent through translations into several languages. Garner later summarized and extended the gist of his dissertation in such papers as Garner (1947 and 1968), and continued with his historical research in numerous publications. In this connection, one might mention Zeff (1987) that offers a profile of 14 former leaders of the accounting profession. To return to the period under discussion, Haynes and Jackson (1935), Montgomery (1939), Webster (1941), Claire (1945) and others also published on various historical accounting topics.

11.5 Conclusion

The research and publications here discussed ought to be viewed in the light of the rise of academic accounting in America. The industrial and financial expansion of America during the first half of the twentieth century was in full swing and exerted a pressure on the education system to provide academically trained commercial and economic experts. Although the Wharton School of Finance and Economy (University of Pennsylvania) was founded as early as 1881. By 1900, other business schools had been established at New York University, at Dartmouth College, at the University of Chicago and at Vernon. Above all, in 1908 the Harvard Business School began its prestigious activity. In Great Britain, the London School of Economics and Political Science was established in 1895, but the two leading universities of Great Britain (Oxford and Cambridge) lagged behind for a long time as far as business education was concerned. The first academic accounting chair at the University of Cambridge was occupied by the economist Richard Stone (later Nobel laureate). Yet, he made his mark in national income accounting rather than business accounting.

12 Accounting research in the English language area

Second half of the twentieth century[1]

In Europe humanism lingers on;
In America science has triumphed.
Yet, what is science without a human face?

R.M.

12.1 Introduction

Accounting as a scientific undertaking, in the more rigorous sense, is the achievement of the second half of the twentieth century. During this time the 'scientific approach' to accounting – strongly influenced by other disciplines like economics, finance, operations research, the behavioural sciences, even philosophy and history (including archaeology) has greatly matured. It brought forth an immense number of scholarly publications in the English tongue, of which the more important ones we discuss in this chapter. This chronological presentation (here deliberately preferred to a purely 'functional' one) emphasizes first the new 'revolutionary' trends of the 1950s and 1960s: the introduction of analytical and empirical-statistical tools to accounting, the pioneering work in computer application and simulation of spreadsheets, the refinements in current value and inflation accounting, as well as the dispute over the correct valuation basis.

Then, we outline the consolidation of these achievements during subsequent decades, stressing the increasing attention given to the empirical-statistical as well as informational-agency aspects. Furthermore, we draw attention to 'positive accounting theory' and the reaction to it from the British 'critical-interpretive camp'. A major part is concerned with academic accounting research during the last two decades and the alleged crisis that accounting faced at the turn of the millennium. There can be little doubt that the Anglo-American accounting literature dominated the world scene during the second half of the twentieth century.

However, progress in academic accounting research during the entire century has, despite innumerable publications, been moderate in comparison to the enormous changes in other scientific and technological fields during this time. Yet, comparing the present state of affairs in this discipline with that in 1950, it becomes obvious that many innovations did occur. Changes in life style and standards of living in the industrialized and many developing countries, no less than the expansion of capital markets or the general scientific and technological achievements, have had an inevitable impact upon accounting and its research efforts – even if the latter did not always influence practice to the extent desired or expected. Indeed, accounting research generated many novel ideas, partly out of an internal impetus, partly due to the application of other fields to this area. However, accounting as a normative or applied discipline, greatly depends on pragmatic, legal, ethical, economic, social and political considerations. All too often, scientific and logical aspects had to be subordinated to these other forces. To accept this fact is one of the first conditions for comprehending not only the practice but also the 'theory' of accounting.

After the Second World War, several sub-areas emerged where research and theory have had a notable impact on accounting *practice*. First, the introduction of the 'flow-of-funds statement' (statement of changes in financial position) as the third pillar in the presentation of financial statements (Anton 1953; Horngren 1956). Second, the application of statistical methods (including sampling and hypotheses testing) to auditing. Third, the simulation and computerization of accounting spreadsheets and similar devices (Mattessich 1964b). Fourth, the supplementation of historical cost by current entry-values in income statements (and occasionally other financial statements) or other inflation accounting procedures (Edwards and Bell 1961). Although from a practical point of view, this item had only temporary success during the inflationary period of the late 1970s and early 1980s. At this time, the USA, and to some extent the UK, Canada and some Commonwealth countries, introduced or considered legislation for *supplementary* inflation adjustments in financial statements. And, finally, fifth, various attempts by professional accounting bodies and other institutions to develop a conceptual framework of accounting (FASB 1974) – if this item too is still controversial, it may have been less due to the underlying research than to the practitioners' execution of research recommendations.

On the other hand, fundamental questions, predominantly those of valuation and accounting measurement, repeatedly raised during the last 100 years or so, have still not found generally accepted answers. This may be surprising in the face of the enormous research output generated during those five decades.[2] Does this prove the inferiority of accounting researchers, particularly when compared to the ingenuity of researchers in the physical and biological sciences? Admittedly, academic accounting does not attract the geniuses occasionally found in the hard sciences; but there are other factors that limit the progress in our field. First, accounting is a discipline incomparably more difficult to treat scientifically than any 'hard' science because it deals with the actions of human beings rather then the more predictable behaviour of atoms and molecules. Second, research funding in accounting is relatively modest. Third, a long-standing dilemma of accounting research lies in the perennial tension between accounting practice (often resisting theoretical insights and their applications) and academic accounting (often alienating practitioners by abstract models beyond their grasp). Finally, the political forces of specific interest groups may defy any effort by academics or institutions to materialize truly meaningful and socially just accounting and auditing standards or accountability systems – despite repeated attempts by the American Institute of Certified Public Accountants (1953, 1954) and the American Accounting Association (1957, 1966, 1977) as well as individuals (e.g., Blough 1957).

Indeed, serious problems arose in practice: fiscal deficits (exponentially growing, decade after decade) and gigantic frauds, as well as bankruptcies in private industry did cast immense shadows, not only over leading public accounting firms but onto the entire discipline. Can academia be blamed for such a trend? Certainly not entirely, but perhaps accountants did allocate too much of their energy, time and other resources to sophisticated statistical and other mathematical techniques while not paying enough attention to ethical and other normative aspects.

Accounting research in the Anglophone literature during this period was overwhelmingly rich, and we can offer only a sweeping view of it (for more details, see Mattessich 1984). This is bound to disregard innumerable studies and subtle details. For a full understanding of its history, precisely those insights are crucial. Just as one cannot judge belles-lettres merely from the plots of the most notable fictions, so it is impossible to convey all its variety or the many subtleties of this research in a mere sketch. On the other side, by concentrating too much on details one loses the overall picture. Hence, such a survey may fill a latent need to see the main trends, no less than the goals and controversies of accounting research in the English language area during the last half-century.[3]

12.2 The 1950s: emergence of a new academic spirit

This decade formed a transition from the traditional concerns of accounting to a more 'scientific' approach, dominated by the introduction of elements of modern mathematics and the social sciences. An example of this transition is Vatter's book, *The fund theory of accounting* (1947). Although written towards the end of the first half of the twentieth century (see Chapter 11), it rather exercised influence in the 1950s (Anton 1953; Horngren 1956). On one side, Vatter's book still looks back to the pre-war controversy but rejects the proprietorship theory as well as entity theory as inadequate in specific situations; it rather pleads for various 'funds' to establish localized entities in controlling particular activities of administration. Although actual practice did not accept the resulting recommendations, the theory may have influenced the wide-spread use of the flow-of-funds (financial position) statement as the new and third element besides the balance sheet and the profit and loss statement in financial reporting.

Vatter's theory may also have had some impact on the ensuing controversy of cash-flow versus profit analysis and on some aspects of modern budgeting; finally, it may have foreshadowed some aspects of conditional-normative methodology (see later) which, like Vatter's approach, opposes single-value theories. But he is also remembered for another reason. Devine (1950a) and Vatter (1950) pioneered the change of cost accounting (for inventory valuation and concern with past costs) to managerial accounting (oriented more towards decision making and future costs). After those publications, most texts on cost accounting had a managerial emphasis (e.g. Schillinglaw 1961; Horngren 1962).

12.2.1 Introduction of statistical and analytical techniques, and other issues

More characteristic for the new trend towards modern scientific methods were the attempts by Vance (1950 – see also our Chapter 1), Trueblood and Cooper (1955), Vance and Neter (1956), Cyert and Trueblood (1957) and others to apply modern statistical methods to accounting and particularly to auditing. Furthermore, there were the econometric studies of cost behaviour by managerial economists like Dean (1951), as well as the contributions of operations research experts (e.g. Charnes and Cooper 1957, 1961) to cost and managerial accounting. In the area of general accounting theory, the *search for the pragmatic foundations* of our discipline (in the form of accounting postulates or axioms and related mathematical approaches) found an early manifestation during this time (Chambers 1957; Mattessich 1957) – in contrast to the search for 'mere' rules or principles of accounting, as found, for example, in Sanders *et al.* (1938), Littleton (1953), Grady (1965), Kohler (1966) and Blough (1967). Those postulational and axiomatic efforts became more prominent during the subsequent periods (see subsections 12.3.2, 12.4.1 and 12.5.6).

Mattessich (1957, 1964a) also tended towards a *common basis of micro- and macro-accounting*. Such a trend was then in the air (cf. Cooper 1949; Kohler 1952; Bray 1953; Edey and Peacock 1954; Powelson 1955) and continued during the 1960s. Later, most accountants seem to have lost interest in dealing with micro- and macro-accounting under a common umbrella – with the exception of scholars in France (e.g. Pérochon 1971) and, above all, in Japan (where Harada's 1978 pertinent book won the Award of the Japanese Accounting Society, and where previous attempts can be encountered – see Chapter 14, particularly subsection 14.3.1). One might count to these methodological efforts an English book by a renowned German scholar, namely Kosiol's (1978) effort to promote his 'pagatoric accounting' (a version of cash flow accounting) in America.

A very different work revealing the features of this transition period was Littleton's (1953) book, *The structure of accounting theory* (and its 'sequel' in Littleton and Zimmerman 1962). Littleton aimed at a scientific approach, yet did not go much beyond such traditional principles as historic costs and the matching of efforts and accomplishments. His book was widely read, but also heavily criticized – not merely for failing to reflect the scientific process but also for its limited view of accounting (cf. Previts and Merino 1979: 292). However, this only reflects the perennial struggle of twentieth-century accounting theorists to find a place somewhere between two extremes. On one side, the need of accounting practice for simple and conservative principles (as are 'lower of cost or market values', 'realization at point of sale', 'cost and revenue matching', nominal capital maintenance, income smoothing, etc.). On the other side, the longing for more basic assumptions and theorems, better justifiable from an economic and managerial point of view (such as present values or replacement values or exit values, real financial or even physical capital maintenance, comprehensive income and clean surplus statements, etc.). This search was an honest one and ought not to be derided. But futile controversies could have been avoided had theorists emphasized that accounting is an *applied* science (instead of a *pure* or *positive* one) with many tasks, each of which requires different means to satisfy its particular end.

Rapid price increases in the first post-war years led to enhanced interest in *inflation accounting* that prompted pertinent academic research (cf. Baxter 1949; May 1949; Alexander 1950; Jones 1956). It prepared the path for the valuation debate of the 1960s and beyond. In the area of cost or management accounting there was a rising demand for proper cost accounting systems to facilitate managerial decision making (beyond mere inventory valuation for financial statement presentation). This brought forth a number of publications (apart from the path-breaking texts by Devine 1950a, and Vatter 1950, mentioned above), even from the quarters of operations research (e.g. Churchman and Ackoff 1955). Furthermore, there were anthologies on costing issues (e.g. Solomons 1952) or *historical* studies, either on cost accounting, as in Garner (1954), or in R. de Roover (1955) on new perspectives of accounting history. Accounting history on a broader basis is found in Littleton and Yamey (1956) – containing important historical papers, as, for example, de Sainte Croix (1956) on 'Greek and Roman accounting'.

Closely related to these problems were those of capital maintenance, still debated today. In management accounting, conceptual problems and studies on depreciation and other allocation problems, as well as on pricing policy, were no less prevalent (e.g. Devine 1950b; Anthony 1957). Even the first steps towards more rigorous empirical-behavioural accounting research belong to this early period, as evidenced by Argyris' (1952) study on *budgeting* (later pursued in the award-winning dissertation by Stedry 1960).

12.3 The 1960s: a golden age of a priori accounting

12.3.1 Current value, inflation accounting and other valuation issues

The first prominent work of the 1960s was the study on current value accounting (CVA) by Edwards and Bell (1961), *The theory and measurement of business income*. Its basic ideas were developed since the early 1920s in a series of articles and books by Schmidt (e.g. 1921). Edwards and Bell, unfamiliar with German, had only limited access to Schmidt's ideas. They developed their theory independently, and went well beyond Schmidt's work. On the other hand, they also misinterpreted several of its features:

1   Edwards and Bell's profit determination took *specific* as well as *general* price-level changes into systematic consideration (a major advance over Schmidt's 1921 theory). Schmidt concentrated on specific changes, and

when he occasionally took general price-level changes into consideration, it was in a confused and unsystematic way.

2   Edwards and Bell's theory aimed at the determination of the 'real business profit', consisting of 'current *operating* profit' adjusted by real *realized* and *realizable* holding gains (i.e. cost savings as well as capital gains). Similarly, Schmidt's *Gesamterfolgsrechnung* (account of total gains) consists of the *Normalumsatzgewinn* (normal operating profit) supplemented (separately) by such items as financial gains, and speculative gains (from outside capital and, separately, from owner's capital). Although Schmidt is willing to include net monetary holding *losses* in his normal operating profit, he did not do so for net monetary holding *gains* (regarding them as speculative gains, financed by debt equity). For Edwards and Bell the global concept of 'real business profit' is the pivot, while for Schmidt it is the restricted concept of 'normal operating profit'.

3   As either theory was based on replacement values, they both assured the maintenance of *physical* capital. Since Edwards and Bell's theory also incorporated general price-level indices, it was suited for maintaining '*real financial* capital' as well (for detail, see Mattessich 1995: Chapter 6; and for a comparison with Schmidt's theory, see Mattessich 1986).

4   Furthermore, Edwards and Bell distinguished clearly between various types of *holding gains* (monetary vs. non-monetary, real vs. fictitious, realized vs. unrealized) and present a more subtle conceptual apparatus than did Schmidt.

For other well-known publications of this period, dealing with income analysis or accounting for price-level adjustments and related problems, see Mathews (1960), Solomons (1961), Bedford (1965), Gynther (1966) and Dyckman (1969) – as well as Holzer and Schoenfeld (1963a, 1963b), as far as Germany and France are concerned, and Johansson (1965), referring to the situation in Sweden. Edwards and Bell's influential book – which, in the late 1970s, ultimately led to the current price-level legislation of the Financial Accounting Standards Board (FASB) (1974, 1979) and later publications (FASB 1994, 1997) – already belongs to what Nelson (1973: 4) called 'a golden age of *a priori* research in accounting'. This expression also refers to the attempts of searching for a postulational or axiomatic basis. As pointed out, such attempts already began in the late 1950s; they stimulated the accounting community to devote more thought to foundational research (for a survey, see Zeff 1982a). For publications on inflation accounting during the 1970s and early 1980s, see our subsection 12.4.2.

12.3.2 Continuing interest in axiomatic and postulational issues of accounting theory, and its spin-off

Maurice Moonitz, the unofficial leader of the 'Berkeley School', was invited around 1960 by the American Institute of Certified Public Accountants (AICPA) to become temporarily its Research Director and to organize a series of 'Accounting Research Studies', focusing on foundational issues. The first of those studies was authored by Moonitz (1961) himself, and was widely referred to. Under the title *The basic postulates of accounting*, it formulated a total of 14 basic propositions (quantification, exchange, identification of entities, time period, unit of measure, financial statements, market prices, structure of entities, tentativeness, continuity, objectivity, consistency, stable unit and disclosure) and generated a wide interest in this kind of research. A subsequent AICPA Accounting Research Study, co-authored by Sprouse and Moonitz (1962) was, as its title suggested, expected to *deduce* a set of broad accounting principles from the Moonitz postulates. However, as the 'Comments of Leonard Spacek' (contained in Sprouse and Moonitz 1962: 77–9) pointed out, 'there is very little attempt to demonstrate how these principles flow from or are based on the postulates set forth in the previous study'. This concise sentence proved to be prophetic for the failure of all subsequent *postulational* accounting studies (including some of the 'conceptual frameworks') which – in contrast to the *axiomatic* research – attempted to forego a rigorous mathematical-logical approach (as first applied to macro-accounting by Aukrust 1955).

Spacek's (1962) insight was in conformity with the axiomatic experiments of Mattessich (1957) that presented theorems (supported by mathematical proofs) based on matrix algebra and set theory. These thoughts were further developed and presented in the form of an axiomatic conceptual framework (Mattessich 1964a), though ultimately aimed towards pragmatic goals. This work tried to introduce rigorous mathematical and logical thinking to the whole gamut of accounting (ranging from micro- to macro-accounting) as indicated by its title. Apart from applying S.S. Stevens' measurement theory and other mathematical techniques to accounting, this book (together with its companion volume, Mattessich 1964b) introduced financial simulation by means of computerized spreadsheets. It thus prepared the ground for the best-selling spreadsheet programmes, like VisiCalc, Lotus 1–2–3, and others that became immensely popular in accounting practice two decades later (for comments, see McHaney 2000; Jelen 2005: 6–7).

As to the further pursuit of accounting postulation and axiomatization, the following contributions were to be particularly significant: *Accounting, evaluation and economic behavior* by Chambers (1966) and *The foundations of accounting measurement* by Ijiri (1967). Apart from the many subtle conceptual and foundational details, the following highlights may be mentioned. Chambers' work attempted to provide a comprehensive postulational framework in non-mathematical fashion, formulating numerous propositions (premises and, what are claimed to be, conclusions, though merely with vague hints instead of proofs) not only for accounting but also for relevant neighbouring disciplines such as economics, sociology and psychology. This book may well have foreshadowed and stimulated the interest in behavioural accounting that developed in the 1970s and 1980s, though the later developments were based on a more rigorous empirical basis. The book might also be regarded as the starting point for Chambers' later publications that pleaded for current *exit*-values (e.g. Chambers 1967, 1980) such as potential resale or liquidation prices (net realizable value or 'current cash equivalent'). But as to *current cash equivalent* (Chambers' term for exit-values), Leftwich (1969: 248) concludes that 'the universal validity of current cash equivalent as an accounting measure is not established by the arguments employed by Chambers because those arguments are based on several behavioural assumptions which are in open conflict with the environment'. Indeed, the greatest weakness of Chambers theory lies in neglecting the fact that, first, the exit-value approach is valid only under the restricted conditions of 'complete and perfect' markets, and second that, lacking those conditions, other valuation approaches have to be considered to secure fair value accounting (cf. Barth 1980; Barth and Landsman 1995).

Chambers was honoured with separate profiles in prominent historical publications by Gaffikin (1994) and Clarke and Dean (1996). In France, Colasse characterized Chambers in the following manner:

> Chambers is undeniably one of the greatest authors of the twentieth century; yet, paradoxically, he is perhaps less a researcher of the end of the twentieth century than a thinker of the nineteenth century ... . And his main contribution consists in proposing a framework capable of perfecting accounting practice, to make it more rigorous, more 'scientific'. Yet he devotes little effort to validate this framework, considering implicitly that the thorough criticism (inspired by economics) from which he proceeds offers logical justification. In this, he is close to a pundit-missionary of the nineteenth century whose ambition is to transform society.
>
> (Colasse 2005a: 212, translated)

Indeed, Chambers' major idea, that *only* exit values (current cash equivalents, etc.) are meaningful in accounting, seems to reflect an unrealistic disregard for the versatility and the practical needs of our discipline. No doubt, there are situations where exit values are appropriate, but there are many more where this is not the case. Actual practice (past as well as current), so much criticized by Chambers, would more often now, than in the past, yield grossly misleading results if Chambers' valuation doctrine were ever to be realized.

Ijiri's (1967) work too presented a postulational or, more correctly, an axiomatic approach (cf. his set-theoretical formulations in the appendix), but in contrast to Chambers, it promoted, from the very outset, an *historical cost* approach. As Dyckman's (1968) review indicated, the

> importance of this book, does not stem directly from the newness of the material contained ... . Rather this volume combines, elaborates and synthesizes these ideas towards a 'better understanding of the foundations of accounting as it is' ... . Ijiri, specifically is not concerned in this book with what accounting ought to be.

It was this book and further important works by Ijiri, which secured him the leadership in analytical accounting for over a decade.

Further contributions of the 1960s to the issues of accounting postulates and principles were made by Bray (1966) and some American authors, while the problem of 'realization' was dealt with by Davidson (1966). Closely related to all those problems was the issue of 'accounting objectives' (see also later sections); some of the earlier of these studies were that by Backer (1966b) and a more methodologically oriented one by Buckley *et al.* (1968). Related to this is the concern with accounting principles, the search of which has been summarized by Storey (1964); and the relation to the postulate controversy was explored by Zeff (1982a).

12.3.3 *Analytical thinking in managerial accounting*

This mathematical trend in accounting was reinforced by a series of other books like those by Williams and Griffin (1964), and Ijiri (1965a, 1965b) in the area of *management accounting*, as well as by a host of papers on *matrix accounting* and *linear programming applications* (e.g. Corcoran 1964; Demski 1967). To this area also belong the attempts of mathematically improved break-even analysis as well as the budgeting process (e.g. Jaedicke 1961; Charnes *et al.* 1963). Further notable research in management accounting of this decade (though of a non-mathematical nature) can be found in several publications. For example, on transfer pricing, as in Solomons' (1965) book and the paper by Goetz (1967); on methodological problems of income measurement, as in Gordon (1960) and Solomons (1961); on overhead costs in income measurement, as in Ferrara (1961); on cost–volume–profit analysis, as in Jaedicke and Robichek (1964); on standard costs and probabilistic control, as in Zannetos (1964); and on measuring operating efficiency, as in Amey (1969).

The 1960s also contributed to the topic of marginal costing versus full (or absorption) costing (see Weber 1966). Furthermore, Sorter and Horngren (1962) introduced the notion of 'relevant costing' that took the specific costing purpose into consideration (e.g. internal control vs. external reporting). It also integrated management accounting with capital budgeting issues – though some experts might count the latter as part of investment theory rather than cost accounting.

12.3.4 *Philosophical-methodological aspects, and further valuation issues*

A first contribution to the 'philosophy of auditing' was made at the beginning of this period by Mautz and Sharaff (1961). Later Boutell (1965) began to study the impact of computers on auditing. Among other examples of methodological accounting studies are Devine (1960) and Zeff (1963), and the book by Goldberg (1965).

But at this time, concern with the variety of different viewpoints on valuation became particularly prominent. One group, Edwards and Bell (1961) and

Sprouse and Moonitz (1962), were primarily in favour of *current entry values*. The monograph of the American Institute of Certified Public Accountants (1963) recommended *general price-level* adjustments. Chambers (1967, 1980) – later also Sterling (1970) and Thomas (1969, 1974) – regarded *current-exit values* as the only proper valuation basis for accounting. Ijiri (1967, 1975) favoured the traditional *historical cost valuation*.

Also, there was increasing interest in the application of the 'economic' or 'present value' approach (discounting expected dividends or net cash or income flows) to accounting. Proponents of this view consisted of scholars like Alexander (1950), Lemke (1966), Corbin (1962) and Brief (1968, 1969) in America; Honko (1959) in Finland; Hansen (1962) in Denmark; Albach (1965) and Seicht (1970) in the German language area. Later, Beaver (1981), Ohlson (1987a), the FASB (1994, 1997) and many others used *present values* extensively or, at least, were in favour of its occasional application in accounting.

Obviously, there was bewilderment over the question 'which of these competing values really fits the bill? As to the related postulational research, Dopuch (1989a: 42) asserted that 'although each work seemed to take off from the same set of basic postulates, each was still able to arrive at a different destination'. This may have been misleading. As indicated, those individual approaches vary greatly in their assumptions, particularly as far as valuation is concerned. Related to this issue is the need for establishing 'objectives' in financial statement presentation – for this, and various views on accounting principles, respectively, see Rappaport (1964, 1965).

Some publications – e.g. Vatter (1947), Mattessich (1964a), the American Accounting Association's (1966: 9–10, 28–31) *A statement of basic accounting theory* (ASOBAT) – favoured a *multi-value* approach. But, to launch it methodically, a theoretical basis was required. For example, the notion of *value to the owner* (often called 'deprival value', see also Lee 1975) – accepting one or the other of the above-mentioned values, depending on the circumstances – has been promoted by what some call the 'LSE Triumvirate'. Indeed, these three scholars, Edey (1963, 1970), Solomons (1966) and Baxter (1967, 1975) of the London School of Economics, promoted a systematic choice of the appropriate but *relative* deprival value (for a revival of the deprival value in the 1990's, see the 'Forum on Deprival Value Accounting' in the March 1998 issue of *Abacus*). Among these three British scholars, Solomons (active in the USA) was honoured with a comprehensive profile (by Chantiri-Chaudemanche 2005) in Colasse's (2005b) book on *Les grands auteurs en comptabilité* (and Solomons as well as Baxter were ultimately inducted into the Accounting Hall of Fame).

Many scholars, at various times and in different countries, pleaded for relative values or some kind of *purpose-oriented* accounting. From the Anglophone literature one may list the following examples: Backer (1966b), Heinen (1978) and Devine (1985). But there may be a more fundamental methodology for attaining this: Mattessich (1964a) distinguished in the set of basic assumptions (the majority of which are, contrary to common belief, of empirical nature) a separate category (surrogate assumptions) that are empirically empty but hold the place for specific pragmatic or instrumental hypotheses (formalized means–end relations). Such an approach, general yet flexible, was little understood and disregarded by the majority of accountants. Indeed, the search of academics for the Holy Grail – i.e. for the one and only *true* or *neutral* accounting valuation basis – continued unabatedly. However, one cannot ignore the fact that different managerial or political goals require different capital maintenance concepts (nominal, financial, real, etc.) as confirmed in Lemke (1982); nor can one deny the need for 'different costs for different purposes'.

12.3.5 Other trends of the 1960s

Further notable research of this period was concern with such topics as changing depreciation methods (Archibald 1967), as well as planning horizons and future cash flows (e.g. Bailey and Gray 1968). Towards the end of this decade, Sorter (1969) presented his 'events approach' to basic accounting theory, recommending the disaggregation of the accounting system into specific building stones to be recombined according to different needs.

Two more significant trends were on the way – though they burst forth in all their vigour only during the next period. The first of these was a shift in analytical accounting from the 'axiomatic approach' to the application of information economics, which ultimately led to a 'fusion' of this accounting-informational work with agency theory, that had at least as much significance for managerial accounting as for financial accounting. Three Berkeley dissertations, submitted by Butterworth (1967), Feltham (1967) and Mock (reflected later in Mock 1969, and other publications), constituted the starting point of a trend that pivots on information economic issues of accounting. Subsequent work by Feltham and Demski (for details, see Chapter 19) proved to be path breaking and led to garnering one of the most prestigious accounting awards (see next section). In addition to these, another but related information theoretic approach to accounting was presented two years later by Lev (1969). Managerial accounting was preoccupied in the 1960s with 'direct (variable or marginal) costing' and the 'contribution margin' approach.

The other trend preparing itself in the 1960s was the influence of finance theory upon accounting (e.g. Staubus 1961) and the quest for rigorous statistical-empirical methods first manifested in finance but soon spilling over into accounting. Representative publications were: Schrader (1962) on the inductive approach, Dopuch and Drake (1966) on accounting for non-subsidiary investments, Dyckman (1968) on investment analysis, Benston (1967), on corporate accounting data and stock prices. Above all, Ball and Brown's (1968) paper 'An empirical evaluation of accounting income numbers', and Beaver's (1968) 'Information content of annual earnings announcements', proved to be revolutionary for empirical accounting. The paper by Ball and Brown (1968) was originally rejected by *The American Accounting Review.* Yet, it was accepted by the *Journal of Accounting Research* (of the 'Chicago School' that had pioneered an empirical trend since the early 1960s), and in 1986 this paper received the most prestigious AAA Award for Seminal Contribution to Accounting Theory – three years later, in 1989, the same award was given to Beaver's (1968) paper. Beyond this, there also emerged interest in such problems as 'lease vs. acquisition' of assets, manifesting itself in Vatter (1966) and continuing into the last decade of the century (e.g. Karen and Herbst 1990).

As regards accounting history, there was (in comparison to later decades) relatively little activity during the 1960s – the *Accounting Historians Journal* began its publication only in 1974. There was the book by Edwards (1960) on the history of public accounting in the US, another book by Littleton and Zimmerman (1962) on the continuity and change of accounting theory, and (in Great Britain) that by R.H. Parker (1969) on the history of management accounting. Furthermore, there emerged a series of anthologies: for example, Baxter and Davidson (1962) on accounting theory, Moonitz and Littleton (1965) on significant accounting essays, Chatfield (1968) on studies in the evolution of accounting thought, and Buckley (1969) on corporate accounting and its environment. The anthology edited by Backer (1966a) on modern accounting theory, had less of an historical orientation, but offered a survey of accounting theory that became quite influential in subsequent decades.

12.4 The 1970s and the new direction of accounting research

Sterling's (1970) *Theory and measurement of the enterprise income* may be, due to its delayed publication, considered a latecomer to *a priori* research; it thus belongs to the preceding decade. It too examined foundational issues but, as pointed out, it is one of the major works pleading for current exit-values (i.e. exit prices as a valuation basis). The two monographs by Thomas (1969, 1974), mainly concerned with accounting allocation issues also promoted current exit-values (for another allocation study, see Jensen 1977); and the book by Mautz (1970) deals with *Financial reporting by diversified companies*.

12.4.1 Continuing interest in foundational and measurement issues

The search for accounting postulates or axioms continued but, as time went by, it became peripheral to the mainstream approach. Nevertheless, interest in postulational and axiomatic accounting issues spread internationally (see, for example, subsection 4.2.6).

This search continued in Germany and other European countries as well as in America and Japan. It manifested itself, for example, in Ijiri (1975) and Saito (1972, 1973). Towards the end of the decade, interest in axiomatization manifested itself in several ways. For example, in a doctoral dissertation by Orbach (1978), a paper by Tippett (1978) and some books in Italian by Onida (1970) and, particularly, Galassi (1978), as well as a series of papers in Spain by such authors as Buenos-Campos (1972), Garcia Garcia (1972) and Requena-Rodriguez (1972) – axiomatization efforts also continued into the 1980s and

1990s (see next section). But this area no longer occupied centre stage, and we refer the reader to Balzer and Mattessich (2000) for further details and a summary. The publications by Ijiri (1989) and, in a certain way, the one by Wells (1971) ought to be counted to this postulational-axiomatic literature.

Related to such foundational problems were measurement issues as, for example, dealt with by Mock (1976), or Anderson (1976) or Beaver and Demski (1979), who focused on income and wealth measurement. We may also add the search for acceptable accounting standards, as in Moonitz (1974).

12.4.2 *The inflationary period of the 1970s (and early 1980s)*

The inflationary tendencies during the 1970s (particularly in America and some Commonwealth countries) boosted research and publications in current value and general price-level adjustments. Typical examples were: Gynther (1970), Ross (1969), Hanna (1972), Rosen (1972), Moonitz (1973), Revsine (1973), Revsine and Weygandt (1974), Basu and Hanna (1975), Sunder (1975), Bromwich (1977a, 1977b), Davidson and Weil (1978), Falk (1979), Zimmerman (1979), and many others. For similar *English* publications about the Netherlands and Germany, see for example, van Seventer (1975), and Coenenberg and Macharzina (1976), respectively. For a historical survey and anthology of price-level accounting (including some *English* publications by Fritz Schmidt), see Zeff (1976). There also appeared an important anthology on capital mainte-nance, edited by Sterling and Lemke (1982).

Most importantly, various countries introduced proposals, guidelines or quasi-legislations to make one version or the other of *supplementary* current value accounting *compulsory* for financial statement presentation. Interest in Edwards and Bell (1961) re-affirmed itself, and ultimately led to various current price-level legislations. The most successful among these (as regards actual materialization) was that of the USA (FASB 1979). Serious attempts were also made in some Commonwealth countries such as Great Britain (e.g. Sandilands 1975; Institute of Chartered Accountants of England and Wales 1980),[4] Canada (e.g. CICA 1981, 1982), Australia (e.g. Australian Society of Accountants 1974; Australian Accounting Standards Committee 1975; Australian Accounting Research Foundation 1980), New Zealand (New Zealand Society of Accoun-tants 1976, 1978, 1982) and Mexico (Instituto Mexicano de Contadores Público 1975). However, in the early years of the 1980s, when inflation ebbed away, interest in such experiments vanished. Though, most of these institutions still recommended replacement value accounting as a *voluntary* supplement in finan-cial statements.

A new approach towards financial statement analysis was presented by Lev (1974), and so was an investigation into the structure of accounting theory by Yu (1976). A survey of publications on international accounting literature (for the late 1970s) was made available by the American Accounting Associ-ation (1979). International accounting became increasingly prominent during the 1970s (see, for instance, Holzer and Tremblay 1973; Mueller and Walker 1976).

12.4.3 *Statistical-empirical accounting and positive accounting theory*

However, as the modern trends gained momentum, the so-called *a priori approach*,[5] in general, was subject to growing criticism through several papers contained in the book by Dopuch and Revsine (1973) – particularly the one by Nelson (1973), to which Wells (1976) responded in fervent opposition. Empirical accounting research, on one side, and agency-information research, on the other, began to dominate academic accounting, and assumed during the 1970s the character of *normal* science (in contrast to the *revolutionary* accounting research of the 1960s), to use Kuhn's (1962) terminology.[6] Indeed, empirical-statistical accounting began to spread rapidly in many countries of English language, but much slower in others. The end of this decade brought forth 'positive accounting theory' (PAT), a radical methodology for empirical research, that (according to Jeanjean 2005: 274) is, above all, a 'political-contractual' approach. It was first disseminated in two papers by Watts and Zimmerman (1978, 1979), 'Towards a positive theory of the determination of accounting standards' and 'The demand and supply of accounting theories: the market for excuses', respectively. Later, the book *Positive accounting theory* (Watts and Zimmerman 1986) summarized and consolidated this theory. Despite the great popularity of these publications, the approach became increasingly controversial and encountered reaction, as indicated below. Nevertheless, the international impact of this direction was profound enough to earn Watts and Zimmerman a joint profile (by Jeanjean 2005) in *Les grand auteurs en comptabilité* (edited by Colasse), as well as the Award for Seminal Contribution to Accounting Theory (2004 – for their 1978 paper), the most prestigious prize of the AAA. Major academic journals published further papers on 'positive accounting' during the last half of this decade than during the first. The anthology by Frecka (1989) summarizes a good deal of this and related research.

Yet, apart from the general criticism of empirical research (mentioned in the previous section), it became obvious in the mid-1980s that a *direct* influence of PAT upon accounting policy appeared to many of having fallen short of its expectations. Thus, growing opposition to PAT manifested itself in publications such as Laughlin *et al.* (1982), Tinker *et al.* (1982), Christenson (1983), Kelly (1983), Lowe *et al.* (1983), Schreuder (1984), Peasnell and Williams (1986), Whittington (1987), Demski (1988), Whitley (1988), Hines (1988), Mouck (1989), Sterling (1990), Boland and Gordon (1992), Schneider (1992) and Chambers (1993). Those papers range from mild misgivings to vehement rejection of PAT. Indeed, one might ask, who does honestly believe that such thoroughly normative disciplines as engineering, medicine, law and accounting can sufficiently be embraced by 'positive theories' and represented as pure sciences? Is this view only held by those plagued with the inferiority complex that 'serving an *applied* science is not good enough'? Ought not the applied disciplines be particularly appreciated, as they are the ones confronted with the *moral choices* so crucial for the future of mankind? Would the eliminating of value judgements from accounting theory (instead of exposing and analysing them through *means–ends* relations) not undermine the very essence of discipline?

Although Watts and Zimmerman (1990) reacted to some of their opponents, the response is still a point of controversy. In this paper, the authors also emphasize that their theory has revealed the following regularities and explanations: (1) the *bonus plan hypotheses* (i.e. in bonus plans, the probability is higher that management selects an accounting method which reports a relatively higher earning figure); (2) the *debt/equity hypothesis* (i.e. management is more likely to select such an 'income increasing' method, the higher a firm's debt/equity ratio is); (3) the *political cost hypothesis* (i.e. management is more likely to select the other method, the 'income decreasing' one, if the firm is relatively large). The variables chosen for those 'choice hypotheses' usually are: managerial compensation, other incentives, firm size, leverage, risk, interest coverage as well as limitations on dividends. As a major argument in favour of PAT, Watts and Zimmerman (1990: 140) mentioned 'the lack of an alternative model with greater explanatory power'.

Empirical accounting research, in general, comprises many aspects, and brought forth an immense number of publications. Above all, it asserted that security prices provide a measure of information content for such events as changes in statement presentation, accounting regulations, earnings announcements, etc. The official AAA (1977) evaluation of the 'state of the art', the *Statement on accounting theory and theory acceptance* (SATTA), attempted to summarize this and related research. But it was pessimistic as to the possibility of a general accounting theory – by way, this study proved to be less influential than the corresponding AAA (1966 or ASOBAT) of the preceding decade. The major new areas discussed in SATTA were: first, *earnings research*, dealing with such topics as the relationship between share prices and 'abnormal earnings' and, second, research in *earnings forecasts* as well as the *information content* of such forecasts, etc. (e.g. Crichfield *et al.* 1978; Givoly and Lakonishok 1979). Since most of these problems stem from financial accounting, managerial accounting aspects were primarily examined by experimental and behavioural-organizational research (see penultimate paragraph of this section, and the next section). Finally, studies on assessing the risks of industries, as in Falk and Heintz (1978) and Falk and Gordon (1978), may also be counted to this line of empirical investigation.

The major *results* of this first phase of non-experimental empirical studies may be summarized as follows: (1) earnings announcements bear information content; (2) the market appears to rely on the firm's earnings forecasts; (3) other financial data of the financial statements are not highly associated with unexpected returns; (4) there seem to be no major correlations between changes in accounting methods on a voluntary basis and unexpected returns (apart from auditing changes related to changes in expected cash flows); (5) the market appears to see through 'cosmetic changes' in financial statements, and FASB regulations seem not to affect stockholders' wealth or earning power.

Irrespective of the provisional nature of those results, they seem to be modest and disproportionate to the extensive effort of highly sophisticated research. Indeed, most empirically oriented scholars themselves admit this freely. But considering the vacuum of rigorous (i.e. statistical) empirical research before the late 1960s, one might see the results in a different light. Nevertheless, empirical accounting research was subjected to further criticism (for example, by Daley 1994: 44) on two points: (1) the repetitiveness of studying the same phenomenon, and (2) documenting phenomena far removed from actual observations. Beyond this, one may add that there were few attempts to examine means–end relations from an empirical point of view (despite an undeniable concern of empirical accountants with policy issues, as manifested, for example, by Ball and Smith 1992). The results of empirical accounting, and its effect on the 'philosophy of financial statement presentation', as well as its relation to informational aspects ('security price research' up to the end of the 1970s) has found its most representative manifestation and summary in Beaver (1981 – see next section).

As to research on adaptive behaviour relating to managerial control and information analysis, there is the publication by Itami (1977), and among experimental studies – particularly as regards earnings vs. cash flows and purpose-orientation, as well as the functional fixation involved – Abdel-khalik and Keller (1979). For an annotated bibliography on cost benefit analysis, see Wood and Campbell (1970) and, for a study on empirical methodology, Abdel-khalik and Ajinkya (1979). Zero-based budgeting (Reckers and Stagliano 1977) emerged in the late 1970s and 'focused on a highly-disciplined, detailed examination of service functions and discretionary costs' (Horngren 1995: 283) – meanwhile, zero-based budgeting seems to have lost its popularity.

Furthermore, empirical and other research of the 1970s tried to clarify accounting objectives and information goals: e.g. the so called 'Trueblood Report' by the AICPA (1973) and its implementation problems, as in Beaver and Demski (1974), Cyert and Ijiri (1974) and other contributions – particularly in special issues on *Studies in financial accounting objectives*, 1974, of the *Journal of Accounting Research*. A special focus of empirical research was on behavioural aspects, including human resource accounting, as well as on economic consequences of standard setting, earnings forecasts and stock price behaviour. For the latter, see, for example, Patell (1976) and, on accounting systems choice, see Uecker (1978) – for work on decision styles, contingency frameworks, see Tiessen and Baker (1977) as well as Waterhouse and Tiessen (1978). As the individual contributions are too numerous to be listed here, one may refer to the following reviews and anthologies: Bruns and DeCoster (1969), Hakansson (1973), Gonedes and Dopuch (1974), Abdel-khalik and Keller (1978), Dyckman *et al.* (1978) and Dyckman and Zeff (1984).

Of particular importance, from a more traditional viewpoint, was the 'Wheat Report' (AICPA 1972), recommending the establishment of the FASB. This, in turn, brought forth a long series of statements, among which was FASB (1979), 'legislating' compulsory, though supplementary, current cost and price-level adjustments to income statements of larger corporations. The latter resulted in lengthy discussions and some reactions (e.g. Dopuch and Sunder 1980).

12.4.4 Early information economic research in accounting

Almost as prominent as empirical accounting research, became the endeavour to apply information economics and agency theory to our discipline (see also subsection 12.5.3; but due to the potential future of the 'information perspective of accounting', we have devoted the entire closing chapter to details about it). The early efforts by Feltham (e.g. 1967, 1972), and other students of the 'Berkeley School' in the application of information economics to accounting were extended and greatly elaborated in a series of publications (e.g. Feltham and Demski 1970; Demski and Feltham 1972), mainly by these two authors, either individually or in cooperation with each other. The most prominent of these joint publications are Demski and Feltham (1976), *Cost determination – a conceptual approach*, and Demski and Feltham (1978), *Economic incentives in budgetary control systems* – the latter received in 1994 the prestigious AAA Award for Seminal Contribution to Accounting Theory. Both authors received many other honours, and Demski was profiled (by Antle 1996) in Chatfield and Vangermeersch's encyclopaedic work, while Feltham was profiled (by Cormier and Magnan 2005) in Colasse's French book on the great authors of accounting.

At first, this direction consisted in an application of information economics (concerned with the probability distribution and value of additional information: e.g. Feltham 1968; Mock 1969, 1971; Baiman 1975) to accounting problems, or with information inductance (Prakash and Rappaport 1977). In the second half of the 1970s, when these issues seemed to be exhausted, it was noticed that descriptive agency theory (Jensen and Meckling 1976) – dealing with the contractual relation between 'principal' and 'agent', various agency costs, risk-sharing and incentive problems – lends itself excellently to a fusion with information economic aspects, thus resulting in what might be called 'analytical agency (or contract) theory' (for pertinent survey articles, see Baiman 1982, 1990; and Feltham 1984). It is remarkable that this approach reinstated *stewardship* as the central paradigm of accounting (cf. Gjesdal 1981), despite the previous attempts of making *investment decision making* the pivot of our discipline. Furthermore, agency theory has been related to issues of ethics (see Noreen 1988).

To these efforts may be added the examination of auditing in the light of modern accounting theory (e.g. Arens *et al.* 1970; Ijiri and Kaplan 1971; Scott 1975; Joyce 1976; Gibbins 1977; Moonitz and Stamp 1978; Ng and Stoeckenius 1979), as well as the application of Brunswik's 'lens model' to auditing by Ashton (1974). One might also mention publications on the history of auditing as, for example, Adelberg (1975).

12.4.5 Behavioural and organizational accounting

Another significant direction emerged during the 1970s in Great Britain (e.g. Hopwood 1972, 1978; Gambling 1974) that gained growing attention in the subsequent decade in America as well as in Continental Europe. Much of its research is associated with the journal *Accounting, Organization and Society* and deals, as its title suggests, with the societal and organizational aspects of our discipline (see also next section). One might even relate this trend to the cost and management accounting in Continental Europe (e.g. Adam 1970; Magnusson 1974; Schoenfeld 1974) and the exploration of a 'contingency theory of managerial accounting' (Hayes 1977) in North America. This trend is further related to the emerging theory of human resource accounting, as proposed, for example, by Flamholtz (1972).

A special place assumes Briloff (1972), with his renowned *Unaccountable Accounting* (and subsequent publications), as one of the earlier manifestations of the 'ethical trend' in American accounting. However, towards the end of the 1970s and the beginning of the 1980s a group of British accounting academics, Hopwood (1978), Burchell *et al.* (1980) and Burchell *et al.* (1985), announced a more radical accounting programme (opposed to neo-classical economics), often addressed as the critical-interpretive (or interpretative) view (see next section).

The American Accounting Association (1979) issued a survey of publications on literature of 'international accounting' for the late 1970s. Indeed, this topic became increasingly prominent during the 1970s (see, for instance, Holzer and Tremblay 1973; Mueller and Walker 1976). Of particular importance was the beginning trend towards 'harmonization' of accounting standards within the European Community after the Fourth EEC Directive) – but this trend came into its own during the 1980s and 1990s.

12.5 The 1980s and 1990s: diversification, consolidation and model building

This period is unparalleled when it comes to the diversification and volume of accounting research. The number of English-language academic accounting journals has more than *trebled* in the 1980s alone, and accounting literature has expanded – one is tempted to say 'exploded' – into many directions. The result is not merely a great richness of contemporary research, but a bewildering variety that is difficult to survey concisely. The former generation, relatively unsophisticated in modern mathematics, statistics, probability and investment theory, was followed by a generation much better trained in these areas. Originally, some of the younger academics seem to have aimed for a complete break with the past; but during the 1990s those persons had entered their fifties and were acquiring wisdom beyond mere cleverness. Slowly some of them began to realize the debt to their predecessors and, what is more important, to see that no science, particularly not an applied one, can be restricted to the Procrustes bed of mere formalization and statistical testing. There are indications that the contempt for, and the utter rejection of research beyond mathematical or statistical 'model building', by this particular group, appears to be waning.

12.5.1 *Flourishing of empirical accounting research*

In the empirical area, it was *Financial reporting: an accounting revolution* by Beaver (1981) that reviewed and summarized the research of the preceding decades (particularly with regard to the 'philosophy of financial reporting' and the information function), manifesting its future aspirations. Above all, this work shows that for perfect and complete markets, *economic income* (based on the discount of net future cash flows) is 'virtually unassailable'. Yet, where these ideal conditions do not hold, there is as yet no way of determining the scientifically correct income concept.

Similarly, the book *Positive accounting theory* by Watts and Zimmerman (1986) recapitulated and consolidated the previous endeavour of those authors. Empirical accounting research continued to flourish in innumerable studies from the economic consequences of accounting choices (Holthausen and Leftwich 1983) to those of price changes and dividend policies, etc. (Holthausen and Verrecchia 1988; Richardson *et al.* 1988), including methodological and historical research (e.g. Zeff 1972; Abdel-khalik and Ajinkya 1979; Zimmerman 1979; Ball and Foster 1982; Kaplan 1984). Also research in the area of information content continued extensively (e.g. Baran *et al.* 1980; Beaver *et al.* 1980; Beaver *et al.* 1982; Beaver and Landsman 1983; Freeman 1983; Schaefer 1984; Lakonishok and Ofer 1985; Hopwood and McKeown 1985; Samuelson and Murdoch 1985; Hoskin *et al.* 1986; Bernard and Ruland 1987; Bernard 1987, 1989; Bowen *et al.* 1987; Freeman and Tse 1989; Hopwood and Schaefer 1989), as well as related studies on earnings forecasts and earnings announcements (e.g. Ajinkya and Gift 1984; Atiase 1985). One of the most important sub-areas of empirical studies goes under the name of 'market-based accounting research' (MBAR). Its preliminary results were characterized in Lev and Ohlson (1982), and may be summarized as follows:

1   While earnings information is confirmed to be useful, the 'usefulness' of non-earning information remains uncertain.
2   As regards some voluntary changes in accounting methods, the *rational* reaction of investors is no longer confirmed, and irrational tendencies are suspected; furthermore accounting changes can have some *real* effect.
3   Research assessing stock market reactions to financial regulations seems to be consistent with: (i) replacement cost accounting, (ii) oil and gas accounting and (iii) lines-of-business information.
4   MBAR has contributed to finance in two different ways. First, it has forced researchers to reconsider the capital asset pricing model as well as the market efficiency hypothesis by investigating evidence that might be inconsistent with either or both. Second, MBAR has presented evidence linking basic variables of the firm to the systematic risk of common stocks (cf. Beaver *et al.* 1970). Furthermore, several studies have confirmed that the market is able to recognize and discount 'cosmetic' changes in financial statements (cf. Dopuch 1989a). Thus, one concluded that pertinent

regulations by the FASB or other professional bodies would not affect stockholders' wealth.

Another area was concerned with issues of *income smoothing* (cf. Ronen and Sadan 1981; Lilien *et al.* 1988) and other income measurement issues (e.g. Linsmeier *et al.* 1995), or even with lobbying activity (Watts and Zimmerman 1979; Puro 1984; King and O'Keefe 1986; Abdel-khalik *et al.* 1989). As to explaining the level and type of *executive remuneration*, the evidence for the reliability of accounting data is mixed (cf. Watts and Zimmerman 1978; Healy 1985; Antle and Smith 1986). A good deal of 'financial accounting research' concentrated on *standard setting* and regulation: e.g. Abdel-khalik (1980) and Schipper (1994) in the USA; Stamp (1980, 1984), Basu and Milburn (1982) and Skinner (1987) in Canada. On a more general level, standard setting and accounting principles were investigated by Peasnell (1982a) in England, and Fujita (1991) in Japan. As to research on corporate governance and accountability, see Benston (1982a, 1982b), Ijiri (1983) and, with emphasis on public accounting, Gibbins and Newton (1995).

Further notable publications were by Thornton (1983, 1988a) and Courtis (1985–86) on contingencies, uncertainties and risk; see, above all, Dyckman and Morse (1986). Gonedes and Dopuch (1989) dealt with capital markets and their efficiency. Atiase *et al.* (1989) and G.D. Richardson (1989) investigated the firm size effect and timeliness of earnings announcements. Hughes and Ricks (1987) studied earnings forecast errors in relation to stock returns, while other studies on the forecasting of earnings came from Collins and Hopwood (1980), Jensen (1983) and Brown *et al.* (1984). Buchanan and Gaumnitz (1987) were concerned with insider trading; Richardson and Gibbins (1988) with behavioural problems in the use of financial statements; and Sorter and Ingberman (1987) on aspects of the events approach. Furthermore, the problems of 'earnings vs. cash flow' received considerable attention: e.g. Lee (1984, 1985), Egginton (1985), Lawson (1985) and Charitou and Katz (1990).

As to financial reporting in general, such publications as Abdel-khalik (1983) and the anthology by Lee and Parker (1994) reflect major concerns of this period. The search for alternative approaches of relating accounting information to the change of security prices may have helped to *explain* those prices by means of fundamental variables of accounting and finance. For a standard work on financial statement analysis, see Foster (1986). Cross-sectional perspective of valuation (as contrasted to the *standard 'returns'* model of Ball and Brown 1968) received impetus through such articles as Lev and Ohlson (1982) – for an overview, see Atiase and Tse (1986). Another notable survey article in this area is Lev (1989). It not only offered evidence that the *earnings usefulness approach* is rather weak but blamed this weakness on the deficiencies in accounting measurement, on valuation principles, and on data manipulation by management. Above all, the paper called for a reorientation of accounting capital market research, and for more emphasis on valuation and measurement methodology. In this way, Lev (1989) offered some insight into empirical accounting research and its relation to corporate 'earnings'. On the other hand, the study by Beaver *et al.* (1980) on information content of security prices may have led to better specifications of price-earnings relations, as did the study by Kormendi and Lipe (1987). This relates to research by Ou and Penman (1989a, 1989b), showing data in financial statements, not only reveal current price movements, it might also help in predicting such future movements.

As far as *accounting policy research* is concerned, Dopuch (1989b) warned of the continuing erosion of policy publications during the late 1980s (with the exception of such papers as Schipper and Thomson 1985; Underdown and Taylor 1985; Lev 1988), particularly when compared with research in the early 1980s and before, as executed by May and Sundem (1976), Foster (1980), Maher (1981) and others. The criticism of the FASB's conceptual framework continued, for example, in Agrawal (1987) and Archer (1993). For research in accounting objectives, see Dopuch and Sunder (1980) and Arthur Andersen & Co. (1984). The literature on valuation, price-level issues and current cost accounting was particularly rich. Typical examples are: Chambers (1980), Mine- mura (1980), Watts and Zimmerman (1980), Macharzina and Coenenberg (1981), Enthoven (1982), Frishkoff (1982), Freeman (1983), Milburn (1988), Brief (1983), Whittington (1983), Bloom and Debessay (1984), Tweedie and Whittington (1984), Zéghal (1984, in French, published in Canada), Espahbodi and Hendrickson (1986), Mattessich (1986), Thornton (1986, 1988a), Solomons (1987), Tippett and Whittington (1988), Beechy (1989), Espahbodi and Tehran- ian (1989) and Tremblay and Cormier (1989, in French, published in Canada).

Particularly influential in this area was the book by Beaver and Landsman (1983), asserting that historical cost accounting is at least as informative as other valuation methods (cf. Ijiri's 1981 continuing defence of the historical cost approach). This study was commissioned by the FASB and published shortly before the Board decided (apparently by the majority of *a single vote*) to abandon the compulsory current price-level adjustments for income statements of large American corporations. For a reaction to, or even disagreement with, Beaver and Landsman (1983), see Bublitz *et al.* (1985), Lakonishok and Ofer (1985), Samuelson and Murdoch (1985), Buzby (1986), Peasnell *et al.* (1987), Stark (1987), Swanson and Shriver (1987), Espahbodi and Tehranian (1989), Sami *et al.* (1989), Lobo and Song (1989) and others.

12.5.2 *Foundational issues of the 1980s and 1990s*

As to foundational work, two publications assumed particular eminence during the second half of the 1980s. The first was Devine (1985), *Essays on accounting theory*, a collection of articles written during the previous three decades or so. They deal with theory construction, behavioural accounting (of which Devine may be regarded as an early forerunner), income theory and related issues. This monumental work of five volumes not only presents the author's philosophical view of many important issues, but also offers a picture of major efforts of theory development during past decades. The second work was Ijiri's (1989) highly original *Momentum accounting and triple-entry bookkeeping: exploring the dynamic structure of accounting measurements*, which also grew out of previous research efforts. Its basis is *triple-entry* bookkeeping; but it also exploits analogies with the help of terminology from physics to represent the dynamics of accounting, and its central ideas are as follows.

1   The notion of *income momentum* (shortly 'momentum' = growth-rate of wealth per time unit), corresponding in physics to the linear momentum (mass × velocity = mass – distance per time).
2   *Force* or better *income force* (growth-rate of income momentum per time unit), corresponding to physical force (mass × acceleration = growth rate of linear momentum).
3   *Impulse* (or *income impulse*, i.e. the increase in income momentum growth rate), corresponding somewhat to impulse in mechanics (increase in momentum = force × time). In contrast to most other studies during this period, Ijiri's is not a derivative from finance but grew out of accounting proper; in other words, it *internalizes* and incorporates managerial-behavioural features into the framework of accounting proper. Other recent theories more or less abandoned this framework, converting accounting either into a kind of economics or finance, or into a branch of the behavioural sciences, hence *externalizing* our discipline.

The category of foundational work includes a series of papers concerned with *reality issues* (e.g. Tomkins and Groves 1983; Abdel-khalik and Ajinkya 1983; Morgan 1983; Willmott 1983) and the closely related question whether income, capital, etc., are notions backed by reality or are mere fiction – see Heath (1987), countered by Thornton (1988b). Here, Sterling (1979) might again be mentioned; his book not only deals with valuation and measurement problems, it also claims 'the primary problem of accounting is that our figures do not have empirical referents' (p. 213). Such 'reality questions' became prominent in the 1980s and early 1990s (e.g. Lukka 1990), continuing into the 2000s (see Macintosh *et al.* 2000). In a related context, a book by Mattessich (1978) explored the epistemology of the applied sciences in general, and another book as well as subsequent paper (Mattessich 1995, 2003) showed that much futile accounting controversy arises from 'category mistakes', that is to say, the failure of clearly distinguishing between:

1   the conceptual representation of *physical* versus *social* realities;
2   the *ontological* vs. the *epistemological* vs. the *methodological* problems posed by accounting representation; and
3   the *real* vs. the *conceptual* vs. the *semantic* aspects of such representation.

Finally, there is the long-standing question of whether accounting is a normative or positive discipline, or to which extent it is one and the other, and how a proper integration could come about (e.g. Hakansson 1969; Hilton 1980;

Ryan 1982; Tinker *et al.* 1982; Schreuder 1984; Waller and Jiambalvo 1984; Zebda 1987; Shapiro 1998). For further philosophical discussions, see Archer (1998).

The 1980s and 1990s brought forth a series of texts surveying the theory of accounting (e.g. Hendriksen 1982; Most 1984; Wolk *et al.* 1984; Belkaoui 1985a; Kam 1986). Among these, the most enduring (with many editions) was the AAA award-winning book by Hendriksen.

Mathematical model-building (see Verrecchia 1982) and analytical accounting research of the 1980s made further contributions. For example, the contractual basis of accounting valuation was examined by John Hughes (1984); or the application of asymmetric information aspects to the LIFO/FIFO choice by Hughes and Schwartz (1988). This and related articles also illustrate the relatively rare but important giving and taking between empirical accountants, on the one side (Sunder 1976; Abdel-khalik 1985; Brown 1980; Morse and Richardson 1983; Hunt 1985; Dopuch and Pincus 1988; Johnson and Dhaliwal 1988) and analytical accountants (Jung 1985; Amershi and Sunder 1987), on the other side.

12.5.3 *Further advances of analytical accounting*

Analytical accounting research during the 1980s and 1990s shifted increasingly from deterministic to stochastic model building. Apart from this shift, one of the fundamental problems was to find the necessary and sufficient conditions for *public information* to possess value. Hakansson *et al.* (1982) solved this problem for *pure exchange economies*; then Kunkel (1982) included also *production activity*, but under most restrictive conditions; finally Ohlson (1988) appears to have stated these conditions on a more general basis. For centralization with regard to communication, see Melumad and Reichelstein (1987); for multiple agencies, Amershi and Butterworth (1988); and for signalling under asymmetric information, P.J. Hughes (1986); for the decentralization of monitoring systems, Demski *et al.* (1984); for communication of private information, Feltham and Hughes (1988); for voluntary disclosure, Wagenhofer (1990); for multi-task efforts in agency analysis, see Feltham and Xie (1994), as stimulated by Holmström and Milgrom (1991), as well as Bushman and Indjejikian (1993).

Of special historical interest is the paper by Coase (1990), reasserting this Nobel laureate's pioneering work. Coase (1937, 1938, 1960) was originally teaching accounting at the London School of Economics. In the 1930s, Coase emphasized opportunity costs in accounting, and pointed out that in Marshall's economic theory the firm is but a 'black box'. This contrasts with actual practice where 'the distinguishing mark of the firm is the "supersession" of the price mechanism' (Coase 1937: 389). This seminal paper anticipated important features (such as 'transaction costs') of modern management by several decades.

A series of publications by Ohlson (1983, 1987a, 1987b, 1989, 1990, 1991, 1995) dealt with incentives in multi-task or multi-date settings and other aspects of capital market theory, leading him to formulate his 'theory of clean surplus' (for details and Ohlson's teamwork with Feltham, see Chapter 19). This was a return to a more traditional basis. This approach reformulated basic thoughts on the accountants' comprehensive income statement – previously analysed by Preinreich (1938, 1996), Peasnell (1981, 1982b) and others (see also Brief and Peasnell 1996) – and used stochastic formulations to draw new mathematical inferences.

Ohlson (1987b) demonstrated that income measurement demands a connection to welfare without any other requirement, such as shareholders' unanimity (apparently in contrast to Beaver and Demski 1979). Ohlson also showed that Beaver's and Demski's *rejection* of the 'measurement perspective of accounting' was mistaken. In other words, even where the conditions of perfect competition, complete markets and stockholders' unanimity are *not* fulfilled, income measurement may remain a meaningful and fundamental objective of accounting. He saw in accounting much more than the 'cost-effective communication procedure' of Beaver and Demski, and pleaded for combining the *informational aspect* with the *measurement aspect* of accounting. Furthermore, Ohlson (1991) showed that the paper by Ball and Brown (1968) falls short of 'an equilibrium model linking value with earnings through expectations (or information)', and that Ball and Brown's notion of unexpected earnings 'appears to have the status of a "folklore concept" with limited economic content'. All this necessitated a rigorous theory, the starting point for which he saw in the 'clean surplus equation' (change in book value of owners' equity + dividends = earnings) as a basis for security valuation. Ohlson also showed why this equation need not be a tautology but can be explained in economic and empirical terms (i.e. each of the three variables of the clean surplus equation act as an independent information component, leading in the long-run to an *equilibrium* in the empirical sense).

There were many other analytical contributions. A favourite area was agency theory (e.g. Atkinson and Feltham 1982; Feltham 1984; Feltham *et al.* 1988; Berg *et al.* 1990), including problems of moral hazard (e.g. Kanodia 1985; Matsumura 1988), or risk aversion and asymmetry in budgeting (e.g. Young 1985) and other budgeting issues (e.g. Samuelson 1986), or the relevance to government accounting (e.g. Beedle 1981; Reichelstein 1992), or an overview of stock valuation and accounting information (e.g. Atiase and Tse 1986). Closely related to agency theory is the contracting theory of Sunder (1996), which offers a 'micro-theory' as well as (what he calls) a 'macro-theory' of accounting and control – while the former is to present an income notion that would supply different information to various constituents, the latter concentrates on the relation between accounting and the economic interests of various agents. We offer more details on the 'information perspective' of accounting (including further aspects of agency theory and the clean surplus theory) in the more future-oriented Chapter 19.

12.5.4 Auditing research

Research in *auditing and the economics of auditing* continued to keep its prominence (e.g. Ashton and Brown 1980; Evans 1980; Lewis 1980; Rappaport 1980; Simunic 1980, 1984; Johnson *et al.* 1981; Joyce and Biddle 1981; DeAngelo 1981b; Mock and Turner 1981; Antle 1982; Duke *et al.* 1982, 1985; Gaumnitz *et al.* 1982; Hylas and Ashton 1982; Joyce and Libby 1982; Kinney and Uecker 1982; Schultz and Reckers 1981; Solomons 1982; Ashton 1983; Campbell 1985; Boritz *et al.* 1987; Mock and Vertinsky 1985; Robinson and Fertuck 1985; Amershi 1986; Blazenko and Scott 1986; Simunic and Stein 1987, 1996; Biggs *et al.* 1989). Research using the so-called 'direct assessment technique' (e.g. R. Weber 1980; Libby and Frederick 1990) showed that auditors, by gaining experience in analytical reviews, steadily improve their handling of errors. There also appeared a 'Discussion of industry differences in the production of auditing services' by Kao (1994).

In the area of business *auditing research*, there emerged some excellent surveys such as Felix and Kinney (1982), Scott (1984, 1988), Ashton *et al.* (1987), Zéghal (1989) and Pincus (1990), as well as such books as Cushing and Loebbecke (1986) and Herbert (1987). Furthermore, we found two anthologies from Great Britain, and two from America, respectively: Hopwood *et al.* (1982) and Kinney (1986), and Lee (1988) and Abdel-khalik and Solomon (1988). Pertinent articles are: Evans (1980), Gaumnitz *et al.* (1982) and Gibbins and Wolf (1982). Finally, there were papers on auditor independence such as Falk and Frucot (1997) and Gordon and Loeb (1997b); and books on auditing in an electronic environment by Cornick (1981) and Davis and Weber (1983).

A particularly fascinating branch of auditing, 'forensic accounting', investigates the *fraudulent* possibilities and activities of accounting. For some of the earlier publications in this area, see Dykeman (1982) and Bologna and Lindquist (1987); for a host of more recent publications, see the *Journal of Forensic Accounting*. Wyatt (2004) offered a profound insight into the ethical development of the public accounting profession. He vividly illustrated how the auditing profession was originally dominated by the 'auditing partners' (with their traditional ethical standards), but from the 1980s onwards the more lucrative consulting business became increasingly important to public accounting firms. Apparently, the 'consulting partners' – that may have lacked the ethical training of the auditors – dominated vital decisions that involved undue moral risks for the sake of higher profits. For further ethical aspects of the accounting profession, see the next subsection 12.5.5.

12.5.5 The behavioural and the critical-interpretive trends of the 1980s and 1990s

Behavioural and organizational accounting is another area (rooted in the previous decade) that assumed particular prominence during the 1980s (for an overview, see Burgstahler and Sundem 1989). Chua (1986) distinguished three sub-areas:

(1) Behavioural accounting (mainstream behavioural research): For an overview see Gibbins and Hughes (1982), Gibbins and Newton (1987) and Libby (1989). This sub-area is dominated by traditional methodology and is more often encountered in America. It includes publications such as Libby's (1981) *Accounting and human information processing: theory and applications*, Ashton's (1982) *Human information processing in accounting* and Ashton's (1984) *The evolution*

of behavioral accounting research: an overview or, for example, the paper by Gibbins and Wolf (1982) on the auditors' subjective decision environment. Swieringa and Weick's (1987) 'Management accounting and action' focused on the dynamic and motivational aspects of managerial accounting, and dealt with organizational as well as behavioural aspects; this paper also indicated that such notions and procedures as 'return on investment', 'cost–volume–profit analysis' and 'variance analysis' may cause a short-run point of view among management. The paper by Kren and Liao (1988), 'The role of accounting information in the control of organizations: a review of the evidence', offered a survey of the pertinent literature with some ties to agency theory.

The remaining two sub-areas of this trend were predominantly promulgated by accountants trained in Great Britain and constitute the major counterweight to the methodology of positive accounting theory. This 'critical-interpretive view' has been ignored rather than refuted by the disciples of PAT, but was also attacked from other quarters (e.g. in Schneider 1992).

Related to, though not identical with, the critical-interpretive trend was Briloff's (1981, 1986, 1990) continuing effort of awakening ethical awareness among accountants. Furthermore, DeAngelo (1981a, 1981b), Antle (1984) and Sweeney and Roberts (1997) examined the auditor's independence and related aspects. To these have to be added several attempts towards a theoretical foundation for the ethics of accounting and auditing by Gaa (1988, 1994), Shaub (1988), as well as Ponemon and Gabhart (1993) and, above all, Clarke *et al.* (1997). The latter book demonstrates, by means of a series of corporate failures in Australia, that (i) the reporting of traditional book values permits management excess borrowing, and (ii) consolidated financial statements enable management to hide losses of poorly performing subsidiaries. Those authors conclude that consolidated statements are irrelevant or worthless; they also regard the present standard-setting process unethical, and call for inflation adjusted, desegregated financial reporting. Other articles worth mentioning in this connection are those by Flamholtz *et al.* (1985), exploring a framework for organizational control, Waller and Jiambalvo (1984), as well as Mozes (1992) who discussed the use of normative models in human information processing and normative accounting research, respectively.

(2) Organizational accounting (interpretative perspective and the 'critical-interpretive' view) began with such publications as Burchell *et al.* (1980), on the roles of accounting in organizations and society, and the book by Hopwood (1988), *Accounting from the outside: the collected papers by Anthony G. Hopwood*, as well as a series of publications, as for example D.J. Cooper (1983), Hopper and Powell (1985). Many of these authors followed the work of European sociologists, social philosophers, constructionists and deconstructionists. This branch is occasionally more oriented towards managerial accounting than the behavioural research discussed above, and relies on different assumptions (see Chua 1986) than the related areas mentioned under item 1 or even under item 3. Some of the pertinent papers were critical and emphasized the 'ritualistic significance' of much of accounting. Among the major books of this trend is the

anthology by Cooper *et al.* (1983), *Management accounting research and practice*, and the book by Macintosh (2002), *Accounting, accountants and accountability: poststructuralist positions*. Some interesting papers in this area are: Hopwood's (1987: 230) 'The archaeology of accounting systems', which examined changes of accounting systems during the last 150 years or so, and the preconditions for such changes by 'sorting through the sediments of organizational history (however recent) to reconstruct the ways in which the present emerged from the past'. A special version of interpretive organizational accounting by Roberts and Scapens (1985), under the title 'Accounting systems and systems of accountability', laid special emphasis on the interdependence between a system and its structure. A related direction, under the title of 'social constructionism' (cf. Lukka 1988), seems to deny the existence of any reality beyond our mental and social constructions.

The leading and most prominent personality of this general trend has been Anthony G. Hopwood. Not only as an original thinker, but also as founder and enduring editor of the journal *Accounting, Organizations, and Society*, and a co-creator of the *European Accounting Review* and other organizations, he has been characterized by Richard in Colasse's classic, *Les grand auteurs en comptabilité*, as follows:

> Educated at [the university of] Chicago, he revealed himself paradoxically as a pioneer in social, organizational and behavioural research of accounting practice and theory. Eminently British, he has been a determined and persistent builder of institutions supporting European accounting researchers.
>
> (Richard 2005: 268, translated)

(3) Critical radicalism (critical perspective): To this sub-area belongs a relatively small group of vociferous accountants of the Marxian tradition. Representatives publications of this trend are those by Tinker *et al.* (1982), Tinker (1984), Tinker's book (1985) *Paper prophets: a social critique of accounting*, Chua (1986) and possibly Lowe *et al.* (1983), as well as Hopper *et al.* (1987) and Puxty *et al.* (1987). Their philosophic basis is to be found primarily in Habermas, Marcuse and other Marxist writers. For the basic epistemic and ontological premises of this camp, and the other two modern organizational theories, see the pertinent tables presented in Chua (1986).

Those authors hold the view that accounting is *not* a neutral or passive but an active instrument involved in social class conflict. They see accounting research as a social critique, emphasizing the inseparability of social, economic and political interest. Chua, however, admitted that, in using such an approach, it still is debatable what does and does not constitute an acceptable theory or explanation. The major author of this radical direction, Tony Tinker, has also been profiled (by Chabrak 2005) in Colasse's *Les grand auteurs en comptabilité*.

Although the critical-interpretive perspective may be the most prominent British contribution to modern accounting research and methodology, it is by no means the only one. Beattie, in discussing recent UK contributions to financial accounting research, makes the following remarks:

> While most research is seen to follow the highly quantitative, economics-based US tradition, a significant amount of UK research adopts a more qualitative approach, and distinctive UK contributions are evident in a number of areas (in particular, the disclosure process, and corporate social reporting). There are signs that UK researchers are helping researchers in other countries contribute to the global body of scholarly knowledge.
>
> (Beattie 2005: 85)

12.5.6 Revived interest in the axiomatic-postulational approach, accounting standards and valuation issues

Although the 1980s were dominated by empirical and positive accounting theory, this period too brought forth a series of contributions to accounting axiomatization (though again on the side-lines). There was Carlson and Lamb (1981), who employed first-order predicate logic (instead of set theory) to accounting, Deguchi and Nakano (1986) from Japan and Avilà *et al.* (1988) in Argentine. From the English language area there was De Pree (1989), concerned with the conceptual framework and Willett (1985, 1987, 1988), who emphasized the distinction between 'measurement' (for *decision making*) vs. 'disclosure' (for *stewardship*) of accounting information. Furthermore, there was a dissertation by Nehmer (1988) that addressed accounting information systems as an algebraic system as well as a system of first order formulas (this dissertation uses 'model theory' and presents a comparison with 'organizational communication theory'). Ijiri (1989: 104–6 – see above) too contains three postulates (reconciliation, conservation and attribution of momentum). In a special way Anthony's (1985) *Reference guide to essentials of accounting* also belongs to the postulational literature. A different and 'linguistic' approach can be found in Tanaka (1982, in English). As to measurement issues, they too were resumed in the 1980s (e.g. Bromwich and Wells 1983; Staubus 1985).

Perhaps surprisingly, axiomatic interests continued even in the 1990s: for example, Herde (1992, in German) evaluated and analysed various axiomatic systems (i.e. those by Carlson and Lamb 1981; Willett 1987, 1988; Balzer and Mattessich 1991). Herde converts each of those three attempts into a logic of higher order (i.e. formalizing the *object-language*, where one argues about the *scientific* objects as well as the *meta-language*, in which the *logical* objects and the pertinent 'object-language' are formulated). Such an approach facilitated a *comparison* of those three axiomatic models. Further 'axiomatic papers' were those by Gutiérrez (1990, 1992) and Gutiérrez and Whittington (1997), as well as a note (in Portuguese) on the axiomatization of accounting by the Brazilian academic Lopes de Sá (1995). Finally, the paper by Balzer and Mattessich (2000) summarized most of the attempts of accounting axiomatization and ventured into further refinements and formalizations based on epistemic structuralism (a philosophic trend originating with Joseph Sneed and greatly extended and elaborated by such philosophers as Stegmüller, Balzer and others – for details, see Mattessich 1995: 126–33).

Discussion and research on *accounting standards and principles* continued into the 1990s – not merely by professional accounting bodies, and not only on the American continent (e.g. Vangermeersch 1981; Wyatt 1988: Hill and Ingram 1989) or in the UK (Whittington 1989) – but also in Europe. For Germany, see Ballwieser and Kuhner (1994) and Baetge *et al.* (1995), both in English; for other countries, see pertinent chapters.

Research on *valuation problems* were revived. They found response in actual practice, often under the term 'mark-to-market accounting', or by pleading directly for exit-values, as in Cheung (1990). Some industries, particularly banking and the financial sector in general, felt the need to supplement or substitute (under certain circumstances and for specific assets) the traditional 'acquisition costs' by the more relevant 'market value' (e.g. Beaver and Wolfson 1992; Hempel and Simonson 1992; Morris 1992; Marker 1995), usually in collaboration with other authors (e.g. Barth *et al.* 1992, 1998) virtually made a whole career out of this mark-to-market approach in combination with the discussion of disclosure and problems on hedging and risk-adjustment, as also contained in various publications by the FASB (e.g. 1994, 1997). Of special interest in this connection is the practical experience of Denmark that introduced some kind of mark-to-market legislation for financial institutions. Bernard *et al.* (1995) studied this situation and found that in Denmark the mark-to-market accounting generated value numbers more reliable than the traditional historical cost figures. Furthermore, the notion of 'value added' has also gained increasing importance (cf. Belkaoui 1999).

In the new millennium, the debate about accounting standards continues. There is, for example, an interesting paper by Schipper (2003), examining to what extent US-GAAP are based on principles derived from the FASB's *Conceptual Framework*, and to what extent they are 'rule-based'. Also, there was the attempt by the FASB, in its 'Proposal for a principles-based approach to US standard setting' (http://www.fasb.org), to tighten its conceptual framework (for a comparison with Germany, see subsection 4.2.6).

12.5.7 Crisis and renaissance of management accounting

During preceding decades the influence of finance theory strongly promoted research in financial accounting and auditing, while other areas, like managerial accounting, were somewhat neglected. Busse von Colbe (1996: 422) even speaks of 'stagnation' in management accounting with regard to the German literature. Nevertheless, in America, interest in the analytical aspects of management accounting research never ceased during the 1970s. But there, new attention was paid during this time to the more practical aspects of managerial accounting (cf. Holzer 1980; Kaplan 1983; Kaplan and Atkinson 1989). This area received a particular boost after publication of Johnson and Kaplan's (1987) *Relevance lost: the rise and fall of management accounting.* Anthony (1975), Kaplan (1978) and Hayes (1983) foreshadowed some of those ideas. Other publications followed in a similar vein (e.g. Ferris and Livingstone 1987; Antle and Demski 1988; Foster and Horngren 1988; Magee 1988). It seemed, the time was ripe to reassess this area. This was done by a series of relevant, sometimes award-winning, publications (e.g. Hayes 1983; Tiessen and Waterhouse 1983; Armitage 1985; Bromwich and Hopwood 1986; Atkinson 1987a, 1987b; Bruns and Kaplan 1987; Ferris and Livingstone 1987; Staubus 1987).

This 'renaissance' of managerial accounting brought forth new concepts and revived old notions, such as 'strategic cost management', 'activity accounting', etc. In some instances, tried to combine financial management and investment theory with management accounting (e.g. Banerjee 1984; Küpper 1985), or generated a series of progressive (sometimes more or less revised) texts or reference works: e.g. Mepham (1980), Magee (1986), Balachandran *et al.* (1987), Bruns and Kaplan (1987), Kaplan and Atkinson (1989), Cooper and Kaplan (1991), Anthony *et al.* (1992), Shank and Govindarajan (1993), Horngren *et al.* (1994), Bhimani (1996), Schoenfeld (1992), Noreen and Burgstahler (1997), as well as the survey article on 'New directions in management accounting research' by Atkinson *et al.* (1997).

Occasionally this research brought about a surprising shift in methodology, namely a *revival or revision of the case method* (cf. Smith *et al.* 1988), originally pioneered by the Harvard Business School. One hoped this new version, called the 'clinical and field-based research', would help in overcoming the loss of relevance, and improve industrial productivity – at least in the short run. Analytical and behavioural-statistical research might then find long-run solutions. Yet, whether clinical or non-clinical, the new trend of management accounting aimed at replacing traditional overhead allocation procedures (e.g. the direct labour basis) by new ones (e.g. set-up times). Why, for instance, do industrial giants, such as the Siemens Co., abandon separate cost accounting systems in favour of integrating them into (or even reducing them to) financial accounting (see Pfaff 1994; Ziegler 1994)?

Towards the end of the 1990s, Foster and Young (1997: 63) asserted that in 'the last 10 years, management accounting research has made dramatic strides in relevance and vigour'. This optimism seems to be justified when looking at the research *input*. Consider, for example, the development of activity-based costing (ABC) and its spin-off, activity-based cost management (ABCM), as well as various success measures (see Foster and Swenson 1997; Ittner *et al.* 1997; Hicks 1999). ABC tries to select the most relevant cost allocation basis (often multi-bases) for different cost drivers;[7] it has received much attention for its ability to explain cost behaviour of non-volume-related activities.[8] However, the optimism may not necessarily be justified when looking at the *output* or *practical results* in general. Indeed, Foster and Young express the following concerns:

Much of the management accounting literature (broadly defined) concerns proposals for new costing systems, new performance evaluation systems, new budget systems and so on. Typically, it is argued that the proposed systems are *better* than existing systems. What is strikingly absent from the research literature is any systematic analysis of what *better* means, how better should be measured, and what challenges are encountered in making these measures ... . The MAR literature does not have agreed standards regarding how to document whether (say) an ABC system is better than a traditional system. Indeed, many management accounting disputes appear to continue *ad nauseam* over many decades. Consider the long-standing argument whether variable or full absorption costing is superior.

(Foster and Young 1997: 75–6)

Such thoughts may reinforce the plea for a better research focus on specific purposes and the means–end relations. The idea of controlling cost as far 'upstream' as possible and to juxtapose the curve of 'committed costs' to that of 'actual expenses' goes back to Blanchard (1978). Other innovative ideas of the ABC variety derived from a paper by Berliner and Brimson (1986) and subsequently dispersed under the abbreviation of CAM-I (for 'Computer Advanced Manufacturing International' a consulting consortium of the same name). Pierre Mévellec, in his award-winning paper, makes the following statement:

The CAM-I model presented in 1986 as the result of one of its working parties, was the synthesis of several of the most innovative practices in use in North American companies ... . Their recommendation concerned a new information system which would take into account all information, financial as well as non-financial, necessary for making operational and strategic decisions. Such a system would be built on four key concepts: continuous improvement, characterization of the enterprise as a network of activities, benchmarking, and improvement in traceability of costs relative to management objectives ... . Although never stated as such in the CAM-I model, its real aim is to change the way the operation of an enterprise is viewed and to identify the necessary evolution of management techniques which derive from such a change. Such new techniques would inevitably require a new approach to cost calculation.

(Mévellec 1993, quoted from the English translation by Michael Adler: 4–5)

Related ideas of reforming management accounting emerged during the last two decades of the twentieth century: for example, the Japanese 'target costing' (Sakurai 1989; Ansari *et al.* 1997), the 'functional analysis method' (Yoshikawa *et al.* 1989), 'strategic cost management' or SCM (Shank and Govindarajan 1993), and 'product life cycle costing' or PLC (Czyzewski and Hull 1991) and its further extensions (cf. Norman and Ramirez 1993; Porter 1996). Apart from such innovations, the 'balanced score-card', promoted by Kaplan and Norton (1992), has become a crucial and internationally praised tool for systematically examining the organizational conditions (and weaknesses) of the production process of firms.

But management accounting also continued to deal with traditional topics such as *transfer pricing* (e.g. Manes and Verrecchia 1981–82; Swieringa and Waterhouse 1982; Eccles 1985; Amershi and Cheng 1990), and cost–volume relations under uncertainty (Kim and Ibrahim 1997), as well as the relation to organization theory. Furthermore, several researchers, endeavouring to apply information economics and agency theory to accounting, have shown considerable interest in management accounting (for an overview, see Namazi 1985). Yet most of this research was based on highly simplified and unrealistic assumptions; though rigorous and theoretically valuable, this kind of research seems to be predominantly of academic interest.[9] Another deficiency of MAR, as pointed out by Foster and Young (1997: 76), is that none of its recent papers concern the function of managerial accounting either under globalization or in start-up companies – two important but risky areas to investigate.

12.5.8 Publications on accounting history in the 1980s and 1990s

Another area, which gathered renewed interest during this period, was *accounting history*. Apart from the many papers in various journals of accounting history and such earlier historical books as those by Chatfield (1978), Previts and Merino (1979) and Previts (1980), there is, for example, the posthumous English book by Kojima (1995) on *Accounting history*, and that by Someya (1996) on *Japanese accounting: a historical approach*; or Walton (1995), as well as Fleischman and Tyson (1993) on cost accounting during the industrial revolution. Primary archival studies seem to have found special favour (cf. Brown *et al.* 1989). Furthermore, there are innumerable papers in various historical accounting journals such as *The Accounting Historians Journal* (founded in 1974 by the Academy of Accounting Historians, which greatly improved its image during the 1980s) and other historical journals, like *Accounting, Business and Financial History* (UK) and *Accounting History* (Australia and New Zealand). Finally, World Conferences of Accounting Historians (held every four years, changed to every two years in the new century) increased in popularity, and a host of historical books on different accounting aspects are occasionally published by Routledge, London, and by Garland Publishing, Inc., New York. One of those earlier publications was by Gaffikin and Aitken (1982), *The development of accounting theory: significant contributors to accounting thought in the twentieth century*, another was the paper by Brief (1987) on corporate financial reporting at the turn of the century. Gaffikin and Aitken (1982) dealt only with English-language accounting literature, but Edwards' (1994) *Twentieth century accounting thinkers* discussed accounting literature on a broader, international level. It contains 19 chapters with numerous personal and research profiles about authors of English as well as of foreign tongues. The same holds for Chatfield and Vangermeersch (1996), the award-winning book *The history of accounting: an international encyclopedia*. For another historical antholog, see T.A. Lee (1990), *The closure of the accounting profession* (two volumes), and some memoirs on foundational accounting research by Mattessich (1995/2007). A further pertinent historical work is the four volume anthology *A history of accounting: critical perspectives on business and management*, compiled and edited by Edwards (2000) as well as the three volumes of *Accounting History*, edited by Fleischman (2005).

In a more specialized vein, are historical books such as Zeff (1982a), *The accounting postulates and principles controversy of the 1960s*; Klemstine and Maher (1983), *Management accounting research: 1926–1983*; Kinney (1986), *Fifty years of statistical auditing*; Moonitz (1986), *History of accounting at Berkeley*; Yamey (1989), *Art and accounting*; Dean and Clarke (1990), *Replacement costs and accounting reform in post World War I Germany*; Graves (1991), *The costing heritage: studies in honour of S. Paul Garner*; Flesher (1991), *The third-quarter century of the American Accounting Association, 1966–1991*; Zeff (1991), *The American Accounting Association – Its first 50 years 1916–1966*; Murphy (1993), *A history of Canadian accounting thought and practice*; and Bedford (1997), *A history of accountancy at the University of Illinois at Urbana-Champaign*.

Among the pertinent papers, we might mention: Clarke (1980), Galassi (1980), Murphy (1980), Zeff (1982b), Dyckman and Zeff (1984), Brief (1987), Edwards (1987), Clarke and Dean (1990, 1996); Sundem (1987), Burgstahler and Sundem (1989), Falk (1989), Mouck (1989), Sundem *et al.* (1990), Schneider (1992), Yamey (1994), Zan (1994), Hernández Esteve (1995) and Horngren (1995). One might mention the University of South Africa's 'Reader' compiled by Saenger (1992), and for a concise survey of different methodologies of accounting history, the paper by Luft (1997).

Attention has also been paid to the *archaeology of accounting*; for example, in a series of publications by the archaeologist Schmandt-Besserat (e.g. 1977, 1978, 1992). This research disclosed overwhelming evidence that accounting with clay tokens developed from 8000 BC to 300 BC in the Middle East. This *token accounting* did not merely precede writing and 'abstract counting', it gave the major impetus to those crucial cultural achievements. For the subsequent development of archaic accounting in the third millennium BC, see Nissen *et al.* (1993). As to the history of Chinese accounting, contributions can be found in Lin (1992) and Guo (1996). Furthermore, Bhattacharyya (1988) submitted evidence that the modern distinction between operating income and holding gains (due to price-level changes) may be traced back to the ancient Indian treatise of *Arthaśāstra* by Kautilya (*c.* 300 BC). In this connection it should be pointed out that it may have been an accounting idea which promoted the acceptance of *negative numbers*. Indeed, the first known use of negative numbers in mathematics has been found by Brahmagupta (AD 628) whose early Indian commentators argued that debts (liabilities) are negative assets, thus offering their first justification for the usefulness of negative numbers on *realistic* grounds (see Colebrooke 1817/1973: 131, footnote 2, 132, footnote 3). Several of these developments are being discussed and interpreted in Mattessich (2000), *The beginnings of accounting and accounting thought: accounting practice in the*

Middle-East (8000 BC to 2000 BC) and accounting thought in India (c.300 BC and the Middle Ages).

12.6 The best-selling spreadsheet programs for the personal computer

From a purely practical point of view, one of the most significant events of the 1980s may have been the introduction of *spreadsheet-simulation for the personal computer* (PC). Such budgeting and financial practices were originally handled 'manually', later by mainframe computers and ultimately through ready-made programmes for personal computers. The electronic spreadsheet has its roots in Mattessich (1961, 1964a, 1964b) – for details, see Mattessich and Galassi (2000). Those publications of the 1960s were not only the first to use accounting matrices (spreadsheets) for simulating financial events but, more importantly, they represented entries by algebraic formulas (not merely by individual numbers) and exploited the interdependence of individual accounting entries. In the 1980s this approach received an immense boost through the development of personal computers and the concomitant use of such best-selling spreadsheet programs as *Visi-Calc* and *Super-Calc* and, later, various versions of *Lotus 1–2–3* and Microsoft's *Excel*. Other computer and systems-related accounting literature can be found in Benbasat and Dexter (1979), McCarthy (1979, 1982), Babad and Balachandran (1989) and Wand and Weber (1989); and the relation between accounting (including auditing) and artificial intelligence is investigated in Vasarhelyi (1989).

12.7 Tax accounting, international accounting, governmental accounting and some specialized areas

Finally, some areas we mention only fleetingly. Tax accounting, still occupied with issues of deferrals and certain allocation problems as reflected foremost in professional publications such as the *Journal of Accountancy*, *The Journal of the American Taxation Association* and the annual issues of *Advances in Taxation.* Furthermore, there are pertinent papers by Davidson and Weil (1978), one paper on deferred tax credits by Davidson *et al.* (1984), other papers by Robbins and Swyers (1984), Stepp (1985) or Sommerfeld and Easton (1987). Finally, there are the books by Sinning (1986), Scholes and Wolfson (1992) and Thornton (1993).

Of further prominence became comparative international taxation issues (e.g. Kirkham and Loft 1993; Fogarty 1997) and studies on the impact which different cultural attitudes have on accounting and its standards (e.g. Gray and Vint 1995). As to the importance of Segment Statements in modern accounting, Ijiri (1995 and 1996) draws attention to it; and for divisional performance evaluation, see Kelly (1997).

Another sub-area, here pretty much neglected, is governmental and municipal accounting (including its auditing); for recent publications see: Beedle (1981), Baber (1983), Berry and Harwood (1984), Ives (1987), Dittenhofer (1988) and

Lapsley (1988). Or the related area of non-profit institutions as, for example, Amernic's (1989) publication on *Accounting and collective bargaining in the not-for-profit sector.*

International accounting became especially prominent during this period due to the continuing growth and globalization of capital markets (cf. Cooper *et al.* 1998). Mueller (1963) has been a major pioneer in international accounting, and research standards have greatly expanded, as testified by the books by Most (1984), Choi and Mueller (1984, 1985), Belkaoui (1985b, 1988) and Afterman (1995). More specialized anthologies are those by Nobes and Parker (1981), Gray (1983) and Holzer (1984), or papers like Daley and Mueller (1982) on accounting in world politics.

As to the harmonization of EEC countries and internationalization in general, the literature is more concentrated in Europe, as for example in the English papers by Busse von Colbe and Pohlmann (1981), Hopwood and Schreuder (1984) and Macharzina (1988). In comparing Continental European financial accounting with that in the UK and the USA, it has to be taken into consideration that in Continental Europe, particularly in Germany, the financial statements are used (apart from debtor protection and taxation basis) foremost to determine distributable profits (Moxter 1982, 1984) – in contrast to the countries of English tongue, where the focus is more on meaningful information to shareholders and creditors. For an English comparison of accounting practice in the USA vs. Korea vs. Japan, see Kim and Song (1990). A more general comparison, from the viewpoint of Italy, is offered in Viganò (1994); or Cooke and Kikuya (1992) in *Financial Reporting in Japan.* For the effects of different generally accepted accounting principles (GAAP) in the USA vs. Canada, see Bandyopadhyay *et al.* (1994) or on comparative disclosure practices between the USA and the UK, see Frost and Pownall (1994). On the implications of alternative general accepted standards, see Murphy (1987); and on the setting of international accounting standards, see Gorelik (1994). Publications in this field span a wide gamut, and the monograph by Scott and Troberg (1980) facilitates the survey by distinguishing seven categories of pertinent subjects: (1) exchange rates and translations, (2) accounting standards, (3) auditing, (4) inflation accounting, (5) performance evaluation, (6) information control systems and (7) taxation.

Other books on international accounting are: Enthoven (1977), Samuels and Piper (1985), some books by Belkaoui (e.g. 1985a, 1988, 1989) and a monograph by Most (1984), all offering a wide spectrum of major topics in international accounting. For a survey paper, see Bindon and Gernon (1987); for an annotated bibliography (from 1972 to 1981), see Agami and Kollaritsch (1983); and for national differences in consolidation accounting, see Parker (1984). Special area of *international auditing* and its standards are dealt with by Moonitz and Stamp (1978), as well as in the anthologies by Campbell (1985) and Needles (1985). As far as international standards for government accounting and their future are concerned, see also, Enthoven (1988).

Oil and Gas Accounting has made great strides in the 1980s, and continues to challenge the historical cost method as well as other traditional standards: see

Dhaliwal (1980), Collins *et al.* (1981), Collins *et al.* (1982), Lilien and Pastena (1982), Larcker and Revsine (1983), Dharan (1984), Lys (1984), Butterworth and Falk (1986) and Magliolo (1986) – also in respect of tax problems (e.g. Wolfson 1985) – and many publications in the *Journal of Petroleum Accounting*.

Pension accounting has gained attention during this decade and representative contributions can be found in Skinner (1980), Schipper and Weil (1982), Pesando and Clarke (1983), Daley (1984), Landsman (1986), Francis and Reiter (1987), Kemp (1987) and others, as well as in the survey article by Stone (1982).

Research in the important area of environmental and socio-economic accounting is still insufficiently developed, but such publications as Belkaoui (1984) and Koguchi (1990), and more recently Epstein (1996), Abdolmohammadi *et al.* (1997), Gordon and Loeb (1997a), Yu *et al.* (1997) and Parker (1998) offer important insights and references to this literature. As an afterthought, the reader may be reminded that in 1984 an economist, Richard Stone (e.g. 1986), turned 'social accountant', was awarded the Nobel Memorial Prize. This might be of particular significance to those who regard national income accounting and other social accounting aspects as belonging to accounting.

Even more underdeveloped is the area of *expert systems* for accounting and auditing purposes – see, Abdolmohammadi (1987), Borthick and West (1987), Connell (1987) and Thierauf (1990), which offer an overview of applications during the 1980s. As to the use of expert systems for tax shelter and estate planning, see Michaelsen (1987, 1988); and as to the relation of expert systems to the problem of materiality, see Steinbart (1987); for information technologies in general, see Simon (1990). As far as 'gender issues' in accounting are concerned, there is, for example, the paper by Fogarty (1997) as well as the section 'Gender issues – work life balance' of the American Accounting Association.

Finally, research in accounting education ought to be mentioned. Typical publications in this area are: Amernic and Beechy (1984), Anderson and Previts (1984), Reider and Saunders (1988), Williams *et al.* (1988), Schultz (1989), Sundem *et al.* (1990), Banerjee (1994) and Gainen and Locatelli (1995). Furthermore, there are several specialized journals: *Accounting Educator's Journal, Accounting Education, Issues in Accounting Education, International Journal of Accounting Education and Research*, and the *Journal of Accounting Education*. Finally, recent anthologies, such as Burns and Needles (1994) and Gibbins (1994), reflect the increasing concern with the educational aspects of accounting.

13 Accounting research in Finland, the Netherlands and the Scandinavian countries during the entire twentieth century[1]

13.1 Accounting research in Finland

13.1.1 Early reputation of Finnish research and accounting education

Finland has a formidable accounting tradition, and for a relatively small country, its scholars have manifested a remarkable interest and activity in accounting research. Apart from the text on single-entry bookkeeping by Lilius (1862 – the first Finnish textbook on bookkeeping), there was another nineteenth-century personality who exercised considerable influence – even on an international level. It was the renowned Finnish scholar Kovero [1877–?], who published not only in Finnish (e.g. Kovero 1905, 1907–16, 1910, 1911b, 1926, 1931, 1932, 1935) but also prominently in German (1911a, 1938) as well as in English (1933, 1959).[2] His publications on replacement valuation and non-realized gains, as well as on the relation between valuation and taxation, respectively (Kovero 1911a), particularly drew wide attention in some countries (e.g. Japan and Germany) but has been neglected in the Anglophone literature.[3] This outstanding pioneering work is more than a mere forerunner of Limperg's as well as Schmidt's versions of *current replacement value* accounting (cf. our sections 2.4.3 and 12.2, as well as note 2 of the Introduction).

In the wake of Finland's beginning industrialization (1860–1917) several business schools emerged. First, a business school (teaching in Finnish as well as Swedish) in Oulu, later the Commercial College of the Association of Finnish Businessmen (1898), and the Higher Swedish Commercial School (1909, later converted to university level under the name of the Swedish School of Economics, now in Helsinki and Vaasa). Although the Imperial Alexander University of Helsinki taught bookkeeping already in the 1870s, the first university accounting education started in Finland with the founding of the Helsinki School of Economics in 1911. Later, in 1927, the Turku School of Economics and the Helsinki Swedish School of Economics, as well as the Academy of Economics-Åbo (or 'Turku' in Finnish), all became prominent in accounting and business education. After the Second World War, further higher business schools were established: the Turku School of Economics in 1950, and the Vaasa School of economics (now University of Vaasa). Furthermore, both the University of Tampere and the University of Jyväskylä maintain departments of business studies.

Lukka *et al.* (1984: 17–18) points out that during the period from 1911 to 1938 the major influence came from Germany, not least due to the fact that Kovero studied in Germany and published his doctoral dissertation in Berlin (though it was defended at the Alexander University in Helsinki). Other prominent accounting publications influenced by German research were those by I.V. Kaitilia (1921a), Brommels (1928) and Nurmilhati (1937). As S. Näsi and J. Näsi (1997: 203) point out: the initial course literature for accounting was mostly German, with names such as Calmes, Lehmann, Penndorf, Schmalenbach, Schubitz, Tremponau, though the influence of English literature did already play some role in Finnish accounting during the first half of the century. I.V. Kaitilia (1921a, 1921b, 1928, 1940), though still influenced by German authors, became well known as an author of a series of prominent accounting texts (from bookkeeping and financial accounting to cost accounting). The German influence manifested itself also through the adoption of the *portemanteau* discipline of 'business economics' (in Swedish *företagseconomi*, similar to the German *Betriebswirtschaftslehre*).

It is interesting to note that most of the early Finnish accounting research was manifested in doctoral dissertations: e.g. Kovero (1911a), I.V. Kaitilia (1921a), Brommels (1928), Nurmiahti (1937), Virkkunen (1951), Jägerhorn (1965), Jaaskeläinen (1966), K. Virtanen (1979), etc. This fact may also speak for the relatively high standards of Finnish doctoral students and their investigations in such areas as financial accounting and its statements, balance sheet valuation and depreciation problems, all with a predominantly practical slant. Factory accounting trailed behind in importance, and cost accounting seems to have taken off only in the 1940s. Indeed, the majority of truly academic research came to the fore after the Second World War, beginning with the work of Virkkunen (1951, 1954, 1961).

13.1.2 The second generation of Finnish scholars and the German influence

Later on Saario (1945, 1949, 1959, 1965) pursued a Finnish tradition by shifting his interest from the balance sheet to the income statement as the actual dynamic element (partly manifesting Schmalenbach's influence, partly reacting to it). Saario's main goals were two. On one side, Saario relates depreciation to realized income (defending the principles of matching and realization) and, on the other side, he reflected the monetary flow in accounting. The latter feature still forms the legalistic and academic basis of Finnish accountancy – though towards the end of the century, the trend towards European accounting harmonization conflicted with some of Saario's ideas. He also envisaged a 'priority ranking' in which depreciation and profit distribution are the *last* items to be charged against revenues.

In the second half of the century, Artto (1968) applied Saario's 'model of priority costs' to finance theory and its systematization, and later examined cash-flows and profitability of Finnish enterprises; he also compared the financing of profit distribution in various industries. In the late 1960s and the 1970s Lethovouri (1969, 1972) continued Saario's research and laid the foundations of modern Finnish accounting theory (cf. Lukka *et al.* 1984: 19).

Apart from Saario's (1945) dissertation on income measurement and depreciation, there were other prominent accounting scholars of the 'second generation' that continued to create pioneering works through their doctoral research. Apart from Grandell's (1944) historical exploration (see subsection 13.13), the most important publications were E. Kaitila's (1940, 1945) studies on cost accounting and his theoretical analysis on cost–volume ratios, respectively, and U. Virtanen's (1949) thesis on the costs structure of Finnish industry. After the Second World War, Virtanen (1959) concerned himself with behavioural accounting issues and emphasized the need for business ethics – then, hardly a particularly popular theme.

Virkkunen's (1954) text on management accounting became another highly influential work that promoted accounting as a tool in the service of Finnish management, its planning, control and information requirements. As in the English-speaking world, Finnish business demanded growth, diversification and better control over productivity and a better future orientation. Other important work in cost and managerial accounting was previously produced by Kaitila (1940), Saario (1949), Virtanen (1949) and Virkkunen (1951) himself. Especially Saario's notion that costs are not proportionally to be covered by revenues, but rather in an 'ideal' *priority order*, influenced Finnish accounting significantly. This idea combined the priority expressed in the LIFO principle with the view that the 'smaller the number of products, the higher the priority order of the cost' (Lukka *et al.* 1984: 18).

13.1.3 Later generations of Finnish scholars and international orientation

Another prominent Finnish accountant and finance expert is Jaakko Honko (1955, 1959, 1963); he mainly focused on investment problems (including investment planning) and applied the present value approach to accounting valuation and income determination. Lukka *et al.* (1984: 18) points out that 'One of the most important aspects of his [Honko's] study is the idea that accumulated residual annual income can be considered a contribution to cover expenditure on fixed assets and profit distribution, thus avoiding the depreciation problem'. Some of Honko's studies were considered pioneering efforts and became prominent beyond Finland.

From the 1960s onwards, the international influence on Finnish accounting research began to make itself felt, as manifested in Jägerhorn's (1965) study on the information content of Finnish annual reports. Although this publication emphasized auditing and empirical aspects, it might have been a *precursor* to the first

American accounting study in the information area (e.g. G.A. Feltham's doctoral dissertation on *A Theoretical Framework for Evaluating Changes in Accounting Information for Managerial Decisions*, Berkeley, 1967 – see Chapter 19).

Other studies were those by Kettunen (1974) on the profitability of Finnish firms, and on the application of mathematical methods to planning by Jääskeläinen (1966), to taxation by Meyer (1971), to growth and productivity models by Ruuhela (1972), as well as to the *simultaneous planning* of investment, production and marketing suggested by Lindström (1972). During the inflationary times of the later half of the 1970s and early 1980s, a series of studies appeared concerning inflation adjustments and related measurement problems, for example: Riistama (1971, 1978), Jägerhorn (1975) and Aho (1981a, 1981b). Furthermore, in Lehtovuori (1973) and Kettunen (1974, 1980) methodological problems and discussions of the scientific aspects of accounting became more prominent.

According to Näsi and Näsi (1997), Finnish academics distinguished between various methodological alternatives. The first one, the 'conceptual' approach (possibly corresponding in Anglo-American literature to the 'analytical-philosophic' approach in a wide sense) was represented in the area of financial accounting by Pihlanto (1978), Majala (1974, 1987, 1992) and Näsi (1980a, 1980b, 1981). While in the area of management accounting this approach was chosen by Virtanen (1979) and Vehmanen (1992, 1994).

The other methodology was the so-called 'nomothetical' (or 'positive-empirical') approach. It still is predominant in Finland, and its early authors were Prihti (1975), Majala (1987, 1992), Neilimo (1975), Tamminen (1976, 1992, 1993), Laitinen (1980), Mäkinen (1980), Neilimo and Näsi (1980) and others in financial accounting and accounting theory, as well as Lehtonen (1976) and Mäkinen (1976) in management accounting.

The third methodology, the 'decision-oriented' approach (corresponding, more or less, to the 'decision-usefulness' approach in America) was pursued in financial accounting by Salmi (1975) and Riistama (1978), and in management accounting by Wallenius (1975), Reponen (1977) and Wallin (1978).

Finally, the fourth methodology, the 'action-oriented' approach (related to the 'critical-interpretive' approach of Great Britain) – represented by Philanto (1978, 1988a, 1988b, 1992, 1994), possibly Majala (1982), Lukka (1991) and others – seems to have been the fastest growing methodology during the 1990s. It became particularly popular among the younger generation. This last direction emphasized philosophical aspects (e.g. the leaning of Lukka 1990, towards the *social constructivist* point of view, asserting that all reality is but a human construct – for details to a similar view from Macintosh and others, see Mattessich 2003: 447, note 7). Finnish accounting researchers seem to have special appreciation of philosophical reflections and sociological accounting studies. Here, the following publications may be mentioned: Neilimo's (1981) and, above all, Majala's (1982) study on corporate *social accounting*; Näsi's (1995) and Niskala and Näsi's (1995) discussions of the 'stakeholder theory' (taking not only shareholders but many other parties or 'stakeholders' into consideration – a topic particular popular in Europe); studies in public administration, as those in Kovero (1959) and Pitkänen (1969); ethical issues by Virtanen (1959) and Brunsson (1981); and the illumination of cybernetic aspects of accounting as a control and information system in Paasio (1981). Finally, the reader will find a series of Finnish *financial* (price-earnings and related) studies, in the *European Accounting Review* of the late 1990s.

13.1.4 Historical accounting research in Finland

Finnish scholars invested a considerable amount of energy in historical accounting research. Typical examples are: Grandell's (1944) study on older accounting models in Finland; Virrankoski (1975) on Finnish economic history; Salmi (1976, 1978), reviewing Finnish accounting and business dissertations (see also Näsi *et al.* 1993), and the selection of subjects, respectively; Rasila (1982) on Finnish economic history and industrialization; Tainio *et al.* (1982) on an historical review of Finnish business economics; Kettunen's (1984, 1986) two probes into the origin and development of Finnish business research; Lukka *et al.* (1984) on accounting research in Finland; Näsi and Näsi (1985, 1997) on accounting research in Finland from the 1940s onwards (as reflected in doctoral dissertations), and on the Finnish accounting and business economics tradition, respectively; Näsi (1990) on the development of accounting thought from the middle of the last century to the end of the 1980s; Pihlanto and Lukka (1993) on Martti Saario and his legacy. Among later historically oriented Finnish accounting studies one might mention Näsi's (1990, 1994) examination of the development in accounting thought (from the 1850s to end of the 1980s), and his study on the evolution of cost accounting in Finland (from the 1800s to the 1960s).

13.1.5 Cost and managerial accounting in Finland

Among the more recent textbooks on management accounting there is, above all, Riistama and Jyrkkiö (1970) that attained over a dozens editions. Alaluusua (1982) and Lukka (1988) examined budgeting issues. During the 1990s, a series of interesting cost studies came forth from Finland: Kasanan *et al.* (1991, with an English version in 1993), presenting a 'constructive approach' to management accounting research; Lumijärvi (1993a, 1993b) a book and paper discussing activity-based costing and management in Finland; the book by Kasanen and Malmi (1994) comparing traditional cost accounting with activity-based costing; Granlund (1994) examining the relation between management accounting and the corporate crisis; and Virtanen *et al.* (1996) studying the 'drivers' of cost accounting in Finland. Above all, there is Lukka and Granlund's (1996) examination of Finnish cost accounting practices that confirmed such trends as the decreasing proportion of labour costs, changing strategies and operating environment, but continuing problems with cost allocation. It also revealed that new cost accounting methods were less frequently applied than expected – and this despite increasing interest in activity-based costing or the fact that Finnish industry kept fairly up-to-date and is worthy of an advanced industrial country.

13.2 Accounting research in the Netherlands[4]

13.2.1 Early developments in the Netherlands

Accounting research in the Netherlands is closely tied to the name of Theodore Limperg [1879–1961] who was Professor of Accounting at the University of Amsterdam (from 1922 to 1949) and has not only been the father of Dutch accounting (particularly a version of replacement value accounting) but also of its *bedrijfseconomie* (business economics).[5] The latter, though related to the German *Betriebswirtschaftslehre*, does not imply a dependence on German research. On the contrary, the accounting scholars of the Netherlands were always anxious to stress and maintain their independence from their western neighbour. Particularly in *current value* (replacement cost) accounting, where Limperg (1917, 1918) may have been a step ahead of the Germans when he outlined his theory of replacement value (in a couple of papers). He did this a few years before Fritz Schmidt (1921 – see our subsection 2.4.3) presented a book with a fairly well developed theory of replacement value. Limperg (1964–68: Part 1B, 223) always dismissed this resemblance, stressing the economic basis of his theory and asserting that Schmidt's theory was a purely artificial response to inflationary conditions (cf. Klaassen and Schreuder 1984: 130, note 5). But such a view may be rather the result of a psychological reaction than a scholarly judgement.

Klaassen and Schreuder (1984: 117) offer an interpretation of some aspects of Limperg's replacement value theory (as presented below). However, this is in terms of Solomons (1966: 125) concise notation, containing concepts (e.g. Bonbright's notion of value to the owner) that Limperg is unlikely to have used:

Let: NRV = net realizable value of asset; PV = present value of expected net receipts; RC = replacement cost of asset; VO = value of asset value to the owner (similar to the deprival value in the English literature – cf. Camfferman 1998).

1   If RC > NVR > PV, then VO = NRV, and asset should be sold.
2   If NRV > PV > RC, then VO = RC, and asset should be bought for resale.
3   If NRV < PV > RC, then VO = RC, and asset should be held for use and replaced if consumed or lost.
4   If NRV < PV < RC, then VO = PV, and asset should be held for use but not be replaced if consumed or lost.
5   If NRV < PV, then VO is either equal to RC or to PV, whichever is the lower.

If this is, indeed, a precise interpretation of Limperg's original theory, it may have afforded a special explanatory power as regards managerial investment decisions were concerned. Although Schmidt (1921: 61–2) did consider present values and other values beside the replacement value, the above-state interpretation of Limperg's theory may go beyond Schmidt's conception. However, Limperg's as well as Schmidt's approach were not merely concerned with balance sheet values but equally so with income determination, and both raised questions of capital maintenance, deferred taxes, income distribution, and many other aspects.

Besides, both Limperg's, as well as Schmidt's efforts were anticipated by the excellent replacement value approach of the Finnish scholar Ilmari Kovero (1911a – see our subsection 13.1.1). But the latter's pioneering contribution remained unmentioned by Schmidt and, apparently, also by Limperg. Finally, neither Limperg's nor Schmidt's approach can match the breadth and depth of Edwards and Bells' (1961 – see our subsection 12.3.1) theory as to comprehensiveness, clarity of presentation, as well as conceptual richness and subtly. This may be an unfair comparison, as more than four decades of accounting research lies between the early current value theories and the later one of Edwards and Bell (1961).

Apart from the 'competition' between Limperg and Schmidt, there also existed tensions between Dutch accountants. As pointed out above, the more pragmatic or less dogmatically oriented professors of the Rotterdam school were opposed to Limperg's 'revolutionary' current value doctrine (cf. van Seventer 1996: 385) and to *his* 'Amsterdam School' (that gradually declined in importance and later disappeared – cf. Camfferman and Zeff 1994: 128).

As to Limperg's major publications (e.g. 1917, 1918, 1932–33, 1937) almost all of them are in Dutch; and relatively few are internationally known (and if known, mainly through indirect sources). This may have contributed to the uncertainty about some features of his contributions – even though there exists a seven volume posthumous Dutch 'compilation' of Limperg's (1964–68) works on various topics of accounting and business economics, as well as a posthumous English translation of Limperg's (1985) essays on auditing theory.

However, there are several difficulties. Apart from the priority claim (resting on a couple of papers by Limperg in 1917 and 1918), a great mystery still surrounds the question: 'What did Limperg's theory actually say, and what has been added by his disciples in interpreting and extending his theory?' The explanations in Limperg's own publications, and the fact that he virtually limited himself to Dutch, greatly contributed to this dilemma. All this stands in stark contrast to Schmidt's clear publication record in several languages (cf. Clarke and Dean 1992: 292–6).

Another exigency lies in the confusion about where the theories of Limperg and Schmidt essentially differ. Clarke and Dean (1992: 292–6) examined the major differences as claimed by various scholars, but found many contradictions in their views and interpretations. There is little doubt that under both theories non-monetary assets were valued at replacement values, and that the resulting adjustments were *not* recorded in the profit and loss account, but went directly to a *special* capital account. Furthermore, *general price-level adjustments* were *not* part of either system, though Schmidt recommended to keep monetary (or even all 'circulatory') assets and debts as much as possible in balance (something that indicates an acute awareness that such systems harbour a major flaw that has to be minimized – cf. the discussion of Edwards and Bell 1961, in our subsection 12.3.1).

There were also some *differences* between Limperg's and Schmidt's theories. First, Schmidt treated increases and decreases of replacement cost *equally*, while Limperg did not. While Schmidt (as well as previously Kovero) recognized unrealized gains as well as unrealized losses, it seems that this symmetry was not part of Limperg's system. Second, although both authors claimed their theories to be 'organic' in relation to the larger picture of business and the economy, Schmidt's emphasis may have gone beyond the individual business entity to macro-economic issues (e.g. to economic business cycles). Yet, these are minor differences that today hardly seem worthy of a dispute.

A third predicament, this time concerning Limperg's writing habits and the posthumous collection of lecture notes, has been described by Clarke and Dean in the following passages:

> In that seven volume collection [of Limperg's (1964–68)], however, no bibliography is provided. Although the collection is stated to be a synthesis of his unpublished manuscripts, 'in the form of detailed lecture notes,' if Limperg's published articles had contained substantive and systematically developed ideas then it is unlikely that the editors would have to state, 'that prior to Limperg's death in 1969, December 1961, 'a complete version of his system or theory has never been written or that his theories are far less widely known than at first sight would appear to be the case.' Van Seventer notes [note ommitted] 'Limperg has never published a full presentation of his theory ... and his writings are limited to number of articles and essays' ... '[Limperg] was throughout his career, entirely sensitive to criticism ...'
>
> (Clarke and Dean 1992: 290)

Nevertheless, in the Anglophone accounting literature Limperg and his approach to replacement values were widely known and discussed (e.g. May 1966; van Seventer 1969, 1975, 1996; Burgert 1972; MacDonal 1977; Ashton 1981; van Sloten 1981; Cattella 1983; Enthoven 1983; Clarke and Dean 1990, 1992; Camfferman and Zeff 1994). In the French accounting literature Limperg's theory has been discussed, for example, by Perridon (1956–57). More recently, Limperg has been profiled (as one of *Les grands auteurs en comptabilité*) in a separate chapter by Camfferman (2005), while Fritz Schmidt had to share a chapter with Veit Simon and Eugen Schmalenbach.

13.2.2 Financial accounting in the Netherlands since the 1950s

Dutch accounting, due to the 'Limperg tradition', maintained a strong bias towards financial accounting. Indeed, even in the second half of the twentieth century, replacement value accounting continued to be a particularly important topic in the Netherlands. Another well know Dutch author, also concerned mainly with valuation problems, was Meij (1948, 1954, 1960). A further relatively early publication, that by van Straaten (1957), analysed the limits of the income concept; and several Dutch authors tried to extend Limperg's theory. For example, Nederstigt (1952) analysed the need for deferred taxation in connection with revaluations; Scheffer (1962) introduced the notion of gearing adjustment; and van der Schroeff (1975) critically examined the limitations of Limperg's capital maintenance notion, as well as other features of his income determination approach.

There also exist some papers by Burgert (1967, 1972) with details on some *reservations* about replacement value accounting, re-iterating M.J. Clarks notion of different costs for different purposes. Thereby, Burgert opted for a stepwise income statement that would reveal *different* income concepts (something anathema to Limperg's disciples – cf. Klaassen and Schreuder 1984: 123). Another paper, by Enthoven (1976), posed the question whether 'replacement value' accounting might be the wave of the future (something that seemed quite plausible during the inflationary years of the late 1970s or even for some future period of monetary instability).

But, as Klaassen and Schreuder (1984: 113) emphasized, Dutch accounting research 'has broadened beyond the traditional foci', and the literature has expanded to most of the fashionable topics, from descriptive studies of accounting practice and court cases to normative analysis, empirical research and harmonization with accounting standards of the EEC and other countries (e.g. Schoonderbeek 1987). Indeed, the connection of theory and practice has always been relatively close in Dutch accounting (possibly related to the relative relaxed attitude of the Dutch accounting legislation during the past).

Nonetheless, Bouma and Feenstra (1997: 181) emphasized that in general Dutch accounting researchers have shown a preference for axiomatic reasoning, though the situation is gradually changing towards a more empirical attitude. Although these contain some laboratory studies (e.g. Feenstra 1985; van de Poel 1986), ordinary inductive studies (e.g. as those contained in Dijksma 1986–90; and Buijink 1992) were much more frequent. Among other well-known pertinent publications in financial accounting of the Netherlands (either in Dutch or English) are: Pryut (1954) and Bouma and Werkema (1965), both on subjective aspects of income determination; or a co-authored book by Hoogedorn and Bijl (1992) and a paper by Hoogendorn (1993), both on financial reporting; or a series of publications on statement presentation and related topics by Klaassen and Schreuder (1980) and Klaassen (1975, 1991, 1993). In recent years a user approach to financial accounting has been preferred; thereby the emphasis is not only on shareholders but, as customary in Europe, on *stakeholders* (i.e. including employees, customers, government agencies, etc.).

Recently the publications by Kees Camfferman (e.g. 1996a, 1996b, 1997, 1998) became particularly noteworthy. They include a book on voluntary financial reporting in the Netherlands, and a series of papers that span a variety of topics, mainly on Dutch accounting. He also presented a series of publications in co-authorship with others; for example a book with Zeff *et al.* (1992), and a paper with Zeff *et al.* (1999), and others (see last subsection on historical accounting research in the Netherlands).

13.2.3 *Auditing in the Netherlands*

As far as auditing is concerned, Limperg (1926, 1932–3) essentially contributed to this area, although in a less known and fairly unconventional way. He was opposed to the traditional auditing process of mere routine verification, but recommended an approach that demanded greater social responsibility and ethical awareness on the part of the auditor. Much later the book by Maijoor (1991) analysed the economics of accounting regulation; and the paper by Biggs *et al.* (1994) dealt with aspects of the auditing profession as a response to Bindenga's (1993) publication on Dutch accounting and auditing. The latter complained of the gap between theory and practice, while the former rejected such a danger as far as auditing was concerned. Quadackers *et al.* (1996) also investigated auditing and the planning for audit risk assessment in some Dutch firms, while the paper by Hassink (2000) dealt with accounting and auditing contracts. In the Netherlands, according to Bouma and Feenstra (1997: 182), the solving of design and adaptation of financial accounting systems (as integrated in financial reporting systems) has become a 'prerogative' of the audit and law professions, rather than of accounting academics.

13.2.4 Cost accounting in the Netherlands

As to cost and management accounting, it seems that Limperg (similar to Zappa in Italy – see our sections 4.4 and 5.4) has cast a shadow over this area. Bouma and Feenstra emphasized that in Limperg's view the principle of continuity would be violated if only *variable* costs (instead of *total* replacement costs) would be allocated to products. Thus direct costing, for example, was a taboo in this theory. Since

> Limperg and his adherents have been very intolerant of dissenters … it is obvious that management accounting in the Netherlands was not able to be developed in a harmonious and consistent way during many decades. Many potential management accounting theorists and researchers looked for an academic shelter with economists
>
> (Bouma and Feenstra 1997: 182)

Here is another striking example of how a dogmatic attitude by a dominant accounting personality may impede the local development of a discipline. Indeed, Bouma and Feenstra (1997: 186) reveal that not only Dutch cost and managerial accounting, but also other accounting aspects (e.g. some of those emphasized in the foreign literature) were hampered by the narrow orientation of Dutch replacement value theory.

Although managerial accounting has meanwhile taken its proper place in the Netherlands, the pertinent publications mentioned in the survey literature are still few. For example, there are two books (in Dutch), one by Meer-Kooistra (1993) and Bouma and van Helden (1994) both tying management accounting to aspects of organization theory, as well as the paper (in English) by van Helden (1997) on cost allocation and product costing in Dutch local government. Apart from such publications, there are also managerial cost topics among Dutch doctoral dissertations (of which the reader will find concise discussions in the *European Accounting Review*, 1966, Vol. 5, No. 1: 149–52).

In addition, we should mention some publications on social and personal accounting (e.g. Dekker 1981; Schreuder 1981; and possibly Bouma and Feenstra 1975), though in the 1990s this area has lost ground in the Netherlands. However, another aspect to be mentioned is the rich literature generated by Dutch-American accountants (particularly by Enthoven, Hendriksen, Vangermeersch and van Seventer – see Chapter 12), some of those publications refer to the Netherlands, but many deal with a broader range of other topics.

13.2.5 Historical accounting research in the Netherlands

As far as historical publications in Dutch are concerned, we refer the reader to Camfferman (1997) that offers a detailed discussion and comprehensive bibliography of close to 200 publications. Beyond this, several publications ought to be pointed out: the books by de Waal (1927) and ten Have (1933), both on the teaching of bookkeeping in the Netherlands during the seventeenth and eighteenth century. Later, Kraayenhofen (1955) – a notable Dutch auditor who also had some influence on financial reporting in the Netherlands – wrote a survey of the accounting profession. Considerable historical research has been done on Limperg and the accounting school of the Netherlands, as, for example, van Seventer's (1969, 1975, 1996) three publications on Dutch accounting issues of the past, or in the last case, on Theodore Limperg himself. Other publications in English and French on Limperg were previously mentioned (Camfferman and Zeff 1994; Camfferman 2005). Furthermore, there are publications, such as Bouma (1966) on enterprise target, Bouma and Feenstra (1975) on changes in personal policies of Dutch firms from 1970 to 1973, Klaassen and Schreuder (1984) on accounting research in the Netherlands, or Hoogendoorn and Bijl (1992) that offers an anthology on *financial reporting in the 1990s, or* Bouma (1992) on management accounting after Limperg.

Furthermore, two Australian authors, Clarke and Dean (1992), made a comparison between Limperg's and Schmidt's versions of replacement value theory. And Enthoven (1982), as well as Brink (1992), examined the accounting practice and policies of Philips (probably the best known Dutch company). Zeff (1993) dealt with the historical development of financial reporting, and Camfferman (1996b) wrote on past accounting in the Netherlands; and in Camfferman and Cooke (2001) he and his co-author offered an overview of Dutch accounting in Japan (1605–1850).

13.3 Accounting research in the Scandinavian countries[6]

13.3.1 Early developments in Scandinavia

The Scandinavian countries supplied an impressive array of renowned economists and Nobel laureates; but among the earlier business economists, it seems that two names have become widely known abroad. One is Oskar Sillén [1885–1965], a former student of Eugen Schmalenbach, who held the Chair of

Business Economics at the Stockholm School of Economics from 1913 to 1950, and was chairman of the *Föreningen Auktoriserade Revisorer* (association of chartered auditors) from 1923 to 1941. His paper on the history of valuation theory in Sweden (Sillén 1929 – published in German) gained international reputation. He also published a book in German on auditing (Sillén 1926) and several works in Swedish. Sillén's work, mainly in financial accounting and auditing, though practically oriented, was theoretically sound. His achievements have been honoured in a book by Wallerstedt (1988). Other auditing aspects were later dealt with by Eilifsen (1998).

The other name is that of Albert ter Vehn [1900–97], a former student of Fritz Schmidt, who (allegedly upon Schmalenbach's recommendation) attained in 1926 the chair at the Gothenburg School of Economics (that merged in 1971 with the University of Gothenburg) where he stayed until 1967. His book (in German) on the development of accounting theory up to the enactment of the German Commercial Code (ter Vehn 1929), and his Swedish work on the standardization of full cost accounting (ter Vehn 1936) are widely known. Indeed, his main interest became the rigorous study of cost and managerial accounting as well as the structuring of charts of accounts (so popular in Continental Europe, yet so alien to the English speaking world). One might also add the names of two economists Ingvar Ohlsson (e.g. 1953) and Aukrust (1955). But apart from the fact that they belong to the next generation, they are 'national income accountants' – and those were all too often excluded from the 'accounting fraternity'.

13.3.2 Scandinavian managerial accounting research after 1950

In the second half of the twentieth century, one of the special interests of Scandinavian accounting research was budgeting and its various aspects. This activity manifested itself in Denmark with Madsen (1959, 1970) in two normative and theoretical works that subsequently stimulated empirical investigations in budgeting; Polesie (1976a, 1976b) dealt with 'goal-budgeting' (emphasizing the link between budgeting and ex-post accounting records) and budgeting by objectives, respectively. A further work by Madsen and Polesie (1981) examined behavioural elements in budgeting, apparently to a larger extent than elsewhere. In Sweden, there emerged publications by Samuelson (1973) and Magnusson (1974) on budgetary control, as well as by Gavatin (1975) on budget simulation. As Östman (1984: 32) pointed out: 'Although these projects contained empirical data and analyses of application problems, a certain emphasis was given to conceptual questions'.

Other facets of management accounting were hardly less popular, particularly after a major shift in interest that occurred in the early 1970s. The following publications offer representative Scandinavian research during and after this time: Riise (1969), on cost calculations for decisions and control; Arvidsson's (1971, 1973) two studies on transfer prices; Jennergren's (1971, 1980) Stanford dissertation on the mathematical theory of decentralized resource allocation, and his paper on accountings impact on a firms profit, respectively; Provstgaard's

(1972, 1976) analysis of the profit function of accounting; Östman's (1977, 1980) empirical study on accounting measures for management control, and his behavioural accounting, respectively; Ljungkvist (1982) on price changes and management control; the English survey of Swedish manufacturing by Ask and Ax (1992) analysing the development of product costing; Frenckner and Samuelson (1984) on industrial product costing; Jönsson (1996a) on accounting as a means for general improvement; Östman (1977) on control by means of accounting measures; Samuelson's (1989, 1990) paper and book on the development of models of management control and accounting information systems in Sweden, and Ask *et al.* (1996) on cost management in Sweden.

Committee and teamwork with industrial associations proved useful in promoting management accounting research. Apart from a concern with the designing of cost and related reports (Hedberg and Jönsson 1978), one discussed, experimented, and applied direct or marginal costing since the 1950s (Freckner and Samuelson 1984; Jönsson 1991). Ask and Ax (1992) reported that some 40 per cent of Swedish industry used marginal costing *as well as* full or absorption costing. As time progressed, management accounting has been increasingly influenced by behavioural and computer research (Polesie 1976a, 1976b; Östman 1973, 1977; Grönlund and Jönsson 1990; Jönsson 1996a, 1996b). A related concern was public sector management accounting (Oson 1983; Jönsson 1982; Brunsson 1989). An anthology edited by Engwall and Gunnarsson (1994) deals with *Management studies in an academic context.*

13.3.3 Financial and social accounting in Scandinavia

In financial accounting and accounting theory the following Scandinavian research has been mentioned in the literature: above all, there is the prominent book by Palle Hansen (1962), analysing the accounting concept of profit from an economic angle. One might also mention Sven-Erik Johansson's (1965) work on the Swedish system of investment reserves – even if its subject matter rather belongs to the theory of finance. Furthermore, there is Kinserdal's (1972) analysis of information contained in the annual reports of Norwegian industry; Östman's (1973) empirical study of the use and design of accounting reports; Eriksson's (1974) book on the information in consolidated financial statements; Kedner's (1975) study on bankruptcy problems; Jönsson's (1988, 1991, 1994) publications on various topics such as (i) accounting regulation and elite structures, (ii) the role making for accounting while the state is watching, and (iii) changing accounting regulatory structures in the context of a strong government.

Among special branches of financial accounting there were studies on inflation accounting during the 1970s, as, for example, that by Åkerblom (1975) on business firms in inflationary times; by Widebäck (1976) on inflation accounting and budgeting; Brööms and Rundfelt (1979) inflation accounting: an approach to price-adjusted annual reports on pension accounting. There also is a conceptual study on inflation accounting by Östman (1980). As to public service accounting, one might mention Oson's (1983) book on the development and use of a municipal accounting information system; and Jönsson's (1982) English paper on a case study of budgetary behaviour in local government (for details, see Östman 1984); aspects of pension accounting were dealt with by Jönsson-Lundmark (1976). As to social accounting, Östman (1984: 38) lists explicitly only the study by Gröjer and Stark (1978) that is far-reaching and research-oriented and was applied in two Swedish companies (Östman also hints at other pertinent studies, but without specific references).

Furthermore, Scandinavian accounting research made notable contributions to various parts of the Anglophone accounting literature, either by residents of Scandinavian countries or, even more so, by Scandinavians living in the English language area. Most prominent among the latter are the numerous and path-breaking publications (e.g. on the refinement of the 'clean surplus theory' and other topics) by the Norwegian-American scholar James A. Ohlson (e.g. 1987, 1988, 1995) of which only a few can here be mentioned (for details see Chapters 12 and 19). Another example is the widely known paper Froystein Gjesdal (1981) on accounting for stewardship. Above all, there are two crucial texts on the information perspective of accounting, co-authored by two Danish scholars. The first text is by J.A. Christensen and Demski (2003), the other is a two-volume work by P.O. Christensen and Feltham (2003, 2005). In both cases, these Danish co-authors were former students of Demski and Feltham, respectively. Indeed, the doctoral dissertation of J.A. Christensen (1979 – or parts of it) on agency theory also seems to have been published. Finally, we might mention Skaer-baek's (1998) paper on 'The politics of accounting technology in Danish central government' and an empirical study on accountability by Tornquist (1999).

13.3.4 Research of accounting history in Scandinavia

Apart from the three publications mentioned above (by Sillén 1929, on the history of valuation theory in Sweden, and the book by ter Vehn 1929, on the development of accounting theory, as well as the book on Sillén by Wallerstedt 1988), the following works might be listed under historical accounting research in Scandinavia: a book by Carlson (1986) on the captains of Swedish industry; and another by Engwall (1992) on early business economics in Sweden and its protagonists; a book by Gunnarsson (1994) on Anders Berch, the founding father of the Swedish economic sciences. Furthermore, there are two English papers, one by Östman, L. (1984) on accounting research in the Scandinavian countries, the other by Jönsson (1996b) on accounting and the business economics tradition in Sweden. In talking about Swedish accounting history, one cannot fail to mention the financial wizard Ivar Kreuger, his industrial empire, and the enormous impact its bankruptcy had. It affected not only the relatively small Swedish auditing profession, and subsequent legislations, but also had an impact on the political future of this small country. This crash even jolted the New York Stock Exchange and, apparently, influenced American accounting legislation as well (cf. Flesher and Flesher 1986).

14 Accounting publications and research in twentieth-century Japan[1]

14.1 Introduction

Japan's interest in modern accounting began in the late nineteenth century with Alexander Shand [1844–1930].[2] The Japanese translation of Shand's (1873) *Bank bookkeeping* proved to be so important that his system of bank accounting became legally obligatory for the newly established banking system of the Meiji era. In the same year, Fukuzawa (1873–74) published a Japanese translation of Bryant and Stratton's (1871) textbook, *Common school bookkeeping*. Yukichi Fukuzawa [1835–1901], a prominent Japanese scholar and the founder of Keio Gijuku University, was no professional accountant but his translation proved to be most influential in improving accounting practice and in spreading the idea of double-entry in schools as well as in private Japanese companies beyond the banking sector. Finally, Naotaro Shimono [1866–1939] introduced his *Boki seiri* (Shimono 1895/1982), an authentic Japanese text of double-entry accounting. For details about early Japanese cost accounting applications, we referred in section 2.7 to Kimizuka (1991).

Japanese accounting research in the twentieth century is characterized by two eras divided by the Second World War. Before and during this war, German accounting exercised great influence on Japanese scholars; while after the war, Anglo-American accounting became dominant. In the late 1960s a new epoch of academic accounting began when the English publications by Chambers, Mattessich, Ijiri and others became known in Japan. But here, we discuss first the contributions of the following eminent Japanese accounting scholars: Tetsuzo Ohta, Kiyoshi Kurosawa, Wasaburo Kimura and Iwao Iwata. Later, other and more recent scholars (Kenji Aizaki, Nobuko Nosse, Fujio Harada and Yuji Ijiri) and publications are mentioned.

14.2 Early contributions in the twentieth century

Tetsuzo Ohta [1889–1970] was undoubtedly one of the leading Japanese accounting scholars in the early twentieth century. Ohta's (1922) 'Kaikeijo no shisan' was the earliest paper that brought a *dynamic* theoretical point of view to Japanese accounting and its revenue–expense matching approach – perhaps even independently from Schmalenbach's work in Germany. Ohta defined assets as an accumulation of expenditures, expected to yield future income or to save costs. This required a historical cost basis for asset evaluation (in contrast to the current cost basis); it also marked the departure from the static accounting theory that dominated the Japanese Commercial Code and Tax Code at the time. Further details can be gathered from the autobiographical essay by Ohta (1968), describing his 60-year experience (from 1907 onwards) as an academic and professional accountant.

Kiyoshi Kurosawa [1902–90], originally trained in sociology, was probably Japan's most prolific and eminent accounting scholar, with a wide range of interests in a variety of accounting fields. He played a crucial role in the major phases of Japanese accounting regulations, from the rationalization of industry in the crisis years of the 1930s, to the economic state control during wartime and, finally, the economic democratization during the rehabilitation of the postwar years (cf. Chiba 1994: 194).

Kurosawa authored or edited more than 100 books (including dictionaries and manuals), and has some 600 papers to his credit. His major contributions may be summarized by the following three themes: (1) the establishment of Japanese Business Accounting Principles and their influence; (2) promoting a scientific (instead of a purely legalistic) approach to accounting, particularly the theoretical integration of micro- and macro-accounting, and (3) pioneering research for a political or normative accounting able to cope with social and ecological–environmental problems – Fujita and Garcia (2005) emphasize related traits of Kurosawa's work. They point at Kurosawa's attempt to create an 'ideal' accounting system for pursuing social–political and collective goals, yet based on strong financial and economic principles (in contrast to the previously legalistic approach). On the other hand, they deem Kurosawa's earlier references to Karl Marx simplistic (though Kurosawa's views tended more towards J.R. Commons than Marx) and criticize his system as fragmentary. But they admit the immense influence of Kurosawa's work on Japanese accounting.

In an early paper Kurosawa (1932: 16–17) emphasized already the need for at least three different types of balance sheets (one satisfying accounting requirements, another for management purposes, and a third for legalistic purposes), thus foreshadowing the desirability of purpose-oriented financial statements. Kurosawa (1933) was his first book on accounting theory, and the most comprehensive theoretical text at that time. It described the historical development of various fields of accounting, both in the German and English language areas, and attempted to establish accounting as an academic discipline beyond a mere practical tool. Kurosawa highly valued the idea of Schmalenbach's (1927/31/38/53) *Kontenrahmen* (chart of accounts) and the *kontenmäßiges Denken* (thinking in terms of accounts) thereby manifested. The latter did not so much express the technical aspects of double-entry but reflected the methodological foundations common to all areas, ranging from micro- to macro-accounting. In its 1939 revised version, Kurosawa discussed in great detail the idea of a national balance sheet (as proposed by Schluter *et al.* 1933 and Ischboldin 1936), as well as the welfare economics approach to valuation theory (originally promoted by Scott 1925, 1931).

Kurosawa (1934) explored the major theories of double-entry bookkeeping developed in Italy, Germany and France, as well as the USA and the UK, and continued to investigate the foundations of *kontenmäßiges Denken*. This way of thinking enabled him to compare various forms of double-entry bookkeeping, and to explain their development under different economic circumstances. This was the first and most comprehensive presentation of the history of double-entry bookkeeping in Japanese. Yet, surprisingly Kurosawa did not consider Pacioli's approach as a fully-fledged double-entry system, as it lacked the balance sheet and did not *insist* on the periodic closing of the accounts (merely recommending it). Kurosawa rather viewed the French '*Ordonnance de Commerce*' (1673) as reflecting the first 'complete' or 'proper' double-entry system (cf. Tanaka 1990: 238). For Kurosawa, *periodic* income determination was the crucial requirement for a fully functioning double-entry system.

Kurosawa (1938) was his first book on cost accounting; it was based on field studies of Japanese companies, particularly of the cotton spinning industry. He regarded cost accounting as one of the applications of the *Kontenrahmen* as well as an indispensable tool for business management.

The Japanese Business Accounting Principles were announced in 1949. Here too, Kurosawa, together with Iwata, was most influential in drafting those principles. Kurosawa (1951a) explained their theoretical foundations, and made comparisons with the publications of the American Accounting Association (1936) and the book by Sanders *et al.* (1938).

Kurosawa also planned to write a history of the development of modern accounting thought and practice in Japan. He began this project in 1987, and Kurosawa (1990) was its first part. It covered the period from the introduction of double-entry to Japan in 1873, through Shand and Fukuzawa, to the establishment of the Business Accounting Principles in 1949. Kuroswa's death in 1990 prevented the completion of this project. In honouring the outstanding contributions of Kurosawa, Aizaki (1999) dedicated a collection of 12 papers to him. This anthology contains, among others, a paper by Harada (1999) on the development of Kurosawa's accounting thoughts, another by Chiba (1999) on Kurosawa's contributions for modernizing Japanese accounting, and one by Kawano (1999) on Kurosawa's introduction of macro-accounting and ecological accounting to Japanese accounting academia.

Wasaburo Kimura [1902–73] was another prolific academic with a wide range of interests in a variety of accounting fields (from financial and cost accounting to bank bookkeeping – for the latter, see Kimura 1935). The publication by Tsuji and Okano (1996: 361) points out that 'Kimura introduced in the 1930s the axiology of Marxist economics to accounting' and was, during the war, ostracized as a war opponent. Even later, he continued to base his accounting analysis on the value and capital cycle theory. Apart from numerous publications (some written after 1952, when his eyesight was failing), he is said to have translated several books into Japanese (cf. Yamagata 1994: 199). He had a special interest in accounting history (see Kimura 1954, 1972) as well as in American accounting theory. Indeed, he subjected the works of such scholars as Hatfield (1918/71), and particularly of Paton and Littleton (1940/53) to intensive scrutiny. Kimura's theory puts special stress on the social and environmental-economic aspects of business activity, as well as on the dependence of accounting on those forces.

Kimura (1954) took issue with the basic tenets of Paton and Littleton (1940/53) by criticizing their almost exclusive reliance on the historical cost basis, and the concomitant neglect of other valuation methods. Although these authors admitted general price-level adjustments in inflationary times, Kimura sided rather with Paton and Littleton in favour of current costing and specific (instead of general) price-level adjustments. He also called into question Paton's and Littleton's claim to accounting objectivity, and believed that accountants cannot avoid subjectivity in their valuation and income measurements. For him the crucial issue of valuation was the sudden and often radical changes of individual prices (not only of general price-levels in times of inflation), and the reliance on the accountant's judgment.

Nowadays we might extend this kind of thinking by arguing that objectivity is a matter of degree, and if the accountant's judgement is sound, he will be able to sense which means fit a particular end. And in this process of matching means to ends properly, there lies all the objectivity that accountants can attain at the present state of knowledge (cf. Mattessich 1995a: 161–2, 187–210). As a possible response to the axiomatic and postulational experiments during the 1960s and 1970s in America and Europe, as well as Japan, Kimura believed that accounting theory can get along with merely two postulates, the first referring to the 'accounting entity', the second to the 'accounting period'. But this seems to be a tenuous point. As to Kimura's contributions to cost accounting and historical studies, see below.

The youngest of the major pioneers of Japanese accounting was Iwao Iwata [1905–55]. He too was interested in the scientific advancement of accounting as well as the reform of Japanese accounting and auditing standards – though most of his time was devoted to the latter. He was strongly influenced by both German accounting theory and American auditing. Indeed, he is considered to be a founder of the audit system as used by the certified public accountants in Japan. *Kaikeishi-kansha* (1954a) and *Kaikei-gensoku to Kansa-kijun* (1955) were his major works (written under the influence of American auditing) that laid the foundations for modernizing Japanese auditing by emphasizing the accountability principle.

Although profoundly influenced by German scholars, particularly Schmalenbach's (1919/38/50) dynamic accounting, he reacted to the one-sided view of the latter by proposing two completely *separate* models of income determination (though he ultimately combined them to supplement each other). The first model, the *Zaisan-ho* (net-worth method), was assumed to measure income based on a comparison of subsequent year-end amounts of owner's equities ascertained by the inventory method. This required the year-end amounts of owner's equities to be calculated by adjusting the owner's equity for additional capital paid-in (including possible dividends). Yet, this approach did not reveal the income sources; it had to be supplemented by a second, *dynamic* model, the *Son-eki-ho* (revenue and expense method) based on the *income statement* (in contrast to Schmalenbach's *dynamic* approach that was based on the *balance sheet*).[3]

This second model required the determination of revenues and expenses (on the basis of the physical quantities purchased, consumed and sold, as well as their proper valuation) by means of double-entry. However, Iwata's system supplied only receipts and payments rather than revenues and expenses. And it was the auditing process that was expected to adjust the former to the latter by taking adequate inventory (i.e. the procedures required by the first model).

The most characteristic feature of Iwata's accounting theory was its reliance on inventory taking and periodic re-valuation instead of a continuous recording within the double-entry system. This may explain why Morita (1994: 175) believed that ultimately the *static* objective dominated Iwata's system and that his idea of a 'dual structure of income determination' – i.e. income determination by combining static accounting (Zaisan-ho) with dynamic accounting (Son-eki-ho), as envisaged by Iwata (1954b) – failed to explain or satisfy modern business accounting. Iwata may have realized this but hoped that his theory would be more adaptable to auditing (see Iwata 1954a, 1955) – or, at least, to 'internal' auditing – where such activities as physical inspection, confirmation, observation and checking the accuracy of accounting records predominate (cf. Iwata 1956: 167).

14.3 Later developments in general accounting theory

Financial reporting, particularly accounting principles or standards, became in time a major concern of Japanese accounting. This was reflected in many publications, such as:

1   *Rijun-keisan-genri* (Iwata 1956, in Japanese) contains his collected papers (published posthumously) dealing mainly with the principles of income determination as encountered in the German literature. It examined, the theories of Schmalenbach, Geldmacher and Nicklisch, etc., and proposed the dual structure of income determination.

2   The translation of *An introduction to corporate accounting standards* (Paton and Littleton 1940/53) by Nakajima was later followed by *Kaisha kaikei kijun josetsu kenkyu* (Nakajima 1979). The latter contained mainly commentaries on individual chapters of the Paton–Littleton work. It praised the rigorous definitions as well as its coherent, coordinated and consistent body of doctrine, thus enhancing a correct understanding of this classical work.

3   *Kaikei-kojun-ron* (Arai 1969) and an anthology of the Accounting Standards Research Committee (1970) of Japan reflected the strong interest in accounting postulates and standards. These together with preceding American publications (from Paton, Gilman and Moonitz to ASOBAT) cemented

the foundation of our discipline, and enhanced the understanding of the postulates and their relationship to principles.

4   Choi and Hiramatsu's (1987, in English) *Accounting and financial reporting in Japan.*
5   Cooke and Kikuya's (1992, in English) *Financial reporting in Japan – regulation, and on practice and environment.*
6   *Kaikei kijun-ron* (Hirose 1995, in Japanese) examined, among others, the FASB's conceptual framework to choose desirable accounting principles for Japan from purely a normative point of view. It emphasized five concepts for standard setting; measurement of disposable profit, information for investment decision, stewardship responsibility, accounting policy and international harmonization.
7   Sunder and Yamaji's (1999, in English) *The Japanese style of business accounting.*

Above all, a series of empirical accounting research has been accumulated in Japan. It was inspired by positive or empirical accounting research that emerged in the USA since the late 1960s. Only the major publications can be mentioned here. *Jissho: kaikeijoho to kabuka* (Ishizuka 1987) resulted after ten years of research activity by Ishizuka and his team. It applied and examined the efficient market hypothesis and the capital asset pricing model (CAPM) to the companies listed on the Tokyo Stock Exchange (TSE). Above all, it compared the results with preceding American studies for the New York Stock Exchange (NYSE). According to the analysis of the Ishizuka team, the stock price behaviour at the TSE showed, in general, a reaction similar to that at the NYSE. It also suggested that the TSE was not misled by the deliberate changes of accounting methods (i.e. companies' share price manipulation) – that means, it ignored them as meaningless.

Sakurai's (1991) empirical analysis proved the usefulness of financial accounting information to investors of the TSE by adopting portfolio theory, and Watts and Zimmerman's two-period CAPM. It confirmed the information relevance of financial accounting to investors.

Another study, by Suda (2000), also inspired by Watts and Zimmerman (1986), examined the decision informativeness and contract-implementation functions of accounting in Japanese stock markets, including Tokyo, Osaka and Nagoya. This kind of empirical research – adopting the models and analytical methods developed by American accounting academics – is expected to open the door to a broader development of 'scientific' accounting research in Japan beyond the traditional descriptive approach.

Further empirical studies re-evaluated the usefulness of traditional financial accounting. For example, Saito (1984) reconsidered the historical cost principle. And Ito (1996) explored a way of redesigning Japanese accounting standards suitable for the changing society of the twenty-first century. He focused on the relationship between accounting standards and company laws. Since Japanese accounting standards have been strongly restricted by the Commercial Code, the

Securities Exchange Act and the Tax Code, Ito criticized this system as undesirably rigid. In this endeavour he examined the historical relationship between GAAP and company laws in ten States of the USA. He then compared the American and Japanese experiences in the setting of accounting standards to find a suitable solution for restoring the independence and dynamism of Japanese accounting standards.

In the 1960s many foundational and methodological works were translated into Japanese. The 'golden age of a priori research' of American accounting was a major influence in Japan. Apart from the publications of the American Accounting Association, there were such well-known authors as Bedford, Chambers, Ijiri, Mattessich, Moonitz, Sprouse and Sterling. Sociological and linguistic writings of America and Great Britain, and possibly its critical-interpretive direction, also exercised some influence on Japanese accounting research. Typical examples are: Inoue's (1984) *Sociological accounting* influenced by Talcott Parsons' structural-functional action analysis, or the linguistic approach of Tanaka's (1982/86) *The structure of accounting language* influenced by Noam Chomsky's theory of transformational generative grammar. Probably the earliest Japanese author pioneering the linguistic approach in accounting is Aoyagi (e.g. 1958, 1991) who interpreted 'accounting as a language of business' and regarded its essence as consisting of a series of conventions.

14.3.1 A general theory for macro- and micro-accounting

One of the major characteristics of Japanese accounting research and education during the second half of the twentieth century was the intensive concern with macro-accounting (including national income accounting) and its integration with micro-accounting. Kurosawa (1937, 1939, 1941a, 1951b) was the forerunner, followed by Kenji Aizaki, Nobuko Nose and Fujio Harada. All of them emphasized consistently the importance of Kurosawa's notion of incorporating macro-accounting into the research, as well as the teaching of it. Kurosawa intensively studied the leading works on macro-accounting (e.g. Kurosawa 1941a; see also Stone 1947; Bray 1949a, 1949b, 1951, 1953, 1957; Clark 1923; Fisher 1906) as well as the works by Schluter *et al.* (1933) and Ischboldin (1936). He unwaveringly held the view that in order to make accounting an integral part of the economic sciences, it was necessary to *integrate* micro- and macro-accounting.

Kenji Aizaki [1921–98] played a vital role in promoting and drawing attention to macro-accounting research. For him, accounting was an essential cultural factor of our society, particularly in relationship with economics and philosophy (in his case with Thorstein Veblen's institutionalism). Furthermore, he held in high regard the theory of economic accounting by Bray (e.g. 1949a, 1949b, 1951, 1953, 1957), and wrote a number of works discussing his theory (e.g. Aizaki 1957, 1962a, 1962b, 1963a, 1963b, 1966, 1971). The essence of Bray's theory was that the Keynesian macroeconomic equations represented the structure of every economic activity ranging from an individual company to a national economy. Hence, business accounting should be redesigned, based on the basis of Keynesian macroeconomics. Bray, in cooperation with Richard Stone (later Nobel laureate), proposed a specific system of accounts to be applicable both to micro-accounting and macro-accounting in order to integrate both areas. Aizaki accepted Bray's approach as a promising basis for a scientific theory of accounting.

Meanwhile, Aizaki, with his graduate student Fujio Harada [1931–2002], began to study Mattessich (1964) and, in *Shakaikagaku to shiteno kaikeigaku* (Aizaki 1966) and *Kigyokaikei to shakaikaikei* (Aizaki and Nosse 1971) promoted his ideas in Japan. He also compared the accounting philosophies of Bray (1949a, 1951, 1957), Mattessich (1957, 1964) and Yu (1966), all of whom explored the possibility of a 'general' theory of accounting. One may even say that Aizaki devoted his life to investigating the scientific foundation of accounting based on those ideas.

However, the researcher most preoccupied with these problems was Harada [1931–2002]. He elucidated the essence of Mattessich (1957, 1964) through a number of publications at a fairly early stage (e.g. Harada 1966a, 1966b, 1967a, 1967b, 1967c, 1968). In 'Kaikeiriron no hoho' (Harada 1974) he made a comparative analysis of the five axiomatic accounting theories presented by Aukrust (1966), Mattessich (1957, 1964), Churchman (1961), Eaves (1966) and Ijiri (1967/68). He was particularly enthusiastic about Mattessich's system because of the generality and flexibility made possible by integrating placeholder hypotheses into the axiomatic system. Inspired by the works of Mattessich and Ijiri (see subsection 14.3.3), Harada (1978) re-examined the foundation of accounting from the viewpoint of modern measurement theory. This work contained a comprehensive explanation of the mathematical structure and application of the measurement theories presented by Campbell, the experimental physicist, Stevens, the psychologist and the philosophers Suppes and Zinnes.

Both Aizaki and Harada taught macro-accounting at Chuo University during their academic careers, and both insisted on the significance of macro-accounting for the evolution of our discipline (including its educational aspects). These scholars actively promoted Mattessich's experiments of a general theory of accounting based on an axiomatic approach, and invited him to write his professional memoirs (published in Japanese as well as in English – see Mattessich 1992–93/1995b/2007).

Nobuko Nosse [1926–98] was another committed macro-accountant who undertook a number of empirical analyses on inflation accounting, income distribution and capital maintenance. She too stressed the close relationship between micro- and macro-accounting. Her first book (Nosse 1961a) had the following three objectives: (1) explaining the development and structure of social accounting by emphasizing the relationship to its economic foundation (i.e. Keynesian economics), (2) analysing the isomorphism between micro- and macro-accounting, especially in reference to the works of Bray (1949a, 1953) and Mattessich (1957), and (3) clarifying the practical implications of macro-accounting for economic policy and for the reconstruction of business accounting. This was the first fairly comprehensive academic publication on macro-accounting focusing on the transition from national income statistics to the system of national accounting designed by Richard Stone. Nosse (1961b), discussed at the annual meeting of the Japan Accounting Association some works by Bray and Mattessich. Indeed, this was the first occasion that those publications were the subject of public comment in Japan.

In 1964 Nosse studied macro-accounting at Oxford University as a research fellow under the guidance of John R. Hicks (another Nobel laureate) and his colleague Gerhart Stuvel; Nosse also published the Japanese translation of Stuvel's (1965/67, 1986/87, 1989/91) work on macro-accounting. During her second visit to Oxford in 1972, she co-authored a book (Hicks and Nosse 1974) that applied Hicks' (1942/61) methodology to the Japanese economy.

Due to the efforts of Kurosawa, Aizaki, Nosse and Harada, as well as Ijiri and Saito (see below), Japanese accounting scholars paid close attention to macro-accounting and the axiomatic approach. But Koguchi (1997a) drew further attention to the pioneering contributions in macro-accounting by Ragnar Frish (the first Nobel laureate in economics – e.g. Frisch 1943). Later, Koguchi presented a Japanese translation of the pioneering work of the Norwegian macro-accountant Odd Aukrust (1955/98), the first rigorous attempt towards an axiomatization of macro-accounting that gave impetus to both Mattessich's and Ijiri's research. Furthermore, Koguchi (1999) characterized Aukrust's axiomatic theory as a Frisch–Stone–Leontief synthesis. This trend presently continues in Japan by applying notions of macro-accounting to environmental issues (see section 14.4).

14.3.2 Reaction to the axiomatization of accounting theory

As to axiomatic or postulational issues, Fujita and Garcia report on Kurosawa's reaction as follows:

> He [Kurosawa] was inspired by a variety of sources, above all by Mattessich, Chambers, Gilman, ... Although Kurosawa searched for an axiomatization of accounting, he recognized the limits of formalization in the social sciences and advocated restraint in its execution. Close to Mattessich's theory, he nevertheless criticized the latter on three accounts: it reveals only a limited knowledge of semiotic concepts, it attempts a complete formalization of accounting, and does not take into consideration the possibility of applying an inductive approach to accounting.
>
> (Fujita and Garcia 2005: 177–8, translated from the French)

But Kurosawa's criticism might have been more appropriate to the paper by Balzer and Mattessich (1991/94 – also mentioned in footnote 40, p. 178, of these French commentators) but seems to have been directed towards Mattessich (1964), as Kurosawa had already died in 1990. Further suggestions to improve Mattessich's axiomatization attempts were made by Saito (1972a, 1972b) with an exchange of ideas and replies by Mattessich (1973a, 1973b), and further replies by Saito (1973a, 1973b).

Ijiri (1979) also tried to extend his original system to make it applicable to macro-accounting; he was particularly influenced by Aukrust (1966) and his axiomatization. Another, more independent axiomatization attempt (based on vector accounting) was made by Deguchi and Nakano (1986).

14.3.3 Ijiri's contributions and his triple-entry and momentum accounting

The youngest among the eight eminent Japanese scholars referred to in our Introduction is Yuji Ijiri. He published five books in Japanese, all of which were slightly revised versions of his original English contributions. *The foundations of accounting measures: a mathematical, economic, and behavioural inquiry* (Ijiri 1967/68) was his first book offering a Japanese version. It aroused in his fatherland strong interest in the axiomatic approach as well as the meta-theoretic approach, set-theoretical formulation of accounting, measurement theory and linguistics. The novelty of his approach quickly gained a wide audience, and his contributions to accounting became well known in his native country. At that time, Aizaki expressed (in a classroom) the radical impact these publications had on Japanese accounting by saying that 'the Ijiri fever is sweeping through Japanese accounting academia'.

Next to be mentioned are the translations of *Management goals and accounting for control* (Ijiri 1965/70) and *Theory of accounting measurement* (Ijiri 1975/76), which were accepted with great enthusiasm. The latter stressed the importance of the 'accountability' approach in contrast to the 'decision-oriented' approach that reflected the mainstream view since the appearance of *A statement of basic accounting theory* (ASOBAT; AAA 1966). According to Ijiri, only the former approach can suitably explain the role of the three parties involved in accounting (i.e. the 'accountor', the 'accountee' and the 'accountant'), quite apart from the significance of the record-keeping function underlying the financial statements. This view took firm roots in Japanese accounting academia. Stimulated by the efforts of introducing 'modern measurement theory' to accounting by Ijiri and, previously, by Mattessich, Japanese research in accounting measurement flourished during the 1970s. Indeed, Jaedicke *et al.* (1966/74/76), i.e. AAA's collected papers on accounting measurement, was translated into Japanese in two volumes in 1974 and 1976, respectively. Furthermore, Ijiri (1981) presented, in dialogue form, his views on the close relationship between double-entry and the historical cost principle.

Subsequent to those works, Ijiri (1982/84) challenged the hypothesis of double-entry by extending it to – or even replacing it by – a multi-entry, particularly a triple-entry approach. In the English original of this book (p. 39) Ijiri claimed that 'there is another important approach to accounting which may be called the *accountability* approach. The pros and cons of implementing a triple-entry system must therefore be considered from this standpoint, too'.

In *Triple-entry bookkeeping and income momentum* (Ijiri 1982/84) Ijiri incorporated as an appendix his Japanese lecture on American accounting practices in the 1970s (as presented at the annual meeting of the Japan Accounting Association in 1983). Ijiri (1989/90) extended his accountability approach and triple-entry bookkeeping to what he called 'momentum accounting'. It is based on drawing parallels between physics and accounting, and may well be Ijiri's most *original* contribution to accounting research.

14.4 Ecological or environmental accounting

Another significant contribution of the latter half of the twentieth century was the development of environmental accounting. The early interest in environmental issues in Japan is natural for a country not only densely populated but also highly industrialized. In the 1960s, Japan experienced severe pollution problems caused by rapid economic growth. Here again, it was Kurosawa who challenged the problems. In 'Seitai-kaikeigaku' (Kurosawa 1972a), he proposed the term 'ecological accounting' for the first time in Japan, and established a course at Yokohama National University in 1974. This course was taught by Aizaki (who held the first chair in this subject). Kurosawa (1972b: 6) argued from the outset that 'to make environmental accounting meaningful it is important to study environmental issues from the following three points of view: (a) the financial information system, (b) the management information system and (c) the macro-accounting system'.

Thus it appears that a major characteristic of Japanese accounting research (compared to other countries) is a more integrated perspective of micro- and macro-accounting. The first and most comprehensive Japanese work on environmental accounting written from this perspective was that by Kawano (1998). It explained the structure of the United Nation's macro-environmental accounting, i.e. SEEA (UN 1993) and the estimation of the main aggregates of SEEA by the Japanese government. It also offers a description of the theory and practice of micro-environmental accounting in relation with the Environmental Management System (EMS) as proposed by the International Organization for Standardization (ISO). Finally, it discussed the possible integration of micro- and macro-environmental accounting. Another notable contribution to environmental accounting was made by Kimio Uno (1995). It examined (i) the feasibility of the proposals of SEEA, (ii) estimated the so-called 'green GDP' and (iii) discussed the Japanese experience gathered in environmentally-related areas such as energy conservation, pollution prevention and a radical change in lifestyle. Koguchi (1990, 1997b, in English) proposed a meso (i.e. regional) environmental accounting system to secure the sustainability of water resources.

There also appeared a series of publications in the area of *corporate* environmental accounting, among which the anthology (of some 17 papers) by Yamagami and Kikuya (1995) should be mentioned. Its first part ('Environmental protection and business accounting'), was a search for the foundations of environmental accounting and the comparison with the methodology of traditional business accounting. The second part ('Environmental reporting in various countries') surveyed the present state of environmental reporting in European countries. Most of its contributors were strongly influenced by the ideas contained in such publications as *The greening of accountancy: the profession after Pearce* (Gray 1990) and *Accounting for the environment* (Gray et al. 1993).

Another book, worth mentioning, is *Kankyo kaikei* (Kokubu 1998). It proposed a framework for corporate environmental accounting from the stakeholders' point of view. There, the author suggested the integration of internal and external environmental accounting; he also emphasized the necessity of reporting the costs and benefits arising from the environment protection activities of a corporation. Kokubu (1999) extended these ideas by taking a fresh look at the notion of accountability. His publications too, were influenced by the methodology and philosophy of Gray (cf. Yamagami and Kikuya 1995) and Hopwood (e.g. 1988).

14.5 Cost and managerial accounting

Cost accounting received attention early on from Kurosawa (1938, 1941b, 1952), and was followed by studies of depreciation and cost accounting by Kimura (1943, 1947) and Kimura and Kojima (1960). Later it was Ijiri's (1965/70) goal programming that attracted the interest of accountants and business men. Then followed studies on sequential choice under moral hazard (e.g. by the Japanese-American Matsumura 1988), and on adaptive behaviour of management control and information analysis (Itami 1977). A further development was the advent of matrix accounting, first made popular in Japan by Koshimura (1968, 1969). The latter publication is a collection and translation of pertinent essays by Mattessich, Richards, Goetz and Corcoran.

A compendium of *Research on information and accounting for managerial decision and control in Japan* was offered by Sato et al. (1982). More recent major achievements of Japanese managerial accounting was the conception of such ideas as 'target costing', '*kaizen* costing', and the 'just in time' (JIT) approach. Target costing is a market-oriented costing concept aiming at cost reduction in the development and design phase of a new product. It starts with the question 'How much is the customer willing to spend for a specific product?' Deducting from this target price the target costs (that must not be exceeded) yields the target profit. *Kaizen* costing, on the other hand, concerns the manufacturing phase where its main goal is cost reduction in a variety of ways. It concentrates on value-adding cost drivers, tries to reduce or eliminate cost drivers that do not add value, and aims at correcting cost-overruns at an early stage, etc.

In the 1960s Toyota introduced another innovative manufacturing method, the JIT manufacturing system that comprises, together with the 'lean production' programme, a management and costing philosophy that essentially reflects the Japanese attitude of economy and discipline. It emphasizes the avoidance of waste on all levels, pleads for minimum inventories, as well as a demand-pull system where production is strictly synchronized with demand, non-confrontational attitudes with workers and suppliers, and many other features. Monden (1983/85) described the JIT system in great detail, promoting its dispersion all over the world. Most of these simple but revolutionary ideas (later greatly elaborated) arose in the Japanese auto industry, but ultimately spread to many industrial and commercial sectors (some of them even to banking). Scholars at the Massachusetts Institute of Technology undertook a five-year project of investigating a new Japanese 'lean production' system. The results were published in Womack *et al.* (1990a) and introduced with the following words:

> we've become convinced that the principles of lean production can be applied equally in every industry across the globe and that the conversion to lean production will have a profound effect on human society – it will truly change the world.
>
> (Womack *et al.* 1990a: 7–8)

Such ideas have greatly stimulated the managerial accounting literature of many countries, and one can find numerous pertinent publications not only in Japanese, but even more so in English, German, French, Spanish, Portuguese and other languages. For details see the collection of essays by Monden and Sakurai (1989) on *Japanese management accounting: a world class approach to profit management*. This title is no exaggeration but well characterizes the international significance of this methodology.

Other pertinent publications were the papers by Sakurai (1989) on how to use target costing, by Sakurai and Huang (1989), discussing a Japanese survey of factory automation and its impact on management control systems, as well as *Japanese cost management* by Monden (2000), dealing with cost management in various Japanese companies under organizational and humanistic aspects of cost reduction practices. There were also two German papers by Hiromoto (1989, 1991) on management accounting and its difficulties. Furthermore, there were two books by Monden, one *Cost reduction systems: target costing and Kaizen costing* (1994/95/97, in Japanese and English, respectively), the other, *Japan target-costing system of parts supplier committed to the development phase of the automaker* (1996). Further, to mention only a few pertinent publications are: *Nissan Motor Company, Ltd.: target costing system* (Cooper 1994); *Japanese language literature on target costing: an abstract of key ideas* (Ishizaki *et al.* 1995); *Target costing for effective cost management: product cost planning at Toyota Australia* (International Federation of Accountants 1999); 'Determinants of effective product cost management during product development: opening the black box of target costing' (Koga 1999).

14.6 Historical accounting studies

Japanese scholars always showed a keen interest in accounting history, publishing in Japanese, as well as in the English language. Early examples of the latter were the publications by Shimme (1937) and Nishikawa (1956), both on the beginning of double-entry bookkeeping in Japan. Later examples of such historical studies (also in English) were by Fujita (1968/91) on the development and nature of accounting principles in Japan, by Someya (1989, 1996) on 'accounting revolutions in Japan' and on an historical approach to Japanese accounting, respectively, and Kojima's (1987/95) work on 'accounting history'. Regrettably, this history does not go much beyond the early nineteenth century (apart from its silence on such important French authors as Jaques Savary, Mathieu de la Porte, Edmond Degrange, etc.). Also, there are some profiles on Iwao Iwata [1905–55], Kiyoshi Kurosawa [1902–90] and Wasaburo Kimura [1902–73] by Morita (1994), Chiba (1994) and Yamagata (1994), respectively (all in Edwards' 1994 book *Twentieth-century accounting thinkers*).

Furthermore, there is a comparison between accounting practice in the USA, Korea and Japan by Kim and Song (1990), as well as Chiba's (1996) examination of Japanese accounting controls over the corporate sector during the Second World War, and Chiba (1991a, 1998) on the modernization process of Japanese accounting research, and on the evolution of Japan's modern accounting system, respectively. There is also Iwanabe's (1996) entry on 'Japan' in Chatfield and Vangermeersch's (1996) encyclopaedic work on accounting history; in this same work there are separate profiles of Kojima by Hirabayashi (1996) and of Kimura by Tsuji and Okano (1996) – surprisingly, there is no such profile on the famous Kurosawa in this encyclopaedic work. However, the latter has been profiled at length by Fujita and Garcia's (2005) 'Kiyoshi Kurosawa: le premier samuraï de la compatibilité' in Colasse's (2005) *Les grand auteurs en comptabilité*.

There exists, of course, a host of historical accounting publications in Japanese language of which some deal with *Izumo* bookkeeping, indigenous to Japan (e.g. Hirai 1936; Yamashita 1936). Among the more important archival studies are two monumental works: one by Ogura (1962), examining the documents of the merchant house of Nakai in Goshu; the other by Noboru Nishikawa (1993) dealing with the house of Mitsui (predecessor of the present Mitsui Group). Both revealed that these big merchant houses of the Edo period had, by the mid-eighteenth century, already highly advanced management accounting systems (for performance evaluation, capital maintenance, branch accounting, motivating employees and internal control). Furthermore, there were two publications in commemoration of the first centennial of modern accounting in Japan (Aoki 1976; Japan Accounting Association 1978).

A host of Japanese publications deal with Luca Pacioli and early Italian accounting, such as the books by Kojima (1961), Yoshio Kataoka (1956) and his son Yasuhiko Kataoka (1988, 1998). Above all, there is a series of papers (Nakanishi 1973, 1974) by Akira Nakanishi [1905–2005], who received various government honours in Italy, as well as a translation (by Nakanishi and Taniguchi) of a renowned book on Pacioli by Ricci (1940/73/77). Finally, it should be noted that Kobe University (1954) released a monumental Japanese *Festschrift* under the title *Studies on Schmalenbach* with contributions by 11 leading Japanese Schmalenbach experts. Apart from Japanese translations of at least eight of Schmalenbach's books, there also exists a translation (by Ichiro Katano [1903–83]) of Littleton's (1933/52) work on accounting history, *Accounting evolution to 1900.* Nakano (1992), inspired by the work of Littleton, explored the development of proprietorship theory from Pacioli to Hatfield. Other publications referring to the USA were, for example, Okamoto (1969), Hiromoto (1993) and Aoyagi (1986). The first dealt with the history of American standard costing; the second with its management accounting; and the third with the evolution of accounting theory in America, examining the works of Hatfield, McKinsey, Paton, Vatter, Littleton, May, Scott, Goetz and Bedford, all of whom were influential to Japanese accounting. For the UK, there was Chiba (1991b) on the history of the British financial accounting system, and for France there is Kishi's (1975) study on the accounting rules of the *Ordonnance de Commerce* of 1673.

Apart from two autobiographical studies by Kurosawa, there was, among his many other historical publications, a paper (Kurosawa 1936) on the accounting theory of D.R. Scott. Kurosawa (1982) also reviewed the papers published in *Kaikei* (the official journal of Japan's Accounting Association) to highlight different Japanese research trends (paradigms). And there was Kurosawa (1987), an anthology that contained discussions on the standardization of financial statements, focusing on the time from the early 1920s to 1949 (together with a presentation of the original texts of those standards). There also was Kurosawa (1990) on the history of Japanese accounting development. Finally, one may mention Tanaka's (1990) anthology on the development of accounting research in Japan, based on interviews with 12 eminent scholars (including Kurosawa, Ijiri, Aoki and Kojima).

14.7 Epilogue

Japanese accounting research in the twentieth century may be characterized by the following five features:

1   The introduction of modern accounting and its standards, including auditing principles by a selective adaptation of theories developed in England, America and Germany and learning from the experience in these countries.
2   Exploring the general foundations of accounting, including macro-accounting as based on an axiomatic approach. In macro-accounting, Japan partly anticipated such research, partly followed it. Its interest in axiomatizing the common basis of both derived from America and Norway. This interest is still much alive in research and education, for example, in the Economics Department of Chuo University in Tokyo that offers both micro- and macro-accounting programmes on the graduate, as well as undergraduate level.
3   Designing environmental accounting on the basis of micro-, meso- and macro-accounting. Although Japanese scholars learned much from the pertinent foreign literature, the Japanese approach to environmental accounting research tends towards a closer integration of micro- and macro-accounting.

4   Introduction of a series of innovations of management accounting and costing procedures (such as target costing, developed by practitioners and engineers in Japanese industry). Here Japan proved its true leadership in modern managerial accounting.

5   Strong interest in Japanese, as well as Western accounting history, and the abundance of Japanese translations of renowned accounting publications in English, German and other languages. These translations made foreign accounting classics accessible to a wide Japanese audience.

As a result of such efforts, a variety of accounting systems have played a crucial role in Japanese society. However, to further pursue this path we must pay heed to the following warning of one of the leading and internationally recognized accounting scholars of our time:

> What could be a dangerous sign for accounting research in the next century is the 'erosion of the common body of knowledge, experience and interest' that binds researchers in the accounting discipline together. When this common body is gone, so is the accounting discipline. This binding force seems to have become weaker and weaker over the past 50 years .... . This point brings up the importance of 'foundational research in accounting'.
>
> (Ijiri 1996: 85)

For Japanese accounting academics this means that foundational research must continue to explore the theoretical framework that comprises micro-, meso- and macro-accounting.

15 Accounting publications and research in twentieth-century Russia[1]

15.1 Introduction

There exist many publications on Russian accounting research in Western literature; for example, the French books by de Sigalas (1936) on the status of government enterprises in the USSR and Gachkel (1946) on the mechanism of Soviet finances; an Italian paper by Amodeo (1945) on cost accounting in the USSR; and a German paper by Rosenkranz (1949) on the organization of industrial accounting in the Soviet Union. In English, the *International Journal of Accounting Education and Research* published a series of papers, among which the best known may be those by Gorelik (1971, 1973, 1974) on changing of profitability measurements in the Soviet Union, on the uniformity of its accounting system, and on Soviet accounting, planning and control, respectively; furthermore there are some papers by Bailey (1977, 1982, 1990) on accounting in Russia and accounting under Stalinism, respectively, and a paper by Lebow and Tondkar (1986) on accounting in the Soviet Union in general.[2] More recently, there is Motyka's (1993, two volumes) bibliography of Russian accounting publications from 1736–1917, the books by Enthoven *et al.* (1992, 1994, 1998) that inform the reader about various accounting, auditing and taxation issues of the 'new' Russian Federation (also offering some short historical remarks), and Sokolov's (1991) books on the history of bookkeeping and accounting, as well as Sokolov and Kovalev's (1996a) entry on 'Russia' in the international accounting encyclopaedia by Chatfield and Vangermeersch, as well as a paper by Liberman and Eidinov (1995) on the development of accounting in Russia (Tsarist as well as Soviet) in the *European Accounting Review*. This journal contains a few more papers on various aspects of Russian accounting and auditing (e.g. Bychkova 1996a). Furthermore, there are some conference presentations on this topic by the latter author (occasionally with co-authors). Finally, there is the paper by Sokolov and Bychkova (2004) on Russian accounting in the twentieth century that also goes beyond Soviet accounting. Yet none of these publications presents a satisfactory insight into Russian 'accounting research', though bits and pieces of such an agenda can be extracted from several of the publications mentioned above.

15.2 Academic accounting in twentieth-century Imperial Russia

Towards the end of the nineteenth century, in Russia there existed three 'native' schools of accounting that rivalled each other: the so-called *Artel*[3] school, the Moscow School and the St Petersburg School.

(1) The leader of the *Artel* School was Feodor Venediktovich Ezersky [1836–1916],[4] who edited the journal *Schetovod* (*Accountant*). This school was known for its 'nationalistic' approach that propagated Russian accounting terminology (e.g. using the equivalent of 'input' and 'output' instead of 'debit' and 'credit'). It also envisioned profit determination after each financial transaction, and emphasized the cash basis as well as the movement of capital through the three stages 'money–goods–money'. According to Sokolov and Kovalev:

> F. Ezersky stressed the importance of a perpetual inventory system, which allowed for profit determination at various time intervals during the year. [And I.F.] Valitsky (1877) focused on prime costs for his 'Cost of Basic Production'. Valitsky designed the methodology of both a national and a firm's balance sheet along the lines of current and noncurrent classification.
>
> (Sokolov and Kovalev 1996a: 508)

Valitsky also showed interest in macro-accounting. But the hallmark of the *Artel* school and its leader was 'triple accounting' (cf. Bailey 1982 – though this must not be confused with 'triple-entry accounting' as advanced by Ijiri 1989). The Russian triple feature rather seems to have been reflected in the use of three accounts or accounts classes, such as 'non-monetary items', 'monetary items' and 'capital items' – an approach that even rejected the customary separation of 'accounts receivable' from 'accounts payable'. According to the historian Masdorov (1972), the dispute between this Russian 'triple accounting' and the Italian 'double-entry accounting' reflected the quarrel between Slavophiles and the Western-oriented accountants (cf. Bailey 1982: 21n). But Lebow and Tondkar (1986: 63) remind us that by '1916, double-entry bookkeeping was well established in the metallurgical industry and mining enterprises operated by the government, in nearly all large private enterprises, and in most government agencies [footnote omitted] … . The use of double-entry, however, did not spread to the merchant classes'.

(2) The St Petersburg School harboured such prominent contemporary Russian accounting academics as Lev (Léon) Gomberg [1866–1936] (1895, 1909),[5] Popov (1910), Sivers (1917)[6] and Blatov (1931), as well as Adolf Markovich Wolf [1854–1920]. The latter was their leader, and the founder of the journal *Schetovodstvo* (*Accountancy*, published from 1888–1904[7] and, under a different editorship, from 1923–30). It promoted the Western double-entry method (later made mandatory in the USSR, except for small enterprises), and promulgated the accounting literature of Germany, Italy and France. But during those uncertain times, it was replaced in 1930 by the journal *Za sotsialistichesky*

uchet, while another, more politically oriented one, *Vestnik Schetovodstva*, was published for an even shorter time (between 1926–28), *Schetovodstvo*. Bailey (1982: 19) pointed out that 'Among the long list of European supporters, named in the journal, were G. Cerboni, F. Hügli, E. Léautey and E. Pisani. The journal featured articles by foreign authors ... and fostered an interest in Continental European accounting theory and practice'.

Although Wolf (1890/1899) may not have been a highly original scholar, he was a remarkable organizer who understood how to gather a circle of prominent accountants. This group favoured an approach that derived the balance sheet from individual *accounts*, based on original vouchers (in contrast to the inventory-based Moscow school, see next item).

Lev (later Léon) Gomberg was undoubtedly the most renowned international member of this group. As to his *Russian* publications, there is an early book by Gomberg (1895) and a series of articles in the journal *Schetovodstvo* (1898: 48–9; 1902: 85; 1903: 229–32), as well as the article 'Schetovodstvo i ego nauchnaya systema' in the *Bulleten Moscowskogo obschestwa buchgalterov* (1909 4: 20). However, Gomberg's best-known works were published in German and French (while he lived in Switzerland). His 'economology' consisted of seven problem-areas: valuation, the inventory, the budget, bookkeeping, (periodic) reporting and control – for further details see Chapters 3 and 4.

Nikolay Ustinovich Popov, who might be counted in the St Petersburg School, employed algebraic methods and demonstrated that different Russian accounting methods were merely different variations of double-entry. He thus concluded that the latter was the major or even only feasible accounting paradigm (cf. Popov 1910).

Evstaphiy Evstaphievich Sivers [1852–1917], another reputed Russian accountant (though, possibly not associated with the journal *Accountancy*) regarded 'exchange' as the core of the economic activity as reflected in double-entry, thus treating all economic operations as exchange transactions. However, Lounsky (1913) opposed this 'exchange theory', raising the objection that not all economic operations are (or may be interpreted as) exchanges. For example, contrary to Sivers, the transfer of income to owner's equity ought not to be regarded as an 'exchange'. Sivers recommended the daily recording of transactions in a special journal, and emphasized the importance of the account for semi-finished products.

Apart from this, Sivers seems to have defended the 'fund theory of depreciation' (apparently corresponding to the 'retirement method' of depreciation that, in the West, 'has now been generally abandoned' – see Cooper and Ijiri (1983: 170); for a better understanding of this method of depreciation and amortization, see the explanation offered (in a later section) in the quotation by Lebow and Tondkar (1986: 72). Sivers was known as an excellent teacher with original educational ideas. Instead of mere techniques, he taught his students to grasp the essence of accounting (see Sivers 1915). Bailey (1982: 21) mentions that Sivers together with Blatov published (from 1908–16) a journal on commercial education: *Kommercheskoe obrazovanie*.

(3) The Moscow School consisted of the following illustrious scholars: Galagan (1918, 1927, 1928a, 1928b, 1930, 1939), Rudanovsky (1913, 1924, 1925), Feldhausen (1888) and Lounsky (1900). In opposition to the St Petersburg school, this group preferred to begin with the *inventory* (and related transactions) in order to derive from this basis the individual accounts (including the profit and loss account) and their closing balances, leading to the balance sheet. These scholars saw the main objective of accounting in the recording and reporting of asset values and equities.

One of their prominent members, Feldhausen (1888) presented an early Russian costing method under the translated name of 'normal factory reporting'. This may be considered to have been a prototype of standard costing (cf. Sokolov and Kovalev 1996a: 508). Feldhausen charged costs on an *estimated* basis, and entered the pertinent variances (between estimated and actual costs) in separate accounts. But this approach caused controversy in Russia: first, because inventories were charged at estimated instead of actual prices, thereby potentially affecting the correct determination of income; and, second, because estimated costs were deemed too unreliable at times of fluctuating prices (cf. *Schetovodstvo* 1889: 227–8).[8] In consequence, this system was limited to situations with minimal variances.

Nikolay Sevastyanovich Lounsky [1867–1956] was the major opponent of Sivers' approach. He regarded himself as the creator of a new accounting methodology, called 'the balance sheet theory' (Lounsky 1913, translated), that attained great popularity in Russia. He defined the balance sheet as 'a table where the property of an enterprise is compared to its sources; the balance sheet represents the economic and legal position of an enterprise at a moment of time' (Lounsky 1913: 238, translated). The novelty of this definition must be understood in its proper context. Traditionally, most of Russian accountants identified the passive side, foremost, as accounts payables or other debts. Owners' equity was merely a 'residual' rather than a 'source' of capital. But by emphasizing owners' equity among the passive items, Lounsky revealed all the '*sources*' of capital of an enterprise. This balance sheet approach is claimed to have lead to a new or different interpretation of the notions of debit and credit.

In Russia, as elsewhere, there existed some prominent economists interested in accounting. The most renowned among them was undoubtedly Wassily Leontief [1906–99], the creator of *input–output* analysis (Leontief 1951 – later called inter-industrial analysis, a special accounting system for the entire economy) who became an American citizen, and was awarded the Nobel Prize in 1973. Yet, his research not only ought to be counted as part of the English macro-accounting literature, but also the second rather than the first half of the twentieth century. But there were other Russia economists with a bent for accounting, for example, Peter Berngardovich Struve [1870–1944] and Mikhail Ivanovich Tugan-Baranovsky [1865–1919]. The former linked accounting to economics, while the latter was concerned with income determination. In Tugan-Baranovsky (1898, with English translation in 1970) he distinguished between the 'income of the enterprise', on one side, and the 'owners' profit', on the other. By doing so, he seems to have regarded the interest expenses on the firm's debt as an income component. For example, in a situation where debt equity was the only equity of the firm and the income covered only the debt's interest, this amounted to the firm's income, and there was no owners' profit. However, if the interest accounted for only one-third of the firm's income, the remaining two-thirds constituted the owners' profit.

For Tugan-Baranovsky the cost of *labour, materials, depreciation* and *other overheads* were genuine expenditures of the firm, but he excluded *interest*, as well as *rent* and *direct taxes* from them. He reasoned that these three kinds of charges do not affect a nation's wealth creation, and thus ought not to be included in the costs of the firm. Indeed, later, when the communists took over, they did not recognize economic costs for the use of capital, land and natural resources. Therefore depletion, rent and interest expenses were viewed as a capitalistic practice of exploitation, and thus were not charged to the enterprise. And since all enterprises are owned by the state, 'goodwill' was not even entered on a Soviet balance sheet (cf. Lebow and Tondkar 1986: 61) – but this is already a leap ahead. Tugan-Baranovsky also developed a notion of 'gross profit' that is of some interest in view of modern ideas on *realization* and *clean surplus.* He defined 'gross profit' in terms of value added.[9]

15.3 Accounting publications and research of Soviet Russia before 1930

Although we are here mainly concerned with accounting publications and research, some peculiar aspects of Soviet accounting *practice* ought to be pointed out. Shortly after the October Revolution of 1917, efforts were made to revise accounting and financial practices. The government decreed on 5 December, 1917 the creation of a Central Accounting Department for the entire Soviet Union. This department was charged to draft periodically a general balance sheet (with accompanying reports) for presentation to the All-Russian Congress for approval by the delegates of the 'Soviet of Workers, Peasants and Soldiers' (cf. Masdorov 1972: 53) – an undertaking hardly accompanied by success.

Another misconceived venture was the attempt to *eliminate* money in general, not merely the *former* monetary currency. Money, the instrument for measuring value, was replaced by the '*tred*', a currency of labour units (based on the 'labour theory of value') – apparently introduced by S.G. Strumilin [1877–1974] (1925). Workers were no longer paid in money but received booklets, each with a specified number of 'work-hours' or corresponding units of the *tred*, that served to pay for goods and services, as far as then available. However, this kind of currency did not work for commerce and industry, though a similar system, based on the '*working day*' (instead of the *tred*), seems to have succeeded temporarily in agriculture. Such drastic changes could not but have a ruinous effect upon accounting and the economic system in general. Originality and productivity were stifled, ledgers were in disarray, entries and financial statements were inaccurate or experienced delays, and inventories, as well as other records were beyond any reasonable control. No wonder that the stewardship function of accounting broke down, and dishonesty became rampant, particularly when the owner was the government (cf. Rudanovsky 1924). Nikolaev (1926: 37, translated) asked: 'Who is able to guess the hundreds of millions and even billions of rubles that have been squandered under such absence of order or, better said, under such disorder?' And Clarkson pointed out that:

> In the absence of financial accounting and control, of profit and loss statements, it was impossible to form a serious idea of the relative conditions of any enterprise .... It was the only occasion in which a modern economy has attempted to get along without accounting, and its absence contributed to the dislocation characterizing those years.
>
> (Clarkson 1961/69: 604; see also Bailey 1982: 26)

And from 'insiders', like Nikolaev (1926: 37, translated), came complaints about the living conditions of accountants at the time: 'A survey of the living conditions of accountants ..., if such surveys were undertaken, would in all likelihood have revealed drastic deviations from the norm as to their physical and mental health, as well as their average life-span'.

By 1920 a number of prominent experts attempted to improve Russian accounting theory (*schetovedenie*) and to restore the traditional ideas of double-entry. One of the first persons to do so was Rakhmily Jakovlevich Veitsman [1870–1936] who propagated ideas developed by German scholars, although he may have been more interested in their methods than in the substance of their ideas. But the general interest in those ideas was manifested by the fact that the following books were made available in Russian translations: Gerstner's *Revisionstechnik* (auditing), Hall's *Die Selbstkostenrechnung und die moderne Organisation von Machinenfabriken* (cost and industrial accounting), Hügli's *Buchhaltungstudien* (studies in accounting) and his *Buchhaltungssysteme und Buchhaltungsformen* (systems and forms of accounting), Schär's *Die Buchhaltung und Bilanz* (accounting and the balance sheet) and his *Methodik der Buchhaltung* (accounting method), as well as Schmalenbach's *Kontenrahmen* (chart of accounts) – cf. Bailey (1982: 26–7).[10] There may well have existed other translations (possibly from one or the other work by H. Nicklisch who enjoyed some popularity in Russia), just as there was a translation from the French of Léautey and Guilbault's *Pricipes généraux de comptabilité* (principles of general accounting).[11] As to the English accounting literature, apparently no publication was translated into Russian at this time – whereby Galagan added that: 'Perhaps not surprising, the work of England's sole professor of accounting, Dicksee, was regarded poorly' (cf. Bailey 1982: 27).

Due to the stifling circumstances, originality in costing and price determination was confined in Soviet Russia to a *special kind* of 'cost accounting' (though not in the sense of Western 'managerial accounting') and to production theory. Bailey

(1982: 26–27), referring to Laktionov (1924), quotes him as criticizing 'the haphazard and old-fashioned production organization found in Russian factories, ... [giving] an exposition of the best practice he had encountered [in Western Europe]'. Laktionov also emphasized that in Western factories the preparation of a *Vorkalkulation* (German for *ex-ante* calculation or cost estimates), a technical specification and a *Nachkalkulation* (German for *ex-post* cost calculation) was required. Bailey (based on further references) continued to point out the eagerness of Russian accountants of this period to learn from the West:

> In 1926, a Soviet delegation attended the International Congress of Accountants held in Amsterdam [footnote omitted]. The delegation was led by Bogorodskii who had translated from the French the book written by A. Guilbault and E. Leautey. Three years later, another Soviet delegation visited a machine accounting exhibition in Paris and six German industrial concerns, including Krupps of Essen, Siemens Sickert, Siemens and Halske (Berlin), and the Allgemeine Electrizität Gesellschaft. At this time, and again in 1934, Schmalenbach received 'visits from Russians who questioned him on inter-firm comparisons, cost behaviour and on the national accounting that he was beginning to advocate'.
>
> (Bailey 1982: 28)

As to Fritz Schmidt's renowned work on 'organic accounting', we could not find out whether his original edition (or a revised version of it) has been translated, but a paper of his (Schmidt 1929) seems to have been translated into Russian (and published in the same year in *Schetovodstvo*). It also appears that the 1924 revaluation for basic production factors in the USSR was stimulated by Schmidt's replacement cost theory.

The followers of this German methodology took the balance sheet as a starting point and derived from it their double-entries. One of those disciples was Nikolay Semenovich Pomazkov [1889–1968]. His *'absolute* balance sheet' (Pomazkov 1929: 249–63, translated) rests on the idea that any classification or partition of balance sheet items is only a particular case of an 'absolute' classification comprising all possible classification schemes. This is a fairly obvious notion, but its explicit formulation may have been prompted by either the disputes on the 'correct' classification scheme, or the insistence of some bureaucrats on one and only one particular classification.

Nikolay Aleksandrovich Blatov [1875–1942] was a follower of Sivers. He supported Sivers' educational ideas and the notion that double-entry reflects an 'exchange of values' based on the flow or circulation principle. Blatov, in continuing the use of Sivers' three basic categories of value exchange (material, money and obligations), devised a scheme revealing the possible categories of economical exchange as mirrored in the double-entry system. This became known as 'Blatov's diagram' (see Blatov 1931: 41–2, reproduced in Sokolov and Bychkova 2004: 486). It contained the following categories: (1) exchange of material values for money (e.g. cash sale of the goods); (2) exchange of money for material values

(e.g. cash purchase of the goods); (3) exchange of material values against an obligation (e.g. credit sale of goods); (4) exchange of an obligation against material values
(e.g. credit purchase of goods); (5) exchange of money for an obligation (e.g. to
lend money to an agent); (6) exchange of an obligation for money (e.g. a customer
paying a debt); (7) exchange of material values for other material values (e.g. disas-
sembling a shack, and using it as fire wood); (8) exchange of an obligation for
another obligation (e.g. taking on a bank debt to finance borrowing by customers).

15.4 Soviet Russia under Stalin: accounting publications and research

The 'exchange theory', though prevailing for a considerable time, engendered
much criticism. Originally, one argued that not all transactions are based on
genuine exchange. After 1930, one objected to the exchange theory with the
argument that it might conceal value added; a criticism that may have failed
since even the Marxists realized that added value resulted from the production
process and its labour input.

Apart from other objections, Blatov's scheme fell short by ignoring a series of
adjustment transactions. And yet, it seems that the exchange theory became an
essential part of Russian accounting literature of this period. In fact, all the theories recognizing the objective character of double-entry (arising out of the asset
movements) were ultimately based on Sivers' and Blatov's ideas. Or, as Losinsky
[1894–1948] asserted: 'Double entry is merely the external registration of the
objective movement of an exchange process' (Losinsky 1938: 34, translated).

But Blatov's influence reached beyond the exchange theory; he is also known
for his classification of the various balances (residuals) arising in various
accounts (we abstain from discussing this classification scheme as it seems
unnecessarily complex, considering the limited insight it offers). Lokshin (1934,
1936), who tried to extend this classification, pointed out that the naive or dema-
gogical call for a 'precise' balance sheet is not only impracticable but profoundly
utopian. He shared the view of the poet Maiakovsky [1893–1930] that accounting
should not be seen as a 'reflecting mirror' but as a 'magnifying glass', as it is
purpose-oriented and based on efficiency and economy. Lokshin also believed
accounting ought to supply only information useful to management; additional
information that cannot influence administrative and managerial decisions need
not be generated. Such thoughts would hardly have been acceptable in a capitalist
society where a good deal of accounting information serves the shareholders.

Nikolaev drew attention to the fact that depreciation and amortization are:

> in essence, two completely incommensurable categories ... *Depreciation*
> results from the physical process of wearing out fixed assets and their losing
> value; *amortization* is a process of accumulation of the financial resources,
> depending on the purposes of a financial policy. And so the sum of depreci-
> ation cannot be identical with the sum of amortization.
>
> (Nikolaev 1926: 56, translated)

This may require the following explanation:

> Soviet practice of capitalizing the expected repairs of assets differs from Western principles, which require such repairs to be either capitalized or expensed ... . The Soviet practice, which capitalizes expected repair costs when a fixed asset is required, is theoretically sound, although different from U.S. practice, because the need to repair assets accumulates as they are used and wear out. Such expenses do not suddenly occur when the repair is made. The estimated capitalized repairs are then amortized over the useful life of the assets.
>
> (Lebow and Tondkar 1986: 72)

Nikolaev's insight greatly influenced accounting theory and practice of Soviet Russia. Indeed, two pertinent accounts were introduced in the Chart of Accounts of 1937. One for the 'depreciation' of fixed assets, the other for 'amortization' of those assets. Yet, the precise use of these accounts was peculiar to Soviet accounting – it is described in some detail in Nikolaev (1926: 56). One may add that only linear depreciation was permitted in the USSR, and that depreciation rates (as well as useful asset lives) were set by government authorities.

Alexander Pavlovich Rudanovsky [1863–1931] believed in the possibility of an *objective* balance sheet; he thought the more perfect an accounting model is, the better it would reflect this objectivity and the economic activity behind it. Yet, the discrepancy between the 'absolute truth' and practical feasibility led him to the following conclusions: (i) only part of the total economic activity of the enterprise is reflected in accounting, the data of which are only of relative value; (ii) an accounting theory should be geared towards generating pertinent models providing the optimal reflection of economic processes.

Furthermore, Rudanovsky distinguished three accounting modes: registration (e.g. dual entries); systematizing (e.g. integration of the real accounts into the balance sheet and a chart of accounts); coordination (e.g. relating data to sources and information); and valuation (e.g. based on the realization principle instead on *ad hoc* rules). He also emphasized more substantive activities, such as funding (financing the operations of the enterprise), allocating reserves (creating financial reserves and making valuation adjustments) and budgeting (recording the process of expected wealth creation) (cf. Rudanovsky 1925: 80). Furthermore, he urged that *all kinds* of obligations of the enterprise should be revealed in its financial statements, a proposal that found approval from neither bureaucrats nor from academics. Today, Rudanovsky and his pupil Galagan are still considered to be the most prominent Russian accountants of this particular era. Rudanovsky is believed to have contributed a wealth of substantive and conceptual ideas (e.g. the emphasis on *realization*, the use of 'funds' rather than 'capital') that prevailed in Russia until the last decade of the twentieth century.

Alexander Mikhailovich Galagan [see Chapter 2] studied in Italy, France and Germany, but returned in 1906 to Russia (cf. Bailey 1982: 20). He may have exercised even more influence than his teacher, Rudanovsky. If the latter was more practice oriented, the former had a theoretical-empirical bent, and pre-ferred to rely on the inductive method (see Galagan 1918, 1928a). In 1930 he developed the 'dialectic-materialistic accounting theory' by trying to interpret double-entry in terms of Hegel's dialectics (see Galagan 1939). Yet, in confor-mity with the former European tradition, his accounting theory relied heavily on classification schemes (even that of Cerboni).

In this sense, Galagan (1928a) distinguished three basic accounting elements. The first was 'subjects', the participants in the economic process, such as employees, proprietors, managers, agents and external 'correspondents' (such as debtors and creditors). The second was 'objects', which were the various kinds of fixed and current assets of the enterprise. And third was *'transactions'* acting upon person and/or values (objects of wealth). He further divided transactions by kinds (according to use in industry, commerce and consumption), also by their effect on the balance sheet (i.e. resulting in changes of balance values, changes in the structure of the balance sheet, as well as by their timing).

Furthermore, Galagan distinguished four kinds of accounting activities: first, 'observation' (determining the general status of an enterprise at a specific point of time, as well as its current performance); second, 'classification' (as carried out by the accounts used in the enterprise); third, 'induction' (resulting 'in the law of double-entry duality') and then 'deducing' the accounts to be debited and credited; fourth, 'synthesis and analysis'. Some of these aspects may seem obscure to modern accountants. Apart from the attempts by Evzlin (1909) and Galagan (1912) to revitalize Cerboni's nineteenth-century logismography (and its synthesis of main journal and ledger) in Russia, these notions are explained by Lebow and Tondkar as follows:

> the standardized accounts are divided into three groupings: synthetic accounts, sub-accounts, and analytical accounts. These accounts are described in Soviet accounting terminology as first-, second-, and third-order accounts. At the highest level, the analytical accounts are subdivided into accounts that detail the economic means, resources, and liabilities (balance sheet accounts) and those that detail the economic process and the results of operations (income statements) for the period. The synthetic income statements accounts can also be subdivided into three functions: procurement, production, and realization. The synthetic balance sheet accounts can be classified into accounts that record the following for the enterprise: (1) legal property, (2) liabilities, (3) reserves, and (4) capital .... The final accounting category is the operational account. Such accounts are nonstandardized accounts that provide complementary information.
>
> (Lebow and Tondkar 1986: 70)

It seems that such ideas arose mainly from the distinction between so-called 'synthetic accounts' that draw on the details found in the so-called 'analytical accounts' (see below). From this basis, Galagan proceeded to transform formal logic into dialectics (though continuing to rely on the principle of duality) in accord with Hegel's *dialectic law* (of conflict and the unity of opposites).[12] Although all this must, at an early stage, have been approved by Soviet authorities, it did not prevent them (in the course of the 1930s) from persecuting Galagan and, to a lesser extent, Rudanovsky as 'bourgeois academics'.[13] Indeed, in time the names of both of these eminent Russian accountants of the Soviet era fell into oblivion in the USSR. And Bailey confirms that:

> Either temporarily or permanently, a number of leading accounting scholars – including V. Andreev, N.A. Blatov, A.M. Galagan, N.A. Kiparisov, N.S. Lunsky, A.P. Rudanovsky, and R.Ya. Veitsman – were forced from public life and their books blacklisted.
>
> (Bailey 1982: 32)

Indeed, after 1929 immense changes occurred in Soviet Russia when all scientific and cultural sectors were put under draconian control. In accounting, Kolman (1931: 74–5, translated), a Czech communist-emigrant, led the major charge; he defamed many accountants with the criticism that 'accounting is based on an economic theory that denies the difference between the USSR and a capitalist country'. Of course, everyone knew that there were great differences between accounting in Soviet Russia compared to that of a capitalistic system. The monopolistic economic system of the state, as owner of all means of production, did simplify many accounting functions. And the substitution of the profit motive by the requirements of fulfilling the production plan was another major shift.

A new political era enabled a new breed of accountants to become prominent. Among these were: J.M. Galperin [see above], N.A. Kiparisov [1875–1956], N.A. Leontiev [1893–1954], I.A. Koshkin [1895–1980], V.I. Stotsky [1894–1941] and M.K. Zhebrak [1889–1962]. The first three of these academics introduced major changes in accounting theory that were more palatable to their political masters, and a new 'official' accounting theory was proclaimed. The focus on a separate balance sheet gave way to a discussion of the 'subject' of accounting, of the proper 'method', and of the 'classification' of accounts. Some accountants put special emphasis on original documents ('source documents') while others denied their importance, arguing that they are a part of accounting technique rather than its method.

According to the first view, the source document would reveal the economic activity that becomes the accounting object. According to the second, accountants neither record economic processes, nor the values of property or obligations, but only generate *information* (thus possibly foreshadowing, in a modest way, an aspect of the modern American 'information perspective'). One argued that from a managerial point of view the recorded economic activities are not crucial, but only the correct information about them (e.g. if a physical count based on a new source document showed a discrepancy with the inventory account, then it is this new information that counts rather than the incorrect account balance). Indeed, it was this view that ultimately prevailed in this era of Soviet accounting. Bailey (1982: 29) summarized all this as follows:

> Based on the experience gained with various accounting systems during the preceding five years, in 1928–1930 the memorial voucher accounting system ... was developed and introduced. The system required the use of memorial vouchers (instead of a memorial book), a registration journal, a cashbook, an annual main ledger, loose-leave sheets and cards for the subsidiary accounts, and a balance sheet into which the ledger accounts were closed. The monthly summarization of the accounts and the extraction of monthly results were in accordance with the practice being advocated by E. Schmalenbach and others in Germany.
>
> (Bailey 1982: 29)

Masdorov (1973: 10–16) also mentions that in 1926 the *Gostorg*, the State Trading Commission, adapted the German *Durchschreibebuchhaltung* (duplication of entries by means of carbon copies) that led to the Russian *Kopiruchet* system. Koshkin (1940), another prominent accountant scholar, also relied to a considerable extent on German theories (of Schmidt, Nicklisch, Schmalenbach and others) and aimed at the analysis and application of those ideas. Although Koshkin was sceptical enough not to overrate the potentials of Soviet accounting techniques, he ultimately influenced the design and structure of the various Charts of Accounts (for different types of enterprises) that became obligatory in the USSR in the 1930s.

However, the greatest advances in Soviet accounting after the year 1930, are claimed to be those made in the peculiar version of cost accounting and cost analysis characteristic for the USSR.[14] It was during this time that intense interest emerged in this field in the Soviet Union, where it dominated our discipline until the mid-1990s. And yet, Lebow and Tondkar (1986: 66) agree with Bailey that:

> During the 1930s, a fierce struggle began between the pro- and anti-Stalinist factions. Accounting theoreticians also waged intense debates in the various accounting publications as to whether the nations accounting system should be based on historical or standard costs. When the Stalinists came to power, debate over accounting matters ended.
>
> (Bailey 1977: 72)

It must be remembered that the term 'cost accounting' when applied to Soviet accounting has a somewhat different connotation. Contrary to the West, where a financial accounting system exists on one side, and a cost accounting system on the other, Soviet accounting recognized only one single standardized system. And as Lebow and Tondkar reminds us that:

> It [i.e. Soviet accounting] is not designed to provide the enterprise managers with the type of information needed for decision making. The enterprise

accounting system is conditioned to provide average cost data for central planners .... Having government-established prices and guaranteed markets does not provide managers with an incentive to produce consistently high-quality goods .... Additionally, any gain or loss from the disposal of fixed assets is not reflected in the operating results of the enterprise. Such gains or losses are charged instead directly to the Ustavnii fund account. Therefore, management has little incentive to use the assets in a responsible manner.

(Lebow and Tondkar 1986: 77–8)

Perhaps this is the reason why many of their costing and pricing notions are difficult to grasp for 'Westerners', particularly decades after all such practices have vanished. Furthermore, Sokolov and Kovalev point out that:

Since October 1, 1929, there has been a compulsory monthly calculation of prime cost of production for all enterprises. On July 29, 1936, the document 'regulation on Accounting Statements and Balance Sheets' declared that only prime cost can be used for valuation of production .... Since 1930, a special accounting system of perpetual inventory cards became the dominant system, following the German system of '*Definitive Kontrollbuchhaltung*'.

(Sokolov and Kovalev 1996a: 509)

During the Stalinist period, financial accounting theory declined,[15] and the most important theoretical as well as practical questions concerned the so-called 'normative accounting', the Russian version of *standard costing*, made popular by Zhebrak. As in any kind of estimated cost scheme, the pivot was the *variance* between standard costs and actual costs, as well as the relation between cost accounting and price calculation. N.G. Chumachenko [1925–], I.A. Basmanov [1917–74] and E.K. Gilde [1904–83] began to discuss pertinent questions during the first half of the 1960s. They emphasized four alternative possibilities: (1) price calculation based on cost accounting; (2) cost accounting based on price calculation; (3) price calculation and cost accounting having the same basis; and (4) price calculation and cost accounting as being independent of each other.

Prominent accountants of previous periods had already promoted estimated costing approaches, for example, Popov (1903) and Blatov (1930), followed much later by Bunimovich (1971). All these authors regarded cost accounting and its analyses as a central issue, but some regarded cost accounting as a mere 'means', and its analysis as the actual 'object'. Others disagreed on the following grounds: (1) costs are based on expenditures but not vice versa; (2) if price calculation determines cost accounting the two might no longer be distinguishable from each other; and (3) if the object of cost accounting is price calculation, the former might get distorted. These controversies may be difficult to grasp from a Western point of view, but they were important in Soviet accounting.

A second cost accounting approach – the most popular in Russian accounting literature – can be traced to the publications of Arnold (1809) and Mudrov (1846). Its twentieth-century disciples were Stotsky (1936), Veitsman (1936),

Zhebrak (1950), Narinsky (1976) and others. The basic idea of this approach is simple: determine first the costs and then the price to be charged, thus considering cost accounting and price determination (calculation) as two distinguished stages. But, for various reasons, objections were raised against this approach as well.

A third approach goes back to a prominent nineteenth-century Russian accountant, Ivanov (1872), whose followers were Guliaev (1905), Bogorodsky (1935), Dodonov (1973), Shchenkov (1973), Margulis (1975), Sopko (1976) and others. Their alleged purpose was to determine the actual costs of finished products, hence considering cost accounting and price determination as a single process.

A fourth approach can be traced back to the work of Korniliev (1862). In the second half of the twentieth century it has been revived by Chumachenko (1965), Gilde (1968), Basmanov (1970), Ivashkevich (1974) and others. It is characterized by the *separation* and juxtaposition of cost accounting and price determination. The authors concentrated on only two alternatives. Either the enterprise has a cost accounting system but no separate pricing system; or the enterprise has a pricing mechanism but no cost accounting system. Obviously, both alternatives are conceivable. Chumachenko (1965) pointed out that a 'general trend in accounting is the gradual transition from controlling the costs of products to controlling costs accumulated in (operational) cost centres'.

Towards the end of the twentieth century, Gilde, a renowned academic, pursued another tradition of Russian accounting. Although recognizing the difference between cost accounting and cost calculation (for product pricing), he concentrated on the former and investigated it by allocating the costs not to cost centres but to various manufacturing processes. This allowed a unified costing system independent from cost centres (it seems to resemble what is called 'process costing' in English terminology). In the beginning, when Gilde started his activity, approximately 58 different industrial branches (each with its own set of instructions) existed in the Soviet Union (cf. Basmanov 1970). This approach made it possible to integrate the accounting charts with individual responsibility centres. Indeed, for each separate technological process there was a matrix that enabled controlling the cost items of each responsibility centre. Such costing matrices reported the economic activities with relatively small time lags, and greatly facilitated the task and decision making of production managers. Ivashkevich (1974) was a major contributor in applying such matrices to cost accounting and cost analysis (for early ideas and applications of computerized spreadsheets and cost accounting matrices in America, see Mattessich 1961, 1964a, 1964b). Further applications led Paly (1975) to the following conclusion:

> Starting from a theoretical premise, it is possible to connect the numerous analytical accounts with each of the corresponding synthetic accounts in such a way as to determine the 'cost price' and the relevant information not only by products and cost items, but also by technical processes, other economic factors and their constituents (i.e. particularly those concerning technical-organizational aspects), and this for self-supporting subdivisions and other facilities required by management.

As to 'accounting history', this topic was reintroduced in 1975 optionally into the accounting curriculum with special permission of the Soviet authorities. The first specialist in this area seems to have been Masdorov (1972, 1973). However, Bailey (1982: 36) warns: 'it should be remembered that published work is expected to be compatible with an approved ideological framework'. Thus some of Masdorov's statements ought to be viewed with caution. Apparently they do not always match with previously made historical remarks in publications such as: Galagan (1927), Galperin (1934), Shchenkov and Leontiev (1938), Losinsky (1939), Kiparisov (1940), Leontiev (1944) and Sumtsov (1940). It must also be added that an early Russian attempt of *historical* writing in accounting was that by Bauer (1911).

15.5 Accounting publications and research in the Russian Federation

Accounting *practice* changed drastically after the disintegration of the USSR. As to accounting *theory*, it is claimed to have been affected to a lesser degree. And yet, both practice and theory were strongly influenced by Anglo-American accounting thought. A significant number of Western (mainly English-language) accounting texts were translated into Russian, for example, Horngren and Foster (1987), Anthony and Reece (1989), Van Horn (1989), Arens and Loebbecke (1991), Mueller *et al.* (1991), Needles *et al.* (1991/94), Hendriksen and Van Breda (1992/97) and Bernstein (1993). Perhaps more English-language accounting texts were translated into Russian than into any other language (with the possible exception of Japanese and Spanish). Furthermore, a great number of Russian accounting students received their training abroad. International accounting conferences, various educational programmes and seminars also contributed to the dispersion of Western accounting thoughts in Russia.

As Enthoven (1999) indicated, shortly after the collapse of the Soviet Union, its unified accounting system for national planning also disintegrated, and an essentially new system emerged. Slowly and painfully, major changes occurred, affecting various accounting regulations as well as the Chart of Accounts. Above all, attempts were made to conform to international accounting standards. This new trend also stimulated foreign authors to write on various aspects of Russian accounting. In the forefront of such activities were such organizations (and their publications) as the Institute of Management Accountants (IMA) that published Enthoven *et al.* (1992, 1998) and the Center for International Accounting Development (CIAD) that jointly with the IMA published Enthoven *et al.* (1994). The first of these books covered 'accounting systems', 'accounting for joint ventures' and 'appraisal of future accounting and auditing', all in respect of the Russian Federation as well as other former Soviet Republics. Since subsequent changes in these countries occurred rapidly, the second of those studies is an update of the extension of the first, while the third is a more in-depth investigation that also captures issues of auditing and taxation in Russia and countries of the former USSR.

15.5.1 Financial accounting and local government accounting in the Russian Federation

Finally, during the 1990s, accounting methods as employed in the West (particularly in America) became popular in Russia. Financial statements (to be prepared quarterly and annually) are still fairly uniform and are regulated by the Russian Ministry of Finance. Statements about the utilization of monetary resources received from the 'official budget' have to be submitted if the firm received financial support from either state, provincial (republic), or local (municipal) governments. Banks and other financial institutions have to fulfil special requirements for accounting and statement presentation. The principal results of the recent transformation of the accounting system are:

- creation and implementation of an essentially new accounting regulation;
- creation of a new national Chart of Accounts consistent with international accounting standards;
- introduction of new financial statements corresponding to the Western formats;
- significant reduction of centralized regulation of accounting practices;
- introduction of a system of independent audit;
- attempts to establish independent professional accounting institutions (Institute of Professional Accountants, national and regional associations of accountants and chambers of auditors);
- attempts to include Russia in the process of European and International accounting harmonization;
- transformation of accounting education and professional certification.

The following publications (among many others) deal with the pertinent problems of financial accounting: Sokolov (1985, 1991, 1996) on some theoretical and historical aspects; Paly and Sokolov (1988) on theoretical issues; Androsov (1995) with considerations on bank accounting; Kovalev (1995, 1998) discussing financial analysis and investment aspects; Richard (1995) on the recent charts of accounting in Russia as well as Romania; Sheremet and Saifylin (1995) also on financial analysis; Sokolov and Kovalev (1996b) defending Russian accounting from recent criticism; Bakaev (1997) discussing the Russian Accounting Act; Kuter (1997) on basic bookkeeping theory; Efimova (1998), again on financial analysis; Enthoven *et al.* (1998: Chapter 7) on form and content of Russian financial statements; and Bourmistrov and Mellemvik (1999) on accounting aspects of the reforms in Russian local governments.

15.5.2 Auditing in the Russian Federation

The paper by Enthoven *et al.* points to an important fact:

> Auditing, as the term is understood in the West, did not exist in the USSR, nor has it ever existed in Russia. The notion of an independent controller

was absolutely alien to the consciousness of administrators, managers, and professionals .... Because Russia was – in fact still is – a country of administrative rather than civil law, where vertical ties have always prevailed over horizontal ones, the concepts of *control* and *controller* were used instead of *audit* and *auditor.* The term 'revision' (inspection) was also widely used.

(Enthoven *et al.* 1998: 79)

All this has slowly changed since the late 1980s. Above all, the big international auditing companies have established a firm foothold in the Russian Federation, they not only cooperate with Russian authorities but also with the World Bank, as their main clientele consists of large American firms investing in Russia. In the English accounting and auditing terminology such terms as 'postulate', 'conceptual framework', etc. have assumed special meaning since the late 1950s (cf. Mautz and Sharaf 1961). But in transferring certain auditing ideas to Russia some modifications were necessary. For this reason Sokolov formulated a special set of such postulates for Russia (outlined in Enthoven *et al.* 1998: 85–6), and in 1993 temporary rules 'Concerning Auditing Activities in the Russian Federation' were officially promulgated.

The problems of auditing activities, annual reports and certifications, licenses, and official, as well as ethical standards, governmental, as well as professional regulatory bodies, and many other general features peculiar to the 'new' Russia have been widely discussed in the local and international literature. In the following, we list a few representative publications characterizing this trend: Sokolov (1994) on Rossi's audit postulates; Smirnova *et al.* (1995) on modern Russian accounting education; Bychkova (1996a, 1996b), Bychkova and Smirnova (1997), all on the status and regulations of Russian auditing; Enthoven *et al.* (1998: Chapter 8) on various aspects of Russian auditing; and Sucher and Bychkova (2001) on auditor independence in Russia; and, above all, the official code of professional ethics of the Chambers of Auditors of Russia (2003).

15.5.3 Cost and management accounting in the Russian Federation

Management accounting in the Western sense exists in Russia only since the advent of *Perestroyka.* It has since become quite popular and was introduced as an important subject in the academic curriculum. The book by Enthoven *et al.* (1998: 127) distinguishes the following three tasks: 'operational accounting', 'cost accounting for finished products and services', and 'analysis of business activity'. It may seem an irony of history, that at a time when in Western countries management accounting is looked at very critically, and a merger with financial accounting was, by some experts, seriously considered (cf. Pfaff 1994), managerial accounting arose in the East like the rising sun.

Before the Gorbachev regime, the task of expense accounting in Russia was the responsibility of accountants while cost and price determination, cost analysis, etc. was attended by administrators, managers and statisticians. But even nowadays Russians are trying to develop their own type of managerial accounting, dominated by a peculiar terminology (particularly in English translation) that can occasionally be confusing to foreigners. It seems what we call 'job-order costing', 'process costing', 'general manufacturing account', 'standard costing', 'transfer payments' and 'joint costs', the Russians call 'calculation by orders' (*pozakasny*), 'calculation by stages' (*poperedelny*), 'account 20', 'norm costing', 'intrafirm payments' and 'complex costs', respectively – with the tendency to translate literally, and apparently with little effort of using proper English translation (see, for example, the terminology used in Enthoven *et al.* (1998: 126–37). Other peculiarities are mentioned in Enthoven *et al.* (1998: 133), as for example, the accounting office of the enterprise computes the so-called internal cost accounting profit for each structural unit. The amount of profit determines the salaries of the employees ... . It may even happen that the company as a whole shows a loss, although its units have earned internal profit. This complication is serious because employee's salaries within units are linked to their salaries.

For further details on general costing issues, we refer the reader to such publications as the following: Sokolov and Kovalev (1991) and Kovalev and Sokolov (1992); Nikolaeva (1993) on direct costing; Van der Vil and Paly (1997) and Enthoven *et al.* (1998: Chapter 9), both on various costing and managerial aspects.

16 Accounting publications and research in Poland and the Ukraine

Mainly twentieth century[1]

16.1 Introduction

To unite in one chapter the discussion of accounting publications and research of Poland *and* the Ukraine may be controversial, but it has at least two justifications. First, during many decades (ending in 1918 or so) parts of present-day Poland and West Ukraine belonged to the Austro-Hungarian Empire (administered as the province of Galicia). The second reason is to be found in the person of Pawel Ciompa, the controller of the Austro-Hungarian Bank in Lwów (or L'vóv in present-day Ukraine) who published (in German) and advanced an original accounting theory (Ciompa 1910), that nowadays is claimed by Polish as well as Ukrainian accountants as a major contribution. While Polish accounting publications are discussed in section 16.2, those of the Ukraine are to be found in sections 16.3 and 16.4.

However, the combination of Poland and the Ukraine in a single chapter is merely a matter of editorial convenience (just as our Chapter 13 covers five different countries, and Chapter 18 covers even more). Thus, it must be emphasized that Poland was an independent country before its several partitions, as well as between the two world wars, no less than after 1945 (even if dominated by the Soviet Union). Furthermore, it possessed charts of accounts since 1946 (similar to those of Germany or France), and in 2004 became a member of the European Union.

16.2 Poland

16.2.1 Political and industrial development

The nineteenth and early twentieth centuries (until 1918) were a very difficult period for the Polish nation, both in socio-political and cultural terms. Poland was partitioned and annexed by three powers: Russia, Prussia and Austria.[2] Industrial revolution reached all these areas, but the pace and scope of economic progress was different in each of the three partitions. Development of the textile industry (Łódź district in the Russian sector), mechanical and chemical industries, metallurgy and mining (in the Prussian sector) and crafts plus commerce in

Cracow and Lvóv (main cities in Galicia, the Austrian sector) contributed to growing importance of accounting as well as increased independence and consolidation of the accounting profession, which now needed specialist knowledge and skills to perform their functions. The demand for a greater number of better qualified accountants (*buchalterzy*) was a driving force of the development of commercial education and accounting textbooks (and related publications) as well as for attempts to establish accounting organizations.

16.2.2 Polish accounting research and publications (c.1900 to 1950)

One would assume that the renowned work by Ciompa (1910) exercised considerable influence on accounting thought in early twentieth-century Poland (as it did in the German language area – for details see sections 3.2 and 16.3). Yet, at this time, accounting was treated in Poland primarily as a practical skill. After 1918 accounting was taught in a growing number of secondary-level commercial schools and in four higher education establishments in Warsaw [1924], Cracow [1925], Lvóv [1922] and Poznań [1926]. The books published on bookkeeping, balance sheet presentation and auditing were mainly practical manuals (cf. Skrzywan 1967). Nonetheless, they played an important role in accounting education, as confirmed by a large circulation and, occasionally, a considerable number of reprints. The authors of major texts were Józef Aseńsko, Tomasz Lulek, Witold Skalski, Franciszek Tomanek, Witold Góra, Witold Byszewski, Marcel Scheffs and Stanisław Skrzywan.

Although advances in accounting theory (from abroad) were largely disregarded (cf. Scheffs 1936; Skrzywan 1964: 205), some theoretical publications are noteworthy. After the First World War a number of publications appeared, calling for reliable financial reporting. One of the first of these contributions was a book by Góra (1920) that explained the significance of well-prepared balance sheets for the assessment of an enterprise by owners, creditors and lenders. Góra presented a model balance sheet with a comparison of analogous models from Germany, the UK and France.

Of special significance were valuation issues, particularly due to inflationary forces (during the period from 1922 to 1927) since the hyperinflation of 1922–23 deprived the figures of the balance sheets of any meaning. Afterwards the situation was stabilized by drastic economic reforms implemented in 1924 and the introduction of a new currency, the Polish zloty.

In response to the inflationary trends in Poland, Lulek (1925) emphasized the importance of balance-sheet revaluations, the effects of changing purchasing power, and Poland's monetary reform of 1924 (cf. Pogodzińska-Mizdrak 2003; Hońko 2003). And in *Normalizacja bilansów*, Lulek (1931) concerned himself with the standardization of balance sheets, while previously, in *Teoretyczne podstawy księgowości kupieckiej* (Lulek 1922), he made an analysis and critical evaluation of the theory of accounts, including Schär's two rows of accounts (see section 3.1), as well as Ciompa's econometric theory of accounting. But Lulek's (1922, 1922–25) major contribution to accounting theory is considered to be his economic classification of accounts. He argued that the theory of double-entry is derived from economics since all basic concepts, such as property, capital, profit and others are of economic rather than of legalistic nature.

Another contribution, promoting the double-entry system, was made by Byszewski (1927) in which the author questioned the personification of accounts and the method of teaching accounting principles prevalent at that time. Although the ideas of Lulek and Byszewski did not go beyond the *static* balance sheet theory, they introduced a number of 'advanced' elements, such as a three-component accounting equations (assets = liabilities + owner's equity), the income function of business assets and the precedence of economic substance over legal form (cf. Kawa 2002: 72).

A further book worth noting was that by Skalski (1928) that explained the main principles and functioning of the balance sheet and its real accounts (compared to nominal accounts). Furthermore, he discussed the links between the general ledger and other books, combining them into one overall system of record keeping.

However, two doctoral dissertations (related to some extent with accounting) were prepared shortly before the Second World War (cf. Skrzywan 1967: 8). One of these dissertations is by A. Bieniek at the Warsaw School of Economics (cf. Skrzywan 1967: 8). And the first accounting 'habilitation' thesis (obligatory for teaching at a Polish university) was completed as late as 1938 (by Hanna Paszkiewicz, using mathematical theorems for explaining many accounting issues).

In the 1930s the situation did improve thanks to publications by Scheffs (1936, 1938, 1939a, 1939b), Aseńko (e.g. 1934), Skalski (1934), Lulek (1937) and Góra (1938). Their works referred to the achievements of European accounting thought, even if they adopted a critical attitude towards certain concepts. Major issues addressed by Polish theorists during the interwar period were:

1   the theoretical foundations of accounting and the theory of accounts;
2   accounting terminology;
3   the structure of the balance sheet and profit and loss account;
4   valuation issues;
5   balance sheet analysis;
6   auditing of accounts and financial statements;
7   explanation and evaluation of extant accounting regulations;
8   historical perspectives on accountancy evolution.

Skalski (1934) discussed such problems as the structure of the balance sheet, rules of inventory-taking, the valuation of fixed and current assets, owner's equity and borrowed capital, reserve capital, hidden provisions, items adjusting the value of assets and capital, as well as the notion of 'real value' (*wartość rzeczywista*) as used in the Commercial Code of 1934.

The most prominent of the Polish accounting theorists of the first half of the twentieth century was Marcel Scheffs (a renowned expert in accounting no less than on banks and cooperatives). In Scheffs (1939b) he expressed his conviction that accounting is not merely a practical skill but part of the economic sciences. Scheff's (1936, 1938, 1939a, 1939b) scientific interests span a broad spectrum, from issues of valuation, intangibles, production costs, capital markets and legislation to auditing and accounting history. To this has to be added his interest in economic and philosophical issues, particularly as related to accounting.

Since 1939 there have been three successive waves of influence in Polish accounting: German, Soviet and Western European. During the Second World War the German system of uniform accounting was enforced in the regions under German occupation. In the Eastern region of Poland that was incorporated into the USSR, the uniform accounting system of the Soviet Union was already introduced during the Second World War.

16.2.3 Polish accounting aspects during the period of 1950 to 1989

The Polish state was re-established in 1944, and the first uniform accounting plan (still inspired by the German model) was established in 1946 by Stanisław Skrzywan and Edward Wojciechowski (cf. Jaruga and Szychta 1997). During the period 1951–53, the mixed economy was replaced by a centrally planned economy, and the adoption of Soviet economic planning and its financial system led to the introduction of Soviet accounting plans and charts of accounts. There were mandatory charts of accounts and a uniform master chart. The charts were reformed and modified several times (i.e. in 1960, 1976 – apart from 1995, after liberation) to adjust them to the objectives of planning and managing the state-owned enterprises.

The Master Chart of Accounts of 1976 was partly influenced by the French uniform master chart. It used a cost classification based towards such macroeconomic purposes as surplus accounting, value added statements and cost flows in two accounting circles (cf. Jaruga 1972, 1988, 1993a, 1993b). As pointed out in Jaruga and Schroeder:

> The Polish accounting system has been under the direct administration of the Ministry of Finance. In place of general principles of accounting, derived from the commercial code and taxation legislation, obligatory and uniform measures of accounting were introduced by financial law ... . The financial statements ... were used for branch and national statistics, performance measurement and price setting within the context of central economic planning.
>
> (Jaruga and Schroeder 2003: 1589)

The role of accounting in a centrally planned economy was that of an administrative instrument for monitoring the implementation of state plans for state enterprises. In this process the 'nominal profitability', i.e. the comparison of the actual outcome and the budgeted figures, was crucial (cf. Dixon and Jaruga

1994). Thus, the primary concern of management decisions was the improvement of 'efficiency', to be monitored by a standard cost accounting system. This enabled internal accountability (called 'responsibility accounting') and the determination of 'correct unit cost' (Jaruga and Ho 2002).

In this period of central planning, cost accounting was not strictly regulated, though its role was limited. Thus, accounting research focused generally on accounting history, costing models, a kind of responsibility accounting, the design of accounting systems and social accounting (macro-accounting). But access to the international accounting literature and, ultimately, economic transformation broadened somewhat the research spectrum in cost and managerial accounting

During this period a considerable amount of Polish cost and managerial accounting literature was created, even if the term 'management accounting' had, for long, been 'banished'. This literature was the result of research conducted from the 1950s by Polish academics in order to meet the growing demand for textbooks and manuals explaining the tenets of cost accounting as laid down in new legislation.

Cost accounting issues and the general theory of accounting constituted two major themes of accounting dissertation (cf. Malc 1964: 211). This resulted in a number of useful publications before 1990. The most noteworthy of them were the monographs and textbooks by S. Skrzywan, W. Malc, Z. Fedak, B. Siwoń, W. Nowaczek, P. Tendera, H. Sobis, T. Wierzbicki, B. Binkowski, A. Jaruga, J. Skowroński, K. Sawicki, J. Matuszkiewicz, E. Burzym and Z. Messner.[3]

Particular interest was generated by a costing model of production factors by Skowroński that combines features of full costing and variable costing for decision making (see Jaruga and Skowroński 1986). Although academic publications stressed cost accounting for decision making and internal economic accountability (see Fedak 1962, 1967; Jaruga 1966; Messner 1967) they had no regulatory impact before the early 1970s (cf. Jaruga 1989: 6–7). The impact of academic research on accounting legislation (particularly on cost accounting regulations), became visible in the 1970s. It was partly due to regulations of the Uniform Plan (Master Chart) of Accounts of 1976, and the pertinent Standard Plans (Charts) of Accounts (for various branches), partly due to modernizing cost accounting principles (Decree of 1983 – see Ministra Finansów 1983: *Zarządzenie Nr 83*). In addition, a number of academics (B. Siwoń, W. Malc, J, Matuszewicz, W. Lewczyński, S. Sudoł, J. Ochman, T. Wierzbiński, Z. Messner, T. Troszczyński, A. Jaruga, J. Skowroński and I. Sobańska) implemented numerous cost and managerial accounting projects (cf. Jaruga and Skowroński 1994: 167).

During the period of centralized planning, cost accounting issues were increasingly included in programmes of institutions of higher learning. Since the 1990s management accounting has gained the status of a separate subject (though at the University of Łodź and other institutions its teaching began as early as 1982). Already during the Cold War, scholars from Poland showed particular interest in 'modern' accounting research. After Wojciechowoski (1962, 1964) introduced his normative accounting theory, Peche (1959, 1963) gave impetus to the 'deductive trend' in Polish accounting research, while Skrzywan (1967) initiated its empirical direction. This close contact with the West was also manifested in a series of papers in English (e.g. Jaruga 1972, 1974, 1976; Berry and Jaruga 1985), and others on various topics concerning accounting in Poland.

16.2.4 Polish accounting publications and research after 1990

Publications such as Jaruga (1991, 1993a, 1993b, 1995) and Jaruga and Szychta (1996) and others continued in the new era. They span from uniform accounting principles and the development of accounting, auditing and charts of accounts to industrial accounting and its re-organization. More recent publications on the statutory development of Polish auditing and the implementation of international accounting standards were presented by Krzywda *et al.* (1998) and Vellam (2004), respectively. A series of pertinent papers can also be found in the major Polish accounting journal *Rachunkowość*. There also exists a bibliography on Polish accounting by Szychta (1989, 1996a) and a book on Mattessich's *Accounting theory* (also by Szychta 1996b).

Since the beginning of the new millennium a series of international accounting research conferences were organized in various cities of Poland. The corresponding proceedings (edited by Dobija 2003; Dobija and Martin 2004, 2005) were published (in English) under the title *General accounting theory* (each year with a different subtitle – also identified as GAT I, GAT II and GAT III). These publications may transgress the period covered in this book, or are not always country-specific, some of their contributions (and their bibliographies) shed light on accounting issues specific to twentieth-century Poland or other East European countries. Typical examples are: Bednarek (2003) comparing local government accounting in Poland with that in the USA; Wędzki (2004) on bankruptcy predictions in Poland; Wójtowicz (2004, 2005) on the influence of IAS on Polish accounting, and on the objectivity of income reporting in Polish companies, respectively; Jaruga *et al.* (2005) on the adoption of IAS/IFRS in Poland; and Szplit and Hnidan (2005) on tax accounting in Poland.

16.3 The 'occupied' Ukraine

In this section we consider Ukrainian accounting, some of its historical aspects, and major publications. Our research is based on three books on Ukrainian accounting history (Butynets 1998, 2001a, 2001b; Mnykh *et al.* 2000; Pushkar *et al.* 2003), as well as on a series of Ukrainian and foreign papers.

16.3.1 Accounting in the 'Western' Ukraine (mid-nineteenth century to 1939)

Ukrainian accounting at the beginning of the twentieth century had developed mainly under the influence of two accounting schools, the German school and the Russian school. The Western part of the Ukraine's present-day territory (the Halychyna) was from 1772 to 1918 part of the Austro-Hungarian monarchy, and developed faster than the eastern and central parts of the Ukraine that joined the Russian Empire. Thus, accounting in the Halychyna was greatly influenced by the German accounting school, one of the most prestigious in Europe at that time.

In 1870 the Halychyna obtained an autonomous government that promoted the development of an economic and social infrastructure. This aided the progress of bookkeeping in commercial banks, cooperatives, unions and companies that flourished in the Halychyna. Later several important institutions were founded: in 1883 the Ukrainian company of 'Public Commerce', in 1884 the first company of Ukrainian handicraft 'Zoria', and in 1892 the first insurance company 'Dnister' (cf. Mnykh *et al.* 2000: 51).

The books published at this time were mainly of a practical nature and concerned themselves with accounting procedures and the preparation of balance sheets (Krasitski 1851; Kormosh 1895, 1912; Gora 1920).[4] The publication of those books arose out of the legal requirement for compulsory accounting and reporting. According to the Austro-Hungarian Law on 'Business Partnerships and Partnerships for Profit' (9 April 1873) such enterprises were obliged to keep accounting records and preserve them for six months after closing the books and presenting the balance sheet (cf. Kormosh 1912).

During the middle of the nineteenth century, accounting theories and various accounting concepts began to appear in the Ukraine – particularly in Lvóv, the capital of the Halychyna. At the beginning of the twentieth century, Ciompa (1910), controller of the Austro-Hungarian Bank in Lvóv, published his renowned study on accounting and 'econometrics' (though that term must not be taken in the modern sense of the word). He introduced it with the following words: 'This part of *economography* I name econometrics; bookkeeping is its practical use on a mathematical level, and vice versa; econometrics is only the theory of bookkeeping' (Ciompa 1910: 5, translated).

Thus, Ciompa defended the economic rather than the juridical approach to accounting. He favoured the context above the form, and expressed his opposition to the juridical (formal) approach of balance sheet presentation in the following words: 'First, we should consider in accounting the business entity from an economic point of view, because its main goal is production; we should not replace economic events with juridical matters' (Ciompa 1910: 70, translated). He later continued to say that: 'it is not clear, why the juridical point of view should be more important than the economic process. Such traditional formalism, imposed upon bookkeeping by law, can only serve artificial and decorative purposes in balance sheets' (Ciompa 1910: 134, translated).

Another important aspect of Ciompa's work was seeing accounting through the prism of property, capital and efficiency: 'The goal of bookkeeping is to calculate mathematically or procedurally the results of the use of property and the efficient handling of capital' (Ciompa 1910: 14, translated). Hence, with the beginning of the twentieth century, the economist Pawel Ciompa supported a management-oriented notion of accounting that focused on economic performance measurement for decision making. Such an approach was highly praised by many local and contemporaneous accounting academics. But even decades before, Krasitski pointed out that:

> Each enterprise, either industrial or agricultural, should keep accounts to record its activity. In such a case each businessman would have, at any time, clear evidence of the results in numerical terms; such that he could make the changes needed. This holds particularly for the fast changes in agricultural activity taking place in the Halychyna. The main adviser of the owner is the account.
>
> (Krasitski 1851: 3, translated)

Later, a managerial approach was promoted and further developed in such books as Góra (1920). A prominent economist, Teofil Kormosh [?–1927] developed at the beginning of twentieth century a Ukrainian version of the German accounting model that pivoted on the notion of capital, as well as on cost classification and standardization. Kormosh (1912) was the first Ukrainian textbook on business administration and accounting for cooperatives.

This author was a proponent of minimizing administrative costs and of creating devices for protecting shareholders' interests. At the beginning of the twentieth century, he was involved in many business and social activities. Kormosh was the co-owner and the leading member of various unions and organizations in Lvóv and Przemysl (cf. Mnykh *et al.* 2000: 52–3).

In the 1920s (at a period of vigorous accounting development in the Western Ukraine), the Revision Movement of Ukrainian Co-operatives (RMUC) played an important role. It issued a weekly magazine, *The Business Co-operative Publication* (1921–44), and a monthly review, *The Co-operative Republic* (1928–39). Unifying more than 3,000 cooperatives, it helped to spread local accounting ideas; it also issued textbooks, books and documentation in Ukrainian language, and organized professional training for bookkeepers (cf. Mnykh *et al.* 2000: 100). One of the most widely used textbooks for trading cooperatives was that by the RMUC inspector (controller), I. Sterniuk (1926), who provided a unified accounting technique for Ukrainian cooperatives. This book and that by Kormosh (1912) were widely used by those Halychynian companies that kept their books in the Ukrainian language.

16.3.2 Accounting in the 'Eastern' Ukraine during the Russian Empire (1900–17) and the entire Ukraine during the Soviet period (1917–91)

During the seventeenth and eighteenth centuries a large part of the Ukraine (except the Halychyna) belonged to the Russian Empire. In 1775, Empress Catherine II terminated autonomy of Zaporizhska Sich – the last island of Ukrainian independency. During the nineteenth and the beginning of the twentieth century most of the territory of the Ukraine, as part of the Russian Empire, had no self-government.

During the last decades of the nineteenth century the Russian Empire experienced rapid economic and industrial growth, and the Ukraine's territory became one of the most powerful industrial regions of Russia. There began the development of sugar, coal and metal industries, as well as railway construction. All these changes enhanced the role of the accounting profession and its members.

At the end of the nineteenth and the beginning of the twentieth century the first professional societies of accountants appeared in the Ukraine. In 1894, the first provincial society of accountants was founded in Kherson; and in 1907 there emerged a union of bookkeepers and accountants in Kiev (cf. Sokolov 1991: 364). During this time, almost all accounting books and magazines were published in Moscow and St Petersburg; only a few such books appeared in the Russian part of the Ukraine (for example, Grass 1899). In 1912–14 the only Ukrainian accounting magazine, *Schetovodstvo i hoziaistvo* (Bookkeeping and business), was published in Kharkov – it was a professional magazine of high quality (cf. Butynets 2001a: 191). Later on, during the first years of Soviet rule such Russian language accounting magazines as: *Uchet i Kontrol* (Accounting and control, Kiev: 1927–28), and *Schetny Rabotnik* (The bookkeeper, Kharkov: 1927–28) were published in the Ukraine. The short life-span of these magazines can be explained by the repressions of progressive accountants that began with the Stalinist period (cf. Butynets 2001a: 195).

In general, the development of accounting during the Soviet period is characterized by significant changes in accounting theory and practice, caused by a reversal of achievements attained by the Russian school of accounting of pre-revolutionary times. The forces of change were rigid government centralization and the dominance of socialistic ideology over economic considerations.

In the 1950s the Soviet-Ukrainian accounting school (the third in importance in the Soviet Union, after the Moscow and the Leningrad schools), was gradually formed.[5] The founder of this Ukrainian school was Professor P.P. Nimchynov [1906–83], known as the author of a new and progressive approach to agricultural accounting and agricultural enterprises (cf. Nimchynov 1976). Others were Igor V. Malyshev [1908–79] and Mykola G. Chumachenko [1925–].

Nimchynov (1976) was the first who attempted to create a pertinent unified classification system of accounts; he also authored some books on accounting theory (e.g. Nimchynov 1977). In total he published nine monographs and more than 200 articles. Other prominent authors of this school were: M.T. Bilukha, A.M. Kuzminsky, O.S. Borodkin, F.F. Butynets, Y.Y. Lytvyn and M.V. Kuzhelny.

Another well-known Ukrainian accountant was Professor Malyshev, who in 1961 headed the Accounting Department of the Ukrainian Agricultural Academy. He was a renowned theoretician as well as practitioner, but his main papers were devoted to accounting theory (Malyshev 1971, 1981).[6]

Furthermore, there is Professor Chumachenko, member of the Ukrainian National Scientific Academy, who authored hundreds of papers, textbooks, monographs and essays. His main works concerned industrial accounting and costing procedures (Chumachenko 1965, 1966) as well as 'normative' accounting, respectively (a Russian version of 'standard costing', not to be confused with normative accounting in the English language area – see note 3 for its originator). During the time from 1960 to 1990, Chumachenko repeatedly worked abroad (e.g. at the University of Illinois), taking part in organizing joint research projects, and cooperating with scientific institutions in the USA, Canada, China and Germany. He was one of the first Soviet scientists to study, thoroughly, accounting research as applied to American industry. In Chumachenko (1971), he began to popularize Western accounting thoughts in the USSR.

Other significant contributions to Soviet accounting theory were made by Valuev (1984), Kuzminsky and Sopko (1984), Kuzminsky (1990), Pushkar (1991); on accounting practice during the last three decades of the twentieth century by such Ukrainian accounting academics as Murashko (1974, 1979); Kuzhelny (1985) on revision and controlling; and by Chumachenko (1960, 1968) and Shkaraban (1988) on activity analysis. Research of these scholars exercised great influence on modern accounting in the Ukraine.

16.4 Formation of modern accounting and auditing in the independent Ukraine (1991 to the beginning of the twenty-first century)

16.4.1 Accounting theory and practice

After the collapse of the USSR in 1991, the Ukraine was proclaimed an independent state. At this time, began the process of gradual harmonization of Ukrainian accounting with international standards. The Ukrainian model – uniting rigid accounting regulation with elements introduced from Western practice – is gradually emerging. This process of liberalization of accounting was accelerated in 1999 when the law 'On Accounting and Financial Reporting of the Ukraine', as well as the new Chart of Accounts, and the National Accounting Standards were enacted.

During recent decades some new textbooks on accounting theory were published (Sopko 1998; Butynets 2000; Kuzhelny and Linnyk 2001). Many papers by Ukrainian accounting scholars deal with various problems of harmonization with the International Financial Reporting Standards (IFRS), for example, Goritskaya (1999), Golov and Kostiuchenko (2001) and Voinarenko (2002). Furthermore, much attention is give to the new Ukrainian financial accounting system (Zavgorodny 1997, 1999; Tkachenko 2000), as well as to accounting for various branches of the economy, such as industry (Sopko *et al.* 1992; Grabova and Dobrovsky 2000), trade (Butynets and Maliuga 2002), agriculture (Butynets 2002), commercial banks (Kindratska 1999) and the public sector of economy (Djoga 2001; Djoga *et al.* 2003; Kaneva 2004).[7]

In 1992, thanks to Kuzminsky's initiative, the first modern Ukrainian accounting journal, *Buchgaltersky oblik i audyt* (Accounting and auditing), was founded. Later, other professional magazines appeared, such as the *Svit buchgalterskogo obliky* (The world of accounting), *Vse pro buchgaltersky oblik* (Everything about accountancy), *Balans* (The balance sheet) and others. Accounting and auditing practitioners began to form professional associations such as the Ukrainian Auditors Union, the Federation of Professional Accountants and Auditors of the Ukraine, the Ukrainian Association of Certified Accountants and Auditors, the Federation of Auditors, Accounting and Financiers of the Agro-Industrial Complex of the Ukraine and the Ukrainian Society of Financial Analysts. These organizations play a significant role in the growth of this country's accounting profession, education, research and legislation.

16.4.2 *Management and cost accounting in the Ukraine*

During the Soviet period, management accounting (as understood in the West) was unknown in the Ukraine. In the Soviet accounting system only some elements of cost accounting (product costing, cost allocation methods, performance measurement) were used; but these were oriented towards a 'command-administrative governance model'.

Only in the beginning of 1990s did Ukrainian accountants get an opportunity to acquaint themselves with Western management accounting practice (cf. Jaruga 1991). After that, management accounting became a major object of accounting research; it engendered hot debates in the Ukraine about the essence of managerial accounting, its concepts and its role in business. Some of the local economists (e.g. Borodkin 1997; Lastovetsky 2003) even denied its *raison d'être*, arguing that it is too artificial a creation, and of little use.

Others, more pro-western oriented accountants, opposed this position and defended management accounting, its development and the need of introducing it to Ukrainian business (e.g. Golov and Efimenko 1996; Pushkar 1995, 1999; Chumachenko 1997, 2000, 2003; Napadovska 2000). The majority of Ukrainian accounting academics and professionals have high regard for the Anglo-American 'school of management accounting'. However, German controlling concepts have also exercised considerable influence on Ukrainian managerial accounting. For example, Pushkar (1999) recommended that Ukrainian accounting should concentrate on *three* parts: financial accounting, management accounting and controlling. Pushkar uses the word 'controlling' in the meaning of 'strategic controlling'. British authors call it 'strategic management accounting'.

Apart from *traditional* management accounting notions, many academics and professionals became, in recent years, interested in such concepts as strategic management accounting, strategic cost management and the Balanced Scorecard. These popular instruments were readily accepted in the Ukraine, particularly after (Russian) translations of important textbooks became available, for example, Ryan (1995), Ward (1992), Shank and Govindarajan (1993) and Kaplan and Norton (1996, 2001). These ideas were reflected in the papers and books of Ukrainian authors, such as Golov (2003) on strategic management accounting, Petrenko (2003) on strategic controlling and Redchenko (2003a, 2003b) on performance measurement and the Balanced Scorecard. Most recently an anthology (intended as a 'textbook') by Dobija and Napadovska (2007), with contributions from the USA, Canada, Poland, Russia and the Ukraine, have been launched.

16.4.3 Auditing in the Ukraine

Auditing obtained official status in the Ukraine only after 1993, when the law on 'Auditing Activity' was passed. At that time the first textbooks for Ukrainian auditing were Robertson (1990) and Arens and Loebbecke (1991). The main feature of the Ukrainian approach to auditing from 1993 onwards was a symbiosis of Western auditing theory and old Soviet 'revision' practice. This situation began to change only in recent years, particularly after the Auditing Chamber of the Ukraine made the decision to accept the International Auditing Standards as the national standards of the Ukraine.

In the second half of the 1990s, many textbooks and monographs on auditing theory (Zubilevych and Golov 1996; Rudnytsky 1998; Dorosh 2001; Redchenko 2001) appeared in the Ukraine; furthermore, guides for auditors and accounting students were published (Bilukha 1994, 1998, 2000; Red'ko 1995; Kuzminsky 1996; Davydov 2001; Goncharuk and Rudnytsky 2002; Gutsailiuk *et al.* 2002). However, the gap between Western and Ukrainian auditing practice continues to be considerable.

17 Accounting books of Argentina

Publications, research and institutional background[1]

17.1 Introduction and methodology

The circumstances of Argentina are very special and have to be taken into consideration when writing an historical survey of its accounting publications and research. First, Argentina is a country that since its origin looked to its mother country for intellectual inspiration and guidance. So, in the early twentieth century, she followed Spain and other Ibero-American countries, where best-selling textbooks were the main stay of accounting 'research'. Yet, Argentina is also a nation that for many years has played a leading intellectual role in Latin America.[2] And this despite the fact that in recent decades it has gone through many economic and political ordeals that left its universities and research institutions in a desperate financial situation (difficult to envisage in prosperous countries). Thus, the rigor and the impact of accounting research are very different in different countries – Tua Pereda (2004), for example, a renowned Spanish scholar, writing for a South American accounting journal, hardly mentions any South American publications in his lengthy and fairly up-to-date paper on the 'evolution and present situation of accounting thought'. Obviously, Argentine accounting publications and research do not compete on the world stage. The dilemma seems to be that, on one side, there is plenty of enthusiasm in Argentina for doing accounting research, on the other side many Argentine academics try to do research in isolation from the trends of leading North American or European universities. Since few if any of those scholars have been trained abroad, they hardly publish in English. The best remedy to break this vicious circle is to provide funds for training young Argentine accounting scholars at first class universities of North America or Europe. The present reaction of intellectuals from Argentina and other South American countries against US politics, might possibly be mitigated by establishing generous US government scholarships for training accounting and possibly other academics from these countries at US universities. Yet, until this is possible, in a global economy there should be sufficient justification to discuss past accounting publications and recent research efforts in Argentina. And this is the task of this paper.

It is for such reasons that we chose a strategy different from that in previous chapters (dealing with other countries). Instead of beginning with prominent accountants, one of us launched an extensive *library* search at Argentine univer-sities and professional institutions (covering some 110 libraries).[3] In our view this proved to be, under the circumstances, the best way to get a rough picture about Argentine accounting publications, and the extent to which foreign publications may have influenced them. Argentina generated a vast accounting literature during the twentieth century, in some cases possibly original. Yet, apart from the works of a few leading experts, we can offer merely representat-ive examples of Argentine accounting publications (here, almost exclusively books). Furthermore, we did not encounter any publication on the *history* of Argentine accounting literature of the twentieth century.[4] Thus, it appears that the present paper is the first attempt in this direction.

An historical sketch of this kind must take into account the impact of Spanish, French and Italian literature in the first half of the twentieth century, as well as the influence of North American accounting literature during the second half. Among the Argentine authors, we encountered several important and pro-lific scholars with publications that often had several editions. In the following, we present our findings about those authors and their influence on accounting theory and practice.

To understand the evolution of accounting literature in Argentina, it may help to be familiar, at least in rough strokes, with the history of its accounting profes-sion, and its academic community together with its publication outlets. There-fore, we devote the subsequent two sections (with a subsection on academic journals) to these topics.

17.2 Evolution of the Argentine accounting profession

The historical backbone of Argentine accounting organizations is the Association of Graduates in the Economic Sciences. The oldest of its member institutions was constituted in 1891 (see Chirom 1985). In those days, the graduates in the eco-nomic sciences from Argentine universities were permitted to act as public accountants. Those professional organizations, still in existence, are designated as *colegios de graduados en ciencias económicas* (in the following, abbreviated as *colegios*), and are constituted as 'legal civil associations' (non-profit institutions). The graduates are free to enter such an association, but these *colegios* do not repre-sent the accounting profession. They usually organize courses for their members and maintain specialized libraries. In addition, there exists the *Federación Argentina de Graduados en Ciencias Económicas* that comprises approximately 20 *colegios* (see Fowler Newton 2001). An important goal of these *colegios* is to advance the professional education of their associates. The *Federación* organized and supports the *Instituto Técnico de Contadores Públicos* that issued legislation or quasi-legislation that ultimately determined Argentine accounting standards.

However, nowadays the professional organizations that are enacted by law to grant and revoke professional registration are the 'provincial' *consejos*. They were created over many decades by provincial laws, and the first of them emerged in the 1940s. Since Argentina is a federal republic, there is an independent *consejo* in each province as well as one in the *Capital Federal*. The latter is the most important one with more than 50,000 members.

Though the state has delegated certain rights and obligations to these organizations, their members elect the management. The Argentine profession of public accountants (anchored in the National Law No. 20488) is autonomous and elects its own directors. Nowadays, the public accountants of Argentina (equivalent to certified public accountant in the USA, or chartered accountants in the British Commonwealth countries) require a university graduation of five years of study. Those graduates neither need any auditing apprenticeship or other additional training – nor do they have to pass a separate professional or state examination in order to *acquire* the right of certifying financial statements.

The *consejos* are entitled by law to grant to its members the right to approve financial statements. Hence, to acquire this right, a graduate accountant has to matriculate with one of the *consejos* that also promulgate accounting and auditing standards, and may impose disciplinarian sanctions on its members. This last prerogative greatly helped to improve the quality of the services provided by accounting professionals. However, one of the most important activities of these institutions is the right to 'legislate' accounting and auditing standards within their jurisdiction.

The *Federación de Consejos Profesionales de Ciencias Economicas* (in the following, abbreviated as *Federación*, and not to be confused with the *Federación de Colegios de Graduados en Ciencias Económicas*) is the mother organization comprising all the provincial *consejos*. It was created in 1972, and organized its own *Centro de Estudios Científicos y Técnicos* (Centre of Scientific and Technical Studies) that makes pronouncements in matters of accounting standards. Before 1969 no accounting association had the right to 'legislate' accounting standards, as there existed only the 'generally accepted accounting principles and technical rules' agreed upon in the Sixth and Seventh National Assembly of Graduates in Economic Sciences (convening in 1962 and 1969 in Buenos Aires). These principles and rules constituted a summary of the common accounting practices at the time.

Since 1973, with the passing of the law (regulating the profession and the organization of the *Federación de Consejos Profesionales*), the first '*resoluciones técnicas*' (accounting standards) were released. Most of the North American accounting literature became better known in Argentina after the Second World War, and then exercised a considerable influence on the organization of the Argentine accounting profession, as well as on the ideas and directions pursued in academic accounting.

17.3 Evolution of the Argentine academic accounting community and its impact on accounting legislation

The *Escuela de Comercio Carlos Pellegrini* (Buenos Aires) was founded in 1890. It still is one of the most prestigious schools of higher business education in Argentina. During the first decade of the twentieth century, several other commercial schools opened in major cities of Argentina. The Faculty of Economic Sciences (of the University of Buenos Aires) was established in 1913 by national law. In 1905, the first Argentine congress of accountants convened, and considered topics such as governmental accounting, auditing, liquidation of insurance contracts, regulation of professional fees, as well as the above-mentioned creation of the Faculty of Economic Sciences (cf. Chirom 1985).

The accounting profession was recognized and regulated by individual *provincial* governments towards the end of the 1940s. However, it received *national* recognition only in 1973 (see above). The 1960s and 1970s showed important growth in the economic sciences and its education, including the establishment of such degrees as the *licenciado en administración de empresas* (graduate in management) and the *licenciado en economía* (graduate in economics). In 1949, the Inter-American Accounting Association was created. Its purpose was to provide a forum for all North and South American accounting associations to be able to discuss accounting issues of common interest. One of the most promising of those activities was the establishment of annual or biennial meetings of the Inter-American Accounting Conference (IAAC). At the seventh conference (in Mar del Plata, Argentina in 1965), some recommendations were accepted that constitute a landmark in the evolution of Argentine accounting thought and practice. This was a proposal (submitted by the Argentine delegation) for 'the unification of criteria related to the application of accounting principles and technical rules for preparing financial statements'.

Furthermore, the Argentine *colegios* organized national assemblies of graduates in economic sciences to discuss professional and theoretical accounting issues. The most important of those assemblies was the seventh, held in 1969 (not to be confused with 7th IAAC Conference, mentioned above). It approved the proposal presented in the seventh Inter-American Accounting Conference as local (i.e. national) accounting standards. This was the first *obligatory* set of accounting principles and rules for preparing financial statements of the Argentine accounting profession.

In 1973, the Center for Scientific and Technical Studies, supported by the *Federación*, began submitting the *resoluciones técnicas* that constitute the Argentine accounting standards. The individual *consejos*, empowered to determine the accounting standards for each jurisdiction, responded in different ways. Some accepted those standards, others made changes or even rejected them.

In 1983, a change in the articles of the commercial law No. 19.550 introduced two regulations for the presentation of financial statements:

- adjustments for changes in purchasing power of the local currency, and
- applying generally accepted accounting principles and standards pronounced by the controlling authority.

These regulations and the possibility to apply them homogeneously in all jurisdictions offered an opportunity for thorough analysis and research.

Therefore, the *Federación* created a Special Commission for the Unification of Accounting Standards, composed of prestigious members of the accounting profession. Thus began the task of preparing rigorous accounting standards. After a period of public exposure, these *resoluciones técnicas* or accounting standards have now been approved and published by the *Federación*. The *consejos* of the capital city and the provinces will have to decide whether to accept or modify them.

In 1998, the *Federación* began to study the harmonizing of Argentine accounting standards with the International Accounting Standards. This project finally resulted (in the year 2000) in the *Resoluciones Técnicas Nr. 16 to 19*, that began to be discussed by the local jurisdictions during 2001. In 2003, the various *consejos* decided on the final unification of accounting standards in Argentina by adopting the *resoluciones técnicas* recently approved by the *Federación*.

17.3.1 Argentine academic accounting journals

In this paper we concentrate more on books (particularly as far as the first half of the twentieth century is concerned). However, academic and professional journals played, and still play, an important role in the development of accounting research in Argentina and other Latin American countries. Beyond the publications discussed in this chapter, the reader will find plenty of pertinent material in the following academic and professional journals (here presented in alphabetical order).

Administración de Empresas (published by Ediciones Contabilidad Moderna, 1970–89) used to be the most prestigious journal of that period in Argentina, publishing papers on such topics as management, planning and budgets, quantitative methods and models, financial and cost accounting, auditing and information technology. The papers on financial accounting were written by Argentine authors such as Enrique Fowler Newton, Arturo Lisdero, Santiago Lazzatti, Horacio Lopez Santiso and William L. Chapman (see section 17.6). This journal also presented occasionally Spanish translations from the English, for example, from publications by R.J. Chambers, Robert Mautz, Yuji Ijiri, Robert Anthony and Stephen Zeff. Furthermore, papers by the Brazilian author Antonio Lopes de Sá, and the Spanish author Vicente Montesinos Julve.

Contabilidad y Auditoría (Instituto de Investigaciones Contables, Universidad de Buenos Aires) publishes financial accounting and auditing research documents, mostly authored by members of the faculty of the University of Buenos Aires.

Costos y Gestión (Instituto Argentino de Profesores Universitarios de Costos, Buenos Aires) publishes only cost accounting and managerial accounting papers authored by academics and professionals. The first issue was published in 1991.

Enfoques: Contabilidad y Administración (Ediciones La Ley. www.laley.com.ar) publishes papers in accounting and management research, and also material intended for professionals, managers and directors (some are Spanish translations of Anglophone papers).

Profesional y Empresaria (Errepar, www.errepar.com). It publishes papers on accounting legislation and professional practice.

Energeia: Revista Internacional de Filosofía y Epistemología de las Ciencias Económicas (Universidad de Ciencias Empresariales y Sociales, Buenos Aires, edited by Eduardo R. Scarano), is a recent journal intended to facilitate an inter-disciplinary exchange of ideas among philosophers, methodologists, social scientists, management experts, economists and accountants.

(*Revista Internacional Legis de*) *Contabilidad & Auditoría* (published by LEGIS for Argentina, Chile, Colombia, Mexico and Peru – this journal was previously called: *Revista Legis del Contador*). It is now one of the leading accounting journals of Latin America, offering a broad spectrum of accounting and auditing research, written by authors not only from South and Middle America but from a wide range of countries (including Spain, the USA, Canada, etc.).

Selección Contable. During the period from 1937 to 1942, this was the most prestigious Argentine accounting journal (published by Estudios Técnico Contables Serau; and from 1951 to 1968 published by Ediciones Selección de Revistas Modernas).[5] A brief inspection of the alphabetical list of authors that wrote for this journal during the 1950s, indicates Argentine authors such as Alberto Arévalo, Francisco Cholvis, Hector R. Bertora and Mario Biondi, Enrique J. Reig (a specialist on taxation issues), William L. Chapman, the well-known Spanish author Boter Mauri, and the important Brazilian author Antonio Lopes de Sá (1956) who wrote on 'the true scientific place of accounting'.[6] Another important feature of this journal was Spanish translations from publications by Erich Schneider, John N. Myer, Robert Ruggles, T.H. Sanders, and others.

Universo Económico (Consejo Profesional de Ciencias Económicas de la Ciudad Autónoma de Buenos Aires) is a professional journal distributed by the *consejos* to its members, who are graduates in *economic sciences* (accountants, economists, graduates in management, etc.). It includes professional news, commentaries on recent conferences, congresses and other academic or professional meetings, activities of the technical committees, etc.

Furthermore, several English language journals are available at some Argentine universities. The Universidad de Buenos Aires subscribed to the *Journal of Accountancy* (from 1937 to 1987) and the *Journal of Accounting Research* (from 1978 to 1986); the National University of Tucumán subscribes to *The Accounting Review* (since 1968); and the library of the Central Bank of the Republic of Argentina subscribes to the *Journal of Accounting and Economics* (since 1979). However, in the twenty-first century modern libraries have access to the electronic publication of accounting journals all over the world by subscribing to huge databases. The Facultad de Ciencias Económicas de la Universidad de Buenos Aires, for example, offers access to 45 international electronic accounting journals (all of them in English, and listed under: www.econ.uba.ar/www/servicios/biblioteca/ejournals).

17.4 Argentine accounting publications and the foreign influence: the first half of the twentieth century

17.4.1 The Spanish influence

Obviously, the Spanish influence, particularly strong before the second half of the twentieth century, has been a dominant force in Argentine accounting. One may infer the influence of individual authors and books by the extent of their representation in Argentine libraries. One of the prestigious Spanish authors of the nineteenth century was Castaño Dieguez (1863/1912); his most important work was on the theory and practice of double-entry accounting (for details of Spanish authors of the first half of the twentieth century, see Carrasco Diaz *et al.* 2004). The work of Castaño Dieguez was originally published in Málaga in 1863 and attained no less than 42 editions, the last one in 1946 (cf. Vlaemminck 1961, 291–3). This may bear witness for its popularity and contribution to accounting knowledge in the Spanish language area (Castaño Dieguez 1912). The University of Buenos Aires possesses a copy of Sacristán y Zavala (1925) on general accounting theory and business administration, another important contribution from the mother country.

Argentine libraries also harbour copies of the following well-known accounting texts from Spain: Goxens Duch (1948, 1950, 1961, 1963, 1979, 1985) on a variety of topics that range from inflation accounting to two encyclopaedic works on accounting. Furthermore, there is the text by Prats y Aymerich (1907) on commercial accounting (with seven editions, of which the original edition is available). Other texts are: Fernández Casas (1931) applied accounting; and two editions of Gardó's (1932) book on industrial accounting. The same author is represented by a series of other works (Gardó 1925a, 1925b, 1926a, 1926b, 1926c). Among these are three pamphlets (of about 30 pages each), dealing with various subjects that range from transportation accounting to accounting for cooperatives and even 'secret accounting'. Finally, these include Gardó's accounting manual for 'workshops'. He certainly was a prolific and versatile author, and his works seemed to have been of great interest in Argentina.

Among the texts from Spain, those by Fernando Boter Mauri are possibly the best represented in Argentina. Of his treatise on general accounting (Boter Mauri 1941) two later editions (the 6th and 11th) are available at the National University of the South in Bahía Blanca (600 kilometres south of Buenos Aires). Further publications by Boter Mauri (1929, 1935, 1942, 1946, 1947, 1949, 1950, 1952) are in our data bank (some of them in several editions). These publications cover a wide variety of topics ranging from industrial accounting to juridical accounting problems as well as auditing – an important topic but relatively rare at the time in Argentina.

Thus, Boter Mauri has had an important presence in Argentina, not only because of the great variety of topics and the number of editions, but also because of his translations of two important French accounting works available in Argentine libraries – namely of Batardon (1933) and Delaporte (1932). Other Spanish authors represented in those libraries include Ruiz Soler (1923, 1924), one of the principal authors referred to by Arévalo (1946). Furthermore, Paret (1942), Cortés y Sabater (1932) and Martínez Pérez (1910).

17.4.2 The French influence

The work of the Frenchman Léon Batardon is widely represented in Argentine libraries. Among the French originals is Bartardon (1913, 1914a, 1914b, 1918, 1929a); and in Spanish translation, we found Batardon (1920, 1928a, 1928b, 1929a, 1929b, 1929c, 1932, 1933, 1944, 1950). One of these publications deals with 'loose leave' bookkeeping (Batardon 1929b), another one with 'commercial corporations' (Batardon 1929c), and a third one with 'current accounts with interest calculations' (Batardon 1950). Each of these are available in Argentina in several editions.

Another renowned French accountant was René Delaporte, though he is represented only by a single copy of his work on banking organization and bookkeeping, translated into Spanish (Delaporte 1932). For more details on French authors of the first half of the twentieth century (though not necessarily available in Argentina), see Degos and Mattessich (2003).

17.4.3 The Italian influence

From the Italian literature of this period, Argentine libraries possess one work by Zappa (1946, in Italian – and not even his *magnum opus*) on balance sheets of commercial enterprises. But these libraries possess three books by Onida (1951a, in Spanish; 1951b; 1970 in Italian). The first two are on balance sheet valuation, and on the development of modern North American accounting theories, respectively. The third one is on balance sheet theory, respectively (for details on these and other Italian accounting literature during the first half of the twentieth century, see Galassi and Mattessich 2004).

The Italian school, particularly the works of Cerboni and Besta, had great influence on the eminent Alberto Arévalo who also owned one of the most important private libraries containing many European and North American books (for a discussion of his work see section 17.5).

17.4.4 The influence of Anglo-American and German literature

On the basis of the books registered in Argentine libraries, the Anglophone literature of this period is represented by Spanish *translations* of such books as: Kester (1939) *Financial accounting theory and practice*; Gillespie (1939) *Introduction to cost accounting*; Finney (1943) *Treatise of accounting*; Paton (1943) *Accountant's manual*; Holmes' (1945) *Auditing*. In the second part of the twentieth century the arrival of English language literature in Argentina became particularly important (see subsection 17.6.1).

From the German accounting literature, we encountered only one representative, namely Erich Schneider's (1949) book on industrial accounting (in Spanish translation). Surprisingly, there seems to be no work available by Schmalenbach or by Fritz Schmidt – the two most prestigious German accountants of the first half of the twentieth century.

Argentine accounting journals had their share of Anglophone papers translated into Spanish, and there were also available several well-known English language journals in different national and private universities during the first and second part of the twentieth century (see sub-section 17.3.1). The prestigious, but more practically oriented *Journal of Accountancy*, for example, has been subscribed by the library of the University of Buenos Aires during a 50-year period (from 1937 to 1987).

17.5 Argentine publications: first half of the twentieth century

Alberto Arévalo was one of the most prestigious and prolific authors among the early Argentine accountants. He is represented in Argentine libraries with some 17 works. His first pamphlets dealt with specialized issues, such as accounting for insurance companies (Arévalo 1917a) and agricultural firms (Arévalo 1917b), Subsequently, he published a work on double-entry and Cerboni's logismographic method (Arévalo 1918).

Later, when already a recognized academic, he published his *magnum opus* on the elements of financial accounting (Arévalo 1946). There, the influence of Italian authors is obvious. The basic concepts are the '*hacienda*' (administrative unit, firm) and the 'administrative activity' (that consisted of directive actions, including leadership and coordination) and 'operative actions'. In the first six chapters, he described the economic and legal aspects of the *hacienda*, its sources of funds, its structure and functioning, as well as the administrative task of accounting in such a setting.

As regards asset valuation, he proposed 'lower of cost or market', based on Hatfield *et al.* (1940). Arévalo also included an interesting chapter on budgets and budgetary control, partly based on the German author Ludwig (1930, in French translation). The latter contained a discussion on planning and control methodology, previously adopted in the United States and Europe.

Arévalo (1946) also analysed the nature of accounting, its relation to management, and to the social sciences, as well as the impact of economic progress. To this he added a short history of accounting. He clearly shared Cerboni's and Besta's view on the mission of accounting. While the task of administration (or management) rests on 'action', that of accounting is to be found in 'illuminating or clarifying'. Then management can choose the optimal actions.

This book also refers to Gino Zappa, the leader of the Italian movement of '*economia aziendale*' that comprises, besides accounting, marketing techniques, organizational and some managerial issues. Zappa founded a new school of thought that considered the '*hacienda*' as its object of research, and 'accounting' as part of a wider discipline. Apart from Zappa, Arévalo refers to the following authors and some of their publications: the Italians, Besta (1909), D'Alvise (1920, 1934), Alfieri (1921), de Gobbis (1931), Vianello (1930); the North Americans, Kester (1939) and Hatfield *et al.* (1940); as well as the Spaniard Ruiz Soler (1923).

Later, Arévalo (1954) presented a book on government accounting. It also revealed Italian influence, particularly the notion of '*hacienda pública*' (governmental enterprise), but dealt primarily with the fundamentals of government administration, and only to a limited extent with accounting problems.

This author, whose work spanned a period of some 56 years (from 1917 to 1973), exercised wide-ranging influence on Argentine accounting theory and practice. In recognition of his contributions, an institute of the University of Buenos Aires was named the *Instituto de Investigaciones Contables 'Alberto Arévalo'*.

Among other early Argentine authors, the following might be mentioned: Galante (1907), with his critical philosophical treatise on accounting; Floriani (1930, 1942, 1960), whose three textbooks deal with 'new' aspects of accounting and bookkeeping, elementary accounting and general accounting, respectively; Pagano (1913, 1915, 1931), who concerned himself with technical-practical aspects of accounting, and with bookkeeping aspects of insurance companies; Zipitria (1914, 1923, 1943), writing on administrative accounting (in his first and last work), and on the elements of accounting; and Quijano (1937), describing the difference between bookkeeping and accounting (including valuation issues).

Other Argentine authors dealt with more specialized applications of accounting. Among those we found: Corti (1918), writing on accounting of state-owned railways; Fernández Romero (1913), dealing with financial and accounting issues of the municipality of Rosario; Coni (1917), on accounting and bookkeeping for agriculture and cattle raising; Vallini (1918) with his treatise on governmental accounting and capital issues; Bórea (1921) on agricultural accounting and production costing; Cassagne Serres (1910, 1912, 1921a, 1921b, 1921c, 1923, 1924), with two books on accounting education, one on accounting of insurance companies, one on accounting of banks, and the others on accounting for capital markets, rural enterprises and finally, one on the operation and accounting of mortgage banking; and Bayetto (1928), dealing also with government accounting. Though Brazilian, the scholar Lopes de Sá (1960a, 1960b, 1962, 1963, 1964, 1969, 1990, 1992, 1994, 1998) also influenced Argentine authors through his books on financial statement analysis, cost accounting, inflation and auditing, all of them translated into Spanish (though many of these books are not available in public Argentine libraries).

17.5.1 Accounting topics, their distribution in Argentina, and the provenance of foreign editions: first half of the twentieth century

According to our library search, in the first half of the twentieth century, the most frequent topics were financial accounting (46 per cent), legal discussions

(13 per cent), cost and managerial accounting (10 per cent), governmental accounting (8 per cent), agricultural accounting (6 per cent), auditing (3 per cent), banking accounting (3 per cent), railways accounting (2 per cent), insurance companies accounting (1 per cent), accounting education (1 per cent), and other topics which represent less than 1 per cent.[7]

As to provenance, the geographic distribution of accounting books shows that some 205 items (or 74 per cent out of a total of 277 books on our list between the years 1900 and 1949) were published in Latin America. The Latin American editions comprise 171 publications (or 62 per cent); they are from Argentina (Buenos Aires, Rosario, Santa Fe, Córdoba, Salta, Tucumán, etc.); 22 (or 8 per cent) from Mexico, four (or 1 per cent) from Uruguay; three from Cuba and five from other countries. The editions published in Mexico (from 1939 onwards), were mostly translations of North American publications, such as Gillespie (1939), Finney (1943), Lawrence (1943), Paton (1943), Himmelblau (1945a, 1945b), Holmes (1945), etc.

As to the editions beyond Latin America, those from Europe were represented with some 25 per cent (68 editions), but those from North America were merely 1 per cent. A proportion that changed dramatically in the second half of the century. The European editions were mostly from Spain (19 per cent) and France (8 per cent), as the language barrier constituted a major obstacle for Argentine accountants during this period. Surprisingly, we found hardly any German publications in our database.

17.6 Argentine publications: second half of the twentieth century and beyond

17.6.1 Distribution, provenance and foreign texts: second half of the twentieth century

In the second half of the century topics diversified, and financial accounting increased its share to 54 per cent of the total books (1,803) registered in our base for the period under consideration. This appears to be the result of an increasing demand for updating the state of the art as well as for a need to improve financial information. Other topics include cost and managerial accounting (20 per cent), auditing (5 per cent), accounting education (4 per cent), governmental accounting (3 per cent), dictionaries and encyclopaedias (2 per cent), economic or national accounting (2 per cent), social accounting (2 per cent), international accounting (1 per cent) and agricultural accounting (1 per cent).

The geographic provenance of the publications indicates the relevance of foreign editions (54 per cent), especially from the United States, Spain and Mexico. The following figures give an inkling: from Argentina 46 per cent (93 per cent of them published in Buenos Aires); from the USA 17 per cent; from Spain 14 per cent; from Mexico 11 per cent; from England 3 per cent; from Colombia 2 per cent; from Switzerland and France 2 per cent; from Italy 1 per cent; and from Chile 1 per cent.

However, the Anglophone accounting textbooks were more important than these figures suggest. One reason is that the Mexican editions are mostly translations from the English language, as, for example, the texts by Kieso and Weygandt (1984, 1987), Horngreen (1966, 1973), Davidson and Weil (1982) and Anthony (1964, reprinted in 1968, 1969, 1976, 1986). More recently, there have been Spanish translations of relevant Anglophone works beyond mere textbooks, such as Mattessich (1964/2002).

17.6.2 General accounting theory

One of the prolific academics in Argentina is García Casella (García Casella 1997, 1998, 1999a, 1999b; García Casella and Rodríguez de Ramírez 2000, 2001, 2002, 2004 – only to mention the more recent publications). Although his work spans a wide range of interests, his concise historical interpretation of modern accounting history (for teaching and other pedagogic purposes) is undoubtedly original. This also holds for two cooperative publications under his direction. The first of these, García Casella (director) (1997) is a research project financed by the *Consejo Nacional de Investigaciones Científicas y Técnicas*, one of the most important national research institutions. The purpose was to critically analyse the status of accounting theory and produce accounting models to enhance the decision-making processes.

The second cooperative effort – that by García Casella and Rodríguez de Ramirez (2000, 2001, 2002, 2004) – is a search for (i) eventual 'hypotheses and laws' of accounting, (ii) alternative models for different segments of the accounting universe (macro- and micro-social accounting, financial accounting, managerial accounting, governmental accounting), and (iii) the foundations and elements of a 'general theory' of accounting.

In both texts, the authors proceeded by examining concisely a considerable number of international publications of accounting theory. The first book attempts to discuss over 80, the second one over 90 publications – most of them published during the last half century or so (but the bibliographies of both refer to relatively few Latin American authors). In a way, the second book is an attempt to extend the first text, offering an even great number of lengthy quotations from well-known international scholars. Here again, the 'new' Anglophone accounting literature plays a decisive role.

García Casella is *profesor consulto* of the University of Buenos Aires (the highest academic position in an Argentine university). He has published some 140 books and papers, and chairs the Research Center on Accounting Models as part of the *Instituto de Investigaciones Contables* of this university. Among several distinctions, he received on three different occasions the '*Premio a la producción científica y tecnológica*' from his university.

His collaborator, María del Carmen Rodríguez de Ramírez, is a professor at the same university, and a co-director of the second joint research project (mentioned above). She focused her own research on financial accounting, investigating recent improvements in financial information provided to third parties. This includes information on intellectual capital, on new ways of distributing business information, as well as widening the scope of the conceptual framework of accounting (Rodríguez de Ramírez 2000, 2001). Most recently, she concerned herself with social accounting and its various ontological postulates (Rodríguez de Ramírez 2004a) and the social responsibility of accounting (Rodríguez de Ramírez 2004b).

Lucio González Bravo presented a doctoral dissertation on epistemological aspects of accounting (1984) and published a book on the methodology of research in the economic sciences, with particular emphasis on accounting (1996). These publications are the fruits of a lengthy academic career at two important Argentine universities. He previously concerned himself with accounting axiomatization and normative problems in several publications (González Bravo 1990a, 1990b; Avilà *et al.* 1988).

Further research can be found in Wirth (2001) who set out to make some revision to modern accounting theory. After describing the central problems, she analysed the way theories are constructed in applied sciences and social technologies. Based on the epistemological model of the Argentine-Canadian philosopher Mario Bunge (1983, 1985, 1996), she presented accounting as a scientific discipline with the characteristics of a 'social technology'.

17.6.3 Financial accounting

In the second half of the twentieth century there were, among other publications, many concerned with inflation accounting and the pertinent adjustments in annual financial statements. Indeed, the number of such publications increased (from the 1960s to the 1990s) considerably, as Argentine wholesale prices increased during the 1960s six-fold, during the 1970s by a factor of 2,192 and between December 1980 and December 1990 by a factor of 23,137,641.

Mario Biondi has been chairman of the previously mentioned *Instituto de Investigaciones Contables 'Profesor Juan Alberto Arévalo'* of the Faculty of Economics at the University of Buenos Aires. Under his direction, different research teams studied the problems of harmonization of accounting standards for the *Mercosur* (a regional economic alliance of several South American countries) (see Biondi 2001). He also examined (in co-authorship) the theoretical basis for the preparation of future-oriented accounting information in Biondi and Viegas (2003). Biondi authored some 18 books on various financial accounting issues (Biondi 1969, 1989), as well as on accounting theory (Biondi 1973a, 1973b, 1976), including his two volume text, Biondi (1984), a treatise of intermediate and advanced accounting.

Enrique Fowler Newton wrote an important treatise of five volumes on financial accounting in Argentina. Its significance lies not merely in the large numbers of volumes, but in presenting a conceptual framework that sustains his entire work. His text begins with a volume on fundamental accounting issues (Fowler Newton 1982a); it continues with accounting basics (Fowler Newton 1977), then with advanced accounting (Fowler Newton 1978) and, finally, with the organization of accounting systems, pivoting on administrative aspects (Fowler Newton 1982b). These books and their later revisions are used as text books in most accounting courses at Argentine universities.

Being an expert on financial accounting in Argentina, Fowler Newton concerned himself also with inflation issues and their impact on accounting. His first book on this subject (Fowler Newton 1976) was written at a time when inflation was officially 'recognized' in Argentina's legislation. And, since 1983, the Argentine Law No. 19,550 makes it obligatory for all firms to adjust their financial statements for inflation (i.e. in constant purchasing power or *moneda constante*). Later, Fowler Newton (1980) analysed the accounting standards promulgated for purchasing power adjustments of the financial statements based on indexation of the non-monetary accounts. Argentine inflation adjustment is based on a general price index called *índice de precios mayoristas internos*, or on a wholesale price index. These adjusted figures constitute the only data of the financial statements and are *not* supplemented by any historical cost or any other figures.

For the period of very low inflation (1995–2001), Argentine accounting standards permitted the omission of such inflationary adjustment. However, this permission was abolished in the year 2002 after a steep increase in prices due to the discontinuation of currency convertibility – a subject that Fowler Newton (2002a) dealt with in a later book. In February 2003, the need for inflationary adjustments was again suspended because of renewed price stabilization.

The different technical and interpretational problems of financial statements analysis are treated as different versions in Fowler Newton (1984, and subsequent editions), namely by examining the information content of different ratios for different contexts. For example, he shows the different information provided by EBITDA (a very common calculation of annual cash flow provided by operations) and the net flow of funds originated in operations (i.e. figures taken from the Cash Flow Statement).

Fowler Newton is a most active scholar as well as a practising accountant, and has received numerous honours. During the years of 2000–01 he was engaged in the evaluation, modification and preparation of the Argentine accounting standards, which now have been aligned with the international standards of the IASB. As a consequence of this, and his participation on the International Accounting Standards Board (IASB), he published another book about the recently approved Argentine accounting standards (Fowler Newton 2002b). He now is engaged in committee work of the *Federación* and the *Consejo Mexicano para la Investigacion y Desarrollo de Normas de Informacion Financiera* (CINIF) in developing a proposal for a new standard on inflation accounting, to be submitted to the IASB.

López Santiso is another author who wrote on inflation accounting and exercised considerable influence on the Argentine accounting profession. He is a professor of the Universidad de Buenos Aires and author of ten books on academic and professional subjects, as well as president of the *Consejo Profesional de Ciencias Económicas de la Ciudad Autonoma de Buenos Aires*.

His first publications (López Santiso 1969, 1986) examined the accounting distortions caused by the erosion of purchasing power. Another book on this subject, but co-authored (López Santiso *et al.* 1988) on financial statements in constant monetary units, has become a classic textbook on inflation adjustments. It clearly defined and systematized the effects of inflation on monetary and non-monetary accounts, and analysed the foundations of inflation accounting with a financial capital maintenance model (based on general price-level adjustments – cf. the 'sophisticated' GPL model in Mattessich 1995: 109–19 – there, the models for general price-level adjustments are presented schematically in simple mathematical terms by means of four 'Tables' together with an explanatory text and further equations). However, it described the application of inflation adjustment by means of the *indirect method* – in contrast to the 'direct' method that does not adjust the non-monetary accounts, and thus is not used for preparing adjusted financial statements. Finally, the book discussed the legal aspects of the information provided by adjusted financial statements.

In 1979, López Santiso led a team of accounting professionals and academics, as well as experts of related disciplines (philosophers, economists, managers and experts in information theory), whose objective was to revise extant accounting theory from a 'scientific' viewpoint to construct a conceptual frame work. The project was undertaken on request of the *Centro de Estudios Científicos y Técnicos*, and its results published in 1980 (see Fortini *et al.* 1980). This work is considered a landmark in Argentine accounting research, and had a considerable impact upon academics. However, it led to vehement debates of the projects' methodology, as well as its results – the more so as it defined accounting as a *technical* discipline focused on *equity valuation* with the ultimate purpose of income determination.

One of the more recent works by López Santiso (2001) is on the epistemological relationship between accounting, administration and the economy. There, he also critically analysed the debate arising from the team's publications during the 1980s.

Another prestigious author, Sánchez Brot (1995, later editions in 2000 and 2004), published a massive compendium on accounting and auditing that analysed accounting standards, their interpretation and application, as well as related issues such as inflation adjustments, etc. It presented, among others, the opinions of prominent accounting academics on problematic issues, including the editor's own interpretation of accounting standards.

Other important academics, including Bértora [1922–94] (1951, 1975) analysed the concept of goodwill, its characteristics and valuation methods, while the contributions of Lazzati (1976, 1978, 1987) referred to problems concerning the auditor's report, and later to inflation and its impact on managerial accounting, respectively. Cholvis was a prolific author who published many textbooks for commercial high-school students, but also wrote on specific topics, such as standard costs, and the preparation of financial statements, respectively (Cholvis 1954, 1955). Two of his more interesting contributions were his study on 'incorrect financial statements' and 'personal frauds in accounting', respectively (Cholvis 1951, 1962).

Arturo Lisdero (1970) analysed the concept and status of the 'balance sheet' in accounting theory, and co-authored a book on accounting and inflation (Lisdero and Outeiral 1973), Sergio García (1983) submitted proposals on the application of current values in equity valuation, while Juan Carlos Viegas *et al.* (1996) analysed the impact of different accounting valuation methods (nominal vs. real value and cost vs. market value) and capital maintenance models (financial vs. physical) on profit measurement. Pahlen Acuña (Pahlen Acuña 1998, 2001; Pahlen Acuña and Campo 2000) directed several teams concerned with the application of models and standards of accounting, as well as textbooks on advanced accounting and applied accounting theory, respectively.

17.6.4 *Auditing*

Apart from occasional contributions on auditing, already mentioned above, William L. Chapman [1922–93] published a book on auditing procedures (Chapman 1965) and another on diverse auditing issues (Chapman 1980). Yet, his foremost concern was the responsibility of professionals, especially accountants, in their position as preparer and auditor of financial statements (Chapman 1979). In the 1980s, he continued these studies elaborating the stewardship issue from the legal and professional aspect to the social perspective (see subsection 17.6.6 on social accounting).

Mario Wainstein, professor at the Universidad de Buenos Aires, specializing in auditing and its research, published a book on auditing of insurance companies (Wainstein 1974, re-edited in 1999), a text on the application of financial statements adjustment for inflation (Wainstein 1980), on the auditor's statement of opinion (Wainstein and Casal 1992), and on diverse auditing issues (Wainstein 1999). More recently, he co-authored a study on the challenging issues of environmental auditing as part of an integrated auditing process (Wainstein and Casal 1996).

Fowler Newton (mentioned above) also concerned himself with fundamental and applied issues of auditing (Fowler Newton 1989 and 1991, respectively, revised version in 2004; both texts later extended and slightly re-named). Other relevant authors published books on diverse auditing issues, such as Lazzati (1976 and previous editions) who dealt with the auditor's statement of opinion as well as with the objectives and procedures of auditing (Lazzati 1981).

Auditing seems to be relatively underdeveloped in Argentina, possibly due to the training of Argentine public accountants (auditors) that is very different from America or the Commonwealth countries. In these countries there used to be an apprenticeship system that later was replaced by intensive in-house training of university graduates. Apart from that, in those countries more funds are available for auditing research. A country like Argentina, with relatively few large corporations, has different auditing needs – something similar may hold for managerial accounting (see below).

17.6.5 Cost and managerial accounting

Herrscher (1967) introduced the concept of managerial accounting in Argentina. This subdiscipline responded to new needs, ideas and concepts of cost accounting, such as management by objectives, results analysis, planning and control, cash flow analysis, etc. Lazzati co-authored a book on managerial accounting and inflation (Lazzati 1969/78) where he analysed the effect of inflation on the information for business decision making.

Carlos Giménez (1979) wrote a textbook on cost accounting that proved to be a classic reference for university students. It not only provided the technical aspect of the subject matter but also a managerial focus. And Vazquez (1971) published a treatise on standard costing, which was also included in university courses.

Oscar Osorio [1927–2001], a prominent professor of the University of Buenos Aires and expert in cost accounting, produced a well-known work on production capacity and production costs (Osorio 1986). There, he analysed the problem of fixed structural costs vs. fixed operational costs in different industries.

Antonio Lavolpe wrote about costs systems for construction firms. He also co-authored a book on cost systems, cost accounting and managerial accounting (Lavolpe *et al.* 1993), and co-authored another on budgetary systems and control (Lavolpe 2000).

Other cost experts who published books on diverse managerial issues were Cascarini who treated the joint costs issue (Cascarini 1985) and analysed the process costing systems (Cascarini 1987), and Perez Alfaro (2000) and Norberto García, from the Universidad Nacional de Córdoba, who also authored books on managerial accounting (García 2003).

17.6.6 Social accounting

William L. Chapman (1965, 1979, 1984b) was professor and dean at the University of Buenos Aires in the 1960s, partner of Price and Waterhouse, and a member of the *Academia Nacional de Ciencias Económicas*. He wrote first on auditing procedures, then on the responsibility of the professionals in the economic sciences (above all, accountants and auditors), as well as on theoretical issues of accounting (see subsection 17.6.3). But his most original works were four papers presented at the *Academia* (Chapman 1982, 1983, 1984a). The first was on the consumer as social beneficiary of economic activity (Chapman 1982); in the second he explored the difficulties of measuring the net social benefit of economic activity of governmental and private organizations (Chapman 1983); in the third paper he considered the firm's responsibility to third parties, including the environmental and human context (Chapman 1984a). Two years later, he presented his 'Principle of fraternity in the economic activity' (Chapman 1986) that was based on Rudolf Steiner's (1919) proposal on human activities in society, as a basis for exploring the foundations of social accounting.

Another prestigious researcher in social accounting is L. Fronti de García. She produced several books on financial accounting and professional issues, but her field of expertise is environmental accounting and environmental auditing (Fronti de García 1998, 1999; Fronti de García and Wainstein 2000). The last of these books is a compilation of the doctrines of several academics (including herself and Mario Wainstein), on such issues as environmental liabilities and contingencies – with special emphasis made to the connections to international and Argentine accounting standards, business policies on environmental control and environmental auditing.

So far, we mainly reported on publications and research activities of professors from the University of Buenos Aires. As to other institutions, a research team of the National University of La Plata, for example, investigates 'social financial statements for non-profit organizations'. From this quarter emerged two books by Fernández Lorenzo *et al.* (1998) and Fernández Lorenzo and Geba (2000). These authors employed the notions of 'accounting by objectives' and 'socio-economic ratios' to constructing social financial statements. These offer information on various aspects of non-profit organizations, relevant to the social objectives of these organizations.

17.6.7 *Governmental accounting*

Governmental accounting is represented in our database by some 21 books (for the period from 1900 to 1949) plus 15 books (for the period from 1950 to 2003). Previously, we also encountered Arévalo's (1954) book on the operative and accounting problems in the *hacienda pública* (see above). Furthermore, Bayetto (1931, 1950) wrote texts on governmental accounting and on budgeting as a fundamental instrument of governmental accounting and control.

In the second part of the twentieth century, Atchabahian and Massier co-authored textbooks on the legal aspects of governmental accounting (1962, 1963). Later, Atchabahian (1996) published an important work on the Argentine legal regulations for operating and controlling governmental entities. Furthermore, Alé (Alé and Goméz 1975; Alé 1983) analysed the governmental accounting law, and later supplemented this work by writing on methods and procedures of governmental accounting in Argentina.

17.7 Concluding remarks

In concluding this brief survey of twentieth-century Argentine authors and researchers, the main feature is a notable increase in accounting literature during the second part of the century, especially in financial accounting that accounts for more than half of the books in our database. Perhaps more importantly, a strong impetus to accounting research came from financial support provided by national universities. For example, the cooperation between the Universidad de Buenos Aires and the Universidad Nacional de La Plata resulted in interesting research on such topics as: (i) accounting theory, its hypothesis, laws and models; (ii) environmental accounting; and (iii) social accounting (including social reports in non-profit organizations and corporate social responsibility). Further features of twentieth-century Argentine accounting literature were:

1   The importance of European publications (mainly from Spain) available in Argentine libraries (25 per cent) compared to those from North American editions (1 per cent) during the first half of the century (probably due to the language barrier).

2   An enormous increase in accounting literature (over 650 per cent) available at Argentine libraries (in the language of origin, as well as Spanish translations) during the second half of the twentieth century. This was mainly due to the growing influence of Anglophone accounting texts and research (particularly on accounting principles and standards, as well as the need for inflation adjustments).

18 Accounting in other countries

Publications and research reports[1]

18.1 Introduction

In previous chapters we have tried to offer a survey of accounting research from a number of industrialized countries and language areas. However, to cover all countries was neither possible nor advisable because of space limitations. Nevertheless, there are some areas where we wish we had succeeded in collecting more material or in securing meaningful cooperation. Unfortunately, this was not possible. The best we could do under those circumstances was to draw the reader's attention to some Anglophone literature about some geographical areas not covered previously.

18.2 Some Eastern European countries, and Israel

For Russia, as well as Poland and the Ukraine, we refer the reader to Chapters 15 and 16. As to other Eastern European countries, one encounters such studies as, for example, McClure (1983) offering an overview of Rumanian accounting; Lakis (1996) on auditing reforms in Lithuania; Illés et al. (1996) on change and choice in Hungarian accounting practice; Rooz and Stanó (1996) on the regulations of joint ventures in Hungary. As regards the Czech Republic, we may mention several studies: Patton and Zelenka (1997) on the notion of disclosure determinants; and Sucher and Jindrichovska (2004) on implementing international accounting standards in this country (as well as Sucher et al. 1996). From the former Yugoslavia, there is the paper by Turk (1976) on professional statements and accounting principles. And from Greece and Cyprus there are such studies as Filios (1984) on transition of systematic accounting from ancient to Byzantine Greece, or Costouros (1975) on accounting education and practice in Greece, and the one by Vafeas et al. (1998) on the usefulness and explanatory power of earnings in the emergent stock market of Cyprus.

We might mention two papers on Israel, one by Markell (1968) on accounting education in Israel and the other by Givoly and Lakonishok (1982) on accounting for construction companies in Israel. However, there are many Israeli scholars in the English language area, doing research and publishing in English. Some of these publications are to be found in Chapter 12.

18.3 The Portuguese language area (Portugal and Brazil)[2]

Although Portuguese and Brazilian accounting academics often rely on Spanish publications, there is no lack of ample accounting literature in the Portuguese language. Again we can offer only a glimpse into major works of this language area. Among the earlier twentieth-century authors, there was Ricardo de Sá [1844–1912] with his book on auditing (Sá 1912) and Jaime Lopes de Amorim [1891–1973] (1929) with his accounting text. Fernando Vieira Gonçalves da Silva [1904–90] (1938), with another accounting text belongs already entirely to the twentieth century. Such efforts were later continued in updated texts (e.g. Amorim 1969, and da Silva 1968), and da Silva (1970) with his historical accounting study; similarly Monteiro (1965a, 1965b) also concerned himself with historical aspects of accounting.

Among contemporary scholars, there is Hernani O. Carqueja, professor at the University of Oporto ('Porto' in Portuguese) and editor of the journal *Revista de Contabilidade e Comercio*. He is a prolific author who dealt with a wide range from historical to theoretical topics (e.g. Carqueja 1975, 1999, 2002). The last of these publications offers to readers of Portuguese a concise survey of academic accounting doctrines from the fifteenth to the beginning of the twenty-first century (though some recent areas are neglected, as, for example, advances in modern information perspective of accounting and related areas). R.M. de Everard Martins (1997) also concerned himself with bibliographical material, particularly of Portuguese accounting. There also exists the book by Santos Feirreira (2002) that summarized and exposed empirical and particularly positive accounting theory to the Portuguese accounting community. There are also some empirical studies as, for example, the one by Neves and Fernández (1998).

As regards Brazil, the book by Américo M. Florentino (1965), on the mathematical foundations of accounting and its educational application to programming and bookkeeping analysis, has raised the attention of some foreign accounting academics. Yet, the internationally best known among the contemporary Brazilian accounting scholars is Antonio Lopes de Sá. He is a most prolific writer and concerned himself early in his career with inflationary problems; later, he wrote on a great variety of topics, from writing a general history of accounting, to axiomatic issues, to compiling an accounting dictionary, to ethical issues and many other topics (e.g. Sá 1960, 1995, 2000a, 2000b, 2002). Occasionally, one encounters in the English literature reports on Brazil, as, for example, McMahon (1972), on the need for improved accounting. Various accounting journals in Portuguese language offer evidence of the 'modern' trend: the *Revista de Contabilidade e Comércio* (founded some 60 years ago) is – besides the *Jornal do Tecnico de Contas e Empresa* – the most prestigious pertinent journal in Portugal; and in Brazil the *Conselho Federal de Contabilidade* (of the federal public accounting body) issues monographs and guidelines on ethics and many other topics. This institution also publishes a monthly journal, the *Jornal do CFC*.

18.4 Some Latin American countries (excluding Argentina and Brazil)

We discussed in Chapter 17 accounting publications in Argentina as representing South America. Yet, Argentina is hardly representative of all Latin American countries, and it is advisable to supplement Chapter 17 with some hints on accounting publications from other Latin American countries. For example, there is the paper by Salas (1967) on accounting education and practice in Spanish Latin America in general; a similar topic is found by Elliot (1972) who wrote on accounting and economic development in Latin America, while Powelson (1967) dealt with national income estimates in Latin America.

As regards Mexico, we encountered two papers; one by Mora (1972) on the accounting profession in Mexico, the other by Wong-Boren and Barnett (1984) on information content and accounting numbers as reflecting Mexican market efficiency. Above all, there is the English publication by the Instituto Mexicano de Contadores Público (1975) on price-level adjustments, and a book (in Spanish) by Rodríguez Alvarez *et al.* (2000) on the origin and the development of accounting in Mexico 1845–2000. The book was designed to celebrate the 150th anniversary of the School of Commerce and Administration (now part of the *Instituto Politécnico National*). Thus, its emphasis is on teaching and institutional matters rather than on accounting research.

As to other Latin American countries, there is a paper by Pena (1976) comparing the accounting profession of Colombia with that in the USA. There are two papers on Peru, the first by Vandendries (1970) on social accounting in Peru, the other by Radebaugh (1975) about the influence of environmental factors on Peruvian accounting practices. And as regards Venezuela, there is a paper by Rivera (1982) on financial aspects of multi-national companies in this country, and another one by Villalobos de Nucete (1984) on the historical development (of accounting) in this country.

Furthermore, there is Chu (1973) on accounting principles and practices in Panama; or by Aguirre and Hagigi (1987) on accounting and other determinants of financial reporting in Guatemala; or the paper by Carmony (1987) on accounting in Uruguay. We may add that some authors from Spain or other language areas contribute (either regularly or occasionally) to the accounting literature of Latin America – be it in the form of reprints or as original contributions, as, for example, Tua Pereda (1988, 1992, 1995), or Mattessich (1964, 2002) and Mattessich and Galassi (2004). As to historical aspects, there are such papers as Jacobsen (1964, 1983) and Orellana (2005), etc. on the 'quipu accounting' of the ancient Incas of Peru (apart from a host of pertinent publications by archeologists – see the Internet under 'quipu', as well as 'khipu') – Jacobsen (1983) also discussed the use of 'quipu accounting' in Hawaii and ancient China.

18.5 Arab and other Moslem countries, as well as some African countries

There are several well-known accounting scholars from Egypt and other Arab countries living on the American continent or in Great Britain who publish in English. Some of their publications may deal with subjects concerning Arab countries, but often enough their subject matter goes beyond a particular country and concerns special accounting and auditing topics. Among these scholars are, just to name a few, the following: A. Rashad Abdel-khalik (see Chapter 12), a prominent Egyptian-American theorist with numerous publications covering a wide spectrum of accounting topics; an Egyptian-Canadian scholar, Moustafa F. Abdel-Magid (1981) with a paper on the theory of Islamic banking. Furthermore, there are the papers by Alhashim (1977) on Egyptian social accounting, by Briston and Ahmed El-Ashker (1984) on the influence of the West on the Egyptian accounting system. Also, there is an eminent and prolific Tunisian-American author, Ahmed Riahi Belkaoui, and Mahmud A. Ezzamel, a prominent English-Arab accounting theorist and historian, occasionally writing on topics of ancient Egypt (e.g. Ezzamel 2002a, 2002b). There are also some papers on accounting aspects in Jordan, as, for example, Abu-nassar and Rutherford (1996) and Naser and Baker (1999). Another well-known Arab-American accounting scholar is Mohammad J. Abdolmohammadi (1990) with his paper on the use of corporate financial reports in Saudi Arabia. Other papers on Saudi Arabia are by Shinawi and Krum (1971) on the emergence of the accounting profession in Saudi Arabia, and by Abdeen and Ugar (1985) on accounting education in Saudi Arabia. Also, there is a paper by Shuaib (1980) on accounting and development planning in Kuwait.

There is the paper by Bait-el-Mal *et al.* (1973) on the accounting development in Tunisia; another study on underdeveloped countries is the paper by Holzer and Tremblay (1973) on the economic development in Thailand and Tunisia, Also, there are two studies by Abdeen (1980, 1984) on the role of accounting in project evaluation and control, and on the impact of accounting practices on tax revenues, respectively, both referring to Tunisia. Furthermore, there are three papers on Turkey, one by Ogan (1978) on Turkish accountancy, another one by Bursal (1984) on the accounting environment in Turkey, and a third one by Cook and Çürük (1996) on accounting and lease transactions. In addition, there is a comparison of accounting in different Arab countries as, for example, by Dhamash (1982). There is also a paper by Foroughi (1981) on accounting in Iran before and after the social crisis, and another one by Qureshi (1973) on private enterprise accounting and economic development in Pakistan.

There are three papers on Nigeria, one by Ogudele (1969) on the accounting profession in Nigeria, another one by Osiegbu (1987) on accounting education in Nigeria, and a third one by Jagetia and Nwadike (1983) on accounting systems in developing countries, emphasizing Nigeria. Another paper, by Ghartey (1978) is on new perspectives for accounting education in Ghana. There is also a paper by Jones and Kinfu (1971) on the birth of the accounting profession in Ethiopia.

18.6 Some countries of the Far East

Babatosh Banerjee is an Indian scholar well known in the West. We might mention Banerjee (1984, 1994) on financial policy and management accounting, and on accounting education in India, respectively. He also edited, in Banerjee (1991), an anthology under the title *Contemporary issues in accounting research* with contributions by Western as well as Indian scholars. Furthermore, there are such papers as Jaggi (1970) on the accounting profession in India, and Singh and Ahuja (1983) on corporate social reporting in India.

As to China, we referred in section 2.7 to Cai Xiyong who is said to have published in 1905 the first Western style double-entry primer (for details on early industrial applications of Western accounting in China, see Guo 1982–89, 1996). In more recent times, there is a paper by Kwang (1966) on the economic accounting system in state enterprises of Mainland China. Another paper by Chu (1969) deals with accounting education in the Republic of China, and one by P.C. Cheng (1970) which deals with accounting in Nationalistic China. There is also the book by Firth (1996), *The diffusion of managerial accounting procedures in the People's Republic of China and the influence of foreign partnered ventures.*

The English language *Asia-Pacific Journal of Accounting and Economics* (formerly *Asia-Pacific Journal of Accounting*), published in Hong Kong, is an important link for conveying current accounting research to Chinese familiar with English, and so is the bilingual journal *China Accounting and Finance Review*. Among the Chinese-language accounting journals, it seems that *Kai Ji Yan* (Accounting research) is the most prominent one. There also exists an English–Chinese dictionary edited by Erxing and Farrell (1985) *Accounting terminologies in use in the People's Republic of China and in the United States.* Furthermore, some English texts have been translated into Chinese, as, for example, Bromwich and Bhimani (2002) on management accounting.

While those books may be of limited use to the non-specialist, the following English-language conference proceedings or anthologies may be of broader interest: first, a joint research study, edited by the Center for International Accounting Development (1987), *Accounting and auditing in the People's Republic of China*; second, Wei *et al.* (1994), *Accounting and finance in China: a review of current practices*; third, Blake and Gao (1995), *Perspectives on accounting and finance in China*; and fourth, Narayan and Reid (2000), *Financial management and governance issues in the People's Republic of China.*

Apart from those books there is the paper by Ji (2000). It offers an evaluation of research in Chinese accounting issues, presenting not merely a fairly complete turn-of-the century survey of major accounting publications, but also of pertinent historical accounting research. This paper lists seven anthologies or proceedings on this topic (containing together over 50 papers), as well as 17 English-language journals (containing in total some 40 papers on Chinese accounting, among which the *International Journal of Accounting* is a major source (with 15 of those papers). There is also a paper on business and accounting developments in China by Hsu (1981).

A paper authored by P.C. Cheng and Jain (1972) deals with accounting practices in South Korea. A paper by Ninsuvannakul (1966) deals with accounting education in Thailand, and Kaocharern (1976) wrote on the development of the security exchange in Thailand (while another paper, partly on the accounting and economic of Thailand, by Holzer and Tremblay 1973, has been mentioned in subsection 18.4). Kim and Song (1990) deal with a comparison of accounting practices in the USA with those in Korea and Japan.

18.7 Publications on developing countries in general

Some pertinent publications do not specify individual countries but deal with accounting problems faced by developing countries in general. One of the experts of accounting in developing countries is Adolf J.H. Enthoven. He has dozens of books to his credit, many of which deal with this topic. One of the first of these works was Enthoven (1973), *Accountancy and economic development policy*, followed by Enthoven (1977), *Accounting systems in third world economies*, again followed by many versions, expansions and variations on those issues. Other publications in this category are the papers by Jaggi (1973) on accounting studies in developing countries, and that by Briston (1978) on the evolution of accounting in developing countries; the paper by Samuels and Oliga (1982) on accounting standards in developing countries, and the one by Gul and Yap (1984) on some aspects of auditing and management services in developing countries, also that by Ndubizu (1984) on accounting standards and economic development.

Another prolific author (occasionally in co-authorship) is Francis B. Narayan. He published for the Asian Development Bank a series of studies dealing with accounting, auditing, or governance issues. For example, Naryan (2000, 2002) on financial governance issues in Cambodia, China, Mongolia, Pakistan, Papua New Guinea, Uzbekistan and Viet Nam, as well as on accounting and auditing in Azabeijan, Fiji Islands, the Republic of Marshall Islands, the Phillipines and Sri Lanka, respectively.

Finally, there exists the series of Research in Emerging Economies (general editor: R.S.O. Wallace [also called Wallacem]) of which several volumes are available (e.g. Wallace *et al.* 1999; Wallace 1995, 2003; Hopper and Hoque 2004), as well as several serial publications dealing with accounting research in the third world or emerging economies (e.g. JAI Press 1990–93, 1995–, as well as various supplements).

19 The information economic perspective and the future of accounting[1]

> If the heart of accounting is 'valuation',
> And its pulse is 'counting',
> Then, 'information' is its mind,
> And 'accountability' its soul.
>
> R.M.

19.1 Introduction

This chapter tries to explain and evaluate major aspects of the information economic perspective of accounting[2] in a non-mathematical way. This seems to be an appropriate conclusion for our historical survey, as pertinent research has steadily grown since the 1960s, and has reached (at the beginning of the twenty-first century) a stage where it may be claimed as the climax of modern accounting research. This is not so much a personal opinion but is based on the many official honours and recognitions that the major pioneers of this approach have received. And yet, the information perspective is still an esoteric mathematical field, presently accessible only to a relatively small minority of academic accountants worldwide (not to speak of practitioners) – hence, the need for some non-mathematical interpretation.

Two major works, each written by one of the two original pioneers of this approach – and each in co-authorship with a former student – summarize the present status of this work. I refer to *Accounting Theory, an Information Content Perspective* by J.A. Christensen and J. Demski (2003), and to *Economics of Accounting*, Vol. I: *Information in Markets* together with Vol. II: *Performance Evaluation* by P.O. Christensen and G.A. Feltham (2003 and 2005, respectively).

Of course, it is impossible to ever attain in the social and behavioural sciences a truly realistic picture through model building. Or as Bell says:

> economic theory should not be taken as a 'model' (or template) of how human beings behave, for these will always be inadequate, but as a 'Utopia', a set of ideal standards against which one can debate and judge different policy actions and their consequences. That, it seems to me, is

the meaningful role of any social 'science' in theorizing about human affairs.

(Bell 1981: 80)

Despite many difficulties and limitations, this approach has succeeded in integrating a number of relevant aspects from financial accounting and auditing to managerial accounting and agency theory. Thus we may speak of a broad synthesis of the information perspective as applied to accounting. And yet, it would be too early to praise these efforts from a practical point of view; so far they are foremost a cultural achievement.

Nevertheless, analytical accountants have good reason to hope that empiricists will attempt to test the hypotheses formulated in analytical models, and possibly succeed in finding some confirmation.[3] Indeed, leading empirical accountants have not only tested some of these hypotheses but have also expressed high regard for several aspects of the information economic perspective (particularly the aspect developed by Feltham and Ohlson 1995). Lee for example points out that:

Five years ago, Bernard (1995) predicted that the Feltham/Ohlson framework would have sweeping effects on the direction of market-based accounting research. Five years later, it is interesting to reflect on the prophetic nature of his statement. By and large, his predictions have been correct.

(Lee 1999: 422)

And more recently Richardson and Tinaikar asserted that:

The 'horserace' literature confirms that without a doubt one need not necessarily undo the accruals in order to estimate intrinsic value. This insight has resulted in the complete rewrite of financial statement analysis text. Such a breakthrough would not have been possible without the foundations laid by the Ohlson and Feltham/Ohlson models.

(Richardson and Tinaikar 2004: 225)

Finally, the mere fact that Beaver (2002), possibly the most prominent of the empirical accounting academics, highly praised information economics and, in particular, the book by Christensen and Demski, might be an additional clue that empirical accountants regard the information perspective as an important supplier of potential hypotheses to be tested factually.

Empirical accounting, in general, is too much dispersed in bits and pieces; it hardly reveals the 'big picture'. Usually, it is driven by data easily available, instead of undertaking the more arduous work of testing hypotheses offered by analytical accounting. Thus, the great hope of the information perspective is to gain an *overall view* of the interrelations of the economic forces impacting on business and accounting. And this awareness is crucial, particularly for the outsider who asks: 'What is all this highly complex conceptual apparatus for?' It simply constitutes the application of a refined version of neo-classical economics (with its *equilibrium* conditions and numerous other 'trappings') to accounting. Or as Christensen and Feltham point out:

> The relevant economic analysis is often referred to as *information economics* ... [but] the information economic analyses conducted by accounting researchers often do not model the specific form of an accounting report. Nonetheless, many generic results apply to accounting reports. Furthermore, the impact of accounting reports depends on the other information received by the economy's participants. Hence, it is essential that accounting researchers have a broad understanding of the impact of publicly reported information within settings in which there are multiple sources of public and private information.
>
> (Christensen and Feltham 2003: xxi)

More bluntly expressed, those who *object* to the premises of neo-classical economics (and its 'recent' extensions) and finance theory are not likely to agree with the application of information economics to accounting. Among those, I suppose, would be some followers of the 'critical-interpretive camp' and other opponents of mainstream economics.

19.2　Recent books by the two pioneers and their collaborators

To some extent, the two texts mentioned above overlap, but in a wider sense they are complementary. Both of them will prove useful in doctoral seminars, but Beaver considers the text by Christensen and Demski (2003) also as 'a "must" for the accounting faculty whose main research interests reside in other areas' (Beaver 2002: 632 – this is one of the rare instances where the book review was published before the book's publishing date – for another review of this book, see Wagenhofer 2003). Indeed, this book comes closer to a *prolegomenon*, if for no other reason than for some pedagogic novelties, and the imaginative sequential numerical illustrations throughout the book. The two volumes by Christensen and Feltham (2003, 2005), on the other hand, are not merely mathematically more demanding and sophisticated, they are also more comprehensive; and their rigorous synthesis approaches a fairly closed overview – in as far as one can speak of 'closure' in such a context.

The text by Christensen and Demski (2003) is an attempt to introduce the 'uninitiated' (though mathematically sophisticated) student to the 'mysteries' of the information perspective by step-wise illustrations and careful explanations. To attain this on an international scale will be no easy task. Perhaps a strategy employing more traditional accounting notions (than presently used in the 'American version' of the information perspective) could remedy this situation. The 'European version' – as presented by Ewert and Wagenhofer (1993, 2003) and Wagenhofer and Ewert (2003) – demonstrates that such an extension to the traditional conceptual apparatus is possible (for a concise discussion of these books, see subsection 19.7.2).[4]

Whereas the text by Christensen and Demski may, at first sight, be preferable from a pedagogic point of view, the work by Christensen and Feltham (although originally based on classroom notes) has more the character of a vast survey. It offers a great wealth of details and goes far beyond an ordinary text book.[5] As important as the work by Christensen and Demski (2003) might be for the pedagogic dissemination of the information perspective among students, the two volumes by Christensen and Feltham (2003, 2005) may prove to be more important in the long run, particularly as a reference work. Although the work of Christensen and Feltham may be used as textbooks (even if lacking the many numerical examples of its 'competitor'), they present the summary of a comprehensive and rigorous 'theory'. They introduce numerous assumptions, formal definitions, and (in Vols I and II together) over 250 propositions (including Lemmas and Corollaries), most of them with rigorous mathematical proofs. This makes the two volumes a fairly self-contained theoretical body that may well become an accounting classic. Taken as an *economic theory of accounting*, it seems to be unmatched by any other extant work dealing with accounting and its economic-informational aspects.

The major hurdle that many accountants (particularly those beyond North America) may encounter in digesting such books might – apart from the rigour and mathematical notation – be the rich conceptual apparatus, considerably different from traditional accounting texts. One may even question whether the title of Christensen and Demski's (2003) book, *Accounting Theory*, is justified. The title of Christensen and Feltham's (2003, 2005) work, *Economics of Accounting*, seems to be more appropriate, considering the lack of major accounting concepts in both of these books, than the title. One may also wonder whether the American version of the information perspective does not contain too many purely conceptual notions that are difficult to relate to the structures encountered in reality.[6] Ideally, most, if not all of the many propositions should, at least in principle, be *refutable* in Popper's sense. But if the theory is 'over-constructed' too many of its variables are 'unobservable' and the related conclusions are difficult if not impossible to confirm (or refute) empirically. Perhaps in future, simpler and more realistic versions of the information perspective will emerge. But this requires a closer cooperation between analytical, empirical and even normative accountants.

Another aspect of these works and the information perspective in general is the intellectual 'extension and integration' that it impacts our discipline. In this regard, there may exist some parallel with the German and Italian attempts in the earlier part of the twentieth century – from Schmalenbach[7] and Zappa (1927) to Gutenberg (1957), who was a later champion of this direction – of creating a *Betiebswirtschaftslehre* and *economia aziendale*, respectively. In all these cases, including the American information perspective, there was an attempt to unify or even integrate different business subjects under a common umbrella. In the first two cases (in contrast to the third one), it was a deliberate attempt to postu-late a kind of super-discipline. While in the third and more recent case, the 'bonding agent' was the all-pervasive concept of information. And the introduc-tion of this notion was the inevitable consequence of a scientific process search-ing to fill certain gaps of hitherto unexplained phenomena.

19.3 Information vs. value?

The information perspective constitutes a challenging paradigm in the Kuhnian sense. In North America it has for some time been accorded high prestige among scholars of elite universities, but it has hardly conquered the minds of many other accounting academics, nor of practitioners. Christensen and Demski (2003) contrast this 'information content perspective' with the more traditional 'valuation perspective' in the following words:

> A popular idiom is that accounting is, or should be, designed to measure value. Ideally the argument goes, assets would be stated at fair value, income would be a fair and true measure of economic accomplishment relative to the net asset employed, ... Once market structure departs from the textbook extreme of a perfect and complete set of markets, the very notion of a well-defined concept of value disappears .... We hasten to add that if valuation is the purpose, accounting is an abject failure on a worldwide basis .... The information perspective, the notion that accounting is designed to provide information, views accounting as using the language and algebra of valuation but for the purpose of conveying information. The distinction is subtle but profound .... The information content school ... views the financial meas-ures as measures of information events, not of value.
>
> (Christensen and Demski 2003: 4–5)

This requires further reflection from an angle unencumbered by mathematical or otherwise strange jargon that the uninitiated frequently suspects as a camouflage to hide the obvious. I shall try to elaborate this by illuminating the essential fea-tures of this perspective and its potentials from a different angle.

If one would accept a distinction (as made by Christensen and Demski) between different *basic attitudes* towards the problem of *accounting valuation*, it would be necessary to distinguish not two but (at least) the following *three* attitudes:

The first one, where *accounting values are meaningful only if they represent a 'true' picture of economic and legalistic reality.* Apart from the need to clarify what one means by 'true' and 'reality' (see Mattessich 2003), this condition is most ideally realized by values in complete markets and under perfect competi-tion. Since these latter or secondary conditions are rarely met in actual practice, this view seems to be fairly unrealistic. However, Chambers (1967), Sterling (1970) and others believed that even in the *absence* of such ideal conditions a *single* valuation approach could reflect all or most situations of accounting reality – namely through valuation based on some version of the *current market exit price.*

Second, the information perspective disagrees with this first view, and regards as its major goal (at least according to Christensen and Demski) the rejection of the valuation perspective (replacing it with an approach that pivots on the *information* function of accounting). This would mean to reveal where and in which way information is produced in accounting and related areas. Thus, one ought to distinguish between accounting information and non-accounting information, and try to illuminate the importance of supplementing one by the other or even integrating the two. But since accounting can hardly operate without the value notion, the disciples of the information perspective had to provide some place to the *value context* within their scheme. Indeed, they regard 'the financial measures as measures of information events'. But this can easily be interpreted (at least by the uninitiated) as an awkward way of admitting that ultimately, modern accounting cannot do without attributing values.

The third view towards accounting valuation is based on a *pragmatic perspective* (e.g. Mattessich 1995, 2003).[8] It agrees with the claim of the information perspective that accounting values often fail to represent reality in any scientific sense. But it argues that such values, if carefully conditioned to a specific purpose, can still be meaningfully applied to accounting, thus refusing to dismiss accounting valuation as 'an abject failure' (see the quote above). It rather tries to understand the pragmatic importance of accounting valuation and its many functions that go far beyond the monetary measurement of prefer-ences. This may include either the assigning of probability functions to most values or using multiple values (cf. the suggestions in Mattessich 1964: 246–50), no less than the *setting of constraints* (e.g. the 'cost or market rule' for preventing dangerous overvaluation), or offering a *guide post* in 'agnostic' situations – for example, where the belief in a fiction (still fulfilling the need for arithmetical accountability) is the only bulwark against total chaos.[9] Such an attitude does (in conformity with the IASB *Framework* and the recent debates over the cost-benefit aspects of 'fair value' and other aspects of accounting policy) regard valuation not as a purpose in itself but as a *means* for providing mainly decision-relevant information. I believe that Edwards and Bell (1961), for example, can be considered as pointing in the direction towards such a pragmatic attitude since this book does not dogmatically insist on a single valuation method but accepts, apart from two versions of the 'preferred' replacement cost method (*nominal*, as well as *real*), also present values and even liquidation values.

To put accounting *valuation* and *information* on the same pedestal may seem heresy to both the disciples of the valuation perspective, as well as to those of the information perspective. Yet, many contradictions between the information perspective and the pragmatic attitude may well disappear if one abandons the pre-conceived maxim that accounting valuation must *either* conform to the rigorous standards of pure science (particularly neo-classical economics) *or* be nothing else but 'an auxiliary to the procurement of information'. Furthermore, if this last phrase (under quotation marks) is interpreted liberally enough (e.g. admitting that *sometimes* valuation may be an auxiliary to information, but *sometimes* the reverse may be the case), the contrast between the pragmatic and the information perspective might vanish as far as the valuation issue is concerned.

Some simple examples may illuminate this. If one has to decide whether a certain share should be sold or kept for short-term speculation purpose. You need two kinds of information: *public information* of its *market value*, let us say $30, and *private information* that the *(subjective) value* is likely to fall within five months to $20. So you decide to sell the share. However, if you have a *long-term purpose* in mind, and your *private information* tells you that in five years the share is likely to rise to a *(subjective) value* of $150, you will keep the share. In other words, in both cases you need not only public and private *information*, but also the resulting *values* – though in these cases the information drives (procures) the values. But suppose a merchant's inventory account shows the total value of his merchandise is $5,000, but the physical count of that inventory shows only a *value* of $3,000. In the absence of any better explanation he may conclude that inventory in the amount or *value* of $2,000 has been pilfered. This latter *information* is derived from the two *values*; thus this *information was value-driven*, in contrast to the former cases where the *values were information-driven*. Yet, in both cases, *valuation* and the procurement of *information* played equally important roles. These examples illustrate two important aspects: first, that both *information*, as well as *values* are dependent on the *purpose* or context, and second, that both, *values* and *information* are required for making economic *decisions*.

It is unlikely that in our discipline 'valuation' will ever become a silent partner to 'information'. In the past it was the latter that played the silent part; in future it is likely that both valuation and information may be regarded as *equally* important notions. Seen on a deeper level, this parity manifests itself already in the information perspective. The latter rests on two major pillars, *expectations* (beliefs) expressed in the form of probabilities, on one side, and *preferences* in form of utilities (and utility functions), on the other side. But since expectations are a consequence of (some kind of) information, and preferences are the basis of values, it appears that both aspects are inherent in, and *equally* important for the information perspective.

As to other pragmatic aspects, the book by Christensen and Demski (2003: 435–43, for example) contains passages alluding to the need for personal or professional judgements in accounting (depending on the specific context) and other features implying means–end relations. Indeed, a conciliatory attitude towards the pragmatic perspective might turn out to be of great advantage to both the pragmatic, as well as the information camp. The former would acquire from the information camp the badly needed conceptual structure to support specific means–end relations, while the latter would be able to shed its bad reputation of throwing overboard most traditional accounting concepts.[10]

It might also be taken as an admission that not only 'accounting' matters (which Christensen and Demski emphasize repeatedly), but also 'traditional accounting'. In other words, that the latter is by no means the thoughtless mechanical routine that some disciples of the information perspective may take it for.

19.4 Methodological differences between the information perspective and traditional accounting theory

Before entering into the more substantial conceptual and theoretical issues (in the next section), let me shortly summarize the *methodology* of the information perspective, and compare it with traditional accounting methodology.[11]

M1 (i.e. the *information perspective and its methodology*) exploits the tools and insights of modern economics, probability and decision theory, operations research and game theory, finance theory as well as their information aspects. Traditional accounting, however, neglects to a great extent such recent developments.

M2 operates with stochastic models, i.e. with statistical expectations expressing objective, as well as subjective beliefs and their changes. Traditional accounting has a more deterministic orientation and rarely operates with complex mathematical or statistical models.

M3 takes individual preferences formally into account through utility functions, while the traditional methodology merely implies them.

M4, as already elaborated above, centres on the notion of information content of accounting events, and on the uncertainty inherent in the decision-making process. In contrast, the traditional methodology takes little *formal* recognition of uncertainty; it rather concentrates on the valuation of assets, equities (foreign and internal), expenses, revenues, etc. At best, rules like 'cost or market value whichever is lower' constitute *informal* safeguards against the uncertainty of risk.

M5 uses a dynamic approach in which several accounting periods and their interactions are taken into consideration simultaneously. This is rarely the case in traditional accounting methodology (an exception is long-term budgeting and capital budgeting), though such interaction is partly or indirectly taken care of through the inter-period allocation process.

M6's agency component (nowadays well-integrated into the information perspective) searches for the optimal contract (depending on prevailing circumstances) between the firm (owner) and management (or between management and his subordinate). It investigates the many aspects of conflict between the two parties of owner and management, and occasionally other parties (like the auditor). In contrast, traditional accounting (particularly cost accounting) concentrates more on the technical than behavioural aspects such as the determination, allocation and control of costs, as well as on the projection of future costs and revenues. In traditional accounting it is the notion of 'stewardship' that points in the direction of agency theory (cf. item T11 below).

M7's conceptual scheme consists of mathematical models with notations borrowed from other disciplines, sequential tables, spreadsheets and a terminology also from other disciplines (often foreign to accountants). Traditional accounting uses the long-established terminology of accounts and their hierarchy, transactions recorded usually in double-entry, summaries in the form of trial balances, income statements, balance sheets, etc.

19.5 Major tenets of the information perspective

This is an attempt to explain, perhaps demystify, the information perspective in a few rough strokes, unencumbered by worries about conceptual precision, completeness, mathematical formulation and similar concerns. But a complete appreciation of this perspective cannot be achieved without a thorough study of its mathematical structure. As mentioned above, the methodology of the information perspective is that of neo-classical economics, but greatly enriched by insights from several related areas. As the information perspective is an analytical theory (where empirical notions are rather based on innumerable assumptions than realistic facts), neither its essence nor many of its subtle results are accessible or even meaningful without an acute awareness of the innumerable conditions, qualifications, artificial limitations of variables and simplifications. To this must be added a fairly esoteric conceptual apparatus, an often unfamiliar notation and, finally, mathematically couched theorems with rigorous proofs (particularly as presented in, for example, Christensen and Feltham 2003, 2005). Hence, offering a survey of the information perspective in a nutshell is not without risk.

Many accountants (even those beyond North America) will be familiar with the ubiquitous notion of *information*,[12] or the names of the major pioneers of this perspective. But beyond that, many academics still seem to be insufficiently familiar with an approach that can hardly be disregarded in the long run. Let me characterize concisely some of its theoretical aspects or implications by means of items T1 to T11 (j).[13]

> T1 – *Accounting* is not (or ought not to be) primarily a tool for measuring or estimating values, but is (or ought to be) a *source of potential information*. This item has been discussed in some detail in a previous section and hardly needs further elucidation. But this view is emphasized in Christensen and Demski (2003) rather than in Christensen and Feltham (2003, 2005). The authors of the latter are more concerned with the overall

survey of the great variety and the many aspects of major information economic models as presented by accountants, investment theorists and economists. Thus, the division between the first and the second valuation attitude (proposed by Christensen and Demski 2003, and discussed above) is not a major focus of the Feltham team;[14] though Feltham would argue that the right information (secured by a sufficiently fine and relevant partition of the system) is bound to result in proper valuation, namely the one that leads to a satisfactory or optimal allocation of resources. Some experts might even favour the providing of information to management than to the public. They argue that the allocations made by shareholders and the stock market in general may change the distribution of wealth but not necessarily increase general welfare, while the resource allocations made by management may have a greater chance of increasing total wealth.

T2 – *Information may not be readily discernable* but has to be separately extracted from the accounting system (or elsewhere). Christensen and Demski (2003) emphasize repeatedly that such information may not accrue automatically to the accountant; he or she will rather have to make a special effort to locate and express it (for more details see T6). Again this is a fairly pragmatic aspect, and not made explicit by Christensen and Feltham (2003, 2005) where it seems to be taken for granted. The latter work rather stresses the distinction between the *decision-facilitating* and *decision-influencing* role of accounting, as stated at the very beginning of Christensen and Feltham (2003: 1).

In its decision-facilitating role, accounting reports provide information that affects a decision maker's beliefs about the consequences of his actions, and accounting forecasts may be used to represent the predicted consequences. On the other hand, in its decision-influencing role, anticipated accounting reports pertaining to the consequences of a decision maker's actions may influence his action choices (particularly if his future compensation will be influenced by those reports).

T3 – Information *content* (in the 'nominal' sense) is based on *uncertainty*, and signifies that a decision maker *acts* upon a *change in her or his future expectation* (belief, probability) due to such information.[15] This holds even where the information offers no trade advantage (cf. Christensen and Demski 2003: 161). In other words: 'no uncertainty, no information content'; and the signal received from an information system at a certain date updates the decision maker's belief about what state can be expected in the future.[16]

T4 – To *compare* different information systems (sources), theorists have introduced the notion of *partition* of the state space (all relevant 'states of nature'), such that an information system corresponding to a *finer* partition is *more informative* than (or at least as informative as) a system corresponding to a less fine partition (though one cannot always compare two information systems by using the notion of partition – see partitions Y″ and Y‴ in Figure 3.1 in Christensen and Feltham 2003: 83).

T5 – To attribute a *value* to an information system, one may compare the maximized expected utilities of this system with that of a simple decision system (based on a probabilistic version of the *states–acts–outcome* matrix, as originally conceived by Savage 1954). An alternative or perhaps equivalent way to determine the value of an information system is to ask how much one is willing to pay for this particular information system.[17]

T6 – To *extract information* from an accounting system, one has to scrutinize such sources as *cash flows, accruals and allocations* (including depreciations), the specific *recognition rules* (e.g. on revenue realization), *deviations* from expectations or budgets and other sources of possible information.[18] One of the major merits of the information perspective is to show that accounting (particular accrual accounting) fulfils an important, even powerful function, and frequently has advantages over other information systems.

T7 – An information *signal* is a specific element of such a partition, indicating the action to be pursued. As pointed out, it is important that accounting academics have a broad understanding of the impact of publicly reported information, particularly where there are multiple sources of public and private information. Thus, the distinction between *public* and *private* information, and the implications of each for financial markets are crucial in the information perspective.

T8 – A *sub-partition* (cf. Christensen and Demski 2003: 86–8) *is finer* than the original partition, thus constitutes an information system at least as preferable as the original information system (provided there are no additional implementation costs). The mathematical notions of partition and sub-partition may irritate the uninitiated; however, they are nothing but a precise way of conveying the possibility of refining information by providing a larger and more relevant array of possible signals.

T9 – Where *multiple information sources* exist (in a specific situation) they and their values are *not separable*. Christensen and Demski (2003: 112–15) are here concerned with the question: 'Can we, in general, concentrate on a single information source when multiple sources are present?' The authors draw a parallel to the *inseparability* of the costs of joint products, and assert a similar *inseparability* for information sources (unless one separates arbitrarily).

T10 – The *clean surplus relation or CSR* (residual income approach) – holding when 'the change in book value of common equity (i.e. the surplus) between any two dates equals the net income minus net dividends'

(Christensen and Feltham 2003: 280)[19] – and the further development of the *clean surplus theory* (CST) by Ohlson (1995) and Feltham and Ohlson (1995) have become an integral part of the information perspective (perhaps initiated through the collaboration of Feltham, the 'information theorist' with Ohlson, the 'clean-surplus theorist'). The major tenets of the CST are:[20]

a   An accounting-value relation that has become more prominent in the information economic literature is that of *residual income* (also called 'abnormal earnings' or 'excess income'). Provided the CSR holds, it can be defined as 'the net income minus a capital charge, which equals the riskless start-of-period interest rate times start-of-period book value' (Christensen and Feltham 2003: Vol. I: 281).

b   *Anticipated dividends* are the proper basis for capitalization of securities, while capitalizing cash flows require (fairly stringent) additional conditions.

c   The extended CST (as based on Feltham and Ohlson 1995) introduces two formal distinctions; one between *operational* and *financial* activities, the other between *unbiased* accounting (based on economic valuation) and *conservative* accounting (based on traditional accounting valuation). Both distinctions, but particularly the latter, constitute an important step in building a *bridge* between the information perspective and traditional accounting. This is reflected in some of the 'propositions' (actually 'theorems') in Christensen and Feltham (2003) dealing with the differences between those two approaches.

T11 – *Agency theory* – with its notions of contracting between principal and agent (most often, between owner and manager), the problems of budgeting, incentives, asymmetric information, moral hazard, risk preference, etc. has also become an integral part of the information perspective (in traditional accounting, the notion of *stewardship* plays a related role). As to the crucial role of incentives, Christensen and Demski emphasize:

> Incentives heavily influence the use and dispersion of information in an organization. Using and controlling the organization's information is a delicate matter that requires close attention to reporting incentives. Additional information might improve contracting with the manager, but not always.
>
> (Christensen and Demski 2003: 276)

The major characteristics and insights of this kind of analysis may be outlined as follows:

a   Christensen and Demski (2003: Chapter 11) distinguish problems of valuation (discussed above) from problems of *evaluation*, namely evaluating management. Labour contracts, particularly those with managers, have features at variance with those in commodity or other service markets. But there too, information is crucial in providing 'the glue' in the labour market for executives. Particularly, the information required to enforce the fulfilment of contractual obligations by the manager (often *not directly observable* from the viewpoint of the owner, and yet an important information source), constitutes a major focus of the information perspective.

b   A major characteristic of employing managers lies in the greater independence of the manager, and the difficulty in controlling the quality of his service (including his honesty of reporting). Hence, the characteristics of an employment contract depend on the manager's job context (e.g. whether his effort is observable to the owner or not). The manager has his own preferences (utility function) as to the benefits, as well as costs arising from his contract. And these preferences are likely to diverge from the preferences of the owners that, in turn, creates (together with difficulties pointed out below) the problem of *moral hazard.* Such a *conflict of interest* makes the incorporation of incentive and *control features* into the agency contract particularly important.

c   A moral hazard problem (a hidden action problem) arises when the self-interested agent (manager) is work averse and the principal (owner) cannot observe the manager's work effort. The self-utility-maximizing behaviour of the manager per se is not a problem if the owner can observe the manager's work effort and can design the contract in such a way that the manager can be penalized if his performance proves inadequate. Furthermore, the non-observability of the manager's effort is no problem as long as the manager is not work-averse. The solution against shirking may be found in the use of an incentive contract (e.g. bonuses) and monitoring (control – e.g. occasional surprise visits to observe the manager's work effort).

d   A related problem arises in situations where *asymmetric information* exists in favour of the manager. The latter is usually much better informed about the operations of the firm than the owner or owners (particularly in cases of publicly held stock companies). The hidden information problem arises when the agent has more information than the principal, and she or he can use this information advantage against the principal. To induce a truthful report, the hidden contract must be designed such that the manager will not be worse off by reporting the truth than by 'misreporting'. Alternatively, an auditor (or other monitor) may be engaged to gather some of the private information the manager has procured for himself.

e   To overcome such difficulties, agency theory is concerned with a variety of different types of managerial contracts and pecuniary *incentive schemes* (e.g. consideration of various contingent contracts instead of offering a fixed salary) to *motivate* the manager. Each of those contracts may be designed for a different situation (also referred to as *designing the contract*). Furthermore, there is the obvious alternative of either hiring an expensive high-powered executive or a less expensive but possibly less competent one. This is another crucial problem that agency theory tries to solve.[21]

f   As previously indicated, also in agency theory, teaching and literature progresses from a relatively simple situation (e.g. of a *perfect labour market* in which most or all of the frictions mentioned above are absent – *first best contract*) to more complicated ones (e.g. more or less *efficient contracts* in *imperfect* markets – a *second best contract*, where some trade frictions are present). In moral hazard models, one usually assumes the principle to be risk neutral (as he or she is more adapt to carry risks) while the manager is assumed to be risk-averse.[22] Under adverse selection models, the manager need not be risk-averse since problems of incentives arise from the manager's private information (misreporting problems) whether the manager is risk-averse or risk-neutral.

g   Such an agency contract would require, first, that it is *acceptable* to the manager (requirement of *individual rationality*) and, second, that the manager *finds it rational to fulfil it*. Basically this *incentive compatibility* is to make sure that the agent cannot attain higher expected utilities by (i) choosing other actions (or work effort levels) than the one the owner desires (under a moral hazard model) or (ii) by misreporting his private information instead of reporting truthfully (under an adverse selection model).

h   More complicated agency models incorporate further extensions. For example *additional information sources* are introduced (beyond *managerial performance*, whether correctly or incorrectly reported). This, in turn, raises the problem of mixing different types or sources of information, and the separation of whatever has been learned from each information source (the problem of *conditional controllability*). Further complications may arise depending on (i) *at which stage does information arrive* (and is acted upon) and (ii) *who receives that information* (owner or manager or both, and in which sequence). The answer to such questions can become crucial for decision making and for evaluating management. Additional extensions include multi-period models and multi-agent models.

i   *Earnings management* (i.e. management's *discretion* to shift earnings from one period to another by means of *intertemporal accruals*, etc.) is another concern of the information perspective. Above all, accruals themselves are used to convey information that, in turn, could be distorted by excessive managerial opportunism. Obviously, 'a delicate game of managed information flow is the norm' (Christensen and Demski 2003: 363).

ii   Similarly, the problem of *intratemporal accruals* (i.e. shifting product costs or divisional costs, etc. within the firm) are important. Such items may, for example, affect the contractual arrangements of two or more managers sharing the same resources. This involves notions such as *decision rights*, the *separation of duties, managerial accounting discretion* and problems of *transfer pricing*.

19.6 Issued beyond the competency of the information perspective

Obviously, the items mentioned above are only a few guidepoints to indicate the direction in which the information perspective has been moving. However, there exist many issues that the information perspective (in the mathematical sense) does not seem able to master. Indeed, the text by Christensen and Demski (2003) delves into some of those 'beyond-issues' (though the more comprehensive work by Christensen and Feltham 2003, 2005 does not). Thus, it is no coincidence that the last two chapters of the former text are virtually bare of model building and mathematical notations. In these chapters, Christensen and Demski deal with such issues as Institutional Considerations (Chapter 19) and Professional Opportunities and Responsibility (Chapter 20). There, it is clearly admitted that in the macro-realm of regulating institutions, the informational perspective (at least, as presently conceived in accounting) is rather helpless (though it might also be helpless in many aspects of the micro-realm):

> This aggregation approach leads us to social choice and Arrow's celebrated impossibility theorem [with four conditions: *universal domain*, the *nondictatorial condition, Pareto optimality, independence of irrelevant alternatives*] .... These conditions are hardly assailable .... The problem is that the four conditions are mutually incompatible. *Any* social choice mechanism, be it voting, market-based allocation, life in a family structure, or the FASB or IASB, violates at least one of those conditions .... At present we see this theme playing out in the international arena where the FASB and the IASB offer competing views of 'global GAAP' .... So at the margin, they offer different partitions, or different information content .... Can we say unequivocally which is preferred or better?
>
> (Christensen and Demski 2003: 430–1)

Other issues pointed out in these last two chapters are problems of governance (including governance of governance institutions), accounting changes induced by technology, by shifting trading patterns and global conditions. Furthermore, these authors discuss additional aspects, such as the need for *professional judgements, purpose-orientation, personal judgement* and related *pragmatic issues, qualitative vs. quantitative considerations* (see Christensen and Demski 2003: 422, 425, 428–37), as well as the *use of representative heuristics, cognitive problems* and so on.

19.7 Opposition and criticism

19.7.1 Resistance to the mathematical-analytical approach

The aversion of many accountants, even academics, to higher mathematics is legendary. In recent years this trend has somewhat abated on the American content, but even there it still festers underground. It is often difficult to distinguish to what extent this resistance is purely emotional, and how far it is rational. The former may be caused by a feeling of being 'left behind' due to either a person's inability or unwillingness (e.g. based on an 'ideological-philosophic' stand against analytical thinking or towards neo-classical economics) to acquire the necessary mathematical knowledge. This attitude and the next may be aggravated by the lack of non-mathematical explanations of essential features of the information perspective.

The second attitude may be rooted in a deep *rational* concern that lies either in a profound misunderstanding of the purpose and benefits of a mathematical analysis or, alternatively, in the purely economic conviction that for accounting education the investment of many years of arduous mathematical training is nothing but a misallocation of resources. Beyond these major reasons or factors there are others that shall shortly be considered.

As to the *emotional* aspects, there is hardly a remedy, save the appeal that an academic should learn to think rationally and put emotions aside when engaged professionally.

As far as the *misconception* of mathematical analysis is concerned, one might try to explain to the objector the advantage of a *mathematical analysis* of social theories. First, it lies in the conciseness of expressing complex conditions, restrictions and other limitations that would otherwise require an immense verbal-descriptive apparatus. Second, and even more importantly, it lies in the greater ease of making *logical deductions*, compared to verbal inferences. Thus the naïve criticism that the use of mathematics cannot be superior to a verbal presentation can easily be dispelled. Wherever mathematical analysis is employed in a *non-trivial* way, it can provide *immense economy in the sheer process of logical reasoning*. The latter is an indispensable part of any scientific activity. The 250 or so propositions in Christensen and Feltham (2003 and 2005), for example, *would have been just as impressive, had they been deduced verbally* (that is to say, *without* mathematics) – though in this case the authors would have been forced to write some *ten tomes* instead of only *two*. Yet, to comprehend the economy of deriving and proving theorems by mathematical instead of verbal means may be difficult to comprehend without delving into the essence of mathematical analysis and its philosophy. And as to the power of mathematical deduction in general, let us not forget, four- and multi-dimensional spaces, as well as black holes were predicted by mathematics a long time before they were discovered empirically.

The other rational objection, the one based on *educational economy*, is much more difficult to dispel. Indeed, I personally would sympathize with this argument, were it not for the fact that you cannot do science without taking risks, and incurring costs that may not pay off. Only the future can show what the real success or failure of the information economic perspective will be. So we have to take chances. But this does not mean every accountant has to become an expert in information economics – an undistorted commonsense view of it is all we can hope for most members of our profession.

Many accountants not trained in the more esoteric techniques object that most authors of the information perspective do not convey their intentions and results in understandable, non-mathematical terms. Practitioners no less than academics all around the globe might be more receptive to the information perspective (and its efforts of pinpointing where and what kind of information is generated in an accounting system) if the experts would at least convey the major conclusions in a way comprehensible to a larger spectrum of accountants. Such an effort would also remove the suspicion that they are confronted with an elite, the major concern of whom is to maintain an exclusive status by keeping ignorant those not conversant in the esoteric language employed. The following statement is but an example of such a very understandable reaction:

> US accounting research that appears in mainstream journals such as the *Accounting Review*, the *Journal of Accounting Research*, and many others is not only irrelevant to practice but unintelligible to practitioners as it is to most of us .... I feel it all to be a conspiracy on the part of faculty at prestigious universities to force their graduate students into duplicating that which got them to the top, so as to perpetuate their elite standing, both individually and institutionally.
>
> (Fleischman 2000: 24)

19.7.2 Neglect of traditional accounting terminology

Banishing traditional accounting terminology from the information perspective, as previously complained about, only aggravates the feelings expressed in the above quote by Fleischman. Some of these obstacles might be overcome, as demonstrated in two German twin texts by Ewert and Wagenhofer (1993/2003) and Wagenhofer and Ewert (2003). Despite the fact that (at this moment) no English translations of these texts exist, they represent a most interesting and original solution in *combining the information perspective* (and a good deal of analytical accounting in general) *with traditional accounting*. These two tomes also offer the additional benefit of relating modern empirical accounting research and its testing possibilities (relating to market efficiency, capital asset pricing models, value relevance, etc., for example, Wagenhofer and Ewert 2003: 103–38) to general accounting and the information perspective.

The first tome (Ewert and Wagenhofer 1993/2003) deals with *cost and managerial accounting* (including budgeting and controlling) with due reliance on decision theory, game theory, information theory and agency theory. Various editions of this book also take into consideration more practice-oriented tools of management accounting, such as 'activity-based costing' (*Aktivitäts-oriented Prozesskostenrechnung*), 'target costing' (*Zielkostenrechnung*), 'life cycle costing' (*Lebenszykluskostenrechnung*), and other relatively new instruments or techniques. Other German texts are also moving somewhat in this direction, at least as far as agency theory and related informational aspects are concerned (e.g. Schweitzer and Küpper 2003).

The second tome is concerned with *financial accounting and auditing*, again under thorough consideration of recent developments in the information perspective. As indicated, the remarkable feature of these twin texts is that (in contrast to the books by Christensen and Demski 2003, as well as Christensen and Feltham 2003, 2005) the German books preserve the terminology, concepts and methodology of traditional accounting, and yet succeed in integrating it with recent developments of the information perspective. Perhaps the most important consequence of this feature is that these texts seem to be much better digestible by accounting students and traditionally trained accountants than the two American books discussed above. One may even claim that the Summaries at the end of each chapter (of those German books) fulfil ideally a maxim attributed to Professor Samuelson.[23]

Apart from those attributes, both tomes are comprehensive enough (658 and 545 pages, respectively) to cover a wide spectrum of traditional as well as modern accounting issues, together with a solid basis of reference works of the English as well as German literature. Other aspects of those texts are no less well designed from a pedagogic point of view. They are complementary twin-texts that possess similar structure. Each chapter tome begins with an 'illustration' (relatively simple discussion of a practical case pertaining to that chapter) followed by a concise discussion of the specific targets. This, in turn, is followed by the text proper together with appropriate mathematical representations, and finally by a summary. Another merit of these texts is that they are among the first to acquaint students of German tongue with a wide spectrum of the information perspective and related mathematical accounting literature. That the information perspective has taken hold not only in America and to some extent in Germany but also in other European countries, is best evidenced by the fact that the co-authors of both texts, that by Demski as well as that by Feltham, are teaching in Denmark. In the German language area, the major merit of disseminating the information perspective to accountants lies with the Austrian Alfred Wagenhofer and the German Ralf Ewert.

19.7.3 Other objections

Occasionally, one hears further objections to the information perspective or to some aspects of it. But most of these seem to be of secondary significance, as they do not hit the general core of the information perspective. Sometimes the objections are directed only against a specific author or publication, or a mere passage of it sometimes implies a somewhat different direction (e.g. Gigler and Hemmer 1998, 2001) than the one pursued by the main stream information perspective.

There also have been complaints from various quarters that the publications of the information perspective make too many simplifying or even controversial assumptions. For example, a well-known academic complained to me that Christensen and Demski (2003) assumes that every member participating in this 'information game' would be able to come up with an identical set of states of nature. States, to which the received information should help match the actions to be chosen. In other words, is it really possible to identify such a truly 'exhaustive' set? This question seems to be particularly pertinent as everyday circumstances and, specifically, present-day financial dealings are so intricate that they threaten to overwhelm the limitations inherent in the information perspective and its set of states.[24]

The same academic made the following remarks after having used the text by Christensen and Demski (2003) in his class room:

> my students found the Christensen–Demski book initially exciting but then rather boring; everything seemed so empty after a while. As one proceeded through the chapters, any kind of information or information setting kept coming back to the same question: What did it reveal about the state partition? No wonder it was able to say so little about the procedures, measurements and institutions of accounting.

Although some *empirical* accountants, like Beaver, have a positive attitude towards the information perspective, this does not hold for all of our 'empiricists'. Some seem to believe that empirical accounting research is in no need of any comprehensive theory like the information perspective, while others might prefer some alternative theory. Of course, the most important criticism by empirical accountants might be the failure to base the information economic premises on *empirical observations* (and not merely on unrealistic or highly simplified assumptions). This is an even more basic aspect than the 'factual confirmation' of the resulting conclusions, as previously mentioned.

Even from the information perspective camp itself one hears complaints or calls for one or the other different variation (in opposition to the mainstream version). Often these 'rebels' are motivated by academic rivalries or disappointments of not being sufficiently regarded or quoted by the main authors of the field – though sometimes their grievance may be legitimate. After all, the information perspective is a broad and complex sub-discipline that encompasses many more aspects (and countless publications) than could be conveyed in a survey.

19.8 Towards a general theory of accounting

A book review of Christensen and Demski (2003) points out: 'It has often been lamented that we do not have a general theory of accounting. That statement may well be true. However, until we have one, if ever, the information content perspective serves as an admirable substitute' (Beaver 2002: 633). Yet, the more traditionally oriented accountants may ask whether the information perspective can even preliminarily fulfil such a task without dealing with such deeply ingrained accounting notions as 'double-entry', 'account', 'profit and loss', 'realization', 'price-level adjustment', 'balance sheet', 'income statement' and so on. The subject index of Christensen and Feltham (2003) lists none of those terms, while that of Christensen and Demski (2003) points at two pages (pp. 57 and 70) where, at least, each of the last two notions is fleetingly mentioned. Although the expression 'double-entry' (or 'double classification') plays no role in either index, it does appear once in Christensen and Demski (2003: 7). Yet, it is in a negative sense; namely, when the authors point out that 'Our focus is on the choice, not on how to do the accounting per se (not on "double-entry matters")'.

In the face of the information perspective's considerable disregard of many other major accounting concepts, traditionalists may wonder whether this 'new' perspective is the messianic approach to a general theory of accounting – or could be a 'substitute' for it. Above all, there is a foundational-methodological aspect at stake. One would expect that even an *economic* theory of accounting would begin at the very basis, namely at such fundamental notions of social reality as *debts* and *ownership rights*, as well as the *transactions* that result from them. These are the main pillars on which the entire construct of accounting rests. This not only holds for a capitalist society, or a modern economy, it even holds for the authoritarian and agricultural environment of the ancient Sumerians, as ancient 'token accounting' bears witness. Second, even if some scholars, like Ewert and Wagenhofer, showed us a way of how to connect the information perspective closer to traditional accounting terminology and its conceptual apparatus, the question raised by Beaver (2002), that of a general theory, still remains to be solved.

As this may possibly be my swansong in accounting *theory*, I take the liberty of relating the information perspective to the theoretical framework, developed more than four decades ago and presented in *Accounting and Analytical Methods* (Mattessich 1964). Although this work (together with such attempts as Ijiri 1965a, 1965b, 1967; and others) revitalized the interest in analytical accounting, these attempts were confined to predominantly *deterministic* models, and definitely adhered to the notion of double-classification. The next stage, and subsequent analytical trend in accounting, however, was preoccupied with *stochastic* representations and the information notion that pretty much ignored the dual aspect and the whole accoutrement that goes with it.

But whether the route of double-classification is chosen or not may be less critical than basing a future theory of accounting on truly fundamental notions, and connecting these with the more far-reaching conceptual scheme of the information perspective. To neglect the first aspect would deprive the theory of the soil that nourishes the roots; to neglect the second would mean to ignore new scientific insights as well as disregard the increasing complexity of economic and financial dealings.

For almost half a century I have held that a general theory of accounting, if feasible, must be a *meta-theory*. That means, it ought to be limited to an overall framework that leaves room for a wide range of specific interpretations or subtheories, each geared towards a different purpose or information objective. Indeed, my meta-theory (Mattessich 1964: 16–45, 446–65; 1995: 75–94) seems to have been the only one of the many axiomatic and postulational frameworks that is flexible enough to serve in such a way. This flexibility permits the application of different valuation models, no less than a variety of premises about realization, classification, etc. – all of which depend on the information.[25]

The reason why such flexibility is possible lies in the 'trick' of providing *place-holder assumptions* for valuation, realization, classification, data input, duration, extension, materiality and allocation. That means these auxiliary propositions hold merely the place for means–end relations (instrumental hypotheses) to be inserted once the specific purpose is known and, of course, as soon as the pertinent means–end relations have been sufficiently established. This latter condition is usually difficult to meet. This may have been the major reason why the notion of place-holder assumptions found no response in the accounting literature and why its potential for the future development of a general accounting theory was not grasped by most of my colleagues.[26] If this was, indeed, a crucial insight for accounting, it will be revived some day. Besides, neither of the two major ingredients forming the basis of such an approach is entirely new. The first ingredient, a broad theory open to a wide range of interpretations, is quite common in many scientific endeavours; and so is the second ingredient, a conditional-normative approach (for determining the proper means–end relations). After all the need for a conditional normative approach did not arise in accounting but in operations research, as confirmed by Luce and Raiffa[27] – though, admittedly, highly simplified mathematical models are better amenable to a conditional-normative treatment than are the more fuzzy accounting relations.

The coming of age of the information perspective, and the claim of its potential for a general accounting theory, leads to an interesting question. Is a marriage between some kind of meta-theory (whether the one I suggested or any other) and the information economic approach, possible? Might it open new vistas for a purpose-oriented accounting – one that relies less on trial and error, vague inferences and intuition, but more on scientific foundations? Is this music *for* the future?

19.9 Conclusion from a wider angle

Whatever this future of the information perspective will be, this sub-discipline is undoubtedly a manifestation that academic accounting does not stand still intellectually. That brings us to a point where we should look at our discipline in the light of a broader, scientific picture. During the second quarter of the twentieth century, quantum theory came about and revolutionized physics by drawing attention to such crucial notions as uncertainty, probability and information. In the course of the second half of this century, those very same notions played an increasingly important role in other disciplines, even in the social sciences, and finally in accounting.

Today, in the twenty-first century, 'uncertainty' and related concepts dominate our scientific outlook – from the string theories of physics to the information perspective of our discipline. Thus, the shift from deterministic to stochastic notions is by no means an isolated case but part of a general trend; it belongs to our modern worldview. This indeterminism is deeply ingrained, not only in the minute world of subatomic particles, but also in the fabric of everyday life where uncertainty seems to be the only certainty. We are living in a stochastic universe, and have finally realized that thinking in probabilistic terms is our 'best bet'. And, to have integrated the humble discipline of accounting into this vast intellectual panorama of modern science should be of some consolation to the members of our brotherhood, otherwise beseeched by numerous financial and accounting scandals (cf. Benston *et al.* 2003). As to competing camps, one might compare the information perspective, at least in some respects, to the physicists' *string theory*[28] – undoubtedly a great intellectual feat of mathematical logic and consistency. So much so, that its proponents consider it 'the theory of everything', whereas many empiricists, who believe that this theory has no chance of ever being confirmed factually, consider it 'the theory of nothing'.

Notes

1 Introduction

1 An exception might be the work by Chatfield and Vangermeersch (1996). But this work is, as its subtitle indicates, actually an encyclopaedia. Its focus on *international accounting research* is more limited than our attempt, but its coverage of 'practical' and 'general' accounting aspects is more far reaching.

2 It is interesting to note that in the German historical accounting literature Limperg's replacement value theory is hardly ever mentioned. There is, for example, no reference to it in Sykora (1949), nor in Seicht (1970), while Schneider (2001) refers to Limperg only shortly in connection with the 'capital procurement and investment theory' derived from Polak and Philip's (1926) German work (Polak taught from 1922 onwards in Rotterdam). Kovero, on the other hand, is mentioned frequently in Sykora (1949), Seicht (1970), and has five entries in Schneider (2001) – see also our subsections 2.4.3, 12.1.1 and 12.2.1).

2 The nineteenth century: an international survey

1 Based in part on Mattessich (2003a).

2 As this paper deals primarily with accounting research rather than accounting practice, I refer the reader to Edwards (1996) as well as his work of four volumes (Edwards 2000) that contains numerous articles on various facets of accounting practice (and occasionally on its research basis) of the nineteenth century (as well as other periods). Further pertinent material can be found in Lee (1982, 1990). A more limited publication (a special issue of the journal *Accounting and Business Research*), restricted to only a few historical and international aspects of accounting institutions and practice (rather than dealing with an 'international history of accounting research'), can be found in Richardson (2002).

3 Originally Edmond Degrange Sr spelled his name without an 's'. According to Nikitin (2005: 52), Degrange Jr changed not only his name but also his father's to 'Degranges', as nowadays occasionally encountered. However, in Colasse's (2005: 39–52) book on *Les grands auteurs en comptabilité*, and in other French publications, it appears as 'Degrange'.

4 Although Queulin's (1840) and Feigneaux's (1827) publications are listed in several sources, none of those I examined indicated the authors' first names or initials; the same also holds for the German author by the name of 'Schüler' (see note 12).

5 It is important to realize that these and the above-mentioned 'pioneering' efforts in cost accounting refer to systematic literature. Pioneers of cost accounting *practice* can already be found in *historical records* from the sixteenth century (e.g. of the firm of Christoffer Plantin – see F. de Roover 1937) to the eighteenth century in Great Britain (cf. Fleischman and Parker 1991), Spain (cf. Gutiérrez *et al.* 2005), and other countries.

6 The American Thomas Jones [1804–89] must not be confused with the Englishman Edward (Thomas) Jones [1767–1833], mentioned previously.

7 Stanisław Budny (1826), exploiting the method of a French author Edmund Degrange, seems to have been the first author of an accounting manual in Polish. The first *original* Polish contribution was the three-volume text by Barciński (1833), though another well-known text was that by Szumłaski (1865). Other Polish authors (publishing mainly in the second half of the nineteenth century) were Novicki, Danielewicz, Veltze, Boleslav Sobieski, Walicki and, at the beginning of the twentieth century, Ciompa. For further details, see Jaruga and Szychta (1996: 465–8).

8 In English, the term 'theories of accounts' is often equated with 'bookkeeping theories' (to distinguish it from 'accounting theories', which has less technical and more scientific implications). Literal translation of such terms into or from other languages is not recommended. In German, for example, the term *Buchhaltungstheorie* is more comprehensive than the corresponding English translation. The competition between various theories of accounts, also the distinction of *personalistic* versus *materialistic* theories, and the further distinction between *proprietary theory* and *entity theory* (see below), all seem to be independent of each other. Yet, Seicht (1970: 57–66) tried to find connecting links between these theories as well as with some German *Bilanztheorien*.

9 But not only Italians, also authors from other countries preferred four- or two-series account theories (e.g. Ziegler 1904). And Galassi (1980: 32, note 7), in discussing Zappa's theory, emphasized that 'the accounting theories which stress *income determination* are all "four (or two times two) series accounts theories"'.

10 Though, Cilloni (2005: 1, 2, 18) points out that Rossi's (1889) book 'raised lively interest' among such scholars as 'Biancardi, D'Alvise, Gagliardi, Hügli, Massa, Sanguinetti and Savigni'.

11 Jackson (1956: 306) called the materialistic or non-personalistic theories 'ownership theories' of accounts. But this expression could be confused with 'proprietary theory' that belongs to an entirely different category (namely that between proprietary vs. entity theory).

12 As for Britain's pioneering effort in developing the accounting *profession*, the reader is referred to R. Brown (1905) and R. Parker (1978).

13 Serra (1999: 281–291) devotes a separate chapter ('*Un secolo di discussioni ideologiche in Italia*') to several such scholarly or 'ideological' disputes that reach from the nineteenth into the twentieth century.

14 Malcolm (1718) and Stephens (1735) had already anticipated certain aspects of the proprietary theory.

15 A different perspective of ethics, namely from the viewpoint of the *public accounting* and auditing profession, was assumed by such American authors as Joseph Sterret (1907) and John A. Cooper (1907).

16 For several reasons the expression 'dynamic accounting' (emphasizing, above all, relevant income determination instead of asset and equity representation, see below) is a better translation of '*dynamische Bilanz*' than 'dynamic Balance Sheet' – above all the latter is a linguistic contradiction. Seicht (1970: 100) regarded von Strombeck, Scheffler, Schüler, Hermann Simon, von Wilmowski (1895), Rehm (1914) and Rudolf Fischer (1909) as having anticipated, in one respect or the other, dynamic accounting. As to the followers of Schmalenbach's dynamic accounting during the *inter-war period*, Sykora (1949: 211) lists Geldmacher, Mahlberg, Haar and Friedrich Leitner (1905). As to the period *after the Second World War*, Seicht (1970: 137–56) and others regarded Ernst Walb's *finanzwirtschaftliche Bilanz* and Kosiol's *pagatorische Bilanz* as the major efforts to further develop dynamic accounting, and to make it formally and materially consistent (though they may not have fully succeeded in doing so).

17 Cameralism went far beyond mere accounting. It flourished in the seventeenth and eighteenth century, but was still influential in the nineteenth century; and traces of it

(particularly in budgeting) can even be found in the twenty-first century. For other notable works on cameralism and cameralistic accounting – like von Sonnenfels (1804), Weber (1819), Rau (1822) and others – see Walb (1926), von Wysocki (1965) and Forrester (1998: 79–102). Government accounting was very important in Italy (e.g. D'Alvise 1912).

18 The decisive passage (originally in awkward legalistic German) of the *Reichsoberlandesgericht* (ROLG judgment of 3.12.1883) may be translated as follows:

> The underlying idea for the balance sheet is a fictitious general realization of all assets and equities [debt and owners' equities]; thereby it has to be assumed that in reality the intention is not the liquidation, but the continuation of the business, and hence that in measuring and determining individual values that aspect has to be neglected which would result in liquidation.
>
> (cf. Seicht 1970: 514; translated from German)

19 Seicht (1977) presented an interesting historical study of cost accounting. However, his book and bibliography (of some 130 publications) contains neither a reference to such American pioneers of cost accounting as Metcalfe, Bastable, Church, Emerson, Longmuir and Whitmore, nor to any of the English pioneers from Babbage to Garcke and Fells, Garry, Bunnell, etc. This shows how parochial accounting history becomes if *hidden* regional and language barriers dominate a study. Something similar can be observed in other excellent historical works on cost accounting; for example, those of Solomons (1968a, 1968b) and Kaplan (1984). Neither of them mentions Schmalenbach's important contributions or those of other German costing pioneers. In some language areas this situation may meanwhile have improved but the example of Schneider (2001) demonstrates that in other places parochialism continues. Schneider's comprehensive historical work, reserving almost 200 pages to the history of accounting up to the end of the twentieth century, for example, fails to mention such internationally eminent names as Dicksee, Hatfield, Paton, Moonitz, Chambers, R. Ball, P.R. Brown, Demski, Feltham, Dopuch, Zeff and others. Hardly any other science (whether pure or applied) could afford to be so out of touch with other countries and language areas.

20 In another publication, Chatfield (1974: 94–5) pointed out that:

> fixed assets purchased from the proceeds of bond and stock issues were capitalized at original cost and never depreciated. Instead, asset replacements as well as repairs were charged directly to expenses; only expenditures for additional and betterments were normally capitalized.

May (1936: 341) suggested that US railroads may not have developed as fast under periodic cost-based depreciation; this may explain why investors in American railroad companies lost immense amounts of money. Brief (1965: 20) confirmed this by pointing out that half the track mileage constructed in the US before 1900 was ultimately placed into receivership. For financial reporting of railroad and other large industrial companies in the UK and USA, see Lee (1982).

21 And Littleton (1929: 102) reported that by 1910 large factories in the USA operated with accounting systems in which financial accounting and cost accounting were well connected. This and, even more so, the pioneering work by Garcke and Fells (1887), would mean a considerable primacy over similar attempts by Schmalenbach's *Kontenrahmen* in the late 1920s.

22 Mathieu de La Port's classification of accounts still influenced such nineteenth-century authors as Vannier (1840), Jaclot (1856) and Sibuet (1867), as well as some authors of the twentieth century.

23 As to the contributions of some nineteenth-century engineers and factory accountants to cost and managerial accounting, as far as not previously mentioned, the following publications should be pointed out: Kirkman (1880), Towne (1885–86), Lewis

(1896), Evans (1911). Out of all this grew the movement of scientific management (or 'Taylorism') in the early twentieth century and a similar trend established by Fayol (1916) in France.

24 For further details on the development of various aspects of accounting and its research, see such historical publications as Penndorf (1913, 1933), Littleton (1933), Meithner (1933), Garner (1940, 1968), Sykora (1949), Melis (1950), Littleton and Yamey (1956), Löffelholz (1970), Chatfield (1974), Previts and Merino (1979), Kaplan (1984), Lee (1990), Chatfield and Vangermeersch (1996), Hernández Esteve (1997) and Forrester (1998). For a series of pertinent studies on nineteenth- and twentieth-century managerial accounting, see: Solomons (1968a, 1968b), Johnson (e.g. 1972, 1981), Kaplan (1984), Johnson and Kaplan (1987), Lee *et al.* (1996) and Lemarchand and Parker (1996). And for an analysis of accounting books kept by 'genteel' and professional *women* from 1700 to 1820, see Vickery (1998).

3 German language area: first half of the twentieth century

1 Based on Küpper and Mattessich (2005).
2 One of the referees of this chapter suggested that we should distinguish between 'leadership in thought and leadership in practice'. There can be little doubt that during much of the nineteenth century, Great Britain led in accounting practice, above all in auditing. Yet, the focus of this chapter is neither on the nineteenth century nor on accounting *practice*; it is on early twentieth-century accounting *research*. And there seems to be little disagreement about the international influence and recognition of German accounting theory during the first half of the twentieth century (see section 3.6). We also believe that the international significance of the various German *Bilanz* theories is well accepted and that, during the first three or four decades of the twentieth century, these theories were unrivalled in subtlety and richness of thought as far as problems of valuation, realization, classification, allocation, stewardship and so on, were concerned.
3 Other names are Gomberg, Sganzini, Schär, Calmes and Käfer (all originally or permanently teaching in Switzerland); furthermore Nicklisch, Rieger, Prion, Osbahr, Passow, Walb, Kalveram, Lion, le Coutre, Geldmacher, Lehmann, Isaac, Mellerowicz, Seÿffert, Beste, Gutenberg, Seischab, Kosiol and Münstermann.
4 However, in the particular context of the English translation of Schmalenbach's *magnum opus*, the title might not quite reflect Schmalenbach's intention of imposing a dynamic function on a basically 'static' balance sheet at the cost of the income statement (for details see subsequent sections).
5 In the French accounting literature, Batardon (1911) submitted also a proposal for a chart of accounts. Furthermore, the *Société Académique de Comptabilité Belgique* seems to have made similar efforts in the early years of the new century (Gomberg 1912).
6 Depending on the preference of its promoter – 'five' was a 'magic number' for account classes, derived from Degrange's famous synoptic system (cf. Mattessich 2003: 127).
7 This is originally a French name, spelled 'Calmès'. Hence, the author's French publications use this spelling (cf. Degos and Mattessich 2003; and Mattessich 2003).
8 For details about the dangers of such confusion, see Mattessich (1995: 43–51).
9 Although Sykora (1949: 91–3) treated Seidel's theory separately.
10 In some respects the expression 'dynamic accounting' (emphasizing, above all, relevant income determination instead of asset and equity representation) is a better translation of '*dynamische Bilanz*' than is 'dynamic Balance Sheet' – above all, the latter is a linguistic contradiction.
11 Specifically, Passow (1910), Fäs (1913), Geldmacher (1920, 1923), von Kast (1920), Klein (1920), Prion (1919, 1921, 1922), Schmalenbach (1921, 1922a, 1922b, 1925),

Schmidt (1921, 1922a, 1922b, 1923a, 1923b, 1924, 1926, 1927a, 1927b, 1927c, 1929, 1930a, 1930b, 1931a, 1931b, 1950), Mahlberg (1920, 1921, 1923, 1925), Walb (1921), Kalveram (1922), Isaac (1924), Leitner (1923, 1924), Dörfel (1925, for Austria) and Haar (1925).

12 Including Bayard, Delavelle, Fain, Faure, Léger, Raffegeau and Lacout, as well as Thomas.

13 Nicklisch is not even profiled in Chatfield and Vangermeersch (1996).

14 Cf. the authors' index of the encyclopaedic work by Küpper and Wagenhofer (2002: cols 2226, 2230, 2232, 2239), where Schmidt has over *twelve* entries, Walb *seven*, Rieger *three* and, almost incredibly, Nicklisch and Schär each have only *two*. Compare this with the first edition of the same work (ed. by Kosiol 1970), where Schmidt has 48 entries, Walb 42, Rieger 36, Nicklisch 20 and Schär 11. This may indicate an increasing anti-historical outlook of the individual contributors, and of the present generation of accounting academics in general. But such an attitude is not confined to Germany. In America, for example, Zeff recently raised the following complaint:

> A few years ago, I made an informal sampling of how many of the leading doctoral programs had even a single course that would acquaint students with the literature before the 1970s. I found virtually none. When I would ask, 'Why?', I would receive the answer, 'We don't have enough time. We use the time we have to explain current research paradigms and methodological approaches'. I think we need to work toward a better balance.
>
> (comments by Zeff contained in Dietrich *et al.* 2002: 74)

15 Schoenfeld, for example, said about Schmalenbach's theory: 'The major emphasis for income and performance measurement, consequently, had to be placed on the income statement'. However, he correctly stated that 'his balance sheet measured assets at various intermediate stages of this conversion [from cash to resources into cash again]; it represents a record of unconsumed resources or, in his words, 'different classes of accruals or prepayments' (Schoenfeld 1996: 515).

16 For a mathematical comparison of different inflation adjustment models (with nominal vs. real, realized vs. unrealized, and monetary vs. non-monetary capital gains) see Mattessich (1995: 97–119).

17 For publications about the *dynamische Bilanz*, see De Motte Green (1937) and Forrester (1987), both in English; and Nicklisch (1921a, 1932), Lion (1928a), W. Lehmann (1932), Rieger (1936), Münstermann (1957, 1966), Muscheid (1957), von Kori (1968a, 1968b), Seicht (1970b) and Kruk *et al.* (1984), in German.

18 While Kosiol's pagatoric theory had its origin in the late 1930s, it had its major impact after the Second World War (for a discussion, see subsection 3.2.1 in this book).

19 For discussions of or critical views on Schmidt's work, see Rieger (1930), Hasenack (1933a), Isaac (1950), Schwantag (1951), Voigtländer (1952), Whittington (1983), Tweedie and Whittington (1984), Mattessich (1986), Clarke and Dean (1986, 1989, 1990).

20 In the English literature by MacNeal, and much later by Chambers, Sterling, and others.

21 Instead of *Betriebswirtschaftslehre* he spoke of *Privatwirtschaftlehre*, thus emphasizing the 'private' (i.e. the profit and business) character of his endeavour.

22 For further details on Rieger's valuation approach, see Jores (1928), Hintner (1930), Engel (1965), and Gümbel (1966) – and for a general examination of the valuation structure for balance sheet presentation, see Gutenberg (1926).

23 Indeed, in the view of some scholars, the profit and loss account is a relative latecomer:

> The profit and loss account was rarely encountered in German ledgers of the 16th century, not even the theoreticians used it. The entry of profits and losses directly

in to the owner's equity account was originally the custom; only later did one use the indirect transfer, namely through a profit and loss account, and from there into the equity account.

(Penndorf 1933a: 137, translation)

24 For example, Jung, Fredersdorff, Ballewski and Tolkmitt (see Dorn 1976; Mattessich 2003).

25 See, for example, Calmes (1906, 1920, 1922), Schmalenbach (1908–09, 1919b, 1924, 1948), Schuchart (1909), Meyerberg (1913), Preiser (1919), Isaac (1921), R.M. Lehmann (1921, 1925, 1928), Beste (1924, 1930), Großmann (1925a, 1925b), Heina (1925), Lohmann (1929), Kosiol (1927, 1944c), Nicklisch (1929–32, 1929), Bouffier (1932), Hasenack (1930, 1933b), Reichskuratorium für Wirtschaftlichkeit (1939–RKW), Mellerowicz (1933), Seidel (1933), Beisel (1936), Funk (1937), Fischer *et al.* (1939), the economist Erich Schneider (1939, 1940, 1951), Michel (1941), Boßhardt (1948), Schnutenhaus (1948), Schwantag (1949), Wolter (1948), Illetschko (1950) and Kalveram (1951). There was also a German report on Soviet cost accounting by Rosenkranz (1949).

26 In 1949, the American Billy E. Goetz made similar proposals, independent of Schmalenbach.

27 This contained, apart from some of his own contributions (e.g. Meithner 1933b), articles by Austrian scholars (like Hatheyer 1933; Kerschagl 1933; Mayer 1933; Nusko 1933; Seidel 1933), accompanied by a galaxy of those from Germany and Switzerland (as, for example, Haar 1926; Gutenberg 1933; Pape 1933; Penndorf 1933a; Schranz 1933; Seischab 1933; Thoms 1933; Töndury 1933). For interesting remarks on Karl Meithner and the 'Viennese School of Business Economics', see Vodrazka (1957) and Schneider (2001: 222 n).

4 German language area: second half of the twentieth century

1 This Chapter, like the previous one, is based on Küpper and Mattessich (2005).

2 For a review of Kosiol's theory, see Gutenberg (1949).

3 For a possible exception to this view, see the 'master thesis' by Schüppenhauer (1965).

4 For some comparison of the similarities and differences between these two crucial works of accounting theory, we refer to subsection 12.3.1 (for further details, see Mattessich 1986).

5 For details, see survey articles by Coenenberg *et al.* (1978), Coenenberg *et al.* (1984), Franzen (1985), Coenenberg and Haller (1993b), Küpper (1993a) and Möller and Hüfner (2002).

6 For different inflation models (general indexation vs. nominal specific indexation vs. real specific indexation) and their corresponding capital maintenance models based on an extension of Edwards and Bell's (1961) theory.

7 As to the situation in Switzerland, see Dellmann (1994).

8 In Germany the formulation of 'accounting principles' can be found as early as 1897 when the *Handelsgesetzbuch* (commercial code) promulgated the *Grundsätze ordnungsmäßiger Buchführung* (principles of orderly accounting).

9 Slaymaker (1996) traced the influence of individual authors (and their publications) on the creation of the FASB's Conceptual Framework (see also Zeff 1982).

10 For a slightly dated comparison between accounting rules and practices in the USA and Germany, see Ballwieser (1996).

11 Or, as Christensen and Demski (2003: 4) state:

> The value school, then, views the task as one of reasonably well approximating value, of designing a financial measurement system that will measure value. The information content school, by contrast, views the financial measures as

measures of information events, not of value. What is being measured, then, differs in a most fundamental sense for the two approaches.

12 A still more sophisticated text of the information economics approach, that by Christensen and Feltham (2003, 2005), does not even contain any references to the issue of standard setting (or such institutions as the FASB) in its Subject Index.
13 As Volume 4 of his comprehensive work on business and micro-economics.
14 For a comparison of 'Fours schools of European accounting taught' before the 1980s, see Filios (1981).
15 The accounting encyclopaedias of the Schäffer-Poeschel Verlag (formerly C.E. Poeschel Verlag) presently consist of two tomes: first, the *Handwörterbuch der Rechnungslegung und Prüfung*, edited by Ballwieser *et al.* (2002); and second, the *Handwörterbuch Unternehmensrechnung und Controlling*, edited by Küpper and Wagenhofer (2002). The latter is the fourth (completely revised edition) of Kosiol's (1970b) *Handwörterbuch des Rechnungswesens* (its second edition appeared in 1981, edited by Kosiol, Chmielewicz and Schweitzer, and its third edition in 1993, edited by Chmielewicz and Schweitzer). Other encyclopaedias of this series each deal with one of the following subjects: business economics, organization, marketing, banking and finance, planning, government administration, export and international business and, finally, German business management. It is a series unmatched in the English business literature. Their closest counterpart in America is *The History of Accounting: An International Encyclopedia* (Chatfield and Vangermeersch 1996), which is however more historically oriented, less massive, organized in a looser form, and often less intimidating. Sometimes it contains personal profiles, and a single author may have several contributions.

5 Accounting research in Italy: first half of the twentieth century

1 Based (with modifications) on Galassi and Mattessich (2004: 62–83).
2 Gino Zappa is the only nineteenth/twentieth-century Italian accounting scholar to whom a separate profile was devoted in the encyclopaedic work of Chatfield and Vangermeersch (1996: 617–18, by Galassi), though Giuseppe Cerboni, Giovanni Rossi, Fabio Besta and other Italians are briefly mentioned in this work and its Index. Something similar holds for the book *Twentieth-Century Accounting Thinkers* by Edwards (1994, and its contribution by Canziani 1994), though, surprisingly, the name of Rossi is absent from the book's Index.
3 This system had a summary account for the 'proprietor' and another one for the 'agents and correspondents'. It used a particular logismographical journal with the possibility of adding further sub-accounts in subsidiary ledgers. It was supposed to reveal the wealth structure on a *daily* basis, and exercised considerable influence in Italy, and occasionally abroad.
4 For a profile of Zappa, see Galassi (1996).
5 For different valuation approaches, see Galassi (1974). For a discussion on Continental versus Anglo-Saxon valuation methodology, see Canziani (1982).
6 These gains and losses were considered as having no time dimension (i.e. they were not identifiable with an income flow over a time period) but manifested themselves at the instant of measurement. Gains and losses, not arising through revenues and costs, were considered changes in the values of equity; they were modifications in economic value of the business entity itself. These changes might have been due to variations in future earning potentials (including price level changes) or to changes in the discount rate.
7 Balance sheets were nothing more than connecting links in successive income statements, a kind of reservoir containing all accounts not belonging to the income statement. Thus, the balance sheet became a repository of 'values in suspense', that

was an account for rest, a sort of receptacle for costs contained in inventories and fixed assets which were to be allocated periodically according to the requirements of periodic income determination. The capital account did not contain, necessarily, the value of the enterprise and a balance sheet was not a means of disclosing this value, but only a system of values reflecting a system of resources and productive conditions.

8 Galassi (1966) discussed these issues. The notion of *re-valued capital* was regarded as being related to a revision process of the firm's 'system of values', particularly, when this system no longer supplied a reliable measure of net income for successive accounting periods.

9 Thus, the value of capital had to be the starting point for income estimation.

10 For a detailed discussion, see Galassi (1980).

11 The *azienda* was considered an open system in its interaction with the external environment in which it operated – i.e. the markets to which it contributed, and the needs of society it had to satisfy (cf. Zappa 1937, 1956–57, 1962: § 13). The *azienda* was compared to a tree from which various interdependent sub-systems branch out on different levels. The first level was that of traditional management, as well as the organizational and data-gathering sub-systems. The second sub-system derived from a different aspect of the entity's functions, for example, from its managerial and organizational control.

12 Zappa saw the balance sheet as a reflection of the future. Basic to his thinking was the Fisherian notion that the value of capital depended on future incomes. Zappa's concept of the balance sheet was based on budgetary considerations, as well as on those of valuation. Future events (values) were discounted to the present day. For Zappa, both sides of the balance sheet referred to the future and not simply to the past.

13 Some Italians argue, for example, that the *Betriebswirtschaftslehre* employs iso-cost and iso-quant curves, while *Economia Aziendale* does not use them because of their 'approximate' and 'static' nature.

14 Yet, this argument is not tight enough. First, the German word *Betrieb* – derived from the verb *betreiben* (to operate) – is at least as generally applicable as the Italian *azienda* (related to the Spanish verb *hacer* and ultimately derived from the Latin *facere*, to make). Second, the English noun 'concern' has a strong *business* connotation. The *Oxford Dictionary* defines it as referring to 'business' or 'business relation'. In short, the attempt to derive the content of such concepts as *economia aziendale*, *Betriebswirtschaftslehre*, business administration, from their etymological roots, opens a Pandora's box.

15 Some works on the development of particular aspects of Italian accounting history belong to the second half of the twentieth century or later: Mazza (1968), Giannessi (1980), Pezzoli (1986), Catturi (1989), Zan (1994), Masi (1997), Serra (1999), (Antonio) Amaduzzi (2001) and Zambon (2002).

6 Accounting research in Italy: second half of the twentieth century

1 Based on Viganò and Mattessich (2007). Valuable references were also found in Viganò (1997) and Canziani (1994); further contributions (mainly referring to bibliographic material) were made by Professor Giuseppe Galassi.

2 However, present-day German accounting has largely shaken off the fetters of Schmalenbach's *monistic* conception of 'dynamic accounting' (dominated by the income notion at the cost of the capital notion), while Italian accounting still seems to follow Zappa's main ideas.

3 A basic idea of this school concerns the logical relationship between the bookkeeping *method* (double-entry) and the *accounting system* within *Economia aziendale*. There, the duality does not grow out of the need for an arithmetical control, but because it reflects economic events from two points of view: that of capital measurement and that

of income measurement. Yet, this too is a misconception because both *income* and *capital* are on the *same side of the balance sheet*. Actually, double-entry arises out of the ingenious combination of three very different dualities: (1) the input–output relation; (2) the debtor–claimant relation; and (3) the relation between an asset and its ownership (cf. Mattessich 1995: 28–30).

4 The neglect of sociology and the behavioural science may be considered serious in the face a sample (from leading academic accounting journals), mentioned in Carmona *et al.* (1999: 476). It showed that some 34 papers, out of 79, were influenced by sociological theories and organizational behaviour.

5 Chatfield review of an anthology of papers by leading Italian accounting scholars (published in English by the *Accademia Nazionale di Ragioneria*, 1974, the forerunner of AIDEA). The review stated that: 'this book is not a valuable addition to the accounting literature, nor is it of much interest to readers of *The Accounting Review*. Most of the articles are insufficiently detailed or documented to be valuable as reference works. The range of topics is too broad. The views expressed are mainly familiar ones, and are largely derivative from readily available American, English and German sources'. (Chatfield 1982: 208–9).

6 For different inflation models (general indexation vs. nominal specific indexation vs. real specific indexation) and their corresponding capital maintenance models based on an extension of Edwards and Bell's (1961) theory, see Mattessich (1995: 97–124).

7 In a way, one might regard Denmark as the European country most advanced in the information perspective of accounting since the co-authors of both, J.A. Christensen and Demski (2003) and P.O. Christensen and Feltham (2003, 2005), are professors in Denmark. However, we have no evidence that these books were translated into Danish.

7 Accounting research in the French language area: first half of the twentieth century

1 Based on Degos and Mattessich (2003).

2 Later, in the second half of the twentieth century, the historical paper by Fortin (1996) and others were collected by Lemarchand and Parker (1996) in a bilingual book (French and English).

3 This link between accounting and economics, already stressed by Proudhon, Léautey and Guilbault, and others, has been a recurrent theme in French accounting.

4 A similar approach was thoroughly developed by Edwards and Bell (1961), and enabled the proper exposition of real business profit and total profit, real and fictitious gains, monetary and non-monetary gains, realizable and non-realizable gains – for a mathematical representation of such concepts, see Mattessich (1995: 98–119).

5 The distinction between 'paper-franc' vs. 'gold-franc' (or 'paper-mark' vs. 'gold-mark') is based on the pertinent index used for adjusting the asset and equity values at a specific point in time. If these values are not adjusted, or adjusted by a country's own price index (cost of living, wholesale, etc.), one may speak of paper-franc value at a specific date. But if the index reflects a gold-based currency (e.g. the US$ in the 1920s) or the price of gold itself, one speaks of a gold-franc (or gold mark) basis. For a survey of the advantages and disadvantages of several inflation adjustment methods and different indices, including gold-based ones, see Schmalenbach (1925).

6 Wasserman devoted some 30 pages to a discussion of some of those details, offering several illustrations. However, he left many questions open, the answers of which would require recourse to the original publications.

7 Regrettably, when talking about *prix de remplacement*, it is often unclear whether Wasserman (1931) – and for that matter various French authors – had a notion in mind that corresponds to that of Kovero (1912) or Limperg (1917) or Schmidt (1921).

One may suspect that in using this expression, some of the French authors referred to cost-items adjusted by a simple *general* inflation index, but neither by a *specific* replacement cost nor one adjusted by a *commodity-specific index*.

8 See also CEGOS (1937), and Danty-Lafrance (1947). The somewhat different notion of 'current sales price' was championed in the English accounting literature by MacNeal (1939), and much later revived by Chambers (1967).

9 Standish (1990: 342) refers to a memorandum of some 15 pages, called '*Circulaire du marechal Goering concernant la tenue des livres comptables*', dealing with, among other subjects, the establishment of an accounting code for manufacturing enterprises. This seems to have given rise to misnaming the German master chart of accounts as the 'Goering Plan', which actually was a much more comprehensive economic plan (not unlike the five-years plan used in the USSR).

10 For some personal notes on Fourastié, see Degos (1997).

11 For further details on the 1942 Plan, see Gabriel (1943), Chardonnet (1946), Standish (1990) and Fortin (1991: 5–8). For additional literature on charts and master charts of accounts, see: Batardon (1950), Berry (1949), Brunet (1948), Gabriel (1947), Horace (1948), Lecompt (1943), Péricauld and Calandreau (1943), Quétard (1950), Richard (1992) and Veyrenc (1950).

12 However, A. Brunet (1951: 254) pointed out that an adaptation of the 1942 Plan was officially used in the aeronautics industry, and unofficially in several larger companies.

8 Accounting research in the French language area: second half of the twentieth century

1 Based on Degos and Mattessich (2006).

2 For details of notable nineteenth-century French accountants, see Chapter 2 or Mattessich (2003: 128, 131, 136, 140, 144–5, 148–9). For French contributions to accounting theory, in general, see also Filios (1987).

3 It is surprising to note that among the 46 bibliographic references of the paper by Hoarau (1997b) on 'Courants et tradition de recherché en comptabilté financière' only a single entry refers to a French publication. However, the references of Bouquin's (1997) paper on 'Aspects transversaux et statut de la comptabilité de gestion' (referring to managerial accounting) are 40 per cent in French and 60 per cent in English.

4 Boussard and Rey (1984: 51) offers the following explanation:

> The 'overall productivity surplus' within a certain period of time equals the change in volume of production minus the change in volume of the factors of production used. Both volumes are expressed in fixed prices. This surplus balances the positive or negative 'advantages' for customers and other business partners. These advantages are measured by the product of two terms: (1) the price change of the factors of production and the **Matrix Methods** production sold, and (2) the quantity of factors used and the production sold. An explanation of the method is given in the first issue of the Documents du CERC (first quarter 1969). [Note: 'CERC' refers to the Centre d'Etudes des Revenus et des Coûts (Centre for Studies on Incomes and Costs).

5 This 'revised' point of view is all the more interesting, as it was in the previous period (i.e. before 1950) that the designers of the French Chart of Accounts rejected Schmalenbach's notion of 'reconciling' or bridging financial and cost accounting aspects (in his chart of account), but insisted on a clear separation between external and internal accounting aspects.

9 Accounting publications and research in Spain: first half of the twentieth century

1 Based on Carrasco Díaz *et al.* (2004). We remind the reader, that in Spain family names are usually double names, sometimes even triple names (e.g. Ballesteros Marín-Baldo or Pérez-Pons Jover).

10 Accounting publications and research in Spain: second half of the twentieth century

1 By Fernández-Feijóo Souto and Mattessich (2006).
2 However, in contrast to the paper by Montesinos Julve (1998), this chapter deals exclusively with Spanish accounting, but not with the super-discipline of *Economía de la Empresa*.
3 One may note that different European countries responded to the impact of Anglo-American research very differently. Spanish academics responded to a fairly wide spectrum of such research. But as to the information perspective of accounting (as initiated by Feltham, Demski and others) – with the possible exception of agency theory – there was hardly any response. In Italy, on the other hand, this spectrum seems to be narrower, but there were several papers and one book, attempting to convey the essentials of the information perspective to Italian accounting academics (cf. Chapter 5).
4 An example of such a mathematical study in agency theory is that by Narayanan and Dávila (1998); another paper by Dávila (2005) on management control systems may here be added. Some experts may count such papers as Spanish contributions to the international accounting literature, as its second co-author seems to be from Spain – though presently he is Assistant Professor at Stanford University, and neither of those papers has a specific Spanish connotation.
5 These journals are: *Abacus*; *Accounting, Auditing and Accountability Journal; Accounting and Business Research*; *Accounting, Organizations and Society*; *The Accounting Review*; *Contemporary Accounting Research*; *Critical Perspectives of Accounting*; *the European Accounting Review*; *Journal of Management Accounting Research*; *Journal of Accounting and Economics*; *Journal of Accounting Research; Journal of Business Finance and Accounting*; and *Management Accounting Research* – for further details see the original paper (Carmona *et al.* 1999).
6 Apart from the translation of Schmalenbach's *magnum opus*, a series of other foreign publications were translated during this period (and later) into Spanish, for example: Vlaemminck (1960), Hansen (1961), Schneider (1969), Ijiri (1972), Mattessich (1958, 1973, 2000, 2002, 2004).
7 For the early evolution and development of the Spanish Chart of Accounts, see Fernández Peña (1984: 192–4).
8 We have tried to include in this section only published historical material directly related to accounting (but not to commercial history in general).

11 Accounting research in the English language area: first half of the twentieth century

1 By Mattessich (previously unpublished) – see Acknowledgements.
2 For profiles on Hatfield, see Moonitz (1986: 7–10), Mills (1994) and Kozub (1996); and for a retrospective on Gilman, see Bloom *et al.* (1990).
3 *Residual income valuation* was used in the USA as early as 1920 (based on a Report of the Internal Revenue Service in evaluating the impact of Prohibition on the business values of breweries).
4 However, Chatfield (1996b: 131) pointed out that 'Corporations have published funds' flow statements since 1862 in Britain and since 1863 in the United States. By 1903 at

least four variants existed: reports summarizing changes in cash and cash equivalents, in current assets, in working capital, and in all financial activities. But there was no agreement about which type of statement was superior or what form it should take'. Though Rosen and DeCoster (1969: 125) believed that 'The Missouri Pacific Railway Company and its subsidiaries, St Louis, Iron Mountain & Southern Railway, seem to have been the first organizations to highlight changes in the balance sheet accounts'. Their reports were called 'Statement showing Resources and their Application during the Year 1893'.

12 Accounting Research in the English language area – second half of the twentieth century

1 Based in part on Mattessich (1996a, 1996b).
2 Particularly the research output during the last two decades has been so overwhelming that even our comprehensive bibliography hardly scratches the surface.
3 For surveys on *general accounting theory*, see: Most (1982), Griffin (1982), Hendriksen (1982), Henderson and Person (1983), Mattessich (1984), Wolk *et al.* (1984), Belkaoui (1985a), Devine (1985), Kam (1986), Brown *et al.* (1989) and Frecka (1989). For more specifically oriented surveys (according to historical periods, geographical areas, journals, etc.), see Onida (1970), Chatfield (1968, 1978), Holzer (1980), Busse von Colbe and Pohlmann (1981), Gaffikin and Aitken (1982), Hopwood and Schreuder (1984), Dyckman and Zeff (1984), L.D. Brown (1987), Gaffikin (1987, 1988), J.R. Edwards (1994, 2000), Ball and Smith (1992), Zan (1994) and Schneider (2001). For general references, see *Kohler's Dictionary for Accountants*, edited by Cooper and Ijiri (1975), as well as the encyclopaedic accounting history by Chatfield and Vangermeersch (1996) and *The Blackwell encyclopaedic dictionary of accounting* by Abdel-khalik (1997).
4 While the Sandilands (1975) proposal took only specific price-level adjustments into consideration (and thus was forced to use the *artificial* 'gearing adjustment' to adjust for financial holding gains or losses), the more complete FASB (1979) approach took, *in addition*, separate adjustments for general price-level changes into consideration. For explanations of the 'gearing (financial) adjustment', see van Hoepen *et al.* (1989) and Gutiérrez (1992).
5 To my understanding, the term 'a priori approach', as used by most accountants, refers to reasoning based on overt or covert normative premises and empirical assumptions without being backed by tested statistical hypotheses – surprisingly, reasoning on the basis of mathematical or formal logical rigour seems not always to be included under this peculiar usage.
6 Several studies have tried to relate Kuhn's (1962) theory of paradigms to accounting: e.g. Wells (1976), AAA (1977), Belkaoui (1985a), Cushing (1989) and Mouck (1993).
7 'Cost drivers' are factors that cause the costs of a specific 'production' activity. The book by Cooper and Kaplan (1991) maintains that costs are caused by activities on the following four different levels (and vary because of them): the *unit level* (volume of units), the *batch level* (volume of batches independent of units), *product-sustaining level* (activity necessary to sustain a production independent of units or batch size), and *facility sustaining* (to maintain a facility independent of all the other factors mentioned previously). The assignments of cost on the basis of such a hierarchy is claimed to explain best the behaviour costs, and to facilitate a more profitable management than other cost allocation bases.
8 Horngren (1995: 284) pointed out that the beginnings of ABC (though under a different name) go back to the book by Longman and Schiff (1955).
9 As to modern research, one easily overlooks two crucial issues: (1) that simplified, and thus, 'unrealistic' models are no idle play but the foundation of every scientific undertaking, and (2) that these models relate to reality only in an idealized way. Reality

itself is, by far, too complex to be captured by them. The perennial disregard of item 2, be it by researchers or practitioners, leads to a *lopsided sophistication* which becomes perilous when practical recommendations are disregarded (or pay only lip service to) the underlying analytical or empirical-statistical assumptions.

13 Accounting research in Finland, the Netherlands and the Scandinavian countries

1 This chapter is authored by Mattessich (previously unpublished) – see Acknowledgements. Since neither the author nor any of the collaborators is competent in the Finnish language, the section on Finnish accounting research is mainly, though not exclusively, based on information conveyed in Lukka *et al.* (1984), Näsi and Näsi (1997) and Lukka (1996) – though the section is very differently organized than any of those sources. Something similar holds for the subsequent sections on the Netherlands and the Scandinavian countries (see notes 4 and 6). For each of the different linguistic areas a separate reference section is provided. We may add two things, first that a considerable number of publications listed in these references (particularly, prominent dissertations) contain English summaries, and second, that there exists a book by Flower (1994) dealing with financial reporting in the 'Northern Countries' *in general.*

2 Note that the WorldCat lists no less than 77 book entries (in Finnish, German and English – some of them later editions) for Ilmari Kovero, while it lists only six book entries for Theodore Limperg (who is better known and frequently cited in the Anglophone accounting literature). Whatever the reason for this discrepancy may be, it seems that Kovero received sufficient attention in Western accounting circles.

3 The WorldCat lists some 19 copies of this book in Japanese libraries, but only nine are available in US libraries.

4 This part of Chapter 13 is based to some extent on Klaassen and Schreuder (1984), Bouma and Feenstra (1997), Camfferman (1996b) and van Seventer (1996) as well as other references (cf. note 1).

5 Bouma and Feenstra (1997: 176) confirm that in recent times ' "bedrijfseconomie" in the traditional sense has fallen apart, and that modern "bedrijfseconomie" and accounting are no longer strongly connected'. And Camfferman and Zeff (1994: 129) pointed out that 'Van der Schroeff, an early Limperg disciple, described in 1970 how he gradually lost his belief in the possibility of constructing an enduring, normative theory as he came to realise that the questions to be addressed by bedrijfseconomie were continually changing and constantly required new approaches' (van der Schroeff 1970: 9–10).

6 For the section on the Scandinavian countries, the main (though not exclusive) sources were Östman (1984) and Jönsson (1996b).

14 Accounting publications and research in twentieth-century Japan

1 By Koguchi and Mattessich (previously unpublished) – see Acknowledgements.

2 Someya (1989: 77) writes about Shand (1873): '[it] became the first work dealing with double-entry bookkeeping to appear in Japan. This work was a five volume translation compiled from proposals by Alexander Allen Shand [1844–1930], a Scotsman who came to Japan at the invitation of the Ministry of Finance … . Yoshikawa, the compiler of this work, describes how this came about'. We also know that Shand was a banker working with the Chartered Mercantile Bank of India, London and China.

3 Though Morita (1994: 172) points out that 'the balance sheet in *Son-eki-ho* is essentially similar to, but more refined than, that of Schmalenbach'.

15 Accounting publications and research of twentieth-century Russia

1 Written by Bychkova, Mattessich and Sokolov (previously unpublished) – see Acknowledgements. The following publications proved valuable sources for this paper: Gorelik (1971), Bailey (1982), Lebow and Tondkar (1986), Motyka (1993), Enthoven *et al.* (1992, 1994, 1998), Sokolov and Kovalev (1996a, 1996b), as well as Sokolov and Bychkova (2004).

   As to the transliteration from Cyrillic writing – that, for example, does not have any letters for either the Latin 'h' (using instead a 'g') nor for our 'w' (using instead 'v') – into the Latin alphabet, there exist many variations. We adhered to the convention that spells proper names according to linguistic origin; hence: 'Feldhausen' instead of 'Feldgauzen', 'Hegel' (the renowned philosopher) and not 'Gegel' and 'Wolf' instead of 'Vol'f'. In the case of other personal names we chose, for example, 'Ezersky' instead of 'Ezerskii', 'Masdorov' instead of 'Mazdorov' and 'Rudanovsky' instead of 'Rudanovskii'. Furthermore, we adhered to 'buchgalterii' (whereby the 'ch', in Cyrillic is 'x') refers to the *guttural* sound (as used in German and some other languages) instead of 'bukgalterii' (both of which are corruptions of the German words 'Buchhaltung' or its derivatives). Furthermore, personal names are occasionally transliterated differently (e.g. 'Jaroslav' as 'Yaroslav', and abbreviated with 'Y', instead of 'J').

2 Other pertinent papers in the *Journal of Accounting Education and Research* are, for example, those by Chumachenko and Bedford (1968), Berry (1982) and Satubaldin (1976).

3 *Artel* means 'Professional Association'.

4 According to Bailey (1982: 20n), some biographical remarks on F.W. Ezersky appeared in the *Soviet Accounting Bulletin* (Winter 1976: 94–7), and Motyka (1993: Vol. I, 360; Vol. 2, 21, 357) reveals that (in sheer number of publications, reprint editions, etc.) Ezersky was by far the most prolific of all Russian accounting authors. Motyka (1993: Vol. 2, 373–4) lists 175 books (including re-editions), all of which were written by Ezersky during the nineteenth century. But his influence reached into the twentieth century when his *Accounting theory* (Ezersky 1902) went into its twelfth edition, and continued with further editions, while the twenty-eighth edition of his book on the Russian triple-accounting system (his most successful work among many) appeared three years later – see Ezersky (1915). He also published books with some co-authors: e.g. Vol. 5 ('Information on commerce') of the *Practical encyclopaedia* (see Ezersky and Shovsky 1906). As an interesting side note: 'Upon his death his estate ... was left to the Accountants' *Artel* (Society) to be used as the country's first convalescent home for ailing accountants' (Motyka 1993: Vol. 1, 78n).

5 Later publications by Léon Gomberg (1908, 1912, 1920) were in French and German when the author lived and taught in Switzerland (for further details, see Küpper and Mattessich 2005).

6 Although Sokolov and Bychkova (2004) count Sivers to the St Petersburg School (see p. 479), they later mention that he did not contribute to the journal *Accountancy* (see p. 482). Sivers was ranked (after F.V. Ezersky) second in the sheer quantity of accounting books published – Motyka (1993: Vol. 2, 386) lists 44 books (including re-editions).

7 According to Veitsman (1978: 69–73) this journal (i.e. its first phase) failed because of insufficient readership (see also Sokolov 1977: 53–6). However, it might be mentioned that Wolf 'disappeared from view at the time of the revolutionary disturbances of 1905, and it is uncertain whether he remained in the country' (Bailey 1982: 20).

8 In Sokolov and Bychkova (2004) a different citation method is used to that customary in the West. In several citations this text refers to the *journal*, instead of the author.

9 This can be illustrated as follows: assume a firm produced 200 units of finished goods per period but sold only 120 of them. Under traditional accounting procedures only 120 units would be considered as income realized while Tugan-Baranovsky would have counted all 200 units as revenues.

10 For the originals of these publications, see Küpper and Mattessich (2005). Surprisingly enough, Motyka (1993) lists only the following translations of well-known authors: Schär (1904), Kheil (1910, 1912), Calmes (1913) and Hügli (1916).

11 For references to these works, see Degos and Mattessich (2003).

12 Already earlier in his activity, Rudanovsky (1924, 1925) tried to explain the structure of the financial report by the dialectic law in such a way that an asset (*activum*) was considered the 'thesis' and an equity (*passivum*) the corresponding 'antithesis', while the profit (or loss) was considered the 'synthesis' that arose out of this 'opposition'.

13 Cf. Laskin's (1931: 70–80) derogatory remarks on Galagan.

14 'Soviet and Russian accounting methodology traditionally has been, uniquely, financial accounting oriented. Internal operational management systems were a collection of very different methods independent of each other. Therefore, it has been difficult until recently to speak about management accounting', although cost accounting and cost analysis have been practised extensively, mostly by enterprise administrators' (Enthoven *et al.* 1998: 125).

15 Voznesensky (in an unpublished manuscript) remarks that: 'It is a misfortune for all students that authors of accounting texts – Leontiev, Gleikh and so on – began by promising to present Soviet accounting theory but expounded Schär's dual series of accounts theory [footnote omitted] and in an inferior manner'. For some remarks on the theory of 'two accounts classes' of Schär and others see the subsection on 'Accounts' in Küpper and Mattessich (2005).

16 Accounting publications and research in Poland and the Ukraine: mainly twentieth century

1 Section 16.2 (on Poland) is co-authored by Jaruga, Szychta, Frendzel and Mattessich (previously unpublished) – see Acknowledgements. Sections 16.3 and 16.4 (on the Ukraine) is co-authored by Redchenko and Mattessich (previously unpublished) – see Acknowledgements.

2 This was the result of division and annexation of the major part of Poland carried out by these countries in three stages: in 1772, 1793 and 1795.

3 Due to space limitations it is not possible to list all those contributions. For details we refer the reader to Malc (1964), Jaruga and Skowroński (1994), Nowak (2003), and the anthology by Gmytrasiewicz and Karmańska (2004).

4 One may note that the majority of academics and professionals from the Halychyna who published in accounting during the second part of nineteenth century and at the beginning of the twentieth were of German or Polish origin. Ukrainians were relatively rare. The result was that most of the accounting literature of this time was in Polish or German.

5 We may note that in the USSR many prominent accountants were of Ukrainian origin; among them were: M. K. Zhebrak, V. B. Ivashkevych, A. S. Margulis, I.I. Poklad, and others. Zhebrak (1931, 1934, 1948), for example, was one of the creators of 'normative' accounting theory (a kind of standard costing).

6 The second textbook (Malyshev 1981) was published posthumous.

7 In business practice (of the Ukraine), one pays more attention to tax accounting than to financial accounting. Such a situation is caused by a rigid taxation policy of the Ukrainian administration. There are numerous tax audits and high penalties, often without good reasons or because of insignificant errors in the accounts or their documentation.

17 Accounting books of Argentina: publications, research and institutional background

1 Based on Wirth and Mattessich (2006). We chose for this paper the spelling of the linguistically more appealing adjective 'Argentine' instead of the orthographically possibly more correct adjective 'Argentinian' (but this did not change the use of the substantive 'Argentina').

2 In accounting, Argentina still seems to be the leading Latin-American country, although Colombia also has a thriving and intellectually interested accounting community, and can boast such journals as *Contaduría* and *(Revista Internacional Legis de) Contabilidad & Auditoría.* Although the latter journal is not limited to Colombia, its head office is there. Mexico also deserves to be mentioned, particularly as an important source of Spanish translations of North American accounting texts.

3 For this purpose, we prepared a data-base in MS Excel, entering any accounting book or monograph registered in those libraries (between 1900 and 2003) in various libraries of Argentina. This may offer a survey of the evolution of accounting literature available at such libraries. The search yielded some 2,088 books registered under '*contabilidad*' (accounting), classified by 'author', 'title', 'editor', 'place of publication', 'year of publication or of subsequent editions or reprints', 'numbers of pages', 'title or topic' and 'libraries holding the item'. Though books on taxation were excluded, we found no less than 277 registered accounting books for the first half of the twentieth century, and 1,804 books for the second half. These figures include some re-editions published in other countries but do not include later editions by the same publisher. Upon request (wirth@udesa.edu.ar) we will supply an 'Appendix' that offers our data-base, arranged by date of publication. Initially the digital collective catalogue 'UNIRED' was utilized; it includes the catalogues of 77 Argentine libraries; but, subsequently we added other digital catalogues not included in UNIRED, totalizing 110 libraries.

4 Though we found two publications that may shed some light on the forces that helped to shape the accounting literature in Argentina. The first, Chirom (1985), dealt with the history of the Argentine accounting profession; the second, Fowler Newton (2001), investigated Argentine accounting institutions and fundamental accounting questions.

5 In the 1960s one could acquire the entire collection of all issues (up to this time) of this journal, bound in '19 volumes with more than 11,500 pages on specialized topics', such as accounting, social laws, taxation, cost accounting and a special section discussing recently published local and foreign books on those subjects.

6 For further information on Lopes de Sá, whose articles were also published in Brazil, Colombia, the United States, Italy, Spain and Portugal, consult his personal site www.lopesdesa.com.br

7 We classified the books on the basis of the subject indicated by its title.

18 Accounting in other countries: publications and research reports

1 By Mattessich (previously unpublished) – see Acknowledgements.

2 Due to the fact that Portuguese accounting literature covers not only Portugal but also Brazil, we use a common section for both of these countries, instead of the discussing Brazil under the Latin American countries.

19 The information economic perspective and the future of accounting

1 Mattessich (2006). I am grateful to Ms Pattarin Adithipyangkul (UBC) and Professor Christian Hofmann (University of Tübingen) for valuable suggestions to this chapter.

2 Also called 'information content perspective' (cf. Christensen and Demski 2003) and in the following shortly addressed as 'information perspective'.

3 Some of the following publications mentioned in Christensen and Feltham (2003) offer examples of establishing relations between this *analytical* endeavour and *empirical* aspects: Feltham *et al.* (1991), Clarkson and Simunic (1994), Datar *et al.* (1991), Begley and Feltham (1999, 2000) and Demski and Sappington (1999). Relevant literature also emphasizes the *empirical* implications of various aspects of the information perspectives, as, for example, Bernard (1995), Lee (1999), Liu and Ohlson (2000), Lo and Lys (2000), Richardson and Tinaikar (2004).

4 It may appear that the books by Ewert and Wagenhofer, despite their importance, have here received short shrift in comparison to those by Feltham or Demski (and their co-authors). But this is hardly the case; first, because a good deal of this chapter is devoted to the information perspective in general, and second, because Feltham and Demski, as the original pioneers of this approach, deserve to be discussed first.

5 Obviously, such a survey has to be selective and cannot include every past publication on this subject. This selectivity is admitted by the authors and is, for example, reflected by opting for the Grossman–Stiglitz rational expectations model (instead of the Hellwig–Verrechia model or the Kyle model that are only shortly mentioned).

6 Such a query is not only justified from the viewpoint of 'social constructivism' but at least as much from that of 'modern realism' (for details see Mattessich 2003).

7 'As the birth of academic *Betriebswirtschaftlehre* one may take the year 1898. In this year schools of higher commercial studies (later to be converted into universities) were opened in Aachen, Leipzig, Vienna, and St. Gallen ... . At first the discipline was called *Handelswissenschaft*. The designation *Betriebswirtschaftslehre*, suggested by Schmalenbach, became popular only after the First World War' (Busse von Colbe and Laßmann 1975: 8, translated). One might here also mention the Dutch attempt by Limperg and his colleagues to create their own brand of 'bedrijfseconomie'. And '[Zappa's] central work, *Tendenze nuove negli studi di ragoneria*, was published in 1927, and presented as a distinct approach the concept of economia aziendale' (Viganò 1998: 384).

8 The 'pragmatic approach' is somewhat related to the 'decision usefulness approach', though the former puts more stress on the need for exploring the long-neglected *means–end relations* of accounting and its normative nature.

9 I have personally experienced such situations in the hyper-inflation of the Greek *drachma* in 1943 when I did *cost accounting* (for a steel construction firm) as a front-engineer in Saloniki. At these times, the value of the currency decreased several times each day. But valuation still maintained its importance as a means of *accountability*, that is to say for rendering evidence of how much cash you received from the bank and how much you paid out to the work force. I think this corresponded precisely to what Christensen and Demski mean when alluding to the fact that in many situations values fulfil an information function rather than expressing a preference in the monetary sense.

10 I have been arguing for some time (see Mattessich 1995) and repeatedly that without a thorough research into *means–end relations*, the pragmatic programme has little chance to become truly scientific. And this may require a re-thinking of empirical research and, possibly, of the information perspective that would enable them to incorporate *means–end relations* into their factual and formal programme.

11 To avoid confusing the numeration of the subsequent methodological items with that of the theoretical items of section 19.5, the former numerals begin with an M, while the later begin with a T.

12 Although the notion of information has become ubiquitous, its meaning in different disciplines is different. In the economic sciences, information is *uncertainty-reducing* (or risk-reducing, also called non-enforcing) that, in turn, may lead to behavioural

changes. But in physics and biology, it is *change-enforcing* (cf. the changes that the information of a photon or a DNA molecule causes). Furthermore, one ought not to identify *information* (to which one may attribute a 'value') with *knowledge* (to which one may attribute a 'truth-value').

13 See note 11 for an explanation of the letter 'T' in front of the numerals in this section.

14 Bernard (1995: 745) even asserts the contrary: 'The Feltham–Ohlson approach [being now part of the information perspective] relies on a "measurement perspective", as opposed to the "information perspective"'.

15 This seems to say that a false (or manipulated) *signal* conveying incorrect information is also considered to have information content, provided it leads to some action.

16 For example, suppose that a decision maker is considering purchasing shares of a certain company for future dividends, and there are four possible states that can occur, say four possible levels of dividends (from the lowest dividend in state 1, to the highest in state 4). The decision maker may originally think that all states are equally likely to occur. The accounting information system provides information that helps the decision maker to determine how many shares to purchase. Suppose the decision maker believes the level of dividend is positively correlated with the level of net income announced. Also, suppose there are two possible signals (two levels of net income), y_1 and y_2, thereby signal y_1 (low net income) means the probabilities that states 3 or 4 will occur are zero and the probabilities that states 1 or 2 will occur are $\frac{1}{2}$ and $\frac{1}{2}$, respectively (and vice versa for signal y_2). Hence, after receiving signal y_1 and the induced change of belief that low levels of dividends are likely to occur, one may take appropriate action (e.g. buy smaller number of shares of the pertinent company).

17 For details about decision theory and its relation to information economics see Mattessich (1978: 197–248).

    To compare the value of different information systems, one first assumes a certain information system. Then one derives the optimal action (or strategy) for that system (i.e. a mapping between the signals received and the actions to take accordingly). Next, one calculates the expected utility resulting from implementing that optimal action plan (in case of risk neutrality, one calculates the expected value in monetary terms). Then one compares the maximized expected utility from the optimal action of each information system. In case the implementing of the information system causes no costs, the system with the higher maximized expected utility (given the optimal action plan) is attributed a higher value.

18 'First, the movement from the accounting income report to the underlying partition is, as usual, a decoding exercise. It presumes we understand the firm's fundamentals and its choice of accounting method' (Christensen and Demski 2003: 130).

19 An alternative definition of the 'clean surplus condition' is offered by Christensen and Demski (2003: 65); it holds when accounting income is taken to be the 'change in accounting value plus cash flow (to or from the owners, again)'.

    The most important feature of the clean surplus relation is that the sum total of a firm's future dividends equals the current book value plus the sum of all future periods' accounting net income – see Christensen and Feltham (2003: 280, equation (9.1)). This is not the case under 'dirty surplus accounting' (often used for such purposes of smoothing the income calculation of several periods).

20 The CST is considered to have created a paradigm-shift away from the empirical or market based accounting research (that began with such revolutionary papers as Ball and Brown 1968; Beaver 1968) to a more analytical approach somewhat closer to traditional accounting.

21 This problem can be categorized as a hidden information problem.

22 Note that if the manager is risk-neutral, and both the owner and the manager have symmetric information, the owner can sell or rent the business to the manager at the price corresponding to the profit that the manager would expect if working diligently.

23 I think it was the Nobel laureate Paul Samuelson who said (and I have to paraphrase) that all his mathematical endeavours are not enough, if he is unable to state its results in such a way that his wife can understand them. This I think is an important lesson that most disciples of the information perspective ought to take to heart. Indeed, one of the major obstacles of the American approach to the information perspective is the fact that most of its achievements are difficult to comprehend outside the context of its own esoteric conceptual framework – or so it seems.

24 The following argument has been added (in this private correspondence): 'Bounded rationality has no part to play in this world; yet even in chess – a very simple set-up compared to real-life decisions – the Grand Masters use heuristic strategies. The kind of formal modelling-based information economics analysed in these two books has not yet succeeded in building a bridge to the other branch of information economics associated with the works of Coase, Demsetz, Stigler and Williamson in economics, and Jensen, Watts and Zimmerman in accounting and finance'. Though in fairness to Christensen and Demski (2003), it has to be admitted that they do consider, or at least mention, the use of a 'representativeness heuristic' (on p. 437).

25 In the Preface to the recent Spanish version of *Accounting and Analytical Methods*, I pointed out that:

> Today I still regard the decision to provide a framework for a truly multi-valued bases, as one of the most important and farsighted strategies for accounting. By formulating the 'valuation axiom' (and other axioms concerning realization, classification, etc.) as a mere place-holder – thus shifting the valuation decision to the time when a specific means-end relation becomes obvious – I tried to create a more flexible and realistic meta-theory that is closer to what accounting practice aims to accomplish.
>
> (Mattessich 2002: xxii)

Although this decision has, on one side, been long ignored (e.g. by the disciples of information perspective) and, on the other side, repeatedly criticized, I am convinced it will ultimately prove to be a viable idea.

26 Other aspects of my framework fared better. They stimulated a considerable literature in America as well as in Europe (for details, see Balzer and Mattessich 2000: 99–101) and found response in specific quarters (e.g. in connection with the FASB conceptual framework – cf. Slaymaker 1996; Zeff 1982).

27 'We belabor this point [of game theory] because we feel that it is crucial that the social scientists recognize that game theory is not *descriptive*, but rather (conditionally) *normative*. It states neither how people do behave nor how they should behave in an absolute sense, but how they should behave if they wish to achieve certain ends' (Luce and Raiffa 1957: 63).

28 *String theory* is an entire group of competing physical theories each of which considers the ultimate building stones of the universe to be strings and loops of energy vibrating at different frequencies in a multi-dimensional space (up to 11 or 12 dimensions, depending on the particular sub-theory). Due to the very nature of those strings (e.g. their almost infinitely small size), many physicists (including at least one Nobel laureate) deem these strings beyond the empirically observable, now and ever (for details, see Greene 1999). As to the last aspect, the comparison with the information perspective of accounting may break down, as the *nature* of the latter does *not* preclude its propositions from empirical confirmation.

References

1 Introduction

Camfferman, K. (1997) 'An overview of recent Dutch-language publications in accounting, business and financial history in the Netherlands', *Accounting, Business and Financial History* 7 (March): 105–37.

Chatfield, M. and Vangermeersch, R. (eds) (1996) *The history of accounting: an international encyclopedia*, New York: Garland Publishing, Inc.

Colasse, B. (ed.) (2005) *Les grands auteurs en comptabilité* (The great authors of accounting), Paris: Corlet Éditions EMS.

Edwards, J.R. (ed.) (1994) *Twentieth-century accounting thinkers*, London: Routledge.

Gaffikin, M.J.R. and Aitken, M.J. (eds) (1982) *The development of accounting theory: significant contributors to accounting thought in the twentieth century*, New York: Garland Publishing, Inc.

Kovero, I. (1911) *Die Bewertung der Vermögensgegenstände in den Jahresbilanzen der privaten Unternehmungen mit besonderer Berücksichtigung der nicht realisierten Gewinne und Verluste* (Valuation of assets in financial statements of firms under special consideration of unrealized gains and losses), Berlin: C. Heymann (Japanese transl., Osaka: Nihon Shoseki, 1974).

Polak, N.J and Philips, R. (1926) *Grundzüge der Finanzierung mit Rücksicht auf die Kreditdauer* (Principles of financing under consideration of credit time). Berlin: Industrieverlag Spaeth & Linde.

Schmidt, F. (1921) *Die organische Bilanz im Rahmen der Wirtschaft* (The organic balance sheet an economic setting), 1st edn, Leipzig: C.A. Gloeckner Verlagsbuchhandlung (2nd edn, 1922, as *Die organische Tageswertbilanz*; 3rd edn, 1929; reprint edition Wiesbaden: Betriebswirtschaftlicher Verlag Dr Th. Gabler, 1953; Japanese translation, *Yukikan taishohyo gakusetsu*, Tokyo: Dobunkan Ltd, 1934).

Schneider, D. (2001) *Betriebswirtschaftlehre, Band 4: Geschichte und Methoden der Wirtschaftswissenschaft* (Business economics, Vol. 4: History and methods of economic science), Munich: R. Oldenbourg.

Seicht, G. (1970) *Die kapitaltheoretische Bilanz und die Entwicklung der Bilanztheorien* (The capital-theoretic balance sheet and the development of balance sheet theories), Berlin: Duncker & Humblot.

Sykora, G. (1949) *Die Konten- und Bilanztheorien – Eine betriebswitschaftlich-historische Untersuchung* (The accounts and balance sheet theories – an historical-economic investigation), Vienna: Industrieverlag Spaeth & Linde.

Tucker, J.J. (1996) 'Statistical sampling', in M. Chatfield and R. Vangermeersch eds, *The history of accounting – an international encyclopedia*, New York: Garland Publishing, Inc.: 557–61.

Vance, L.L. (1950) *Scientific methods for auditing*, Berkeley, CA: University of California Press.

Wyatt, A.R. (2004) 'Accounting professionalism – they just don't get it', *Accounting Horizons* 18 (1, March): 45–53.

2 The nineteenth century: an international survey

Alfieri, V. (1891) *La partita doppia applicata alle scritture delle antiche aziende mercantile veneziane* (The application of double-entry in the ancient Venetian merchant enterprises), Turin.

Amaduzzi, A. (1946) *Ragioneria generale* (General accounting), Vol. 1, Città di Castello e Bari.

Arnold, H.L. (1899) *The complete cost-keeper*, New York: The Engineering Magazine Press.

Augspurg G.D. (1852–55) *Die kaufmännische Buchführung* (Commercial bookkeeping), Parts I and II, Bremen.

Augspurg G.D. (1873) *Die Entwerthung des Geldes, die Steigerung der Preise und die Mittel zur Abhülfe* (nineteenth-century spelling/Devaluation of money, price increases and the means to remedy this), 2nd edn, Bremen (reprinted by Microfilm, CT: Yale University Library, 1992).

Australian Institute of Management (ed.) (1950) *Uniform accounting: a standard classification of accounts*, Sydney: AIFM.

Babbage, C. (1827) *On the economy of machinery and manufactures*, London: Knight (several later editions, as well as reprints, New York: Augustus M. Kelly, 1963).

Bachi, R. (1896) *I bilanci, le scritture e i rendiconti nella monarchia piemontese nel secolo XVIII* (Balance sheets, accounts and accountability in the Piemontese Monarchy of the eighteenth century), Turin.

Ballewski, D. (1877) *Die Kalkulation von Maschinenfabriken* (Cost accounting of engine factories), Magdeburg.

Barciński, A. (1833) *O rachunkowości kupieckiej* (Merchant accounting), Warsaw (later editions 1834 and 1835).

Barduzzi, L. (1880) *Sulla storia della ragioneria* (On the history of accounting), Treviglio.

Bariola, P. (1897) *Storia della ragioneria italiana* (History of Italian accounting), Milan.

Bastable, C.F. (1892) *Public Finance*, London: MacMillan.

Battaille, M. (1804) *Nouveau système de tenue de livres* (New bookkeeping system), Bruxelles.

Battersby, T. (1878) *The perfect double entry bookkeeper (abridged) and the perfect prime cost and profit demonstrator (on the departmental system), for iron and brass founders, machinists, engineers, shipbuilders, manufacturers, etc.*, Manchester.

Beigel, R. (1904) *Rechnungswesen und Buchführung der Römer* (Accounting and bookkeeping of the Romans), Karlsruhe: G. Braun.

Bellini, C. (1883) *La logismografia e le sue forme, ovvero la teorica delle scritture secondo il metodo razionale* (The logismography and its forms, or accounting theory on a rational basis), Reggio Emilia: Stab. Tipografia Artigianelli.

Bennet, J.A. (1820) *The American system of practical book-keeping adapted to the commerce of the United States*, New York.

Bentley, H.C. (1911) *The science of accounts: a presentation of the underlying principles of modern accounting*, 2nd printing, New York.

Bentley, H.C. and Leonard, R.S. (1934–35) *Bibliography of works of accounting by American authors*, 2 vols, Boston, MA: Harry Clark Bentley.

Berényi, P. (1894) *Paciolo Lukácsról. A könyvviteról irt legrégibb mú megjelenésének 400-ik évcfordulójára* (Luca Paciolo …), Sopron.

Berliner, M. (1887) 'Allgemeine Lehrsätze der kaufmännischen Buchhaltung' (General principles about commercial bookkeeping), *Kaufmännische Blätter*.

Berliner, M. (1893) *Schwierige Fälle der kaufmännischen Buchhaltung* (Difficult cases of commercial bookkeeping), Leipzig: Hahn.

Bes, K. (1894) *Leerboek von de theorie en de practijk van het dubbel boekhouden* (Textbook of the theory and practice of double-entry bookkeeping), Amsterdam.

Besta, F. (1891–1916) *La ragioneria* (Accounting theory), 3 vols, Milano: Vallardi (a one-volume work by this author, under the same title, was published in 1880).

Boer, G. (1966) 'Replacement cost: a historical look', *The Accounting Review* 41 (January): 92–7.

Boiko, M.K. (1898) *Luka Pachiolo – Traktat o schetaki i zapisyakh* (Luca Paciolo – his treatise and writings), Moscow.

Bonalumi, F. (1873) *Storia della genesis o dello svolgimento del pensiero logismografico* (History of the genesis or development of logismographic thought), San Remo: Tipografia Ligure.

Borkowsky, R. (1946) *Die Bilanztheorien und ihre wirtschaftlichen Grundlagen* (The balance sheet theories and their economic foundations), Zürich.

Bornaccini, G. (1818) *Idee teoriche e practiche di ragioneria e di doppia registrazione* (Theoretical and practical ideas on accounting and double-entry), Rimini: Marsoner and Grandi.

Bossi, M. (1917) 'Ragionieri e computitsti nello Stato Pontificio' (Accounts and bookkeepers in the Papal State), *Rivista Italiana di Ragioneria*: 43–50.

Bournesien, J. (1917) *Précis de comptabilité industrielle appliqué à la Métallurgie* (Outline of industrial accounting in the metallurgical industry), 2nd edn, Paris: Dunod et Pinat.

Brambilla, G. (1896) *Saggio di storia della ragioneria presso i popoli antichi* (Treatise of accounting history in antiquity), Milan.

Brenkman, N. (1882) *Nieuwe theorie van het dubbel boekhouden* (New theory of double-entry bookkeeping), Gravenhagen: J. Ykema.

Brief, R.P. (1965) 'Nineteenth century accounting error', *Journal of Accounting Research* 3 (1): 12–31.

Brief, R.P. (1966) 'The origin and evolution of nineteenth century asset accounting', *Business History Review* 40: 1–22.

Brief, R.P. (1967) 'A late nineteenth century contribution to the theory of depreciation', *Journal of Accounting Research* 5 (Spring): 27–38.

Brost, J.M. (1825) *Curso completo de teneduria de libros, o modo de llevarlos por partida doble* (Complete course of bookkeeping, or method of double-entry), Madrid: E. Aguado.

Brown, R. (ed.) (1905) *History of accounting and accountants*, Edinburgh.

Bruinier, J. (1908) *Selbskostenberechnung für Maschienfabriken* (Cost calculation for engine factories), Berlin.

Budny, S. (1826) *Buchalterya ulatwiona ułatwiona, czyli sposób utrzymywania ksiąg kupieckich pojedynczego i podwójnego rachunku podług metody Edmond Degrange Sr*

(Bookkeeping facilitated, or keeping accounts by single-entry and double-entry system according to Edmond Degrange Sr), Wilno.

Bunnell, S.H. (1911) 'Standardized factory expenses and cost', *Iron Age* (November 16).

Burrows, G.H. and Syme, B. (2000) 'Zero-based budgeting: origins and pioneers', *Abacus* 36 (June): 226–41.

Campi, V. (1879) *Il ragioniere – appunti storici* (The accountant – historical comments), Rome: Stamperia Reale.

Capparozzo, G. (1880) *Sull' origine della scrittura doppia* (On the origin of double-entry bookkeeping), Vincenza.

Castaño Diéguez, F. (1863) *La verdadera contabilidad, e sea curso completo, teórico y práctico de teneduria de libros por partida doble* (The true accounting, or complete theoretical and practical course on bookkeeping in double-entry) 15th edn (revised by the author's widow and son), Madrid: Viuda e Hija Fuentenebro.

Cazaux, L.F.G., de (1824) *De la comptabilité dans une entreprise industrielle et especialment dans une exploitation rurale* (On accounting in an industrial firm and especially in a rural enterprise), Toulouse.

Cazaux, L.F.G., de (1825) *Elements d'économie privée et publique* (Elements of private and public economics), vol. 2, Paris (its Chapter 3 has been translated as 'On the budget' in the *Journal of Accounting Research* 2, 1962: 264–5).

Ceccherelli, A. (1910) *La logismologia* (The logismology), Milan: F. Vallardi.

Cerboni, G. (1873) *Primi saggi di logismografia* (First exposition of logismography), Florence.

Cerboni, G. (1877) *Quadro di contabilità per le scritture in partita doppia della Ragioneria Generale dello Stato* (General accounting treatise for double-entry in government), Rome.

Cerboni, G. (1878) *Elenco cronologico delle opere di computisteria e ragioneria venute alla luce in Italia* (Chronological survey of the works in bookkeeping and accounting that came to light in Italy), Rome.

Cerboni, G. (1886–94) *La ragioneria scientifica e le sue relazioni con le discipline amministative e sociali* (Scientific accounting and its relations to the administrative and social disciplines), 2 vols, Rome: Loeschner.

Chatfield, M. (1974) *A history of accounting thought*, Hindsdale, IL: Dryden Press (2nd edn, Krieger, 1978).

Chatfield, M. (1996a) 'Capital maintenance', in M. Chatfield and R. Vangermeersch eds, *The history of accounting: an international encyclopedia*, New York: Garland Publishing, Inc.: 95–9.

Chatfield, M. (1996b) 'Jones, Edward Thomas (1867–1833)', in M. Chatfield and R. Vangermeersch eds, *The history of accounting: an international encyclopedia*, New York: Garland Publishing, Inc.: 355–6.

Chatfield, M. (1996c) 'Savary, Jacques (1622–1690)', in M. Chatfield and R. Vangermeersch eds, *The history of accounting: an international encyclopedia*, New York: Garland Publishing, Inc.: 514.

Chatfield, M. and Vangermeersch, R. (eds) (1996) *The history of accounting: an international encyclopedia*, New York: Garland Publishing, Inc.

Child, P. (1891) *Bookkeeping and Accounts*, London.

Christantes y Cañedo, M.V. (1838) *Tratado de cuenta y razon* (Treatise on accounting and [its] reasoning).

Christensen, J. and Demski, J.S. (1995) 'The classical foundations of "modern" costing', *Management Accounting Research* 6: 13–32.

Church, A.H. (1901–02) 'The proper distribution of establishment charges', *The Engineering Magazine* 21: 508–17, 725–34, 904–12; 22: 31–40, 231–40, 367–76 (reprinted in book form under the same title by the same magazine publisher, 1916).

Cilloni, A. (2005) 'La genesi della contabilità matriciale la "ragioneria scientifica" del secolo decimonono' (The genesis of matrix accounting and 'ragioneria scientifica' of the nineteenth century), *De Computis – Spanish Journal of Accounting History* (www.decomputis.org): 4–52.

Coenenberg, A.G. and Schoenfeld, H.-M. (1990) 'The development of managerial accounting in Germany: a historical analysis', *The Accounting Historians Journal* 17 (December): 95–112.

Coffy, R.P. (1832) *Tableau synoptique des principes généraux* (Synoptic table of general [accounting] principles), Paris.

Colasse, B. (1982) 'Review of the re-issue of Eugène Léautey and Adolphe Guilbault: '*La sciences des comptes mise à la porteé de tous*' (Paris: Libraire Comptable et Administrative, 1889, reprinted in New York: Arno Press, 1980)', *The Accounting Historians Journal* 9 (1): 127–9.

Colasse, B. (ed.) (2005) *Les grands auteurs en comptabilité* (The great authors of accounting), Paris: Corlet Éditions EMS.

Cooper, J.A. (1907) 'Professional ethics', *AAPA Year-Book*: 133–45 (reprinted in *Journal of Accountancy* 1907: 81–94).

Cooper, W.W. and Ijiri, Y. (1983) *Kohler's dictionary for accountants*, 5th edn, Englewood Cliffs, NJ: Prentice-Hall, Inc.

Courcelles-Seneuil, J.G. (1867) *Notions préliminaires de comptabilité* (Basic concepts of accounting), Paris: Hachette.

Courcelles-Seneuil, J.G. (1870) *Cours de comptabilité* (Accounting course), 2nd edn, Paris.

Crippa, L.G. (1838) *La scienza dei conti* (The science of accounts), Milano.

Cronhelm, F.W. (1818) *Double entry by single*, London: Longman, Hurst, Rees, Orme and Brown (reprinted New York: Arno Press, 1978).

D'Alvise, P. (1912) *Contabilità del Stato* (Government accounting), Florence.

D'Anastasio, N. (1803) *La scrittura doppia ridotta a scienza* (Double-entry accounting as science), Venice: Glichi.

Degos, J.-G. (2005) 'Eugène Léautey et Adolph Guilbault: la face mathémtique de la comptabilité' (Egène Léautey and Adolphe Guilbault: the mathematical aspect of classical accounting), in B. Colasse ed., *Les grand auteurs en comptabilité*, Paris: Éditions EMS: 55–71.

Degrange Sr, E. (1795) *La tenue des livres rendue facile* (Bookkeeping made easy), Paris.

Degrange Sr, E. (1801) *Supplément à la tenue des livres rendue facile, ou nouvelle méthode pour d'enseignement à l'usage des personnes destinées au commerce, comprenant trois méthodes: l'une pour simplifier la balance génerale, l'autre pour tenir les livres en double partie par le moyen d'un seul registre dont tous les comptes balancent journellement, etc.* (Supplement to bookkeeping made easy or the new instruction method for commerce personnel, consisting of three approaches: one to simplify the general balance sheet, the other for double-entry bookkeeping by means of a single table in which all accounts are balanced, etc.), Paris: Hocquart.

Delaporte, R. (1926) *La comptabilité d'après des principes rationnels basés sur les mouvements des valeurs et les grandeurs arithmétiques* (Accounting based on the rational principles of value flow and mathematical magnitudes), Paris.

Delorme, B. (1808) *Nouveau système de tenue des livres, d'aprés Jones* (New system of bookkeeping, according to Jones), Avignon.

Deplanque, L. (1842) *Tableau synoptique, théoretique, pratique* (Synoptic [accounting] table: theory and practice), Paris.

Dicksee, L.R. (1892) *Auditing: a practical manual for auditors*, London: Gee.

Dicksee, L.R. (1903) *Depreciation, reserves and reserve funds*, London: Gee (5th edn, New York: Arno Press, 1976).

Dicksee, L.R. (1905) *Auditing, authorized American edition*, edited by Robert H. Montgomery, New York: Arno Press (reprinted 1976).

Dicksee, L.R. (1911) *Advanced accounting*, London: Gee & Company (an earlier version of this book appeared by the same publisher in 1903) (reprinted New York: Arno Press, 1976).

Diemer, L.R. (1900) 'The commercial organisation of the machine shop', *The Engineering Magazine* 19 (3): 342–7; (4): 511–17; (5): 705–11; (6): 892–6.

Dumarchey, J. (1914) *Théorie positive de la comptabilité* (Positive accounting theory), Lyon: A. Rey (2nd edn, Lyon: Bibliothèque du Comptabilité, 1933).

Edwards, J.R. (1996) 'Financial accounting practice (1600–1970): continuity and change', in T.A. Lee, A. Bishop and R.H. Parker eds, *Accounting history from the Renaissance to the present*, New York: Garland Publishing, Inc.: 31–90.

Edwards, J.R. (ed.) (2000) *The history of accounting: critical perspectives on business and management*, 4 vols., London: Routledge.

Emerson, H. (1908–09) 'Efficiency as a basis for operation and wages', *The Engineering Magazine* 35 and 36.

Evans, A.H. (1911) *Cost keeping and scientific management*, New York: McGraw-Hill.

Fayol, H. (1916) *Administration industrielle et général*, Paris (first English translation 1925: *General and industrial Administration*; recent bilingual edition Toronto: York University, 1991).

Feigneaux (1827) *Cours théorique et pratique de tenues de livres en parties doubles, demonstré dans ses différentes applications a toutes les branches de commerce* (Theoretical and practical course of double-entry bookkeeping, demonstrated with application to all branches of commerce), Bruxelles: P.-M. De Vroom. (For the lack of initials to the author's name, see note 4 of text).

Ferrara, W.L. (1996) 'Break-even chart', in Michael Chatfield and Richard Vangermeersch eds, *The history of accounting: an international encyclopedia*, New York, NY: Garland Publishing, Inc.: 79–81.

Fischer, R. (1909) *Über die Grundlagen der Bilanzwerte* (On the foundations of balance sheet values), Leipzig: Veit & Co.

Fleischman, R.K. (1996) 'A History of management accounting through the 1960s', in T.A. Lee, A. Bishop and R.H. Parker eds, *Accounting history from the Renaissance to the present*, New York: Garland Publishing, Inc.: 119–42.

Fleischman, R.K. and Parker, L.D. (1991) 'British entrepreneurs and pre-industrial revolution evidence of cost management', *The Accounting Review* 66 (2): 361–75.

Fleming, J. (1854) *Bookkeeping by double entry*, Pittsburgh, PA: W.S. Haven.

Folsom, E.G. (1873) *The logic of accounts*, New York: A.S. Barnes & Company.

Forrester, D.R.F. (1998) *An invitation to accounting history*, Glasgow: Strathclyde Convergencies (also available at http://accfinweb.account.strath,ac.uk/df/aitha.html).

Foster, B.F. (1837) *A concise treatise of commercial book-keeping*, 2nd edn, Boston, MA: Perkins & Marvin.

Foster, B.F. (1852) *The origin and progress of bookkeeping: comprising an account of the works on this subject in the English language, from 1543 to 1852, with remarks, critical and historical*, London.

Fox, W.H. (1887) 'The present and future of accountancy', a lecture delivered before the Chartered Accountants' Students Society of London, London.

Fredersdorff, L.F. (1802) *Praktische Anleitung zu einer Eisenhütten-Oekonomie* (Practical guide to an iron-works business), Bad Pyrmont.

Fukuzawa, Y. (1873) *Choai-no-ho* (Textbook of bookkeeping – a Japanese version of the book by H.B. Bryant and D.H. Stratton, 1871), Tokyo: Keio-Gijuku.

Fulton, J.W. (1800) *British-Indian book-keeping*, London.

Galagan, A.M. (1912) *Noveishie italianskie formy dvoyinoi buchgalterii* (New Italian forms of double-entry bookkeeping), Moscow.

Galassi, G. (1980) 'Capital-income relations: a critical analysis', *Gino Zappa, founder of concern economics*, Bologna: Accademia Italiana di Economia Aziendàle: 25–49.

Garner, P. (1940) *The evolution of elementary cost accounting theories and techniques*, Austin, TX: Dissertation, University of Texas at Austin (2nd edn, 1954).

Garner, P. (1968) 'Highlights in the development of cost accounting', in M. Chatfield ed., *Contemporary studies in the evolution of accounting thought*, Belmont, CA: Sickenson Publishing Co.: 210–21.

Garcke, E. and Fells, J.M. (1887) *Factory accounts: their principles and practice*, New York: McGraw-Hill.

Garry, S. (1903) 'Factory costs', *The Accountant* (July 25): 954–61.

Geijsbeek, J.B. (1914) *Ancient double-entry bookkeeping* (reprinted Houston, TX: Scholars Book Co., 1974).

Gerisher, C. (1817) *Modern book-keeping, by double entry, adapted to commission business as it is conducted in the United States of America*, New York.

Ghidiglia, C. (1895) *Storia della ragioneria, nella voce ragioneria dell 'Encyclopedia di Ammistrazione, Industria e Commercio' diretta dal Cerboni* (History of accounting, in accounting terms from the 'Encyclopaedia of administration, industry and commerce' edited by Cerboni), Milan: Vallardi.

Gitti, V. (1878) *Sulla storia della ragioneria* (On the history of accounting), Turin.

Gneist, R. (1882) *Englische Verfassungsgeschichte* (History of the English Constitution), Berlin.

Godard, M. (1827) *Traité général et sommaire de la comptabilité commerciale* (General treatise and summary of commercial accounting), Paris.

Goddard, F.R. (1872–73) 'The balance sheets of manufacturing firms: their principles and theories viewed analytically', *Proceedings of the (January 1873) Meeting of the Cleveland Institution of Engineers*: 79–113.

Godfroid, H. (1864) *Cours de comptabilité industrielle et commerciale* (Course of industrial and commercial accounting), Charleroi.

Gomberg, L. (1897) *La science de la comptabilité* (The science of accounting), Genéve.

Gomberg, L. (1908) *Grundlegung der Verrechnungswissenschaft* (Foundations of accounting science), Leipzig: Duncker & Humblot (Japanese translation, *Kaikegaku hohoron*, Tokyo: Ganshodoshoten, 1944).

Gomberg, L. (1912) *L' économologique (scientifique comptable) et son histoire* (Scientific accounting and its history), Genéve: Société Général d'Impr.

Guilbault, A. (1865) *Traité de comptabilté et d'administation industrielle avec atlas de 40 planches* (Treatise of accounting and administration with 40 illustrations), Paris: Guillaumin.

Guo, D. (1982–89) *Zhongguo kuaiji shigao* (Accounting history of China), 2 vols, Bejing: China Finance and Economic Press.

Guo, D. (1996) 'China', in M. Chatfield and R. Vangermeersch eds, *The history of accounting: an international encyclopedia*, New York: Garland Publishing, Inc.: 122–3.

Gutiérrez, F., Larrinaga, C. and Nuñez, M. (2005) 'Cost and management accounting in pre-industrial revolution Spain', *Accounting Historians Journal* 32 (1, June): 111–48.

Hagers, J. (1903) *Bowstoffen voor de Geschiedenis von de Boekhouden in de Nederlanden* (Materials for the history of bookkeeping in the Netherlands), Rotterdam.

Hall, H.L.C. (1904) *Manufacturing costs*, Detroit, IL: The Bookkeeper Publishing Company.

Hamilton, R. (1777–79) *Introduction to merchandise*, London.

Hardcastle, J. (1891–92) 'Talks on accounts V', and 'Talks on accounts VI', *Business* 11 (3): 183–5, 12 (3): 48–9.

Hardcastle, J. (1897) 'Logismography', *Business* 17: 203–4, 235–6, 273–5, 303–4, 335–7, 366–70.

Haskins, C.W. (1904) *Business education and accountancy*, New York: Harper & Brothers (reprinted New York: Arno Press, 1978).

Hatfield, H.R. (1909) *Modern accounting: its principles and some of its problems*, New York: Appelton (reprinted in New York: Appelton, 1976; revised as *Accounting: its principles and problems*, New York: Appelton, 1927; reprint edition Lawrence, KS: Scholars Book Co., 1971).

Hautschl, F. (1840) *Anfangsgründe des einfachen und doppelten kaufmännischen Buchhaltens* (Principles of single- and double-entry commercial bookkeeping), Vienna.

Heina, F. (1925) 'Die Bewertung der Anlagen in Bergbaubilanzen einschließlich der steuerlichen Behandlung der Substanzverringerung' (Valuation in the balance sheets of the mining industry, including the taxation of diminishing capital), *Zeitschrift für handelswissenschaftliche Forschung*: 97–138.

Hernández Esteve, E. (1996) 'Spain', in M. Chatfield and R. Vangermeersch eds, *The history of accounting: an international encyclopedia*, New York: Garland Publishing, Inc.: 546–48.

Hernández Esteve, E. (1997) 'Historia de la contabilidad: pasado rumbo al futuro' (History of accounting: the past headed for the future), *Revista de Contabilidade e Comercio* 54 (No. 216, Portugal): 611–90.

Hernández Esteve, E. (1999) 'Literatura contable española 1522–1943', in Communicaciónes presentada en el congreso AECA (Zaragoza, Septiembre, 23–25).

Hess, H. (1903) 'Manufacturing, capital, costs, profits and dividends', *Engineering Magazine* (December): 367–???.

Heykoop, H.L. (1897) *Handelsonderwijs en Handeldverenigingen* (Commercial knowledge and commercial associations), Amsterdam.

Hügli, F. (1887) *Die Buchhaltungs-Systeme und Buchhaltungs-Formen* (Bookkeeping systems and forms of bookkeeping), Bern: K.J. Wyss (3rd edn, Berne, 1923; reprint edition Osaka: Nihon Shoseki, 1977 – see also Chapter 4).

Hügli, F. (1900) *Buchaltungsstudien* (Bookkeeping studies), Berne: K.J. Wyss.

Humbert, G. (1886) *Essai sur les finances et la comptabilité publique chez les Romains* (Essay on the public accounting of the Romans), Paris.

Isler, J. (1809) *Nouvelle mèthode Swiss pour tenire les livres en partie double* (The new Swiss method of double-entry bookkeeping), Bruxelles: Weissenbruch.

Jackson, J.G.C. (1956) 'The history and methods of exposition of double-entry bookkeeping in England', in A.C. Littleton and B.S. Yamey eds, *Studies in the history of accounting*, Homewood, IL: R.D. Irwin, Inc.

Jackson, W. (1801) *Book-keeping in the true Italian form of debtor and creditor by way of double entry*, Philadelphia.

Jaclot, J.-J. (1856) *La tenues des livres* (Bookkeeping), Paris: Maison.

Jäger, E.L. (1874) *Beiträge zur Geschichte der Doppelbuchhaltung* (Contributions to the history of double-entry bookkeeping), Stuttgart.

Jaruga, A. and Szychta, A. (1996) 'Poland', in M. Chatfield and R. Vangermeersch eds, *The history of accounting: an international encyclopedia*, New York: Garland Publishing, Inc.: 465–8.

Jeannin, M. (1829) *Traité de la comptabilité* (Treatise on accounting), Paris.

Johnson, H.T. (1972) 'Early cost accounting for internal management control: Lyman Mills in the 1850s', *Business History Review* (Winter): 466–74.

Johnson, H.T. (1981) 'Towards a new understanding of nineteenth-century cost accounting', *The Accounting Review* 56 (July): 510–18.

Johnson, H.T. and Kaplan, R.S. (1987) *Relevance lost: the rise and fall of management accounting*, Boston, MA: Harvard Business School Press.

Jones, E.(T.) (1796/1816) *English system of bookkeeping by single or double-entry*, Bristol: R. Edwards Publisher (American edition Cincinnati, OH: William A. Drew, Williams & Mason, 1816).

Jones, E.(T.) (1832) *The science of bookkeeping*, 3rd edn, London.

Jones, T. (1841) *Principles and practices of bookkeeping*, New York.

Käfer, K. (1966) *Theory of accounts in double-entry bookkeeping*, Urbana, IL: Center for International Education and Research in Accounting, University of Illinois.

Kaplan, R.S. (1984) 'The evolution of management accounting', *The Accounting Review* 59 (July): 390–418.

Kautilya, V.C. (*c*.300 BC) *Arthaśāstra*, Maghada (India).

Kempin, W. (1910a) *Vom Geist der Buchhaltung* (Of the spirit of bookkeeping), Cologne.

Kempin, W. (1910b) *Entwicklung der Bilanzlehre und der Abschluß Technik* (Development of the balance sheet and closing technique), Düsseldorf: Dobler Peltzer.

Kheil, K.P. (1896) *Über einige ältere Bearbeitungen zur Geschichte des Buchhaltungstraktates von Luca Pacioli – Ein Beitrag zur Geschichte der Buchhaltung* (On some older treatise on the history of the accounting tractatus by Luca Pacioli – a contribution to accounting history), Prague.

Kimizuka, Y. (1991) 'The evolution of Japanese cost accounting to 1945', in F.O. Graves ed., *The costing heritage: studies in honor of S. Paul Garner*, Harrisonburg, VA: The Academy of Accounting Historians (Monograph 6): 74–88.

Kirkman, M.M. (1880) *Railway expenditures: their extent, object, and economy*, Chicago: Railway Age.

Kittredge, A.O. (1896) 'Is bookkeeping progressive?', *Business* 16: 320–1.

Klein-Blenkers, F. (1992) *Die Hochschullehrer der Betriebswirtschaft in der Zeit von 1898–1955* (University teachers of business economics in the period from 1898–1955), Cologne: Wirtschaftsverlag Bachem.

Kreukniet, W. (1896) *Zur Theorie der doppelten Buchführung* (To the theory of double-entry bookkeeping), Rotterdam: Selbstverlage.

Kreukniet, W. (1898) *Handelsonderwijs* (Commercial knowledge), Rotterdam.

Kurzbauer, G. (1850) *Lehrbuch der kaufmännischen Buchhaltung* (Textbook of commercial bookkeeping), Vienna.

Lane, H.M. (1897) 'A method of determining selling price', *Transactions of the American Society of Mechanical Engineers*: 221–7.

Lanfranchi, G. (1891) *Le origini della partita doppia secondo il più recenti indagni* (The origins of double-entry according to recent research), Ferrara: Tipografia Sociale.

Lardner, D. (1850) *Railway economy: a treatise on the new art of transport*, London: Taylor, Walton & Maberly.

Léautey, E. (1897) *Traité des inventaires et des bilans* (Treatise on inventories and balance sheets), Paris: Libairie comptable et administrative.

Léautey, E. (1903) *L'unification de bilan des societés par actions* (The unification of the balance sheet of limited companies), Paris.

Léautey, E. and Guilbault, A. (1889) *La science des comptes mise à la portée de tous – traité théorique et pratique de comptabilité domestique, commerciale, industrielle, financière et agricole* (The science of accounts for everyone – a theoretical and practical treatise of domestic, commercial, industrial, financial and agricultural accounting), Paris: Guillaum (2nd edn, 1899; reprint edition New York: Arno Press, 1980, and Paris: Bibliothèque des science commerciales et économique, 1994).

Léautey, E. and Guilbault, A. (1895) *Principes généraux de comptabilité* (Principles of general accounting), Paris: Berger Levrault.

Lee, G.A. (1996) 'The tithe rent charge: a pioneer in income indexation', *Accounting, Business and Financial History* 6 (3): 301–13.

Lee, T.A. (1982) 'The early history of company financial reporting', *Company Financial Reporting*, New York: Van Nostrand: 79–98 (reproduced in Thomas A. Lee ed., *The closure of the accounting profession*, vol. 2, 1990: 125–44).

Lee, T.A. (1990) *The closure of the accounting profession*, 2 vols, New York: Garland Publishing, Inc.

Lee, T.A., Bishop, A. and Parker, R.H. (eds) (1996) *Accounting history from the Renaissance to the present*, New York: Garland Publishing, Inc.

Lehmann, K. (1895) *Die geschichtliche Entwicklung des Aktienrechts bis zum Code de Commerce* (The historical development of the law of limited companies until the Code of Commerce), Berlin (reprinted Frankfurt, 1968).

Leitner, F. (1905) *Die Selbstkostenrechnung industrieller Betriebe* (Cost calculation of industrial enterprises), Frankfurt.

Lemarchand, Y. and Parker, R.H. (eds) (1996) *Accounting in France /La Comptabilité en France*, New York: Garland Publishing, Inc.

Leuchs, J.M. (1806) *Theorie und Praxis des italienischen Buchhaltens und des Nürnberger Buchhaltens* (Theory and practice of Italian bookkeeping and Nuremberg bookkeeping), Nürnberg.

Lewis, J.S. (1896) *The commercial organisation of factories*, London: E.&F.N. Spon (reprint edition New York: Arno Press, 1978).

Leyerer, C. (1907) *Die Handlungsbücher der Republik Ragusa: Ein Beitrag zur Geschichte der Buchhaltung* (The commercial books of the Republic of Ragusa: a contribution to the history of bookkeeping), Trieste (later edition: Brünn: M. Trill, 1919; reprinted Osaka: Nihon Shoseki, 1975).

Lilienthal, J. (1907) *Fabrikorganisation, Fabrikbuchführung und Selbstkostenberechnung der Firma Loew & Co.* (Factory organization, factory accounting and cost calculation of the firm Ludwig Loewe & Co.), Berlin: J. Springer (later edition, same publisher, 1914).

Littleton, A.C. (1929) 'Die Entwicklung des Rechnungswesens in den Vereinigten Staaten' (The development of accounting in the United States), *Zeitschrift für Handelswissenschaft und Handlungspraxis* (later called *Die Betriebswirtschaft*): 101–6.

Littleton, A.C. (1933) *Accounting Evolution to 1900*, New York: American Institute Publishing (reprinted New York: Russell & Russell, 1966).

Littleton, A.C. and Yamey, B.S. (eds) (1956) *Studies in the history of accounting*, Homewood, IL: R.D. Irwin.

Löffelholz, J. (1970) 'Geschichte der Buchhaltung' (History of accounting), in E. Kosiol ed., *Handwörterbuch des Rechnungswesens*, Stuttgart: Poeschel Verlag: cols 583–90.

Longmuir, P. (1902) 'Recording and interpreting foundry costs', *Engineering Magazine* (September): 887.

López Toral, F. (1878) *Derechos y deberes reciprocos entre comerciantes y dependientes – Teneduria de libros por el método Logismográfico* (Reciprocal claims and obligations between merchants and employees – bookkeeping according to the logismographic method), Zaragoza: El Consultor del Dependiente de Comercio.

Löw, E. (1860) *Theorie des Rechnungswesens und systematische Anleitung zur Buchführung in Staats- Kommual- und Privathaushalte, nebst der Geschichte und Literature des Rechnungswesens* (Theory of accounting and systematic instruction to bookkeeping for government, communal and private entities, as well as the history and literature of accounting), Berlin.

McMillan, K.P. (1998) 'The Science of accounts: bookkeeping rooted in the ideal of science', *Accounting Historians Journal* 25 (December): 1–33 (Winner of the 1997 Vangermeersch Award).

MacNaughton, J. (1899) *Factory bookkeeping for paper mills*, London.

Magelhães Peixoto, A. (1910) *Tratado teorico e practico: Noções garaes de commercio – Contabilidade e escripturação commercial* (Theoretical and practical treatise of commercial concepts – business accounting and bookkeeping), 2nd rev. edn, Lisbon: Editores Verol & Ca.

Maisner, S.G. (1828) *Kurzer und deutlicher Unterricht für unbemittelte Handlungslehrlinge, Handlungsdiener und angehende Kaufleute* (Short and clear instructions of bookkeeping for impecunious apprentices, employees and young merchants), Berlin.

Malcolm, A. (1718) *Treatise on arithmetic and book-keeping*, Edinburgh.

Malot, A. (1841) *Elements de comptabilité rurale* (Elements of agricultural accounting), Paris.

Mann, J. (Sir) (1891) 'Notes on cost records: a neglected branch of accountancy', *The Accountant* (September 5).

Mann, J. (Sir) (1904) 'Cost records or factory accounting', in C. Lisle ed., *Encyclopaedia of accounting*, Vol. 2, Edinburgh.

Marchi, F. (1867) *I Cinquecontisti, ovvero la ingannevole teorica che viene insegnata negli Instituti Tecnici del Regno a fuori del Regno, intorno al sistema della scrittura a partita doppia, e nuovo saggio per la facile intelligenza e applicazione di quel sistema* (The 'five-accounts theorists' or the deceptive theory that is being taught at technical institutions in Italy and abroad ....), Prato: Giachetti.

Marshall, A. (1890) *Principles of economics*, Cambridge (later edition London: Macmillan & Co., 1956).

Massa, G. (1896) *Trattato di ragioneria teoretica* (Treatise on accounting theory), Milan: Office of The Accountant.

Massa, G. (1911) *Opere antiche di ragioneria* (Ancient accounting works), Milan.

Matheson, E. (1884) *The depreciation of factories*, London.

Mattessich, R. (1995) *Critique of accounting: examination of the foundations and normative structure of an applied discipline*, Westport, CT: Quorum Books.

Mattessich, R. (2000) *The beginnings of accounting and accounting thought: accounting praxis in the Middle East (8000 BC to 2000 BC) and accounting thought in India (300 BC and the Middle Ages)*, New York: Garland Publishing, Inc.

Mattessich, R. (2003a) 'Accounting research and researchers of the nineteenth century and the beginning of the twentieth century', *Accounting, Business and Financial History* 13 (2, July): 125–79.

Mattessich, R. (2003b) 'Accounting representation and the Onion Model of Reality: A comparison with Baudrillard's Orders of Simulacra and his Hyperreality', *Accounting, Organization and Society* 28 (5, July): 443–70 (Spanish translation in the form of a separate Monograph under the title *La Representación contable y el modelo de capas-cepola de la realidad: una comparación con las 'Ordenes de Simulacro' de Baudrillard y su 'Hiperrealidad'*, Asociación Española de Contabilidad y Administración de Empresas, Madrid: AECA, 2004).

Mattessich, R. and Galassi, G. (2000) 'History of the spreadsheet: from matrix accounting to budget simulation and computerization', in ASEPUC (and E. Hernández Esteve) eds, *Accounting and history: a selection of the papers presented at the 8th World Congress of Accounting*, Madrid: Asociación Española de Contabilidad y Administración de Empresas – Ediciones Gráficas Ortega: 203–32.

May, G.O. (1936) *Twenty-five years of accounting responsibility, 1911–1936*, vol. 2 (edited by B.C. Hunt), New York: American Institute Publishing Company.

Meithner, K. (ed.) (1933) *Die Bilanzen der Unternehmungen*, 2 vols (Accounting of enterprises), Vienna: Österreichischer Wirtschaftsverlag.

Melis, F. (1950) *Storia della ragioneria – Contributo alla conoscenza e interpretazione delle fonti più significative della storia economica* (History of accounting – contribution to the knowledge and interpretation of the most significant sources of economic history), Bologna: Cesare Zuffi.

Mepham, M.J. (1988) 'Matrix-based accounting: a comment', *Accounting and Business Research* 18 (72, Autumn): 375–8.

Metcalfe, H. (1885) *The cost of manufactures and the administration of workshops*, New York: John Wiley & Sons.

Mézière, L. (1862) *Comptabilité industrielle et manufacturier* (Industrial and manufacturing accounting), 5th edn, Paris.

Ministero per i Beni Cultural e Ambientali (1984) *Mostra bibliografica: Storia della ragioneria* (Bibliographical exhibition: history of accounting), Pisa: Biblioteca Universitaria.

Miranti, P.J. and Goodman, L. (1996) 'Railroad accounting (U.S.)', in M. Chatfield and R. Vangermeersch eds, *The History of accounting: an international encyclopedia*, New York: Garland Publishing, Inc: 487–91.

Mondini, E. (1882) *La ragioneria, storia e considerazioni da F. Marchi alla chiusura del II Congresso* (Accounting, the history of and comments on F. Marchi to the end of the Second Congress), Vol. 5 delle Monografie Contabili Amministrative, Como: Ostinelli.

Monginot, A. (1854) *Elements de comptabilité commercial, industrielle et agricole* (Elements of commercial, industrial and agricultural accounting), Paris.

Montgomery, R.H. (1912) *Auditing theory and pratice*, New York: Ronald Press Co. (with many subsequent editions).

Morgan, A. de (1846) *Elements of arithmetic*, 5th edn, London: Taylor and Walton (translation into Japanese and Chinese, Ekawa-Matchi: Shizukoa Shugakujo, 1872).

Most, K. (1996) 'Sombart, Werner (1863–1941)', in M. Chatfield and R. Vangermeersch eds, *The history of accounting: an international encyclopedia*, New York: Garland Publishing, Inc.: 541–2.

Moxter, A. (1984) *Bilanzlehre*, Band 1: *Einführung in die Bilanztheorie* (Accounting theory, Vol. 1: Introduction into the balance sheet theory), 3rd edn, Gabler Verlag (1st edn, 1974; 2nd edn, 1976).

Nicholson, J.L. (1909) *Factory organization and costs*, New York: Kohl Technical Publishing Co.

Nicklisch, H. (1903) *Handelsbilanz und Wirtschaftsbilanz* (Commercial and economic financial statements), Magdeburg: W. Ochs & Co. (reprinted Glashütten, Taunus: Detlev Auvermann, 1972).

Nicklisch, H. (1912) *Allgemeine kaufmännische Betriebslehre als Privatwirtschaftlehre des Handels und der Industrie* (General business theory as micro-economics of commerce and industry), Leipzig: C.E. Poeschel Verlag.

Nikitin, M. (2005) 'Edmond Degrange père et fils: de la tenue des livres à la comptabilité', in B. Colasse ed., *Les grand auteurs en comptabilité*, Paris: EMS: 21–38.

Nirmheim, H. (1895) *Das Handlungsbuch Vickos von Geldersen* (The merchant book of Vicos von Geldersen), Hamburg.

Norton, G.P. (1889) *Textile manufacturers' bookkeeping for the counting house, mill and warehouse*, London: Simpkin, Marshall, Hamilton & Kent (4th edn, in 1900).

Oliver Castañer, E. (1885) *La partida dobe – estudios teórico-practicos de contabilidad comercial al alcance de todos* (Double-entry – theoretical-practical studies of commercial accounting compcehensible to all), 2 vols, Barcelona: Tipografía y Casa Editorial Viuda de Luis Caso.

Ouvrat, P.C.L. (1835) *Éléments d'idéologie du commerce …* (Theoretical sights on business …), Bruxelles.

Pacioli, L. (1494) *Summa de arithmetica, geometria, proportioni et proportionalità.* Venice: *Paganino de Paganini.*

Packard, S.S. (1881) 'Philosophy in book-keeping', *The Book-Keeper* (December): 131–2.

Parker, R.H. (1965) 'Lower of cost and market in Britain and the United States: an historical survey', *Abacus* 1: 156–72 (reprinted with revisions in R.H. Parker and G.C. Harcourt eds, *Readings in the concepts and measurement of income*, London: Syndics of the Cambridge University Press, 1969: 239–58).

Parker, R.H. (1969) *Management accounting: an historical perspective*, London: Macmillan.

Parker, R.H. (1978) 'British man of account', *Abacus* 15 (1): 53–65.

Paton, W.A. (1922) *Accounting theory: with special reference to the corporate enterprise*, New York: Ronald Press (reprinted Chicago, IL: Accounting Studies Press).

Payen, A. (1817) *Essai sur la tenue des livres d'un manufacturier* (Essay on bookkeeping for a manufacturer), Paris.

Penndorf, B. (1913) *Geschichte der Buchhaltung in Deutschland* (History of bookkeeping in Germany), Leipzig: G.A. Gloeckner Verlag.

Penndorf, B. (1933) 'Die historische Entwicklung der Bilanz' (The historical development of the balance sheet) in K. Meithner ed., *Die Bilanzen der Unternehmungen*, Vol. 1, Vienna: Österreichischer Wirtschaftsverlag: 125–47.

Pholmann, J.H. (1838) *Lärobok uti enkl och dubbla bokhalleriet* (Text on double-entry bookkeeping), Stockholm: N.H. Thomson.

Pisani, E. (1880) *La statmografia applicata alle aziende private* (The statmography applied to private firms), Modica: Piccilto and Antoci.

Pixley, F.W. (1881) *Auditors: their duties and responsibilities under the Joint-Stock*

Companies Act and the Friendly Societies and Industrial and Provident Societies Acts, London: Good (reprinted New York: Arno Press, 1976).

Pollins, H. (1956) 'Aspects of railway accounting before 1868', in A.C. Littleton and B.S. Yamey eds, *Studies in the history of accounting*, Homewood, IL: Richard D. Irwin: 332–55.

Previts, G.J. and Merino, B.D. (1979) *A history of accounting in America*, New York: John Wiley and Sons, Inc. (2nd edn, as: *A History of accountancy in the United States: the cultural significance of accounting*, Columbus, OH: Ohio State University Press, 1998).

Puteani, J. von (1818) *Grundsätze des allgemeinen Rechnungswesens mit Anwendung auf Landwirtschaft, Handlung und Staatswirtschaft* (Foundations of general accounting with applications to agriculture, commerce and the state economy), Vienna.

Queulin (1840) *L'inventaire perpétuel* (Perpetual inventory), Paris. (For the lack of initials to the author's name, see note 4 of text).

Quiney, J.S. (1817/39) *Comptabilité général ou livre de raison* (General accounting or the book of [its] reasoning), Paris.

Rau, K.H. (1822) *Grundriß der Kameralwissenschaft* (Foundations of cameral science), Heidelberg.

Rehm, H. (1914) *Die Bilanzen der Aktiengesellschaften, ...* (The balance sheets of the limited companies ...), 2nd edn, Berlin: J. Schweitzer-A. Sellier (1st edn, 1903).

Reymondin, G. (1909) *Bibliographie méthodologique des Ouvrages en langue française parus de 1543 à 1908 sur la Science des comptes* (Methodological bibliography of works on the science of accounting in French language, appearing between 1534 and 1908) Paris: Société Académique de Comptabilité.

Richard, J. (2005) 'Herman Veit Simon, Eugen Schmalenbach et Fritz Schmidt: "les trios S" de la pensée comptable allemande' (Herman Veit Simon, Eugen Schmalenbach and Fritz Schmidt: the three 'S's of German accounting thought), in B. Colasse ed., *Les grands auteurs en comptabilité*, Paris: Édirions EMS.

Richardson, A. (ed.) (2002) 'Special issue on international accounting history', *Accounting and Business Research* (March issue).

Rieger, W. (1928) *Einführung in die Privatwirtschaftslehre* (Introduction to business theory), Nürnberg: Kirsche Co.

Rigobon, P. (1892) *La contabilità di Stato nella republica di Firenze e nel Gran Ducato di Toscana* (Government accounting in the Republic of Florence and in the Grand Duchy of Toscana), Agrigento: Salvatore Montes.

Riva, M. (1875) *Dell'insufficienza dell'attuale computisteria di Stato e della necessità di riformarla secondo i principi della Logismografia* (On the insufficiency of present-day government accounting and the need to reform it according to the principles of logismography), Rome: Artero & Co.

Roover, F.E. de (1937) 'Cost accounting in the sixteenth century', *The Accounting Review* 12: 226–37 (reprinted in D. Solomons ed., *Studies in costing*, London: Sweet & Maxwell: 53–71).

Rossi, G. (1880) *Saggi di critica logismografica* (Treatise on the critics of logismography), Reggio Emilia: Tipografia Artigianelli.

Rossi, G. (1889) *Lo scacchiere anglo-normanno e la scrittura in partita doppia a forma di scacchiera* (The Anglo-Norman Exchequer and the double-entry chessboard), Roma: Botta.

Rossi, G. (1896) *La computisteria dei Romani e l'invenzione della scrittura doppia a proposito di un opinione dello storico G.B. Niebuhr* (Roman accounting and the invention of double-entry in reference to an opinion of the historian G.B. Niebuhr), Rome.

Rossi, G. (1901) *Teorica matematica della scrittura doppia* (Mathematical theory of double-entry bookkeeping), Genova.

Sá, R. de (1912) *Verificações e examen de escripta* (Verification and auditing), Lisbon: Livraria Ferin-Editora.

Salvador y Aznar, F. (1846) *Manual de teneduria de libros por partida doble, aplicada al comercio, la industria, empresas, banco fondos provinciales y oficinas del estado* (Manual of double-entry bookkeeping, applied to commerce, industry, enterprises, bank funds of provincial and state offices), Madrid (15th edn, Madrid Hernando, 1894).

Sanguinetti, A. (1880) *Ricomposizioni logismografiche* (Logismographical revisions), Turin: Artistico-Librario.

Savary, J. (1675) *Le parfait négoçiant* (The perfect merchant), Paris.

Scandellari, A. (1803) *Sull'importanza della professione di computista* (On the importance of the accounting profession), Bologna: Marsigli ai Celestini.

Schär, J.F. (1890) *Versuch einer wissenschaftlichen Behandlung der Buchhaltung* (Attempt of a scientific treatment of bookkeeping), Basel.

Schär, J.F. (1911) *Allgemeine Handelsbetriebslehre, 1. Teil* (General commercial economics, Part 1), Leipzig: G.A. Gloeckner.

Schär, J.F. (1914) *Buchhaltung und Bilanz* (Bookkeeping and financial statements), 2nd edn, Berlin (many editions, later by J.F. Schär and W. Prion, Berlin: Julius Springer, 1932).

Scherpf, P. (1955) *Der Kontenrahmen* (The master chart of accounts), Munich: Max Huber Verlag.

Schiller, R. (1895) 'Vier Jahrhunderte Buchhaltung: Ein Rückblick auf die Entwicklung der Buchhaltung seit des Erscheinen von Lucas Paciolis "Summa de Arithmetica" im Jahre 1495' (Four centuries of bookkeeping: retrospect on the development of bookkeeping since the appearance of Luca Pacioli's 'Summa Arithmetica' in the year 1494), *Kaufmännische Zeitschrift* (special edition for nos 2–4).

Schmalenbach, E. (1899) 'Buchführung und Kalkulation im Fabrikgeschäft' (Bookkeeping and calculation in manufacturing), *Deutsche Metallindustriezeitung*.

Schmalenbach, E. (1908–09) 'Über Verrechnungspreise' (On transfer prices), *Zeitschrift für handelswissenschaftliche Forschung* 3: 165–85.

Schmalenbach, E. (1911–12) 'Die Privatwirtschaftlehre als Kunstlehre' (Commercial economics as applied science), *Zeitschrift für handelswissenschaftliche Forschung* 6: 304–15.

Schmalenbach, E. (1919) 'Grundlagen der dynamischen Bilanztheorie' (Foundations of dynamic accounting), *Zeitschrift für handelswissenschaftliche Forschung* 13: 1–60, 65–101 (published in book form as *Grundlagen dynamische Bilanzlehre*, Leipzig, 1920; later as *Dynamische Bilanz*, 3rd edn, Leipzig, 1925; English translation as *Dynamic Accounting*, London: Gee and Co., 1959) – see also Chapter 14 (for Japanese translations).

Schneider, D. (1981) *Geschichte betriebswirtschaftlicher Theorie* (History of the theory of business-economics), Munich: Oldenbourg Verlag (3rd edn, 1987). (This book has been greatly expanded to a work of four volumes under the title *Betriebswirtschaftslehre*, Vol. 1: Grundlagen, 1993; Vol. 2: *Rechnungswesen*, 1994; Vol. 3: *Theorie der Unternehmung* and Vol. 4: see below: *Geschichte und Methoden der Wirtschaftswissenschaft*, 2001).

Schneider, D. (2001) *Betriebswirtschaftlehre, Band 4: Geschichte und Methoden der Wirtschaftswissenschaft* (Business economics, Vol. 4: History and methods of economic science), Munich: R. Oldenbourg.

Schrott, J. (1852) *Der österreichische Staatsrechnungsabschluß* (The closing of books in Austrian cameralistic accounting), Vienna.

Schrott, J. (1871) *Lehrbuch der allgemeinen Verrechnungswissenschaft* (Textbook of general accounting science), 2nd edn, Vienna.

Schrott, J. (1882) *Die Logismographie* (Logismography), Vienna.

Seicht, G. (1970) *Die kapitaltheoretische Bilanz und die Entwicklung der Bilanztheorien* (The capital-theoretic balance sheet and the development of balance sheet theories), Berlin: Duncker & Humblot.

Seicht, G. (1977) *Die Grenzbetrachtung in der Entwicklung des betrieblichen Rechnungswesens* (Marginal consideration in the development of cost accounting), Berlin: Duncker Humblot.

Serra, L. (1999) *Storia della ragioneria italiana* (History of Italian accounting), Milan: Giuffrè Edittore.

Sganzini, C. (1908) *Die realistische Theorie der Doppelten Buchhaltung* (The realistic theory of double-entry), St Gallen, Switzerland: Städtische Handelsakademie St Gallen.

Shand, A.A. (1873) *Ginko-boki-seiho* (Complete treatise of bank bookkeeping, translated from English), Tokyo.

Shimono, N. (1895) *Boki seiri* (Complete treatise on bookkeeping), Tokyo.

Sibuet, S. (1867) *Traité théorique et practique de tenue des livres* (Treatise of theoretical and practical bookkeeping), Paris: Mulo.

Sieveking, H. (1898) 'Aus Genueser Rechnungs- und Steuerbüchern' (From accounting and taxation books of Genua), *Sitzungsberichte der Akademie der Wissenschaften in Wien*, Vienna: AdW.

Sillén, O. (1929) 'Zur Geschichte der Bewertungslehre in Schweden' (On the history of valuation theory in Sweden), *Zeitschrift für Handelswissenschaft und Handelspraxis*, (later called *Betriebswirtschaft*): 118–26.

Simon, F.N. (1832) *Méthode complete de la tenue des livres* (Complete method of keeping books), Paris.

Simon, H.V. (1899) *Die Bilanzen der Aktiengesellschaften und Kommanditgesellschaften auf Aktien* (Financial statements of limited and private companies), 3rd edn, Berlin.

Smith, E.J. (1899) *The new trades combination movement*, London, UK.

Sokolov, J.V. and Kovalev, V.V. (1996) 'Russia', in M. Chatfield and R. Vangermeersch eds, *The history of accounting: an international encyclopedia*, New York: Garland Publishing, Inc.

Solomons, D. (ed.) (1968a) *Studies in cost analysis*, London: Sweet & Maxwell.

Solomons, D. (1968b) 'The historical development of costing', in D. Solomons ed., *Studies in cost analysis*, London: Sweet & Maxwell: 3–49 (reprinted in Thomas E. Lee ed., *The closure of the accounting profession*, Vol. 2, New York: Garland Publishing, Inc., 1990: 36–82).

Sombart, W. (1902) *Der moderne Kapitalismus: Historisch-systematische Darstellung des gesamteuropäischen Wirtschaftslebens von seinen Anfängen bis zur Gegenwart* (The modern capitalism: historic-systematic treatment of the entire European economic activity from its beginnings to the present), Munich: Duncker & Homblot (later editions 1919, 1922, 1928, etc.).

Sonnenfels, J. von (1804) *Grundsätze der Policey, Handlung und Finanzen* (Foundations of policy, commerce and finances), 3 vols, Vienna (1st edn, Vienna: 1763–67).

Soulé, G. (1881) *Soulé's new science and practice of accounts*, Paris (7th edn, 1903).

Soulé, G. (1905) *Soulé's manual of auditing*, 6th edn, Paris.

Sprague, C.E. (1880) 'The algebra of accounts', *The Bookkeeper* (20 July): 2–4, (17 August): 35–5, 44, (31 August): 51–3.

Sprague, C.E. (1898) 'Logismography I', (and) 'Logismography II', *Accountics* 2 (4 and 5): 73–5, 117–21.

Sprague, C.E. (1904) *The accountancy of investment*, New York: Business Publishing Co. (rev. edn: Ronald Press, 1914).

Sprague, C.E. (1907–08) 'The philosophy of accounts', *Journal of Accountancy* (January 1907 to January 1908) (reprinted as *The philosophy of accounts*, 4th edn, New York: Ronald Press 1918).

Sterret, J. (1907) 'Professional ethics', *AAPA Year-Book 1907*: 108–33 (reprinted in *Journal of Accountancy*, October 1907: 407–31).

Stephens, H. (1735) *Italian book-keeping reduced into art*, London.

Strachan, W. (1909) *Cost accounting*, London: Stevens & Haynes.

Strieder, J. (1905) 'Die Inventur der Firma Fugger aus dem Jahre 1527' (The inventory of the firm of Fugger from the year 1527), *Zeitschrift für die gesamten Staatswissenschaften* XVII (Vienna).

Swarte, V. de (1885) 'Essai sur l'histoire de la comptabilité publique en France' (Essay on the history of public accounting in France), *Journal de la Société Statistique de Paris* (August).

Sykora, G. (1949) *Die Konten und Bilanztheorien – Eine betriebswirtschaftlich-historische Untersuchung* (Theory of accounts and financial statements – an economic-historical investigation), Vienna: Industrieverlag Spaeth & Linde.

Synnerberg, L.N. (1813) *Svensk contorist eller berakning af utrikes orters mynt, matt och vigt, al pari emot Sverige* (Swedish accounting …), Götheborg.

Szumlaski, A. (1865) *Buchhalterya i rachunkowosc gospodarska: oparta na zasadach podwójnego rachunku i zastosowana do gospodarstw wiesjskich wszelkiego rodzaju …, z dolaczeniem wzorów rejestrów folwarcznych kassowych …* (Economic transactions of bookkeeping and accounting based on the principles of double-entry and adapted to all kinds of rural enterprises including accounting models for agriculture …), Warsaw: J. Ungra.

Taylor, F.W. (1895) 'A piece rate system', *Transactions of the American Society of Mechanical Engineers* 7: 856–83.

Taylor, F.W. (1911) *The principles of scientific management*, New York: Harper & Brothers.

Thaer, A.D. (1809) *Grundsätze der rationellen Landwirtschaft* (Principles of rational farming), Berlin.

Tofani, A. (1910) *Alcune ricerche storiche sull'ufficio e la professione di ragioniere a Firenze al tempo della Republica e Studi affini* (Some historical research on the status and the profession of accountants in Florence during the Republic and related studies), Florence.

Tolkmitt, H. (1894) *Grundriß der Fabrik-Geschäftsführung* (Outline of factory accounting), Leipzig: F. Hirt & Sohn.

Tomkins, C. and Groves, R. (1983) 'The everyday accountant and researching his reality', *Accounting, Organizations and Society* 8 (4): 361–74.

Töndury, H. (1933) 'Die Grundlagen der betrieblichen Verrechnung' (The foundations of managerial accounting), in K. Meithner ed., *Die Bilanzen der Unternehmungen*, Vol. I, Vienna: Österreichischer Wirtschaftsverlag: 95–122.

Tonzig, A. (1857–59) *Trattato della scienza della contabltà dello Stato* (Treatise of the science of government accounting), Venice: Tipografia Narotvich.

Tonzig, A. (1879) *Stratagemmi della logismografia ed analisi critica del suo ordigno*

(Devices of logismography and critical analysis of its functioning), Padova: Tipografia Sachetto.

Towne, H.R. (1885–86) 'The engineer as an economist', *Transactions of the Society of American Engineers* 7 (2): 428–32.

Vangermeersch, R. (1988) *Alexander Hamilton Church – a man of ideas for all seasons*, New York: Garland Publishing, Inc.

Vangermeersch, R. (1996) 'Standard costing', in M. Chatfield and R. Vangermeersch eds, *The history of accounting: an international encyclopedia*, New York: Garland Publishing, Inc.: 550–3.

Vannier, H. (1840) 'Première notions du commerce et de la comptabilité' (Basic concepts of business and accounting), Paris: Colas.

Vianello, V. (1895) 'Antichi codici e libri di computisteria e di scrittura doppia' (Old codes and accounting books of double-entry), *Rivista di amministrazione e contabilità* (May).

Vickery, A. (1998) *The Gentlemen's daughter: women's lives in Georgian England*, London: Yale University Press.

Villa, F. (1840–41) *La contabilità applicata alle amministrazioni private e pubbliche* (Accounting applied to business and public administration), 2 vols, Milan: Angelo Monti.

Vitale, F. (1896) *Storia della ragioneria in Italia dalle origini ai nostri tempi* (History of accounting in Italy from its origin to the present time), Aversa.

Volmer, J.G.Ch. and Rijnberk, C. van (1896) *Paciolo's Verhandeling over Koopmansboekholding in het Nederlandsch overgebracht* (Paciolo's treatise on commercial bookkeeping in the Netherlands' tradition), Rotterdam.

Walb, E. (1926) *Die Erfolgsrechnung privater und öffentlicher Betriebe* (Income accounts of private and public enterprises), Berlin: Spaeth und Linde.

Weber, F.B. (1819) *Entwurf einer Encyklopädie und Methodologie der Kameralwissenschaften* (Sketch of an encyclopaedia and methodology of cameralistic), Berlin.

Whitmore, J. (1908) Shoe factory cost accounts, *Journal of Accountancy* 4 (1): 12–25.

Willame, J.F. (1842) *Nouveau système de comptabilité commerciale* (A New system of accounting), Bruxelle.

Wilmowski, B. von (1895) 'Die Abschreibung für Abnutzung von Gebäuden, Maschinen, Betriebsgerätschaften, u.s.w'. (The depreciation for the usage of buildings, machines, implements, etc.), in *Verwaltungsarchiv – Zeitschrift für Verwaltungsrecht und Verwaltungsgerichtsbarkeit* 3 (June): 366–82.

Wilmowski, B. von (1896) *Das Preußische Einkommensteuergesetz* (The Prussian Income Tax Law), Breslau (2nd edn, 1907).

Woolf, A.H. (1910) *A short history of accountants and accountancy*, London: Gee (also 1912 and 1913, and reprint in co-authorship with Alexander Cosmo, 1970 and 1983).

Worthington, B. (1895) *Professional accountants: an historical sketch*, London.

Wysocki, K. von (1965) 'Kameralistisches Rechnungswesen' (Cameralistic accounting), Stuttgart: Poeschel Verlag.

Yamey, B.S. (1956) 'Edward Jones and the reform of book-keeping, 1795–1810' in A.C. Littleton and B.S. Yamey eds, *Studies in the history of accounting*, Homewood, IL: Richard D. Irwin, Inc.

Yamey, B.S, (1964) 'Accounting and the rise of capitalism: further notes on a theme by Sombart', *Journal of Accounting Research* 2 (Autumn): 117–36.

Zanten, L. van (1890) *Leerboek voor de theorie en de practijk van hat boekhouden naar de nieuwe theorie van N. Brenkman* (Textbook of the theory and practise of bookkeeping according to the new theory of N. Brenkman), Rotterdam/Groningen: Noordhoff.

Zeff, S.A. (1978) *A critical examination of the orientation postulate in accounting with particular attention to its historical development*, New York: Arno Press.

Ziegler, J. (1904) *Beitrag zur Begründung der zwei Kontenreihen in der Buchhaltung* (Contribution to the justification of the two-account series in bookkeeping), in Kayser ed., Separatabdruck aus dem *Jahrbuch der Export-Akademie des k.k. österreichischen Handelsmuseums*, 1902–03.

3 German language area: first half of the twentieth century

Batardon, L. (1911) *La tenue des livres sur feuillets mobiles* (Bookkeeping on loose-leave accounts), Brussels (reprinted in 1918, Paris: H. Dunod and E. Pinat; and later in 1941).

Baxter, W.T. (1949) 'Accountants and the inflation', *Proceedings of the Statistical Society* 9 (February): 1–19.

Baxter, W.T. (1967) 'Accounting values: sales price versus replacement cost', *Journal of Accounting Research* 5 (2): 208–14.

Baxter, W.T. (1975) *Accounting values and inflation*, New York: McGraw-Hill, Inc.

Becker, W. (1914–15) 'Die einheitliche Deutung der Buchungsvorgänge' (The uniform interpretation of accounting entries), *Zeitschrift für Handelswissenschaft und Handelspraxis* 7 (11): 309–10.

Beigel, R. (1904) *Rechnungswesen und Buchführung der Römer* (Accounting and bookkeeping of the Romans), Karlsruhe: G. Braun.

Beisel, K. (1936) *Neuzeitliche Gestaltung des industriellen Rechnungswesens* (Modern formation of industrial accounting), Leipzig: G.A. Gloeckner.

Berliner, M. (1909) *Schwierige Fälle und allgemeine Lehrsätze der kaufmännischen Buchhaltung* (Difficult cases and general principles of commercial bookkeeping), 3rd edn, Hannover: Hahnsche Buchhandlung.

Berliner, M. (1911) *Buchhaltungs- und Bilanzlehre (Theoretischer Teil)* (Theory of bookkeeping and accounting, Vol. II), 3rd edn, Hannover: Hahnsche Buchhandlung (5th and 6th edns, 1920).

Beste, T. (1924) *Die Verrechnungspreise in der Selbstkostenrechnung* (Transfer prices in cost accounting), Berlin: Springer Verlag.

Beste, T. (1930) *Die kurzfristige Erfolgsrechnung* (Short-term income calculation), Leipzig: G.A. Gloeckner (reprinted Cologne: Westdeutscher Verlag, 1962).

Borkowsky, R. (1946) *Die Bilanztheorien und ihre wirtschaftlichen Grundlagen* (Balance sheet theories and their economic foundations), Zürich: E. Lang.

Borkowsky, R. (1949) 'Die Entwicklung der Verrechnungslehre in der Schweiz' (The development of accounting theory in Switzerland), *Industrielle Organisation* 18: 18–22.

Boßhardt, L. (1948) *Leistungsmäßige Kostenrechnung* (Efficient cost accounting), Zürich: Winter.

Bouffier, W. (1932) 'Die Bedeutung des Gleichlaufes der Betriebstätigkeit für die Bewertung' (The influence of an even production on valuation), *Zeitschrift für betriebswirtschaft*: 731–40.

Brunier, J. (1908) *Selbstkostenrechnung für Maschinenfabriken* (Cost accounting for engine factories), Berlin.

Buhl, H. (1929a) *Die geschichtlich begründete Kontentheorie, ein Beitrag zur Geschichte der doppelten Buchhaltung* (The historically based theory of accounts – a contribution to the history of double-entry), Stuttgart: C.E. Poeschel (reprinted in 1929).

Buhl, H. (1929b) 'Anfänge der kameralistischen Buchhaltung – Ein Beitrag zur Geschichte des Rechnungswesens' (Beginnings of cameralistic bookkeeping – a contribution to the history of accounting) and Anfänge der kameralistischen Buchhaltung in Deutschland – Ein weiterer Beitrag zur Geschichte des Rechnungswesens (Beginnings of cameralistic bookkeeping – a further contribution to the history of accounting), *Zeitschrift für Handelswissenschaft und Handelspraxis* 22: 111–16, 211–14.

Buhl, H. (1929c) *Buchhaltungsformen und Verfahren* (Forms of bookkeeping and procedures), Karlsruhe, i. B.: G. Braun.

Busse von Colbe, W. (1996) 'Accounting and business economics tradition in Germany', *European Accounting Review* 5 (3): 413–34.

Calmes, A. (1906) *Die Buchführung, die Selbstkostenrechnung und die Organisation industrieller Betriebe* (Bookkeeping, cost accounting and the organization of industrial plants), St Gallen, Switzerland: Honegger.

Calmes, A. (1910) *Lehrbuch der kaufmännischen Buchhaltung* (Text of commercial bookkeeping), Leipzig: G.A. Gloeckner.

Calmes, A. (1920) *Das industrielle Rechnungswesen* (Industrial accounting), Leipzig: G.A. Gloeckner.

Calmes, A. (1922) *Die Fabrikbuchhaltung* (Factory bookkeeping), Leipzig: G.A. Gloeckner.

Canning, J.B. (1929) *Economics of accountancy, a critical analysis of accounting theory*, New York: Ronald Press.

Carrasco Díaz, D., Hernández Esteve, E. and Mattessich, R. (2004) 'Accounting publications and research in Spain: first half of the twentieth century', presented at the 2003 Congress of the European Accounting Association in Seville (abbreviated version published in the *Review of Accounting and Finance* 3 (3, 2004): 40–58).

Chatfield, M. and Vangermeersch, R. (eds) (1996) *The history of accounting: an international encyclopedia*, New York: Garland Publishing, Inc.

Ciompa, P. (1910) *Grundrisse einer Ökonometrie und die auf der Nationalökonomie aufgebaute natürliche Theorie der Buchhaltung* (Outlines of an 'econometrics' and a natural theory of bookkeeping based on macro-economics), Lemberg: Poeschel Verlag.

Clarke, F.L. and Dean, G.W. (1986) 'Schmidts Betriebswirtschaft Theory' (Schmidts business economics), *Abacus* 22 (September): 65–102 (including two appendices of which Appendix B contains an English translation of K. Schwantag's paper on: 'The academic work of Fritz Schmidt' – see below, under Schwantag 1951).

Clarke, F.L. and Dean, G.W. (1989) 'Conjectures on the influence of the 1920s in Betriebswirtschaftslehre on Henry Sweeney's stabilized accounting', *Accounting and Business Research* 19 (76): 291–304.

Clarke, F.L. and Dean, G.W. (1990) *Contributions of Limperg and Schmidt to the replacement cost debate in the 1920s*, New York: Garland Publishing, Inc.

Clarke, F.L. and Dean, G.W. (1996) 'Schmidt, Julius August Fritz (1882–1950)', in M. Chatfield and R. Vangermeersch eds, *The history of accounting: an international encyclopedia*, New York: Garland Publishing, Inc.: 16–18.

Coenenberg, A.G. and Schoenfeld, H.-M.W. (1990) 'The development of managerial accounting in Germany: a historical analysis', *The Accounting Historians Journal* 17 (December): 95–112.

Coutre, W. le (1921) *Die kaufmännische Bilanz als Grundlage der Besteuerung – Ein Leitfaden für Kaufleute, Juristen und Steuerbeamte* (The commercial balance sheet as taxation basis – a guide for merchants, jurists and officers of public revenue), Berlin: Haude & Spennersche Buchhandlung.

Coutre, W. le (1924) *Grundzüge der Bilanzkunde – Eine totale Bilanzlehre* (Outlines of teaching financial statements – a total accounting theory), Leipzig: G.A. Gloeckner (later edition 1927).

Coutre, W. le (1926) *Praxis der Bilanzkritik* (Practice of the analysis of financial statements), 2 vols, Berlin: Spaeth & Linde.

Coutre, W. le (1939) 'Die Bilanztheorien' (The balance sheet theories), in H. Nicklisch ed., *Handwörterbuch der Betriebswirtschaft* (Encyclopaedic handbook of business economics), Vol. 1, 2nd edn, Stuttgart: Poeschel Verlag: cols 1054–78.

Coutre, W. le (1949) *Einrichtung und Umstellung der Buchhaltung nach dem Kontenrahmen* (Installation and change of bookkeeping on the basis of the master-chart of accounts), 3rd edn, Stuttgart: Muth.

Coutre, W. le (1956) 'Bilanztheorien' (Balance sheet theories), in H. Seischab and K. Schwantag eds, *Handwörterbuch der Betriebswirtschaft* (Encyclopaedic handbook of business economics), Vol. 1, 3rd edn, Stuttgart: Poeschel Verlag (1st edn, 1926): cols 1154–75.

Degos, J.-G. and Mattessich, R. (2003) 'Accounting research in the French language area: the first half of the twentieth century', presented at the 2003 Conference of the European Accounting Association, Seville (under same title, abbreviated version published in the *Review of Accounting and Finance* 2 (4): 112–30).

Dietrich, J.R. (panel chairman), Demski, J.S., Dopuch, N., Mattessich, R.V., Ohlson, J.A. and Zeff, S.A. (2002) 'Accounting research', in D.L. Jensen ed., *Challenge and achievement in accounting during the twentieth century* (A Conference Celebrating the Fiftieth Anniversary of the Accounting Hall of Fame), Columbus, OH: AHF, Ohio State University, Fisher College of Business: 64–83.

Dörfel, F. (1925) *Die Goldbilanz in Österreich* (The gold balance sheet in Austria), Vienna: Spaeth & Linde.

Dorn, G. (1976) 'Geschichte der Kostenrechnung' (History of cost accounting), in E. Kosiol, K. Chmielewicz and M. Schweitzer eds, *Handwörterbuch des Rechnungswesens* (Lexicon of accounting), 2nd edn, Stuttgart: Poeschel: cols 630–7.

Edwards, E.O. and Bell, P.W. (1961) *The theory and measurement of business income*, Berkeley, CA: University of California Press.

Enderlen, E. (1936) *Nominale und reale Bilanz* (Nominal and real balance sheet), Stuttgart: W. Kohlhammer.

Engel, D. (1965) *Wilhelm Riegers Theorie des 'heutigen Wertes' und sein System der Privatwirtschaftslehre* (Wilhelm Riegers 'current value' and his system of commercial theory), Berlin: Duncker & Humblot.

Engels, W. (1962) *Betriebswirtschaftliche Bewertungslehre im Licht der Entscheidungstheorie* (Valuation theory of business economics in the light of decision theory), Cologne: Westdeutscher Verlag.

Fäs, E. (1913) *Die Berücksichtigung der Wertminderungen des stehenden Kapitals in den Jahresbilanzen der Erwerbswirtschaft* (Consideration of value decline of standing capital in business), Tübingen: H. Laupp.

Financial Accounting Standards Board (FASB) (1979) 'Financial reporting and changing prices', *Statement of financial accounting standards*, No. 33, Stamford, CT: FASB.

Fischer, J., Hess, O. and Seebauer, G. (1939) *Buchführung und Kostenrechnung* (Bookkeeping and cost accounting), Leipzig: G.A. Gloeckner (2nd edn, 1942).

Fischer, R. (1905–08) *Die Bilanzwerte, was sie sind und was sie nicht sind* (Balance sheet values, what they are and what they are not), Berlin: Dieterichsche Verlagsbuchhandlung (Part I, 1905; Part II, 1908).

Fischer, R. (1909) *Über die Grundlagen der Bilanzwerte* (On the Foundations of Balance Sheet Values), Leipzig: Veit & Co.

Forrester, D.A.R. (1987) *Eugen Schmalenbach and German Business Economics*, Glasgow: University of Strathclyde (doctoral dissertation; re-published in New York: Garland Publishing, Inc., 1993).

Funk, H. (1937) *Industrielles Rechnungswesen* (Industrial accounting), Berlin.

Galassi, G. and Mattessich, R. (2004) 'Italian accounting research in the first half of the twentieth century', presented at the 2003 Congress of the European Accounting Association in Seville (abbreviated version published in 2004 in the *Review of Accounting and Finance* 3 (2): 61–82).

Geldmacher, E. (1914) 'Bilanzmäßige Buchführung' (Accounting for balance sheet presentation), *Deutsche Handelsschullehrer-Zeitung* 11: 393–6; 401–4; 425–9.

Geldmacher, E. (1920) 'Bilanzsorgen' (Trouble with balance sheets), *Industrie- und Handelszeitung* 1 (57–63): 364, 378, 392, 398, 406.

Geldmacher, E. (1923) *Wirtschaftsunruhe und Bilanz – Teil I: Grundlagen und Technik der bilanzmäßigen Erfolgsrechnung* (Economic unrest and the balance sheet – Part I: Foundation and balance sheet oriented income determination), Berlin: Springer Verlag.

Geldmacher, E. (1929) 'Grundbegriffe und systematischer Grundriß des betrieblichen Rechnungswesens' (Basic concepts and systematic outline of business accounting), *Zeitschrift für handelswissenschaftliche Forschung* 23: 1–27.

Gerstner, P. (1921) *Bilanz-Analyse* (Balance sheet analysis), Berlin: Paschke Verlag.

Gomberg, L. (1897) *La science de la comptabilité* (The science of accounting), Genéve.

Gomberg, L. (1908) *Grundlegung der Verrechnungswissenschaft* (Foundations of accounting science), Leipzig: Duncker & Humblot (Japanese translation, *Kaikegaku hohoron*, Tokyo: Ganshodoshoten, 1944).

Gomberg, L. (1912) *L' économologique (scientifique comptable) et son histoire* (Scientific accounting and its history), Genéve: Société Général d'Impr.

Gomberg, L. (1927) *Eine geometrische Darstellung der Buchhaltungsmethoden* (A geometrical presentation of bookkeeping methods), Berlin: L. Weiß.

Graves, O.F. (1989) 'Walter Mahlbergs valuation theory: an anomaly in the development of inflation accounting', *Abacus* 25 (1, March): 7–25.

Graves, O.F., Dean, G.W. and Clarke, F.L. (eds) (1989) *Schmalenbach's dynamic accounting and price-level adjustments: an economic consequence explanation*, New York: Garland Publishing, Inc.

Green, D.R. (1960) 'A moral to the direct cost controversy', *The Journal of Business* 33: 218–26.

Großmann, H. (1921) *Einführung in das System der Buchhaltung auf Grundlage der Bilanz* (Introduction to bookkeeping on the basis of financial statements), Berlin: Spaeth & Linde (3rd rev. edn, 1927).

Großmann, H. (1922) *Grundlagen der Bilanzlehre mit Hinweise auf das Steuerrecht* (Foundations of accounting with reference to the taxation law), Berlin: Spaeth & Linde.

Großmann, H. (1925a) 'Die Abschreibungen in ihrer Beziehung zu den betriebswirtschaftlich wichtigsten Werttypen' (Depreciation in relation to the most important types of assets), *Zeitschrift für Betriebswirtschaft* 2: 10–12.

Großmann, H. (1925b) *Die Abschreibungen vom Standpunkt der Unternehmung,* --

insbesondere ihre Bedeutung als Kostenfaktor (Depreciations from the viewpoint of the firm, particularly its significance as cost factor), Berlin: Spaeth & Linde.

Gümbel, R. (1966) 'Die Bilanztheorie Wilhelm Riegers – Eine kritische Analyse' (Wilhelm Rieger's balance sheet analysis – a critical analysis), *Zeitschrift für Betriebswirtschaft* 36: 333–67.

Gutenberg, E. (1926) 'Die Struktur der Bilanzwerte' (The structure of balance sheet values), *Zeitschrift für Betriebswirtschaft* 3: 497–511; 598–614.

Gutenberg, E. (1933) 'Die Bilanzen der Genossenschaften' (Financial statements of cooperatives), in K. Meithner ed., *Die Bilanzen der Unternehmungen*, Vol. 2, Vienna: Österreichischer Wirtschaftsverlag: 78–122.

Haar, A. (1925) 'Die Geldwertveränderung und ihr Einfluß auf die transitorischen Posten und Antizipationen' (The change of money value and its influence on transitory items and anticipations), *Zeitschrift für Betriebswirtschaft* 2: 353–66, 414–33.

Haar, A. (1926) *Das Wesen der tansitorischen Posten und Antizipationen und ihre Behandlung in der Buchhaltung* (On the essence of transitory items and anticipations and their treatment in accounting), Vienna: Selbstverlag (reprint version in K. Meithner edition, *Bilanzen der Unternehmung*, Vol. 1, Vienna: Österreichischer Wirtschaftsverlag, 1933: 341–78).

Hasenack, W. (1930) 'Budgeteinführung und Betriebspsyche' (Introduction of the budget and industrial psychology), *Annalen der Betriebswirtschaft* 3 (4): 381–98.

Hasenack, W. (1933a) 'Krisenbilanz und Tageswertidee' (Accounting for times of crises and the idea of current value), *Zeitschrift für Handelswissenschaft und Handelspraxis* 26: 55–61.

Hasenack, W. (1933b) 'Die Vorschau als Element der kaufmännischen Budgetrechnung' (Anticipation as element of commercial budgeting), *Zeitschrift für Betriebswirtschaft* 10: 11–27.

Hatheyer, E. (1933) 'Reservierungen (Bereitstellungen) und Wertberichtigungen (Abschreibungen)' (Reservations and value adjustments as depreciations), in K. Meithner ed., *Die Bilanzen der Unternehmungen* (Financial Statements of Firms), Vol. 1, Vienna: Österreichischer Wirtschaftsverlag: 281–340.

Hax, K. (1926) *Der Gewinnbegriff in der Betriebswirtschaftslehre* (The income concept in business economics), Leipzig: G.A. Gloeckner.

Hax, K. (1948) Die Gesamtbewertung von Unternehmungen (The total evaluation of firms), *Betriebswirtschaftliche Beiträge*: 97–138.

Heina, F. (1925) 'Die Bewertung der Anlagen in Bergbaubilanzen einschließlich der steuerlichen Behandlung der Substanzverringerung' (Valuation in the balance sheets of the mining industry, including the taxation of diminishing capital), *Zeitschrift für handelswissenschaftliche Forschung* 19: 97–138.

Heinen, E. (1959) *Betriebswirtschaftliche Kostenlehre*, (Cost theory of business economics), Vol. 1, 1st edn, Wiesbaden: Gabler Verlag.

Heinen, E. (1965) *Betriebswirtschaftliche Kostenlehre* (Cost theory of business economics), Vol. 1, 2nd edn, Wiesbaden: Gabler Verlag (6th edn, 1983).

Henzel, F. (1939) *Die Kostenrechnung in der gewerblichen Wirtschaft*, (Cost accounting in small-sized firms), 1st edn, Stuttgart: Muthsche Verlagsbuchhandlung (2nd edn, 1950).

Henzel, F. (1941) *Kosten und Leistung* (Cost and performance), 2nd edn, Bühl-Baden: Konkordia A.G.

Hernández Esteve, E. (1997) 'Historia de la contabilidad: pasado rumbo al futuro', *Revista de Contabilidade e Comercio* 54 (216, Portugal): 611–90.

Hintner, O. (1930) 'Die Riegersche Bilanzlehre, ein Vergleich mit Gesetzgebung und Rechtssprechung' (Riegers balance sheet theory, a comparison with the law and legal pronouncements), *Zeitschrift für das gesamte Handelsrecht und Konkursrecht* 4 (23): 228–69.

Holzer, H. (1936) *Zur Axiomatik der Buchführungs- und Bilanztheorie* (To the axiomatic of bookkeeping), Stuttgart: Kohlhammer.

Hügli, F. (1900) *Buchaltungsstudien* (Bookkeeping studies), Berne: K.J. Wyss.

Hügli, F. (1923) *Die Buchhaltungs-Systeme und Buchhaltungs-Formen* (Bookkeeping systems and forms of bookkeeping), 3rd edn, Berne (for 1st edn, see Chapter 2; reprint edition Osaka: Nihon Shoseki, 1977).

Illetschko, L. (1947) *Der ÖKW-Kontenrahmen* (The master-chart of accounts of the Austrian Committee for Efficiency), Vienna: Ruf.

Illetschko, L. (1950) *Die Wirtschaftsrechnung als Leistungsrechnung* (Cost accounting as efficiency test), Vol. 3, Vienna: Betriebswirtschaftliche Schriftenreihe.

Isaac, A. (1921) *Über das Selbstkostenproblem im Bankbetrieb* (On the problem of cost accounting in banking), Leipzig: G.A. Gloeckner (reprinted or translated, Tokyo: Yushodo, 1980).

Isaac, A. (1923) *Die Entwicklung der wissenschaftlichen Betriebswirtschaftslehre in Deutschland seit 1898* (The development of scientific business economics in Germany since 1898), Berlin: Spaeth & Linde.

Isaac, A. (1924) 'Anschaffungswertbilanz und Tageswertbilanz' (The balance sheet at acquisition costs vs. current values), *Zeitschrift für Betriebswirtschaft* 1: 246–65.

Isaac, A. (1929) *Bilanzen und Bilanztheorien* (Accounting and accounting theories), Wiesbaden: Gabler (later edition 1958).

Isaac, A. (1950) 'Fritz Schmidt, Forscher und Persönlichkeit' (Fritz Schmidt, researcher and personality), *Zeitschrift für handelswissenschaftliche Forschung*, New Series 2: 93–6.

Jores, A. (1928) 'Die Riegersche Bilanzauffassung' (Riegers balance sheet theory), *Archiv für Revisions- und Treuhandwesen* 24: 522–7.

Käfer, K. (1946) 'Zur Bewertung der Unternehmung als Ganzes' (On the evaluation of the firm as an entity), in *Rechnungsführung in Unternehmung und Staatsverwaltung, Festgabe für Otto Juzi*, Zürich: Schulthess & Co. A.G.: 71–98 (reprinted in C. Helbling (ed.) (1966) *Zur Bewertung der Unternehmung – Zum 98. Geburtstag von Karl Käfer*, Zürich: Verlag Schellenberg: 13–42).

Käfer, K. (1947) *Kontenrahmen für Gewerbsbetriebe* (Master-chart of accounts for industrial firms), Bern: Paul Haupt.

Käfer, K. (1966) *Theory of accounts in double-entry bookkeeping*, Urbana, IL: Center for International Education and Research in Accounting, University of Illinois.

Kalveram, W. (1922) *Die kaufmännische Rechnungsführung unter dem Einfluß der Geldentwertung* (Commercial accounting under the influence of inflation), Berlin: Spaeth & Linde.

Kalveram, W. (1951) *Kostenrechnung* (Cost accounting), Wiesbaden: Gabler Verlag.

Kast, G. von (1920) 'Falsche Bilanzierungsmethoden seit der Valutenentwertung' (Wrong accounting methods since devaluation), *Berliner Tageblatt* (September 16).

Kempin, W. (1910a) *Vom Geist der Buchhaltung* (Of the spirit of bookkeeping), Cologne: Verlag Faust.

Kempin, W. (1910b) *Entwicklung der Bilanzlehre und der Abschlußtechnik* (Development of the balance sheet and closing technique), Düsseldorf: Dobler Peltzer.

Kerschagl, R. (1933) 'Volkswirtschaftliche und betriebswirtschaftliche Bilanzen' (Macro-economic and commercial balance sheets), in K. Meithner edition, *Die Bilanzen der Unternehmungen*, Vol. 1, Vienna: Österreichischer Wirtschaftsverlag: 14–28.

Kheil, C.P. (1906) *Benedetto Cotrugli Ragueo* (same in translation), Vienna: Manz.

Kheil, C.P. (1908) *Über amerikanische Buchführung – Ein Beitrag zur Geschichte der französischen Buchhaltungs-Literatur des XIX. Jahrhunderts* (On 'American' book-keeping: a contribution to French bookkeeping literature of the nineteenth century), Vienna: Manz.

Klein, L. (1920) 'Einfluß der sinkenden Kaufkraft des Geldes auf Kalkulation, Bilanz und Steuer' (The effect of declining purchasing power on costing, the balance sheet and taxes), *Zeitschrift für Handelswissenschaft und Handelspraxis* 13 (1): 1–5.

Kohlmann, L. (1902/05 or 1903–1906) 'Die Theorie unserer doppelten Buchhaltung' (Theory of our double-entry bookkeeping), *Zeitschrift für Buchhaltung* 11 and 14 (or 12–15?).

Kori, O. von (1968a) 'Verzeichnis der Arbeiten von Eugen Schmalenbach' (List of the works by Eugen Schmalenbach), *Zeitschrift für betriebswirtschaftliche Forschung* 20: 473–88.

Kori, O. von (1968b) 'Besprechungen zur Dynamischen Bilanz' (Reviews of dynamic accounting), *Zeitschrift für betriebswirtschaftliche Forschung* 26: 485–7.

Kosiol, E. (1927) 'Kostenauflösung und Proportionaler Satz' (Cost determination and marginal principle), *Zeitschrift für handelswissenschaftliche Forschung* 21: 345–58.

Kosiol, E. (1931) 'Elastizität der Kalkulation und Preispolitik' (Elasticity of costing and pricing policy), *Zeitschrift für Betriebswirtschaft* 8: 740–6.

Kosiol, E. (1944a) *Bilanzreform und Einheitsbilanz* (Accounting reform and the uniform balance sheet), 2nd edn, Reichenberg (2nd printing, Wiesbaden, 1949; 3rd edn, Berlin: Deutscher Betriebswirteverlag, 1999).

Kosiol, E. (1944b) 'Der pagatorische Character des Anschaffungswertes in der Bilanz' (The pagatoric nature of the acquisition cost in the balance sheet), *Zeitschrift für handelswissenschaftliche Forschung* 37/38: 47–54.

Kosiol, E. (1944c) *Betriebsbuchhaltung und Kontenrahmen* (Cost accounting and master chart of accounts), Wiesbaden: Gabler Verlag.

Kosiol, E. (1948) 'Der neue Schweizer Kontenrahmen für Gewerbetreibende' (The new Swiss master-chart of accounts for trades people), *Die Wirtschaftsprüfung* 1 (5): 14–25.

Kosiol, E. (1956) 'Pagatorische Bilanz' (Financial statements based on cash flows), *Lexikon des kaufmännischen Rechnungswesens*, 2nd edn, Stuttgart: C.E. Poeschel Verlag.

Kosiol, E. (1962) *Kontenrahmen und Kontenpläne der Unternehmung* (Master charts and charts of accounts of firms), Essen: W. Girardet.

Kosiol, E. (ed.) (1970) *Handwörterbuch des Rechnungswesens* (Lexicon of account-ing), Stuttgart: C.E. Poeschel Verlag (4th edn by H.-U. Küpper and A. Wagenhofer, 2002).

Kovero, I. (1912) *Die Bewertung der Vermögensgegenstände in den Jahresbilanzen der privaten Unternehmungen mit besonderer Berücksichtigung der nichtrealisierten Gewinne und Verluste* (Valuation of assets in balance sheets under special considera-tion of unrealized gains and losses), 2nd edn, Berlin: C. Heymann (doctoral disserta-tion, defended at the Imperial Alexander University in Helsinki – 1st edn, 1911; reprinted in Osaka: Nihon Shoseki, 1974).

Kruk, M., Potthof, E. and Sieben, G. (1984) *Eugen Schmalenbach, Der Mann, Sein Werk, Die Wirkung* (Eugen Schmalenbach, the man, his work, its effect), Stuttgart: Schäffer.

Küpper, H.-U. and Mattessich, R. (2005) 'Twentieth-century accounting research in the German language area', *Accounting, Business and Financial History* (Special issue on *German Accounting*) 15 (3): 345–410.

Küpper, H.-U. and Wagenhofer, A. (eds) (2002) *Handwörterbuch Unternehmensrechnung und Controlling* (Lexicon for accounting and controlling), 4th edn, Stuttgart: Schäffer-Poeschel Verlag.

Lehmann, K. (1895/1968) *Die geschichtliche Entwicklung des Aktienrechts bis zum Code de Commerce* (The historical development of the Law of Limited Companies until the Code of Commerce), Berlin: Heymann (reprinted Frankfurt: Sauer und Auvermann, 1968) – see also Chapter 2.

Lehmann, K. (1898–1904) *Recht der Aktiengesellschaft* (Law of the limited company), Vol. 1 (1898), Vol. 2 (1904), Berlin: Heymann.

Lehmann, M.R. (1921) *Das Rechnungswesen auf Bleihütten: Eine wirtschaftswissenschaftliche Studie* (Accounting in lead foundries: an economic study), Berlin: Emil Ebering (reprint edition Tokyo: Yoshudo, 1980).

Lehmann, M.R. (1925) *Die industrielle Kalkulation* (Industrial cost accounting), Berlin: Spaeth & Linde (4th edn, 1951).

Lehmann, M.R. (1928) Der formelle und materielle Inhalt der Bilanz (The formal and material content of the balance sheet), *Zeitschrift für Handelswissenschaft und Handelspraxis* 21: 253–64; 278–88.

Lehmann, W. (1932) *Die dynamische Bilanz Schmalenbachs – Darstellung, Vertiefung und Weiterentwicklung* (Dynamic accounting of Schmalenbach – presentation, analysis and development), Wiesbaden: Gabler Verlag (later edn, 1963).

Leitner, F. (1905) *Die Selbstkostenrechnung industrieller Betriebe* (Cost calculation of industrial enterprise), Frankfurt: J.D. Sauerländer (2nd edn, 1906; 9th edn, 1930; reprinted Osaka: Nihon-Soseki, 1990).

Leitner, F. (1922a) *Grundriß der Buchhaltungs- und Bilanzkunde* (Outline of bookkeeping and accounting theory), 2 vols, 5th edn, Berlin: G. Reimer (1st edn, 1909).

Leitner, F. (1922b) *Privatwirtschaftslehre der Unternehmung* (Business theory), 4th edn, Berlin: de Gruyter.

Leitner, F. (1923) *Finanz- und Preispolitik bei sinkendem Geldwert* (Financial and pricing policy under declining purchasing power), Frankfurt a.M.: J.D. Sauerländer (Sonderabdruck).

Leitner, F. (1924) *Der Übergang zur Goldbilanz und Goldbuchführung nach den neuesten Bestimmungen* (The transition to the gold-balance sheet and gold-bookkeeping according to the newest regulations), Berlin: C. Heymann.

Leitner, F. (1929) *Bilanztechnik und Bilanzkritik* (Technique and critique of the balance sheets), 8th edn, Berlin: de Gruyter.

Leyerer, C. (1907) *Die Handlungsbücher der Republik Ragusa: Ein Beitrag zur Geschichte der Buchhaltung* (The commercial books of the Republic of Ragusa: a contribution to the history of bookkeeping), Trieste (later edition Brünn: M. Trill, 1919; reprinted Osaka: Nihon Shoseki, 1975).

Leyerer, C. (1919) *Theorie der Geschichte der Buchhaltung* (Theory of bookkeeping history), Brünn: M. Trill.

Leyerer, C. (1922) 'Die historische Entwicklung der Buchhaltung' (The historical development of bookkeeping), *Zeitschrift für handelswissenschaftliche Forschung* 16: 123–52.

Lilienthal, J. (1907) *Fabrikorganisation, Fabrikbuchführung und Selbstkostenberechnung der Firma Loew & Co.* (Factory organization, factory accounting and cost calculation of the firm Loew & Co.), Berlin: Springer Verlag (2nd edn, 1914).

Limperg Jr, T. (1917) 'Kostprijsberekening en kostprijsbeholding' (Current value accounting and current value representation), *Accountancy* 15: 42–4, 55–8, 87–9, 104–5.

Lion, M. (1928a) 'Die dynamische Bilanz und die Grundlagen der Bilanzlehre' (Dynamic accounting and the foundations of balance sheet theory), *Zeitschrift für Handelswissenschaft und Handelspraxis* 21: 253–64; 278–88.

Lion, M. (1928b) 'Geschichtliche Betrachtungen der Bilanztheorie bis zum Allgemeinen Deutschen Handelsgesetzbuch' (Historical considerations of balance sheet theories until the introduction of the General German Commercial Law), *Vierteljahresschrift für Steuer- und Finanzrecht* 2: 401–41.

Littleton, A.C. and Zimmerman, V.K. (1962) *Accounting theory: continuity and change*, Englewood Cliffs, NJ: Prentice-Hall, Inc.

Löffelholz, J. (1935) *Geschichte der Betriebswirtschaft und der Betriebswirtschaftslehre* (History of business economics and business economic theory), Stuttgart: Poeschel Verlag (reprinted Tokyo: Nihon Shoseki, 1981).

Löffelholz, J. (1970) 'Geschichte der Buchhaltung' (History of accounting), in E. Kosiol ed., *Handwörterbuch des Rechnungswesens* (Lexicon of accounting), Stuttgart: Poeschel Verlag: cols 583–90.

Lohmann, M. (1929) *Der Wirtschaftsplan der Unternehmung* (The economic plan of the firm), Berlin: Weiss.

Lohmann, M. (1948) 'Der Schweizer Kontenrahmen' (The Swiss master-chart of accounts), *Der Wirtschaftsprüfer* 5: 134–9.

Lohmann, M. (1950) 'Der französische Kontenrahmen' (The French master-chart of accounts), *Der Wirtschaftsprüfer* 6: 165–8.

Lorentz, S. (1926) 'Die Schmalenbachschen Kostenkategorien' (Schmalenbachs cost categories), *Zeitschrift für Betriebswirtschaft* 4: 311–15.

Mahlberg, W. (1920) 'Wirtschaftsrelativität' (Economic relativity), *Zeitschrift für Handelswissenschaft und Handelspraxis* 13 (9): 133–6.

Mahlberg, W. (1921) *Bilanztechnik und Bewertung bei schwankender Währung* (Accounting technique and valuation at fluctuating currency), Leipzig: G.A. Gloeckner (further editions in 1922 and 1923).

Mahlberg, W. (1923) *Goldkreditverkehr und Goldmarkbuchführung* (Gold-credit extension and gold-mark bookkeeping), Berlin: Springer Verlag.

Mahlberg, W. (1925) *Der Tageswert in der Bilanz* (The current value in the balance sheet), Leipzig: G.A. Gloeckner.

Mattessich, R. (1986) 'Fritz Schmidt (1892–1950) and his pioneering work in current value accounting in comparison to Edwards and Bells theory', *Contemporary Accounting Research* 2 (Spring): 157–78.

Mattessich, R. (1995) *Critique of accounting: examination of the foundations and normative structure of an applied discipline*, Westport, CT: Quorum Books.

Mattessich, R. (2000) *The beginnings of accounting and accounting thought: accounting practice in the Middle East (8000 BC to 2000 BC) and accounting thought in India (300 BC and the Middle Ages)*, New York: Garland Publishing, Inc.

Mattessich, R. (2003) 'Accounting research and researchers of the nineteenth century and the beginning of the twentieth century', *Accounting, Business and Financial History* 13 (2, July): 125–79.

Mayer, L. (1933) 'Bilanznormung (standardization of financial statements)', in K. Meithner ed., *Die Bilanzen der Unternehmungen*, Vol. 1, Vienna: Österreichischer Wirtschaftsverlag: 444–73.

Meithner, K. (ed.) (1933a) *Die Bilanzen der Unternehmungen* (Financial statements of firms), 2 vols, Vienna: Österreichischer Wirtschaftsverlag.

Meithner, K. (1933b) 'Das Kapital in der Bilanz' (The capital in the balance sheet), in K. Meithner ed., *Die Bilanzen der Unternehmungen*, Vol. 1, Vienna: Österreichischer Wirtschaftsverlag: 148–91.

Melis, F. (1950) *Storia della ragioneria-contributo alla conoscenza e interpretazione delle fonti più significativi della storia economica* (History of accounting-contribution to the knowledge and interpretation of the most significant sources of economic history), Bologna: Cesare Zuffi.

Mellerowicz, K. (1933) *Kosten und Kostenrechnung* (Costs and cost accounting), Berlin: W. de Gruyter (reprinted, same publisher, 1936, 1951 and 1963).

Mellerowicz, K. (1949) 'Aufgaben und Bildungsgesetze des Einheitskontenrahmens der Industrie' (Tasks and formation principles of the unified master-chart of accounts), *Der Wirtschaftsprüfer* 2 (6): 161–72.

Meyerberg, F. (1913) *Einführung in die Organisation von Maschinenfabriken* (Introduction into the organization of engine factories), Berlin.

Michel, E. (1941) *Handbuch der Plankostenrechnung* (Handbook of standard cost accounting), 2nd edn, Berlin: Otto Elsner Verlagsgesellschaft (1st edn, 1937).

Möller, H. (1941) *Kalkulation, Absatzpolitik und Preisbildung* (Costing, sales policy and price formation), Vienna: Springer.

Motte Green, C. de (1937) *The dynamic balance sheet: a German theory of accounting*, New York: Arno Press.

Müller, G. (1915) *Die kaufmännische Erfolgs-Rechnung* (Commercial profit and loss accounting), Berlin: Springer.

Müller, H. (1949) 'Standard- und Plankostenrechnung im betrieblichen Rechnungswesen' (Standard cost accounting and budgeting in business), Stuttgart: C.E. Poeschel Verlag.

Münstermann, H. (1957) 'Schmalenbachs "Dynamische Bilanz"' (Schmalenbach's 'dynamic accounting'), *Zeitschrift für handelswissenschaftliche Forschung* 9: 265–72.

Münstermann, H. (1966) 'Dynamische Bilanz: Grundlagen, Weiterentwicklung und Bedeutung der neuesten Bilanzdiskussion' (Dynamic accounting: foundation, development and significance of the newest accounting discussion), *Zeitschrift für betriebswirtschaftliche Forschung* 18: 512–31.

Murphy, G.W. and Most, K.S. (1959) *Translators note to Eugen Schmalenbachs dynamic accounting* (see also below under Schmalenbach, 1959), London: Gee and Co. Ltd: 5–6.

Muscheid, W. (1957) *Schmalenbachs Dynamische Bilanz-Darstellung, Kritik und Antikritik* (Schmalenbach's dynamic accounting-presentation, critique and anti-critic), Cologne: Westdeutscher Verlag.

Napier, C.J. (1996) 'Accounting and the absence of a business economics tradition in the United Kingdom', *European Accounting Review* 5 (3): 449–81.

Nicklisch, H. (1903) *Handelsbilanz und Wirtschaftsbilanz* (Commercial and economic balance sheets), Magdeburg: W. Ochs & Co. (reprinted Glashütten, Taunus: Detlev Auvermann, 1972).

Nicklisch, H. (1912) *Allgemeine kaufmännische Betriebslehre als Privatwirtschaftslehre des Handels und der Industrie* (General business theory as micro-economics of commerce and industry), Leipzig: C.E. Poeschel Verlag.

Nicklisch, H. (1921a) 'Dynamik' (Dynamic), *Zeitschrift für Handelswissenschaft und Handelspraxis* 13 (11): 241–6.

Nicklisch, H. (1921b) 'Buchbesprechung zu Schigut E' (Book review of E. Schigut), *Zeitschrift für Handelswissenschaft und Handelspraxis* 14 (2): 45.

Nicklisch, H. (1929–32) *Die Betriebswirtschaft* (Business economics), 3 vols, Stuttgart: C.E. Poeschel.

Nicklisch, H. (1929) 'Budgetierung und Rechnungswesen' (Budgeting and accounting), *Zeitschrift für Handelswissenschaft und Handelspraxis* 22: 50–5.

Nicklisch, H. (1932) 'Die Entthronung der Bilanz' (The dethroning of the balance sheet), *Die Betriebswirtschaft* 25: 2–5.

Nicklisch, H. (1939) 'Kosten' (Costs), in H. Nicklisch ed., *Handwörterbuch der Betriebswirtschaft* (Encyclopaedic handbook of business economics), Vol. 2, 2nd edn, Stuttgart: Poeschel Verlag: cols 674–83.

Nissen, H.J., Damerow, P. and Englund, R.K. (1993) *Archaic bookkeeping: early writing techniques and economic administration in the ancient Near East*, Chicago: University of Chicago Press (translated and edited from the original by H.J. Nissen, *Frühe Schrift und Techniken der Wirtschaftsverwaltung im alten Vorderen Orient – Informationsspeicherung und -verarbeitung vor 5000 Jahre*, Bad Salzdetfurth: Verlag Franzbecker, 1990).

Novak, A. (1902) 'Über die Gleichung der doppelten Buchhaltung' (On the equation of double-entry bookkeeping), *Zeitschrift für Buchhaltung* 11: 25–31; 49–54.

Nusko, H. (1933) 'Bilanz und Recht' (Balance sheet and the law), in K. Meithner ed., *Die Bilanzen der Unternehmungen* (Financial statements of firms), Vol. 1, Vienna: Österreichischer Wirtschaftsverlag: 749–75.

Osbahr, W. (1913) *Die Bilanzen vom Standpunkt der Unternehmung* (Balance sheets from the viewpoint of the enterprise), Berlin: G.A. Gloeckner (Haude & Spennerschen Buchhaltung, 2nd edn, 1919; 3rd edn, by W. Osbahr and H. Nicklisch, 1923).

Pantaleoni, M. (1909) 'Alcune osservazioni sulle attribuzioni di valori in assenza di formazioni di prezzi di mercato' (Some observations on valuation in the absence of market values), *Scritti varii di economica, Serie seconda*, Milano.

Pape, E. (1920) *Grundriß der doppelten Buchführung* (Outline of double-entry bookkeeping), Leipzig: G.A. Gloeckner.

Pape, E. (1925) 'Zur Frage des Bilanzbegriffes' (To the question of the concept of balance sheets), *Zeitschrift für Handelswissenschaft und Handelspraxis* 18: 200–7.

Pape, E. (1933) 'Der Begriff Gewinn (Verlust) und Rentability' (The notion of profit [loss] and rentability), in K. Meithner ed., *Die Bilanzen der Unternehmungen*, Vol. 1, Vienna: Österreichischer Wirtschaftsverlag: 53–65.

Passow, R. (1910) *Die Bilanzen der privaten Unternehmungen* (Balance sheets of private enterprises), (expanded in later editions to a work in 2 vols: *Die Bilanzen der privaten und öffentlichen Unternehmungen* (The balance sheets of private and public enterprises), Leipzig: B.G. Teubner (3rd edn, 1921)).

Penndorf, B. (1913) *Geschichte der Buchhaltung in Deutschland* (History of bookkeeping in Germany), Leipzig (abbreviated and amended as: Die historische Entwicklung der Bilanz, in K. Meithner ed., *Die Bilanzen der Unternehmungen*, Vol. 1, Vienna: Österreichischer Wirtschaftsverlag, 1933: 125–47).

Penndorf, B. (1929) 'Luca Pacioli: Aus seinem Leben und seinem Werk' (Luca Pacioli: on his life and his work), *Zeitschrift für Handelswissenschaft und Handelspraxis* 22 (4): 106–8.

Penndorf, B. (1933a) 'Die historische Entwicklung der Bilanz' (The historical development of the balance sheet), in K. Meithner ed., *Die Bilanzen der Unternehmungen*, Vol. 1, Vienna: Österreichischer Wirtschaftsverlag: 126–47.

Penndorf, B. (1933b) 'Die Anfänge der Betriebsbuchhaltung' (The beginning of cost accounting), *Zeitschrift für handelswissenschaftliche Forschung* 24: 627–31.

Peters, F. (1927) 'Über Industriekalkulation und Preispolitik in den Vereinigten Staaten von Amerika' (On cost accounting and pricing policy in the United States of America), *Zeitschrift für handelswissenschaftliche Forschung* 21: 1–32; 97–144.

Preiser, H. (1919) *Grundlagen der Betriebsrechnung in Maschinenbauanstalten* (Foundations of cost accounting in engine factories), Berlin (2nd edn, 1923).

Prion, W. (1919) *Inflation und Geldentwertung* (Inflation and devaluation), Berlin: Springer.

Prion, W. (1921) *Die Finanzierung und Bilanz wirtschaftlicher Betriebe unter dem Einfluß der Geldentwertung* (Financing and the business balance sheet under the influence of monetary devaluation), Berlin: Julius Springer Verlag.

Prion, W. (1922) 'Die Finanzpolitik der Unternehmung im Zeichen der Scheingewinne' (Financial policy of firms – in the face of fictitious gains), in E. Schmalenbach and W. Prion eds, *Zwei Vorträge über Scheingewinne*, Jena: Julius Springer Verlag.

Rehm, H. (1914) *Die Bilanzen der Aktiengesellschaften, ...* (The Balance Sheets of the Limited Companies, ...), 2nd edn, Berlin: J. Schweitzer-A. Sellier (1st edn, 1903).

Reichskuratorium für Wirtschaftlichkeit (RKW) (1939) *Allgemeine Grundsätze der Kostenrechnung* (General principles of cost accounting), Berlin: RKW.

Rieger, W. (1928) *Einführung in die Privatwirtschaftslehre* (Introduction to business theory), 3rd edn, Erlangen: Palm & Enke.

Rieger, W. (1930) 'Die organische Tageswertbilanz' (Organic current value accounting), *Archiv für Sozialwissenschaft und Sozialpolitik* 64: 136–54.

Rieger, W. (1936) *Schmalenbachs dynamische Bilanz* (Schmalenbachs dynamic accounting), Stuttgart: W. Kohlhammer (reprinted 1954).

Rosenkranz, K. (1949) 'Die Organisation der Betriebsbuchführung in der Sowjetunion' (The organization of cost accounting in the Soviet Union), *Zeitschrift für handelswissenschaftliche Forschung* (New Series) 1 (3): 101–25.

Rummel, K. (1934) *Grundlagen der Selbstkostenrechnung* (Foundations of cost accounting), Düsseldorf: Stahleisen.

Rummel, K. (1939) *Kostenrechnung auf der Grundlage der Proportionalität der Kosten* (Uniform costing on the basis of proportional cost), 2nd edn, Düsseldorf: Stahleisen.

Schär, J.F. (1890) *Versuch einer wissenschaftlichen Behandlung der Buchhaltung* (Attempt of a scientific treatment of bookkeeping), Basel.

Schär, J.F. (1911) *Allgemeine Handelsbetriebslehre, 1. Teil* (General commercial economics, Part 1), Leipzig: G.A. Gloeckner.

Schär, J.F. (1914) *Buchhaltung und Bilanz* (Bookkeeping and financial statements), 2nd edn, Berlin (many editions, later by J.F. Schär and W. Prion, Berlin: Julius Springer, 1932).

Scherpf, P. (1955) *Der Kontenrahmen* (The chart of accounts), Munich: Max Huber Verlag.

Schmalenbach, E. (1899) 'Buchführung und Kalkulation im Fabrikgeschäft' (Bookkeeping and calculation in manufacturing), *Deutsche Metallindustriezeitung*.

Schmalenbach, E. (1908–09) 'Über Verrechnungspreise' (On transfer prices), *Zeitschrift für handelswissenschaftliche Forschung* 3: 165–85.

Schmalenbach, E. (1917–18) 'Die Werte von Anlagen und Unternehmungen in der Schätzungstechnik' (The values of fixed assets and firms in the valuation technique), *Zeitschrift für handelswissenschaftliche Forschung* 12: 1–20.

Schmalenbach, E. (1919a) 'Grundlagen der dynamischen Bilanztheorie' (Foundations of dynamic accounting), *Zeitschrift für handelswissenschaftliche Forschung* 13: 1–60, 65–101 (published in book form as *Grundlagen dynamische Bilanzlehre*, Leipzig,

1920; later as *Dynamische Bilanz*, 3rd edn, Leipzig, 1925; English translation as *Dynamic Accounting*, London: Gee and Co., 1959) – see also Chapter 14 (for Japanese translations).

Schmalenbach, E. (1919b) 'Selbstkostenrechnung' (Cost accounting), special reprint of the *Zeitschrift für handelswissenschaftliche Forschung* 13: 257–356 (later editions Cologne: Westdeutscher Verlag, 1956, etc. – under the title *Kostenrechnung und Preispolitik*).

Schmalenbach, E. (1921) 'Geldwertausgleich in der bilanzmäßigen Erfolgsrechnung' (Monetary adjustment in the balance-based income calculation), *Zeitschrift für handelswissenschaftliche Forschung* 15: 401–17 (translated into English as: Monetary stabilization in profit- and loss-accounting, in O.F. Graves, G.E. Dean and F.L. Clarke eds, *Schmalenbachs dynamic accounting and price-level adjustment*, New York: Garland Publishing, Inc.: 3–20).

Schmalenbach, E. (1922a) 'Die steuerliche Behandlung der Scheingewinne' (Tax treatment of fictitious gains), *Mitteilungen der Gesellschaft für wirtschaftliche Ausbildung* 1 (Special volume 1 and 2; also in E. Schmalenbach and W. Prion eds, *Zwei Vorträge über Scheingewinne*, Jena: Julius Springer Verlag).

Schmalenbach, E. (1922b) *Goldmarkbilanz* (Goldmark balance sheet – taken over into the 3rd and 4th edn of his *Dynamische Bilanz*), Berlin: J. Springer Verlag (English translation as: Gold-mark accounting, in O.F. Graves, G.E. Dean and F.L. Clarke eds, *Schmalenbach's dynamic accounting and price-level adjustment*, New York: Garland Publishing, Inc.: 23–80).

Schmalenbach, E. (1924) *Grundlagen der Selbstkostenrechnung und Preispolitik* (Foundations of cost accounting and pricing policy), 2 vols, Leipzig: G.A. Gloeckner (2nd edn, 1925; 8th edn, Cologne: Westdeutscher Verlag, 1963).

Schmalenbach, E. (1925) *Einfluß der Geldwertschwankungen auf die Gewinnrechnung* (The effect of monetary value fluctuations on the income calculation), 3rd edn, Leipzig: G.A. Gloeckner (reprinted as: The effect of changing prices on profit calculation, in O.F. Graves, G.E. Dean and F.L. Clarke eds, *Schmalenbach's dynamic accounting and price-level adjustments*, New York: Garland Publishing, Inc.: 83–166).

Schmalenbach, E. (1927) *Der Kontenrahmen* (The master chart of accounts), Leipzig: G.A. Gloeckner (later editions in 1930 and 1935) – for Japanese translations, see Chapter 14.

Schmalenbach, E. (1938) *Kontenpläne und Kontentabellen* (Master charts and tables of accounts), Leipzig: G.A. Gloeckner.

Schmalenbach, E. (1948) *Pretiale Wirtschaftslenkung* (Price-guiding of companies), 2 vols, Bremen-Horn: Industrie und Handelsverlag Walter Dorn.

Schmalenbach, E. (1956) *Kostenrechnung und Preispolitik* (Cost accounting and pricing policy), 7th edn, Cologne: Westdeutscher Verlag.

Schmalenbach, E. (1959) *Dynamic accounting* (English translation by G.W. Murphy and K.S. Most of the 3rd edn of the *Dynamische Bilanz*, Cologne: Westdeutscher Verlag, 1925), London: Gee and Co.

Schmandt-Besserat, D. (1992) *Before writing*, Vol. 1, *From counting to Cuneiform;* Vol. 2, *A catalogue of Near Eastern tokens*, Austin, TX: University of Texas Press.

Schmidt, F. (1921) *Die organische Bilanz im Rahmen der Wirtschaft* (The organic balance sheet in an economic setting), 1st edn, Leipzig: G.A. Gloeckner Verlagsbuchhandlung (2nd edn, 1922, *Die organische Tageswertbilanz*, Leipzig; 3rd edn, 1929, reprint, Wiesbaden: Betriebswirtschaftlicher Verlag Dr T. Gabler, 1953; Japanese translation, *Yukikan taishohyo gakusetsu*, Tokyo: Dobunkan Ltd, 1934).

Schmidt, F. (1922a) 'Gewinn und Scheingewinn der Unternehmung' (Profits and nominal gains in business), *Zeitschrift für das gesamte Aktienwesen* 32: 50–6.

Schmidt, F. (1922b) 'Bilanzberichtigung durch Indexziffern (Goldmarkbilanz)' (Accounting adjustment through indexing: gold-mark balance sheet), *Zeitschrift für das gesamte Aktienwesen* 32: 484–92.

Schmidt, F. (1923a) *Der Wiederbeschaffungspreis des Umsatztages in Kalkulation und Volkswirtschaft* (The current replacement value in cost accounting and the national economy), Berlin: Spaeth & Linde.

Schmidt, F. (1923b) 'De winst van der onderneming' (The profit of the enterprise). *De Naamlooze Vennootschap Roermond* 15 (February): 301–4; (March): 332–4.

Schmidt, F. (1924) *Bilanzwert, Bilanzgewinn und Bilanzumwertung* (Accounting value, profit and balance sheet revaluation), Berlin: Spaeth & Linde.

Schmidt, F. (1926) 'Profit and balance sheet value', *Proceedings, Het International-aal Accountantscongres*, Purmerend: J. Muuses (reprinted New York: Arno Press, 1980).

Schmidt, F. (1927a) 'Die Industriekonjunktur – ein Rechenfehler' (The business cycles – a calculation error), *Zeitschrift für Betriebswirtschaft* 4: 1–29; 87–114; 165–99 (revised under the title *Betriebswirtschaftliche Konjunkturlehre*, Berlin: Spaeth & Linde (reprinted 1933)).

Schmidt, F. (1927b) 'Bilanzberichtigung durch Indexziffern – Goldmarkbilanz' (Balance sheet adjustment through index figures – gold-mark balance sheet), *Zeitschrift für Aktienwesen* 32: 474–82.

Schmidt, F. (1927c) 'Indexziffern' (Index figures), in H. Nicklisch edition, *Handwörter-buch der Betriebswirtschaft* (Encyclopaedic handbook of business economics), 1st edn, Stuttgart: C.E. Poeschel Verlag: cols 274–82.

Schmidt, F. (1929) 'The valuation of fixed assets in financial statements', *The accountant* 16 (November): 616–29.

Schmidt, F. (1930a) 'The basis of depreciation charges', *The Harvard Business Review* (April): 257–64.

Schmidt, F. (1930b) 'The importance of replacement value', *The Accounting Review* (September): 235–42 (reprinted in S.A. Zeff ed., *Asset appreciation, business income and price level accounting 1918–1955*, New York: Arno Press, 1976).

Schmidt, F. (1931a) 'Is appreciation profit?', *The Accounting Review* (September): 289–93 (reprinted in S.A. Zeff ed., *Asset appreciation, business income and price level accounting 1918–1955*, New York: Arno Press, 1976).

Schmidt, F. (1931b) 'Budgeting simplified by separating fixed and variable costs', *The American Accounting Review* 16 (February): 40–5.

Schmidt, F. (1950) *Allgemeine Betriebswirtschaftslehre* (General business economics), Wiesbaden: Gabler.

Schneider, D. (1981a) *Geschichte betriebswirtschaftlicher Theorie* (History of business-economics theory), Munich: Oldenbourg Verlag (3rd edn, 1987).

Schneider, D. (1981b) 'Geschichte der Buchhaltung und Bilanzierung' (History of book-keeping and accounting), in E. Kosiol, K. Chmielewicz and M. Schweitzer eds, *Hand-wörterbuch des Rechnungswesens* (Lexicon of accounting), 2nd rev. edn, Stuttgart: C.E. Poeschel Verlag: cols 616–30.

Schneider, D. (2001) *Betriebswirtschaftslehre*, Vol. 4: *Geschichte und Methoden der Wirtschaftswissenschaften* (History and methods of the economic sciences), Munich: R. Oldenbourg Verlag (previous volumes were Vol. 1: *Grundlagen*, 1993; Vol. 2: *Rechnungswesen*, 1994; Vol. 3: *Theorie der Unternehmung*, 1997).

Schneider, E. (1939) *Grundfragen des industriellen Rechnungswesens* (Basic questions about industrial accounting), Copenhagen: Hos & Gad.

Schneider, E. (1940) 'Grundsätzliches zur Planung und Standardkostenrechnung' (Basic thoughts to planning and standard cost accounting), *Zeitschrift für handelswissenschaftliche Forschung* 34: 235–69.

Schneider, E. (1951) *Wirtschaftlichkeitsrechnung* (Efficiency accounting), Tübingen: Mohr.

Schnutenhaus, O.R. (1948) 'Neue Grundlagen der "esten" Kostenrechnung' (New foundations of 'fixed' cost accounting), in *Die Betriebsstrukturkostenrechnung*, Berlin: Deutscher Betriebswirte-Verlag.

Schoenfeld, H.-M. (1996) 'Schmalenbach, Eugen (1873–1955)', in M. Chatfield and R. Vangermeersch eds, *The history of accounting: an international encyclopedia*, New York: Garland Publishing, Inc.: 514–16.

Schranz, A. (1933) 'Die gesetzliche Verankerung der Bilanzrevision in den wichtigsten Staaten Europas' (The legal foundation of auditing in major European countries), in K. Meithner ed., *Die Bilanzen der Unternehmungen*, Vol. 2, Vienna: Österreichischer Wirtschaftsverlag: 853–83.

Schuchart, A. (1909) *Die Selbstkostenrechnung für Hüttenwerke, insbesondere für Eisen- und Stahlwerke* (Cost accounting for foundries, particularly for iron- and steel-works), Düsseldorf.

Schulze, G. (1933) *Urkunden zur Geschichte der deutschen Wirtschaftsprüfung* (Documents to the history of German public accounting), Leipzig.

Schwantag, K. (1949) *Zins und Kapital in der Kostendrechnung* (Interest and capital in cost accounting), Bad Oeynhausen.

Schwantag, K. (1951) 'Fritz Schmidts wissenschaftliches Werk' (The scientific work of Fritz Schmidt), *Zeitschrift für Betriebswirtschaft* 21: 1–14 (translated by F.L. Clarke and G.W. Dean in *Abacus* (September) 1986: 90–9).

Schweitzer, M. (1972) *Struktur und Funktion der Bilanz* (Structure and function of financial statements), Berlin: Duncker & Humblot.

Schweitzer, M. (1995) 'Eugen Schmalenbach as the founder of cost accounting in the German-speaking world', in A. Tsuji and P. Garner eds, *Studies in Accounting History: Tradition and Innovation for the Twenty-First Century*, Westport, CT: Greenwood Publishing Group, Inc.: 29–43.

Seicht, G. (1970a) *Die kapitaltheoretische Bilanz und die Entwicklung der Bilanztheorie* (The capital-theoretic balance sheet and the development of accounting theory), Berlin: Duncker & Humblot.

Seicht, G. (1970b) 'Die Unhaltbarkeit der dynamischen Bilanztheorie' (The untenability of the dynamic balance sheet theory), *Zeitschrift für Betriebswirtschaft* 40: 589–612.

Seicht, G. (1977) *Die Grenzbetrachtung in der Entwicklung des betrieblichen Rechnungswesens* (Marginal consideration in the development of cost accounting), Berlin: Duncker & Humblot.

Seidel, K. (1933) 'Die Bilanzen der Handels- und Industrie-Unternehmungen' (Financial statements in commercial and manufacturing firms), in K. Meithner ed., *Die Bilanzen der Unternehmungen*, Vol. 2, Vienna: Österreichischer Wirtschaftsverlag: 205–69.

Seidler, G. (1901) 'Die theoretische Grundlage der doppelten Buchhaltung' (The theoretical foundation of double-entry bookkeeping), *Zeitschrift für Volkswirtschaft, Sozialpolitik und Verwaltung* 10: 53–65.

Seischab, H. (1933) 'Die Funktionen der Bilanz' (Functions of financial statements), in K. Meithner ed., *Die Bilanzen der Unternehmungen*, Vol. 1, Vienna: Österreichischer Wirtschaftsverlag: 379–405.

Sellien, R. and Sellien, H. (eds) (1956) *Dr. Gablers Wirtschafts-Lexikon* (Dr Gablers economic lexicon), 2 vols, Wiesbaden: Betriebswirtschaftlicher Verlag Gabler.

Sewering, K. (1925) *Die Einheitsbilanz, die Überbrückung des Gegensatzes zwischen statischer und dynamischer Bilanzlehre* (Reconciled accounting, overcoming the differences between 'static' and 'dynamic' accounting), Leipzig: G.A. Gloeckner.

Seÿffert, R. (1938) 'Betriebswirtschaftslehre, Geschichte' (Business economics, history), in H. Nicklisch ed., *Handbuchwörterbuch der Betriebswirtschaft* (Encyclopaedic handbook of business economics), Vol. 1, 2nd edn, Stuttgart: Poeschel Verlag: cols 932–56.

Sganzini, C. (1906) 'Die realistische Theorie der doppelten Buchhaltung' (Foundation of the realistic theory of bookkeeping), *Zeitschrift für Buchhaltung* 15, St Gallen, Switzerland.

Sganzini, C. (1908) *Zur Grundlegung der realistischen Theorie der Doppelten Buchhaltung* (On the foundations of the realistic theory of double-entry), St Gallen, Switzerland: Städtische Handelsakademie St Gallen.

Sganzini, C. (1910) 'Die Grundirrtümer der materialistischen Zweikonten Theorie' (The basic errors of the materialistic two-accounts theory), *Zeitschrift für Buchhaltung* 19: 246–51; 282–90.

Sieveking, H. (1901) 'Aus venezianischen Handelsbüchern – Ein Beitrag zur Geschichte des Großhandels im 15. Jahrhundert' (From Venetian commercial books – a contribution to the history of wholesale of the fifteenth century), *Gustav Schmollers Jahrbuch für Gesetzgebung, Verwaltung und Volkswirtschaft im Deutschen Reich* 25 (4).

Sieveking, H. (1902) *Bestand an Handels- und sonstigen Geschäftsbüchern großer italienischer Archive* (Inventory of commercial and other business books of great Italian archives), Vienna: Verlag A. Hölder.

Sieveking, H. (1905) *Die Handlungsbücher der Medici* (The commercial books of the Medici), Vienna: Verlag A. Hölder.

Sieveking, H. (1909) 'Aus Genueser Rechnungs- und Steuerbüchern – Ein Beitrag zur mittelalterlichen Handels- und Vermögensstatistik' (From Genoese accounts and taxation records – a contribution to the commercial and capital statistics), *Sitzungsberichte, Kaiserliche Akademie der Wissenschaften* CLXII, Vol. 2, Philosophical Class.

Sillén, O. (1929) 'Zur Geschichte der Bewertungslehre in Schweden' (To the history of valuation theory in Sweden), *Zeitschrift für Handelswissenschaft und Handelspraxis* 22: 118–26.

Simon, H.V. (1910) *Die Bilanzen der Aktiengesellschaften und Kommanditgesellschaften auf Aktien* (Financial statements of limited and private stock companies), 4th edn, Berlin: Gutentag.

Skokan, K. (1914) 'Die Dreikontentheorie der doppelten Buchhaltung' (The three-accounts theory of double-entry bookkeeping), *Zeitschrift für Buchhaltung* 23: 25–35.

Skokan, K. (1918) *Buchhaltung und Bilanz auf wirtschaftstheoretischer Grundlage* (Bookkeeping and accounting on the basis of economic theory), Vienna: Pichler (reprinted 1924).

Sommerfeld, H. (1926) 'Bilanz (eudynamische)' (The 'eudynamic balance sheet') in H. Nicklisch ed., *Handwörterbuch der Betriebswirtschaft* (Encyclopaedic handbook of business economics), Vol. 1, 1st edn, Stuttgart: C.E. Poeschel Verlag: cols 1340–6.

Stackelberg, H. von (1932) *Grundlagen der reinen Kostentheorie* (Foundations of pure cost theory), Vienna: Springer Verlag.

Strieder, J. (1905) 'Die Inventur der Firma Fugger aus dem Jahr 1527' (The inventory of the firm of Fugger from the year 1527), *Zeitschrift für die gesamten Staatswissenschaften* XVII, Vienna.

Sweeney, H.W. (1927) 'Effects of inflation on German accounting', *Journal of Accountancy* (March): 178–91.

Sweeney, H.W. (1928) 'German inflation accounting', *Journal of Accountancy* (February): 104–16.

Sweeney, H.W. (1936) *Stabilized accounting*, New York: Harper & Brothers.

Sykora, G. (1949) *Die Konten und Bilanztheorien – Eine betriebswirtschaftlich-historische Untersuchung* (Theory of accounts and financial statements – an economic-historical investigation), Vienna: Industrieverlag Spaeth & Linde.

ter Vehn, A. (1924) 'Gewinnbegriff der Betriebswirtschaft' (Profit notion of business economics), *Zeitschrift für Betriebswirtschaft* 1: 361–75.

ter Vehn, A. (1929) *Entwicklung der Bilanzauffassung bis zum AHGB* (Development of accounting theory up to the general commercial codex), Berlin.

Thoms, W. (1933) 'Die Bewertung des Vermögens' (The valuation of assets), in K. Meithner ed., *Die Bilanzen der Unternehmungen*, Vol. 1, Vienna: Österreichischer Wirtschaftsverlag: 192–227.

Thoms, W. (1936) *Kameralistische und kaufmännische Buchführung – Ein Beitrag zum Rechnungswesen kommunaler Betriebe* (Cameralistic and commercial bookkeeping – a contribution to the accounting of communal enterprises), Berlin: Verlag für Organisationsschriften.

Töndury, H. (1933) 'Die Grundlagen der betrieblichen Verrechnung' (The foundations of managerial accounting), in K. Meithner ed., *Die Bilanzen der Unternehmungen*, Vol. 1, Vienna: Österreichischer Wirtschaftsverlag: 95–122.

Tweedie, D. and Whittington, G. (1984) *The debate of inflation accounting*, Cambridge: Cambridge University Press.

Ullmann, J. von (1904) 'Aufstellung einer einheitlichen Buchhaltungsregel' (Setting a uniform bookkeeping rule), *Zeitschrift für Buchhaltung* 13.

Vodrazka, Karl (1957) 'Karl Meithner', in E. Obermeyer-Marnach ed., *Österreichisches Biographisches Lexikon 1815–1950*, Vol. VI, Graz: Böhlaus Nachf: 203ff.

Voigtländer, D. (1952) 'Bibliographie: Das wissenschaftliche Werk von F. Schmidt' (Bibliography: the works of F. Schmidt), *Zeitschrift für Betriebswirtschaft* 22 (January): 182–5.

Wagenhofer, A. (1986) *Bilanzierung und Bilanzanalyse – Theoretische Grundlagen und praktische Anwendung* (Accounting and statement analysis – theoretical foundations and practical application), Vienna: Industrieverlag Peter Linde.

Walb, E. (1921) *Das Problem der Scheingewinne* (The problem of fictitious gains), Freiburg i. Br.: Momber.

Walb, E. (1924) 'Die Bilanz als Mittel der Erfolgsrechnung' (The balance sheet as a means for income determination), *Zeitschrift für Betriebswirtschaft* 1: 34–44.

Walb, E. (1926) *Die Erfolgsrechnung privater und öffentlicher Betriebe* (Income accounts of private and public enterprise), Berlin: Spaeth & Linde.

Walb, E. (1933) 'Zur Dogmengeschichte der Bilanz von 1861–1910' (To the history of the balance sheet from 1860–1919), in *Festschrift für Eugen Schmalenbach*, Leipzig: G.A. Gloeckner: 1–64 (reprint edn, Scientia Verlag, 1975).

Walb, E. (1948) *Die Finanzwirtschaftliche Bilanz* (The financial balance sheet), 2nd edn, Duisburg: Visser.

Walther, A. (1947) *Einführung in die Wirtschaftslehre der Unternehmung*, Vol. 1: Der Betrieb (Introduction to business economics, Part I: The firm), Zürich: Schulthess.

Weber, C.(K.) (1966) *The evolution of direct costing*, Urbana-Champaign, IL: Center for International Education and Research in Accounting, University of Illinois.

Weitenauer, A. (1931) *Venezianischer Handel der Fugger nach der Musterbuchhaltung des Matthäus Schwarz* (Venetian trade of the Fuggers according to the exemplary accounting of Matthäus Schwarz), Munich: Duncker & Humblot.

Whittington, G. (1983) *Inflation accounting: an introduction to the debate*, Cambridge: Cambridge University Press.

Wieser, R. von (1884) *Über den Ursprung und die Hauptgesetze des wirtschaftlichen Werthes*, Vienna.

Wilmowski, B. von (1895) 'Die Abschreibung für Abnutzung von Gebäuden, Maschinen, Betriebsgerätschaften, u.s.w'. (The depreciation for the usage of buildings, machines, implements, etc.), in *Verwaltungsarchiv – Zeitschrift für Verwaltungsrecht und Verwaltungsgerichtsbarkeit* 3 (June): 366–82.

Wilmowski, B. von (1896) *Das Preußische Einkommensteuergesetz* (The Prussian Income Tax Law), Breslau (2nd edn, 1907).

Wolter, A. (1948) *Das Rechnen mit fixen und variablen Kosten* (Accounting with fixed and variable costs), Cologne: Westdeutscher Verlag.

Ziegler, J. (1904) *Beitrag zur Begründung der zwei Kontenreihen in der Buchhaltung* (Contribution to the justification of the two account series in bookkeeping), in Kayser ed., *Separatabdruck aus dem Jahrbuch der Export-Akademie des k.k. österreichischen Handelsmuseums*, 1902–03.

Ziegler, J. (1930) 'Die natürliche Bilanz' (The natural balance sheet), *Betriebswirtschaftliche Blätter* 1.

4 German language area: second half of the twentieth century

Adam, D. (1969a) *Produktionsplanung bei Sortenfertigung: ein Beitrag zur Theorie der Mehrproduktunternehmung* (Production planning at patch production: a contribution to the theory of the multiple-product enterprise), Wiesbaden: Gabler Verlag.

Adam, D. (1969b) 'Koordinationsprobleme bei dezentralen Entscheidungen' (Coordination problems at decentralized decisions), *Zeitschrift für Betriebswirtschaft* 39: 615–32.

Adam, D. (1970) *Entscheidungsorientierte Kostenbewertung* (Decision-oriented costing), Wiesbaden: Gabler Verlag.

Albach, H. (1962) *Investition und Liquidität: die Planung des optimalen Investitionsbudgets* (Investment and liquidity), Wiesbaden: Gabler Verlag.

Albach, H. (1965) 'Grundgedanken einer synthetischen Bilanztheorie' (Basic thoughts to a synthetic balance sheet theory), *Zeitschrift für Betriebswirtschaft* 35: 21–31.

Albach, H. (1974) 'Innerbetriebliche Lenkpreise als Instrument dezentraler Unternehmensführung' (Internal pricing as instrument of decentralized management), *Zeitschrift für betriebswirtschaftliche Forschung* 26: 216–42.

Antle, R. and Eppen, G.D. (1985) 'Capital rationing and organizational slack in capital budgeting', *Management Science* 31: 163–74.

Baetge, J. (1970) *Möglichkeiten der Objektivierung des Jahreserfolges* (Possibilities of objectifying annual income), Düsseldorf: IDW-Verlag.

Baetge, J. (1984) *Grundsätze ordnungsmäßiger Abschlußprüfung für Forderungen* (Principles of orderly auditing of obligations), Düsseldorf: IDW-Verlag.

Baetge, J. (1987) 'Die neuen Ansatz- und Bewertungsvorschriften' (New approaches to valuation legislation), *Zeitschrift für betriebswirtschaftliche Forschung* 39: 206–18.

Baetge, J. (2002) 'Grundsätze ordnungsmäßiger Buchführung' (Principles of orderly accounting) in H.-U. Küpper and A. Wagenhofer eds, *Handwörterbuch Unternehmensrechnung und Controlling* (Lexicon for accounting and controlling), 4th edn, Stuttgart: Schäffer-Poeschel Verlag, cols 635–47.

Baetge, J. and Apelt, B. (1992) 'Bedeutung und Ermittlung der Grundsätze ordnungsmäßiger Buchführung (GoB)' (Significance and determination of principles for orderly accounting), in K. von Wysocki and J. Schulze-Osterloh eds, *Handbuch des Jahresabschlusses in Einzeldarstellungen*, 2nd edn, Cologne: Verlag Dr Otto Schmidt: Abt. I/2: 3–54.

Baiman, S. and Demski, J.S. (1980) 'Economically optimal performance evaluation and control systems', *Journal of Accounting Research* 18, Supplement: 184–220.

Ballwieser, W. (1985a) 'Informationsökonomie, Rechnungslegungstheorie und Bilanzrichtlinien-Gesetz' (Information economics, accounting theory, and the *Bilanzrichtlinien-Gesetz*), *Zeitschrift für betriebswirtschaftliche Forschung* 37: 47–66.

Ballwieser, W. (1985b) 'Ergebnisse der Informationsökonomie zur Informationsfunktion der Rechnungslegung' (Results of information economics as regards the information function of accounting), in S. Stöppler ed., *Information und Produktion – Beiträge zur Unternehmenstheorie und Unternehmensplanung, Festschrift für Waldemar Wittmann*, Stuttgart: Poeschel: 21–40.

Ballwieser, W. (1987a) 'Grundsätze der Aktivierung und Passivierung' (General principles of balance sheet presentation), in E. Castan, G. Heymann, E. Müller, D. Ordelheide and E. Scheffler eds, *Becksches Handbuch der Rechnungslegung*, Munich: Verlag C.H. Beck, Abschnitt B 131.

Ballwieser, W. (1987b) 'Grundsätze ordnungsmäßiger Buchführung und neues Bilanzrecht' (Principles of orderly accounting and the new accounting legislation), *Zeitschrift für Betriebswirtschaft* (Supplementary Issue 1 on the *Bilanzrichtlinien Gesetz*): 3–24.

Ballwieser, W. (1993) 'Die Entwicklung der Theorie der Rechnungslegung in den USA' (Development of accounting theory in the USA), *Zeitschrift für betriebswirtschaftliche Forschung* (Special Issue), in F.W. Wager ed., *Ökonomische Analyse des Bilanzrechts*: 107–38.

Ballwieser, W. (1996) *US-amerikanische Rechnungslegung: Grundlagen und Vergleiche mit dem deutschen Recht* (US accounting: foundations and comparison with German law), Stuttgart: Schäffer-Poeschel Verlag.

Ballwieser, W., Coenenberg, A.G. and von Wysocki, K. (2002) *Handwörterbuch der Rechnungslegung und Prüfung* (Lexicon of accounting and auditing), 3rd rev. edn, Stuttgart: Schäffer-Poeschel Verlag.

Baxter, W.T. (1949) 'Accountants and the inflation', *Proceedings of the Statistical Society* 9 (February): 1–19.

Betz, S. (1995) 'Die Berücksichtigung von technischem Fortschritt im Konzept investitionstheoretisch fundierter Abschreibungen' (The effect of technological progress upon the concept of investment-oriented depreciation), *Zeitschrift für Betriebswirtschaft* 65: 425–44.

Böcking, H.-J. and Orth, C. (1998) 'Neue Vorschriften zur Rechnungslegung und Prüfung durch das KonTraG und das KapAEG – Ergebnisse eines kapitalmarktinduzierten Reformzwangs' (New standards of accounting and auditing through the KonTraG and the KapAEG – results of enforced legislation as a result of the capital market), *Der Betrieb* 58: 1241–6.

Böhm, H.-H. (1957) 'Die Programmplanung mit Hilfe der Standard-Grenzpreise' (Cost and price planning by means of standard marginal pricing), in *Taschenbuch für den Betriebswirt*, Berlin, Stuttgart: Deutscher Betriebswirte-Verlag: 93–136.

Böhm, H.-H. (1959) *Nichtlineare Programmplanung* (Nonlinear cost and price planning), Wiesbaden: Gabler Verlag.

Böhm, H.-H. and Wille, F. (1974) *Deckungsbeitragsrechnung, Grenzpreisrechnung und Optimierung* (Contribution margin costing, variable costing and optimization), 5th edn, Munich: Verlag Moderne Industrie.

Börner, D. (1961) *Direct Costing als System der Kostenrechnung* (Direct costing), Munich: Fotodruck Mikrokopie.

Bredt, O. (1956) *Die Krise in der Betriebswirtschaftslehre* (The crisis of business economics), Düsseldorf: Verlagsbuchhandlung des Instituts der Wirtschaftsprüfer.

Breid, V. (1994) *Erfolgspotentialrechnung. Konzeption im System einer finanztheoretisch fundierten, strategischen Erfolgsrechnung* (Accounting for potential profit: conception within the system of a financed-oriented cost accounting), Stuttgart: Schäffer-Poschel Verlag.

Brockhoff, Klaus K.L. (1975) *Zur externen gesellschaftsbezogenen Berichterstattung deutscher Unternehmen* (Society-oriented reporting of German enterprises), Cologne: Hanstein.

Bucher, J.H. (1980) 'Grundlagen einer inflationsgerechten Kalkulation' (Foundations of inflation accounting), *Kostenrechnungspraxis* 24: 7–14.

Busse von Colbe, W. (1966) 'Aufbau und Informationsgehalt von Kapitalflussrechnungen' (Structure and information content of flow of funds accounting), *Zeitschrift für Betriebswirtschaft* 36 (Special Issue): 82–114.

Busse von Colbe, W. (1968) 'Kapitalflußrechnungen als Berichts- und Planungsinstrument' (Flow of funds accounting as instrument of reporting and planning), in H. Jacob ed., *Schriften zur Unternehmensführung*, Vol. 6/7, Wiesbaden: Gabler: 9–28.

Busse von Colbe, W. (1984) 'Financial accounting research in Germany: some socio-economic determinants', in A.G. Hopwood and H. Schreuder eds, *European contributions to accounting research: the achievements of the last decade*, Amsterdam: Free University Press: 103–12.

Busse von Colbe, W. (1990) 'Funds flow statement', in E. Grochla, E. Gaugler and H.E. Büschgen eds, *Handbook of German Business Management*, Vol. 1, Stuttgart: Poeschel and Berlin, New York: Springer: cols 1000–16.

Busse von Colbe, W. (1993) 'Kapitalflußrechnung' (Flow of funds accounting), in K. Chmielewicz and M. Schweitzer eds, *Handwörterbuch des Rechnungswesens* (Lexicon of accounting), 3rd edn, Stuttgart: Schäffer-Poeschel Verlag: cols 1074–85.

Busse von Colbe, W. (ed.) (1994) *Lexikon des Rechnungswesens* (Lexicon of accounting), 3rd edn, Munich: Oldenbourg Verlag.

Busse von Colbe, W. (1996) 'Accounting and business economics tradition in Germany', *European Accounting Review* 5 (3): 413–34.

Busse von Colbe, W. and Ordelheide, D. (1969) *Konzernabschlüsse* (Consolidated financial statements), Wiesbaden: Gabler (6th edn, 1993).

Canning, J.B. (1929) *Economics of accountancy, a critical analysis of accounting theory*, New York: Ronald Press.

Chambers, R.J. (1957) 'Detail for a blueprint', *The Accounting Review* 32 (April): 206–15.

Chambers, R.J. (1966) *Accounting, evaluation and economic behaviour*, Englewood Cliffs, NJ: Prentice-Hall, Inc. (reprinted in *Accounting Classics Series*, Houston, TX: Scholars Books Co., 1975).

Chatfield, M. and Vangermeersch, R. (eds) (1996) *The history of accounting: an international encyclopedia*, New York: Garland Publishing, Inc.

Chenery, H.B. (1948) Engineering production functions, *The Quarterly Journal of Economics* 63: 507–31.

Chmielewicz, K. (1972) *Integrierte Finanz- und Erfolgsplanung: Versuch einer dynamis-chen Mehrperiodenplanung* (Integrated financial and profit planning), Stuttgart: Poeschel.

Chmielewicz, K. (1979) *Forschungskonzeptionen der Wirtschaftswissenschaft* (Research notions of economic science), 2nd edn, Stuttgart: Poeschel Verlag.

Chmielewicz, K. and Caspari, B. (1985) 'Zur Problematik von Finanzrechnungen' (To the problem of financial accounting), *Die Betriebswirtschaft* 45: 156–69.

Chmielewicz, K. and Schweitzer, M. (eds) (1993) *Handwörterbuch des Rechnungswe-sens* (Lexicon of accounting), 3rd edn, Stuttgart: Schäffer-Poeschel Verlag.

Christensen, J.A. (1981) 'Communication in agencies', *Bell Journal of Economics* 12: 661–74.

Christensen, J.A. and Demski, J.S. (2003) *Accounting theory: an information content perspective*, New York: McGraw-Hill, Irwin.

Christensen, P.O. and Feltham, G.A. (2003) *Economics of accounting*, Vol. 1: *Informa-tion in markets*, Boston, MA: Kluwer Academic Publishers.

Christensen, P.O. and Feltham, G.A. (2005) *Economics of accounting*, Vol. 2: *Perfor-mance evaluation*, Boston, MA: Kluwer Academic Publishers.

Coenenberg, A.G. (1974) 'Jahresabschlußinformation und Kapitalmarkt. Zur Diskussion empirischer Forschungsansätze und – ergebnisse zum Informationsgehalt von Jahresabschlüssen für Aktionäre' (Financial reporting and the capital market: to the discussion of principles and results of empirical research concerning the information content), *Zeitschrift für betriebswirtschaftliche Forschung* 26: 647–57.

Coenenberg, A.G. (1992) *Kostenrechnung und Kostenanalyse* (Cost accounting and cost analysis), Landsberg: Moderne Industrie.

Coenenberg, A.G. (1995) 'Einheitlichkeit oder Differenzierung von internem und externem Rechnungswesen: Die Anforderungen der internen Steuerung' (Uniformity and differenciation of internal and external accounting: demands of internal manage-ment), *Der Betrieb* 55: 2077–83.

Coenenberg, A.G. and Fischer, T.M. (1991) 'Prozeßkostenrechnung – strategische Neuorientierung in der Kostenrechnung' (Process cost accounting – strategic reorienta-tion of cost accounting), *Die Betriebswirtschaft* 51: 21–38.

Coenenberg, A.G. and Haller, A. (1993a) 'Empirische Forschung' (Empirical research), in K. Chmielewicz and M. Schweitzer eds, *Handwörterbuch des Rechnungswesens* (Lexicon of accounting), 3rd edn, Stuttgart: Schäffer-Poeschel: cols 506–17.

Coenenberg, A.G and Haller, A. (1993b) 'Externe Rechnungslegung' (External account-ing), in J. von Hauschildt and O. Grün eds, 'Ergebnisse empirischer betrieb-swirtschaftlicher Forschung' (Results of empirical research in business economics), *Festschrift to Eberhard Witte*, Stuttgart: Schäffer-Poeschel Verlag: 557–600.

Coenenberg, A.G. and Schmidt, F. (1978) 'Kapitalflussrechnung' (Flow of funds accounting), *Zeitschrift für Betriebswirtschaft* 48: 507–16.

Coenenberg, A.G. and von Wysocki, K. (eds) (1983) *Handwörterbuch der Revision* (Lexicon on auditing), Stuttgart: Schäffer-Poeschel Verlag (2nd edn, 1992).

Coenenberg, A.G., Möller, P. and Schmidt, F. (1984) 'Empirical research in financial accounting in Germany, Austria and Switzerland', in A.G. Hopwood and H. Schreuder eds, *European contributions to accounting research: the achievements of the last decade*, Amsterdam: Free University Press: 61–82.

Coenenberg, A.G., Schmidt, F. and Werhand, M. (1983) 'Bilanzpolitische Entschei-dungen und Entscheidungswirkungen in manager- und eigentümerkontrollierten Unternehmungen' (Accounting policy decisions and their effects in enterprises controlled by managers of proprietors), *Betriebswirtschaftliche Forschung und Praxis* 35: 321–43.

Coenenberg, A.G., Berndsen, H., Möller, P., Schmidt, F. and Schönbrodt, B. (1978) 'Empirische Bilanzforschung in Deutschland' (Empirical accounting research in Germany), *Die Betriebswirtschaft* 38: 495–507.

Dellmann, K. (1994) 'Schweiz' (Switzerland), in W. Busse von Colbe ed., *Lexikon des Rechnungswesens* (Lexicon on accounting), 3rd edn, Munich: Oldenbourg Verlag.

Dellmann, K. and Franz, K.-P. (eds) (1994) 'Neuere Entwicklungen im Kostenmanagement' (New developments in the management of costs), Bern: Verlag Paul Haupt.

Dellmann, K. and Kalinski, R. (1986) 'Die Rechnungslegung zur Finanzlage der Unternehmung' (Accounting for the financial position of an enterprise), *Die Betriebswirtschaft* 46: 174–87.

Demski, J.S. and Feltham, G.A. (1976) *Cost determination: a conceptual approach*, Ames, IO: Iowa State University Press.

Demski, J.S. and Feltham, G.A.. (1978) 'Economic incentives in budgetary control systems', *The Accounting Review* 53: 336–59.

Dinkelbach, W. (1964) 'Zum Problem der Produktionsplanung in Ein- und Mehrproduktunternehmen' (To the problem of production planning in one and multi-product firms), *Würzburg*, Vienna: Physica-Verlag.

Dinkelbach, W. and Rosenberg, O. (1994) *Erfolgs- und umweltorientierte Produktionstheorie* (Production theory oriented towards profit and the environment), Berlin: Springer (2nd edn, 1997).

Dörner, E. and Kloock, J. (1984) 'A survey of management accounting research from a German view', in A.G. Hopwood and H. Schreuder eds, *European contributions to accounting research: the achievements of the last decade*, Amsterdam: Free University Press: 83–102.

Drumm, J. (1972a) 'Theorie und Praxis der Lenkung durch Preise' (Theory and practice of pricing policy), *Zeitschrift für betriebswirtschaftliche Forschung* 24: 253–67.

Drumm, J. (1972b) 'Probleme der Kalkulation und Bestandsbewertung bei Lenkungs- und Verrechnungspreisen' (Problems of costing and inventory valuation under transferpricing), *Zeitschrift für Betriebswirtschaft* 42: 471–92.

Dyckhoff, H. (1992) *Betriebliche Produktion. Theoretische Grundlagen einer umweltorientierten Produktionswirtschaft* (Commercial production, theoretical foundations of an environmentally-oriented production system), Berlin, Heidelberg, New York: Springer (2nd edn, 1994).

Edwards, E.O. and Bell, P.W. (1961) *The theory and measurement of business income*, Berkeley, CA: University of California Press.

Edwards, J.R. (ed.) (1994) *Twentieth-century accounting thinkers*, London: Routledge.

Eiff, W. von (ed.) (1985) *Kompendium des Krankenhauswesens: Beiträge zu ökonomischen, technischen u. rechtlichen Problemen im Krankenhaus* (Compendium on health care: contributions to the economic, technical and legal problems of hospitals), Bad Homburg: Bettendorf Verl.-Ges.

Engels, W. (1962) *Betriebswirtschaftliche Bewertungslehre im Licht der Entscheidungstheorie* (Valuation theory of business economics in the light of decision theory), Cologne: Westdeutscher Verlag.

Ewert, R. (1986) *Rechnungslegung, Gläubigerschutz und Agency Probleme* (Accounting, debtor protection and agency problems), Wiesbaden: Gabler.

Ewert, R. (1987) 'The financial theory of agency as a tool for an analysis of problems in accounting', in G. Bamberg and K. Spremann eds, *Agency theory, information and incentives*, Berlin: Springer Verlag: 281–309.

Ewert, R. (1990) *Wirtschaftsprüfung und asymmetrische Information* (Auditing and asymmetrical information), Berlin: Springer Verlag.

Ewert, R. (1997) 'Target Costing und Verhaltenssteuerung' (Target costing and behavioural direction), in C.-C. Freidank, U. Götze, B. Huch and J. Weber eds, *Kostenmanagement – Neuere Konzepte und Anwendungen*, Berlin: Springer: 299–321.

Ewert, R. and Ernst, C. (1999) 'Target costing, coordination and strategic cost management', *European Accounting Review* 8: 23–49.

Ewert, A. and Wagenhofer, A. (1993/2003) *Interne Unternehmensrechnung* (Internal business accounting), Berlin: Springer Verlag (5th edn, 2003).

Ewert, A. and Wagenhofer, A. (2000) 'Neuere Ansätze zur theoretischen Fundierung von Rechnungslegung und Prüfung' (Novel attempts to a theoretical foundation of accounting and auditing), in L. Lachnit and C.-C. Freidank eds, *Investororientierte Unternehmenspublizität: neue Entwicklungen von Rechnungslegung, Prüfung und Jahresabschlussanalyse*, Wiesbaden: Gabler: 31–60.

Fandel, G. (1987) *Produktion* (Production), Berlin: Springer (5th edn, 1996).

Fickert, R. (1983) *Inflation Accounting – Theorien, Methoden, Formen* (Inflation accounting – theories, methods and forms), Zürich: Schulthess Polygraphischer Verlag A.G.

Filios, V.P. (1981) 'Four schools of European accounting thought', *Accounting Historians Journal* 8 (2): 61–78.

Financial Accounting Standards Board (FASB) (1978) 'Objectives for financial reporting by business enterprises', *Statement of financial accounting concepts* No. 1, Stamford, CT: FASB (for subsequent releases on the Conceptual Framework see FASB website: www.fasb.org).

Fischer, T.M. (1993) *Kostenmanagement strategischer Erfolgsfaktoren: Instrumente zur operativen Steuerung der strategischen Schlüsselfaktoren Qualität, Flexibilität und Schnelligkeit* (Cost management of strategic profit factors), Munich: Vahlen.

Fischer, T.M. (2000) *Kosten-Controlling: neue Methoden und Inhalte* (Cost controlling: new methods and contents), Stuttgart: Schäffer-Poeschel.

Fischer-Winkelmann, W.F. (1971) *Methodologie der Betriebswirtschaftslehre* (Methodology of business economics), Munich: W. Goldmann.

Fischer-Winkelmann, W.F. (1980) *Gesellschaftsorientierte Unternehmensrechnung* (Society-oriented accounting), Munich: Vahlen Verlag.

Fisher, I. (1906) *The nature of capital and income*, New York: Macmillan Company.

Franke, R. (1972) *Betriebsmodelle. Rechensysteme für Zwecke der kurzfristigen Planung, Kontrolle und Kalkulation* (Business models. Accounting systems for short-term planning, control and accounting), Düsseldorf: Bertelsmann.

Franz, K.-P. and Kajüter, P. (1997) *Kostenmanagement: Wettbewerbsvorteile durch systematische Kostensteuerung* (Cost management: through systematic costing policy), Stuttgart: Schäffer-Poeschel (2nd edn, 2002).

Franzen, W. (1985) *Entscheidungswirkungen von Kosteninformationen* (The effect of decisions on cost information), Frankfurt a.M.: O. Lang.

Freidank, C.-C., Götze, U., Huch, B. and Weber, J. (1997) *Kostenmanagement: aktuelle Konzepte und Anwendungen* (Cost management: up-to-date concepts and applications), Berlin: Springer.

Glaser, H. (1992) 'Prozeßkostenrechnung: Darstellung und Kritik' (Process cost accounting: discussion and critique), *Zeitschrift für betriebswirtschaftliche Forschung* 44: 275–88.

Göx, R.F. (1998) 'Pretiale Lenkung als Instrument der Wettbewerbsstrategie' (Pricing policy as instrument of competitive strategy), *Zeitschrift für betriebswirtschaftliche Forschung* 50: 260–88.

Göx, R.F. (1999) *Strategische Transferpreispolitik im Duopol* (Strategic transfer policy in the Duopol), Wiesbaden: Gabler.

Grossman, S.J. and Hart, O.D. (1983) 'An analysis of the principal–agent problem', *Econometrica* 51: 7–45.

Gümbel, R. (1988) 'Haben die Vollkostenrechner wirklich unrecht? Theoretische Grundlagen der Kostenrechnung' (Are those using process costing really wrong? Theoretical foundations of cost accounting), in W. Lücke eds, *Betriebswirtschaftliche Steuerungs- und Kontrollprobleme*, Wiesbaden: Gabler: 81–90.

Gutenberg, E. (1949) *Buchbesprechung zu Erich Kosiol: Bilanzreform und Einheitsbilanz* (Review of Kosiol: balance sheet reform and uniform accounting), *Zeitschrift für handelswissenschaftliche Forschung* (New Series) 33: 533–6 (reprinted under same title in book form: Berlin: Deutscher Betriebswirte-Verlag, 1952).

Gutenberg, E. (1951) *Grundlagen der Betriebswirtschaftslehre*, Vol. 1: *Die Produktion* (Foundations of business economics, Vol. 1: Production), Berlin: Springer Verlag.

Halbinger, J. (1980) *Erfolgsausweispolitik: Eine empirische Untersuchung zum bilanzpolitischen Verhalten deutscher Aktiengesellschaften* (Policy of profit reporting: an empirical investigation to the financial statement policy of German stock companies), Berlin: Schmidt.

Haller, A. (1995) 'International accounting harmonization', *European Accounting Review* 4 (2): 235–47.

Hansen, P. (1962) *The accounting concept of profit: an analysis and evaluation in the light of the economic theory of income and capital*, Amsterdam: North Holland Publishing Co.

Hax, H. (1964) 'Investitions- und Finanzplanung mit Hilfe der linearen Programmierung' (Investment and financial planning by means of linear programming), *Zeitschrift für betriebswirtschaftliche Forschung* 16: 430–46.

Hax, H. (1965a) *Die Koordination von Entscheidungen* (The coordination of decisions), Cologne.

Hax, H. (1965b) 'Kostenbewertung mit Hilfe der mathematischen Programmierung' (Costing by means of mathematical programming), *Zeitschrift für Betriebswirtschaft* 35: 197–210.

Hax, H. (2002) 'Integration externer und interner Unternehmungsrechnung' (Integration of external and internal accounting), in H.-U. Küpper and A. Wagenhofer, eds, *Handwörterbuch Unternehmensrechnung und Controlling* (Lexicon for accounting and controlling), Stuttgart: Schäfer-Poeschel Verlag: 758–67.

Hax, K. (1957) *Die Substanzerhaltung der Betriebe* (Capital maintenance of firms), Cologne: Westdeutscher Verlag.

Heinen, E. (1965) *Betriebswirtschaftliche Kostenlehre* (Cost theory of business economics), Vol. 1, 2nd edn, Wiesbaden: Gabler Verlag (6th edn, 1983).

Herde, G. (1992) *Präzisierung dreier axiomatischer Theorien des Rechnungswesens in einer formalen Typentheorie* (Making three axiomatic theories of accounting more precise by means of a formal theory of types), Bamberg: doctoral dissertation (published), Otto-Friedrich-Universität.

Hofmann, C. (2001) *Anreizorientierte Controllingsysteme* (Incentive-oriented control systems), Stuttgart: Schäffer-Poeschel Verlag.

Holmström, B. (1979) 'Moral Hazard and Observability', *Bell Journal of Economics* 10: 74–91.

Holzer, H.P. (1959) 'Corporate financial reporting in West Germany', *The Accounting Review* 34 (3): 399–402.

Holzer, H.P. and Schoenfeld, H.-M. (1963) 'The German solution to the post-war price level problem', *The Accounting Review* 38 (2): 67–80.

Homann, K., Meyer, M. and Waldkirch, R. (2002) 'Ethik und Unternehmensrechnung' (Ethics and accounting), in H.-U. Küpper and A. Wagenhofer eds, *Handwörterbuch Unternehmensrechnung und Controlling* (Lexicon for accounting and controlling), 4th edn, Stuttgart: Schäffer-Poeschel Verlag: cols. 495–504.

Honko, J. (1959) *Yrityksen Vuositulos: the annual income of an enterprise and its determination* (with English summary), Jakaia: Liietaloustieteellinen Tutkimuslaitos.

Horváth, P. (2003) *Controlling* (meaning approximately 'Managerial accounting'), 9th edn, Munich: Vahlen (1st edn, 1979).

Horváth, P. and Mayer, R. (1989) 'Prozeßkostenrechnung – Der neue Weg zu mehr Kostentransparenz und wirkungsvolleren Unternehmensstrategien' (Process cost accounting – the new road to greater cost transparency and a more efficient managerial strategy), *Controlling* 1 (4): 214–19.

Horváth, P. and Mayer, R. (1993) 'Prozeßkostenrechnung – Konzeption und Entwicklungen' (Process cost accounting), *Kostenrechnungspraxis* (Special Issue 2): 15–28.

Horváth, P., Kieninger, M., Mayer, R. and Schimank, C. (1993) 'Prozeßkostenrechnung – oder wie die Praxis die Theorie überholt' (Process cost accounting – or, how practice overtakes theory), *Die Betriebswirtschaft* 53: 609–28.

Hotelling, H. (1925) *Three-dimensional manifolds of states of motion*, Princeton, NJ.

Ijiri, Y. (1965) 'Axioms and structures of conventional accounting measurement', *The Accounting Review* 40 (January): 36–53.

Ijiri, Y. (1967) *The foundations of accounting measures*, Englewood Cliffs, NJ: Prentice-Hall, Inc.

Ijiri, Y. (1971) 'Axioms for historical cost valuation: a reply', *Journal of Accounting Research* 9 (1): 181–7.

Jäger, W. and Vogelsang, M. (1973) 'Konzernrechnungslegung von Aktienbanken' (Consolidated statements of stock companies), *Die Wirtschaftsprüfung* 26: 389–400, 421–8.

Käfer, K. (1967) *Kapitalflussrechnungen – Statement of Changes in Financial Position, Liquiditätsnachweis, Bewegungsbilanz als dritte Jahresrechnung der Unternehmung* (Flow of funds accounting – statement of changes in financial position, liquidity determination, statement of changes as the third annual financial statement type of the enterprise), Stuttgart: Poeschel Verlag (2nd edn, 1984).

Kilger, W. (1958) *Produktions- und Kostentheorie* (Production and cost theory), Wiesbaden: Gabler.

Kilger, W. (1961) *Flexible Plankostenrechnung* (Flexible cost planning), Köln: Westdeutscher Verlag (9th edn, 1988, under the title *Flexible Plankostenrechnung und Deckungsbeitragsrechnung* (Flexible cost planning and accounting with contribution margins), Wiesbaden: Gabler (11th edn by W. Kilger, J. Pampel and K. Vikas, 2002)).

Kilger, W. (1976) 'Kostentheoretische Grundlagen der Grenzplankostenrechnung' (Cost-theoretical foundations of marginal cost planning), *Zeitschrift für betriebswirtschaftliche Forschung* 28: 679–93.

Kistner, K.-P. (1981) *Produktions- und Kostentheorie* (Production and cost theory), Heidelberg: Physica (2nd edn, 1993).

Kistner, K.-P. and Luhmer, A. (1981) 'Zur Ermittlung der Kosten der Betriebsmittel in der statischen Produktionstheorie' (To the determination of operating resources in the static production theory), *Zeitschrift für Betriebswirtschaft* 51: 165–80.

Klein-Blenkers, F. (1992) *Die Hochschullehrer der Betriebswirtschaft in der Zeit von*

1898–1955 (University teachers of business economics in the time from 1898–1955), Cologne: Wirtschaftsverlag Bachem.

Kloock, J. (1969) *Betriebswirtschaftliche Input-Output-Modelle* (Input–output models in business economics), Wiesbaden: Gabler.

Kloock, J. (1981) 'Mehrperiodige Investitionsrechnungen auf der Basis kalkulatorischer und handelsrechtlicher Erfolgsrechnungen' (Multi-period investment calculation based on financial income and cost accounting), *Zeitschrift für betriebswirtschaftliche Forschung* 33: 873–90.

Kloock, J. (1992) 'Prozeßkostenrechnung als Rückschritt und Fortschritt der Kostenrechnung' (Process cost accounting as a step backwards and forwards in cost accounting), Parts 1 and 2, *Kostenrechnungspraxis* 36 (4): 183–93; (5): 237–45.

Kolb, J. (1978) *Industrielle Erlösrechnung* (Industrial profit calcultation), Wiesbaden: Gabler.

Koopmans, T.C. (1951) *Analysis of production as an efficient combination of activities, activity analysis of production and allocation*, New York, London, Sydney.

Kosiol, E. (1937) 'Jahresabschluß der Aktiengesellschaften' (Year-end closing of limited companies), *Zeitschrift für Betriebswirtschaft* 14: 225–64.

Kosiol, E. (1944a) *Bilanzreform und Einheitsbilanz* (Accounting reform and the uniform balance sheet), 2nd edn, Reichenberg (2nd printing, Wiesbaden, 1949; 3rd edn, Berlin: Deutscher Betriebswirteverlag, 1999).

Kosiol, E. (1944b) 'Der pagatorische Character des Anschaffungswertes in der Bilanz' (The pagatoric nature of the acquisition cost in the balance sheet), *Zeitschrift für handelswissenschaftliche Forschung* 37/38: 47–54.

Kosiol, E. (1956) Pagatorische Bilanz (Financial statements based on cash flows), *Lexikon des kaufmännischen Rechnungswesens*, 2nd edn, Stuttgart: C.E. Poeschel Verlag.

Kosiol, E. (1970a) 'Zur Axiomatik der Theorie der Pagatorischen Erfolgsrechnung' (On the axiomatization of the theory of cash flow earnings statement), *Zeitschrift für Betriebswirtschaft* 40: 135–62.

Kosiol, E. (ed.) (1970b) *Handwörterbuch des Rechnungswesens* (Lexicon of accounting), Stuttgart: C.E. Poeschel Verlag (4th edn by H.-U. Küpper and A. Wagenhofer, 2002).

Kosiol, E. (1978) *Pagatoric theory of financial income determination*, Urbana, IL: Center for Education and Research in Accounting.

Kosiol, E., Chmielewicz, K. and Schweitzer, M. (eds) (1981) *Handwörterbuch des Rechnungswesens* (Lexicon of accounting), 2nd edn, Stuttgart: C.E. Poeschel Verlag.

Kreikebaum, H. (1996) *Grundlagen der Unternehmensethik* (Foundations of entrepreneurial ethics), Stuttgart: Schäffer-Poeschel.

Küpper, H.-U. (1979) 'Dynamische Produktionsfunktion der Unternehmung auf der Basis des Input-Output-Ansatzes' (Dynamic production functions of the enterprise based on the input–output approach), *Zeitschrift für Betriebswirtschaft* 49: 93–106.

Küpper, H.-U. (1980) *Interdependenzen zwischen Produktionstheorie und der Organisation des Produktionsprozesses* (Interdependence between production theory and the organization of the production process), Berlin: Duncker & Humblot.

Küpper, H.-U. (1983) 'Der Bedarf an Kosten- und Leistungsinformationen in Industrieunternehmungen – Ergebnisse einer empirischen Erhebung' (Information demand for cost and performance data in industrial firms), *Kostenrechnungspraxis* 27: 169–81.

Küpper, H.-U. (1984) 'Kosten- und entscheidungstheoretische Ansatzpunkte zur Behandlung des Fixkostenproblems in der Kostenrechnung' (Cost and decision theoretic treatment of the problem of fixed costs in cost accounting), *Zeitschrift für betriebswirtschaftliche Forschung* 36: 794–811.

Küpper, H.-U. (1985a) 'Investitionstheoretische Fundierung der Kostenrechnung' (Investment theoretical foundations of cost accounting), *Zeitschrift für betriebswirtschaftliche Forschung* 37: 26–46.

Küpper, H.-U. (1985b) 'Structure, applications and limits of dynamic production functions of the firm based on the input–output approach', *Engineering Costs and Production Economics* 9: 129–34.

Küpper, H.-U. (1988a) 'Gegenstand und Ansätze einer dynamischen Theorie der Kostenrechnung' (Object and approaches of a dynamic costing theory), in H. Hax, W. Kern and H.-H. Schröder eds, *Zeitaspekte in betriebswirtschaftlicher Theorie und Praxis*, Stuttgart: Poeschel: 43–59.

Küpper, H.-U. (1988b) 'Investitionstheoretische versus kontrolltheoretische Abschreibungen: Alternative oder gleichartige Konzepte einer Entscheidungsorientierten Kostenrechnung?' (Depreciations: investment-theoretical vs. control-theoretical-alternative or equivalent concepts of decision-oriented cost accounting), *Zeitschrift für Betriebswirtschaft* 58: 397–415.

Küpper, H.-U. (1991) 'Multi-period production planning and managerial accounting', in G. Fandel and G. Zäpfel eds, *Modern production concepts: theory and applications*, Berlin, Heidelberg, New York: Springer: 46–62.

Küpper, H.-U. (1992) 'Unternehmensethik – ein Gegenstand betriebswirtschaftlicher Forschung und Lehre' (Entrepreneurial ethics – a subject for research and teaching), *Betriebswirtschaftliche Forschung und Praxis* 44: 498–518.

Küpper, H.-U. (1993a) 'Internes Rechnungswesen' (Cost accounting), in J. Hauschild and O. Grün eds, *Ergebnisse empirischer betriebswirtschaftlicher Forschung. Zu einer Realtheorie der Unternehmung, Festschrift to Eberhard Witte*, Stuttgart: Schäffer-Poeschel: 601–31.

Küpper, H.-U. (1993b) 'Kostenrechnung auf investitionstheoretischer Basis' (Costing based on investment theory – to the re-orientation of cost accounting), in J. Weber ed., *Zur Neuausrichtung der Kostenrechnung. Entwicklungsperspektiven für die 90er Jahre*, Stuttgart: Schäffer-Poeschel: 79–136.

Küpper, H.-U. (1995) 'Unternehmensplanung und -steuerung mit pagatorischen oder kalkulatorischen Erfolgsrechnungen?' (Business planning and directing through pagatoric accounting vs. cost accounting?), in T. Schildbach and F.W. Wagner eds, *Unternehmensrechnung als Instrument der internen Steuerung*, Special Issue 34 of the Zeitschrift für betriebswirtschaftliche Forschung, Düsseldorf: Verlags-Gruppe Handelsblatt: 19–50.

Küpper, H.-U. (2000) 'Hochschulrechnung auf der Basis von doppelter Buchführung und HGB?' (Accounting for universities based on double-entry bookkeeping and the German commercial code), *Zeitschrift für betriebswirtschaftliche Forschung* 52: 348–69.

Küpper, H.-U. (2001) *Controlling. Konzeption, Aufgaben und Instrumente* (Controlling: conception, tasks and instruments), 3rd edn, Stuttgart: Schäffer-Poeschel Verlag (1st edn, 1995).

Küpper, H.-U. (2002) 'Konzeption einer Perioden-Erfolgsrechnung für Hochschulen' (The concept of periodic performance accounting for universities), *Zeitschrift für Betriebswirtschaft* 72: 929–51.

Küpper, H.-U. and Mattessich, R. (2005) 'Twentieth-century accounting research in the German language area', *Accounting, Business and Financial History* (Special issue on German Accounting) 15 (3): 345–410.

Küpper, H.-U. and Picot, A. (1999) 'Gegenstand der Unternehmensethik' (The subject of the ethics of the firm), in W. Korff ed., *Handbuch der Wirtschaftsethik*, Vol. 3: *Ethik wirtschaftlichen Handelns*, Gütersloh: Gütersloher Verlagshaus: 132–48.

Küpper, H.-U. and Wagenhofer, A. (eds) (2002) *Handwörterbuch Unternehmensrechnung und Controlling* (Lexicon for accounting and controlling), 4th edn, Stuttgart: Schäffer-Poeschel Verlag.

Laßmann, G. (1968) *Die Kosten- und Erlösrechnung als Instrument der Planung und Kontrolle in Industriebetrieben* (Cost and profit calculation as instrument of planning and control in industrial enterprises), Düsseldorf: Stahleisen.

Laßmann, G. (1973) 'Gestaltungsformen der Kosten- und Erlösrechnung im Hinblick auf Planungs- und Kontrollaufgaben' (Forms of cost and profit calculation from the viewpoint of planning and control), *Die Wirtschaftsprüfung* 26: 4–17.

Laßmann, G. (1980) 'Neue Aufgaben der Kosten- und Erlösrechnung aus der Sicht der Unternehmensführung' (New tasks of cost and profit calculation from the viewpoint of the management), in D. Hahn ed., *Führungsprobleme industrieller Unternehmungen*, *Festschrift to the 60th Birthday of Friedrich Thomée*, Berlin, New York: de Gruyter: 327–47.

Laux, H. (1995) *Erfolgssteuerung und Organisation* (Profit policy and organization), Berlin: Springer.

Leffson, U. (1964) *Die Grundsätze ordnungsmäßiger Buchführung* (Principles of orderly accounting), Düsseldorf: IDW-Verlag (4th edn, 1976; 7th rev. edn, 1987).

Leontief, W. (1966) 'Input–output analysis', in W. Leontief ed., *Input–output economics*, New York: Oxford University Press: 134–55.

Leuz, C. (1998) 'The role of accrual accounting in restricting dividends to shareholders', *European Accounting Review* 7 (4): 579–604.

Loitlsberger, E. (ed.) (1963) *Empirische Betriebswirtschaftslehre* (Empirical business economics), Wiesbaden: Gabler Verlag.

Lücke, W. (1955) 'Investitionsrechnungen auf der Grundlage von Ausgaben und Kosten' (Investment calculation based on expenditures and costs), *Zeitschrift für handelswissenschaftliche Forschung* 7: 310–24.

Lücke, W. (1965) 'Die kalkulatorischen Zinsen im betrieblichen Rechnungswesen' (Imputed interests in cost accounting), *Zeitschrift für Betriebswirtschaft* 35: 3–28.

Lücke, W. (1969) *Produktions- und Kostentheorie* (Production and cost theories), Würzburg, Vienna: Physica-Verlag (2nd edn, 1970; 3rd edn, 1976).

Luhmer, A. (1980) 'Fixe und variable Abschreibungskosten und optimale Investitionsdauer – Zu einem Aufsatz von Peter Swoboda' (Fixed and variable depreciation costs and optimal investment time), *Zeitschrift für Betriebswirtschaft* 50: 897–903.

Magee, R.P. (1980) 'Equilibria in budget participation', *Journal of Accounting Research* 18: 551–73.

Mahlert, H. (1976) *Die Abschreibungen in der entscheidungsorientierten Kostenrechnung* (Depreciations in decision-oriented cost accounting), Opladen: Westdeutscher Verlag.

Männel, W. and Küpper, H.-U. (eds) (1999) 'Integration der Unternehmensrechnung' (Integration of enterprise accounting), *Kostenrechnungspraxis* (Special Issue 3): 119–32.

Mattessich, R. (1957) 'Towards a general and axiomatic foundation of accountancy: with an introduction to the matrix formulation of accounting systems', *Accounting Research* 8 (October): 328–355 (reprinted in S.A. Zeff ed., *The accounting postulates and principles controversy of the 1960s*, New York: Garland Publishing, Inc., 1982; Spanish translation in *Technica Economica* (April 1958): 106–27).

Mattessich, R. (1964) *Accounting and analytical methods: measurement and projection of income and wealth in the micro- and macro-economy*, Homewood, IL: R.D. Irwin, Inc. (reprinted in the 'Accounting Classics Series', Houston, TX: Scholars Book Co., 1977; also in the 'Series of Financial Classics' of Reprints on Demand, Ann Arbor, MI: Microfilms International, 1979, still available; Japanese translation under the direction of Shinzaburo Koshimura, *Kaikei to Bunsekiteki-Hoho Jokan*, 2 vols, Tokyo: Dobunkan, Ltd, Vol. 1: 1972, Vol. 2: 1975; Spanish translation, by Carlos Luis García Casella and Maria del Carmen Ramírez de Rodríguez, Buenos Aires: La Ley, 2002).

Mattessich, R. (1970) *Die wissenschaftlichen Grundlagen des Rechnungswesens* (The scientific foundations of accounting), Düsseldorf: Bertelsmann Universitätsverlag.

Mattessich, R. (1986) 'Fritz Schmidt (1892–1950) and his pioneering work in current value accounting in comparison to Edwards and Bells theory', *Contemporary Accounting Research* 2 (Spring): 157–78.

Mattessich, R. (1996a, 1996b) 'Academic research in accounting: the last 50 years'; and 'Accounting research: response to commentators', both *Asia-Pacific Journal of Accounting* 3 (1, June): 3–81, 109–35.

Mattessich, R. (2002) 'Accounting schism or synthesis? A challenge for the conditional-normative approach', *Canadian Accounting Perspective* 1 (2): 185–216.

Mattessich, R. (2003) 'Accounting research and researchers of the nineteenth century and the beginning of the twentieth century', *Accounting, Business and Financial History* 13 (2, July): 125–79.

Mattessich, R. and Küpper, H.-U. (2003) 'Accounting research in the German language area: first half of the twentieth century', paper presented at the 26th Congress of the European Accounting Association in Seville. Abbreviated version published in the *Review of Accounting and Finance* 2 (3): 106–37.

Maus, S. (1996) *Strategiekonforme Kostenrechnung* (Cost accounting in conformity with business strategy), Stuttgart: Schäffer-Poeschel.

Möller, H.P. and Hüfner, B. (2002) 'Empirische Forschung' (Empirical research), in H.-U. Küpper and A. Wagenhofer eds, *Handwörterbuch Unternehmensrechnung und Controlling* (Lexicon for accounting and controlling), 4th edn, Stuttgart: Schäffer-Poeschel Verlag: cols 351–9.

Möller, P. (1983) 'Probleme und Ergebnisse kapitalmarktorientierter empirischer Bilanz-forschung in Deutschland' (Problems and results of capital market oriented accounting research in Germany), *Betriebswirtschaftliche Forschung und Praxis* 35: 285–302.

Moonitz, M. (1961) *The basic postulates of accounting*, New York: AICPA.

Moxter, A. (1966) 'Die Grundsätze ordnungsmäßiger Bilanzierung und der Stand der Bilanztheorie' (Principles of orderly financial statement presentation and the status of accounting theory), *Zeitschrift für betriebswirtschaftliche Forschung* 18: 28–59.

Moxter, A. (1974) *Bilanzlehre* (Theory of financial statements), Wiesbaden: Gabler Verlag (2nd edn, 1976; 3rd edn, Band 1: *Einführung in die Bilanztheorie*, Vol. 1: *Introduction to accounting*, 1984 – see also Chapter 12).

Moxter, A. (1976) *Grundsätze ordnungsmäßiger Unternehmensbewertung* (Principles of orderly valuation of a business), Wiesbaden: Gabler Verlag (2nd rev. edn, 1983).

Moxter, A. (1980) 'Die handelsrechtlichen Grundsätze ordnungsmäßiger Buchführung und das neue Bilanzrecht' (The commercial priniciples of orderly accounting and the new accounting legislation), *Zeitschrift für Unternehmens- und Gesellschaftsrecht* 9: 254–76.

Moxter, A. (1985) 'Das System der handelsrechtlichen Grundsätze ordnungsmäßiger Bilanzierung' (The system of commercial principles of orderly statement presentation), in G. Gross ed., *Der Wirtschaftsprüfer im Schnittpunkt nationaler und internationaler*

Entwicklung, Festschrift to the 60th Birthday of Klaus von Wysocki, Düsseldorf: IDW-Verlag: 17–28.

Moxter, A. (1989) 'Zur wirtschaftlichen Betrachtungsweise im Bilanzrecht' (The economic view of accounting legislation), *Steuer und Wirtschaft* 19 (66): 232–41.

Moxter, A. (1993) *Bilanzrechtsprechung* (Juridical accounting judgements), 3rd edn, Tübingen: Mohr (1st edn, 1982).

Neus, W. (1997) 'Verrechnungspreise – Rekonstruktion des Marktes innerhalb der Unternehmung' (Transfer prices – a reconstruction of the market within the firm), *Die Betriebswirtschaft* 57: 38–47.

Ordelheide, D. (1993) 'True and fair view: a European and a German perspective', *European Accounting Review* 2 (2): 81–90.

Ordelheide, D. (1996) 'True and fair view: a European and a German perspective II', *European Accounting Review* 5 (3): 495–506.

Ossadnik, W. (1998) 'Considering interrelationship in strategic decisions', *European Accounting Review* 7 (2): 315–21.

Pack, L. (1966) *Die Elastizität der Kosten. Grundlagen einer entscheidungsorientierten Kostentheorie* (The elasticity of costs. Foundations for a decision-oriented cost theory), Wiesbaden: Gabler.

Pellens, B. (1989) *Der Informationswert von Konzernabschlüssen – eine empirische Untersuchung deutscher Börsengesellschaften* (The information value of consolidated financial statements – an empirical investigation of German enterprises listed on stock exchanges), Wiesbaden: Gabler Verlag.

Pfaff, D. (1993) *Kostenrechnung – Unsicherheit und Organisation* (Cost accounting-uncertainty and organization), Heidelberg: Physica-Verlag.

Pfaff, D. (1994) 'Zur Notwendigkeit einer eigenständigen Kostenrechnung-Anmerkungen zur Neuorientierung des internen Rechnungswesens im Hause Siemens' (On the necessity of an independent cost accounting – remarks to the new orientation at the House of Siemens), *Zeitschrift für betriebswirtschaftliche Forschung* 46 (December): 1065–84.

Plaut, H.-G. (1951) 'Die Plankostenrechnung in der Praxis des Betriebes' (Plan costing in business practice), *Zeitschrift für Betriebswirtschaft* 21: 531–43.

Plaut, H.-G. (1953) 'Die Grenzplankostenrechnung' (Marginal plan-costing), *Zeitschrift für Betriebswirtschaft* 23: 347–63, 402–13.

Plaut, H.-G. (1955) 'Die Grenzplankostenrechnung' (Marginal plan-costing), *Zeitschrift für Betriebswirtschaft* 25: 25–39.

Plaut, H.-G. (1958) 'Die Grenzplankostenrechnung in der Diskussion und ihrer weiteren Entwicklung' (Discussion on marginal plan costing and its development), *Zeitschrift für Betriebswirtschaft* 28: 251–66.

Plaut, H.-G. (1987) 'Die Entwicklung der flexiblen Plankostenrechnung zu einem Instrument der Unternehmensführung' (The development of flexible plan costing to an instrument of management), *Zeitschrift für Betriebswirtschaft* 57: 355–66.

Preinreich, G.A.D. (1937) 'Valuation and amortisation', *The Accounting Review* 12: 209–24.

Preinreich, G.A.D. (1940) 'The economic life of industrial equipment', *Econometrica* 8 (1): 12–44.

Pressmar, D.B. (1971) *Kosten- und Leistungsanalyse im Industriebetrieb* (Cost and performance analysis in the industrial enterprise), Wiesbaden: Gabler.

Riebel, P. (1959) 'Das Rechnen mit Einzelkosten und Deckungsbeiträgen' (Calculation with unit costs and contribution margins), *Zeitschrift für handelswissenschaftliche Forschung* (New Series) 11: 213–38.

Riebel, P. (1964a) 'Die Preiskalkulation auf der Grundlage von "Selbstkosten" oder von relativen Einzelkosten und Deckungsbeiträgen' (Price calculation based on 'total cost' vs. relative unit costs and contribution margins as instrument for market analysis), *Zeitschrift für betriebswirtschaftliche Forschung* 16: 549–612.

Riebel, P. (1964b) *Deckungsbeitragsrechnung als Instrument der Absatzanalyse* (Accounting with contribution margins as instrument for market analysis), Baden-Baden: Verlag für Unternehmensführung.

Riebel, P. (1972) *Einzelkosten- und Deckungsbeitragsrechnung: Grundfragen einer markt- und entscheidungsorientierten Unternehmensrechnung* (Costing with unit costs and contribution margins: basic questions of a market and decision oriented accounting), Opladen: Westdeutscher Verlag (2nd rev. edn, 1976; 7th edn, 1994, Wiesbaden: Gabler).

Riebel, P. (1983) 'Thesen zur Einzelkosten- und Deckungsbeitragsrechnung' (Theses to unit costing and contribution margin costing), in K. Chmielewicz ed., *Entwicklungslinien der Kosten- und Erlösrechnung*, Stuttgart: C.E. Poeschel: 21–47.

Riebel, P. (1994) Core features of the 'Einzelkosten- und Deckungsbeitragsrechnung', *European Accounting Review* 3 (3): 515–43.

Riebel, P. and Sinzig, W. (1982) Einsatzmöglichkeiten relationaler Datenbanken zur Unterstützung einer entscheidungsorientierten Kosten-, Erlös- und Deckungsbeitragsrechnung (Application potential of relational data banks in support of decision-oriented cost accounting), in P. Stahlknecht ed., *EDV-Systeme im Finanz- und Rechnungswesen. Anwendergespräch*, Osnabrück, Berlin, Heidelberg, New York: Springer: 93–125.

Rieger, W. (1928) *Einführung in die Privatwirtschaftslehre* (Introduction to business theory), 3rd edn, Erlangen: Palm & Enke.

Riegler, C. (1996) *Verhaltenssteuerung durch Target Costing* (Behavioural guidance through target costing), Stuttgart: Schäffer-Poeschel.

Riegler, C. (2000) *Hierarchische Anreizsysteme im wertorientierten Management: eine agency-theoretische Untersuchung* (Hierarchical incentive systems in value-oriented management: an agency-oriented investigation), Stuttgart: Schäffer-Poeschel Verlag.

Rieper, B. (1986) 'Die Bestellmengenrechnung als Investitions- und Finanzierungsproblem' (Calculating order quantities as a problem of investment and finance), *Zeitschrift für Betriebswirtschaft* 56: 1230–55.

Roski, R. (1987) 'Planungsrelevante Aggregatskosten' (Aggregated costs for planning), *Zeitschrift für Betriebswirtschaft* 57: 526–45.

SAP (2000) *Whitepaper: Integriertes Produkt- und Prozess-Engineering mit mySAP.com*, Walldorf: SAP Discrete Industries.

Scheer, A.-W. (1981) 'Einsatz von Datenbanksystemen im Rechnungswesen – Überblick und Entwicklungstendenzen' (The use of data bank systems in accounting – survey and developmental trends), *Zeitschrift für betriebswirtschaftliche Forschung* 33: 490–507.

Scheffler, E. (1999) 'Der Deutsche Standardisierungsrat – Struktur, Aufgaben und Kompetenzen' (German council on standardisation – structure, tasks and responsibilities), *Betriebswirtschaftliche Forschung und Praxis* 51: 407–17.

Scheffler, E. (2002) 'Deutsches Rechnungslegungs Standards Committee (DRSC)' (The German Accounting Standards Board), in W. Ballwieser, A.G. Coenenberg and K. von Wysocki eds, *Handwörterbuch der Rechnungslegung und Prüfung* (Lexicon of accounting and auditing), 3rd rev. edn, Stuttgart: Schäffer-Poeschel Verlag: cols 528–37.

Schierenbeck, H. (2001) *Ertragsorientiertes Bankmanagement* (Profit oriented bank management), 2 vols, 7th edn, Wiesbaden: Gabler-Verlag (1st edn, 1985).

Schildbach, T. (1979) *Geldentwertung und Bilanz: kritische Analyse der Eignung ver-*

schiedener Erhaltungs- und Bewertungskonzeptionen in Zeiten steigender Preise auf der Grundlage der Aufgaben von Erfolgsbilanzen sowie auf der Basis des Konsumstrebens als Ziel der Wirtschaftssubjekte (Inflation and accounting: a critical analysis of the usefulness of different capital maintenance and valuation methods in times of rising prices ...), Düsseldorf: IDW-Verlag.

Schildbach, T. (1984) 'Inflation Accounting I and II' (in German language), *Das Wirtschaftsstudium* 13 (4): 122–5; 215–20.

Schildbach, T. (1987) 'Die neue Generalklausel für den Jahresabschluß von Kapitalgesellschaften – zur Interpretation des Paragraphen 264 Abs. 2 HGB' (The new legal summary for financial statement presentation of stock companies – to the interpretation of ...), *Betriebswirtschaftliche Forschung und Praxis* 39: 1–15.

Schildbach, T. (1990) 'Inflation accounting', in Erwin Grochla managing editor, *Handbook of German business management*, Vol. 1, Stuttgart: Verlag C.E. Poeschel/Springer Verlag: 1118–29.

Schiller, U. (1999) 'Information management and transfer pricing', *European Accounting Review* 8 (4): 655–73.

Schiller, U. (2000) *Informationsorientiertes Controlling in dezentralisierten Unternehmen* (Information oriented controlling in decentralized enterprises), Stuttgart: Schäffer-Poeschel Verlag.

Schipper, K. (2003) 'Principles-based accounting standards', *Accounting Horizons* 17 (1): 61–73.

Schmidt, F. (1921) *Die organische Bilanz im Rahmen der Wirtschaft* (The organic balance sheet in an economic setting), 1st edn, Leipzig: G.A. Gloeckner Verlagsbuchhandlung (2nd edn, 1922, *Die organische Tageswertbilanz*, Leipzig; 3rd edn, 1929; reprint, Wiesbaden: Betriebswirtschaftlicher Verlag Dr T. Gabler, 1953; Japanese translation, *Yukikan taishohyo gakusetsu*, Tokyo: Dobunkan Ltd, 1934).

Schneider, D. (1961) *Die wirtschaftliche Nutzungsdauer von Anlagegütern als Bestimmungsgrund der Abschreibungen* (Economic usefulness of fixed assets as determination of depreciation), Cologne: Westdeutscher Verlag.

Schneider, D. (1968) 'Ausschüttungsfähiger Gewinn und das Minimum an Selbstfinanzierung' (Distributable profit and minimal self-financing), *Zeitschrift für betriebswirtschaftliche Forschung* 20: 1–29.

Schneider, D. (1981) *Geschichte betriebswirtschaftlicher Theorie* (History of business-economics theory), Munich: Oldenbourg Verlag (3rd edn, 1987).

Schneider, D. (1984) 'Entscheidungsrelevante fixe Kosten, Abschreibungen und Zinsen zur Substanzerhaltung – Zwei Beispiele von 'Betriebsblindheit' in Kostentheorie und Kostenrechnung' (Decision relevant costs, depreciations and interests at capital maintenance – two examples of managerial blindness in cost theory and cost accounting), *Der Betrieb* 37: 2521–8.

Schneider, D. (1990) 'Unternehmensethik und Gewinnprinzip in der Betriebswirtschaftslehre' (Entrepreneurial ethics and the profit principle in business economics), *Zeitschrift für betriebswirtschaftliche Forschung* 42: 869–91.

Schneider, D. (1991) 'A critique of the "New school in the history of accountancy"', in *Accounting history: the paradigms of depreciation and price calculation* – Proceedings of the Accounting Research Methodology Conference, Oxford.

Schneider, D. (1992) 'Theorien zur Entwicklung des Rechnungswesens' (Theories to the development of accounting), *Zeitschrift für betriebswirtschaftliche Forschung* 44 (1): 3–31.

Schneider, D. (1996) 'Germany', in M. Chatfield and R. Vangermeersch eds, *The history of accounting: an international encyclopedia*, New York: Garland Publishing, Inc.: 278–9.

Schneider, D. (2001) *Betriebswirtschaftslehre*, Vol. 4: *Geschichte und Methoden der Wirtschaftswissenschaften* (History and methods of the economic sciences), Munich: R. Oldenbourg Verlag (previous volumes were Vol. 1: *Grundlagen*, 1993; Vol. 2: *Rechnungswesen*, 1994; Vol. 3: *Theorie der Unternehmung*, 1997).

Schneider, E. (1951) *Wirtschaftlichkeitsrechnung* (Efficiency accounting), Tübingen: Mohr.

Schoenfeld, H.-M. (1972) 'Development and present state of cost theory in Germany', *International Journal of Accounting Education and Research* 9 (1): 43–65.

Schoenfeld, H.-M. (1996a) 'Micro economics in Germany', in M. Chatfield and R. Vangermeersch eds, *The history of accounting: an international encyclopedia*, New York: Garland Publishing, Inc., 416–20.

Schoenfeld, H.-M. (1996b) 'Schmalenbach, Eugen (1873–1955)', in M. Chatfield and R. Vangermeersch eds, *The history of accounting: an international encyclopedia*, New York: Garland Publishing, Inc.: 514–16.

Schoenfeld, H.-M. (1996c) 'Zimmerman, Vernon K. (1928–)', in M. Chatfield and R. Vangermeersch eds, *The history of accounting: an international encyclopedia*, New York: Garland Publishing, Inc., 619.

Schüppenhauer, J. (1965) *Die Bilanzauffassung von Edwards and Bell, insbesondere ihre Beziehung zur organischen Bilanztheorie* (Edwards and Bells view of accounting, particularly its relation to organic accounting), Saarbrücken: University of Saarbrücken (Diplomarbeit, approximately master thesis).

Schweitzer, M. (1970) 'Axiomatik des Rechnungswesens' (Axiomatic of accounting), in E. Kosiol ed., *Handwörterbuch des Rechnungswesens* (Lexicon of accounting), 1st edn, Stuttgart: Poeschel Verlag: cols 83–90.

Schweitzer, M. (1972) *Struktur und Funktion der Bilanz* (Structure and function of financial statements), Berlin: Duncker & Humblot.

Schweitzer, M. (1990) 'Zur Geltung produktionstheoretischer Aussagen in der Industrie, Führungsorganisation und Technologiemanagement' (On the validity of production theoretical statements in industry, management, organizations and technology management), in R. Bühner ed., *Festschrift to the 65th Birthday of Friedrich Hoffmann*, Berlin: Duncker & Humblot: 231–56.

Schweitzer, M. (1995) 'Eugen Schmalenbach as the founder of cost accounting in the German-speaking world', in A. Tsuji and P. Garner eds, *Studies in accounting history: tradition and innovation for the twenty-first century*, Westport, CT: Greenwood Publishing Group, Inc.: 29–43.

Schweitzer, M. and Küpper, H.-U. (1974) *Produktions- und Kostentheorie der Unternehmung* (Production and cost theory of the firm), Reinbek bei Hamburg: Rowohlt (2nd edn, 1997, Wiesbaden: Gabler).

Schweitzer, M. and Küpper, H.-U. (2003) *Systeme der Kosten- und Erlösrechnung* (Systems of cost and profit accounting), 8th edn, Munich: Verlag Franz Vahlen (1st edn, *Systeme der Kostenrechnung* (Systems of cost accounting), Munich: Verlag Moderne Industrie, 1975; 7th edn, 1998).

Seicht, G. (1970) *Die kapitaltheoretische Bilanz und die Entwicklung der Bilanztheorie* (The capital-theoretic balance sheet and the development of accounting theory), Berlin: Duncker & Humblot.

Seicht, G. (1977) *Die Grenzbetrachtung in der Entwicklung des betrieblichen Rechnungswesens* (Marginal consideration in the development of cost accounting), Berlin: Duncker & Humblot.

Seidenschwarz, W. (1993) *Target costing: marktorientiertes Zielkostenmanagement* (Target costing: market oriented target management), Munich: Vahlen.

Siegel, T. (1994) 'Das Realisationsprinzip als allgemeines Periodisierungsprinzip?' (The realization principle as general periodization criterion), *Betriebswirtschaftliche Forschung und Praxis* 46: 1–24.

Sinzig, W. (1983) *Datenbankorientiertes Rechnungswesen. Grundzüge einer EDV-gestützten Realisierung der Einzelkosten- und Deckungsbeitragsrechnung* (Data bank oriented accounting. Basic principles of a computer-based realization of accounting with unit costs and contribution margins), Berlin, Heidelberg, New York, Tokyo: Springer.

Slaymaker, A.E. (1996) 'Conceptual framework', in M. Chatfield and R. Vangermeersch eds, *The history of accounting: an international encyclopedia*, New York: Garland Publishing, Inc.: 150–4.

Sprouse, R.T. and Moonitz, M. (1962) *A tentative set of broad accounting principles for business enterprises*, New York: AICPA.

Steinmann, H. and Löhr, A. (1994) *Grundlagen der Unternehmensethik* (Foundations of enterpreneurial ethics), 2nd edn, Stuttgart: Schäffer-Poeschel Verlag.

Steven, M. (1991) 'Umwelt als Produktionsfaktor' (The environment as production factor), *Zeitschrift für Betriebswirtschaft* 61: 509–23.

Steven, M. (1993) *Produktion und Umweltschutz* (Production and environmental protection), Wiesbaden: Gabler.

Steven, M. (1994a) 'Dynamische Analyse des Umweltfaktors in der Produktion' (Dynamic analysis of environmental factors in factories), *Zeitschrift für Betriebswirtschaft* 64: 493–513.

Steven, M. (1994b) 'Die Einbeziehung des Umweltfaktors in die Gutenberg- Produktionsfunktion' (Consideration of environmental factors in the production function of Gutenberg), *Zeitschrift für Betriebswirtschaft* 64: 1491–512.

Swoboda, P. (1979) 'Die Ableitung variabler Abschreibungskosten aus Modellen zur Optimierung der Investitionsdauer' (Derivation of variable depreciation costs from models for the optimization of investment time), *Zeitschrift für Betriebswirtschaft* 49: 565–80.

Troßmann, E. (1983) *Grundlagen einer dynamischen Theorie und Politik der betrieblichen Produktion* (Basics of a dynamic theory and policy of commercial production), Berlin: Duncker & Humblot.

Ulrich, P. (1998) *Integrative Wirtschaftsethik* (Integrative economic ethics), 2nd edn, Bern: Paul Haupt (1st edn, 1996).

Vikas, K. (1989) *Controlling im Dienstleistungsbereich mit Grenzplankostenrechnung* (Controlling in service industries with marginal plan costing), Wiesbaden: Gabler.

Vikas, K. (1996) *Neue Konzepte für das Kostenmanagement* (New concepts of cost management), 3rd edn, Wiesbaden: Gabler.

Wagenhofer, A. (1990) 'Voluntary disclosure with a strategic opponent', *Journal of Accounting and Economics* 12 (4): 341–63.

Wagenhofer, A. (1992a) 'Verrechnungspreise zur Koordination bei Informationsasymmetrie' (Divisional pricing for the coordination in case of information asymmetry), in K. von Spremann and K. Aeberhard eds, *Controlling-Grundlagen, Informationssysteme, Anwendungen*, Wiesbaden: Gabler Verlag: 637–56.

Wagenhofer, A. (1992b) 'Abweichungsanalysen bei der Erfolgskontrolle aus agencytheoretischer Sicht' (Variance analysis with profit control from the viewpoint of agency theory), *Betriebswirtschaftliche Forschung und Praxis* 44: 319–38.

Wagenhofer, A. (1994) 'Transfer pricing under asymmetric information', *European Accounting Review* 3: 71–104.

Wagenhofer, A. (1995a) 'Verursachungsgerechte Kostenschlüsselung und die Steuerung dezentraler Preisentscheidungen' (Causation rights, cost allocation, and decentralized transfer pricing), in T. Schildbach and F.W. Wagner eds, *Unternehmensrechnung als Instrument der internen Steuerung*, Special Issue 34 of the *Zeitschrift für betriebswirtschaftliche Forschung*, Düsseldorf: Verlags-Gruppe Handelsblatt: 81–118.

Wagenhofer, A. (1995b) 'Verhaltenssteuerung durch Verrechnungspreise' (Behavioural policy through transfer pricing), in A.-W. Scheer ed., *Rechnungswesen und EDV, 16. Saarbrücker Arbeitstagung 1995*, Heidelberg: Physica: 281–301.

Wagenhofer, A. (1997) 'Kostenrechnung und Verhaltenssteuerung' (Cost accounting and behavioural policy), in C.-C. Freidank, U. Götze, B. Huch and J. Weber eds, *Kostenmanagement – Neuere Konzepte und Anwendungen*, Berlin: Springer: 57–78.

Wagenhofer, A. (1999) *International Accounting Standards: Bilanzierung und Bewertung; Auswirkungen auf den Jahresabschluß* (International accounting standards: statement presentation and valuation: effects upon financial statements), 2nd edn, Vienna: Ueberreuter.

Wagenhofer, A. (2006) 'Management accounting research in German-speaking countries', *Journal of Management Accounting Research* 18: 1–19.

Wagenhofer, A. and Ewert, R. (2003) *Externe Unternehmensrechnung* (Financial accounting and auditing), Berlin: Springer Verlag.

Wagner, F.W. (1982) 'Zur Informations- und Ausschüttungsbemessungsfunktion des Jahresabschlusses auf einem organisierten Kapitalmarkt' (On the information and distribution function of statement presentation in a capital market), *Zeitschrift für betriebswirtschaftliche Forschung* 34: 749–71.

Wagner, F.W. (ed.) (1993) *Ökonomische Analyse des Bilanzrechts: Entwicklungslinien und Perspektiven; Tagung des Ausschusses Unternehmensrechnung im Verein für Socialpolitik am 12. und 13. März 1993 in München* (Economic analysis of accounting legislation: …), Düsseldorf: Verl.-Gruppe Handelsblatt.

Wartmann, R. (1963) 'Rechnerische Erfassung der Vorgänge im Hochofen zur Planung und Steuerung der Betriebsweise sowie der Erzauswahl' (Accounting of blast furnace processes for planning and managing as well as the selection of iron ores), *Stahl und Eisen* 83: 1414–26.

Weber, C.(K.) (1966) *The evolution of direct costing*, Urbana-Champaign, IL: Center for International Education and Research in Accounting, University of Illinois.

Weber, J. (1987) *Logistikkostenrechnung* (Logistic-based cost accounting), Berlin: Springer.

Wedekind, H. and Ortner, G.E. (1977) 'Der Aufbau einer Datenbank für die Kostenrechnung' (Installing a data bank for cost accounting), *Die Betriebswirtschaft* 37: 533–42.

Weilenmann, P. (1981) 'Kapitalflußrechnungen als Führungsinstrument (unter besonderer Berücksichtigung schweizerischer Unternehmungen)' (Cash flow accounting as directional instrument – under particular consideration of Swiss enterprises), in E. Rühli and J.-P. Thommen eds, *Unternehmungsführung aus finanz- und bankwirtschaftlicher Sicht*, Stuttgart: Poeschel: 387–96.

Wieland, J. (1994) 'Warum Unternehmensethik?' (Why an ethics for business?), in S. Blaschke, W. Köhler and P. Rohs eds, *Markt und Moral: Die Diskussion um die Unternehmensethik*, Bad Homburg and Bern: Paul Haupt: 215–39.

Wittenbrink, H. (1975) *Kurzfristige Erfolgsplanung und Erfolgskontrolle mit Betrieb-smodellen* (Short-term profit and revenue planning and control by means of business models), Wiesbaden: Gabler.

Wittmann, W. (1968) *Produktionstheorie* (Production theory), Berlin, Heidelberg, New York: Springer.

Wysocki, K. von (1969) *Konzernrechnungslegung in Deutschland* (Accounting of con-solidated statements in Germany), Düsseldorf: Institut der Wirtschaftsprüfer (4th edn, by K. von Wysocki and K. Wohlgemuth, 1996).

Wysocki, K. von (1976) 'Ergebnisse empirischer Untersuchungen über das Publiz-itätsverhalten deutscher Unternehmen' (Results of empirical studies on the disclosure behaviour of German enterprises), *Zeitschrift für betriebswirtschaftliche Forschung* 28: 744–55.

Zeff, S.A. (ed.) (1982) *The accounting postulates and principles controversy of the 1960s*, New York: Garland Publishing, Inc.

Ziegler, H. (1994) 'Neuorientierung des internen Rechnungswesen für das Unternehmens-Controlling im Hause Siemens' (Re-orientation of cost accounting for business controlling in the House of Siemens), *Zeitschrift für betriebswirtschaftliche Forschung* 46: 175–88.

5 Accounting research in Italy: first half of the twentieth century

Adamoli, G. (1940) 'Gli studi aziendali nel mondo: Germania' (Accounting studies in the world: Germany), *Rivista Italiana di Ragioneria* 33 (7–8): 181–4.

Alfieri, V. (1912) 'La scrittura nel controllo economico' (Recording and economic control, in monographs in honour of Fabio Besta), *Monografie edite in onore di Fabio Besta*, Rome: Tipografia G. Bertero.

Alfieri, V. (1914) *Ragioneria generale* (General accounting), 2nd edn, Rome: Società Editrice Dante Alighieri (1st edn, 1907).

Alfieri, V. (1915) 'La ragioneria dalle antiche alle moderne aziende mercantili, discorso inaugurale pronunciato il 19 Nov. 1914 nel Regio Istituto Superiore di Studi Commer-ciali in Roma' (Accounting from antiquity to the modern mercantile firms, an inau-gural presentation of 19 November 1914 at the Higher Royal Institute of Commercial Studies in Rome), *Inaugural presentation of 1915*, Caserta: Tipografia della Libreria Moderna (also in the *Rivista Italiana di Ragioneria* 8 (2): 57–69).

Alfieri, V. (1918a) 'Le regole, le classificazioni ed i concetti filosofici nelle opere italiane di ragioneria' (Rules, classifications and philosophical concepts in the Italian works of accounting), *Rivista Italiana di Ragioneria* 11 (3): 59–72.

Alfieri, V. (1918b) *Lezioni di ragioneria applicata* (Lectures of applied accounting), Città di Castello: Unione arti grafiche.

Alfieri, V. (1921) *La ragioneria applicata* (Applied accounting), Milan: Soc. Ed. Albrighi.e. Segati.

Alfieri, V. (1928) 'A proposito dei nuovi studi di ragioneria' (On novel accounting studies), *Rivista Italiana di Ragioneria* 21 (6): 222–25.

Amaduzzi, Aldo (1936) *Aziende di erogazione. Primi problemi di organizzazione, ges-tione, rilevazione* (Consumption entities. Basic problems of organization, management and recording), Milan: Principato.

Amaduzzi, Aldo (1949) *Ragioneria generale* (General accounting), 3rd edn, Vol. 1, *Economia generale delle aziende* (General economics of entities), Florence: Macrì (1st edn, 1942).

Amaduzzi, Aldo (1950) *Ragioneria generale* (General accounting), Vol. II: *I procedimenti della rilevazione* (Recording methods), Florence: Casa Edit. Dr L. Macrì.

Amaduzzi, Aldo (1955) *Sulla variabilità del processo produttivo dell'azienda industriale* (On the variability of production process of industrial enterprises), 2nd edn, Rome: Signorelli (1st edn, 1939).

Amaduzzi, Aldo (1956) *Il sistema dell'impresa nelle condizioni prospettiche del suo equilibrio* (The business system and its equilibrium conditions), 3rd edn, Rome: Signorelli (1st edn, 1947).

Amaduzzi, Antonio (2001) *Storia della ragioneria. Uomini, aziende, contabilità* (History of accounting: personalities, entities and accounting), Bergamo: Collegio dei Ragionieri di Bergamo.

Amodeo, D. (1938) *Contributo alla teoria delle valutazioni dei bilanci d'esercizio* (Contribution to the theory of the valuations of financial statements), Naples: Italia imperiale.

Amodeo, D. (1941) *I costi comuni nell'aspetto funzionale* (Functional aspects of overhead costs), Milan: A. Giuffrè.

Amodeo, D. (1945a) *La contabilità dei costi nell' U.R.S.S.* (Cost accounting in the Soviet Socialist Republics Union), Economia aziendale 2.

Amodeo, D. (1945b) 'The development of modern cost accounting in Italy', *N.A.C.A. Bulletin* XVIII: 855–62.

Amodeo, D. (1950a) *Costanza e variabilità dei costi nelle aziende industriali* (Constancy and variability of costs in industrial enterprises), Naples: Giannini.

Amodeo, D. (1950b) *La unificazione della contabilità* (The standardization of accounting), Naples: Giannini.

Amodeo, D. (1953) *A proposito di un antico bilancio del Vicereame di Napoli* (On an ancient financial statement of Naples Vice-royalty), Naples: Giannini.

Antoni, T. (1946) 'Il bilancio di una compagnia mercantile del Trecento' (The balance sheet of a commercial enterprise of the fourteenth century), *Rivista del Diritto Commerciale* 44 (11–12): 2–11.

Ardemani, E. (1940) *Costi e prezzi nelle concerie al cromo* (Costs and prices in chrome tanneries), Milan: Vita e Pensiero.

Ardemani, E. (1944) *Costi e risultati di esercizio nelle grandi imprese meccaniche a produzione varia* (Costs and production results in big mechanical enterprises of various manufacturing activites), Milan: Vita e Pensiero.

Argenziano, A. (1910) *Il prezzo di costo nelle aziende industriali* (The price of costing in industrial enterprises), Parma.

Armuzzi, V. (1902) *La ragioneria di una tenuta condotta a mezzadria. Studio di amministrazione e contabilità agraria* (Accounting of an estate at lease – A study of administration and accounting in agriculture), Ravenna: Tipografia Ravegnana (new edition 1941, edited by Prof. E. Boncinelli, Milan: A. Mondadori Editore).

Armuzzi, V. (1906) *Finalità ed ordinamento della contabilità agraria* (Aims and organization of the agricultural accounting), Rome: Tip. Agostiniana.

Armuzzi, V. (1940) *Le liquidazioni ereditarie* (Probate liquidations), new rev. edn, by Prof. Ettore Boncinelli, Milan: A. Mondadori Editore (1st edn, Milan: Giovanni Massa Editore, 1889).

Astuti, G. (1934) *Il libro dell'entrata e dell'uscita di una compagnia mercantile senese del secolo XIII (1277–1282)* (The book of revenue and expenditure of a Sienese mercantile company of the thirteenth century, 1277–1282), Turin: Lattes.

Battara, A. (1911) 'La contabilità industriale e sua applicazione all'industria chimica'

(Cost accounting and its application to the chemical industry), *Monografie di ragioneria applicata*, Milan: Monitore dei ragionieri: 1–79.

Belardinelli, G. (1936) 'I principì logismologici di Cerboni, Besta e Zappa' (The logismological principles of Cerboni, Besta and Zappa), *Rivista Italiana di Ragioneria* 29 (2): 12–20.

Bellini, C. (1908) *Trattato di ragioneria applicata alle aziende private con una appendice sulle funzioni speciali del ragioniere* (Accounting treatise applied to private entities with an appendix on the accountant's special functions), Milan: Hoepli.

Bellini, C. (1914a) *La scrittura doppia americana detta a giornale mastro* (American double-entry as a journal-ledger), 2nd edn, Milan: U. Hoepli.

Bellini, C. (1914b) 'Il pensiero e l'opera di Giuseppe Cerboni', *Conferenze intorno alla vita e alle opere di Giuseppe Cerboni'* (The thought and the work of Giuseppe Cerboni. In Lectures about the life and the works of Giuseppe Cerboni), Rome: Tipografia Cartiere Centrali.

Bellini, C. (1924a) 'Le nostre riviste di ragioneria in questi ultimi cinquant'anni. Reminiscenze e riflessioni' (Our reviews on accounting during the last fifty years. Reminiscences and reflections), *Rivista Italiana di Ragioneria* 17 (5): 217–20.

Bellini, C. (1924b) 'La professione di ragioniere nella sua secolare tradizione e i tempi nuovi' (The accountant profession in its secular tradition and the new times), *Rivista Italiana di Ragioneria* 17 (7): 337–42.

Bellini, C. (1927) 'Nel 1° centenario della nascita di Giuseppe Cerboni' (To the first centenary of Giuseppe Cerboni's birth), *Rivista Italiana di Ragioneria* 20 (6): 225–34.

Bergamin-Barbato, M., Collini, P. and Quagli, A. (1996) 'Management accounting in Italy: evolution within tradition', in A. Bhimani ed., *Management accounting: European perspectives*, Oxford: Oxford University Press: 140–63.

Besta, F. (1880) *La ragioneria – prolusione letta nella solenne apertura degli studi per l'anno 1880–81 alla R. Scuola Superiore di Commercio in Venezia* (Accounting – opening lecture for the academic year 1880–81 at the Royal Superior School of Commerce in Venice), Venice: Colletti.

Besta, F. (1900) *Lezioni di contabilità di Stato* (Lessons in government accounting), Venezia: Litografia Arnanti.

Besta, F. (1910) *Lezioni di ragioneria. Trattati speciali* (Lessons in accounting. Special treatises), Padua: La Motolitotipo.

Besta, F. (1922) *La ragioneria* (Accounting theory), 3 vols, 2nd edn, Milan: Vallardi (1st edn, 1891–1916; a one volume work by this author, under the same title, was published in 1880 as mentioned above; a revised edn, of the three volumes was published in Milan: Vallardi, 1932).

Bianchi, T. (1984) 'The founding of concern economics: the thought of Gino Zappa', *Economia Aziendale* 3: 255–72.

Biondi, Y. (2002) *Gino Zappa e la rivoluzione del reddito. Azienda, moneta e contabilità nella nascente economia aziendale* (Gino Zappa and the income revolution. The entity, currency and accounting in the rising economia aziendale), Padua: Cedam.

Bodrito, A. (1937–38) 'Sulla elasticità dei costi' (On the elasticity of costs), *Annuario di studi.e. ricerche della Facoltà di Economia e Commercio dell'Università degli Studi di Genova*, Anno III, No. 3, Messina: Principato.

Bossi, M. (1912) 'Note storiche sulle finanze dello Stato pontificio ed in particolare sull'amministrazione di Gregorio XVI' (Historical notes on the finances of the Papal State and particularly of the administration of Gregory XVI), *Rivista Italiana di Ragioneria* 5 (8): 351–8; 5 (9): 398–402; 5 (10): 442–50; 5 (11): 503–7; 5 (12): 544–9.

Bossi, M. (1914) 'I processi del controllo economico nelle leggi.e. nei bilanci pubblicati dallo Stato Pontificio (1832–1860)' (The processes of economic control in the laws and published balance sheets of the Papal State (1832–1860)), *Rivista Italiana di Ragioneria* 7 (2): 49–59; 7 (3): 118–24; 7 (4): 183–8; 7 (5): 207–12; 7 (6): 246–50; 7 (7): 305–8; 7 (8): 348–58; 7 (9): 395–405.

Bossi, M. (1917) 'Ragionieri.e. computisti nello Stato Pontificio' (Accountants and book-keepers in the Papal State), *Rivista Italiana di Ragioneria* 10 (2): 43–50.

Botarelli, A. (1945) 'Storia della ragioneria italiana dalla seconda metà del secolo XIX ai giorni nostri. Uno sguardo d'insieme al passato' (History of Italian accounting from the second half of nineteenth century until the present. A holistic view of the past), *Rivista Italiana di Ragioneria* 38 (1–6): 47–57.

Brambilla, G. (1901) *Storia della ragioneria italiana* (History of Italian accounting), Milan: Tip. A. Boriglione.

Brambilla, G. (1905) *Aristotile e la contabilità di Stato in Atene* (Aristotle and government accounting in Athens), Milan: Tip. Sociale Opizzi.

Bruni, E. (1914) *Contabilità generale dello stato* (General government accounting), 4th edn, Milan: Hoepli.

Cantoni, C. (1905) *Storia della ragioneria, con appendice bibliografica* (History of accounting, with a bibliographical appendix), Milan: Sonzogno.

Canziani, A. (1982) 'Measurements and calculations in accounting: a note on Continental v. Anglo-Saxon methodology', *Economia Aziendale* 1: 58–71.

Canziani, A. (1987) 'Sulle premesse metodologiche della rivoluzione zappiana, in *Saggi di economia aziendale per Lino Azzini*' (On the methodological premises of Zappa's revolution, in essays of 'economia aziendale' in honour of Lino Azzini), Milan: A. Giuffrè Editore, 142–65.

Canziani, A. (1994) 'Gino Zappa (1879–1960): accounting revolutionary', in J. Richard Edwards ed., *Twentieth-century accounting thinkers*, London: Routledge, in association with the Institute of Chartered Accountants of England and Wales.

Caprara, U. (1923) *La teoria della partita doppia nella concezione della nostra scuola* (Double-entry theory according to our school), Milan: Copisteria fotografica.

Cassandro, P.E. (1941) *Sulle teorie aziendali di Eugenio Schmalenbach* (On business theories by Eugen Schmalenbach), Bari: Cressati.

Cassandro, P.E. (1950a) *L'incidenza dei fattori produttivi a lungo termine sul risultato economico di periodo nelle imprese* (The influence of long-term production factors on the periodic economic result of enterprises), Bari: Cacucci.

Cassandro, P.E. (1950b) *I problemi della rilevazione nelle aziende agrarie* (The accounting problems in agricultural concerns), Bari: Cacucci.

Castagnoli, A. (1940) 'La ragioneria nel mondo romano' (Accounting in the Roman world), *La ragioneria* 2 (3–4).

Catturi, G. (1989) *Teorie contabili e scenari economico-aziendali* (Accounting theories and various scenarios of economic entities), Padua: Cedam.

Ceccherelli, A. (1910) *Le scritture commerciali delle antiche aziende fiorentine* (Commercial recordings of 'ancient' Florentine companies), Florence: Lastrucci.

Ceccherelli, A. (1913) *I libri di mercatura della banca Medici.e. l'applicazione della partita doppia a Firenze nel secolo decimoquarto* (Mercantile books of the Medici bank and the application of double-entry in fourteenth-century Florence), Florence: Bemporad.

Ceccherelli, A. (1914) 'Le funzioni contabili e giuridiche del bilancio nelle società medievali' (The accounting and juridical functions of the financial statement in medieval companies), *Rivista Italiana di Ragioneria* 7 (8): 371–8; 7 (9): 391–5; 7 (10): 436–5.

Ceccherelli, A. (1915) *La logismologia* (The logismology of accounting), Milan: F. Vallardi.

Ceccherelli, A. (1922) *L'indirizzo teorico negli studi di ragioneria* (The theoretical nature of accounting studies), Florence: Ariani.

Ceccherelli, A. (1931) *Le prospettive economiche e finanziarie nelle aziende commerciali* (Economic financial prospects of commercial firms), Florence: Le Monnier.

Ceccherelli, A. (1933) 'In memoria di Fabio Besta' (In memory of Fabio Besta), *Rivista Italiana di Ragioneria* 26 (2): 73–5.

Ceccherelli, A. (1936) *Il problema dei costi nelle prospettive economiche e finanziarie delle imprese* (The problem of costs from the economic and financial viewpoint of firms), Florence: Seeber.

Ceccherelli, A. (1938) 'Intorno ad alcuni antichi libri di conti' (On some ancient books of accounts), *Rivista Italiana di Ragioneria* 31 (3–4): 81–3.

Ceccherelli, A. (1947) *Il linguaggio dei bilanci. Formazione e interpretazione dei bilanci commerciali* (The language of financial statements. Formation and interpretation of the commercial balance sheets), Florence: F. Le Monnier (1st edn, 1939).

Ceccherelli, A. (1948) *Economia aziendale e amministrazione delle imprese* ('Economia aziendale' and business administration), Florence: Barbera.

Ceccherelli, A. (1953) *Le istituzioni di ragioneria* (Accounting institutions), 7th edn, Florence: Le Monnier (1st edn, 1930).

Cerboni, G. (1901) *Il libro maestro logismografico negli ordinamenti.e. riscontri amministrativo-contabili per le aziende economiche di Stato* (The logismographic ledger of accounting and management control of the State enterprises), Rome: Tipografia Elzeviriana.

Cerboni, G. (1902) *Saggio riassuntivo dei concetti filologico-tecnici formanti il sistema grafico-razionale logismografico per le funzioni e pei fatti amministrativi dell'azienda economica* (Recapitulation of the philological-technical concepts of the 'graphical-rational' system of logismography, serving the functions and administrative activities of the firm), Rome: Tipografia Elzeviriana.

Chatfield, M. and Vangermeersch, R. (eds) (1996) *The history of accounting: an international encyclopedia*, New York: Garland Publishing, Inc.

Chianale, A. (1926) *I bilanci dello Stato Pontificio alla vigilia della rivoluzione romana* (The balance sheets of the Papal State at the eve of the Roman revolution), Turin: Mercurio.

Chianale, A. (1928) 'La "Betriebswirtschaftslehre" e la "Science of Business"' (Business economics and the science of business), *Rivista di Ragioneria e Studi Affini* 25 (7–9).

Chianale, A. (1935) *Il patrimonio degli enti pubblici nei conti e nei bilanci* (The wealth of public bodies in the accounts and balance sheets), Turin: Giappichelli.

Chianale, A. (1939) 'Note sulla contabilità egiziana del III secolo avanti Cristo' (Notes on Egyptian accounting of the third century BC), *La ragioneria* 1 (1).

Chiaudano, M. (1927) *Il bilancio sabaudo nel secolo XIII* (The balance sheet of Savoy in the thirteenth century), Turin: Bocca.

Chiaudano, M. (1933–1937) *La finanza sabauda nel secolo XIII* (The finances of Savoy in the thirteenth century), 3 vols, Turin: Soc. Storica Subalpina.

Cinquini, L. and Marelli, A. (2002) 'An Italian forerunner of modern cost allocation concepts: Lorenzo De Minico and the logic of the "flows of services"', *Accounting, Business and Financial History* 12 (1): 95–111.

Colletti, N. (1945) *Introduzione allo studio dell'economia aziendale. Calcolo aziendale*

(Introduction to the study of *Economia aziendale*. Business calculus), Palermo: Industrie Riunite Editoriali Siciliane.

Colletti, N. (1947) *Problemi economico-aziendali determinati dalle rivalutazioni per adeguamento monetario* (Problems of business economics caused by revaluations for price-level changes), *Annali della Facoltà di Economia e Commercio, Anno I, N. 1*, Palermo: Lilia.

Colletti, N. (1954) *Il 'numero' in economia aziendale* (The 'number' and the *Economia aziendale*), Palermo-Roma: Abbaco (1st edn, 1941).

Corsani, G. (1917) 'I criteri di valutazione della ricchezza presso i fondaci toscani del secolo XIV' (The criteria of wealth valuation in fourteenth-century tenements of Tuscany), *Rivista Italiana di Ragioneria* 10 (2): 1–7.

Corsani, G. (1922) *I fondaci e i banchi di un mercante pratese del Trecento. Contributo alla storia della ragioneria e del commercio* (Stores and banks of a Prato merchant in the fourteenth century. Contribution to the history of accounting and commerce), Prato: La Tipografica.

Cova, G. (1926) *Compendio di ragioneria applicata alle aziende publiche* (Compendium of accounting applied to the public entities), 9th edn, Milan: Tamburini.

D'Alvise, P. (1912) *Contabilità di Stato* (Government accounting), Florence: Barbera.

D'Alvise, P. (1920) *Nozioni fondamentali di ragioneria* (Fundamental notions of accounting), Vol. I, Padua: Stabilimento Tipografico del Messaggero.

D'Alvise, P. (1932a) 'Sullo sviluppo del pensiero logismologico italiano negli ultimi cento anni' (On the development of the Italian logismologic thought in the last one hundred years), *Rivista Italiana di Ragioneria* 25 (3): 49–55.

D'Alvise, P. (1932b) *Principi.e. precetti di ragioneria per l'amministrazione economica delle aziende* (Accounting principles and assumptions for the economic administration of an entity), Padua: Cedam.

D'Alvise, P. (1932c) 'A dieci anni dalla perdita di Fabio Besta' (Ten years after the loss of Fabio Besta), *Rivista Italiana di Ragioneria* 25 (10–12): 309–12.

D'Alvise, P. (1933) 'Reminiscenze ed attualità nel campo degli studi ragionieristici' (Reminiscences and novelties in accounting research), *Rivista Italiana di Ragioneria* 26 (3–4): 101–9.

D'Alvise, P. (1936) 'Contributo alla unificazione internazionale del linguaggio in ragioneria' (Contribution to the international standardization of accounting terminology), *Rivista Italiana di Ragioneria* 29 (2): 37–42.

D'Alvise, P. (1939) 'Per chiarimenti su punti di "Contabilità di Stato"' (Explanations on government accounting), *Rivista Italiana di Ragioneria* 32 (7–8–9): 217–21.

D'Alvise, P. (1940) *Studio sintetico di ragioneria statale italiana* (A 'synthetic' study of Italian government accounting), Padua: R. Zannoni.

De Brun, A. (1911) *Contabilità dello Stato* (Government accounting), Milan: Società Editrice Libraria.

De Dominicis, U. (1937) *Le negoziazioni di quote di capitale delle società commerciali* (The transactions of shares of commercial companies), Turin: Utet.

De Dominicis, U. (1950a) *Il reddito dell'impresa ed il suo sistema contabile* (Business income and its accounting system), Cuneo: Ghibaudo.

De Dominicis, U. (1950b) *La ragioneria quale tecnica dell'economia politica* (Accounting as a technique of political economy), Cuneo: Ghibaudo.

De Gobbis, F. (1915) *Ragioneria privata* (Private accounting), 2nd edn, 2 vols, Rome: Albrighi.e. Segati.

De Gobbis, F. (1927) 'Il problema dei bilanci delle società anonime in correlazione alla svalutazione ed alla rivalutazione della moneta' (The problem of stock companies' financial statements in relation to the depreciation and revaluation of currency), *Rivista Italiana di Ragioneria* 20 (12): 433–45.

De Gobbis, F. (1931) *Il bilancio delle società anonime* (Financial statements of limited companies), 2nd edn, Rome: Società Editrice Dante Alighieri.

De Gobbis, F. (1934a) 'Tendenze nuove negli studi di ragioneria?' (New trends in accounting research?), *Rivista Italiana di Ragioneria* 27 (3): 129–37.

De Gobbis, F. (1934b) *Ragioneria generale. Corso teorico-practico* (General accounting. Theoretical-practical course), 20th edn, Rome: Società Editrice Dante Alighieri.

De Gobbis, F. (1939) 'Vecchio stile e stile nuovo negli studi di ragioneria' (The old approach and the new approach to accounting research), *La ragioneria* 1 (1).

Della Penna, F. (1922) *Il contenuto scientifico e la partizione della ragioneria teorica* (The scientific content and structure of accounting theory), Città di Castello: Unione Arti Grafiche.

Della Penna, F. (1937) *I fondamenti della Ragioneria*. Reprint (The foundations of accounting), Catania: Studio Editoriale Moderno (1st edn, 1931).

Della Penna, F. (1946–1950) *Le istituzioni contabili* (Accounting institutions), 2 vols, Rome: Casa Editrice Castellani.

De Minico, L. (1927) *Le riserve nelle imprese* (The 'reserves' in the enterprises), Naples: Majo.

De Minico, L. (1931) *Rinnovamento e liquidità del capitale nelle imprese industriali* (Restatements and capital liquidity in industrial enterprises), Naples: Casa Editrice Rondinella.

De Minico, L. (1935) *Elasticità e relazioni dinamiche dei costi nelle imprese industriali* (Elasticity and the dynamics of costs in industrial enterprises), Naples: Casa Editrice Rondinella.

De Minico, L. (1946) *Lezioni di ragioneria – i fondamenti economici della rilevazione del reddito* (Accounting lessons – the economic foundations of income determination), 2nd edn, Naples: Pironti (1st edn, 1944).

De Minico, L. and Amodeo D. (1942) *Saggi di economia delle aziende* (Essays on the economics of 'entities'), Milan: Giuffrè.

D'Ippolito, T. (1932) *La contabilità sistematica nelle imprese industriali.e. mercantili* (Systematic accounting of industrial and mercantile enterprises), Milan: Istituto di ricerche economico-aziendali.

D'Ippolito, T. (1935a) *I costi di produzione nelle aziende industriali* (Production costs of industrial enterprises), Milan: A. Giuffrè.

D'Ippolito, T. (1935b) *Costi.e. prezzi nelle aziende industriali. Casi concreti di rilevazion.* (Costs and prices of industrial enterprises. Cases of cost determination), Milan: A. Giuffrè.

D'Ippolito, T. (1937) *Scritture e bilanci nelle aziende divise* (Accounting entries and financial statements of divisionalized enterprises), Milan: A. Giuffrè.

D'Ippolito, T. (1940) *Le discipline aziendali. L'azienda corporativa* (Business disciplines. The corporative entity), Milan: A. Giuffrè.

D'Ippolito, T. (1945) *La contabilità e il bilancio delle aziende di produzione* (Accounting and financial statement of production entities), Milan: A. Giuffrè.

D'Ippolito, T. (1946a) *La valutazione delle aziende in avviamento* (The valuation of going concerns), Milan: A. Giuffrè.

D'Ippolito, T. (1946b) *I costi di produzione nelle aziende industriali* (Production costs of manufacturing entities), Milan: A. Giuffrè.

D'Ippolito, T. (1952) *L'unificazione contabile* (On the standardization of accounting), Palermo: Abbaco.

D'Ippolito, T. (1963) *Il 'quadro' dei conti in partita doppia, sistema duplice e le scritture tipiche relative* (The 'chart' of accounts and double-entry – the dual system and its recording process), 6th edn, Palermo: Abbaco.

D'Ippolito, T. (1967) *Determinazioni di produttività, di rendimenti, di inefficienze e di cicli a quantità fisico-tecniche* (Determining productivity, efficiency, inefficiency and the quantitative flows), 4th edn, Palermo: Abbaco (1st edn, 1951).

Edwards, J.R. (ed.) (1994) *Twentieth-century accounting thinkers*, London: Routledge.

Einaudi, L. (1907) *Le entrate pubbliche dello Stato Sabaudo nei bilanci.e. nei conti dei tesorieri durante la guerra di successione spagnola* (Public revenues of the State of Savoy and its treasury's balance sheets and accounts during the Spanish War of Succession), Turin: Editrice Fratelli Bocca.

Einaudi, L. (1908) *La finanza Sabauda all'aprirsi del secolo XVIII.e. durante la guerra di successione spagnola* (The finance of Savoy at the beginning of eighteenth century and during the Spanish War of Succession), Turin: Officine Grafiche della S.T.E.N.

Fanfani, A. (1935) *Un mercante del trecento* (A merchant of the fourteenth century), Milan: A. Giuffrè.

Galagan, A.M. (1912) 'Le nuove forme della ragioneria italiana, Logismografia, Statmografia' (The new forms of Italian accounting, logismography, statmography), *Rivista di Amministrazione e Contabilità*.

Galassi, G. (1966) 'Il postulato della "realizzazione" nella dottrina aziendale nord-americana' (The 'realization' postulate in the North American business doctrine), *Studi e ricerche della Facoltà di Economia e Commercio dell'Università degli Studi di Parma*, Vol. III, Parma: La Nazionale Editrice.

Galassi, G. (1974) *Misurazioni differenziali, misurazioni globali.e. decisioni d'azienda* (Differential measurements, global measurements and business decisions), Milan: A. Giuffrè.

Galassi, G. (1980) 'Capital-income relations: a critical analysis', *Gino Zappa, founder of concern economics*, Bologna: Accademia Italiana di Economia Aziendale: 25–49.

Galassi, G. (1996) 'Zappa, Gino (1879–1960)', in M. Chatfield and R. Vangermeersch eds, *The history of accounting: an international encyclopedia*, New York: Garland Publishing, Inc.: 617–18.

Galassi, G. and Mattessich, R. (2004) 'Italian accounting research in the first half of the twentieth century', *Review of Accounting and Finance* 3 (2): 62–83.

Germani, G. (1914) *La ragioneria come scienza moderna* (Accounting as a modern science), Torino: F.lli Bocca Editori (reprinted in Biblioteca Storica di Economia Aziendale, diretta da Antonio Amaduzzi, Vol. 5, Bari: Cacucci, 1989).

Ghidiglia, C. (1906) *Corso di ragioneria applicata* (Course of applied accounting), Rome: Albrighi.e. Segati.

Ghidiglia, C. (1909a) *Compendio di ragioneria generale* (Compendium of general accounting), Leghorn: Giusti.

Ghidiglia, C. (1909b) *La contabilità di Stato nei suoi fini.e. nei suoi rapporti con le altre discipline* (Government accounting, its aims and its relations with other disciplines), Padua: Crescini.

Ghidiglia, C. (1911) 'Le attinenze della ragioneria con le scienze economiche e giuridiche' (The relations of accounting to the economic and juridical sciences), *Rivista Italiana di Ragioneria* 4 (10): 441–54.

Ghidiglia, C. (1912) 'La scienza delle finanze e gli studi di ragioneria' (The science of finance and accounting studies), *Rivista Italiana di Ragioneria* 5 (7): 292–5.

Ghidiglia, C. (1913–15) *Ragioneria applicata* (Applied accounting), 3 vols, Milan: Soc. Ed. Dante Alighieri.

Giannessi, E. (1935) *I costi di produzione nelle imprese tessili cotoniere* (Production costs of cotton mills), Florence: Libreria internazionale Seeber.

Giannessi, E. (1937) 'Il problema dei costi nel pensiero di Alberto Ceccherelli' (The problem of costs in Alberto Ceccherelli's theory), *Rivista Italiana di Ragioneria* 30 (2): 49–59.

Giannessi, E. (1943) *Costi e prezzi-tipo nelle aziende industriali* (Standard costs and prices of industrial firms), Milan: A. Giuffrè.

Giannessi, E. (1944) 'Impossibilità della determinazione analitica dei costi dei singoli prodotti' (Impossibility of an analytical determination of single products costs), *Rivista Italiana di Ragioneria* 37 (1–12): 14–15.

Giannessi, E. (1980) *I precursori in Economia Aziendale* (The forerunners of 'economia aziendale'), 4th rev. edn, Milan: A. Giuffrè Editore.

Giovannini, P. (1935) *L'azienda nello Stato corporativo* (The concern in the corporate state), Messina: Casa Editrice Giuseppe Principato.

Giovannini, P. (1936) *La ragioneria nell'economia aziendale generale corporativa* (Accounting in the general corporate *Economia aziendale*), Messina: Principato.

Giovannini, P. (1938–39) *Costi, prezzi, politica corporativa e indagini aziendali* (Costs, prices, corporate politics and business investigations), *Annuario di studi e ricerche della Facoltà di Economia e Commercio dell'Università degli Studi di Genova*, Vol. IV, No. 4, Genova: Società Editrice Dante Alighieri.

Giovannini, P. (1942) *Amministrazione aziendale generale-corporativa. Gestione, ragioneria ed organizzazione delle aziende in genere nello Stato corporativo* (General administration of corporative entities. Management, accounting and organization of entities in the corporative state), Milan: Hoepli.

Gitti, V. (1915) *Ragioneria* (Accounting), 6th rev. edn, Milan: Hoepli (1st edn, 1883).

Gomberg, L. (1908) *Grundlegung der Verrechnungswissenschaft* (Foundations of accounting science), Leipzig: Duncker & Humblot (Japanese translation, Kaikegaku hohoron, Tokyo: Ganshodoshoten, 1944).

Guatri, L. (1951) *Il costo di produzione. L'efficienza* (Production costs and efficiency), Milan: A. Giuffrè.

Guidetti, R. (1910) 'Saggio di registro a partita doppia del 1387 per il Comune di Reggio Emilia' (Essay of double-entry bookkeeping in 1387 of the Municipality of Reggio Emilia), *Rivista dei ragionieri* 6 (2): 645–7.

Jannaccone, P. (1904) *Il costo di produzione* (The production cost), Biblioteca dell'economista, Series IV, Vol. IV, Part II, Turin (reprint edition Turin: Utet, 1956).

Lorusso, B. (1906) *La Ragioneria come arte e come scienza, Discorso inaugurale dell'anno accademico 1905–06 nella R. Scuola Superiore di Commercio di Bari* (Accounting as an art and a science, inaugural lecture of the academic year 1905–06 at the Higher Royal School of Commerce in Bari), Bari: Stabilimento Tipografico Alighieri.

Lorusso, B. (1911) *Calcolo e documenti commerciali* (Calculus and commercial documents), Turin: Paravia.

Lorusso, B. (1912) *La contabilità commerciale* (Commercial accounting), 3rd edn, Bari: Laterza.

Lorusso, B. (1922) *Ragioneria generale, basata sulle funzioni di controllo economico* (General accounting, based on the functions of economic control), 2nd edn, Bari: Laterza.

Lorusso, B. (1924) *La partita doppia nelle scritture generali dello Stato* (Double-entry bookkeeping in the general accounting system of the state), Milan: De Silvestri.

Marcantonio, A. (1942) *I costi di produzione nell'economia di guerra* (Production costs in the war economy), Milan: A. Giuffrè.

Marcantonio, A. (1950) *L'azienda dello Stato* (Government business), Milan: A. Giuffrè.

Marchi, A. (1911) *La ragioneria nella sua evoluzione storica* (Accounting in its historical evolution), Camerino: Egidio Marchi.

Marchi, A. (1912) *La ragioneria nella sua funzione sociale* (Accounting as a social function), Camerino: Egidio Marchi.

Masetti, A. (1901) *Sulla teoria matematica del conto e dei metodi di scrittura* (On the mathematical theory of the account and accounting methods), Rome: Bottero.

Masi, V. (1935) *Battaglie e conquiste in economia aziendale* (Battles and victories in *Economia aziendale*), Udine: Edizioni Accademiche.

Masi, V. (1937) *Ragioneria applicata alle aziende pubbliche* (Accounting applied to governmental institutions), Padua: Cedam.

Masi, V. (1938) *La ragioneria nelle società commerciali* (Accounting in commercial companies), 2 vols, Padua: Cedam.

Masi, V. (1939a) 'La vecchia e la nuova ragioneria' (The old and the new accounting), *Rivista Italiana di Ragioneria* 32 (2): 145–8.

Masi, V. (1939b) *Analisi finanziarie e reddituali in relazione al capitale di gestione nelle imprese* (Economic financial analyses of the 'balance sheet' capital of enterprises), Milan: Vallardi.

Masi, V. (1943) *La ragioneria come scienza del patrimonio* (Accounting as the science of wealth), Padua: Cedam (1st edn, 1927).

Masi, V. (1945) *Statica Patrimoniale* (A static picture of wealth), 2nd edn, Vol. 2, Padua: Cedam.

Masi, V. (1946a) *Statica patrimoniale* (A static picture of wealth), 3rd edn, Vol. 1, Padua: Cedam (1st edn, 1938).

Masi, V. (1946b) 'Fabio Besta e la storia della ragioneria' (Fabio Besta and the history of accounting), *Rivista Italiana di Ragioneria* 39 (2): 57–9.

Masi, V. (1946–47) *Dinamica patrimoniale* (The dynamics of wealth), 2 vols, Padua: Cedam.

Masi, V. (1947) *La ragioneria negli enti pubblici* (Accounting of public institutions), Padua: Cedam.

Masi, V. (1997, posthumously published) *La ragioneria nell' età moderna e contemporanea, Testo riveduto e completato da Carlo Antinori* (Accounting of the modern and contemporaneous age. Revised and extended text by Carlo Antinori), Milan: A. Giuffrè.

Masini, C. (1947a) *Economia delle imprese industriali e rilevazioni d'azienda* (Economics of industrial enterprises and recordings in entities), Milan: A. Giuffré.

Masini, C. (1947b) *I grafici nelle rilevazioni di azienda* (Charts and business recordings), Milan: A. Giuffrè.

Massa, G. (1905–08) *Trattato completo di ragioneria* (Complete treatise of accounting), 12 vols, Milan: (various publishers) Gelmetti (Vols 1–5); Monitore dei Ragionieri (Vols 6–8 and 12), Galimberti Politti (Vols 9–11).

Massa, G. (1907) *Storia e bibliografia* (History and bibliography), Vol. 12 of the Trattato completo di ragioneria – see above), Milan: Monitore dei Ragionieri.

Massa, G. (ed.) (1911) *Opere antiche di ragioneria* (Ancient works of accounting), Milan: Monitore dei Ragionieri.

Mattessich, R. (2003) 'Accounting research and researchers of the nineteenth century and the beginning of the twentieth century: an international survey of personalities, ideas and publications', *Accounting, Business and Financial History* 13 (1, March): 1–46.

Matteucci, R. (1908) *L'identità sostanziale dei tre sistemi scritturali italiani. Studio critico* (The virtual identity of the three Italian accounting systems. A critical study), Genova: Stabilimento Tipografico G.B. Mazzano.

Mazza, G. (1968) *Premesse storico-sistematiche negli studi di ragioneria* (Systematic-historical premises of accounting research), Milan: A. Giuffrè.

Melis, F. (1940) 'Prospetti storici di ragioneria' (Historical tables of accounting), *Rivista Italiana di Ragioneria* 33 (10–11): 238–49.

Melis, F. (1946) 'Un mastro toscano del '200: le "raiçone de Cambio Detaccomando et Johannes suo frate"' (A Tuscan ledger of the thirteenth century: the 'exchange rates of Detaccomand and his brother Johannes'), *Rivista Italiana di Ragioneria* 39 (2): 51–6.

Melis, F. (1947) 'Di un libro delle spese del Comune di Amandola (Ascoli Piceno) del XIV secolo' (About a fourteenth-century book of expenditures of the Amandola municipality, Ascoli Piceno), *Rivista Italiana di Ragioneria* 40 (7–9): 168–74.

Melis, F. (1948) *La ragioneria nella civiltà minoica* (Accounting at the Minoan civilization), Casa Editrice della Rivista Italiana di Ragioneria.

Melis, F. (1950a) *Storia della ragionerìa – contributo alla conoscenza e interpretazione delle fonti più significative della storia economica* (History of accounting – a contribution to the knowledge and interpretation of the most significant sources of economic history), Bologna: Cesare Zuffi.

Melis, F. (1950b) *La scrittura contabile alla fonte della storia economica* (Accounting as a source of economic history), Bologna: Zuffi Editore.

Mondini, E. (1910) *Aritmetica applicata all'amministrazione* (Arithmetic applied to administration), Como: Bertolini Nani.e. C.

Mondini, E. (1911) 'La ragioneria e le altre scienze e dottrine' (Accounting and the other sciences and theories), *Rivista di Amministrazione e Contabilità*.

Mondini, E. (1912) *L'elemento giuridico nei conti* (The juridical element in accounting), Como: Tipografia Editrice Ostinelli.

Mondini, E. (1916a) *Ragioneria teorica* (Theoretical accounting), 9th edn, Como: Tipografia Editrice Ostinelli.

Mondini, E. (1916b) *Ragioneria applicata* (Applied accounting), 9th edn, Como: Tipografia Editrice Ostinelli.

Monetti, U. (1926) *Le amministrazioni contabili dello Stato e l'ordinamento dei controlli* (The administration of centralized government accounting and the exercise of control) Monograph No. 1 of the Library of Applied Accounting 'Rota', Turin: Utet.

Monetti, U. (1937) *Corso di contabilità di Stato* (Course in government accounting), Rome: Casa Editrice della Rivista Italiana di Ragioneria.

Onida, P. (1926) *I costi comuni nelle imprese industriali. I costi medi e i costi supplementari* (Overhead costs in industrial enterprises. Average costs and full costs), Milan: Stab. tip.-lit. G. Tenconi.

Onida, P. (1927) *Elementi di ragioneria commerciale svolti nel sistema dell'economia aziendale* (Elements of commercial accounting developed in the system of *Economia aziendale*), Milan: Soc. An. Istituto Editoriale Scientifico.

Onida, P. (1931) *I finanziamenti iniziali d'impresa* (The initial financing of an enterprise), Milan: Istituto Editoriale Scientifico.

Onida, P. (1935) *Il bilancio delle aziende commerciali* (The financial statement of business enterprises), Milan: A. Giuffré (published as *Il bilancio d'esercizio nelle imprese*, 1945).

Onida, P. (1944) *Le dimensioni del capitale di impresa – Concentrazioni, trasformazioni, variazioni di capitale* (The dimensions of the capital of a firm – concentrations, transformations and variations of the capital), Milan: A. Giuffré.

Onida, P. (1945) *Il bilancio d'esercizio nelle imprese* (Financial statements of a firm's operations), Milan: A. Giuffré.

Onida, P. (1947a) *La logica e il sistema delle determinazioni quantitative d'azienda* (The logic and the system of quantitative measurement of the enterprise), Milan: A. Giuffré.

Onida, P. (1947b) *Elementi di ragioneria con particolare riguardo all'impresa* (Elements of accounting with particular reference to the enterprise), Milan: A. Giuffré (1st edn, 1927).

Onida, P. (1947c) *Le discipline economico-aziendali. Oggetto e metodo* (The disciplines of 'economia aziendale'. Object and method), 1st edn, Milan: A. Giuffré (later edn, 1951).

Onida, P. (1951) *Il bilancio di esercizio nelle imprese. Significato economico del bilancio. Problemi di valutazione* (The balance sheet of enterprises ...), Milan: Giuffré (1st edn, 1945; translated into Spanish as *El balance de ejercicio en las empresas*, 2 vols, Buenos Aires: El Ateneo).

Pacces, F.M. (1934) *I costi industriali* (Industrial costs), Turin: Istituto Aziendale Italiano.

Pagnano, S.U. (1943) *Le rilevazioni amministrative dell'unitario processo produttivo d'impresa* (Administrative recording of an enterprise's entire production process), Catania: Azienda Poligrafica Editoriale.

Pagnano, S.U. (1944) *Aspetti tipici della gestione nelle imprese mercantili.e. industriali* (Typical managerial aspects of mercantile and industrial enterprises), Catania: Azienda Poligrafica Editoriale.

Palumbo, P. (1906) *Il libro maestro nella ragioneria del Monte di Pietà di Palermo* (The ledger of the accounting system of the Pawnbroker's Shop of Palermo), Palermo: Ed. Gazzetta Commerciale di Palermo.

Pellerano, B. (1909) *La ragioneria scientifica di G. Cerboni. Appunti critici* (The scientific accounting system of G. Cerboni. Critical remarks), Genova: Associazione Ligure Ragionieri.

Pezzoli, S. (1986) *Profili di storia della ragioneria* (Profiles of accounting history), Padua: Cedam.

Pisani, E. (1901a) *Elementi di ragioneria generale* (Elements of general accounting), Roma: Società editrice Dante Alighieri.

Pisani, E. (1901b) *L'unificazione dei metodi contabili.e. la contabilità di Stato in rapporto al problema finanziario* (The unification of accounting methods and government accounting with reference to financial problems), Modica: Tipografia Carlo Papa.

Pisani, E. (1903) *La verità della Storia e i perfezionamenti nel campo statmografico. In risposta al saggio riassuntivo del Comm. Cerboni* (Historical truth and improvements in statmographic accounting. In reply to the review essay by Commendatore Cerboni), Rome: Tipografia Nazionale.

Pisani, E. (1909) *Studi e proposte sulla riforma della Legge della Contabilità dello Stato* (Studies and proposals on the reform of the Government Accounting Law), Rome: Tipografia della Camera dei Deputati.

Pivato, G. (1942) *I bilanci delle imprese di servizi pubblici* (The financial statements of public utility enterprises), Milan: A. Giuffré.

Pivato, G. (1946) *Rilevazioni contabili e bilanci nelle aziende di servizi pubblici* (Accounting recordings and financial statements of public utility enterprises), Milan: A. Giuffrè.

Ravenna, E. (1903) *La funzione del rendiconto nell'amministrazione dello Stato* (The function of the balance sheet in the State administration), Palermo: Vizzì.

Ravenna, E. (1909–22) *Trattato teorico-pratico di ragioneria commerciale* (Theoretical-practical treatise of commercial accounting), 3 vols, Palermo: A. Reber.

Riccardi, T. (1915) *Il bilancio presso la colonia di Pompei. Note archeologiche-critiche di ragioneria* (The balance sheet in the colony of Pompei. Critical archeological notes of accounting), Rome: Stabilimento Tipografico Befani.

Riera, A. (1935) *Lineamenti di contabilità di Stato* (Outline of government accounting), Siracusa: Istituto di Ragioneria 'F. Besta'.

Riera, A. (1938) *Saggio sul Tractatus de Computis et Scripturis* (Essay on the Tractatus de Computis et Scripturis), Siracusa: Istituto di Ragioneria 'F. Besta'.

Riera, A. (1942) *I costi generali delle imprese manifatturiere* (Overhead costs of manufacturing firms), Padua.

Riera, A. (1949) *I costi industriali* (Industrial costs), 2nd edn, Catania (first edn, 1946).

Rigobon, P. (1902) *Studii antichi e moderni intorno alla tecnica dei commerci* (Ancient and modern studies in commercial techniques), Bari: Tipografia Avellino.

Rigobon, P. (1912) 'Alcuni appunti storico-bibliografici intorno alla partita doppia sintetica applicata alle aziende mercantili, in *Monografie edite in onore del Prof. Fabio Besta*' (Some historic-bibliographical notes on 'synthetic' double-entry accounting as applied to mercantile enterprises, in *Monographs in honour of Prof. Fabio Besta*), Rome: Tipografia G. Bertero.

Rigobon, P. (1914) 'Intorno all'opera di Giuseppe Cerboni, in *Conferenze intorno alla vita e alle opere di Giuseppe Cerboni*' (On the work of Giuseppe Cerboni, in *Lectures on the life and the works of Giuseppe Cerboni*), Rome: Tipografia Cartiere Centrali.

Rigobon, P. (1920) *Tecnica dei commerci* (Commercial techniques), Padua: La Litotipo.

Riparbelli, A. (1943) *Aspetti tecnico-contabili delle disposizioni del nuovo Codice civile in materia di bilanci di società per azioni* (Technical accounting aspects of the regulations of the new civil code for financial statements of stock companies), Florence: Coppini.

Riparbelli, A. (1951–52) *Il primato italiano nelle applicazioni della ragioneria e negli studi economico-aziendali. Prolusione tenuta nell'Università degli Studi di Catania il 29 gennaio 1952* (The Italian pre-eminence in accounting applications and in studies of *Economia aziendale*. Opening lecture, University of Catania, 29 January 1952), Catania: Pubblicazioni della Facoltà di Economia e Commercio.

Rossi, G. (1901a) *Teoria matematica della scrittura doppia italiana* (Mathematical theory of Italian double-entry bookkeeping), Reggio Emilia: Tipografia Popolare.

Rossi, G. (1901b) *Il bilancio finanziario* (The financial balance sheet), Rome: Società Editrice Dante Alighieri.

Rossi, G. (1905) *Le scritture metodiche della Ragioneria Generale dello Stato. Memoria* (Methodical recordings of the General State Accounting Office. A Memoir), Reggio Emilia: Stab. Cromo–tip. S. Cuore di Gesù Cristo.

Rossi, G. (1906) *Nuove osservazioni sul rendiconto patrimoniale dello Stato* (New remarks on the financial statements of the State's treasury), Modena: Tip. della Società Tipografica.

Rossi, G. (1907a) *Nuovi studi di Ragioneria e battaglie critiche* (New accounting studies and critical controversies), Reggio Emilia: Società Tipografica–Editrice S. Ferraboschi.

Rossi, G. (1907b) *Classificazione degli enti economico-amministrativi* (Classification of economic-administrative entities), Reggio Emilia: Ferraboschi.e. C.

Rossi, G. (1908) *Teoria economica delle scritture metodiche computistiche* (Economic theory of methodical accounting entries), Macerata: Libreria Editrice Marchigiana.

Rossi, G. (1909a) *Forme tipiche degli organismi amministrativi. Memorie di Giovanni Rossi* (Typical forms of administrative entities – Memoirs of Giovanni Rossi), Reggio Emilia: Cooperativa Lavoranti Tipografi.

Rossi, G. (1909b) *I metodi di contabilità prescritti per il bilancio finanziario italiano, esaminati in base ai principi della Ragioneria* (Accounting methods prescribed for the Italian financial balance sheet, examined on the basis of the accounting principles), Reggio Emilia: Cooperativa Lavoranti Tipografi.

Rossi, G. (1910a) *I nuovi principi regolatori del bilancio finanziario italiano* (The new regulating principles of the Italian financial balance sheet), Macerata: Stabilimento Tipografico Fratelli Mancini.

Rossi, G. (1910b) *Analisi e ricomposizione di un bilancio finanziario dello Stato eseguito in nuova forma e con la scorta di alcuni nuovi principi regolatori*, Parts 1–3 (Analysis and changes of a government financial balance sheet, executed in a new way and on the basis of some new regulating principles), Reggio Emilia: Cooperativa Lavoranti Tipografi ed. Affini.

Rossi, G. (1912a) 'La ragioneria naturale, in *Monografie edite in onore del Prof. Fabio Besta*' (Natural accounting, in *Monographs in honour of Prof. Fabio Besta*), Rome: Tipografia G. Bertero.

Rossi, G. (1912b) 'Sul nuovo riassunto delle scritture della Ragioneria Generale dello Stato' (On the new accounting summary of the General State Accounting Office), *Monitore dei Ragionieri*, Milan, August.

Rossi, G. (1917) *Studi e lavori sui maggiori problemi tecnici della Ragioneria Superiore di Stato* (Studies and works on major technical problems of the Superior State Accounting Office), Macerata: Tipografia Economica.

Rossi, G. (1921) *Trattato di ragioneria scientifica* (Treatise of scientific accounting), Vol. 1, Reggio Emilia: Cooperativa Lavoranti Tipografi.

Rossi, N. (1949) *Scritture doppie in imprese mercantili, bancarie ed industriali* (Double entries in mercantile, banking and industrial enterprises), Milan: A. Giuffrè.

Rossi, N. (1950a) *Rilevazioni d'impresa nella industria meccanica* (Business recordings in mechanical industries), Milan: A. Giuffrè.

Rossi, N. (1950b) *Le previsioni d'impresa* (Business forecasting), Milan: A. Giuffrè.

Rossi-Passavanti, E. (1935) *La contabilità di Stato o l'economia di Stato nella storia* (Government accounting or government economics in history), Turin: G. Giappichelli.

Ruffini, G. (1924) *La contabilità di Stato in Francia al tempo di Napoleone I* (Government accounting in France under Napoleon I), San Felice sul Panaro: Tipografia e Cartoleria Vescovini.

Salzano, A. (1936) *Lineamenti della partita doppia applicata al sistema del reddito* (Outline of double-entry accounting applied to income system), Naples: Iodice.

Salzano, A. (1941a) *Il 'Monte dei denari' e il 'Monte del grano' a Spoleto nella seconda metà del Quattrocento* (The 'Money Mountain' and the 'Wheat Mountain' at Spoleto in the second half of the fifteenth century), Spoleto: Tipografia dell'Umbria.

Salzano, A. (1941b) *Le finanze e l'ordinamento amministrativo di Spoleto all'alba del Quattrocento* (The finance and administrative organization of Spoleto at the beginning of the fifteenth century), Spoleto: Tipografia dell'Umbria.

Salzano, A. (1942a) 'Intorno ad alcune opere di Antonio Tonzig' (On some works by Antonio Tonzig), *Rivista Italiana di Ragioneria* 35 (3): 50–8.

Salzano, A. (1942b) 'Relazioni tra valutazioni di bilancio, riserve ed autofinanziamento delle imprese' (Relations between financial statement valuations, reserves and self-financing of enterprises), *Rivista Italiana di Ragioneria* 35.

Salzano, A. (1951) *Orientamenti per la determinazione dei risultati di esercizio e per la rilevazione sistematica nelle imprese* (Introduction to the measurement of periodic results and systematic accounting in business), Rome: Ferri.

Sanguinetti, A. (1901) 'Giovanni Rossi.e. le sue opere' (Giovanni Rossi and his work), *Rivista di Amministrazione e Contabilità*, Como.

Sanguinetti, A. (1902) *Esposizione sommaria dell'opera 'Il bilancio finanziario' di Giovanni Rossi* (Summary exposition of 'The financial balance sheet' by Giovanni Rossi), Modena.

Sanguinetti, A. (1903) *I nuovi orizzonti della Ragioneria italiana* (New horizons of Italian accounting), Parma: Tipografia A. Zerbini.

Sapori, A. (1923) *Le compagnie dei Bardi e dei Peruzzi in Inghilterra nei secoli XIII.e. XIV* (The companies of the Bardi's and Peruzzi's in England during the thirteenth and fourteenth centuries), Florence: Deputazione toscana di storia patria.

Sapori, A. (1928) 'Un bilancio domestico a Firenze alla fine del Dugento' (A domestic balance sheet in Florence at the end of the thirteenth century), *La bibliofilia* 30 (6) (reprinted in *Studi di storia economica medievale*, Vol. 1, 1955: 353–71).

Sapori, A. (1931) 'La registrazione dei libri di commercio in Toscana nell'anno 1605' (The recordings of commercial books in Tuscany in the year 1605), *Rivista del diritto commerciale e del diritto generale delle obbligazioni* 29 (9–10).

Sapori, A. (1932) *Una compagnia di Calimala ai primi del Trecento* (A company of Calimala at the beginning of the fourteenth century), Florence: Olschki.

Sapori, A. (1934) *I libri di commercio dei Peruzzi* (The commerce books of the Peruzzi), Milan: F.lli Treves.

Sapori, A. (1940) *Studi di storia economica medievale* (Studies of medieval economic history), Florence: G.C. Sansoni (3rd edn, 2 vols, 1955).

Sapori, A. (1943) *I libri della ragione bancaria dei Gianfigliazzi* (The books of the Gianfigliazzi bank), Milan: A. Garzanti.

Sapori, A. (1944–45) *Il mercante italiano nel medio evo* (The Italian merchant in the Middle Ages), Florence: Barbera.

Sapori, A. (1947) *La compagnia dei Frescobaldi in Inghilterra. Appunti al volume Tercius Liber Mercatorum de' Frescobaldis* (The Frescobaldi company in England. Notes to volume three of the commerce book of Frescobaldi), Florence: Olschki (reprinted in *Studi di storia economica medievale*, Vol. 2, 1955: 859–926).

Sapori, A. (1952) *I libri degli Alberti del Giudice* (The ledgers of Alberti del Giudice), Milan: Garzanti.

Saraceno, P. (1941) *Il bilancio dell'azienda industriale* (The financial statements of the industrial enterprise), Milan: A. Giuffrè.

Sassi, S. (1939) *Note sull'applicazione della partita doppia nei mastri 'Vecchio Real' e 'Nuovo Real' della Fraterna dei Soranzo* (Notes on the application of double-entry in the ledgers 'Vecchio Real' and 'Nuovo Real' of the brothers Soranzo), Naples: Tipomeccanica.

Sassi, S. (1940) *Il sistema dei rischi d'impresa* (Risk analysis in business), Milan: Vallardi.

Scherpf, P. (1955) *Der Kontenrahmen – Entstehung, Verbreitung, Möglichkeiten* (The master chart of accounts – origin, dispersion, possibilities), Munich: Max Huber.

Schmalenbach, E. (1919) 'Grundlagen der dynamischen Bilanztheorie' (Foundations of dynamic accounting), *Zeitschrift für handelswissenschaftliche Forschung* 13: 1–60, 65–101 (published in book form as *Grundlagen dynamische Bilanzlehre*, Leipzig, 1920; later as *Dynamische Bilanz*, 3rd edn, Leipzig, 1925; English translation as *Dynamic Accounting*, London: Gee and Co., 1959) – see also Chapter 14 (for Japanese translations).

Schneider, D. (1981) *Geschichte betriebswirtschaftlicher Theorie* (History of the theory of business-economics), Munich: Oldenbourg Verlag (3rd edn, 1987). (This book has been greatly expanded to a work of four volumes under the title *Betriebswirtschaftslehre*, Vol. 1: Grundlagen, 1993; Vol. 2: *Rechnungswesen*, 1994; Vol. 3: *Theorie der Unternehmung* and Vol. 4: see below: *Geschichte und Methoden der Wirtschaftswissenschaft*, 2001).

Schneider, D. (2001) *Betriebswirtschaftlehre, Band 4: Geschichte und Methoden der Wirtschaftswissenschaft* (Business economics, Vol. 4: History and methods of economic science), Munich: R. Oldenbourg.

Serra, L. (1999) *Storia della ragioneria Italiana* (History of Italian accounting), Milan: A. Giuffrè Editore.

Terranova, P. (1924) *Il vero posto della ragioneria di fronte alla scienzomania moderna* (The true place of accounting in facing the modern science-mania), Milan: Hoepli.

Tofani, A. (1910) *Alcune ricerche storiche sull' ufficio e la professione di ragioniere a Firenze al tempo della Repubblica* (Some historical research on the duties and the accounting profession in Florence during the time of the Republic), Florence: Tipografia Barbera Alfani e Venturi.

Tognacci, G. (1925) *La contabilità del costo di produzione* (Manufacturing cost accounting), Monograph No. 68 of the Library of Applied Accounting 'Rota', Turin: Utet.

Tognacci, G. (1930) *La contabilità dello Stato* (Government accounting), Monograph No. 1, Part III of the Library of Applied Accounting 'Rota', Turin: Utet.

Verna, A. (1942) *Il bilancio e le scritture di esercizio nelle imprese* (Financial statements and the recordings of the activities of enterprises), Rome: Stabilimento Tiberino.

Verna, A. (1950) *La ragioneria e l'economia aziendale* (Accounting and the 'economia aziendale'), 2nd rev. edn, Rome: Signorelli (first edn, 1936).

Vianello, V. (1914) 'Ancora sulla ragioneria come scienza moderna' (Again on accounting as a modern science), *Rivista Italiana di Ragioneria* 7 (7): 301–5.

Vianello, V. (1924) *Le aziende marittime* (Maritime enterprises), Biblioteca di ragioneria applicata 'Rota', No. 30, Turin: Utet.

Vianello, V. (1925) *L'amministrazione economica e la contabilità di Stato* (Economic administration and government accounting), Turin.

Vianello, V. (1927) 'Deficit patrimoniale ed 'Avanzi' di bilancio nello Stato italiano' (Government deficit and balance sheet 'surplus' of the Italian State), *Rivista Italiana di Ragioneria* 20 (4): 149–55.

Vianello, V. (1928) 'Tendenze nuove negli studi di Ragioneria' (New trends in accounting studies), *Rivista di Ragioneria e Studii affini* 25 (5): 194–201.

Vianello, V. (1932) 'Pensiero in memoria di Fabio Besta' (Thoughts in memory of Fabio Besta), *Rivista Italiana di Ragioneria* 25 (10–12): 316–17.

Vianello, V. (1935) *Istituzioni di ragioneria generale* (Institutions of general accounting), 9th edn, Rome: Società Editrice Dante Alighieri.

Viganò, E. (1998) 'Accounting and business economics tradition in Italy', *European Accounting Review* 7 (3): 381–403.

Virgili, A. (1902) *La Ragioneria è una scienza?* (Is accounting a science?), Venice: Tipografia A. Pelizzato.

Zambon, S. (2002) *Locating accounting in its national context: the case of Italy*, Milan: Franco Angeli.

Zan, L. (1994) 'Toward a history of accounting histories: perspectives from the Italian tradition', *European Accounting Review* 3 (2): 255–307.

Zappa, G. (1910) *Le valutazioni di bilancio con particolare riguardo ai bilanci delle società per azioni* (Balance sheet valuations with particular reference to the financial statements of joint stock companies), Milano: Società Editrice Libraria (reprinted 1927).

Zappa, G. (undated, but between 1915 and 1920) *La tecnica dei cambi esteri. Teoria e pratica dei pagamenti internazionali* (Foreign exchange techniques. Theory and practice of international trade payments), Milan: Società Editrice Libraria.

Zappa, G. (1920–29) *La determinazione del reddito nelle imprese commerciali – I valori di conto in relazione alla formazione dei bilanci* (Income determination in commercial enterprises – accounting values in relation to structuring financial statements), Rome: Anonima Libreria Italiana.

Zappa, G. (1924) *Bilanci di imprese commerciali. Note e commenti* (Notes to and comments on financial statements of commercial enterprises), Milan: A. Giuffrè.

Zappa, G. (1927) *Tendenze nuove negli studi di ragioneria* (New trends in accounting research), Venice: Tipografia Libreria Emiliana.

Zappa, G. (1935a) *Fabio Besta: il maestro* (Fabio Besta: the master), Milan: A. Giuffrè Editore.

Zappa, G. (1935b) *La tecnica della speculazione di borsa. Parte prima: Le operazioni elementari di borsa* (Speculative techniques of the stock exchange. Part one: Basic stock market transactions), Milan: D. Ravezzani Editore.

Zappa, G. (1937) *Il reddito di impresa – Scritture doppie, conti.e. bilanci di aziende commerciali* (The business income – double entries, accounts and financial statements of commercial enterprises), 2nd edn, Milan: A. Giuffrè (3rd printing of 2nd edn, 1950).

Zappa, G. (1946) *La nazionalizzazione delle imprese* (The nationalization of enterprises), Milan: A. Giuffrè Editore.

Zappa, G. (1956–57) *Le produzioni nell'economia delle imprese* (Production activities in the economy of enterprises), 3 vols, Milan: A. Giuffrè Editore.

Zappa, G. (1962, published posthumously) *L'economia delle aziende di consumo* (The economy of consumption entities), Milan: A. Giuffrè Editore.

Zappa, G. and Marcantonio, A. (1954) *Ragioneria applicata alle aziende pubbliche* (Accounting applied to public entities), Milan: A. Giuffrè Editore.

Zappa, G., Azzini, L. and Cudini, G. (1949) *Ragioneria generale* (General accounting), Milan: A. Giuffré.

Zappa, G., Azzini, L. and Cudini, G. (1951) *Ragioneria applicata alle aziende private* (Accounting applied to private enterprises), Milan: A. Giuffré.

Zerbi, T. (1935) *La banca nell'ordinamento finanziario visconteo* (The bank in the financial organization of the Visconti), Como: Casa Editrice Emo Cavalleri.

Zerbi, T. (1936a) *Il mastro a partita doppia di un'azienda mercantile del trecento* (The double-entry ledger of a commercial enterprise of the fourteenth century), Como: Casa Editrice Emo Cavalleri.

Zerbi, T. (1936b) *Aspetti economico-tecnici del mercato di Milano nel trecento* (Technical economic aspects of the market of Milan in the fourteenth century), Como: Casa Editrice Emo Cavalleri.

Zerbi, T. (1940) *Guida brevissima allo studio del sistema del reddito* (Concise guide to the study of the 'income system'), Como: Casa Editrice Emo Cavalleri.

Zerbi, T. (1948) *Indirizzo allo studio del sistema del reddito* (Guide to the study of the 'income system'), Milan: Marzorati.

Zerbi, T. (1952) *Le origini della partita doppia. Gestioni aziendali.e. situazioni di mercato nei secoli XIV e XV* (The origins of double-entry bookkeping. Management operations and markets in the fourteenth and fifteenth centuries), Milan: Marzorati.

Zorli, A. (1911a) *La scienza della ragioneria nel grande albero della filosofia positiva* (The science of accounting on the great tree of positive philosophy), Como.

Zorli, A. (1911b) 'La teorica della valutazione economica' (The theory of economic valuation), *Rivista Italiana di Ragioneria* 4 (6): 251–3.

Zorli, A. (1919) 'Ancora della ragioneria come scienza descrittiva' (Again on accounting as a descriptive science), *Rivista Italiana di Ragioneria* 12 (1): 10–12.

Zorli, A. (1933) 'La ragioneria scienza d'insieme' (Accounting as a unified science), *Rivista Italiana di Ragioneria* 26 (10): 348–9.

Zorli, A. (1939) 'La scienza economica aziendale è la vera unica scienza economica' (The science of *Economia aziendale* is the genuine unique economic science) *Rivista Italiana di Ragioneria* 32 (4): 116–17.

6 Accounting research in Italy: second half of the twentieth century

Accademia Italiana di Economia Aziendale (AIDEA) (1978) *L'inflazione*, Vol. 1: *Problemi.e. risposte per i dirigenti dell'industria, della banca e dell'ammistrazione pubblica;* Vol. 2: *Problemi e risposte per operatori economici delle assicurazioni, della produzione agricola, delle aziende di consumo e patrimoniale familiari* (Inflation, Vol. 1: Problems and responses of the captains of industry, banking and public administration; Vol. 2: Problems and responses from the economic leaders of the sectors of insurance, agricultural production, consumer entities and family estates), Milano: A. Giuffrè.

Accademia Italiana di Economia Aziendale (AIDEA) (1980a) *Pianificazione e controllo della gestione nelle imprese bancarie* (Planning and management control in the banking sector), Bologna: AIDEA.

Accademia Italiana di Economia Aziendale (AIDEA) (1980b) *Gino Zappa, founder of concern economics: papers on the hundredth anniversary of his birth*, Bologna: AIDEA.

Agazzi, E. (1961) *Introduzione ai problemi dell'assiomatica* (Introduction to the problems of axiomatization), Milan: Vita e Pnsiero.

Amaduzzi, Aldo (1955) *Sulla variabilità del processo produttivo dell'azienda industriale* (On the variability of production process of industrial enterprises), 2nd edn, Rome: Signorelli (1st edn, 1939).

Amaduzzi, Aldo (1959) 'L'azienda nel suo sistema e nell'ordine delle sue rilevazioni' (The entity system. An accounting perspective), 3rd edn, Turin: Utet: 111–14.

Amaduzzi, Aldo (1962) 'Sviluppi delle nostre teorie contabili.e. confronto con recenti generalizzazioni' (The development of our accounting theories and the confrontation with recent generalizations), *Rivista dei Dottori Commercialisti: Giuffrè.*

Amaduzzi, Aldo (1965) *Richerche di economia dell'azienda industriale*, Torino: Utet.

Amaduzzi, Antonio (2001) *Storia della ragioneria. Uomini, aziende, contabilità* (History of accounting: personalities, entities and accounting), Bergamo: Collegio dei Ragionieri di Bergamo.

Amodeo, D. (1953) *A proposito di un antico bilancio del Vicereame di Napoli* (On an ancient financial statement of Naples Vice-royalty), Naples: Giannini.

Amodeo, D. (1961a) 'La moderna teoria contabile: dalla contabilità pura alla formulazione matriciale' (Modern accounting theory: from traditional accounting to matrix formulation), in Istituto di economia aziendalem ed., *Saggi di economia aziendale e sociale in memoria di Gino Zappa*, Milan: Università commerciale Luigi Bocconi.

Amodeo, D. (1961b) 'Nuovi orizzonti per la ragioneria' (New horizons for accounting), in Domenico Demarco ed., *Studi in onore di Epicarmo Corbino*, Milan: A. Giuffrè.

Amodeo, D. (1976) *Le gestioni indutriali produttrici di beni* (The management of industrial production), Torino: Utet.

Amodeo, D., Cianniello, A., Curcio, E., Di Meo, W., D'Oriano, R., Mariniello, L., Musto, N., Palombini, S., Potito, L. and Viganò, E. (1975) *La certificazione professionale dei bilanci* (The certification of financial statements), Napoli: Giannini.

Antoni, T. (1970) *Fabio Besta. contributo alla conoscenza degli studi aziendali* (Fabio Besta. Contribution to knowledge of the studies of the *azienda*), Pisa: Colombo Cursi.

Antonelli, V. and Cerbioni, F. (1998) 'L'analisi dei costi alle origini dello sviluppo industriale in Italia: osservazioni sul caso Ansaldo' (Cost analysis at the beginning of the industrial revolution in Italy: in particular in the firm of Asaldo), *Atti del IV Convegno Nazionale di Storia della Ragioneria*, Perugia: CNSR.

Ardemani, E. (1967) *Istituzioni di ragioneria* (Accounting institutions), Milan: Marzorati.

Associazione Industriale Lombarda (AIL) (1980) *La gestione dell'impresa industriale in periodo di inflazione* (Business management in periods of inflation), Milan: AIL.

Azzini, L. (1954) *Investimenti.e. produttività nelle imprese industriali* (Investments and productivity in industrial enterprises), Milan: A. Giuffrè.

Azzini, L. (1957) *Le situazioni d'impresa investigate nella dinamica economia delle produzioni* (Investigation of production dynamics in enterprises), Milan: A. Giuffrè.

Azzini, L. (1964) *I processi produttivi e i rischi di andamento dei prezzi nel tempo* (Production processes and risks of prices variation), Milan: A. Giuffrè.

Azzini, L. (1976) *Composizione e sintesi di esercizio del sistema di valori nelle aziende delle diverse specie, appunti di lezioni* (Composition and synthesis of valuation problems in different kinds of enterprises, lecture notes), Parma: Facoltà di Economia e Commercio.

Bergamin-Barbato, M., Collini, P. and Quagli, A. (1996) 'Management accounting in Italy: evolution within tradition', in A. Bhimani ed., *Management accounting: European perspectives*, Oxford: Oxford University Press: 140–63.

Besta, F. (1922) *La ragioneria* (Accounting theory), 3 vols, 2nd edn, Milan: Vallardi (1st edn, 1891–1916; a one volume work by this author, under the same title, was published in 1880 as mentioned above; a revised edn, of the three volumes was published in Milan: Vallardi, 1932).

Bianchi, T. (1975) *Costi, ricavi e prezzi nelle banche di deposito* (Costs, withdrawals and prices at saving banks), Milan: A. Giuffrè (1st edn, 1967).

Biondi, Y. (2002) *Gino Zappa e la revoluzione del reddito – azienda, moneta e contabilità*, Padova: CEDAM.

Boscarato, E. (1973) *La ragioneria generale: gli assurdi del sistema del reddito secondo le teorie zappiane* (General accounting: the absurdities of income determination according to Zappa's theory), Ancona: CLUA.

Bruni, G. (1996) *Revisione aziendale* (Economic entity auditing), 4th edn, Turin, Utet.

Brusa, L. (1978) *Il sistema budgetario nel sistema organizzativo di impresa* (The budgetary system in the organization of enterprises), Milan: A. Giuffrè.

Brusa, L. and Dezzani, F. (1983) *Budget e controllo di gestione* (Budget and management control), Milan: A. Giuffrè.

Campedelli, B. (1995) *Le analisi di bilancio per la revisione aziendale* (The analysis of financial statement for business auditing), Turin: Giappichelli.

Canziani, A. (1987) 'Sulle premesse metodologiche della rivoluzione zappiana, in *Saggi di economia aziendale per Lino Azzini*' (On the methodological premises of Zappa's revolution, in *Essays of* Economia aziendale *in honour of Lino Azzini*), Milan: A. Giuffrè Editore, 142–65.

Canziani, A. (1988) 'Italy and the seven directives', in S.J. Gray and A.G. Coenenberg eds, *International Group Accounting*, Beckenham: Croom Helm.

Canziani, A. (1990) 'The evolution of Italian accounting regulations'; paper presented at the EIASM Workshop on Accounting in Europe: Past Traditions and Future Issues, Brussels, 14–15 May.

Canziani, A. (1994) 'Gino Zappa (1879–1960): accounting revolutionary', in J.R. Edwards ed., *Twentieth century accounting thinkers*, London: Routledge: 142–65.

Capaldo, P. (1973) 'Il bilancio dello stato nel sistema dalla programmazione economica' (The state balance sheet in the system of economic planning), Milan: A. Giuffrè.

Carmona, S., Guitérrez, I. and Camarra, M. (1999) 'A profile of European accounting research: evidence from leading research journals', *The European Accounting Review* 8 (3): 463–80.

Catturi, G. (1989) *Teorie contabili e scenari economico-aziendali* (Accounting theories and various scenarios of economic entities), Padua: Cedam.

Catturi, G. and Riccaboni, A. (1992) 'The development of Italian accounting theories: their relationship to the economic and business environmental role played by the national culture and the international accounting debate', paper presented at the 15th Annual Congress of the European Accounting Association, Madrid, April.

Cavalieri, E. (1974) *Sulle relazioni tra modelli economico-aziendali e di ragioneria* (On the relations between economic models and accounting), Chieti: Edigrafital.

Chatfield, M. (1982) 'Review of "Papers on business administration"', *Accounting Review* 57 (1): 208–9.

Chianale, A. (1962a) *Ragioneria generale* (General accounting), Turin: Levrotto & Bella.

Chianale, A. (1962b) *Ragioneria applicata alle società commerciali* (Accounting applied to corporations), Turin: Levrotto & Bella.

Christensen, J.A. and Demski, J.S. (2003) *Accounting theory: an information content perspective*, New York: McGraw-Hill, Irwin.

Christensen, P.O. and Feltham, G.A. (2003) *Economics of accounting*, Vol. 1: *Information in markets*, Boston, MA: Kluwer Academic Publishers.

Christensen, P.O. and Feltham, G.A. (2005) *Economics of accounting*, Vol. 2: *Performance evaluation*, Boston, MA: Kluwer Academic Publishers.

Cilloni, A. (1998) 'Economia dell'informazione ed economia dell'agenzia. Un approccio metodologico innovativo alla scienza economico aziendale?' (Information economics and agency economics. A methodological innovative approach to *economia aziendale* science?), *Rivista Italiana di Ragioneria e di Economia Aziendale* (11–12): 587–601.

Cilloni, A. (1999) 'Rilevanza dell'informazione economico-aziendale e riduzione del rischio morale nel rapporto di agenzia 'amministratore-proprietario' (Relevance of business economics information and reduction of moral hazard in the agency relation 'manager-owner'), *Rivista Italiana di Ragioneria e di Economia Aziendale* 1999 (9–10): 471–83.

Cilloni, A. (2004) *Economia dell'informazione e sistemi contabili aziendali* (Information economics and entity accounting systems), Milan: A. Giuffrè.

Cilloni, A. and Marinoni, M.A. (2006) 'Spreadsheet, chessboard and matrix accounting. The origin and development of advanced accounting instruments: an archival research', *Contabilità e Cultura Aziendale – Rivista della Società Italiana di Storia della Ragineria* 6 (1): 95–113.

Cinquini, L. and Marelli, A. (2002) 'An Italian forerunner of cost allocation concepts: Lorenzo de Minico and the logic of the "flows of services"', *Accounting, Business and Financial History* 12 (1, March): 95–111.

Coda, V. (1968a) *I costi di produzione* (Costs of production), Milan: A. Giuffrè.

Coda, V. (1968b) 'In tema di principi contabili generalmente accettati' (On the topic of generally accepted accounting principles), *Rivista dei Dottori Commercialisti* 1 (January–February): 431–7.

Coda, V. and Frattini, G. (1980) *Valutazioni di bilancio* (Balance sheet valuations), Venice: Venice University Press.

Coda, V., Brunetti, G. and Bergamin-Barbato, M. (1974) *Indici di bilancio e flussi finanziari* (Balance sheet ratios and flow of financial funds), Milan: Etas.

Colombo, G.E. (1965) *Il bilancio di esercizio delle società per azioni* (The balance sheet of stock corporations), Padova: Cedam.

Colombo, G.E. (1977) 'La disciplina italiana della revisione' (The discipline of auditing), *Rivista dei Dottori Commercialisti*, Milan: A. Giuffrè.

Colombo, G.E. (1987) *Il bilancio di esercizio. Strutture e valutazioni* (Financial statement. Structures and valuations), Turin: Utet.

Consiglio Nazionale dei Dottori Commercialisti (CNDC) (1977–83) *Commissione per la Statuizione dei Principi Contabili* (Commission for the establishment of accounting principles), Milan: CNDC.

Cossar, L. (1973) *L'analisi dei flussi dei fondi e il 'cash flow'* (Analysis of flow of funds and cash flows), Trieste: Università di Trieste.

De Dominicis, U. (1963–69) *Lezioni di ragioneria generale* (Lessons of general accounting), Vols I–V, Bologna: Azzoguidi.

De Dominicis, U. (1977). Svalutazione monetaria e rendiconto d'esercizio nelle imprese (Inflation and periodic financial statement in the enterprises), *Rivista dei Dottori Commercialisti* 28 (2): 203–85.

Dell'Amore, G. (1978) *Economia delle aziende di credito. Le banche di deposito* (Economics of financial entities. Saving banks), Milan: A. Giuffrè.

Dezzani, F., Pisoni, P., Puddu, L. and Cantino, W. (2000) *Revisione contabile e certificazione del bilancio* (Internal auditing and financial statement auditing), Turin: Giappichelli.

D'Ippolito, T. (1952) *L'unificazione contabile* (On the standardization of accounting), Palermo: Abbaco.

D'Ippolito, T. (1962) *I costi di produzione e di distribuzione* (Costs of production and distribution), Palermo: Abbaco.

D'Ippolito, T. (1963) *Il 'quadro' dei conti in partita doppia, sistema duplice e le scritture tipiche relative* (The 'chart' of accounts and double-entry – the dual system and its recording process), 6th edn, Palermo: Abbaco.

D'Ippolito, T. (1967) *Determinazioni di produttività, di rendimenti, di inefficienze e di cicli a quantità fisico-tecniche* (Determining productivity, efficiency, inefficiency and the quantitative flows), 4th edn, Palermo: Abbaco (1st edn, 1951).

Di Lazzaro, F. (1998) *Le 'frontiere' della ragioneria negli anni trenta* (The boundaries of accounting during the 1930s), Milan: A. Giuffrè.

Edwards, E.O. and Bell, P.W. (1961) *The theory and measurement of business income*, Berkeley, CA: University of California Press.

Ewert, R. and Wagenhofer, A. (1993/2003) *Interne Unternehmensrechnung* (Managerial accounting), Berlin: Springer Verlag (5th edn, 2003).

Fanni, M. (1971) *Modelli analitici di programmatazione aziendale* (Analytical models for business planning), Trieste: Istituto di Ragioneria dell'Università di Trieste.

Fanni, M. and Cossar, L. (1994) *Il modello contabile* (The accounting method), Rome: NIS.

Ferraris-Franceshi, R. (1978) 'L'indagine metodologica in economia aziendale' (Methodological investigations of *economia aziendale*), Milan: A. Giuffrè.

Ferraris-Franceshi, R. (1994) *Il percorso scientifico dell'economia aziendale* (The scientific path of *economia aziendale*), Torino: Giappichelli.

Ferrero, G. (1966) *La valutazione economica del capitale d'impresa* (The economic valuation of business capital), Milan: A. Giuffrè.

Ferrero, G. (1968) *Instituzione di economia aziendale*, Milano: A. Giuffrè.

Ferrero, G. (1977) Bilanci e contabilità per l'inflazione (Balance sheets and accounting for inflation), Milano: A. Giuffrè.

Ferrero, G. (1988) *La valutazione del capitale di bilancio*, Milan: A. Giuffrè.

Galassi, G. (1978) *Sistemi contabili assiomatici.e. sistemi teorici deduttivi* (Axiomatic accounting systems and theoretical deductive systems), Bologna: Pàtron Editore.

Galassi, G. (1980) 'Capital-income relations: a critical analysis', in *Gino Zappa, founder of concern economics*, Bologna: Accademia Italiana di Economia Aziendale: 25–49.

Galassi, G. (1984) 'Accounting research in Italy: past, present and future', in A. Hopwood and H. Schreuder eds, *European contributions to accounting research: the achievements of the last decade*, Amsterdam: VU Uitgeverii/Free University Press: 163–87.

Galassi, G. (1987) 'Economia dell'informazione ed economia della conoscenza. Recenti sviluppi metodologici' (Information economics and knowledge economics. Recent methodological developments), in *Scritti di economia aziendale per Egidio Giannessi*, Pisa: Pacini: 617–35.

Galassi, G. (1991) 'Economia dell'agenzia ed economia dell'informazione: un approccio integrato' (Agency economics and information economics: an integrated approach), in *Studi in onore di Ubaldo De Dominicis*, Trieste: Lint: 86–101.

Galassi, G. (1994) 'Teoria dell'informazione ed economia dell'informazione. Considerazioni critiche' (Information theory and information economics. Critical remarks), in M. Morelli and M. Tangheroni eds, *Leonardo Fibonacci. Il tempo, le opere, l'eredità scientifica*, Pisa: Pacini: 137–65.

Galassi, G. (1996a) 'Italy, after Pacioli', in M. Chatfield and R. Vangermeersch eds, *The history of accounting: an international encyclopedia*, New York: Garland Publishing, Inc.: 347–50.

Galassi, G. (1996b) 'Pacioli, Luca (c. 1445–1517)', in M. Chatfield and R. Vangermeersch eds, *The history of accounting: an international encyclopedia*, New York: Garland Publishing, Inc.: 445–7.

Galassi, G. (1996c) 'Zappa, Gino (1879–1960)', in M. Chatfield and R. Vangermeersch eds, *The history of accounting: an international encyclopedia*, New York: Garland Publishing, Inc.: 617–18.

Galassi, G. and Mattessich, R. (2004) 'Italian accounting research in the first half of the twentieth century', presented at the Congress of the European Accounting Association, Seville (abbreviated version published in the *Review of Accounting and Finance* 4 (2): 62–82).

Giannessi, E. (1960) *Interpetazioni del concetto di aziend publica*, Pisa: Colombo Cursi.

Giannessi, E. (1982) *Il 'Kreislauf' tra i costi e prezzi* (The 'circulation' between accounts and prices), Pisa: Colombo Cursi.

Guarini, A. (1977) *Il bilancio degli entity pubblici* (The balance sheet of public entities), Milan: Angeli.

Guatri, L. (1951) *Il costo di produzione. L'efficienza* (Production costs and efficiency), Milan: A. Giuffrè.

Guatri, L. (1954) *Il costo di produzione* (The production cost), Milan: A. Giuffrè.

Guatri, L. (1981) *La valutazione delle aziende* (Valuation of economic entities), Milan: A. Giuffrè.

Guglielmi, M. (1997) 'Contabilità dei costi e competitività aziendale nel settecento Veneziano: le fàbbriche Tron' (Cost accounting and competitive enterprises in eighteenth century Venice: the Tron factory), Venice: paper presented at the AIDEA June Workshop.

Kaplan, R.S. (1984) 'The evolution of management accounting', *The Accounting Review* 59 (3, July): 390–418.

Marchi, L. (1988) *Strategie di revisione aziendale* (Strategies of business auditing), Milan: Ipsoa.

Marcon, G. (1978) *Bilancio, programmazione e razionalità delle decisione pubbliche* (The balance sheet, planning and rationality in public decision making), Milan: Angeli.

Masi, V. (1961) *Filosofia della ragioneria* (Philosophy of accounting), Bologna: Tamari Editore.

Masi, V. (1963) *La ragioneria nella preistoria e nell'antichità* (Accounting in prehistoric and ancient times), Bologna: Tamari.

Masi, V. (1964) 'Ragioneristi Greci.e. Romani' (Greek and Roman accountants), *Rivista Italiana di Ragioneria* 7–8: 155–65.

Masi, V. (1997, posthumously published) *La ragioneria nell' età moderna e contemporanea, Testo riveduto e completato da Carlo Antinori* (Accounting of the modern and contemporaneous age. Revised and extended text by Carlo Antinori), Milan: A. Giuffrè.

Masini, C. (1963) *La dinamica economica nei sistemi dei valori d'azienda: valutazioni.e. rivalutazioni* (The economic dynamics in the valuation of the firm: valuation and valuation adjustments), Milan: A. Giuffrè (1st edn, 1959).

Masini, C. (1978) *Il sistema dei valori di aziende* (The value system of the economic entity), Milan: A. Giuffrè.

Mattessich, R. (1964) *Accounting and analytical methods: measurement and projection of income and wealth in the micro- and macro-economy*, Homewood, IL: R.D. Irwin, Inc. (reprinted in the 'Accounting Classics Series', Houston, TX: Scholars Book Co., 1977; also in the 'Series of Financial Classics' of Reprints on Demand, Ann Arbor, MI: Microfilms International, 1979, still available; Japanese translation under the direction of Shinzaburo Koshimura, *Kaikei to Bunsekiteki-Hoho Jokan*, 2 vols, Tokyo: Dobunkan, Ltd, Vol. 1: 1972, Vol. 2: 1975; Spanish translation, by Carlos Luis García Casella and Maria del Carmen Ramírez de Rodríguez, Buenos Aires: La Ley, 2002).

Mattessich, R. (1995) *Critique of accounting: examination of the foundations and normative structure of an applied discipline*, Westport, CT: Quorum Books.

Mazza, G. (1968) *Premesse storico-sistematiche negli studi di ragioneria* (Systematic-historical premises of accounting research), Milan: A. Giuffrè.

Melis, F. (1950) *Storia della ragioneria – Contributo alla conoscenza e interpretazione delle fonti più significativi della storia economica* (History of accounting – contribution to the knowledge and interpretation of the most significant sources of economic history), Bologna: Cesare Zuffi.

Mella, P. (1995) *Contabilità e bilancio* (Accounting and the balance sheet), Turin: Utet.

Miolo Vitali, P. (1978) *Problemi ecologici nella gestione delle aziende* (Ecological problems in business management), Milan: A. Giuffrè.

Montesinos Julve, V. (1998) 'Accounting and business economics in Spain', *European Accounting Review* 7 (3): 357–80.

Mulazzani, M. (1978) *Ragioneria pubblica* (Government accounting), Padova: Cedam.

Olivotto, L. (1983) *La valutazione economica dell'impresa* (Economic valuation of the enterprise), Milan: Isedi.

Onida, P. (1960) *Economia d'azienda* (Business economics), Turin: Utet.

Onida, P. (1970) *I moderni sviluppi della dottrina contabile nord-americana e gli studi economia aziendale*, Milan: A. Giuffrè (English version as a monograph under the title *Modern developments of the North American accounting doctrine and the studies of business economics*, Milan: A. Giuffrè, 1974).

Onida, P. (1973a) 'Alcuni punti di dissenso di R.J. Chambers, espressi in una mia pubblicazione del 1970' (Some points of disagreement with R.J. Chambers, expressed in one of my publications of the 1970s), *Rivista dei Dottori Commercialisti* 24 (6, November–December): 995–1000.

Onida, P. (1973b) 'Replica all articolo di R.J. Chambers', *Rivista dei Dottori Commercialisti* 24 (6, November–December): 1023–33.

Peragallo, E. (1971) 'A commentary on Viganò's historical development of ledger balancing procedures, adjustments and financial statements during the fifteenth, sixteenth and seventeenth centuries', *The Accounting Review* 46 (3): 529–34.

Perotta, R. (1983) *Le valutazioni di fusione* (Valuations in mergers), Milan: A. Giuffrè.

Pezzoli, S. (1977) *Profili di storia della ragioneria* (Profiles in accounting history), Padova: Cedam.

Pisoni, P. (1995) *Il bilancio consolidato* (The consolidated balance sheet), Milan: Giuffrè (3rd edn, 2000).

Quagli, A. (1997) 'Tendenze evolutive nel controllo dei costi di produzione in Piaggio & C. s.p.a'. (Evolutionary trends in production cost control at Piaggio & C. s.p.a.), Venice: paper presented at the AIDEA June 13, Workshop.

Rinaldi, L. (1990) *Il bilancio consolidato* (The consolidated balance sheet), Milan: A. Giuffrè

Riparbelli, A. (1951–52) *Il primato italiano nelle applicazioni della ragioneria e negli studi economico-aziendali. Prolusione tenuta nell'Università degli Studi di Catania il 29 gennaio 1952* (The Italian pre-eminence in accounting applications and in studies of *Economia aziendale*. Opening lecture, University of Catania, 29 January 1952), Catania: Pubblicazioni della Facoltà di Economia e Commercio.

Rossi, N. (1950) *Rilevazioni d'impresa nella industria meccanica* (Business reporting in manufacturing industries), Milan: A. Giuffrè.

Russo, A. and Siniscalco, F. (1984) 'The Fourth Directive in Italy', in S.J. Gray and A.G. Coenenberg eds, *EEC Accounting harmonization: implementation and impact of the Fourth Directive*, Amsterdam: North-Holland.

Salzano, A. (1951) *Orientamenti per la determinazione dei risultati di esercizio e per la rilevazione sistematica nelle imprese* (Introduction to the measurement of periodic results and systematic accounting in business), Rome: Ferri.

Serra, L. (1999) *Storia della ragioneria italiana* (History of Italian accounting), Milan: A. Giuffrè Editore.

Superti Furga, F. (1976) *Le valutazioni di bilancio* (Valuation in financial statements), Milan: Ised.

Superti Furga, F. (1987) *Reddito e capitale nel bilancio di esercizio* (Income and capital in the balance sheet), Milan: A. Giuffrè.

Terzani, M. (1992) *Il bilancio consolidato* (The consolidated balance sheet), Padova: Cedam.

Took, L. (1993) 'Totemism, nationalism and Gino Zappa: founder of *economia aziendale*', paper presented at the 16th Annual Congress of the European Accounting Association, Turku, Finland, 30 April.

Viganò, A. and De Cicco, R. (1983) *La revisione del bilancio di esercizio* (Auditing of the annual financial statement), Milan: A. Giuffrè.

Viganò, E. (1968) *La Tecnica del bilancio di cerifcazione nell'opera dei primi trattatisti* (ed. by Domenico Amodeo), Naples: Francesco Giannini & Figli.

Viganò, E. (1972) 'The accounting problem of financial leasing', *Management International Review* 14 (6): 99–107.

Viganò, E. (1993) *L'impresa e il bilancio europeo* (The firm and European financial statements), Padova: Cedam.

Viganò, E. (1997) 'L'economia aziendale e la ragioneria. Evoluzione – prospettive internazionali (with a special summary in English added to the Italian text: 'Accounting and *economia aziendale* in an international perspective'), Padova: Cedam (modified English version as: 'Accounting and business economics', *The European Accounting Review* 7: 3, 1998: 381–403).

Viganò, E. and Mattessich, R. (2007) 'Accounting research in Italy: second half of the twentieth century', *Review of Accounting and Finance* 6 (1): 24–41.

Walb, E. (1948) *Die finanzwirtschaftliche Bilanz* (The financial balance sheet), 2nd edn, Duisburg: Visser.

Wagenhofer, A. and Ewert, R. (2003) *Externe Unternehmensrechnung* (Financial accounting), Berlin: Springer Verlag.

Zambon, S. (1995) 'Italy', in D. Alexander and S. Archer eds, *European accounting guide*, 2nd edn, San Diego: Harcourt Brace: 379–533.

Zambon, S. and Saccon, C. (1993) 'Accounting change in Italy: fresh start or Gattopardo's revolution?', *The European Accounting Review* 3 (20): 245–84.

Zan, L. (1994) 'Toward a history of accounting histories: perspectives from the Italian tradition', *European Accounting Review* 3 (2): 255–307.

Zan, L. and Hoskin, K. (1996) 'Il discorso del maneggio' (Accounting and the production of management discourse at the Venice Arsenal, 1580–1650), Venice: Ateneo Veneto 11–12.

Zappa, G. (1950) *Il reddito d'impresa* (The income of the economic entity), 3rd printing of 2nd edn, Milan: A. Giuffrè (for 1st edn, see Zappa, G. 1937).

Zappa, G. (1955–57) *Le produzioni nell'economia delle imprese* (Production activities in the economy of enterprises), 3 vols, Milan: A. Giuffrè Editore.

Zappa, G. (1962, published posthumously) *L'economia delle aziende di consumo* (The economy of consumption entities), Milan: A. Giuffrè.

Zappa, G. and Marcantonio, A. (1954) *Ragioneria applicata alle aziende pubbliche* (Accounting applied to public entities), Milan: A. Giuffrè.

Zappa, G., Azzini, L. and Cudini, G. (1951a) *Ragioneria applicata alle aziende private*, 2nd edn, (Accounting applied to private enterprises), Milan: A. Giuffré (1st edn, 1949).

Zappa, G., Azzini, L. and Cudini, G. (1951b) *Ragioneria applicata alle aziende private* (Accounting applied to private entities), Milan: A. Giuffré.

Zerbi, T. (1952) 'Le origini della partita doppia. Gestioni aziendali.e. situazioni di mercato nei secoli XIV e XV' (The origins of double-entry bookkeping. Management operations and markets in the fourteenth and fifteenth centuries), Milan: Marzorati: 88–121.

7 Accounting research in the French language area: first half of the twentieth century

Batardon, L. (1911) *La tenue des livres sur feuillets mobiles* (Bookkeeping on loose-leaf accounts), 2nd edn, Brussels (reprinted Paris: Publications de la société académique de comptabilité, 1941).

Batardon, L. (1950) 'Le plan comptable et le progrès de la technique' (The chart of accounts and technical progress), *La comptabilité et les affaires* (July/August).

Bayard, P. (1926) *Les effets de l'inflation – le bilan au point de vue fiscal* (The effects of inflation: the balance sheet from a fiscal point of view), Paris: Sirey.

Beaupère, L. (1927) *Les troubles monétaire et la vie des entreprises* (Monetary difficulties and the life of firms), Paris: Jouve.

Berry, W.C. (1949) 'Uniform accounting in France: le Plan Comptable', *The Accountant* (February 26): 157–61, (March 5): 176–80.

Bisson, A. (1926) *Le bénéfice réel en période de déprécation monétaire* (The real profit in times of monetary inflation), Paris: Sirey.

Blairon, H. (1926) *Cours complet de comptabililté des industries manufacturières* (Complete course of industrial cost accounting), Bruxelles.

Boukovetzki, A. (1947) Le financement de l'entreprise industrielle de l'U.R.S.S. (The financing of industrial enterprises of the URSS), *Connaissance de l'U.R.S.S. Paris:* Connaissance de l'U.R.S.S.

Bouquin, H. (1995) 'Rimailho revisité' (Rimailho revisited), *Comptabilité, contrôle, audit*, 1 (2, September): 5–33.

Bournisien, J. (1917) *Précis de comptabilité industrielle appliquée à la Métallurgie* (Outline of industrial accounting in the metallurgical industry), 2nd edn, Paris: Dunod et Pinat.

Bournisien, J. (1919) *Essai de philosophie comptable* (Essay of accounting philosophy), Paris.

Brunet, A.T. (1947) *Rapport général présenté au nom de la commission de normalisation des comptabilités* (General report presented on behalf of the accounting standardization commission), Paris: Imprimerie Nationale.

Brunet, A.T. (1951) *La normalisation comptable au service de l'entreprise, de la science et de la nation* (Accounting standardization in the service of business, science and the nation), Paris: Dunod.

Brunet, C. (1940) *La comptabilité industrielle dans le plan comptable moderne* (Industrial accounting in the modern chart of accounts), Paris: Éditions CCC.

Brunet, C. (1948) *Les principes d'établissement d'un plan comptable universel* (The principles for establishing a universal chart of accounts), Paris: Société d'éditions professionnelles et techniques.

Brunet, C. (1951) La normalisation de l'entreprise de la science et de la nation, Paris: Dunot.

Calmès, A. (1922) *La comptabilité industrielle* (Industrial accounting), Paris: Payot (later edn, 1927).

Calmès, A. (1925) *Administration financière des entreprises et des sociétés* (Financial administration, of firms and companies), Paris: Payot (later edition 1928).

Caujolle, P. (1942) *Principes généraux de comptabilité, et ce qu'il faut savoir sur le bilan* (General accounting principles, and what one has to know about the balance sheet), Paris: Centre de Documentation Universitaire.

Caujolle, P. (1943) Discours (Discussions), *Bulletin de l'Ordre national des experts comptables et des comptables agrées* 1 (October): 7–10.

Caujolle, P. (1949) Introduction to *Le plan comptable: Elément de progrès économique* (Introduction to the chart of accounts: A step in economic progress), Paris: Institut d'observation économique.

Cauvin, R. (1949) 'Historique et critique du plan comptable général' (History and critique of the master chart of accounts) in E. Archavlis ed., *Le plan comptable général*, Marseille: Édition du Conseil Regional de l'Ordre national des experts comptables et comptables agréés: 19–36.

Chambers, R.J. (1967) 'Continuously contemporary accounting – additivity and action', *The Accounting Review* 42 (October): 751–7.

Chardonnet, L. (1946) *Traité théorique et pratique de comptabilité industrielle en harmonie avec le plan comptable* (Theoretical and practical treatise on industrial accounting in conformity with the master chart of accounts), Bordeaux: Éditions Delmas.

Chezleprêtre, J. (1940) 'Normalisation des comptabilités' (Standardization of accounting activities), *Rapport présenté à la Commission de la Normalisation des Comptabilités*, Paris: Mimeo.

Chezleprêtre, J. (1943) *Raison d'être et modalités d'un plan comptable général* (Justification for and modalities of a general chart of accounts), Paris: Conférence faite à la Sorbonne.

Colasse, B. (ed.) (2005) *Les grands auteurs en comptabilité* (The great authors of accounting), Paris: Corlet Éditions EMS.

Colasse, B. and Durand, R. (1994) 'French accounting theorists of the twentieth century', in J.R. Edwards ed., *Twentieth-century accounting thinkers*, London: Routledge: 41–59 (reprinted in T. Lemarchand and R.H. Parker eds, *Accounting in France – La Comptabilitié en France*, New York: Garland Publishing, Inc.: 379–401).

Comité National de l'Organisation Français (CNOF) (1944/46) *Le plan comptable et la normalisation des comptabilités* (The chart of accounts and the standardization of accounting activities), Proceedings of the CNOF meetings held on 17–18 November 1944 and 18 March 1946). Paris: CNOF.

Commission générale d'organisation scientifique (CEGOS) (1937) *Une méthode uniforme de calcul des prix de revient: Pourquoi? Comment?* (A uniform method for calculating replacement costs. Why and how?), Paris: CEGOS.

Cordoliani, A. (1947) *L'Ordre national des experts-comptables* (The national association of public accountants), Paris: Sirey.

Croizé, A. and Croizé, H. (1907) 'De l'inventaire commercial' (On commercial inventory), Paris: Librairie Comptable Pigier.

Danty-Lafrance, J. (1947) *Le prix de revient conforme au plan comptable général de 1947* (Replacement cost in accord with the master chart of 1947), Paris: Foucher.

Deaubresse, L. (1908) *Comptabilité industrielle* (Industrial accounting), Paris.

Degos, J.-G. (1997) 'Jean Fourastié: diachronie d'une pensée comptable' (Jean Fourastié: Chronicle of an accounting scholar), *Comptabilité, contrôle, audit* 3 (1).

Degos, J.-G. (1998) *Histoire de la comptabilité* (History of accounting), Paris: Presses universitaires de France.

Degos, J.-G. (2000) 'Plan comptable: une réforme bien venue et bien conçue' (Chart of accounts: a welcome and well executed reform), *La Revue du Financier* 64–72.

Degos, J.-G. (2005) 'Eugène Léautey et Adolph Guilbault: Le face mathématique de la comptabilté', in B. Colasse ed., *Les grand auteurs en comptabilité*, Paris: Éditions EMS: 55–71.

Degos, J.-G. and Mattessich, R. (2003) 'Accounting research in the French language area: the first half of the twentieth century,' *Review of Accounting and Finance* 2 (4): 110–28.

Delaporte, R. (1926) *La comptabilité d'après des principes rationels basés sur les mouvements des valeurs et les grandeurs arithmetiques* (Accounting based on the rational principles of value flow and mathematical magnitudes), Paris: published by the author.

Delaporte, R. (1930) *Concepts raisonnés de la comptabilité économique* (Logical concepts of economic accounting), Neuilly: Delaporte.

Delaporte, R. (1931) 'La comptabilité est elle une science?' (Accounting, is it a science?), *La comptabilité et les affaires* 21 (June).

Delaporte, R. (1936) *Méthode rationnelle de la tenue des comptes* (Rational method of bookkeeping), Paris: Société Française d'éditions littéraires et techniques.

Delavelle, E. (1924) *La comptabilité en francs-or* (Accounting in gold-francs), Paris: Nouvelle Librairie Nationale.

Detoeuf, A. (1941) *Exposé sur le plan comptable* (Exposé on the chart of accounts), Paris: Centre d'information interprofessionelle.

Dumarchey, J. (1914) *La théorie positive de la comptabilité – suivi d'une étude critique sur l'établissement des bases scientifiques de la comptabilité* (The positive theory of accounting – an attempt of a critical study on establishing scientific bases of accounting), Lyons: Rey (reprinted Lyons: Bibliothèque du Comptable, 1933).

Dumarchey, J. (1925) *La comptabilité moderne: Essai de constutition rationnelle d'une discipline comptable du triple point de vue philosophique, scientifique et technique* (Modern accounting: essay on the rational structure of accounting from a three-dimensional point of view, a philosophic, scientific and technical one), Paris: Gauthier-Villars.

Dumarchey, J. (1926) *Théorie scientifique du prix de revient* (Scientific theory of replacement cost), Paris: Experta.

Dupont, A. (1925) 'Contribution à l'histoire de la comptabilité: "Luca Pacioli", l'un de ses fondateurs' (Contribution to accounting history: 'Luca Pacioli' one of its founders), *Conférence faite à la Société de Comptabilité de France*, Paris: Société de Comptabilité de France.

Dupont, A. (1926) *La partie double avant Pacioli, Les origines et le développement de la méthode* (Double-entry before Luca Pacioli – the origins and the development of the method), Paris: Société de Comptable de France.

Dupont, A. (1927) *Les successeurs de Paciolo en Italie au XVIᵉ siècle* (The successors of Luca Paciolo in the Italy of the sixteenth century), Paris: Société de Comptable de France.

Dupont, A. (1928) *Formes des comptes et manière de compter dans l'ancien temps* (Forms and ways of counting in ancient times), Paris: Société de Comptable de France.

Dupont, A. (1930) *Les auteurs comptables du XVIᵉ siècle dans l'empire germanique et les Pays-Bas* (The accounting authors of the sixteenth century in the German empire and the Netherlands), Paris (previous edition 1920; later reprint, Paris: Société de Comptabilité de France).

Durand, R. (1926) 'Le fisc dans ses rapport avec les entreprises avant adopté une comptabilité en francs-or' (Taxes in respect to enterprises before adopting accounting in gold-francs), *Mon Bureau* 150 (April): 513–14.

Edwards, E.O. and Bell, P.W. (1961) *The theory and measurement of business income*, Berkeley, CA: University of California Press.

Fages de Latour, E. de (1924) *Les concepts fondamentaux de la comptabilité* (Basic concepts of accounting), Paris: L. Eyrolles.

Fain, G. (probably around middle of the 1920s; but no year of publication indicated) *Comment se défendre contre l'inflation?* (How to protect oneself from inflation?) Paris: Compagnie des Chefs de Comptabilité de la Region Paris.

Fain, G. (1927) 'Amortissements industriels' (Industrial depreciations), *La comptabilité et les affaires* 87 (March): 74–8.

Faure, G. (1905) *Traité de comptabilité générale* (Treatise on general accounting), Paris: Masson.

Faure, G. (1917) *Amortissements. Considérations sur l'amortissement financier et sur l'amortissement comptable*, Paris: Société de comptabilité de France.

Faure, G. (1919) *Comptabilité générale* (General accounting), Paris: Masson.

Faure, G. (1921) 'Quelque points de théorie et pratique de comptabilité' (Some aspects of the practice and theory of accounting), *La comptabilité et les Affaires* (June).

Faure, G. (1926) *Bilans et comptes en francs-or* (Balance sheets and accounts in gold-francs), Paris: Nouvelle Librairie Nationale.

Fayol, H. (1916) *Administration industrielle et générale*, Paris: Dunod (first English translation 1925: *General and Industrial Administration*; recent bilingual edition Toronto: York University, 1991).

Fortin, A. (1991) 'The 1947 French accounting plan: origins and influence on subsequent practice, *Accounting Historians Journal* 18 (2): 1–23 (reprinted in Y. Lemarchand and R.H. Parker eds, *Accounting in France/La Comptabilité en France*, New York: Garland Publishing, Inc., 1996: 279–303).

Fortin, A. (1996) 'France', in M. Chatfield and R. Vangermeersch eds, *The history of accounting: an international encyclopedia*, New York: Garland Publishing, Inc.: 259–62.

Fourastié, J. (1943) *La comptabilité* (Accounting), Paris: Presses Universitaires de France.

Fourastié, J. (1944) *Comptabilité générale conforme au plan comptable général* (General accounting in accord with the master chart), Paris: Pichon-Durand-Auzias (also Paris: Librairie générale de droit et de jurisprudence, 1943 and 1945).

Gabriel, C. (1943) *Le plan comptable à la portée des petites et moyennes entreprises – adaption pratique* (The master chart of accounts as applied to small and medium firms – practical application), Reims.

Gabriel, C. (1947) *Le plan comptable, 1947* (The chart of accounts of 1947), Paris.

Gachkel, S. (1946) *Le mécanisme des finances soviétiques – monnaie, prix, crédit, budget* (The mechanism of Soviet finances – money, price, credit, budget), Paris: Payot.

Garnier, P. (1942) *La méthode comptable: traité de comptabilité générale* (The accounting method: treatise of general accounting), Paris: Dunod (previous edition 1940).

Garnier, P. (1947) *Technique comptable approfondie – la comptabilité algèbre du droit et méthode d'observation des sciences économiques* (Higher accounting techniques – algebraic accounting of the law and behavioural methods of economic science), Paris: Dunod.

Gomberg, L. (1912) *L' econologique (scientifique comptable) et son histoire* (Scientific accounting and its history), Geneva: Société Général d'Impr.

Gomberg, L. (1929) *Histoire critique de la théorie des comptes* (Critical history of the theory of accounts), Geneva and Berlin: Weiss, 1929 (also translated into Japanese and Russian).

Horace, A. (1948) 'Doctrine: Art. 5202, Le Plan comptable officiel de 1947 *Prononce-ment: Article 5002*' (The official chart of accounts of 1947), *Journal des Sociétés Civiles et Commerciales* (July–October): 201–40.

Howard, S.E. (1932) 'Public rules for private accounting in France, 1673–1807', *The Accounting Review* 7 (June): 91–102.

Julhiet, E. (1920) *Cours de finance et comptabilité dans l'industrie* (Course of finance and accounting in industry), Paris: Librairie de l'Inseignement Technique (later edition 1930).

Kovero, I. (1912) *Die Bewertung der Vermögensgegenstände in den Jahresbilanzen der privaten Unternehmungen mit besonderer Berücksichtigung der nichtrealisierten Gewinne und Verluste* (Valuation of assets in balance sheets under special considera-tion of unrealized gains and losses), 2nd edn, Berlin: C. Heymann (doctoral disserta-tion, defended at the Imperial Alexander University in Helsinki – 1st edn, 1911; reprinted in Osaka: Nihon Shoseki, 1974).

Lamson, J. (1950) *Principes de comptabilité économique* (Principles of economic accounting), Paris: Dunod.

Léautey, E. (1903) *L'unification des bilans des sociétés par actions* (The unification of the balance sheet of limited companies), Paris: Librairie comptable et administra-tive.

Léautey, E. and Guilbault, A. (1889) *La science des comptes mise à la portée de tous – traité théorique et pratique de comptabilité domestique, commerciale, industrielle, financière et agricole* (The science of accounts for everyone – a theoretical and practi-cal treatise of domestic, commercial, industrial, financial and agricultural accounting), Paris: Guillaumin (2nd edn, 1899; reprinted in New York: Arno Press, 1980; and Paris: Bibliothèque des science commerciales et économique, 1994).

Lecompt, R. (1943) *Projet préparatoire à l'adaption du "plan comptable national"*, Reims: privately published.

Leford, R. (1926 [or 1925?]) 'Essai de didactique de comptabilité' (Didactical essay on accounting), *La comptabilité et les Affaires* (May/June).

Léger, F. (1926) *Le redressement des bilans en francs-papier* (Adjustment for financial statements in paper-francs), Paris: Edition Experta.

Lemarchand, Y. and Parker, R.H. (eds) (1996) *Accounting in France/La Comptabilité en France*, New York: Garland Publishing, Inc.

Limperg Jr, T. (1917) 'Kostprijsberekening en Kostprijsbeholding' (Current cost accounting and current cost representation), *Accountancy* 15: 42–4, 55–8, 87–9, 104–5.

Lucas, M. (1931) 'Fixation d'une doctrine comptable' (Formulation of an accounting doctrine), *La comptabilité et les Affaires* (February).

MacNeal, K.F. (1939) *Truth in accounting*, Philadelphia, PA: University of Pennsylvania Press.

Mahlberg, W. (1921) *Bilanztechnik und Bewertung bei schwankender Währung* (Accounting technique and valuation at fluctuating currency), Leipzig: G.A. Gloeckner (further editions in 1922 and 1923).

Mahlberg, W. (1923) *Goldkreditverkehr und Goldmarkbuchführung* (Gold-credit exten-sion and gold-mark bookkeeping), Berlin: Springer Verlag.

Mattessich, R. (1995) *Critique of accounting: examination of the foundations and norma-tive structure of an applied discipline*, Westport, CT: Quorum Books.

Michaïlesco, C. (2005) 'Jean Dumarchey: une contribution á la théorie du bilan et de valeur' (Jean Dumarchey: a contribution to the theory of accounting and value), in B. Colasse ed., *Les grand auteurs en comptabilité*, Paris: Éditions MES: 90–110.

Penglaou, C. (1929) *Introduction à la technique comptable* (Introduction to the technique of accounting), Paris: Les Presses Universitaires de France.

Penglaou, C. (1933) 'Réflexion sur les essais "doctrinaux" en matière de comptabilité' (Reflections on the 'doctrinal' essays about accounting), *La comptabilité et les Affaires* (March).

Penglaou, C. (1947) 'De l'incidence des doctrines sur la pratique comptable' (On the doctrines of accounting practice), *Revue d' Economie Politique* (May/June).

Péricauld, J. and Calandreau, A. (1943) *Le plan comptable dans les entreprises* (The chart of accounts in the enterprises), Paris: Le Commerce.

Quétard, M. (1950) 'Synthèse du plan comptable 1947' (Synthesis of the chart of accounts of 1947), *La comptabilité et les affaires* (article series, beginning July/August).

Raffegeau, P.C. and Lacout, A. (1926) *Établissement des bilans en francs-or* (Establishing the gold-franc balance sheet), Paris: Taylor.

Ratier, A.E. (1927) 'L'évolution du point de vue fiscal en matière d'amortissements' (The evolution of the fiscal viewpoint on matters of depreciation), *Experta* 33 (June): 32–3.

Reymondin, G. (1909) *Bibliographie méthodologique des Ouvrages en langue française parus de 1543 à 1908 sur la Science des comptes* (Methodological bibliography of works on the science of accounting in French language, appearing between 1534 and 1908), Paris: Société Académique de Comptabilité.

Reymondin, G. (1928) *La vérité comptable en marche* (Accounting truth in action), Paris: Experta.

Richard, J. (1992) 'De l'histoire du plan comptable français et de sa réforme éventuelle' (On the history of the French chart of accounts and its eventual reform), in R. Duff and J. Allouche eds, *Annales de management*, Paris: Economica (reprinted in Y. Lemarchand and R.H. Parker eds, *Accounting in France/La Comptabilité en France*, New York: Garland Publishing, Inc., 1996: 307–20).

Rimailho E., (1935) *Organisation à la française* (Organization from a French point of view), 3 vols, Paris: Delmas.

Roover, R. de (1928a) 'Jan Ympyn – contribution à l'histoire de la comptabilité' (Jan Ympyn – a contribution to accounting history), *Bulletin d'études de l'Ecole superieure de commerce Saint-Ingnace*, Anvers: Secrétariat de l'Association des Licenciés de Saint-Ignace.

Roover, R. de (1928b) *Jan Ympyin – essai historique et technique sur le premier traité flamand de comptabilité, 1543* (Jan Ympyn – historical essay and technique of the first Flemish accounting treatise, 1543), Amberes.

Roover, R. de (1937) 'Aux origines d'une technique intellectuelle: La formation et l'expansion de la comptabilité à partie double' (Of the origin of an intellectual technique: the formation and spread of double-entry accounting), *Annales d'histoire économique et sociale* IX. (not to be confused with the English paper by R. de Roover 1937 on 'early cost accounting' – in Chapter 2).

Satet R. (1936) *Le contrôle budgétaire* (Budgetary control), 2 vols, Paris: Delmas.

Satet, R. (1942) *Le contrôle budgétaire* (Budgetary control), Cours de l'EOES, Paris: CNOF.

Sauvegrai, L. (1937) *Logique et comptabilité* (Logic and accounting), Paris.

Schär, J.F. (1911) *Allgemeine Handelsbetriebslehre, 1. Teil* (General commercial economics, Part 1), Leipzig: G.A. Gloeckner.

Scherpf, P. (1955) *Der Kontenrahmen* (The chart of accounts), Munich: Max Hueber Verlag.

Schmalenbach, E. (1921) 'Geldwertausgleich in der bilanzmäßigen Erfolgsrechnung' (Monetary adjustment in the balance-based income calculation), *Zeitschrift für handelswissenschaftliche Forschung* 15: 401–17 (translated into English as: Monetary stabilization in profit- and loss-accounting, in O.F. Graves, G.E. Dean and F.L. Clarke eds, *Schmalenbachs dynamic accounting and price-level adjustment*, New York: Garland Publishing, Inc.: 3–20).

Schmalenbach, E. (1922) *Goldmarkbilanz* (Goldmark balance sheet-taken over into the 3rd and 4th edn of his *Dynamische Bilanz*), Berlin: J. Springer Verlag (English translation as: Gold-mark accounting, in O.F. Graves, G.E. Dean and F.L. Clarke eds, *Schmalenbach's dynamic accounting and price-level adjustment*, New York: Garland Publishing, Inc.: 23–80).

Schmalenbach, E. (1925) *Einfluß der Geldwertschwankungen auf die Gewinnrechnung* (The effect of monetary value fluctuations on the income calculation), 3rd edn, Leipzig: G.A. Gloeckner (reprinted as: The effect of changing prices on profit calculation, in O.F. Graves, G.E. Dean and F.L. Clarke eds, *Schmalenbach's dynamic accounting and price-level adjustments*, New York: Garland Publishing, Inc.: 83–166).

Schmidt, F. (1921) *Die organische Bilanz im Rahmen der Wirtschaft* (The organic balance sheet in an economic setting), 1st edn, Leipzig: G.A. Gloeckner Verlagsbuchhandlung (2nd edn, 1922, *Die organische Tageswertbilanz*, Leipzig; 3rd edn, 1929; reprint, Wiesbaden: Betriebswirtschaftlicher Verlag Dr T. Gabler, 1953; Japanese translation, *Yukikan taishohyo gakusetsu*, Tokyo: Dobunkan Ltd, 1934).

Sigalas, A., de (1936) *Le statut des entreprises gouvernementales en U.R.S.S.* (The status of government enterprises in the USSR), Paris.

Standish, P. (1990) 'Origins of the Plan comptable général: a study of cultural intrusion and reaction', *Accounting and Business Research* 20 (80): 337–51 (reprinted in Y. Lemarchand and R.H. Parker eds, *Accounting in France/La Comptabilité en France*, New York: Garland Publishing, Inc., 1996: 261–75).

Thomas, L. (1927) *La tenue des comptabilités en période d'instabilité monétaire* (Doing accounting in periods of monetary instability), Paris: Éditions Experta.

Veyrenc, A. (1950) *Exposé pratique du plan comptable général 1947* (Practical exposé of the general chart of accounts of 1947), Paris: Éditions G. Durassié et Compagnie.

Vlaemminck, J.H. (1956) *Histoire et doctrines de la comptabilité* (History and doctrines of accounting), Bruxelles: Éditions Dunod et Truremberg, (reprinted Vesoul: Éditions Pragnos, 1979; Spanish translation as *Historia y doctrinas de la contabilidad*, Madrid, 1961).

Wasserman, M. (1931) Accounting practice in France during the period of monetary inflation, *The Accounting Review* 6 (March): 1–32.

8 Accounting research in the French language area: second half of the twentieth century

Akoka, J. and Augustin, G. (1983) 'Le modèle comptable multidimensionnel l'approche entité-relation' (The multidimensional accounting model ...), *Revue Française de Gestion* 41.

Archer, S., Delvaille, P. and MacLay, S. (1995) 'De la mesure de l'harmonisation comptable internationaux, *Actes du Congrès de l'AFC'* (On the progress of the international accounting standardization, *Actes du Congrès de l'AFC*), Paris: Dauphine, T1.

Association Française de Comptabilité, ed. (1997a) *Cahier No. 2 de la A.F.C. – May 1997: Evolution de la recherche comptable et sciences de gestion* (Evolution of research in accounting and managerial economics), Christian Hoarau ed., Paris: AFC.

Association Française de Comptabilité, ed. (1997b) *Hommes, savoirs et pratiques de la comptabilité* (Persons, scholars and practices of accounting) M. Lagon: AFC and Laboratoire des Gestion des Organisations des Nantes, Faculté des Science économiques et de gestion.

Atkinson, R.N., Hamburg, J. and Ittner, C. (1994) 'Linking quality to profits', *Quality based cost management*, Milwaukee, WI: ASQC Press and IMA.

Augustin, G. (1985) 'De la théorie événementielle aux comptabilités multidimensionnelles' (From events theory to multidimensional accounting), *Revue Française de Gestion* (156, April).

Augustin, G. (1986) *La comptabilité et la révolution informatique* (Accounting and the data processing revolution), Paris: Masson.

Augustin, G. (1990) 'Temps et comptabilité: temps, valeurs et principes comptables' (Time and accounting: time, values and accounting principles), *Revue de Droit Comptable* 90 (4): 45–69.

Barrett, M. (1976) 'Annual reporting practices: disclosure and comprehension in an international setting', *Journal of Accounting Research* 14 (1, Spring): 10–26.

Batardon, L. (1950a) 'Le plan comptable et le progrès de la technique' (The chart of accounts and technical progress), *La comptabilité et les affaires* (July/August).

Batardon, L. (1950b) *L'inventaire et le bilan* (Inventory and balance sheet), Paris: Dunod.

Bernheim, Y. (1997) *L'essentiel des US GAAP* (Essentials of US GAAP), Paris: Mazars et Guérard.

Blind, S. (1967) *Démystification des bilans de sociétés* (Demystification of social balance sheets of corporations), Paris: Les Editions d'Organisations.

Blind, S. (1977) *Le bilan social et mesure du rôle social de l'entreprise* (The social balance sheet and measures of the social tasks of firms), Paris: L'Editions d'Organisation.

Bouquin, H. (1995) 'Rimailho revisité' (Rimailho revisited), *Comptabilité – Contrôle–Audit*, 1 (2, September): 5–33.

Bouquin, H. (1997) 'Courants et traditions de recherche en comptabilité financière' (Currents and traditions in financial accounting research), in Christian Hoarau ed., *Cahier No. 2 de la A.F.C*, Paris: AFC: 29–35.

Boussard, D. (1983) *Comptabilité et inflation: méthodes et applications* (Accounting and inflation: methods and applications), Paris: Masson.

Boussard, D. and Rey, F. (1984) 'Accounting institutions and accounting research in France', in A.G. Hopwood and H. Schreuder eds, *European contributions to accounting research: the achievements of the last decade.* Amsterdam: VU Uitgeverij/Free University of Amsterdam.

Brunet, A.T. (1951) *La normalisation comptable au service de l'entreprise, de la science et de la nation* (Accounting standardization in the service of business, science and the nation), Paris: Dunod.

Burlaud, A. (1979) *Comptabilité et inflation* (Accounting and inflation), Paris: Cujas.

Burlaud, A. (1997) 'Recherche comptable et profession comptable' (Accounting research and the accounting profession), in C. Hoarau ed., *Cahier No. 2 de la A F.C.*, Paris: AFC: 41–56.

Burlaud, A. and Simon, C. (1981) *Analyse des coûts et contrôle de gestion* (Cost analysis and management control), Paris: Vuilbert.

Burlaud, A., Messina, M. and Walton, P. (1996) 'Depreciation: concepts and practices in France and the UK', European Accounting Review 5 (2): 299–317.

Capron M. (1995) 'Vers un renouveau de la comptabilité des ressources humaines' (Towards renewed human resource accounting), *Revue Française de Gestion* 106 (November/December): 46–5.

Capron M. and Grey, R. (2000) 'Experimenting with assessing corporate social responsibility in France: an exploratory note on an initiative by social economy firms', *The European Accounting Review* 9 (1, May): 99–110.

Casta, J.F. (2000) 'Théorie positive', in Colasse, B. ed., *Encyclopédie de comptabilité, contrôle de gestion et audi*, Paris: Economica.

CERC (Centre d'Etudes des Revenus et des Coûts or Centre for Studies on Incomes and Costs) – see reference in Boussard and Rey (1984): 51.

Chalayer, S. (1995) 'Le lissage des résultats: éléments explicatifs avancés dans la littérature' (The smoothing of results: some explanations presented in the literature), *Comptabilité – Contrôle – Audit* 2 (1): 89–104.

Chalayer, S. and Dumontier, P. (1996) 'Pérformances économique et manipulations comptables: une approche empirique' (Economic performance and window dressing: an empirical approach), *Actes de l'AFC* 2: 803–18.

Chatfield, M. and Vangermeersch, R. (eds) (1996) *The history of accounting: an international encyclopedia*, New York: Garland Publishing, Inc.

Chevalier, J. (1976) *Le Bilans Social de l'Entreprise* (The social balance sheet for the firm), Paris: Institut de L'Entreprise and Masson.

Choi, F.D.S. (1974) 'European disclosure: the competitive disclosure hypothesis', *Journal of International Business Studies* 5 (Fall): 15–23.

Christensen, J.A. and Demski, J.S. (2003) *Accounting theory: an information content perspective*, New York: McGraw-Hill, Irwin.

Cibert, A. (1968a) *Comptabilité analytique* (Cost accounting), Paris: Dunod.

Cibert, A. (1968b) *Comptabilité general* (General accounting), Paris: Dunod.

Cibert, A. (1986) 'La technique et la science comme idéologie de la formation comptable', in Y.-A. Côté ed., *L'enseignement et le recherche face aux sciences comptables en mutation*, Montreal, Quebec: École des Hautes Études Commerciales de Montréal: 291–304.

Colasse, B. (1973) *La rentabilité: analyse, prevision, et contrôle* (Profitability, forecast, and control), Paris: Dunod.

Colasse, B. (1986) 'La technique et la science comme idélogie de la formation comptable' (Technique and science as ideology in the formation of accounting), in Y.-A. Côté ed., *L'enseignement et la recherche face aux sciences comptables en mutation*, Montreal, Quebec: École des Hautes Études Commerciales de Montréal: 291–304.

Colasse, B. (ed.) (1988) *Comptabilité general* (General accounting), Paris: Económica (several subsequent editions).

Colasse, B. (1989) 'Les trios âge de la comptabilité' (The three phases of accounting) *Revue Française de Gestion* (82, September–October – Fondation Nationale pour l'Enseignement de la Gestion).

Colasse, B. (1992) 'Funds-flow statements and cash-flow accounting in France', *European Accounting Review* 1 (1, Issue 2): 229–54.

Colasse, B. (1997) 'La politique editorial de "*Comptabilité – Contrôle – Audit*"', C. Hoarau ed., *Cahier No. 2 de la A.F.C.*, Paris: AFC: 57–62.

Colasse, B. (ed.) (2000) *Encyclopédie de Comptabilité* (Encyclopaedia of accounting), Paris: Economica.

Colasse, B. (ed.) (2005) *Les grands auteurs en comptabilité* (The great authors of accounting), Paris: Corlet Éditions EMS.

Colasse, B. and Durand, R. (1994) 'French accounting theorists of the twentieth century', in J. Richard Edwards ed., *Twentieth-century accounting thinkers*, London: Routledge: 41–59 (reprinted in T. Lemarchand and R.H. Parker eds, *Accounting in France – la comptabilitié en France*, New York: Garland Publishing, Inc.: 379–401).

Colasse, B. and Standish, P. (2001) 'State versus market: contending interests in the struggle to control French accounting standardisation', in S. McLeay and A. Riccaboni eds, *Contemporary issues in accounting regulation*, Boston, MA: Kluwer Academic Publishers.

Conseil National de la Comptabilité (1986) *Plan comptable general* (General chart of accounts), Paris: LCNC.

Cooper, William W. (1949) 'Social accounting: an invitation to the accounting profession', *The Accounting Review* 24 (July): 233–8.

Cormier, D. and Magnan, M. (1995) 'La gestion stratégique des résultats: le cas des firmes publiant une prévision lors d'un premier appel public à l'épargne' (Strategic income management: the case of firms issuing forecasts prior to an initial public offering), *Comptabilité – Contrôle – Audit* 1 (1): 46–61.

Cormier, D. and Magnan, M. (2005) 'Gerald Feltham: l'information comptable vue dans une perspective économique', in B. Colasse ed., *Les grands auteurs en comptabilité*, Paris: Éditions EMS: 239–53.

Cormier, D., McDonough, H. and Raffournier, B. (1990) 'The evolution of inflation accounting in France since 1960', *Research in Accounting Regulation* 4: 21–42.

Corre, J. (1969) *La consolidation des bilans* (Consolidation of financial statements), Paris: Dunod.

Cossu, C. (1975) 'Description de la scripture productive de la firme multiproduits et constructions des modèles comptables du coûts' (Description of productivity measures of the multi-product firm and the construction of cost accounting models), Paris: University of Paris I (unpublished thesis).

Cossu, C. (1997) 'Mésopotamie' (Mesopotamia), in Association Français de Comptabilité ed., *Hommes, savoirs et pratiques de comptabilité*, Paris: Assóciation Française de Comptabilité.

Côté, Y.-A. (ed.) (1986) *L'enseignement et le recherche face aux sciences comptables en mutation*, Montreal, Quebec: École des Hautes Études Commerciales de Montréal.

Danziger, R. (1983) *Le bilans social. Outil d'information et de gestion* (The social balance. A managerial information tool), Paris: Dunod.

Degos, J.-G. (1985) 'Les grands précurseurs de la comptabilité' (The forefathers of accounting), *Revue Française de comptabilité* (161): 34–41.

Degos, J.-G. (1991) 'Histoire de la comptabilité matricielle' (History of the accounting matrix), *Revue Française de Gestion* 83.

Degos, J.-G. (1997) 'Jean Fourastié: diachronie d'une pensée comptable' (Jean Fourastié: Chronicle of an accounting scholar), *Comptabilité, contrôle, audit* 3 (1).

Degos, J.-G. (1998) *Histoire de la comptabilité* (History of accounting), Paris: Presses universitaires de France.

Degos, J.-G. (2000) 'Plan comptable: une réforme bien venue et bien conçue' (Chart of accounts: a welcome and well executed reform), *La Revue du Financier* 64–72.

Degos, J.-G. and Leclère, D. (1990) *Méthodes matricielles de gestion comptable approfondie* (Matrix methods in advanced accounting), Paris: editions Eyrolles.

Degos, J.-G. and Mattessich, R. (2003) 'Accounting research in the French language area: the first half of the twentieth century', *Review of Accounting and Finance* 2 (4): 110–28.

Degos, J.-G. and Mattessich, R. (2006) 'Accounting research in the French language area: second half of the twentieth century', *Review of Accounting and Finance* 5 (4): 423–42.

Delmas-Marsalet, J. (1976) *La réévaluation des bilans* (Re-valuation of financial statements), Paris: La Documentation Française.

Depoers, F. (2000) 'A cost–benefit study of voluntary disclosure: some empirical evidence from French listed companies', *European Accounting Review* 9 (2, July): 245–64.

Ding, Y., Stolowy, H. and Tenenhaus, M. (2003) '"Shopping around" for accounting for practices: the financial statement presentation of French groups', *Abacus* 39 (1): 42–65.

Dumontier, P. and Labelle, R. (1998) 'Accounting earnings and firm evaluation: the French case', *Europen Accouting Review* 7 (2, July): 163–84.

Dumontier, P. and Raffournier, B. (1998) 'Why firms comply voluntarily with AIS: an empirical analysis with Swiss data', *Journal of International Management and Accounting* 9 (3): 216–45.

Dupuis, M. (1969) *La consolidation des bilans* (Consolidation of financial statements).

Durand, R. (1992) 'La séparation des comptabilités, origines et consequences' (The division of accounting systems, its source and consequences), *Revue Française de Comptabilité* 240 (December): 72–81.

Evraert, S. (1997) 'Normalisation international et recherché comptable', in Christian Hoarau ed., *Cahier No. 2 de la A.F.C*, Paris: AFC: 37–40.

Ferchiou, R. (1986) 'L'orientation de la stratégie en sciences comptables et en gestion international dans les grandes écoles du Maghreb', in Y.-A. Côté ed., *L'enseignement et le recherche face aux sciences comptables en mutation*, Montreal, Quebec: École des Hautes Études Commerciales de Montréal: 329–35.

Filios, V.P. (1987) 'French contributions to the theory of accounting', *Advances in International Accounting*: 137–51.

Fortin, A. (1991) 'The 1947 French accounting plan: origins and influence on subsequent practice, *Accounting Historians Journal* 18 (2): 1–23 (reprinted in Y. Lemarchand and R.H. Parker eds, *Accounting in France/La Comptabilité en France*, New York: Garland Publishing, Inc., 1996: 279–303).

Fortin, Anne (1996) 'France', in M. Chatfield and R. Vangermeersch eds, *The history of accounting: an international encyclopedia*, New York: Garland Publishing, Inc.: 259–62.

Gajewski, J.-F. and Quéré, B.P. (2001) 'The information content of earnings and turnover announcements in France', *European Accounting Review* 10 (4, December): 679–704.

Gensse, P. (1983) 'Le renouvellement du modèle comptable: évolution ou révolution?' (The renewal of the accounting model: evolution or revolution), *Revue Française de Comptabilité* (139, Octobre): 374–83.

Gray, J. and Pesqueux, Y. (1993) 'Evolutions actuelles des systèmes de tableaux de bord' (Evolution of the 'tableaux de bord'), *Revue Française de Comptabilité* (242, February): 61–70.

Harada, F. (1978) *Joho Kakei Ron* (Accounting in a new informational society), Tokyo: Dobunkan, Ltd.

Hoarau, C. (1991) 'L'analyse financière par les flux: a-t-on besoin de modèles?' (The analysis of financial flows: do we need models?), *Analyse Financière* (1st semester): 54–62.

Hoarau, C. (1995) 'L'harmonisation comptable internationale: vers la reconnaissance mutuelle normative?', *Contabilité – Contôle – Audit* 1 (2): 75–88.

Hoarau, C. (ed.) (1997a) *Les cahiers de récherchei de l'A.F.C. – Cahier No. 2 – Mai 1997: Evolution de la recherche comptable et sciences de gestion*, Paris: Association Français de Comptabilité.

Hoarau, C. (1997b) 'Courants et traditions de recherché en comptabilité financière', in C. Hoarau and Association Française de Comptabilité eds, *Cahier No. 2 de la A.F.C. – May 1997: Evolution de la recherche comptable et sciences de gestion*, Paris: AFC: 19–27.

Holzer, H.P. and Schoenfeld, H.-M. (1983) 'The French approach to the post-war price-level problem', *The Accounting Review* 38 (2, April): 382–8.

Houery, M. (1977) *Mesurer la productivité – les comptes de surplus* (Productivity measures – the 'surplus accounts'), Paris: Dunod.

Jeanjean, T. (2004) 'La théorie positive de la comptabilité: une revue des critiques' (Positive accounting theory: a review of its critiques), *Cahier 99–12 du CEREG* 1–35.

Jouanique, P. (1995) *Traité des comptes et des écritures, Luca Pacioli* (Luca Pacioli's treatise on counting and writing), Paris: Ordre des Experts Comptables.

Jouanique, P. (1996) 'Un classique de la comptabilité au siècle des lumières – la science des négociants de Matthieu de la Porte' (An accounting classic of the age of Enlightenment – the 'Science des Négociants' by Matthieu de la Port), in R.H. Parker and Y. Lemarchand eds, *Accounting in France* (in English and French), New York: Garland Publishing, Inc.: 67–87.

Kaplan, R.S. and Norton, D.P. (1992) 'The balanced score-card: measures that drive performance', *Harvard Business Review* 70 (1, January–February): 71–9.

Lamson, J. (1950) *Principes de comptabilité économique* (Principles of economic accounting), Paris: Dunod.

Lassègue, P. (1959) *Comptabilité et gestion de l'entreprise* (Accounting and the management of the firm), Paris: Dalloz.

Lassègue, P. (1962) 'Esquisse d'une épistémologie de la comptabilité' (Outline of an epistemology of accounting), *Revue d'Economie Politique* 3 (May–June): 314–25.

Lauzel, P. (1965) *Le Plan comptable français* (The French chart of accounts), Paris: Presse Universitaires de France.

Lauzel, P. and Cibert, A. (1959a) *Des ratios au tableau de bord* (From ratios to management reporting), Paris: Entreprise moderne d'édition (reprint in 1962).

Lauzel, P. and Cibert, A. (eds) (1959b) *Le Plan comptable commenté* (The chart of accounts with comments), 5 vols, Paris: Foucher (later edition 1969).

Leclère D. and Degos, J.-G. (2000) 'La comptabilité matricielle' (Matrix accounting), in B. Colasse ed., *Encyclopédie de Comptabilité, Contrôle de Gestion et Audit*, Paris: Economica: 383–94.

Lecointre, G. (1977) *La comptabilité d'inflation* (Inflation accounting), Paris: Dunod.

Leech, S.A. (1986) 'The theory and the development of a matrix-based accounting system', *Accounting and Business Research* 16 (64): 327–41.

Lemarchand, Y. (1992) 'Werner Sombart, quelques hypothèses à l'épreuve des faits' (Werner Sombart, some hypotheses to be proven by facts), *Cahier d'Histoire de la Comptabilité* 2: 37–56.

Lemarchand, Y. (1993) *Du dépérissement à l'amortissement – Enquête sur l'histoire d'un concept et de sa traduction comptable* (On depreciation – meeting on the history of traditional accounting), Nantes: Ouest Éditions.

Lemarchand, Y. (1995) 'Les contes d'armement revisités' (The accounts of the defence ministry revisited), Les particulierités comptables des sociétés quirataires à Nantes au XVIIe siècle, *Revue d'Histoire Moderne et Contemporaine* 42 (3): 435–53.

Lemarchand, Y. and Parker, R.H. (eds) (1996) *Accounting in France /La Comptabilité en France*, New York: Garland Publishing, Inc.

Lequin, Y. (1977) 'Form, content and effect of social accounting and its publication', *Revue Française de Comptabilité* (March).

Lönning, H. (1995) 'A la recherche d'une culture européenne en comptabilité et contrôle de gestion', *Comptabilité – Contrôle – Audit* 1 (1): 81–97.

McHaney, R. (2000) 'Spreadsheets', in R. Rojas (ed. in chief), *Encyclopedia of computers and computer history*, Vol. 2 (M-Z), Chicago: Fitzroy Dearborn Publishers: 728–9.

Mangenot, M. (1976) *La comptabilité en service du capital* (Accouting in the service of 'capital'), Paris: Jean-Pierre Delarge.

Marques, E. (1973) *Comptabilité des ressources humaines* (Human resource accounting), Paris Edition Hommes et Techniques.

Marques, E. (1978) *Le bilan sociale, l'homme, l'entreprise et la cité* (Social accounting, man, the firm and the city), Paris: Dalloz.

Marshal, J. and Lecaillon, J. (1958) *La répartition du revenue national* (The classification of the national product), Paris: Cujas.

Mattessich, R. (1957) 'Towards a general and axiomatic foundation of accountancy: with an introduction to the matrix formulation of accounting systems', *Accounting Research* 8 (October): 328–355 (reprinted in S.A. Zeff ed., *The accounting postulates and principles controversy of the 1960s*, New York: Garland Publishing, Inc., 1982; Spanish translation in *Technica Economica* (April 1958): 106–27).

Mattessich, R. (1964) *Accounting and analytical methods: measurement and projection of income and wealth in the micro- and macro-economy*, Homewood, IL: R.D. Irwin, Inc. (reprinted in the 'Accounting Classics Series', Houston, TX: Scholars Book Co., 1977; also in the 'Series of Financial Classics' of Reprints on Demand, Ann Arbor, MI: Microfilms International, 1979, still available; Japanese translation under the direction of Shinzaburo Koshimura, *Kaikei to Bunsekiteki-Hoho Jokan*, 2 vols, Tokyo: Dobunkan, Ltd, Vol. 1: 1972, Vol. 2: 1975; Spanish translation, by Carlos Luis García Casella and Maria del Carmen Ramírez de Rodríguez, Buenos Aires: La Ley, 2002).

Mattessich, R. (2000) *The beginnings of accounting and accounting thought: accounting praxis in the Middle East (8000 B.C. to 2000 B.C.) and accounting thought in India (300 B.C. and the Middle Ages)*, New York: Garland Publishing, Inc.

Mattessich, R. (2003) 'Accounting research and researchers of the nineteenth century and the beginning of the twentieth century', *Accounting, Business and Financial History* 13 (2, July): 125–79.

Mattessich, R. and Galassi, G. (2000) 'History of the spreadsheet: from matrix accounting to budget simulation and computerization', in ASEPUC (and E. Hernández Esteve) eds, *Accounting and history: a selection of the papers presented at the 8th World Congress of Accounting*, Madrid: Asociación Española de Contabilidad y Administración de Empresas – Ediciones Gráficas Ortega: 203–32.

Mévellec, P. (1993) 'Plaidoyer pour une vision française de la méthode ABC' (translated by Michael Adler as 'Activity-Based Costing: a call for a French approach' in a paper available directly from the author: mevellec@iae.univ.nantes.fr), *Revue Française de Comptabilité* (251): 36–44 (this paper received the 'FMAC Prix de Concours 1994' and resulted from a project funded by a FNEGE–AFC research contract).

Mévellec, P. (2001) 'Whole life cycle costs: a new approach, *WLCC Pise*' (June – available directly from the author: mevellec@iae.univ.nantes.fr): 1–19.

Mikol, A. and Standish, P. (1998) 'Audit independence and non-audit services: a comparative study in differing British and French perspectives', *The European Accounting Review* 7 (3, September): 541–70.

Momen, H. (1957–58) *Le Plan comptable international* (The international chart of accounts), Vols 1 and 2, Brussels: Cambel.

Montagnier, G. (1981) *Principes de comptabilité publique* (Principles of governmental accounting), Paris: Dalloz.

Navarro, J.-L. (2000) *Guide technique et théorique du plan comptable généneral 1999* (Technical and theoretical guide to the General Chart of Accounts of 1999), Paris: Gualino éd.

Nikitin, M. (1992) *La naissance de la comptabilté industrielle en France*, Paris: Université de Paris Dauphine (doctoral dissertation).

Nioche, J.-P. (1992) 'Institutionalizing evaluation in France: skating on thin ice?', in J. Maine ed., *Advancing public policy administration: learning from public experiences*, Amsterdam: Elsevier.

Nioche, J.-P. and Pesqueux, Y. (1997) 'Accounting, economics, and management in France: the slow emergence of an "accounting science"', *The European Accounting Review* 6 (2): 231–50.

Norman, R. and Ramirez, R. (1993) 'From value chain to value constellation: designing interactive strategy', *Harvard Business Review* 71 (4, July–August): 65–78.

OECD (1986) *Harmonization of Accounting Standards*, Paris: OECD.

Ordre des Experts Comptables (OEC) (1993) *La profession comptable* (The accounting profession), Paris: OEC 123 (March 26).

Panglaou, C. (1962) 'Une épistémologie de la comptabilité est-elle possible et souhaitable?' (An epistemology of accounting. It is possible and desirable?), *Journal de la société de statistique de Paris* 4.

Panglaou, C. (1978) 'La réévaluation des bilans' (The re-valuation of the balance sheet), *Revue d'Economie Politique* (1st semester).

Parker, R.H. (1966) 'A note on Savary "le Parfait Négociant"', *Journal of Accounting Research* 4 (2): 260–1.

Percival, C.T., Donaghy, P.J. and Laidler, J. (1993) *European charts of accounts with English translation/France: plan comptable general/Germany: Industrie Kontenrahmen/Spain: Plan general de contabilidad*, Durham: Flambard (European).

Pérochon, C. (1971) *Comptabilité national et comptabilité d'entreprise* (National accounting and business accounting), Paris: Université de Paris (doctoral dissertation).

Pérochon, C. (1974) *Comptabilité general* (General accounting), Paris: Foucher.

Petit, B. (1963) *La technique comptable supérieure* (Advanced accounting techniques), Paris: Licet.

Pinceloup, C.C. (1993) *Histoire de la comptabilité et des comptables* (History of accounting and accountants), 2 vols, Nice: Edi-Nice.

Powelson, J.P. (1955) *Economic accounting*, New York: McGraw-Hill Book Co.

Prada, M. and Sonrier, A. (1985) *La comptabilité publique* (Governmental accounting), Paris: Berger Levrault.

Quétard, M. (1950) 'Synthèse du plan comptable 1947' (Synthesis of the chart of accounts of 1947), *La comptabilité et les affaires* (article series, beginning July/August).

Raffournier, B. (1990) 'La théorie positive de la comptabilité: une revue' (The positive theory of accounting: a review), *Economie et Société: série science de gestion* 16: 137–66.

Raffournier, B. (1995) 'The determinants of voluntary financial disclosure by Swiss listed companies', *European Accounting Review* 4 (2): 261–80.

Rey, F. (1978) *Introduction á la comptabilité sociale* (Introduction to social accounting), Paris: Entreprise Moderne d'Edition.

Rey, F. (1979) *Développements récents de la comptabilité* (Recent developments of accounting), Paris: EME.

Richard, J. (1982) 'Essai sur l'histoire des pratiques comptables internationals' (Essay on the history of international accounting practices), *AFC Annales* 3: 177–226 (also CEREG, Université de Paris-Dauphine, Cahier de recherche no. 8203).

Richard, J. (1992) 'De l'histoire du plan comptable français et de sa réforme éventuelle' (On the history of the French chart of accounts and its eventual reform), in R. Duff and J. Allouche eds, *Annales de management*, Paris: Economica (reprinted in Y. Lemarchand and R.H. Parker eds, *Accounting in France/La Comptabilité en France*, New York: Garland Publishing, Inc., 1996: 307–20).

Richard, J. (1993) 'Les origines du plan comptable français de 1947: les influences de la doctrine comptable allemande' (Origin of the French chart of accounts of 1947: the influence of German accounting theory), *Cahier de recherche No. 9302*, CEREG, Université Paris 9 – Dauphine.

Richard, J. (2000) 'Plans comptables' (Charts of accounts), *Encyclopédie de comptabilité, contrôle de gestion et Audit*, Paris: Economica: 943–59.

Roover, R. de (1990) 'Sur les problèmes poses aux comptables du XIXe siècle par l'évolution du Droit des Sociétés' (On the problems posed to nineteenth-century accountants through the evolution of the Companies Act), *Comptabilité et pluridiscipinarité – Actes du XIe Congrès de l'AFC*, Vol. 1, Paris: Val-de-Marne.

Sauvy, A. (1970) 'Historique de la comptabilité' (History of accounting), *Economie et Statistique* 15 (September): 19–32 (reprinted in Y. Lemarchand and R.H. Parker eds, *Accounting in France/La Comptabilité en France*, New York, NY: Garland Publishing, Inc.: 323–78).

Scheid, J.-C. (1986) 'Situation présente de la profession comptable et de la recherche en France', in Y.-A. Côté ed., *L'enseignement et le recherche face aux sciences comptables en mutation*, Montreal, Quebec: École des Hautes Études Commerciales de Montréal: 122–37.

Scheid, J.-C. (1997) 'Recherche et profession en comptabilité' (Research and profession in accounting), in Christian Hoarau ed., *Cahier No. 2 de la A.F.C.*, Paris: AFC: 49–56.

Scheid, J.C. and Standish, P. (1989) 'La normalisation comptable: sa perception dans le monde Anglophone et en France' (Accounting standardization: its perception in the English language area and in France), *Revue Française de la Comptabilité* (May).

Schmandt-Besserat, D. (1977) 'An archaic recording system and the origin of writing', *Syro-Mesopotamian Studies* 1 (2): 1–32.

Schmandt-Besserat, D. (1978) 'The earliest precursor of writing', *Scientific American* 238 (6): 50–9.

Schmandt-Besserat, D. (1992) *Before writing*, 2 vols (Vol. 1: From counting to cuneiform; Vol. 2: A catalogue of Near Eastern tokens), Austin, TX: University of Texas Press.

Shank, J.K. (1972) *Matrix methods in accounting*, Reading, MA: Addison-Wesley Publishing Company.

Shank, K.K. and Govindarajan, V. (1993) *Strategic cost management: a new tool, for competitive advantage*, New York: The Free Press.

Sorter, G. (1969) 'An event approach to basic accounting theory', *The Accounting Review* 44 (1, January), 12–19.

Standish, P. (1990) 'Origins of the plan comptable général: a study of cultural intrusion and reaction', *Accounting and Business Research* 20 (80): 337–51 (reprinted in Y. Lemarchand and R.H. Parker, eds, *Accounting in France/La Comptabilité en France*, New York: Garland Publishing, Inc., 1996: 259–75).

Stevelinck, E. (1970) *La comptabilité à travers les ages* (Accounting throughout the ages), Brussels: Bibliothèque Royal (second edition Vesoul: Pragnos, 1977).

Stevelinck, E. (1994) 'De la comptabilité à la literature' (From accounting to literature), *Revue Belge de la Comptabilitè* 1 (March): 65–8.

Stevelinck, E. and Haulotte, R. (1958) 'Les études historiques et théoriques de la comptabilité' (Historical and theoretical studies of accounting), *Le comptable et la comptabilité*, Brussels: Exposition international et universelle de Bruxelles, UNPC.

Stolowy, H. (1989) *Les Tableaux de Financement* (cash-flow statements), Paris: Presses Universitaires de France.

Stolowy, H. and Ding, Y. (2003) 'Regulatory flexibility and management opportunism in the choice of alternative accounting standards: an illustration based on large French groups', *The International Journal of Accounting* 38 (2): 195–213.

Stolowy, H. and Jeny, A. (2001) 'International accounting disharmony: the case of intangibles', *Accounting, Auditing and Accountability Journal* 14 (4): 477–96.

Suzuki, T. (2003) 'The epistemology of macroeconomic reality: the Keynesian revolution from an accounting point of view', *Accounting, Organization and Society* 28 (5, July): 471–517.

SYNTEC (1976) *Regards sur le bilan social* (Concerning the social balance sheet), Paris: Hommes et Techniques.

Teller, R. (1997) 'Evolution des travaux de recherche en comptabilité financière' (Evolution of research activity in financial accounting), in C. Hoarau ed., *Cahier No. 2 de la A.F.C.*, Paris: AFC: 5–18.

Tremblay, D. (1986) 'Les recherches en théorie comptable: La comtabilité, une science à paradigme multiples', in Y.-A. Côté ed., *L'enseignement et le recherche face aux sciences comptables en mutation*, Montreal, Quebec: École des Hautes Études Commerciales de Montréal: 103–19.

Tremblay, D. and Cormier, D. (1989), *Théories et models comptables – voies de recherché* (Theories and models of accounting – from a research viewpoint), Sillery, Quebec: L'Université du Québec.

Veyrenc, A.T. (1950) *Exposé pratique du plan comptable général 1947* (Practical exposé of the general chart of accounts of 1947), Paris: Editions G. Durassié et Compagnie.

Vincent, A. (1968) *La measure de la productivité* (The measurement of productivity), Paris: Dunod.

Vlaemminck, J.H. (1955) *Considération sur la pensée comptable* (Examining accounting thought), *Revue de la comptabilité* (Organe de la compagnie des chefs de comptabilité).

Vlaemminck, J.H. (1956) *Histoire et doctrines de la comptabilité* (History and doctrines of accounting), Bruxelles: Éditions Dunod et Truremberg, (reprinted Vesoul: Éditions Pragnos, 1979; Spanish translation as *Historia y doctrinas de la contabilidad*, Madrid, 1961).

Wieser, F., von (1876/1929) 'Über das Verhältnis der Kosten zum Wert' (On the relation of cost to value) (written in 1876, but first published in 1929), in J.C.B. Mohr ed., *F. von Wieser: Gesammelte Abhandlungen*, Tübingen: 377–404.

Windsor, F. (1982) 'L'Ordre des Expert Comptables, sa contribution à l'information économique, comptables et financière' (The Association of Public Accountants, its contribution to economic, accounting and financial information), *Courrier des Statistiques* (April): 3–6.

Zeff, S.A. (1972) *Forging accounting principles in five countries*, Champaign, IL: Stripes Publishing.

Zéghal, D. (1984) *La comptabilité en periodes de changements de prix* (Accounting in periods of changing prices), Vancouver, BC: The Canadian Certified General Accountants' Research Foundation.

Zéghal, D. (1989) *Le marché de la vérification au Canada* (The auditing market in Canada), Vancouver, BC: The Canadian Certified General Accountants' Research Foundation.

9 Accounting publications and research in Spain: first half of the twentieth century

Readers not accustomed to *Spanish surnames* are reminded that they *usually* consist of two parts, a *paternal* as well as a *maternal* surname (sometimes one even encounters triple names). Neither of them must be confused with a 'first' name. For further accounting literature from Spain, see also Chapter 10, and Chapter 17 (on Argentina).

Aced y Bartrina, F. (1916) *Curso de contabilidades oficiales. Estado, provincia, municipio* (Official accounting course for government, province and city), Madrid: Hermanos Reus.

Ballesteros Marín-Baldo, L. (1924) *Tratado completo de contabilidad. Obra escrita para consulta del comercio, de la banca y de la industria* (Complete treatise of accounting …), Barcelona: Librería Bosch.

Ballesteros Marín-Baldo, L. (1927) *Tratado elemental de contabilidad general, comercial y bancaria. Escrita para uso de las escuelas de comercio* (Elementary treatise of general accounting …), 1st edn, Barcelona: Librería Bosch (see below, 8th edn, 1947, Barcelona: Librería Hispano Americana).

Ballesteros Marín-Baldo, L. (1947) *Tratado elemental de contabilidad general comercial y bancari'* (Elements of general accounting for trade and banking), Barcelona: Librería Hispano Americana.

Boter Mauri, F. (1924) *Curso de Contabilidad. Obra escrita y publicada en idioma catalá'* (Accounting course …), 1st edn, Barcelona: Sociedad General de Publicaciones (later edition in Catalán, Barcelona: Sociedad General de Publicaciones, 1934).

Boter Mauri, F. (1935) *Precio de coste industrial* (Industrial costing), Barcelona: Editorial Juventud, S.A.

Boter Mauri, F. (1941a) *Nociones fundamentales de contabilidad* (Fundamental accounting concepts), Madrid: José Zendrera, and Barcelona: Editorial Juventud, S.A.

Boter Mauri, F. (1941b) *Tratado de contabilidad general* (Treatise on general accounting), Madrid: Jose Zendrera and Barcelona: Editorial Juventud, S.A.

Boter Mauri, F. (1943) *Revisión de contabilidades y balances* (Auditing of accounts and balance sheets), Madrid: José Zendrera and Barcelona: Editorial Juventud, S.A. (for later edition, see Chapter 17, under Boter Mauri 1952).

Boter Mauri, F. (1959) *Las doctrinas contables* (Accounting doctrines), Barcelona: Juventud, S.A.

Brost, J.M. (1825) *Curso completo de teneduría de libros o modo de llevarlos por partida doble* (Complete bookkeeping course or the double-entry method), Madrid: Imprenta de E. Aguado.

Bruño, G.M. (1919) *Contabilidad y prácticas mercantiles* (Accounting and commercial practices), Barcelona: Juan de Gasso, Editor.

Campo Recio, E. (1928) *Contabilidad por partida doble* (Accounting by double-entry), Madrid: Imprenta de C. Falquina.

Cañizares Zurdo, J.M. (1905) *Prolegómenos de contabilidad de empresas* (Introduction to enterprise accounting), Málaga: Imprenta Calvente y Castro.

Cañizares Zurdo, J.M. (1933) *Ensayo histórico sobre contabilidad* (Historical essay on accounting), Málaga: Imprenta del asilo de San Bartolomé (facsimile edition of the original, edited and with introductory commentary by D. Carrasco Díaz and F. González Gomila, Madrid: Asociación Española de Contabilidad y Administración de Empresas, and el Ilustre Colegio Oficial de Titulados Mercantiles y Empresariales de Madrid, 1996).

Cardús Rosell, C. (1950) *La dirección y vigilancia del negocio a través de la contabilidad* (Management and business control by accounting), Madrid: Editorial Enciclopédica.

Carrasco Díaz, D. and González Gomila, F. (see Cañizares Zurdo 1933).

Carrasco Díaz, D., Hernández Esteve, E. and Mattessich, R. (2004) 'Accounting publications and research in Spain: first half of the twentieth century', *Review of Accounting and Finance* 3 (2): 40–58.

Casas Gaspar, E. (1944) *Contabilidad general* (General accounting), Barcelona: Juan Bruguer, Editor.

Castaño Diéguez, F. (1864/1876) *La verdadera contabilidad o sea curso completo, teórico y práctico de teneduría por partida doble* (Genuine accounting or complete theoretical and practical course in double-entry bookkeeping), 5th edn, Madrid: Imprenta de Alejandro Gómez Fuentenebro.

Cavanna Sanz, R. (1929) *Lecciones de contabilidad* (Accounting lessons), Madrid: Imprenta de La Enseñanza.

Fernández Casas, J. (1926) *Generalidades y prolegómenos de contabilidad industrial* (General introduction to industrial accounting), Madrid: Imprenta Gráfica Universal.

Fernández Casas, J. (1931) *Contabilidad aplicada* (Applied accounting), Barcelona: José Montesó, Editor.

Fernández Pirla, J.M. (1960) *Un ensayo sobre teoría económica de la contabilidad. Introducción contable al estudio de la economía de la empresa* (An essay on the economics of accounting ...), Madrid (1st edn, 1957).

Gardó Sanjuán, J. (1925) *Interpretación de balances* (Analysis of the balance sheet), Barcelona: Editorial Cultura.

Gardó Sanjuán, J. (1929) *Contabilidad por moneda oro* (Gold money based accounting), Barcelona.

Goxens Duch, A. (1944) *Revisión de contabilidades y examen de negocios* (Auditing and examining the accounting of firms), Barcelona: Juan Bruguer.

Goxens Duch, A. (1948) *Inflación, deflación y tributos en la contabilidad de las empresas* (Inflation, deflation and taxes in entrepreneurial accounting), Madrid: M. Aguilar.

Hernández Esteve, E. (1999) 'Literatura contable española, 1522–1943' (Spanish accounting literature 1522–1943), Presentation at the Xth Congreso AECA, Zaragoza, 23–25 September.

Junco y Reyes, J.J. del (1943) *Contabilidad general* (General accounting), Jerez: Editorial 'Jerez Gráfico'.

Lázaro y López, D. (1935) *Curso de contabilidad general* (Course of general accounting), Guernica: Imp. Goitia y Ormaechea.

López y López, F. (1926–27) 'Apuntes para constituir la historia de la contabilidad por partida doble' (Outlines for designing a history of double-entry accounting). *Administración y Contabilidad* 19: 393; 20: 403.

Lluch y Capdevila, P. (1950) *Introducción a la teoría general de la contabilidad* (Introduction to the theory of general accounting), Barcelona: Editorial Lux.

Martínez Pérez, E. (1910) *Contabilidad y teneduría de libros aplicadas a los negocios agrícolas, industriales y comerciales, en grande y pequeña escala, y a los de empresas da banca, seguros, navieras, de ferrocarriles y minas* (Accounting and bookkeeping applied to …), Madrid: Establecimiento Tipográfico.

Martínez Pérez, E. (1920) *Contabilidad elemental y superior* (Elementary and higher accounting), Madrid: V.H. Sanz Calleja, Editores y Impresores.

Montesinos Julves, V. (1998) 'Accounting and business economics in Spain', *European Accounting Review* 7 (3): 357–80.

Oliver Castañer, E. (1904) *Guía de peritos y contadores mercantiles para la revisión judicial o extrajudicial de libros de contabilidad del comercio* (Auditing guide for commercial experts and accountants …), Barcelona: José Espasa.

Pérez-Pons Jover, F. (1934) *Contabilidad elemental* (Elementary accounting), 1st edn, Bilbao: Pérez Malumbres.

Piqué Batlle, R. (1935) *Revisió de comptabilitats* (The auditing of accounts), Barcelona: Artes Gráf. F. Camps Calmet.

Piqué Batlle, R. (1936) *Revisión técnica de contabilidades* (The technique of auditing accounts), Barcelona: Tipogr. Galve.

Piqué Batlle, R. (1939) *Cómo se lee y examina un balance* (How to read and examine a balance sheet), Barcelona: Librería Bosch.

Rodríguez Pita, E. (1945) *Curso de contabilidad general* (Course of general accounting), Barcelona: Gráficas Alfa, S.A.

Rodríguez Pita, E. and Rodríguez Flores de Quiñones, J.M. (1956) *Ciencia de la contabilidad. Técnica, práctica y organización* (The science of accounting. Technique, practice and organization), Barcelona.

Ruiz Soler, L. (1917) *Tratado elemental teórico-práctico de contabilidad general* (Theoretical-practical treatise of general accounting), 1st edn, San Sebastián: Tip. Y Lib. De A. Bueno Oliván (at least five editions; the 5th edn corrected and extended, San Sebastián: Imprenta de la Diputación de Guipúzcoa, 1950).

Ruiz Soler, L. (1924) *Elementos de administración y contabilidad de empresas* (Administrative elements and accounting for enterprises), Irún: J. Sagarzazu.

Sacristán y Zavala, A. (1918) *Teorías de contabilidad general y de administración privada* (Theory of general accounting and administration), Madrid: Hijos de Reus.

Salvador y Aznar, F. (1846) *Manual de teneduría de libros por partida doble, aplicada al comercio, la industria, empresas, bancos, fondos provinciales y oficinas del Estado* (Manual of double-entry bookkeeping …). Madrid: Imprenta de la Sociedad.

Torrents y Monner, A. (1895) *Tratado de teneduría de libros para uso de los alumnos de 1a y 2a enseñanza, escuelas de comercio y de artes y oficios* (Treatise on bookkeeping for students of the first and second grade …), Barcelona: Imprenta de la Casa P. de Caridad.

Torrents y Monner, A. (1910) *Curso de hacienda pública y su aplicación teórico-práctica a la hacienda y contabilidad municipal y provincial* (Course of taxation and public finance ...), Barcelona: Imprenta de Bayer, Hijos, Hermanos y Cía.

Vlaemminck, J.-H. (1960) *Historia y doctrinas de la contabilidad* (History and doctrines of accounting), Spanish version, translated, revised and extended by José María González Ferrando, Madrid, 1960 (see also Chapter 8 References).

10 Accounting publications and research in Spain: second half of the twentieth century

Alcarria Jaime, J. (1998) *Problemática contable de los instrumentos derivados* (Accounting questions of financial derivatives), Madrid: Instituto de Contabilidad y Auditoría de Cuentas.

Alcocer Chillón, F.J. (1956) 'Aplicación de los modelos de Leontief a la contabilidad social y a la economía de la empresa' (Application of the models of Leontief to social accounting and business economics), *Revista Técnica Económica* 3rd period I (1): 23–30.

Aldaz Isanta, J. (1971) *Teoría unitaria de la información económica* (General theory of economic information), Madrid: Instituto de Censores Jurados de Cuentas.

Almela Díez, B. (1987) *Análisis metodológico del control y auditoría internos de la empresa* (Methodological analysis of the control and internal audit of the firm).

Alvarez López, J. (1970) *Análisis e interpretación de balances* (Analysis and interpretations of balance sheets), San Sebastián: Editorial Donostiarra.

Alvarez López, J. and Carrasco Díaz, D. (2000) *El cálculo del beneficio en las empresas constructoras* (Income determination in construction enterprises), Madrid: Centro de Estudios Financieros.

Alvarez López, J. and López Caso, M.D. (1981) 'Conceptuación doctrinal de la contabilidad' (Doctrinal concepts of accounting), *Técnica Contable* XXXIII (393): 335–53.

Alvarez Melcón, S. (1978) *Grupos de sociedades, cuentas consolidadas. Imposición sobre el beneficio* (Parent and subsidiary companies, consolidated accounts. Corporate taxes), Madrid: Instituto de Planificación Contable, Ministerio de Economía y Hacienda.

Alvira Martín, F. and García López, J. (1976) 'La veracidad contable en España en opinión de los profesores, asesores y funcionarios' (Truth in Spanish accounting – the opinion of professionals, assessors and government officials), *Revista Hacienda Pública Española* (39): 83–109.

Aparisi Caudeli, J.A. and Ripoll Feliu, V.M. (2000) 'El Cuadro de Mando Integral: una herramienta para el control de gestión' (Balanced scorecard: a tool for management control), *Partida Doble* (114): 54–63.

Aparisi Caudeli, J.A., Malonda Martí, J. and Ripoll Feliu, V. (2000) 'Unidad para la contabilidad de gestión de los nuevos sistemas de información' (Uniformity of management accounting in the new information systems), *Técnica Contable* (615): 177–88.

Apellániz Gómez, P. and Labrador Garrafón, M. (1995) 'El impacto de la regulación contable en la manipulación del beneficio. Estudio empírico de los efectos del PGC de 1990' (The influence of accounting standards on income determination. An empirical study of the effects of the 1990 General Chart of Accounts), *Revista. Española de Financiación y Contabilidad* XXIV (82): 13–40.

Arderiu Gras, E. (1980) *El balance social: integración de objetivos sociales en la empresa* (Social accounting: incorporating social goals of the firm), Barcelona: Real Academia de Ciencias Económicas y Financieras.

Argüello Reguera, C. and Aracil Martín, J. (1974) 'Funciones múltiple de un sistema moderno de contabilidad pública' (Multiple functions of a modern government accounting system), *Revista Hacienda Pública Española* (31): 119–37.

Arthur Andersen Co. (1998) *Cómo leer las cuentas de una empresa* (How to read the accounts of an enterprise), Madrid: Invesor Ediciones.

Asociación Española de Contabilidad y Administración de Empresas (AECA) (1981–2004) *Principios contables* (Accounting principles), Madrid: AECA.

Asociación Española de Contabilidad y Administración de Empresas (AECA) (1990) *Principios y normas de contabilidad en España* (Accounting principles and standards in Spain), Madrid: AECA.

Asociación Española de Contabilidad y Administración de Empresas (AECA) (1990–2004) *Principios de contabilidad de gestión* (Principles of management accounting), Madrid: AECA.

Asociación Española de Contabilidad y de Administración de Empresas (AECA) (2004) *Marco Conceptual de la Responsabilidad Social Corporativa* (Conceptual framework of corporate social responsibility), Madrid: AECA.

Balagué Doménech, J.C. (1986) Metodología de la auditoría (Audit methodology), *Técnica Contable* XXXVIII (447): 123–32.

Ballestero Pareja, E. (1975) *La nueva contabilidad* (The new accounting), Madrid: Alianza Universidad Editorial.

Banegas Ochovo, R. (1997) Coste de capital: una metodología contable (Cost of capital: an accounting methodology), *Revista de Contabilidad y Tributación* (167): 141–204.

Banegas Ochovo, R. and Nevado Peña, D. (1999) 'Propuestas para la renovación del control de gestión en la empresa' (Proposals for the revision of management control of firms), *Revista de Contabilidad* 2 (3): 19–49.

Beascoechea Ariceta, J.M. (1980) *Planeamiento y desarrollo de las empresas industriales* (Planning and development of industrial firms), Madrid: Instituto de Planificación Contable, Ministerio de Economía y Hacienda.

Beascoechea Ariceta, J.M. (1982) *Contabilidad de costes clásica y moderna (análisis del Grupo 9 del Plan General de Contabilidad)* (Traditional and modern cost accounting: analysis of Group 9 of the General Chart of Accounts), Madrid: Instituto de Planificación Contable, Ministerio de Economía y Hacienda.

Bisbe Viñas, J. and Otley, D. (2004) 'The effects of the interactive use of management control systems on product innovation', *Accounting, Organizations and Society* 29 (8): 709–37.

Blanco Dopico, M.I., Aibar Guzmán, B. and Cantora Agra, C. (1999) 'El enfoque conductal contable en su reflejo en un cuadro de mando integral' (Behavioural accounting and its effect on the scorecard), *Revista Española de Financiación y Contabilidad* XXVIII (98): 77–105.

Borrás Pamies, F. (1999) *Contabilización de los Derivados Financieros* (Accounting for financial derivatives), Madrid: Instituto de Contabilidad y Auditoría de Cuentas.

Boter Mauri, F. (1959) *Las doctrinas contables* (Accounting doctrines), Barcelona: Juventud.

Brio González, E. (1998) 'Efecto de las salvedades de los informes de auditoría sobre el precio de las acciones en la Bolsa de Madrid' (Conditional audit reports and their effect on share prices on the Madrid stock exchange), *Revista Española de Financiación y Contabilidad* XXVII (94): 129–70.

Bueno Campos, E. (1972a) 'La contabilidad multi-dimensional como instrumento de medida y valoración en la concentración de empresas' (Multidimensional accounting as an instrument for measuring and valuation in consolidated enterprises), *Técnica Contable*: 321–31, 360, 374–81.

Bueno Campos, E. (1972b) 'Análisis conceptual de la planificación contable (I) y (II)' (Conceptual analysis of Chart of Accounts, Parts I and II), *Revista Española de Financiación y Contabilidad* I (1): 73–94; I (2): 219–58.

Bueno Campos, E. (1974) *Los sistemas de información en la empresa* (Information systems of the firm), Madrid: Confederación Española de Cajas de Ahorro.

Bueno Campos, E. and Cañibano Calvo, L. (1978) *Cash-Flow: Autofinanciación y tesorería* (Cash-flow: self-financing and cash control), Madrid: Editorial Pirámide.

Bueno Campos, E., Cañibano Calvo, L. and Fernández Peña, E. (1980) *Contabilidad analítica: Comentarios y casos prácticos* (Cost accounting: comments and practical examples), Madrid: Instituto de Planificación Contable, Ministerio de Economía y Hacienda.

Busto Marroquín, B. (1992) 'Método contable adoptado en la Universidad vallisoletana en la centuria del dieciocho' (Accounting methods adopted in the University of Valladolid in the eighteenth century), *Cuadernos de Investigación Contable* 4 (1–2).

Busto Marroquín, B. and Niño Amo, M. (1990) 'Tratamiento de las diferencias de cambio en moneda extranjera en el proyecto del nuevo Plan general de contabilidad' (Treatment of foreign currency exchange problems in the new Chart of Accounts), *Técnica Contable* XLII: 19–26.

Calafell Castelló, A. (1960–61) 'Concepto y contenido actual de la ciencia de la contabilidad' (Concepts and the present status of accounting theory), *Revista Técnica Económica* 3rd period, V (10): 344–6; V (11): 370–9; VI (1:) 21–7; VI (2): 85–90; VI (3) 117–24; V (4) 146–54; VI (5) 181–7.

Calafell Castelló, A. (1967a) 'Fundamentos de la teoría lineal de la contabilidad' (Basics of the application of 'linear algebra' to accounting), *Revista Técnica del Instituto de Censores Jurados de Cuentas*, Año I, (3): 90–4.

Calafell Castelló, A. (1967b) 'Sistemas de cálculo y control de costes' (Systems of cost accounting and control), *Técnica Contable* XIX, (222): 241–50.

Calleja Meso, D. (1961) *Contabilidad pública* (Government accounting), Madrid.

Camaleón Simón, C. (1997) 'Deficiencias e imperfecciones del modelo ABC' (Shortcomings and imperfections of the ABC model), *Técnica Contable*, XLIX, (578): 91–109.

Cañibano Calvo, L. (1974) 'El concepto de contabilidad como programa de investigación' (The notion of accounting as a research programme), *Revista Española de Financiación y Contabilidad* III, (7): 33–45.

Cañibano Calvo, L. (1975/79) *Teoría actual de la contabilidad* (Modern accounting theory), Madrid: Editorial ICE (later edition 1979).

Cañibano Calvo, L. (1991) *Curso de auditoría contable* (An auditing course), Madrid: Pirámide.

Cañibano Calvo, L. (1998) 'Información contable y responsabilidad corporativa en España' (Accounting information and corporate responsibility in Spain), *La contabilidad en el siglo XXI*, Madrid: Técnica Contable: 445–55.

Cañibano Calvo, L. and Cea García, J.L. (1971) *Los grupos de empresa: consolidación y censura de sus estados financieros* (Company groups: consolidation and revision of their financial statements), Madrid: Instituto de Censores Jurados de Cuentas.

Cañibano Calvo, L. and Cea García, J.L. (1999) 'Chapter 11: Spain', in S. McLeay ed., *Accounting regulation in Europe*, London: MacMillan.

Cañibano Calvo, L. and Giner Inchausti, B. (1994) 'Análisis de Estados Financieros: perspectiva europea' (Financial statements analysis: European perspective), *Cuadernos de Derecho y Comercio* (4): 297–319.

Cañibano Calvo and Gonzalo Angulo, J.A. (1995) 'Los programas de investigación en contabilidad' (Research programmes of accounting), Primera Jornada de Trabajo Sobre Teoría de la Contabilidad. ASEPUC-Universidad de Cádiz: 23–60.

Cañibano Calvo, L. and Mallo Rodríguez, C. (1974) 'El cálculo de los costes de la producción conjunta' (Cost calculations in joint production), *Revista Española de Financiación y Contabilidad* III (8): 305–31.

Cañibano Calvo, L. and Mora Enguidanos, A. (eds) (1997) *La regulación de la información contable-financiera en la Unión Europea: Países del sur de Europa* (Regulation of financial accounting information in the European Union: countries of Southern Europe), Madrid: Instituto de Contabilidad y Auditoría de Cuentas.

Cañibano Calvo, L., García-Ayuso Corvasí, M. and Sánchez Muñoz, P. (1999) 'La relevancia de los intangibles para la valoración y gestión empresarial. Revisión de la literatura' (The relevance of intangibles for valuation and managerial administration – a revised viewpoint), *Revista Española de Financiación y Contabilidad* XXVIII, (100): 17–88.

Cañibano Calvo, L., García-Ayuso Corvasí, M. and Sánchez Muñoz, P. (2000a) 'La valoración de los intangibles: Estudios de innovación vs. información contable financiera en España' (The valuation of intangibles: studies in innovation vs. financial accounting information in Spain), *Análisis Financiero* (80): 6–24.

Cañibano Calvo, L., García-Ayuso Corvasí, M. and Sánchez Muñoz, P. (2000b) 'Shortcomings in the measurement of innovation: implications for accounting standard setting', *Journal of Management and Governance* 4, (4): 1–24.

Capella San Agustín, M. (1975) *Concentración de empresas y consolidación de balances* (Concentration of companies and consolidated financial statements), Barcelona: Editorial Hispano Europea.

Cardús Rosell, C. (1950) *La dirección y vigilancia del negocio a través de la contabilidad* (Management and business control through accounting), Madrid: Editorial Enciclopédica.

Carmona Moreno, S. (1993) *Cambios tecnológicos y contabilidad de gestión* (Technical changes and managment accounting), Madrid: Instituto de Contabilidad y Auditoría de Cuentas.

Carmona Moreno, S., Carrasco Fenech, F. and Fernández-Revuelta Pérez, L. (1993) 'Un enfoque interdisciplinario de la contabilidad del medio ambiente' (An interdisciplinary approach to environmental accounting), *Revista Española de Financiación y Contabilidad* XXII (75): 277–305.

Carmona Moreno, S., Guitérrez Calderón, L. and Cámara de la Fuente, M. (1999) 'A profile of European accounting research: evidence from leading research journals', *The European Accounting Review* 8 (3): 463–80.

Carrasco Díaz, D. (1997) 'Estructura y funcionamiento del proceso de cálculo del coste en los servicios hospitalarios: una experiencia empírica' (Structure and operation of the process of cost calculation in hospital services: an empirical study), *Revista de Contabilidad* 0 (0): 97–123.

Carrasco Díaz, D. and González Gomila, F. (eds) (1996) *Cañizares Zurdo, J.M. 1933. Ensayo histórico sobre contabilidad* (Cañizares Zurdo, J.M. 1933: historical essay of accounting), Málaga: Imprenta del Asilo de San Bartolomé (facsimile edition of the original, edited with introductory commentary by the editors, Madrid: Asociación

Española de Contabilidad y Administración de Empresas, and the Ilustre Colegio Oficial de Titulados Mercantiles y Empresariales de Madrid).

Carrasco Díaz, D., Hernández Esteve, E. and Mattessich, R. (2004) 'Accounting publications and research in Spain: first half of the twentieth century' (an abbreviated version of an invited paper presented at the 26th Congress of the European Accounting Association), *Review of Accounting and Finance* 3 (3): 40–58.

Casanova Ramón, M. (1983) 'La valoración de acciones: proposición de una metodología' (Share valuation: a proposal for a methodology), *Técnica Contable* XXXIV (412): 121–31.

Casanovas Parella, I. (1976) *Representación contable de flujos económicos y financieros* (Accounting representation of economic and financial flows), Barcelona: Editorial Hispano Europea.

Castelló Taliani, E. (1992a) 'Análisis conceptual del "Activity Based Costing" (ABC)' (Conceptual analysis of Activity Based Costing, ABC), *Partida Doble* (27): 22–35.

Castelló Taliani, E. (1992b) 'Marco conceptual de la gestión de la empresa a través de las actividades' (Conceptual framework of company administration for various tasks), *Actualidad Financiera* Week 31 (August–September) C: 385–95.

Castelló Taliani, E. (1993) *Nuevas tendencias en contabilidad de gestión. Implantación en la empresa española* (New tendencies in management accounting. Application in the Spanish firm), Madrid: Asociación Española de Contabilidad y Administración de Empresas.

Castelló Taliani, E. (2000) 'Incidencia del ABM en el proceso de presupuestación empresarial: el control a través del activity based budgeting' (Application of ABM in the company budgetary process: control through the activity based budgeting), *Actualidad Financiera*, Año V, Monográfico 4/00: 41–51.

Castelló Taliani, E. and Lizcano Alvarez, J. (1994) *El sistema de gestión y de costes basado en las actividades* (Activity based cost and management system), Madrid: Instituto de Estudios Económicos.

Castrillo Lara, L., Calderón Monge, E., García Marín, M., Ortiz Alonso, J. and Pérez Arnaiz. M.J. (1995) 'Análisis multivariante del comportamiento ético de los auditores españoles (Multivariant analysis of ethical behaviour of Spanish auditors), *Revista Española de Financiación y Contabilidad* XIII (84): 667–96.

Cea García, J.L. (1974) 'La información contable ante la variación del poder adquisitivo del dinero' (Accounting information and changing purchasing power), *Revista Española de Financiación y Contabilidad* III (8): 143–98.

Cea García, J.L. (1979) *Modelos de comportamiento de la gran empresa* (Behavioural models for the larger enterprise), Madrid: Instituto de Planificación Contable, Ministerio de Economía y Hacienda.

Cea García, J.L. (1980) *La teoría del Balance Social* (Social Balance Sheet Theory), Cuadernos Universitarios de Planificación Empresarial. Universidad Autónoma de Madrid: Volumen VI.

Cea García, J.L. (1987) *Análisis contable de los contratos de futuros* (Accounting analysis of 'futures'), Madrid: Instituto de Planificación Contable, Ministerio de Economía y Hacienda.

Cea García, J.L. (1990) 'Los contratos de permute financiera (SWAPS)', Madrid: ICAC.

Cea García, J.L. (1995) 'Panorámica contable de los nuevos instrumentos financieros' (The accounting panorama of new financial instruments), *Perspectivas del Sistema Financiero* (50): 142–79.

Cea García, J.L. (1996) *La búsqueda de la racionalidad económico-financiera. Impera-tivo prioritario para la investigación contable* (In search of economic-financial ratio-nality. On the urgency and high priority of accounting research), Madrid: Instituto de Contabilidad y Auditoría de Cuentas.

Cea García, J.L. (1997) 'Las operaciones en moneda extranjera. Las sombras de la regu-lación contable española' (Dealings in foreign currency. Reflections of Spanish accounting regulation), *Revista de Contabilidad y Tributación* (176): 139–212.

Céspedes, J. (1993) 'Ecología y principios contables' (Ecology and accounting princi-ples), *Revista Española de Financiación y Contabilidad* XXII (75) 307–15.

Chauveau, B. (1995) 'The Spanish *Plan General de Contabilidad*: agent of development and innovation', *European Accounting Review* 4 (1): 125–38.

Crespo Domínguez, M.A. (1993) *El principio contable de correlación de ingresos y gastos* (The matching principle of costs and revenues), Madrid: Instituto de Contabili-dad y Auditoría de Cuentas.

Cuadrado Ebrero, A. and Valmayor López, L. (1992) *Organismos contables Americanos emisores de normas* (American accounting organizations' standards setting), Madrid: Instituto de Contabilidad y Auditoria de Cuentas, Ministerio de Economía y Hacienda.

Cuadrado Ebrero, A. and Valmayor López, L. (1999) *Teoría contable: Metodología de la investigación contable* (Accounting theory: research methodology of accounting), Madrid: McGraw-Hill/Interamericana de España, SAU.

Cubillo Valverde, C. (1967) *Regularización de balances: La incorporación de la cuenta de capital* (Revaluation of balance sheets: incorporation of the capital account), Madrid: Editorial ICE.

Cubillo Valverde, C. and Fernández Peña, E. (1974) *Regularización de balances: dis-posiciones legales y comentarios* (Revaluation of balance sheets: legal regulations and comments), Madrid: Editorial ICE.

Cuervo García, A. and Rivero Torre, P. (1986) 'El análisis económico-financiero de la empresa' (Economic and financial analysis of companies), *Revista Española de Finan-ciación y Contabilidad* XXV (49): 15–34.

Dávila, A. (2005) 'An exploratory study on the emergence of management control systems: formalizing human resources in small growing firms', *Accounting, Organiza-tions, and Society* 30 (3, April): 223–48.

Donoso Anes, R. (1992) 'Bartolomé Salvador de Solórzano, primer autor de un libro de contabilidad por partida doble en España o cuatrocientos años de reconocimiento teórico de la contabilidad por partida doble en España' (Bartolome Salvador de Solórzano, the first author in Spain to write a book on double-entry bookkeeping, or four-hundred years of the theoretical treatment of double-entry in Spain), *Cuadernos de Investigación Contable* 4 (1–2): 171–203.

Donoso Anes, R. and Donoso Anes, A. (eds) (1998) *Disertación critica y apologética del arte de llevar cuenta y razón por Sebastián Jócano y Madaria* (Critical and apologetic treatise of the art of bookkeeping by Sebastián Jócano y Madaria – facsimile reproduc-tion of the original, published in Madrid in 1793), Madrid: Asociación Española de Contabilidad y Administración de Empresas.

Donoso Anes, R. and García-Ayuso Covarsí, M. (1993) 'La historia de la contabilidad a debate: una encuesta a los académicos españoles' (Discusson on accounting history: a survey of Spanish academics), *Revista Española de Financiación y Contabilidad* XXII (77): 737–56.

EMVI (2006) *Encyclopedia de economia en CD-Rom* (www.eumed.net/emvi.htm).

Escobar Pérez, B., García-Ayuso Corvasí, M. and Pérez López, J.A. (2000) 'Financial accounting and reporting in extractive industries: evidence from Spanish oil bompanies', *Petroleum Accounting and Financial Management Journal* 19 (2): 1–11.

Fernández Blanco, M. (1989) 'El precio de los opciones y la teoría financiera' (Option pricing and finance theory), *Revista Española de Financiación y Contabilidad* XVIII (60): 733–70.

Fernández de Caso, E. (1981) *Las amortizaciones: su incidencia en la productividad y en el nivel de empleo* (Depreciations: their impact on productivity and employment level), Madrid: Universidad Autónoma.

Fernández-Feijóo Souto, B. (1994) *La contabilidad de gestión de las entidades financieras bajo la perspectiva de un modelo informático normalizado* (Management accounting of financial entities from the perspective of a regular computer model), Vigo: Universidad de Vigo.

Fernández-Feijóo Souto, B., Gago Rodríguez. S. and Urrutia de Hoyos, I. (2003) 'El cuadro de mando integral en las PYMES: Un instrumento para su contabilidad estratégica' (A Balanced Scorecard for SMS enterprises: an instrument for strategic accounting), *Partida Doble* (145): 40–53.

Fernández-Feijóo Souto, B. and Mattessich, R. (2006) 'Accounting research in Spain: second half of the twentieth century and beyond', *De Computis* 5: 7–38.

Fernández Peña, E. (1957/65) *Integración de balances* (Integration of accounts), Madrid: Semsa Distribuciones Epresariales, 1957 (later edition 1965).

Fernández Peña, E. (1977) 'Los tantos de propiedad y de participación y el control en grupos de sociedades' (Percentages of ownership and stock holdings, and the control of companies groups), *Técnica Contable* XXIX (346): 361–6.

Fernández Peña, E. (1984) 'Developments in accounting research in Spain', in A. Hopwood and H. Schreuder eds, *European contributions to accounting research: the achievements of the last decade*, Amsterdam: VU Uitgeverij/Free University Press: 189–209.

Fernández Peña, E. (1989) 'Introduction to *La contabilidad en España en la segunda mitad del siglo XX*' (Introduction to the book *Accounting in Spain in the middle of the twentieth century*), *Técnica Contable*, Madrid: Edit: 9–20.

Fernández Peña, E. (1992) 'Accounting in Spain in the twentieth century', in J.A. Gonzalo Angulo ed., *Accounting in Spain 1992*, Madrid: Asociación Española de Contabilidad y Administración de Empresas: 39–56.

Fernández Peña, E. (1993) 'Hacia la auditoria contemporánea' (Towards contemporary auditing), *Revista Técnica del Instituto de Auditores-Censores Jurados de Cuentas de España*, 3rd period (3): 61–9.

Fernández Pirla, J.M. (1957) *Teoría económica de la contabilidad – introducción contable al estudio de la economía* (Economic theory of accounting – an accounting introduction to the study of business), Madrid: Editorial ICE (10th edn, 1986).

Fernández Pirla, J.M. (1960) *Un ensayo sobre teoría económica de la contabilidad – introducción contable al estudio de la economía de la empresa* (An essay on the economic theory of accounting – accounting introduction to the study of business), Madrid: Editorial E.J.E.S. (also later editions).

Fernández Pirla, J.M. (1963) *Comentarios a la ley de regularización de balances: Su problemática económica, contable y fiscal* (Comments on financial statement regulations, their economic, accounting and fiscal implications), Barcelona: Editorial Ariel.

Fernández-Revuelta Pérez, L. and Ask, U. (2001) 'Diseño e implantación del cuadro de mando estratégico: el caso de tres empresas multinacionales' (Design and installation of the strategic balanced scorecard: the case of three multinational companies), *Revista Española de Financiación y Contabilidad* XXX (109): 743–64.

Fernández-Revuelta Pérez, L. and Robson, K. (1999) 'Ritual legitimation, de-coupling and the budgetary process: managing organizational hypocrisies in a multi-national company', *Management Accounting Research* 10: 383–407.

Fernández Rodríguez, F. (1980) 'Responsabilidad social de la empresa y balance social. El caso del Banco de Bilbao' (Social responsibility of the company, and social accounting: the case of the Bank of Bilbao), *Cuadernos universitarios de planificación empresarial y marketing,* Universidad Autónoma de Madrid (3): 405–16.

Fernández Sevillano, J. (1995) 'ABC y sistemas convencionales de costes: una reflexión desde el enfoque socióeconómico' (ABC and conventional costing systems: reflections on a socio-economic approach), *Actualidad Financiera,* Week 20 (12, 26 March): C 509–16.

Ferrer Jeremias, M.A. and Alamán Sales, F. (1992) *Contabilidad pública local* (Accounting for local governments), Madrid: Ediciones Valbuena-Adams.

Flores Caballero, M. (1992) 'Metodología del informe sobre las cuentas anuales (I) and (II) aspectos estructurales y financieros del balance de situación' (Methodology of the annual reports (I) and (II) structural and financial aspects of the balance sheet), *Técnica Contable* XLIV (521): 295–318; (526): 627–38; (527): 749–60.

Gabás Trigo, F. (1991) *El marco conceptual de la contabilidad financiera* (The conceptual framework of financial accounting), Madrid: Asociación Española de Contabilidad y Administración de Empresas.

Gabás Trigo, F. and Apellániz Gómez, P. (1994) 'Capacidad predictiva de los componentes del beneficio: flujos de tesorería y ajustes corto-largo plazo' (Forecast capacity of profit components: cash flows and short- and long-term adjustments), *Revista Española de Financiación y Contabilidad* XXIII (78): 107–42.

García-Ayuso Corvasí, M., Moreno Campos, I. and Sierra Molina, G. (2000) 'Fundamental analysis and human capital: empirical evidence on the relationship between the quality of human resources and fundamental accounting variables', *Journal of Human Resources, Costing and Accounting* 5 (1): 45–57.

García Benau, M.A. (1995) *Armonización de la información financiera en Europa* (Harmonization of financial information in Europe), Madrid: Instituto de Contabilidad y Auditoría de Cuentas.

García Benau, M.A. (1997) 'Algunas consideraciones internacionales sobre la controversia entre teoría y práctica contable' (Some international considerations on the controversy between the theory and practice of accounting), *Revista Española de Financiación y Contabilidad* XXVI (90): 264–79.

García Benau, M.A. and Humphrey, C. (1992) 'Beyond the audit expectations gap: learning from the experience in Britain and Spain', *The European Accounting Review* 1 (2): 75–103.

García Benau, M.A., Humphrey, C., Moizer, P. and Turley, S. (1993) *La auditoría y sus expectativas: los casos de España y Reino Unido* (Auditing and expectations: the cases of Spain and the UK), Madrid: Instituto de Contabilidad y Auditoría de Cuentas.

García Benau, M.A., Ruiz Barbadillo, E., Humphrey, C. and Al Hussain, W. (1999) 'Success in failure: reflections on the changing Spanish audit experience', *The European Accounting Review* 8 (4): 701–30.

García Benau, M.A., Ruiz Barbadillo, E. and Vico Martínez, A. (1998) *Análisis de la estructura del mercado de servicios de auditoría en España* (Analysis of the market structure for auditing services in Spain), Madrid: Instituto de Contabilidad y Auditoría de Cuentas.

García Díez, J., Martínez Arias, A. and Rubín Fernández, I. (1996) 'Los informes de auditoría en las entidades de depósito' (Audit reports in financial institutions), *Revista Técnica del Instituto de Censores Jurados de Cuentas*, 3rd period (9): 42–51.

García García, M. (1972) 'Modernas tendencias metodológicas en contabilidad' (Modern methodological accounting trends), *Revista Española de Financiación y Contabilidad* I (1): 23–44.

García García, M. (1974) *Contabilidad general: Introducción al análisis circulatorio de la realidad económica* (General accounting: introduction to the analysis of the circulation of economic reality), Madrid: Escuela Superior de las Cajas de Ahorros de la CECA.

García García, M. (1975) 'El paradigma de la partida doble en la ciencia contable' (The paradigm of double-entry in academic accounting), *Revista Española de Financiación y Contabilidad* IV (12–13): 341–64.

García García, M. (1980) *Contabilidad social: Del sistema de la circulación económica a los sistemas de cuentas nacionales* (Social accounting: from the economic cycle to the systems of national accounts), Madrid: Instituto de Planificación Contable. Ministerio de Economía y Hacienda.

García García, M. (1983) 'Ultimas tendencias de la metodología de la Contabilidad' (Recent trends of accounting methodology), *Técnica Contable* XXXV (415): 253–7.

García Martín, V. (1978) *El balance bancario. Una hipótesis para el análisis financiero de la economía* (The bank balance sheet. A hypothesis for the financial analysis of the economy), Málaga: Universidad de Málaga.

García Martín, V. (1980) 'El balance del sistema crediticio y la metodología microcontable convencional' (The balance sheet of financial institutions and the methodology of conventional micro-accounting), *Revista Española de Financiación y Contabilidad* IX (32): 413–25.

Giménez Cassina, A. (1980) 'Experiencia de balance social en Metalúrgica de Santa Ana, S.A.' (Application of social accounts in the Metalúrgica de Santa Ana, S.A.), *Cuadernos universitarios de planificación empresarial y marketing*, Universidad Autónoma de Madrid VI (3): 417–22.

Giner Inchausti, B. (1995) *La divulgación de la información financiera: una investigación empírica* (Publication of financial accounting information: an empirical study), Madrid: Asociación Española de Contabilidad y Adminsitración de Empresas.

González Ferrando, J.M. (1960) *Estudio interempresas en la industria del calzada* (An inter-company study in the shoe industry), Madrid: Comisión Nacional de Productividad Industrial.

González Ferrando, J.M. (1992) 'El sevillano Luis de Luque y Leyva, "reintroductor" de la partida doble en la bibliografía española' (Luis de Luque y Leyva of Sevilla who 're-introduced' double-entry accounting to Spanish literature), *Cuadernos de Investigación Contable* 4 (1–2).

González Ferrando, J.M. (1993) 'La contabilidad de la Casa Real del príncipe Don Juan, heredero de los Reyes Católicos' (Accounting in the royal household of Don Juan, heir to the Catholic Kings), *Revista Española de Financiación y Contabilidad* XXII (77): 713–57.

Gonzalo Angulo, J.A. (1979) *Modelos normativos para el calculo y control de costes en la empresa* (Normative models for cost accounting of the firm – doctoral dissertation), Reprinted in Madrid: Instituto de Contabilidad y Auditoría de Cuentas.

Gonzalo Angulo, J.A. (ed.) (1992) *Contabilidad en España 1992* (Accounting in Spain 1992), Madrid: Instituto de Contabilidad y Auditoría de Cuentas.

Gonzalo Angulo, J.A. (1995) 'La auditoría, una profesión en la encrucijada de los noventa' (Auditing, a profession on the cross-road of the 1990s), *Revista Española de Financiación y Contabilidad* 24 (84): 595–629.

Gonzalo Angulo, J.A. and Tua Pereda, J. (1981) *Normas y recomendaciones de auditoría y contabilidad* (Auditing and accounting standards and recommendations), Madrid: Instituto de Censores Jurados de Cuentas.

Gonzalo Angulo, J.A. and Tua Pereda, J. (eds) (1993) 'Marco conceptual para la elaboración y presentación de estados financieros (IASB)' (A conceptual framework for the elaboration and presentation of financial statements, IASB), in *Normas Internacionales del IASC*, Madrid: Instituto de Auditores-Censores Jurados de Cuentas de España.

Goxens Duch, A. (1954) *La contabilidad y la política económica* (Accounting and economic policy), Barcelona: Real Academia de Ciencias Económicas y Financieras.

Goxens Duch, A. (1974) *Investigación de la evolución doctrinal de la contabilidad en Barcelona entre 1795 y 1901* (Examination of the evolution of accounting doctrines in Barcelona between 1795 and 1901), Barcelona: Universidad de Barcelona.

Goxens Duch, A. (1993) Evolución del profesional de la contabilidad (Evolution of the accounting profession), *Técnica Contable* XLV (531): 177–85.

Gutiérrez Ponce, H. (1991) Los actuales instrumentos de control de costes (Modern tools of cost control), *Actualidad Financiera*, Week 8 (15, 14 April): 81–139.

Hansen, P. (1961) *Contabilidad interna de la industria* (Internal accounting of industry), Madrid: Editorial Aguilar (translated from Danish by Franck Suarez of *Industriens interne regnskabsvaesen*, Copenhagen: Hark, 1951).

Hernández Diosdado, R. (1976) *Optimización presupuestaria a través del balance y la contabilidad matricial* (Budgetary optimization through balance sheet and accounting matrix), Málaga: Universidad de Málaga.

Hernández Esteve, E. (1981) *Contribución al estudio de la historiografía contable en España* (A contribution to the study of accounting historiography in Spain), Madrid: Banco de España, Servicio de Estudios.

Hernández Esteve, E. (1982) 'La historia de la contabilidad y los primeros tiempos de la partida doble en España' (The history of accounting and the beginnings of double-entry bookkeeping in Spain), *Revista Técnica Económica* 3rd period, XI (1): 103–22.

Hernández Esteve, E. (1988) *Contribución al estudio de las ordenanzas de los Reyes Católicos sobre la contaduría mayor de hacienda y sus oficios* (Contribution to the study of the by-laws of the Catholic Kings on the accounting of major estates and their dealings), Madrid: Banco de España, Servicio de Estudios.

Hernández Esteve, E. (1993) 'Quinto centenario de la publicación del tratado de contable de Luca Pacioli' (Venecia, 1494) (To the 500 years' celebration of the accounting treatise of Luca Pacioli, Venice 1494), *Técnica Económica* (145): 4–10.

Hernández Esteve, E. (1994a) *Luca Pacioli – de las cuentas y las escrituras* (Luca Pacioli – on accounts and recordings), Madrid: Asociación Española de Contabilidad y Administración de Empresas.

Hernández Esteve, E. (1994b) 'Luca Pacioli's treatise De Computis et Scripturis: a composite or a unified work?', *Accounting, Business and Financial History* 4 (1): 67–82.

Hernández Esteve, E. (1995) 'A review of recent Spanish publications in accounting and financial history', *Accounting, Business and Financial History* 5 (2): 237–69.

Hernández Esteve, E. (1996) 'Spain: history of accounting and accounting thought', in M. Chatfield and R. Vangermeersch eds, *The history of accounting: an international encyclopedia*, New York: Garland Publishing, Inc.: 546–8.

Hernández Esteve, E. (2000) *Los libros de cuentas y la jurisdicción privata mercantil en España. El caso del consulado de comercio de Barcelona y su instrucción contable de 1766* (Account books and legal regulations for private merchants in Spain – the case of the chamber of commerce in Barcelona and its accounting rules of 1766), Barcelona: Real Academia de Ciencias Económicas y Financieras.

Iglesias Sánchez, J.L. (coord.) (1996) *Avances y practicas empresariales en contabilidad de gestión* (Advances and entrepreneurial applications of management accounting), Madrid: Asociación Española de Contabilidad y Administración de Empresas.

Ijiri, Y. (1972) *Análisis de objetivos y control de gestión,* Madrid: ICE (translated from *Goal-oriented models for accounting and control,* Amsterdam: North-Holland, 1965).

Jouanique, P. (1994) 'Benedetto Cotrugli reencontrado' (A new introduction to Benedetto Cotrugli), *Técnica Contable* XLVI (543): 205–17.

Keller, R. and Serrano, J. (1980) 'El balance social de la empresa publica. La experiencia del INI' (Social accounting in public companies: the experience of INI), *Cuadernos universitarios de planificación empresarial y marketing,* Universidad Autónoma de Madrid VI (3): 395–403.

Lainez, J.A. and Callao, S. (2000) 'The effect of accounting diversity on international financial analysis: empirical evidence', *The International Journal of Accounting* 35 (1): 65–83.

Larrañetta, J.L., Onieva, D. and Lozano Díaz, A. (1991) 'Inteligencia artificial aplicada a la planificación, programación y control de calidad' (Artificial intelligence applied to planning, programming and quality control), *Alta Dirección* 26 (155): 101–8.

Larriba Díaz-Zorita, A. (1979) *La dilución de las acciones y los derechos de la suscripción* (Share dilution and subscription rights), Madrid: Universidad Autónoma de Madrid.

Larriba Díaz-Zorita, A. (1990) 'Diferencias de cambio en moneda extranjera' (Problems in foreign currency exchanges), *Revista Española de Financiación y Contabilidad* XIX (64): 625–64.

Larrinaga González, C. and Bebbington, J. (2001) 'Accounting changes or institutional appropriations? A case study of the implementation of environmental accounting', *Critical Perspectives* 12: 269–92.

López Aldea, J. (1995) *Análisis práctico de las salvedades en el informe de auditoría* (Practical analysis of conditional audit reports), Zaragoza: Grupo Trae y Fair.

López Pérez, M.V. and Rodríguez Ariza, L. (2002) 'Aplicación del enfoque cognitivo a la metodología contable' (On the cognitive value of accounting methodology), *Revista Española de Financiación y Contabilidad* XXXI (112): 461–93.

López Viñegla, A. (1998) *El cuadro de mando y los sistemas de información para la gestión empresarial* (Balanced scorecard and information systems for the management of firms), Madrid: Asociación Española de Contabilidad y Administración de Empresas.

Luna Luque, J. (1974) *Teoría y práctica contable en España durante el siglo XVI* (Accounting theory and practice in Spain during the sixteenth century), Madrid: Universidad Autónoma de Madrid.

Mallo Rodríguez, C. (1979) *Contabilidad analítica: costes, rendimientos, precios y resultados* (Cost accounting: costs, profitability, prices and income), Madrid: Instituto de Planificación Contable, Ministerio de Economía y Hacienda (also later editions).

Mallo Rodríguez, C. and Merlo Bataller, J. (1995) *Control de gestión y control presupuesto* (Management control and budget control), Madrid: McGraw-Hill.

Martínez Arias, A. (1993) 'El cuadro de financiación visto por los auditores y por las empresas auditadas' (The financial scorecard seen from the viewpoints of auditors and the audited companies), *Revista Técnica del Instituto de Censores Jurados de Cuentas* 3rd period (3): 55–63.

Martínez García, F.J. (1996) 'Materialidad y riesgo en auditoria – su análisis como factores condicionantes de la calidad técnica de la actividad de auditoria' (Materiality and the auditing risk – its analysis as conditional factors for the quality of auditing services), Madrid: Instituto de Contabilidad y Auditoría de Cuentas.

Martínez Vilches, R. (1990) 'Panorama actual de la contabilidad de gestión en la empresa bancaria' (On the current situation of management accounting for banking), *Actualidad Financiera*, Week 2 (14, 8 April): C 882–908.

Mattessich, R. (1958) 'Hacia una fundamentación general y axiomática de la ciencia contable – introducción a la formulación matricial de los sistemas contables', *Revista Técnica Económica* 3rd period, III (4): 106–27 (for the English original, see Mattessich 1957 – in Chapter 4).

Mattessich, R. (1973) 'Recientes perfeccionamientos en la representación axiomática de los sistemas contables' (Recent improvements in the axiomatic representation of accounting systems), *Revista Española de Financiación y Contabilidad* II (4): 443–65.

Mattessich, R. (1995) *Critique of accounting: examination of the foundations and normative structure of an applied discipline*, Westport, CT: Quorum Books.

Mattessich, R. (2000) 'Hitos de la investigación en contabilidad – segunda mitad del siglo' (Highlights of modern accounting research – the last half century), *Revista de Contabilidad* 3 (5): 19–66 (reprinted in *Revista Legis del Contador*, April–June: 9–86, Bogotá, Colombia).

Mattessich, R. (2002) 'The theory of clean surplus and its evolution: survey and recent perspectives', *Energeia – Revista Internacional de Filosofía y Epistemología de las Ciencias Económicas* 1 (2): 9–79 (Universidad de Ciencias Empresariales y Sociales, Buenos Aires, invited paper, with Spanish text translation on: 49–79).

Mattessich, R. (2004) *La representación contable y el modelo de capas-cebolla de la realidad: una comparación con las 'Ordenes de Simulacro' de Baudrillard y su Hiperrealidad*, Monograph of the Asociación Española de Contabilidad y Administración de Empresas, Madrid (translated by Belén Fernández-Feijóo Souto from: 'Accounting representation and the Onion Model of Reality: a comparison with Baudriallard's Orders of Simulacra and his hyperreality', *Accounting, Organization and Society* 28/5, July 2003: 443–70).

Medina Hernández, V., Hernández García, M.C. and Hernández Concepción, C.A. (1997) 'Los informes de auditoría a través de una muestra de empresas' (Audit reports through an entrepreneurial sample), *Partida Doble* (78): 55–63.

Merlo Sánchez, J. (1995) 'Modelos inductivos de reparto y distribuciones de costes – I: Centros de servicios, and II: El modelo ABC' (Inductive models of the allocation and distribution of costs – Part I: Cost centres; Part II: The ABC model), *Partida Doble* (56): 39–45, (57): 40–9.

Montero Perez, A. (1980) 'El balance social en la Caja de Ahorros y Monte de Piedad de Madrid' (The social balance sheet in the savings bank and pawn shop of Madrid), *Cuadernos universitarios de planificación empresarial y marketing*, Universidad Autónoma de Madrid VII (1): 127–41.

Monterrey Mayoral, J. (1998) 'Un recorrido por la contabilidad positiva' (A recapitulation of positive accounting theory), *Revista Española de Financiación y Contabilidad* 27 (95): 427–67.

Montesinos Julve, V. (1975) 'La contabilidad en la formación y manifestación de las expectativas empresariales' (Accounting and the formation and manifestation of managerial expectations), *Seguros*: 259–87.

Montesinos Julve, V. (1978) 'Formación histórica, corrientes doctrinales y programas de investigación en contabilidad' (Historical development, doctrinal currents and research programmes of accounting), *Técnica Contable* XXX (347): 81, 135, 171, 219, 253, 285, 351, 373.

Montesinos Julve, V. (1980) *Las normas de contabilidad en la Comunidad Económica Europea* (Accounting standards in the European Economic Community), Madrid: Instituto de Planificación Contable, Ministerio de Economía y Hacienda.

Montesinos Julve, V. (1993) 'Análisis de la información contable pública' (Analysis of publicly available accounting information), *Revista Española de Financiación y Contabilidad* XXII (76): 683–722.

Montesinos Julve, V. (1994) 'La normalización en la auditoría del sector público' (Standardization of auditing for the public sector), *Revista Española de Financiación y Contabilidad* XXIII (79): 433–62.

Montesinos Julve, V. (1998) 'Accounting and business economics in Spain', *European Accounting Review* 7 (3): 357–80.

Montesinos Julve, V., Pina Martínez, V., Torres Pradas, L. and Vela Bargues, J.M. (1998) 'Análisis comparado de los principios y prácticas contables de los sistemas contables públicos de los países de la OCDE: una aproximación empírica' (Comparative analysis of the accounting principles and practices of public accounting systems of the countries of the OECD: an empiric approach), *Revista Española de Financiación y Contabilidad* XXVII (96): 787–821.

Morala Gómez, B. (1990) *Información contable para la gestión pública* (Accounting information for governmental administration), Oviedo: Universidad de Oviedo.

Muñoz Colomina, C.I. (1994) 'La eficiencia en los entes públicos no empresariales' (Efficiency in non-entrepreneurial public entities), *Revista Española de Financiación y Contabilidad* XXIII (81): 983–1013.

Narayanan, V.G. and Dávila, A. (1998) 'Using delegation and control systems to mitigate the trade-off between the performance-evaluation and belief-revision uses of accounting signals', *Journal of Accounting and Economics* 25 (3, June): 255–82.

Navarro Galera, A. (1998) *El control económico de la gestión municipal: Un modelo basado en indicadores* (Economic control of municipal management: a model based on statistical indicators), Valencia: Sindicatura de Comptes de la Generalidad Valenciana.

Nuñez Lozano, P. (1989) *El régimen jurídico de la auditoría de cuentas en el derecho español* (Legal auditing statutes in Spanish law), Sevilla: Consejería de Hacienda y Planificación. Intervención General, Junta de Andalucía.

Ortigueira Bouzada, M. (1977) *Contabilidad de recursos humanos: una introducción* (Human resource accounting: an introduction), Sevilla: Servicio de Publicaciones de la Universidad de Sevilla.

Pedraja García, P. (1995) 'Soluciones contables a los problemas del tipo de cambio' (Accounting solutions to problems of foreign exchange), *Partida Doble* (53): 23–32.

Pina Martínez, V. (1993) 'El cuadro de financiación del borrador del plan general de contabilidad pública' (The funds statement in the draft for the governmental chart of accounts), *Revista Española de Financiación y Contabilidad* XXII (77): 808–33.

Pina Martínez, V. (1994) 'Principios de análisis contable en la administración pública' (Accounting principles of public administration), *Revista Española de Financiación y Contabilidad* XXIII (79): 379–432.

Pina Martínez, V. and Torres Pradas, L. (1995) 'Indicadores de output para el análisis de eficiencia de las entidades no lucrativas. Aplicación en el sector público español' (Output indicators for the efficiency analysis of non-profit entities. Application in the Spanish public sector), *Revista Española de Financiación y Contabilidad* XXIV (85): 969–91.

Pinilla Monclús, V.J. (1975) 'Un nuevo sistema contable: el modelo circulatorio de flujos de renta y agragados de riqueza' (A new accounting system: the circulatory model of income flows and wealth aggregates), *Revista Española de Financiación y Contabilidad* IV (12–13): 409–38.

Pique Batlle, R. (1960) *Un nuevo balance. Contribución al estudio de la financiación empresarial* (A new accounting. Contribution to the study of business finance), Barcelona: Real Academia de Ciencias Económicas y Financieras.

Poveda Maestre, J.P. (1995) 'Valoración de los objetivos de control por los auditores informáticos españoles' (Evaluation of control objectives by Spanish computer auditors), *Partida Doble* (56): 50–7.

Prado Lorenzo, J.M. (1993) 'La norma de auditoría sobre la aplicación del principio de empresa en funcionamiento. Consideraciones de los auditores' (The audit standard for applying the going concern principle. The auditors' point of view), *Revista Técnica del Instituto de Censores Jurados de Cuentas* 3rd period (3): 30–45.

Prado Lorenzo, J.M., González Bravo, L. and Martín Jiménez, D. (1995) 'La situación de la auditoría en España desde la perspectiva de los auditores' (The situation of the audit in Spain from the auditors' point of view), *Revista Española de Financiación y Contabilidad* XXIV (84): 631–67.

Prieto Moreno, B. and Pérez Arnáiz, M.J. (1992) 'La teoría de contabilidad positiva en el transcurso de una década' (A decade of the theory of positive accounting), *Actualidad Financiera* Week 21 (47, 27th December): C 645–54.

Ramos Díaz, F.J. (1969) 'La normalización en el campo de la contabilidad de la empresa' (Standardization in the area of corporation accounting), *Revista Técnica del Instituto de Censores Jurados de Cuentas* III (1): 9–19.

Ramos Stolle, A. and Fernández-Feijóo Souto, B. (1994) 'Tratamiento de las diferencias de cambio de valores de renta fija, créditos y débitos: Sistemas actuales y una alternativa' (On the treatment of foreign exchange for interest bearing debits and credits: present situation and alternative), *Actualidad Financiera* Week 4 (32, 11th March): C 639–63.

Requena Rodríguez, J.M. (1967) 'Metodología de la contabilidad' (Accounting methodology), *Técnica Contable* XIX (214): 448–53.

Requena Rodríguez, J.M. (1972) 'Teoría de la contabilidad: Análisis dimensional' (Accounting theory: multidimensional analysis), *Revista Española de Financiación y Contabilidad* I (1): 45–53.

Requena Rodríguez, J.M. (1974) 'El resultado interno' (The internal result), *Revista Española de Financiación y Contabilidad* III (8): 229–52.

Requena Rodríguez, J.M. (1977) *La homogeneización de magnitudes en la ciencia de la contabilidad* (Uniform valuation in accounting), Madrid: Ediciones ICE.

Rivero Menéndez, M.R. (2000) *La formación de los registros contables en Mesopotamia* (The development of keeping accounting records in Mesopotamia), Guadalajara: Gráficas Minaya, S.A.

Rivero Torre, P. (1977) 'Coste de depreciación, expansión de la empresa, inestabilidad monetaria y política de amortizaciones' (Depreciation costs, company expansion, monetary instability, and amortization policies), *Técnica Contable* XXIX (337): 1–8; (338): 41–55.

Rodríguez Pita, E. and Rodríguez Flores de Quiñones, J.M. (1956) *Ciencia de la contabilidad – técnica práctica y organización* (Accounting theory – practical techniques and organization), Barcelona: [s.n.] Graf. Alfa.

Rodríguez Rodríguez, A. (1979) *Ensayo sobre contabilidad de la liquidez* (An accounting study of liquidity), Madrid: Instituto de Censores Jurados de Cuentas.

Ruiz Barbadillo, E. (1997) *Los objetivos del informe de auditoría* (Objectives of the audit report), Madrid: Instituto de Contabilidad y Auditoría de Cuentas.

Ruiz Barbadillo, E., Humphrey, C. and García Benau, M.A. (2000) 'Auditors versus third parties and others: the unusual case of Spanish audit liability crisis', *Accounting History* 5 (2): 119–46.

Sáez Torrecilla, A. (1982) *Costes empresariales: su estructura contable* (Company costs: their accounting structure), Madrid: Instituto de Planificación Contable, Ministerio de Economía y Hacienda.

Sáez Torrecilla, A. and Corona Romero, E. (1991) *Análisis sistemático y operativo del plan de contabilidad* (Systematic and operative analysis of the chart of accounts), Madrid: McGraw-Hill.

Sánchez-Mayoral García-Calvo, F. (1997) *La medida contable de la equidad intergeneracional en el sector público* (Accounting measurement in the public sector: intergenerational aspects), Madrid: Instituto de Contabilidad y Auditoría de Cuentas.

Sánchez Muñoz, P., Chaminade Domínguez, C. and Olea de Cárdenas, M. (2000) 'Management of intangibles: an attempt to build a theory', *Journal of Intellectual Capital* 1 (4): 312–28.

Schmalenbach, E. (1954) *Balance dinámico* (Dynamic accounting), Madrid: Instituto de Censores y Jurados de Cuentas de España (translated from the German original of *Die Dynamische Bilanz* – see, Schmalenbach 1919a – in Chapter 2).

Schneider, E. (1969) *Contabilidad industrial*, Madrid: Editorial Aguilar (translated from *Industrielles Rechnungswesen: Grundlagen und Grundfragen*, Tübingen: Mohr, 1954 – see also E. Schneider 1939 – in Chapter 3).

Serra Salvador, V. (1978) 'Un planteamiento de los modelos contables en relación con los criterios de valoración' (Accounting models and valuation criteria), *Técnica Contable* XXX (350): 41–54.

Sierra Molina, G. and Bonsón Ponte, E. (1992) 'Audi Expert: Un sistema experto para la elaboración del informe de auditoría' (Audi expert: an expert system for providing the audit report), *Partida Doble* (28): 45–52.

Sierra Molina, G. and Orta Perez, M. (1997) 'Una responsabilidad básica del auditor: El control de calidad de la auditoría' (The auditor's basic responsibility: controlling the audit quality), *Revista de Contabilida* 0 (0): 185–227.

Snozzi, E.G. (1969) *Verificación de balances* (Verification of balance sheet data), Madrid: Rialp.

Soldevilla García, E. (1978) *El control crítico de la gestión económica* (Effective control of business management), Barcelona: Real Academia de Ciencias Económicas y Financieras.

Soler Amaro, R. (1980) 'Un modelo para la mecanización del Plan General de Contabilidad' (A model for routine application of the General Chart of Accounts), *Técnica Contable* XXXII (374): 41–7.

Torres Pradas, L. (1991) 'Indicadores de gestión para entidades públicas' (Management indicators for public entities), *Revista Española de Financiación y Contabilidad* XX (67): 535–58.

Tua Pereda, J. (1982) *Principios y normas de contabilidad: historia, metodología y entorno de la regulación contable* (Principles and accounting rules: history, methodology and environment of accounting regulation), Madrid: Universidad Autónoma de Madrid (doctoral dissertation).

Tua Pereda, J. (1983a) *Memoria sobre concepto, método, fuentes y programa de teoría de la contabilidad* (Monograph on the concept, method, sources and programmes of accounting theory), Madrid: Universidad Autónoma de Madrid.

Tua Pereda, J. (1983b) *Principios y normas de contabilidad. Historia, metodología y entorno de la regulación contable* (Principles and accounting rules. History, methodology and environment of the accounting regulation), Madrid: Instituto de Planificación Contable, Ministerio de Economía y Hacienda (publication of the above-mentioned dissertation).

Tua Pereda, J. (1991) *La investigación empírica en contabilidad. La hipótesis de eficiencia del Mercado* (Empirical research in accounting. The hypothesis of market efficiency), Madrid: Instituto de Contabilidad y Auditoría de Cuentas.

Tua Pereda, J. (2004) 'Evolución y situación actual del pensamiento contable' (Evolution and present situation of accounting thought), *Revista Internacional Legis de Contabilidad & Auditoria* (October–December): 41–128.

Tua Pereda, J. and Bellostas Pérez-Grueso, A.J. (eds) (2000) *El marco conceptual para la información financiera* (Conceptual framework for financial information), Madrid: Asociación Española de Contabilidad y Administración de Empresas.

Urias Valiente, J. (1987) *Auditoría financiera* (Financial auditing), Madrid: Tébar Flores.

Urias Valiente, J. (1990) *El objetivo de relevancia en el informe del auditor independiente* (The objective of materiality in the independent auditor's report), Madrid: Instituto de Contabilidad y Auditoría de Cuentas.

Vallverdú Calafell, J. (2003) 'La responsabilidad social de la empresa: una aportación contable' (The social responsibility of business: an accounting contribution), *Papeles de Etica, Economía y Dirección*: N.8.

Vela Bargues, J.M. (1991) 'La contabilidad pública frente a la contabilidad empresarial: algunas reflexiones en torno a la interpretación de sus diferencias' (Governmental accounting versus business accounting: some reflections on viewing their differences), *Revista Española de Financiación y Contabilidad* XX (68): 581–621.

Vela Bargues, J.M. (1992) 'La nueva contabilidad de las entidades locales y los principios contables públicos (I) y (II) significado y antecedentes de los principios contenidos en el Documento de la I.G.A.E'. (The new accounting of local entities and governmental accounting principles (I) and (II). Interpretation and antecedents of principles in the document of the I.G.A.E.), *Revista Española de Financiación y Contabilidad* XXI (71): 369–91; (72): 653–73.

Vela Bargues, J.M. (1994) 'Contabilidad pública y normalización contable: una especial referencia al caso español' (Public accounting and accounting standards: special reference to the Spanish case), *Revista Española de Financiación y Contabilidad* XXIII (79): 309–34.

Vereda Espada, J. (1977) *El nivel óptimo de reservas* (The optimum level of reserves), Madrid: Universidad Autónoma.

Verges Mamé, E. (1998) 'Los servicios relacionados con la auditoría' (Services connected to auditing), *Revista Técnica del Instituto de Censores Jurados de Cuentas* XXXI (13): 6–23.

Vidal Blanco, C. (1977) *El leasing* (Leasing), Madrid: Instituto de Planificación Contable, Ministerio de Economía y Hacienda.

Vlaemminck, J.H. (1960) *Historia y doctrinas de la contabilidad* (History and doctrines of accounting), Spanish version, translated from French, revised and extended by J.M. González Ferrando, Madrid: E.J.E.S.

11 Accounting research in the English language area: first half of the twentieth century

American Accounting Association (AAA) (1941a) *Accounting principles underlying corporate Financial statements*, AAA.

American Accounting Association (AAA) (1941b) *Accounting concepts and standards underlying corporate financial statements*, AAA.

American Association of University Instructors in Accounting (later: American Accounting Association) (1936) 'A tentative statement of accounting principles underlying corporate financial statements', *The Accounting Review* (June): 187–91.

Arnold, H.L. (1903) *The factory manager and accountant*, New York: Engineering Magazine Co.

Arthur Andersen & Co. (1970) *Behind the figures: addresses and articles by Arthur Andersen, 1913–1941*, Chicago, IL: Arthur Andersen & Co.

Backer, M. (1973) *Current value accounting*, New York: Financial Executives Research Foundation.

Baxter, W.T. (1937) *Income tax for professional students*, London: Pitman.

Baxter, W.T. (1949) 'Accountants and the inflation', *Proceedings of the Manchester Statistical Society* 9 (February): 1–19.

Bedford, Norton (1965) *Income determination theory*, Reading, MA: Addison-Wesley Publishing Co.

Bentley, H.C. (1911) *The science of accounts: a presentation of the underlying principles of modern accounting*, 2nd printing, New York.

Bentley, H.C. and Leonard, R.S. (1934–35) *Bibliography of works by American authors*, 2 vols, Boston, MA: Harry Clark Bentley.

Bloom, R. (1996) 'Gilman, Stephen (1887–1959)', in M. Chatfield and R. Vangermeersch eds, *The history of accounting: an international encyclopedia*, New York: Garland Publishing, Inc.

Bloom, R., Collins, M. and Debessay, A. (1990) 'Gilman's contributions to accounting thought: a golden anniversary retrospective', *Accounting History* 2 (2): 107–23.

Blough, C.B. (1937) 'Some accounting problems of the Security and Exchange Commission', *The New York Certified Public Accountant* (April): 3–14 (reprinted in W.G. Shenkir ed., *Carman G. Blough: his professional career and accounting thought*, New York: Arno Press, 1978).

Blough, C.B. (1948) 'The accountants view: replacement costs and depreciation policy', *National Industrial Conference Board*: 8–11 (reprinted in W.G. Shenkir ed., *Carman G. Blough: his professional career and accounting thought*, New York: Arno Press, 1978).

Bonbright, J.C. (1937) *The valuation of property: a treatise on the appraisal of property for different legal purposes*, New York: McGraw-Hill Book Co.

Bray, F.S. (1947) *Precision and design in accountancy*, London: Gee & Co.

Bray, F.S. (1949) *Social accounts and the business enterprise sector of the national economy*, Cambridge: Cambridge University Press.

Brief, R.P. (1980) *Dicksee's contribution to accounting theory and practice*, New York: Arno Press.

Brief, R.P. and Peasnell, K.V. (eds) (1996) *Clean surplus: a link between accounting and finance*, New York: Garland Publishing, Inc.

Brown, F.D. (1927a) 'Centralized control with decentralized responsibilities', *Annual Convention Series, No. 57*, New York: American Management Association: 3–24.

Brown, F.D. (1927b) 'Pricing policy in relation to financial control', *Management and Administration* (February): 195–8, (March): 283–6.

Brown, R. (ed.) (1905) *History of accounting and accountants*, Edinburgh.

Bunnell, S.H. (1911) 'Standardized factory expenses and cost', *Iron Age* (November 16).

Burns, T.J. and Coffman, E.N. (1991) *The accounting hall of fame: profiles of fifty members*, 3rd edn, Columbus, OH: College of Business, Ohio State University.

Canning, J.B. (1929) *Economics of accountancy, a critical analysis of accounting theory*, New York: Ronald Press.

Carman, E.A. (1930) *Standard costs: installation and procedure*, New York: The International Congress of Accounting 1929.

Castenholz, W.B. (1918) 'Is interest on invested capital a cost?', *Journal of Accountancy* (April 18): 248–54.

Chambers, R.J. (1967) 'Continuously contemporary accounting: additivity and action', *The Accounting Review* 42 (October): 751–7.

Chatfield, M. (1974) *A history of accounting thought*, Hindsdale, IL: Dryden Press (2nd edn, Huntington, New York: R.E. Krieger Publishing Co., 1977).

Chatfield, M. (1996a) 'An introduction to corporate accounting standards', in M. Chatfield and R. Vangermeersch eds, *The history of accounting: an international encyclopedia*, New York: Garland Publishing, Inc.: 43–4.

Chatfield, M. (1996b) 'Dickinson, Arthur Lowes (1859–1935)', in M. Chatfield and R. Vangermeersch eds, *The history of accounting: an international encyclopedia*, New York: Garland Publishing, Inc.: 203–4.

Chatfield, M. (1996c) 'Harrison Norman G. Charter (1881–)' in M. Chatfield and R. Vangermeersch eds, *The history of accounting: an international encyclopedia*, New York: Garland Publishing, Inc.: 291–2.

Chatfield, M. and Vangermeersch, R. (eds) (1996) *The history of accounting: an international encyclopedia*, New York: Garland Publishing, Inc.

Chiera, E. (1921) *Selected temple accounts from Telloch, Yokha, and Drehem*, Philadelphia, PA: University of Pennsylvania.

Church, A.H. (1901–02) 'The proper distribution of establishment charges', *The Engineering Magazine* 21: 508–17, 725–34, 904–12; 22: 31–40, 231–40, 367–76 (reprinted in book form under the same title by the same magazine publisher, 1916).

Church, A.H. (1908) *The proper distribution of expense burden*, London: Works Management Library, The Engineering Magazine.

Church, A.H. (1910) *Production factors in cost accounting and works management*, New York: Industrial Management Library, The Engineering Magazine Co.

Church, A.H. (1917) *Manufacturing costs and accounts*, New York, NY: McGraw-Hill (2nd edn, 1929).

Claire, R.S. (1945) 'Evolution of corporate reports', *Journal of Accountancy* 79 (January): 39–51.

Clark, J.M. (1923) *Studies in the economics of overhead costs*, Chicago, IL: University of Chicago Press.

Coase, R.H. (1937) 'The nature of the firm', *Economica* 4 (November): 386–405.

Coase, R.H. (1938) 'Business organizations and the accountant', *The Accountant*

(1 October–17 December) (reprinted in D. Solomons ed., *Studies in costing*, London: Sweet & Maxwell Ltd, 1952: 105–58).

Cochran, G. (1950) 'The auditor's report: its evolution in the U.S.A.', *Accountant* 123 (November 4): 448–60.

Cole, W.M. (1908) *Accounts, their construction and interpretation*, Boston, MA: Houghton and Mifflin (2nd edn, 1915).

Cole, W.M. (1910) *Accounting and auditing*, New York: Cree Publishing Co.

Cooper, W.W. (1996) 'Kohler, Eric Louis (1892–1976)', in M. Chatfield and R. Vangermeersch eds, *The history of accounting: an international encyclopedia*, New York: Garland Publishing, Inc.: 362–3.

Cooper, W.W. and Ijiri, Y. (eds) (1979) *Eric Louis Kohler: accounting's man of principles*, Reston, VA: Reston Publishing.

Degos, J.-G. and Previts, G.P. (2005) 'A.C. Littleton et W.A. Paton: la normalization comptable entre induction et deduction' (A.C. Littleton and W.A. Paton: accounting standardization through induction and deduction), in B. Colasse ed., *Les grands auteurs en comptabilité*, Paris: Éditions EMS: 145–62.

Deinzer, H.T. (1965) *Development of accounting thought*, New York: Holt, Reinhart and Winston, Inc.

Devine, C.T. (1944) 'Depreciation and income measurement', *The Accounting Review* 19 (January): 39–46.

Devine, C.T. (1950) 'Cost accounting and pricing policies', *The Accounting Review* 25 (October): 384–9.

Dickinson, A.L. (1908) *Accounting practice and procedure*, New York: Ronald Press (2nd edn, 1908, later edition 1917; reprint edition Houston, TX: Scholars Books, 1975).

Dicksee, L.R. (1892/1902) *Auditing: a practical manual for auditors*, London: Gee (1st edn, 1892; 5th edn, 1902).

Dicksee, L.R. (1903) *Depreciation, reserves and reserve funds*, London: Gee (5th edn, New York: Arno Press, 1976).

Dicksee, L.R. (1905) *Auditing: authorized American edition*, edited by R.H. Montgomery, New York (1st edn, 1892; reprint edition New York: Arno Press, 1976).

Dicksee, L.R. (1910) 'Auditing with special reference to the accounts of local authorities', *The Accountant* 13 (August).

Dicksee, L.R. (1911) *Advanced accounting*, London: Gee & Co, California Press (1st edn, 1903; reprint edition New York: Arno Press, 1976).

Diem, E. van (1929) 'The development of professional accounting in Continental Europe', *Accountant* 81: 409–17, 439–48.

Edey, H.C. (1950) 'Published accounts as an aid to investment', *The Accountant* 18 (February): 163–8.

Edwards, E.O. and Bell, P.W. (1961) *The theory and measurement of business income*, Berkeley, CA: University of California Press.

Edwards, J.D. and Salmonson, R.F. (1961) *Contributions of four accounting pioneers: Kohler, Littleton, May, Paton*, East Lansing, MI: Bureau of Business and Economic Research, Michigan State University.

Edwards, R.S. (1937a) *Survey of the French contributions to the study of cost accounting dring the nineteenth century*, London: McGee.

Edwards, R.S. (1937b) 'Some notes on the early literature and development of cost accounting in Great Britain', *Accountant* 47: 193–5, 225–31, 253–5, 283–7, 313–16, 343–4.

Edwards, R.S. (1938a) 'The rational of cost accounting', in A. Plant ed.: 277–99 (reprinted in D. Solomons ed., *Studies in costing*, London: Sweet & Maxwell: 87–104).

Edwards, R.S. (1938b) 'The nature and measurement of income', *The Accountant* (July–October) (reprinted in W.T. Baxter ed., *Studies in accounting*, 1950; in abridged form in W.T. Baxter and S. Davidson, eds, London: Institute of Chartered Accountants of England and Wales, 1962 and 1977: 96–140).

Elbourne, E.T. (1914) *Factory administration of accounts*, London.

Emerson, H. (1908–09) 'Efficiency as a basis for operation and wages', *Engineering Magazine* (July 1908 to March 1909).

Esquerré, P.J. (1925) 'Resources and their applications', *Journal of Accountancy* (May): 424–30.

Fells, J.M. (1919) 'Some principles governing the ascertainment of cost', *Incorporated Accountants' Journal* (November): 34f.

Fells, J.M. (1922) 'Industrial economics', *The Incorporated Accountants' Journal* (February): 123–5.

Ferrara, W.L. (1996) 'Break-even chart', in M. Chatfield and R. Vangermeersch eds, *The history of accounting: an international encyclopedia*, New York: Garland Publishing, Inc.: 79–81.

Finney, H.A. (1925) 'The statement of application of funds: a reply to Mr. Esquerré', *Journal of Accountancy* (June): 497–511.

Finney, H.A. (1930) *Principles of accounting*, New York: Prentice-Hall, Inc. (many later editions and versions, co-authored with H. Miller, under the title *Finney and Miller's principles of accounting*).

Fisher, I. (1906) *The nature of capital and income*, London: Macmillan & Co., Ltd.

Fisher, I. (1911) *The purchasing power of money*, New York: Macmillan & Co., Ltd.

Fisher, I. (1925) *The money illusion*, New York: Macmillan & Co., Ltd.

Fitzgerald, A.A. (1952) 'Current cost accounting trends', Sydney: Butterworth & Co. (Australia), Ltd.

Fleischman, R.K. and Tyson, T.N. (2000) 'Parallels between US and UK cost accountancy during the World War I era', *Accounting, Business and History* 10 (July): 191–212.

Forrester, D.A.R. (1982) *Frank Sewell Bray: master accountant, 1906–1979: a selection and assessments of his work*, Glasgow: Strathclyde Convergencies.

Fowler, R.F. (1934) *The depreciation of capital*, London: King.

Gaines, M.W. (1905) 'Tabulating machine cost-accounting for factories of diverse producers', *Engineering Magazine* 30.

Gantt, H.L. (1915) *Evolution of cost accounting to 1925* (reprinted Tuscaloosa, AL: University of Alabama Press, 1954).

Gantt, H.L. (1916) 'The relation between production and costs', *Transactions: American Society of Mechanical Engineers* 38.

Garner, S.P. (1940) *Evolution of cost accounting to 1925* (doctoral dissertation, by published University of Alabama, Tuscaloosa, AL: University of Alabama Press, 1954; reprinted 1976; translated into Japanese and Chinese; freely available on the Internet by the Academy of Accounting Historians under: http://weatherhead.cwru.edu/accounting/pub/garner/index.html).

Garner, S.P. (1947) 'Historical development of cost accounting', *The Accounting Review* 22 (October): 385–9.

Garner, S.P. (1968) 'Highlights in the development of cost accounting', in M. Chatfield, ed., *Contemporary studies in the evolution of accounting thought*, Belmont, CA: Sickenson Publishing Co.

Garry, S. (1903) 'Factory costs', *The Accountant* (July 25): 954–61.

Geijsbeek, J.B. (1914) *Ancient double-entry bookkeeping* (reprinted Houston, TX: Scholars Book Co., 1974).

Gilman, S. (1939) *Accounting concepts of profits*, New York: Ronald Press.

Goldberg, L. (1965) *An inquiry into the nature of accounting*, Sarasota, FA: American Accounting Association.

Grady, P. (1962) *Memoirs and accounting thought of George O. May*, New York: Ronald Press.

Graham, W.J. (1949) 'Changing price levels and the determination, reporting and interpretation of income', *The Accounting Review* 24 (January): 15–26.

Grier, E. (1934) *Accounting in the Zenon papyri*, New York: Columbia University Press.

Hall, H.L.C. (1904) *Manufacturing costs*, Detroit, IL: The Bookkeeper Publishing Company.

Harris, J.N. (1936) 'What did we earn last month?', *N.A.(C.)A. Bulletin*.

Harrison, G.C. (1918–19) 'Cost accounting to aid production', *Industrial Management* (October/June).

Harrison, G.C. (1920) 'Scientific basis for cost accounting', *Industrial Management* (March): 237–42.

Hatfield, H.R. (1908) 'Review: *The philosophy of accounts* by Charles E. Sprague ...', *Journal of Accountancy* 6: 67–9.

Hatfield, H.R. (1909) *Modern accounting: its principles and some of its problems*, New York: Appelton, 1909 (revised edition as *Accounting: its principles and problems*, New York: Appelton, 1927; reprinted in Laurence, KA: Scholars Book Co., 1971, and in New York: Arno Press, 1976).

Hatfield, H.R. (1924) 'An historical defence of bookkeeping', *Journal of Accountancy* (April): 241–53 (originally presented on 29 December 1923 at the American Association of University Instructors in Accounting, later: AAA).

Hatfield, H.R. (1936). 'What they say about depreciation', *The Accounting Review* 11 (March): 19.

Haynes, B.R. and Jackson, H.P. (1935) *A history of business education in the United States*, New York: South-Western Publishing Co.

Hein, L.W. (1959) 'L. Lee Nicholson: pioneer cost accountant', *The Accounting Review* 34 (1): 106–11.

Hess, H. (1903) 'Manufacturing, capital, costs, profits and dividends', *Engineering Magazine* (December): 367–???.

Hicks, J.R. (1931) 'Uncertainty and profit', *Economica* (May) (reprinted in J.R. Hicks, *Money, interest and wages: collected essays on economic theory*, Vol. II, Oxford: Basil Blackwell, 1982: 11–27).

Hicks, J.R. (1938) *Value and capital: an inquiry into some fundamental principles of economic theory*, Oxford: Clarendon Press.

Ijiri, Y. (1975) *Theory of accounting measurement*, Sarasota, FA: American Accounting Association.

Jones, R.C. (1949) 'Effects of inflation on capital and profits: the record of nine steel companies', *Journal of Accountancy* (January): 9–27.

Judd, H.C. (1914) 'Fixed and fluctuating on-cost', *Accountants' Magazine* (March): 134–46.

Kester, R.B. (1916) *A study in valuation of the commercial balance sheet*, New York: doctoral dissertation, Columbia University.

Kitchen, J. and Parker, R.H. (1994a) 'Laurence Robert Dicksee (1864–1932), in J.R. Edwards ed., *Twentieth-century accounting thinkers*, London: Routledge: 206–24.

Kitchen, J. and Parker, R.H. (1994b) 'Frederic Rudolph Mackley de Paula (1882–1954)', in J.R. Edwards ed., *Twentieth-century accounting thinkers*, London: Routledge: 225–73.

Knoeppel, C.E. (1920) *Graphic production control*, New York: Engineering Magazine Co.

Kohler, E.L. (1935) 'Standards: a dialogue', *The Accounting Review* 10 (4): 370–8.

Kohler, E.L. (1938) 'Some tentative propositions underlying consolidated reports', *The Accounting Review* 13 (1): 63–72.

Kozub, R.M. (1996) 'Hatfield, Henry Rand (1866–1945)', in M. Chatfield and R. Vangermeersch eds, *The history of accounting: an international encyclopedia*, New York: Garland Publishing, Inc.: 293–4.

Lane, F.C. (1945) 'Venture accounting in medieval business management', *Bulletin of the Business Historical Society* 62: 164–73.

Littleton, A.C. (1933) *Accounting evolution to 1900*, New York: American Institute Publishing (reprinted New York: Russell & Russell, 1966).

Littleton, A.C. and Zimmerman, V.K. (1962) *Accounting theory: continuity and change*, Englewood Cliffs, NJ: Prentice-Hall, Inc.

Longmuir, P. (1902) 'Recording and interpreting foundry costs', *Engineering Magazine* (September): 887.

McHenry, W.E. (1914) 'Cost per ton', *Engineering Magazine:* 791–.

McHenry, W.E. (1916) 'Is your cost system scientific?', *Engineering Magazine* 681–3.

McKinsey, J.O. (1922) *Budgetary control*, New York: Ronald Press.

McKinsey, J.O. (1924) *Managerial accounting*, Chicago, IL: University of Chicago Press.

MacNeal, K.F. (1939) *Truth in accounting*, Philadelphia, PA: University of Philadelphia Press, 1939.

Mann, J. (Sir) (1904) 'Cost records or factory accounting', in C. Lisle ed., *Encyclopaedia of accounting*, Vol. 2, Edinburgh.

Marshall, A. (1905a) 'Education for business men', *The Times* 23 (November): 4.

Marshall, A. (1905b) 'Letter to the Editor: "Education for business men"', *The Times* 29 (December): 5.

Marshall, A. (1919) *Industry and trade*, London, Macmillan.

Mason, P.E. (1937) *Principles of public utility depreciation*, New York: American Accounting Association.

Mathews, R. and Grant, J.M. (1962) *Inflation and company finance*, Sydney: The Law Book Company of Australia, Pty, Ltd.

Mattessich, R. (1964) *Accounting and analytical methods: measurement and projection of income and wealth in the micro- and macro-economy*, Homewood, IL: R.D. Irwin, Inc. (reprinted in the 'Accounting Classics Series', Houston, TX: Scholars Book Co., 1977; also in the 'Series of Financial Classics' of Reprints on Demand, Ann Arbor, MI: Microfilms International, 1979, still available; Japanese translation under the direction of Shinzaburo Koshimura, *Kaikei to Bunsekiteki-Hoho Jokan*, 2 vols, Tokyo: Dobunkan, Ltd, Vol. 1: 1972, Vol. 2: 1975; Spanish translation, by Carlos Luis García Casella and Maria del Carmen Ramírez de Rodríguez, Buenos Aires: La Ley, 2002).

May, G.O. (1936) *Twenty-five years of accounting responsibility, 1911–1936*, vol. 2 (edited by B.C. Hunt), New York: American Institute Publishing Company.

May, G.O. (1937) 'Eating peas with your knife', *Journal of Accountancy* (January): 15–22.

May, G.O. (1943) *Financial accounting: a distillation of experience*, New York: MacMillan & Co.

May, G.O. (1949) *Business income and price levels: an accounting study*, New York: Study Group on Business Income.

Mead, J.E. and Stone, J.N.R. (1941) 'The construction of tables of national income, expenditure, savings and investment', *The Economic Journal* (June–September): 216–33.

Middleditch, L. (1918) 'Should accountants reflect the changing value of the dollar treat?', *The Journal of Accountancy* 24 (2, February): 114–20 (reprinted in S.A. Zeff ed., *Asset appreciation, business income and price-level accounting*, New York: Arno Press, 1976).

Mills, P.A. (1994) 'Henry Rand Hatfield (1866–1945): life and humour in the dust of ledgers', in J.R. Edwards ed., *Twentieth-century accounting thinkers*, London: Routledge: 293–308.

Montgomery, R.H. (ed.) (1905) *Auditing: a practical manual for auditors by Robert Dicksee* (authorized American edition), New York (reprint edition New York: Arno Press, 1976).

Montgomery, R.H. (1912) *Auditing theory and pratice*, New York: Ronald Press Co. (with many subsequent editions).

Montgomery, R.H. (1927) 'Book Review of *Accounting: its principles and problems* by Henry Rand Hatfield', New York, D. Appleton and Company (reprinted in M.J.R. Gaffikin and M.J. Aitken eds, *The Development of accounting theory: significant contributors to accounting thought in the twentieth century*, New York: Garland Publishing, Inc., 1982: 14–19).

Montgomery, R.H. (1939) 'Fifty years of accountancy', New York: The Ronald Press Co. (reprint edition New York: Arno Press, 1978).

Moonitz, M. (1944) *The entity theory of consolidated statements*, Bloomington, IN: AAA (several reprint editions, e.g. New York: Arno Press, 1978).

Moonitz, M. (1948) 'Adaptations to price-level changes', *The Accounting Review* 23 (April): 137–47.

Moonitz, M. (1986) *History of accounting at Berkeley*, Berkeley, CA: Schools of Business Administration.

Moonitz, M. (1994) 'Carman G. Blough (1895–1981)', in J.R. Edwards ed., *Twentieth-century accounting thinkers*, London: Routledge: 319–33.

Neuner, J.J.W. (1939) *Cost accounting: principles and practice*, Chicago, IL: Business Publications, Inc.

Nicholson, J.L. (1909) *Factory organization and costs*, New York: Kohl Technical Publishing Company.

Parker, R.H. (1969) *Management accounting: an historical perspective*, London: Macmillan.

Paton, W.A. (1918) 'The significance and treatment of appreciation in accounts', in G.H. Coons ed., *Michigan Academy of Science, twentieth annual report* (reprinted in S.A. Zeff ed., *Asset appreciation, business income and price-level accounting*, New York: Arno Press, 1976).

Paton, W.A. (1920a) 'Depreciation, appreciation and productive capacity', *The Journal of Accountancy* 30 (1, July): 1–11 (reprinted in S.A. Zeff ed., *Asset appreciation, business income and price-level accounting*, New York: Arno Press, 1976).

Paton, W.A. (1920b) 'Some current value accounts', *The Journal of Accountancy* 30: 335–50.

Paton, W.A. (1922) *Accounting theory, with special reference to the corporate enterprise*, New York: Ronald Press, 1922 (reprint edition New York: Russell & Russell, 1966).

Paton, W.A. and Littleton, A.C. (1940) *An introduction to corporate accounting standards*, New York: American Accounting Association.

Paula, F.R.M. de (1914) *The principles of auditing*, London: Pittman (14th edn by F.R.M. de Paula and F.C. de Paula as *Principles of auditing: a practical manual for students and practitioners*, London: Pitman, 1970).

Paula, F.R.M. de (1943) 'The future of the accountancy profession', *Accountant* (May 8): 239–42.

Paula, F.R.M. de (1948) *Developments in accounting*, London: Pitman (reprinted New York: Arno Press, 1970).

Peragallo, E. (1938) *Origin and evolution of double-entry book-keeping, a study of Italian practice from the fourteenth century*, New York: American Institute Publishing Co.

Peragallo, E. (1941) 'Origin of the trial balance', *Journal of Accountancy* 72: 448–54 (reprinted in *The Accounting Review* 31, 1956: 389–94).

Pixley, F.W. (1881) *Auditors: their duties and responsibilities under the Joint-Stock Companies Act and the Friendly Societies and Industrial and Provident Societies Acts*, London: Good (reprinted New York: Arno Press, 1976).

Plant, A., Eatwell, J., Milgate, M. and Newman, P. (eds) (1987) 'Coase, R.H'., *The New Palgrave: a dictionary of economics*, Vol. 3, London: Macmillan: 891.

Preinreich, G.A.D. (1938) 'Annual survey of economic theory: the theory of depreciation', *Econometrica* 6 (January): 219–41.

Preinreich, G.A.D. (1939) 'Economic theories of goodwill', *Journal of Accountancy* 64 (September): 169ff.

Preinreich, G.A.D. (posthumously edited by Richard B. Brief) (1996) *A landmark in accounting theory: the work of Gabriel A.D. Preinreich*, New York: Garland Publishing, Inc.

Previts, G.J. and Merino, B.D. (1979) *A history of accounting in America: an historical interpretation of the cultural significance of accounting*, New York: John Wiley & Sons.

Previts, G.J. and Robinson, T.R. (1994) 'William A. Paton (1889–1991): theorist and educator', in J.R. Edwards ed., *Twentieth-century accounting thinkers*, London: Routledge: 309–18.

Radcliff, T.A. and Munter, P. (1981) *Complete handbook of inflation accounting*, Englewood Cliffs, NJ: Prentice-Hall, Inc.

Rappaport, A. (1965) 'Seminar research on uniformity', *The Accounting Review* 40 (3, July): 643–8.

Rautenstrauch, W. (1922) 'The budget as a means of industrial control', *Chemical and Metallurgical Engineering* 27: 415–16.

Revsine, L. (1973) *Replacement cost accounting*, Englewood Cliffs, NJ: Prentice-Hall, Inc.

Richardson, A. (1996) 'Canada', in M. Chatfield and R. Vangermeersch eds, *The history of accounting: an international encyclopedia*, New York: Garland Publishing, Inc.: 89–92.

Rogers, D.M. (1932) 'Development of the modern business budget', *Journal of Accountancy* 53: 186–205.

Roover, F.E. de (1937) 'Cost accounting in the sixteenth century', *The Accounting Review* 12: 226–37 (reprinted in D. Solomons ed., *Studies in costing*, London: Sweet & Maxwell: 53–71).

Roover, F.E. de (1941) 'Partnership accounts in twelfth century Genua', *Bulletin of the Business Historical Society* 15: 87–92.

Roover, R. de (1938) 'Characteristics of bookkeeping before Paciolo', *The Accounting Review* 13 (2): 140–8.

Roover, R. de (1944) 'Early accounting problems of foreign exchange', *The Accounting Review* 19 (4): 381–406.

Rorem, C.R. (1928) *Accounting method*, Chicago, IL: University of Chicago Press.

Rosen, L.S. (1972) *Current value accounting and price level restatements*, Toronto: Canadian Institute of Chartered Accountants.

Rosen, L.S. and DeCoster, D.T. (1969) 'Funds statements: a historical perspective', *The Accounting Review* 44 (January): 124–36.

Rowland, S.W. (1936) 'Some modern difficulties in the measurement of profit', in A. Plant ed., *Some modern business problems*, London: Longmans.

Rowland, S.W. (1938) 'The nature and measurement of income: a rejoinder – II', *The Accountant* 15 (October): 519–22.

Roy, G.D. (1963) *A survey of accounting ideas*, Calcutta: Alpha Publishing Concern.

Salmonson, R.F. (1969) *Basic financial accounting theory*, New York: Wadsworth.

Sanders, T.H., Hatfield, H.R. and Moore, U. (1938) *A statement of accounting principles*, New York: American Accounting Association.

Schmidt, F. (1930a) 'The impact of replacement value', *The Accounting Review* 5 (September): 235–42.

Schmidt, F. (1930b) 'The basis of depreciation charges', *Harvard Business Review* 8 (April): 257–64.

Schmidt, F. (1931) 'Is appreciation profit?', *The Accounting Review* 6 (December): 289–93.

Shenkir, G. (ed.) (1978) *Carman G. Blough: his professional career and accounting thought*, New York: Arno Press.

Scott, D.R. (1925) *Theory of accounts*, New York: Henry Holt & Co.

Scott, D.R. (1931) *The cultural significance of accounts*, New York: Henry Holt & Co.

Skinner, R.M. (1972) *Accounting principles: a Canadian viewpoint*, Toronto: Canadian Institute of Chartered Accountants.

Solomons, D. (1948) 'Income: true and false', *The Accountants Journal* (October): 366–70.

Solomons, D. (1968) 'The historical development of costing', in D. Solomons ed., *Studies in cost analysis*, London: Sweet & Maxwell: 3–49 (reprinted in Thomas E. Lee ed., *The closure of the accounting profession*, Vol. 2, New York: Garland Publishing, Inc., 1990: 36–82).

Soulé, G. (1900) *Soulé's manual of auditing, suggestions to auditors, receivers, and liquidators, and points on higher and expert accounting*, New Orleans, LA: published by the author (6th edn, 1905; later edition 1982).

Sprague, C.E. (1904) *The accountancy of investment*, New York: Business Publishing Co. (revised edition Ronald Press, 1914).

Sprague, C.E. (1907–08) 'The philosophy of accounts', *Journal of Accounting* (January) (reprinted as *The philosophy of accounts*, 4th edn, New York: Ronald Press, 1918, 1920; reprint edition Houston, TX: Accounting Classics Series, Scholars Book Co., 1972).

Sprouse, R.T. and Moonitz, M. (1962) *A tentative set of broad accounting principles for business enterprises*, New York: AICPA.

Stamp, J. (1921) 'The relation of accountancy to economics', *The Incorporated Accountants' Journal*, November: 41–52.

Stamp, J. and Nelson, C.H. (1924) *Business statistics and financial statements*, London: Modern Business Institute.

Staub, W.A. (1942) *Auditing developments during the present century*, Cambridge, MA: Harvard University Press.

Staubus, G.J. (1996) 'Moonitz, Maurice (1910–)' in M. Chatfield and R. Vangermeersch eds, *The history of accounting: an international encyclopedia*, New York: Garland Publishing, Inc.: 423–4.

Sterling, R.R. (1970) *Theory of the measurement of enterprise income*, Lawrence, KA: University Press of Kansas.

Sterret, J. (1907) 'Professional ethics', *AAPA Year-Book 1907*: 108–33 (reprinted in *Journal of Accountancy*, October: 407–31).

Stone, J.R.N. (1947) 'Definition and measurement of the national income and related totals, Appendix to *Measurement of national income and the construction of social accounts*', Report of the Sub-Committee on National Income Statistics of the League of Nations Committee of Statistical Experts (Studies and Reports on Statistical Methods No. 7). Geneva, United Nations.

Strachan, W. (1909) *Cost accounting*, London: Stevens & Haynes.

Sweeney, H.W. (1927) 'Effects of inflation on German accounting', *The Journal of Accountancy* (March): 180–91.

Sweeney, H.W. (1936) *Stabilized accounting*, New York: Harper & Brothers, 1936 (reprint edition, with a Foreword by W.A. Paton, New York: Holt, Reinhart & Winston, 1964).

Taggart, H.-F. (ed.) (1964) *Paton on accounting: selected writings of W.A. Paton*, Ann Arbor, MI: University of Michigan.

Theiss, E.L. (1937) 'The beginnings of business budgeting', *The Accounting Review* 12: 43–55.

Thomas, A.L. (1969) *The allocation problem in financial accounting*, Chicago, IL: American Accounting Association.

Thompson, J.E. (1996) 'Paton, William Andrew (1889–1991)', in M. Chatfield and R. Vangermeersch eds, *The history of accounting: an international encyclopedia*, New York: Garland Publishing, Inc.: 453–4.

Vance, L.L. (1943) 'The authority of history in the inventory valuation', *The Accounting Review* 18 (July): 219–27.

Vance, L.L. (1950) *Scientific methods for auditing*, Berkeley, CA: University of California Press.

Vangermeersch, R. (1988) *Alexander Hamilton Church: a man for all seasons*, New York: Garland Publishing, Inc.

Vangermeersch, R. (1996) 'Standard costing', in M. Chatfield and R. Vangermeersch, eds, *The history of accounting: an international encyclopedia*, New York: Garland Publishing, Inc.: 550–3.

Vatter, W.J. (1947) *The fund theory of accounting and its implications for financial reports*, Chicago, IL: University of Chicago Press.

Vatter, W.J. (1950) *Managerial accounting*, New York: Prentice-Hall.

Veblen, T. (1899) *Theory of the leisure class: an economic study of the evolution of institutions* (re-edited by Stuart Chase, New York: The Modern Library, 1934).

Walton, S. (ed.) (1918) 'Student's Department: "Increase in Market Price of Fixed Assets"', *The Journal of Accountancy* (November): 393.

Webster, N.E. (1941) 'Accountancy organizations 1882–1900', *The New York Society of Accountants, Bulletin* 19 (4, December): 2–7.

Whitmore, J. (1906–07) 'Factory accounting as applied to machine shop', *Journal of Accountancy* (August 1906–January 1907).

Whitmore, J. (1908) 'Shoe factory cost accounts', *Journal of Accountancy* 4 (1): 12–25.

Whittington, G. (1994) 'The LSE Triumvirate and its contribution to price change accounting', in J.R. Edwards ed., *Twentieth-century accounting thinkers*, London: Routledge: 252–73.

Wildman, J.R. (1926) 'A research program', *The Accounting Review* 1: 43–54.

Woolf, A.H. (1912) *A short history of accountants and accountancy*, London: Gee (reprint: Osaka: Nihon Soseki, 1974).

Yamey, B.S. (1940) 'The functional development of double-entry bookkeeping', *Accountant* 103: 333–42.

Yamey, B.S. (1944) 'Edward Jones's "English system of bookkeeping"', *The Accounting Review* 19: 407–16.

Yamey, B.S. (1949) 'Scientific book-keeping and the rise of capitalism', *Economic History Review*, 2nd series, 1: 99–113 (reprinted in T.W. Baxter ed., *Studies in Accounting*, London: Sweet & Maxwell: 13–30.

Zeff, S.A. (ed.) (1974) 'A profile of F.R.M. De Paula', *Accounting Historians Journal* 1 (1–4): 31.

Zeff, S.A. (ed.) (1982) *Accounting principles through the years: the views of professional and academic leaders, 1938–1954*, New York: Garland Publishing, Inc.

Zeff, S.A. (1987) 'Leaders of the accounting profession: 14 who made a difference', *Journal of Accountancy* (May): 91–137.

Zeff, S.A. (1994) 'Truth in accounting: the ordeal of Kenneth MacNiel (1895–1972)', in J.R. Edwards ed., *Twentieth-century accounting thinkers*, London: Routledge: 334–63 (originally published in *The Accounting Review* 57, July 1982: 528–53).

Zeff, S.A, Demski, J. and Dopuch, N. (eds) (1979) 'Essays in honor of William A. Paton: pioneering accounting theorist', Ann Arbor, MI: Research Division, Graduate School of Business Administration, University of Michigan.

12 Accounting research in the English language area – second half of the twentieth century

Abdel-khalik, A.R. (1980) *Government regulation of accounting*, Accounting Series, No. 11, University Press of Florida.

Abdel-khalik, A.R. (1983) *Financial reporting by private companies: analysis and diagnosis*, Stamford, CT: Financial Accounting Standards Board.

Abdel-khalik, A.R. (1985) 'The effects of LIFO-switching and firm ownership on executives' pay', *Journal of Accounting Research* (Autumn 1985): 427–47.

Abdel-khalik, A.R. (1997) *The Blackwell encyclopedic dictionary of accounting*, Cambridge, MA: Blackwell Business Series,

Abdel-khalik, A.R. and Ajinkya, B.B. (1979) *Empirical research in accounting: a methodological point of view*, Sarasota, FA: American Accounting Association (AAA).

Abdel-khalik, A.R. and Ajinkya, B.B. (1983) 'An evaluation of "the everyday accountant" and researching his reality', *Accounting, Organizations and Society* 8 (4): 375–84.

Abdel-khalik, A.R. and Keller, T.F. (eds) (1978) *The impact of accounting research on practice and disclosure*, Durham, NC: Duke University Press.

Abdel-khalik, A.R. and Keller, T. F. (1979) *Earnings or cash flows: an experiment on functional fixation and the value of the firm*, Sarasota, FA: AAA.

Abdel-khalik, A.R. and Solomon, I. (eds) (1988) *Research opportunities in auditing: the second decade*, Sarasota, FA: AAA.

Abdel-khalik, A.R., Regier, P.R. and Reiter, S.A. (1989) 'Some thoughts on empirical research in positive theory', in T.J. Frecka ed., *The state of accounting research as we enter the 1990s*, Urbana-Champaign, IL: University of Illinois, Department of Accountancy: 153–80.

Abdolmohammadi, M.J. (1987) 'Decision support and expert systems in auditing: a review and research directions', *Accounting and Business Research* 17 (Spring): 173–85.

Abdolmohammadi, M.J., Burnaby, P., Greenlay, L. and Thibodeau, J. (1997) 'Environmental accounting in the United States: from control and prevention to remediation', *Asian Pacific Journal of Accounting* 4 (December): 199–217.

Adam, D. (1970) – see Chapter 4.

Adelberg, A.H. (1975) 'Auditing on the march: ancient times to the twentieth century', *Internal Auditor* (November/December): 35–47.

Afterman, A.B. (1995) *International accounting, financial reporting, and analysis: a U.S. perspective*, Boston, MA: Warren, Gorham & Lamont.

Agami, A.M. and Kollaritsch, F.P. (1983) *Annotated international accounting bibliography: 1972–1981*, Sarasota, FA: AAA.

Agrawal, S.P. (1987) 'On the conceptual framework of accounting', *Journal of Accounting Literature* 6: 165–78.

Ajinkya, B.B. and Gift, M.J. (1984) '"Corporate managers" earnings forecasts and symmetrical adjustments of market expectations', *Journal of Accounting Research* 22 (Autumn): 425–44.

Albach, H. (1965) 'Grundgedanken einer synthetischen Bilanztheorie' (Basic thoughts to a synthetic accounting theory), *Zeitschrift für Betriebswirtschaft* 35: 21–31.

Alexander, S.S. (1950) 'Income measurement in a dynamic economy', *Five monographs on business income*, New York: Study Group on Business Income, American Institute of Accountants.

American Accounting Association (AAA) (1957) *Accounting and reporting standards for corporate financial statements and preceding statements and supplements*, Madison, WI: AAA.

American Accounting Association (AAA) (1966) *A statement of basic accounting theory*, Evanston, IL: AAA.

American Accounting Association (AAA) (1977) *A statement on accounting theory and theory acceptance*, Sarasota, FA: AAA.

American Accounting Association (AAA) (1979) *Notable contributions to the periodical international accounting literature, 1975–1978*, Sarasota, FA: AAA.

American Institute of Certified Public Accountants (AICPA) (1953) 'Restatement and revision of research bulletins' *Accounting Research Bulletin* No. 43, New York: AICPA.

American Institute of Certified Public Accountants (AICPA) (1954) *Generally accepted auditing standards: their significance and scope*, New York: AICPA.

American Institute of Certified Public Accountants (AICPA) (1963) *Reporting financial effects of price-level changes*, New York: ICPA.

American Institute of Certified Public Accountants (AICPA) (1972) *Establishing financial accounting standards: report on the establishment of accounting principles* (Wheat Report), New York: AICPA.

American Institute of Certified Public Accountants (AICPA) (1973) *Objectives of financial statements: report of the study group on the objectives of financial statements* (Trueblood Report), New York: AICPA.

Amernic, J.H. (1989) *Accounting and collective bargaining in the not-for-profit sector*, Hamilton, ON: Society of Management Accountants of Canada (French translation as *La comptabilité et la négociation collective dans les organismes sans but lucrative*, Hamilton, ON: SMAC, 1989).

Amernic, J.H. and Beechy, T.H. (1984) 'Accounting students' performance and cognitive complexity: some empirical evidence', *The Accounting Review* 59 (April): 300–13.

Amershi, A.H. (1986) 'Discussion: a model of standard setting in auditing', *Contemporary Accounting Research* 3 (Fall): 93–101.

Amershi, A.H. and Butterworth, J.E. (1988) 'Explorations in the theory of single and multiple agents agencies', in G.A. Feltham, A.H. Amershi and W.T. Ziemba eds, *Economic analysis of information and contracts*, Norwell, MA: Kluwer Academic Press: 197–219.

Amershi, A.H. and Cheng, P. (1990) 'Intrafirm resource allocation: the economics of transfer pricing and cost allocation in accounting', *Contemporary Accounting Research* 7 (Fall): 61–99.

Amershi, A.H. and Sunder, S. (1987) 'Failure of stock prices to discipline managers in a rational expectations economy', *Journal of Accounting Research* 25 (Autumn): 177–95.

Amey, L.R. (1969) *The efficiency of business enterprises*, London: George Allen and Unwin, Ltd.

Anderson, J.A. (1976) *A comparative analysis of selected income measurement theories in financial accounting*, Sarasota, FA: AAA.

Anderson, J.T. and Previts, G.J. (1984) 'Accounting accreditation and schools of accountancy in the United States', *Advances in Accounting* 1: 89–104.

Ansari, S.L., Bell, J. and the CAM-I Target Cost Core Group (1997) *Target costing, the next frontier in strategic cost management*, Homewoold, IL: Irwin Professional Publications.

Anthony, R.N. (1957) 'Cost concepts for control', *The Accounting Review* 32 (April): 229–34.

Anthony, R.N. (1975) 'The rebirth of cost accounting', *Management Accounting* 57 (4): 13–16.

Anthony, R.N. (1985) *Reference guide to essentials of accounting*, Reading, MA: Addison-Wesley Publishing Co.

Anthony, R.N., Dearden, J. and Govindarajan, V. (1992) *Management control systems*, 7th edn, Boston, MA: Richard D. Irwin, Inc.

Antle, R. (1982) 'The auditor as an economic agent', *Journal of Accounting Research* 20 (Autumn, Part II): 503–27.

Antle, R. (1984) 'Auditor independence', *Journal of Accounting Research* 22 (1): 1–20.

Antle, R. (1996) 'Demski, Joel S. (1940–)', in M. Chatfield and R. Vangermeersch eds, *The history of accounting: an international encyclopedia*, New York, NY: Garland Publishing, Inc.: 196–7.

Antle, R. and Demski, J. (1988) 'The controllability principle in responsibility accounting', *The Accounting Review* 63 (October): 700–18.

Antle, R. and Smith, A. (1986) 'An empirical investigation of the relative performance evaluation of corporate executives', *Journal of Accounting Research* 24, (1): 1–39.

Anton, Hector R. (1953) *A critical evaluation of techniques of analysis of the flow of business funds*, PhD dissertation, University of Minnesota (published in revised version as *Accounting for the flow of funds*, New York, NY: Houghton and Mifflin, 1962).

Archer, S. (1993) 'On the methodology of constructing a conceptual framework for financial accounting', in M.J. Mumford and K.V. Peasnell eds, *Philosophical perspectives on accounting: essays in honour of Edward Stamp*, London: Routledge: 62–122 (see also *Accounting, Business and Financial History* 2, September 1992 and March 1993: 199–228 and 81–108, respectively).

Archer, S. (1998) 'Mattessich's "Critique of accounting": a review article', *Accounting and Business Research* 28 (3): 297–316.

Archibald, T.R. (1967) 'The return to straight-line depreciation: an analysis of a change in accounting method', *Journal of Accounting Research* 5 (Supplement): 164–80.

Arens, A.A., May, R.G. and Dominiak, G. (1970) 'A simulated case for audit education', *The Accounting Review* 45 (July): 573–8.

Argyris, C. (1952) *The impact of budgets on people*, Ithaca: School of Business and Public Administration, and Controllership Foundation.

Armitage, H.M. (1985) *Linking managerial accounting systems with computer technology*, Hamilton, ON: The Society of Management Accountants.

Arthur Andersen & Co. (1984) *Objectives of financial statements for business enterprises*, Chicago, IL: Arthur Andersen & Co.

Ashton, R.H. (1974) 'An experimental study of internal control judgments', *Journal of Accounting Research* 12 (1): 143–57.

Ashton, R.H. (1982) *Human information processing in accounting*, Sarasota, FA: AAA.

Ashton, R.H. (1983) *Research in audit decision making: rationale, evidence and implications*, Vancouver, BC: Canadian CGA's Research Foundation.

Ashton, R.H. (ed.) (1984) *The evolution of behavioral accounting research: an overview*, New York: Garland Publishing, Inc.

Ashton, R.H. and Brown, P.R. (1980) 'Descriptive modeling of auditors' internal control judgments: replication and extension', *Journal of Accounting Research* 18 (Spring): 269–77.

Ashton, R.H., Willingham, J.W. and Elliott, R.K. (1987) 'An empirical analysis of audit delay', *Journal of Accounting Research* 25 (2): 275–92.

Atiase, R.K. (1985) 'Predisclosure information, firm capitalization, and security price behavior around earnings announcements', *Journal of Accounting Research* 23 (1): 21–36.

Atiase, R.K. and Tse, S. (1986) 'Stock valuation models and accounting information: a review and synthesis', *Journal of Accounting Literature* 5: 1–34.

Atiase, R.K., Bamber, L.S. and Tse, S. (1989) 'Timeliness of financial reporting, the firm size effect, and stock price reactions to annual earnings announcements', *Contemporary Accounting Research* 5 (Spring): 526–52.

Atkinson, A. (1987a) *Intra-firm cost and resource allocations: theory and practice*, Toronto, ON: The Canadian Academic Accounting Association.

Atkinson, A. (1987b) *Cost estimation in management accounting: six case studies*, Hamilton, ON: The Society of Management Accountants of Canada.

Atkinson, A. and Feltham, G.A. (1982) 'Agency theory research and financial accounting standards', in S. Basu and A.J. Milburn eds, *Research to support standard setting in financial accounting: a Canadian perspective*, Toronto, ON: Clarkson Gordon Foundation: 260ff.

Atkinson, A., Bakakrishnan, R., Booth, R.P., Cote, J.M., Groot, T., Malmi, T., Roberts, H., Uliana, E. and Wu, A. (1997) 'New directions in management accounting research', *Journal of Management Accounting Research* 9: 79–108.

Aukrust, O. (1955) *Nasjonalregnskap – teoretiske prinsipper*, Oslo: Statistik Sentralbyrå.

Australian Accounting Research Foundation (1980) *Current cost accounting: omnibus exposure draft*, Melbourne: AARF.

Australian Accounting Standards Committee (1975) *A method of current value accounting committee*, Melbourne: AASC.

Australian Society of Accountants (1974) *Accounting for price and price-level changes*, Melbourne: ASA.

Avilà, H. E., González Bravo, L. and Scarano, E.R. (1988) 'An axiomatic foundation of accounting', working paper, Buenos Aires: Institute of Accounting Research, University of Buenos Aires.

Babad, Y.M. and Balachandran, B.V. (1989) 'Operational matrix accounting', *Contemporary Accounting Research* 5 (Spring): 775–92.

Baber, W.R. (1983) 'Toward understanding the role of auditing in the public sector', *Journal of Accounting and Economics* 5 (December): 213–27.

Backer, M. (ed.) (1966a) *Modern accounting theory*, Englewood Cliffs, NJ: Prentice-Hall, Inc.

Backer, M. (1966b) 'Accounting theory and multiple reporting objectives', in M. Backer ed., *Modern accounting theory*, Englewood Cliffs, NJ: Prentice-Hall, Inc.: 43963.

Baetge, J., Berndt, H., Bruns, H.G., Busse von Colbe, W., Coenenberg, A.G., Korst, H., Lederle, H., Metze, H.A., Ordelheide, D., Pingsten, H.-D., Reinhard, H., Schnicke, C., Schwitters, J., Seeberg, T., Slepe, G., Urban, P., Weber, H., Weismüller, A. and Wysocki, K. (1995) 'Working group on external reporting of the Schmalenbach-Gesellschaft, Deutsche Gesellschaft für Betriebswirtschaft' (Committee on External Reporting of the Schmalenbach Society for Business Economics), *Accounting Horizons* 9 (September): 92–9.

Bailey Jr, A.D. and Gray, J. (1968) 'A study of the importance of the planning horizon on reports utilizing discounted future cash flows', *Journal of Accounting Research* 6 (1): 98–105.

Baiman, S. (1975) 'The evaluation and choice of internal information systems within a multiperson world', *Journal of Accounting Research* 13 (Spring): 1–15.

Baiman, S. (1982) 'Agency research in managerial accounting: a survey', *Journal of Accounting Literature* 1 (Spring): 154–213 (reprinted in Richard Mattessich, ed., *Modern accounting research: history, survey, and guide*, Vancouver, BC: Canadian Certified General Accountants' Research Foundation, 1984: 251–94).

Baiman, S. (1990) 'Agency research in managerial accounting: a second look', *Accounting, Organizations and Society* 15: 341–71 (reprinted in R. Mattessich ed., *Accounting research in the 1980s and its future relevance*, Canadian Certified General Accountants' Research Foundation, 1991: 221–56).

Balachandran, B.V., Li, L. and Magee, R.P. (1987) 'On the allocation of fixed and variable costs from service departments', *Contemporary Accounting Research* 4 (Fall): 164–85.

Ball, R.J. and Brown, P.R. (1968) 'An empirical evaluation of accounting income numbers', *Journal of Accounting Research* 6 (Autumn): 159–78.

Ball, R.J. and Foster, G. (1982) 'Corporate financial reporting: a methodological review of empirical research', *Journal of Accounting Research* 20 (Supplement): 161–234.

Ball, R.J. and Smith Jr, C.W. (eds) (1992) *The economics of accounting policy choice*, New York: McGraw-Hill, Inc.

Ballwieser, W. and Kuhner, C. (1994) *Accounting standards and economic stability*, Bergisch Gladbach: Wohkittel Verlag.

Balzer, W. and Mattessich, R. (1991) 'An axiomatic basis of accounting: a structuralist reconstruction', *Theory and Decision* 30: 213–43.

Balzer, W. and Mattessich, R. (2000) 'Formalizing the basis of accounting', in W. Balzer and C.U. Moulines eds, *Structuralistic knowledge representation: paradigmatic examples*, Amsterdam: Poznan Studies in the Philosophy of the Sciences and the Humanities: 99–126.

Bandyopadhyay, S.P., Hanna, J.D. and Richardson, G. (1994) 'Capital market effects of U.S.–Canada GAAP Differences', *Journal of Accounting Research* 32 (2): 262–77.

Banerjee, B. (1984) *Financial policy and management accounting*, Calcutta: The World Press, Pvt. Ltd.

Banerjee, B. (1994) *Accounting education in India*, Calcutta: DSA in Commerce, University of Calcutta.

Baran, A., Lakonishok, J. and Ofer, A.R. (1980) 'The information content of general price level adjusted earnings: some empirical evidence', *The Accounting Review* 55 (January): 22–35.

Barth, M.E. (1980) 'Fair value accounting: evidence from investment securities and the market valuation of banks', *The Accounting Review* 69 (January): 1–25.

Barth, M.E. and Landsman, W.R. (1995) 'Fundamental issues related to using fair value accounting for financial reporting', *Accounting Horizons* 9 (4, December): 97–107.

Barth, M.E., Beaver, W.H. and Landsman, W.R. (1992) 'The market valuation implications of net periodic pension cost components', *Journal of Accounting and Economics* 15 (March): 27–62.

Barth, M.E., Beaver, W.H. and Landsman, W.R. (1998) 'Relative valuation roles of equity book value and net income as a function of financial health', *Journal of Accounting and Economics* 25 (1): 1–34.

Basu, S. and Hanna, J.R. (1975) *Inflation accounting: alternatives, implementation issues and some empirical evidence*, Hamilton, ON: Society of Industrial Accountants of Canada.

Basu, S. and Milburn, A.J. (eds) (1982) *Research to support standard setting in financial accounting: a Canadian perspective*, Toronto, ON: Clarkson Gordon Foundation.

Baxter, W.T. (1949) 'Accountants and the inflation', *Proceedings of the Statistical Society* 9 (February): 1–19.

Baxter, W.T. (1967) 'Accounting values: sale price versus replacement cost', *Journal of Accounting Research* 5 (2): 208–14.

Baxter, W.T. (1975) *Accounting values and inflation*, New York: McGraw-Hill, Inc.

Baxter, W.T. and Davidson, S. (eds) (1962) *Studies in accounting theory*, Homewood, IL: Richard D. Irwin, Inc.

Beattie, V. (2005) 'Moving the financial accounting research front forward: the UK contribution', *The British Accounting Review* 37 (1): 85–114.

Beaver, W.H. (1968) 'Information content of annual earnings announcements', *Journal of Accounting Research* 6 (Supplement): 67–92.

Beaver, W.H. (1981) *Financial reporting: an accounting revolution*, Englewood Cliffs, NJ: Prentice-Hall, Inc.

Beaver, W.H. and Demski, J.S. (1974) 'The nature of financial accounting objectives: a summary and synthesis', *Journal of Accounting Research* 12 (Supplement): 170–87.

Beaver, W.H. and Demski, J.S. (1979) 'The nature of income measurement', *The Accounting Review* 54 (January): 38–46.

Beaver, W.H. and Landsman, W.R. (1983) *Incremental information content of Statement 33 disclosures*, Stamford, CT: Financial Accounting Standards Board.

Beaver, W.H. and Wolfson, M.A. (1992) 'The role of market value accounting in the regulations of insured depository institutions', in J.R. Barth and R.D. Brumbaugh Jr eds, *The reform of federal deposit insurance*, New York: Harper Business.

Beaver, W.H., Griffin, P.A. and Landsman, W.R. (1982) 'The incremental information content of replacement cost earnings', *Journal of Accounting and Economics* 4 (July): 15–39.

Beaver, W.H., Kettler, P. and Scholes, M. (1970) 'The association between market determined and accounting determined risk measures', *The Accounting Review* 45 (October): 654–82.

Beaver, W.H., Lambert, R. and Morse, D. (1980) 'The information content of security prices', *Journal of Accounting and Economics* 2 (March): 3–28.

Bedford, N. (1965) *Income determination theory*, Reading, MA: Addison-Wesley Publishing Co.

Bedford, N. (1997) *A history of accounting at the University of Illinois at Urbana-Champaign*, Urbana-Champaign, IL: Center for International Education and Research in Accounting.

Beechy, T.H. (1989) *Accounting for changing prices*, Boston, MA: Allyn and Bacon, Inc.

Beedle, A. (1981) *Accounting for local government in Canada: the state of the art*, Vancouver, BC: The Canadian Certified General Accountants' Research Foundation.

Belkaoui, A. (1984) *Socio-economic accounting*, Westport, CT: Quorum Books.

Belkaoui, A. (1985a) *Accounting theory*, 2nd edn, San Diego, CA: Harcourt Brace Jovanovich, Publishers (1st edn, 1981).

Belkaoui, A. (1985b) *International accounting: issues and solutions*, Westport, CT: Quorum Books.

Belkaoui, A. (1988) *The new environment in international accounting: issues and practices*, New York: Quorum Books.

Belkaoui, A. (1989) *The coming crisis in accounting*, New York: Quorum Books.

Belkaoui, A. (1999) *Value added reporting and research: state of the art* (Internet Resource Computer File), Westport, CT: Quorum Books.

Benbasat, I. and Dexter, A. (1979) 'Value and events approaches to accounting: an experimental evaluation', *The Accounting Review* 54 (October): 735–49.

Benston, G.J. (1967) 'Published corporate accounting data and stock prices', *Journal of Accounting Research* 5 (Supplement): 1–14.

Benston, G.J. (1982a) 'Accounting and corporate accountability', *Accounting, Organizations and Society* 7 (2): 87–106.

Benston, G.J. (1982b) 'An analysis of the role of accounting standards for enhancing corporate governance and social responsibility', *Journal of Accounting and Public Policy* 1 (1): 5–17.

Berg, J., Daley, L., Gigler, F. and Kanodia, C. (1990) *The value of communication in agency contracts: theory and experimental evidence*, Vancouver, BC: The Canadian Certified General Accountants' Research Foundation.

Berliner C. and Brimson, J. (1986) *Cost management for today's advanced manufacturing*, Boston, MA: HBS Press.

Bernard, V.L. (1987) 'Cross-sectional dependence and problems in inference in market-based accounting research', *Journal of Accounting Research* 25 (1): 1–48.

Bernard, V.L. (1989) 'Capital markets research in accounting during the 1980s: a critical review', in T.J. Frecka ed., *The state of accounting research as we enter the 1990s*, Urbana-Champaign, IL: University of Illinois, Department of Accountancy: 72–120.

Bernard, V.L. and Ruland, R.G. (1987) 'The incremental information content of historical cost and current cost income numbers: time-series analyses for 1962–1980', *The Accounting Review* 62 (October): 707–22.

Bernard, V.L., Merton, R.C. and Palepu, K.G. (1995) 'Mark-to-market accounting for banks and thrifts: lessons from the Danish experience', *Journal of Accounting Research* 33 (Spring): 1–32.

Berry, L.E. and Harwood, G.B. (1984) *Governmental and nonprofit accounting: a list of readings*, Homewood, IL: R.D. Irwin, Inc.

Bhattacharyya, A.K. (1988) *Modern accounting concepts in Kautilya's Arthaśāstra*, Calcutta: Firma KLM Private Ltd.

Bhimani, A. (ed.) (1996) *Modern cost management, European perspectives*, Englewood Cliffs: Prentice-Hall, Inc.

Biggs, S.F., Mock, T.J. and Watkins, P.R. (1989) *Analytical review procedures and processes in auditing*, Vancouver, BC: Canadian Certified General Accountants' Research Foundation.

Bindon, K.R. and Gernon, H. (1987) 'International accounting research', *Advances in Accounting* 4: 43–68.

Blanchard, B.S. (1978) *Design and manage to Life Cycle Cost*, Oregon: M/A (Japanese version co-authored with I. Miyauchi as: Raifu saikuru kosuto keisan no jissai, Tokyo: Rojisutikusu Gakkai Nihon Shibu, 1949).

Blazenko, G.W. and Scott, W.R. (1986) 'A model of standard setting in auditing', *Contemporary Accounting Research* 3 (Fall): 68–92.

Bloom, R. and Debessay, A. (1984) *Inflation accounting: reporting of general and specific price changes*, New York: Praeger Publishers.

Blough, C.B. (1957) *Practical applications of accounting standards*, New York: AICPA.

Blough, C.B. (1967) 'Development of accounting principles in the United States', *Berkeley symposium on the foundations of financial accounting*, Berkeley, CA: University of California: 1–14 (reprinted in W.G. Shenkir ed., *Carman G. Blough: his professional career and accounting thought*, New York: Arno Press, 1978).

Boland, L.A. and Gordon, I.M. (1992) 'Criticizing positive accounting theory', *Contemporary Accounting Research* 9 (Fall): 142–70.

Bologna, J. and Lindquist, R.J. (1987) *Fraud auditing and forensic accounting*, New York: Wiley.

Boritz, J.E., Gaber, B.G. and Lemon, W.M. (1987) *An experimental study of review of preliminary audit strategy by external auditors*, Toronto, ON: Canadian Academic Accounting Association.

Borthick, A.F. and West, O.W. (1987) 'Expert systems: a new tool for the professional', *Accounting Horizons* 1 (March): 9–16.

Boutell, W.S. (1965) *Auditing with computers*, Berkeley, CA: University of California Press.

Bowen, R.M., Burgstahler, D. and Daley, L.A. (1987) 'The incremental information content of accrual versus cash flows', *The Accounting Review* 62 (October): 723–47.

Brahmagupta (AD 628) *Brahma-Sphuta-Sidd'hánta*, India.

Bray, F.S. (1953) *Four essays in accounting theory*, London: Oxford University Press.

Bray, F.S. (1966) 'Accounting postulates and principles', in M. Backer ed., *Modern accounting theory*, Englewood Cliffs, NJ: Prentice-Hall, Inc.: 28–47.

Brief, R.P. (1968) 'Depreciation theory and capital gains', *Journal of Accounting Research* 6 (1): 149–51.

Brief, R.P. (1969) 'An econometric analysis of goodwill: some findings in a search for valuation rules', *The Accounting Review* 44 (January): 20–37.

Brief, R.P. (1983) 'Valuation, matching and earnings: the continuing debate', in J.F. Gaertner ed., *Selected papers from the Charles Waldo Haskins accounting history seminars of Texas, 1983*, San Antonio, TX: San Antonio University: 15–30.

Brief, R.P. (1987) 'Corporate financial reporting at the turn of the century', *Journal of Accountancy* 163 (5): 142–57.

Brief, R.B. and Peasnell, K.V. (eds) (1996) *Clean surplus: a link between accounting and finance*, New York: Garland Publishing, Inc.

Briloff, A.J. (1972) *Unaccountable accounting*, New York: Harper & Row.

Briloff, A.J. (1981) *Truth about corporate accounting*, New York: Harper & Row.

Briloff, A.J. (1986) 'Standards without standards/principles without principles/fairness without fairness', *Advances in Accounting* 3: 2250.

Briloff, A.J. (1990) 'Accountancy and society, a covenant desecrated', *Critical Perspectives in Accounting* 1: 5–30.

Bromwich, M. (1977a) 'The use of present value valuation models in published accounting reports', *The Accounting Review* 52 (July): 587–96.

Bromwich, M. (1977b) 'The general use of certain "current" value asset valuation bases', *Accounting and Business Research* 7 (Autumn): 242–9.

Bromwich, M. and Hopwood, A.G. (eds) (1986) *Research and current issues in management accounting*, London: Pitman Publishing Ltd.

Bromwich, M. and Wells, M.C. (1983) 'The usefulness of a measure of wealth', *Abacus* 19: 119–29.

Brown, L.D. (ed.) (1987) *The modern theory of financial reporting*, Flano, TX: Business Publications, Inc.

Brown, L.D., Gardner, J.C. and Vasarhelyi, M.A. (1989) *Accounting research directory: the database of accounting literature*, 2nd edn, New York: Markus Wiener Publishing, Inc.

Brown, P.R., Foster, G. and Noreen, E.W. (1984) *Security analysts multi-year earnings forecasts and the capital market*, Sarasota, FL: AAA.

Brown, R.M. (1980) 'Short-range market reaction to changes to LIFO accounting using preliminary earnings announcement dates', *Journal of Accounting Research* 18 (Spring): 38–63.

Bruns Jr, W.J. and DeCoster, D.T. (eds) (1969) *Accounting and its behavioral implications*, New York: McGraw-Hill.

Bruns Jr, W.J. and Kaplan, R.S. (eds) (1987) *Accounting and management: field study perspectives*, Boston, MA: Harvard Business School Press.

Bublitz, B., Frecka, T.J. and McKeown, J.C. (1985) 'Market association tests and FASB Statement No. 33 disclosures: a reexamination', *Journal of Accounting Research* 23 (Supplement): 1–23.

Buchanan II, H. and Gaumnitz, B.R. (1987) 'Accountants and "insider" trading', *Accounting Horizons* 1 (December): 7–12.

Buckley, J.W. (ed.) (1969) *Contemporary accounting and its environment*, Belmont, CA: Dickenson Publishing Co., Inc.

Buckley, J.W., Kircher, P. and Mathews, R.L. (1968) 'Methodology in accounting theory', *The Accounting Review* 43 (April): 274–83.

Buenos-Campos, E. (1972) 'Análisis conceptual de la planificación contable' (Conceptual analysis of accounting planning), *Revista Española de Financiación y Contabilidad* (January/April): 73–94.

Burchell, S., Clubb, C. and A. Hopwood, A.G. (1985) Accounting in its social context: towards a history of value added in the United Kingdom, *Accounting, Organizations, and Society* 10 (4): 381–413.

Burchell, S., Clubb, C., Hopwood, A.G., Highes, J. and Nahapiet, J. (1980) 'The roles of accounting in organizations and society', *Accounting, Organizations, and Society* 5 (1): 5–27.

Burgstahler, D. and Sundem, G. (1989) 'The evolution of behavioral accounting research, 1968–1987', *Behavioral Research in Accounting* 1: 75–108.

Burns, J.O. and Needles Jr, B.E. (eds) (1994) *Accounting education, twenty-first century: the global challenges*, New York: Elsevier Science, Inc. and International Accounting Section of the AAA.

Bushman, R.M. and Indjejikian, R.J. (1993) 'Accounting income, stock price and managerial compensation', *Journal of Accounting and Economics* 16 (January/April/July): 3–23.

Busse von Colbe, W. (1996) 'Accounting and the business economics tradition in Germany', *The European Accounting Review* 5 (3): 413–34.

Busse von Colbe, W. and Pohlmann, P. (1981) 'Contemporary issues in financial accounting: a European review', in F.D.S. Choi ed., *Multinational accounting: a research framework for the eighties*, Ann Arbor, MI: University of Michigan Research Press: 175–87.

Butterworth, J.E. (1967) 'Accounting systems and management decision: an analysis of the role of information in the managerial decision process', doctoral dissertation, Berkeley, CA: University of California.

Butterworth, J.E. and Falk, H. (1986) *Financial reporting: theory and application to the oil and gas industry in Canada*, Hamilton, ON: The Society of Management Accountants of Canada.

Buzby, S.L. (1986) 'Discussion of current cost disclosures and nondisclosures: Canadian evidence', *Contemporary Accounting Research* 3 (Fall): 45–9.

Campbell, L.G. (1985) *International auditing: a comparative survey of professional requirements in Australia, Canada, France, West Germany, Japan, the Netherlands, the U.K. and the U.S.A.*, New York: St Martin's Press.

Canadian Institute of Chartered Accountants (CICA) (1981) 'Reporting the effects of changing prices: re-exposure draft', Toronto, ON: CICA.

Canadian Institute of Chartered Accountants (CICA) (1982) 'Section 4510: reporting the effects of changing prices', *CCA Handbook*, Toronto, ON: CICA.

Carlson, M.L. and Lamb, J.W. (1981) 'Constructing a theory of accounting: an axiomatic approach', *The Accounting Review* 56 (July): 554–73.

Chabrak, N. (2005) 'Tony Tinker: un comptable "radical"' (Tony Tinker: a 'radical' accountant), in B. Colasse ed., *Les grands auteurs en comptabilité*, Éditions EMS: 291–305.

Chambers, R.J. (1957) 'Detail for a blueprint', *The Accounting Review* 32 (April): 206–15.

Chambers, R.J. (1966) *Accounting, evaluation and economic behavior*, Englewood Cliffs, NJ: Prentice-Hall, Inc. (reprinted in Accounting Classics Series, Houston, TX: Scholars Books Co., 1975).

Chambers, R.J. (1967) 'Continuously contemporary accounting: additivity and action', *The Accounting Review* 42 (October): 751–7.

Chambers, R.J. (1980) *Price variation and inflation accounting*, Sydney: McGraw-Hill Co.

Chambers, R.J. (1993) 'Positive accounting and the PA cult', *Abacus* (March): 1–26.

Chantiri-Chaudemanche, R. (2005) 'David Solomons: d'une théorie de l'évaluation en comptabilité à une théorie comptable' (David Solomons: from an accounting theory of valuation to a theory of accounting), in B. Colasse ed., *Les grands auteurs en comptabilité*, Paris: Éditions EMS.

Charitou, A. and Katz, J.E. (1990) 'Valuation of earnings, cash flows, and their components: an empirical investigation', *Journal of Accounting, Auditing and Finance* New Series, 5, (4): 475–500.

Charnes, A. and Cooper, E.W. (1957) 'Management models and industrial applications of linear programming', *Management Science* 4 (October): 38–91.

Charnes, A. and Cooper, W.W. (1961) *Management models and industrial applications of linear programming*, vols 1 and 2, New York: John Wiley & Sons, Inc.

Charnes, A., Cooper, W.W. and Ijiri, Y. (1963) 'Break-even budgeting and programming to goals', *Journal of Accounting Research* 1 (March): 1–41.

Chatfield, M. (ed.) (1968) *Contemporary Studies in the Evolution of Accounting Thought*, Belmont, CA: Dickenson Publishing Co., Inc.

Chatfield, M. (1978) *A history of accounting thought*, 2nd edn, Hindsdale, IL: Krieger, 1978 (1st edn, 1974).

Chatfield, M. and Vangermeersch, R. (eds) (1996) *The history of accounting: an international encyclopedia*, New York: Garland Publishing, Inc.

Cheung, J.K. (1990) 'The valuation significance of exit values: a contingent-claims analysis', *Contemporary Accounting Research* 6 (Part II, Spring): 724–37.

Choi, F.D.S. and Mueller, G.G. (1984) *International accounting*, Englewood Cliffs, NJ: Prentice-Hall, Inc.

Choi, F.D.S. and Mueller, G.G. (eds) (1985) *Frontiers of international accounting*, Ann Arbor, MI: UMI Research Press.

Christenson, C. (1983) 'The methodology of positive accounting', *The Accounting Review* 58 (January): 1–22 (reprinted in R. Mattessich (ed.) (1984) *Modern accounting research: history, survey, and guide*, Vancouver, BC: CCGA Research Foundation: 131–49).

Chua, W.F. (1986) 'Radical developments in accounting thought', *The Accounting Review* 61 (October): 601–32.

Churchman, C.W. and Ackoff, R.L. (1955) 'Operational accounting and operations research', *Journal of Accountancy* 99 (2): 33–9.

Clarke, F.L. (1980) 'Inflation accounting and the accidents of history', *Abacus* 16 (2): 79–99.

Clarke, F.L. and Dean, G.W. (1990) *Contributions of Limperg and Schmidt to the Replacement Cost Debate in the 1920s*, New York: Garland Publishing.

Clarke, F.L. and Dean, G.W. (1996) 'Chambers Raymond John (1917–)', in M. Chatfield and R. Vangermeersch eds, *The history of accounting: an international encyclopedia*, New York: Garland Publishing, Inc.: 109–11.

Clarke, F.L., Dean, G.W. and Oliver, K.G. (1997) *Corporate collapse: regulatory accounting and ethical failure*, Melbourne: Cambridge University Press.

Coase, R.H. (1937) 'The nature of the firm', *Economica* 4: 386–405.

Coase, R.H. (1938) 'Business organizations and the accountant', *The Accountant* (1 October–17 December) (reprinted in David Solomons (ed.) (1952) *Studies in costing*, London: Sweet & Maxwell, Ltd: 105–58).

Coase, R.H. (1960) 'The problem of social cost', *Journal of Law and Economics* 3 (October): 1–44.

Coase, R.H. (1990) 'Accounting and the theory of the firm', *Journal of Accounting and Economics* 12 (January): 3–13.

Coenenberg, A.G. and Macharzina, K. (1976) 'Accounting for price changes: an analysis of current developments in Germany', *Journal of Business Finance and Accounting* 1 (3): 53–8.

Colasse, B. (2005a) 'Raymond John Chambers: pour une comptabilité continuellement actuelle', in B. Colasse ed., *Les grands auteurs en comptabilité*, Paris: Éditions EMS: 197–215.

Colasse, B. (ed.) (2005b) *Les grands auteurs en comptabilité* (The great authors of accounting), Paris: Corlet Éditions EMS.

Colebrooke, H.T. (1817/1973) *Algebra with arithmetic and mensuration from Sanskrit of Brahmegupta and Bháskara*, London: John Murray, 1817 (reprinted in Wiesbaden: Martin Sändig, 1973).

Collins, D.W., Rozeff, M.S. and Dhaliwal, D.S. (1981) 'The economic determinants of the market reaction to proposed mandatory accounting changes in the oil and gas industry: a cross-sectional analysis', *Journal of Accounting and Economics* 3 (March): 37–71.

Collins, D.W., Rozeff, M.S. and Salatka, W.K. (1982) 'The SEC's rejection of SAS No. 19: tests of market price reversal', *The Accounting Review* 57 (January): 1–17.

Collins, W.A. and Hopwood, W.S. (1980) 'A multi-variate analysis of annual earnings forecasts generated from quarterly forecasts of financial analysts and univariate time-series models', *Journal of Accounting Research* 18 (Autumn): 390–406.

Connell, N.A.D. (1987) 'Expert systems in accountancy: a review of some recent applications', *Accounting and Business Research* 17 (Summer): 221–34.

Cooke, T.E. and Kikuya, M. (1992) *Financial reporting in Japan: regulation, practice and environment*, Oxford: Blackwell Publishers, Ltd.

Cooper, D.J. (1983) 'Tidiness, muddle and things: commonalities and divergence in two approaches to management accounting research', *Accounting, Organizations and Society* 8 (3): 269–86.

Cooper, D.J., Scapens, R.W. and Arnold, J. (1983) *Management accounting research and practice*, London: Institute of Management Accountants.

Cooper, D.J., Greenwood, R., Hinnings, B. and Brown, J.L. (1998) 'Globalization and nationalism in a multinational accounting firm: the case of opening new markets in Eastern Europe', *Accounting, Organizations and Society* 12 (5/6): 531–48.

Cooper, R. and Kaplan, R.S. (1991) *The design of cost management systems*, Englewood Cliffs, NJ: Prentice-Hall, Inc.

Cooper, W.W. (1949) 'Social accounting: an invitation to the accounting profession', *The Accounting Review* 24 (July): 233–8.

Cooper, W.W. and Ijiri, Y. (1975) *Kohler's dictionary for accountants*, 2nd edn, Englewood Cliffs, NJ: Prentice-Hall, Inc.

Corbin, D.A. (1962) 'Revolution in accounting', *The Accounting Review* 37 (October): 626–35.

Corcoran, A.W. (1964) 'Matrix bookkeeping', *Journal of Accountancy* 117 (3): 60–6.

Cormier, D. and Magnan, M. (2005) 'Gerald Feltham: l'information comptable vue dans une perspective économique', in B. Colasse ed., *Les grands auteurs en comptabilité*, Paris: Éditions EMS: 239–53.

Cornick, D.L. (1981) *Auditing in the electronic environment: theory, practice and literature*, Mt Airy, MD: Lomon Books.

Courtis, J.K. (1985–86) 'An investigation into annual report readability and corporate risk–return relationships', *Accounting and Business Research* 16 (64): 285–94.

Crichfield, T., Dyckman, T. and Lakonishok, J. (1978) 'An evaluation of security analysts' forecasts', *The Accounting Review* 53 (April): 651–68.

Cushing, B.E. (1989) 'A Kuhnian interpretation of the historical evolution of accounting', *The Accounting Historians Journal* 16 (Fall): 1–41.

Cushing, B.E. and Loebbecke, J.K. (1986) *Comparison of audit methodologies of large accounting firms*, Sarasota, FA: AAA.

Cyert, R.M. and Ijiri, Y. (1974) 'Problems of implementing the Trueblood objectives report', *Journal of Accounting Research* 12 (Supplement): 29–42.

Cyert, R.M. and Trueblood, R.M. (1957) *Sampling techniques in accounting*, New York: Prentice-Hall, Inc.

Czyzeswski, A.B. and Hull, R.P. (1991) 'Improving profitability with Life Cycle Costing', *Journal of Cost Management* 5 (2, Summer): 20–7.

Daley, L.A. (1984) 'The valuation of reported pension measures for firms sponsoring defined pension plans', *The Accounting Research* 59 (April): 177–98.

Daley, L.A. (1994) 'Measurement, information and academic research', in The Ernst & Young Foundation and University of Waterloo School of Accountancy eds, *Measurement research in financial accounting*, Toronto, ON: The Ernst & Young Foundation: 40–8.

Daley, L.A. and Mueller, G.G. (1982) 'Accounting in the arena of world politics', *Journal of Accountancy* 153 (2): 40–53.

Davidson, S. (1966) 'The realization concept', in Morton Backer ed., *Modern accounting theory*, Englewood Cliffs, NJ: Prentice-Hall, Inc.: 99–116.

Davidson, S. and Weil, R.L. (1978) 'Income tax implications of various methods of accounting for changing prices', *Journal of Accounting Research* 16 (Supplement): 154–233.

Davidson, S., Rasch, S.F. and Weil, R.L. (1984) 'Behavior of the deferred tax credit account, 1973–82', *Journal of Accountancy* 158 (October): 138–42.

Davis, G.B. and Weber, R. (1983) *Auditing advanced EDP systems: a survey of practice and development of a theory*, Altamonte Springs, FA: The Institute of Internal Auditors.

Dean, G.W. and Clarke, F.L. (1990) *Replacement costs and accounting reform in post World War I Germany*, New York: Garland Publishing, Inc.

Dean, J. (1951) *Managerial economics*, New York: Prentice-Hall, Inc.

DeAngelo, L.E. (1981a) 'Auditor independence, "low balling", and disclosure regulation', *Journal of Accounting and Economics* 3 (August): 113–27.

DeAngelo, L.E. (1981b) *The auditor–client contractual relationship: an economic analysis*, Ann Arbor, MI: ULMI Research Press.

Deguchi, H. and Nakano, B. (1986) 'Axiomatic foundations of vector accounting', *Systems Research* 3 (1): 31–9.

Demski, J.S. (1967) 'An accounting system structured on a linear programming model', *The Accounting Review* 42 (4, Ocober): 701–12.

Demski, J.S. (1988) 'Positive accounting theory: a review', *Accounting, Organizations and Society* 13 (6): 623–8.

Demski, J.S. and Feltham, G.A. (1972) 'Forecast evaluation', *The Accounting Review* 47 (July): 533–48.

Demski, J.S. and Feltham, G.A. (1976) *Cost determination: a conceptual approach*, Ames, IO: Iowa State University Press.

Demski, J.S. and Feltham, G.A. (1978) 'Economic incentives in budgetary control systems', *The Accounting Review* 53 (April): 336–59.

Demski, J.S., Patell, J.M. and Wolfson, M.A. (1984) 'Decentralized choice of monitoring systems', *The Accounting Review* 59 (January): 16–34.

Devine, C. (1985) *Essays in accounting theory*, 5 vols, Sarasota, FA: AAA.

Devine, C.T. (1950a) *Cost accounting and analysis*, New York: Macmillan Co.

Devine, C.T. (1950b) 'Cost accounting and pricing policies', *The Accounting Review* 25 (October): 384–9.

Devine, C.T. (1960) 'Research methodology and accounting theory formation', *The Accounting Review* 35 (March): 87–399.

Dhaliwal, D.S. (1980) 'The effect of the firm's capital structure on the choice of accounting methods', *The Accounting Review* 55 (January): 78–84.

Dharan, B.G. (1984) 'Expectation models and potential information content of oil and gas reserve value disclosures', *The Accounting Review* 59 (April): 199–217.

Dittenhofer, M. (1988) 'Research in governmental accounting and auditing', *Advances in International Accounting* 2: 201–3.

Dopuch, N. (1989a) 'The auto- and cross-sectional correlations of accounting research', in T.J. Frecka ed., *The state of accounting research as we enter the 1990s*, Urbana-Champaign, IL: University of Illinois, Department of Accountancy: 40–59.

Dopuch, N. (1989b) 'The impact of regulations on financial accounting research', *Contemporary Accounting Research* 5 (Spring): 494–500.

Dopuch, N. and Drake, D.F. (1966) 'The effect of alternative accounting rules for non-subsidiary investments' (Empirical research in accounting: selected studies), *Journal of Accounting Research* 4 (Supplement): 192–219.

Dopuch, N. and Pincus, M. (1988) 'Evidence on the choice of inventory accounting methods: LIFO versus FIFO', *Journal of Accounting Research* 26 (Spring): 28–59.

Dopuch, N. and Revsine, L. (eds) (1973) *Accounting research 1960–1970: a critical evaluation*, Urbana, IL: Center for International Education and Research in Accounting.

Dopuch, N. and Sunder, S. (1980) 'FASB's statements on objectives and elements of financial accounting: a review', *The Accounting Review* 55 (January): 1–21.

Duke, G.L., Neter, J. and Leitch, R.A. (1982) 'Power characteristics of test statistics in the auditing environment: an empirical study', *Journal of Accounting Research* 20 (Spring): 42–67.

Duke, G.L., Neter, J. and Leitch, R.A. (1985) *Behavior of test statistics in the audit environment*, Sarasota, FA: AAA.

Dyckman, T.R. (1968) 'Review of "Yuji Ijiri, *The foundations of accounting measurement: a mathematical, economic, and behavioral inquiry*"', *The Accounting Review* 43 (January): 199–210.

Dyckman, T.R. (1969) *Investment analysis and general price-level adjustments*, Evanston, IL: AAA.

Dyckman, T.R. and Morse, D. (1986) *Efficient capital markets and accounting: a critical analysis*, 2nd edn, Englewood Cliffs, NJ: Prentice-Hall, Inc.

Dyckman, T.R. and Zeff, S.A. (1984) 'Two decades of the journal of accounting research', *Journal of Accounting Research* 22 (Spring): 225–97.

Dyckman, T.R., Gibbins, M. and Swieringa, R.J. (1978) 'Experimental and survey research in financial accounting: a review and evaluation', in A.R. Abdel-khalik and T.F. Keller eds, *The impact of accounting research on practice and disclosure*, Durham, NC: Duke University Press: 48–105, 99–134 (reprinted in R. Mattessich (ed.) (1984) *Modern accounting research: history, survey and guide*, Vancouver, BC: Canadian Certified General Accountants' Research Foundation: 299–323).

Dykeman, F.C. (1982) *Forensic accounting*, New York: Wiley.

Eccles, R.G. (1985) 'Transfer pricing as a problem of agency', in J. Pratt and R. Zeckhauser eds, *Principals and agents: the structure of business*, Boston, MA: Harvard Business School Press: 151–86.

Edey, H.C. (1963) 'Accounting principles and business reality', *Accountancy* (November): 998–1002 and (December): 1083–8.

Edey, H.C. (1970) 'The nature of profit', *Accounting and business research* (Winter): 50–5.

Edey, H.C. and Peacock, A.D. (eds) (1954) *National income and social accounts*, London: Hutchinson.

Edwards, E.O. and Bell, P.W. (1961) *The theory and measurement of business income*, Berkeley, CA: University of California Press.

Edwards, J.D. (1960) *The history of public accounting in the United States*, East Lansing, MI: Bureau of Business and Economic Research.

Edwards, J.D. (1987) 'The AICPA's century of progress', *Accounting Historians Journal* 14 (1): 111–21.

Edwards, J.R. (ed.) (1994) *Twentieth-century accounting thinkers*, London: Routledge.

Edwards, J.R. (ed.) (2000) *A history of accounting: critical perspectives on business and management*, 4 vols, London: Routledge.

Egginton, D.A. (1985) 'Cash flow, profit and performance measures for external reporting: a rejoinder', *Accounting and Business Research* 15 (58): 109–12.

Enthoven, A.J.H. (1977) *Accounting systems in third world economies*, Amsterdam: North-Holland Publishing.

Enthoven, A.J.H. (1982) *Current value accounting*, Dallas, TX: University of Texas.

Enthoven, A.J.H. (1988) 'The future of international standards in government accounting', *Advances in International Accounting* 2: 205–28.

Epstein, M.J. (1996) *Measuring corporate environmental performance: best practice for costing and measuring an effective environmental strategy*, Chicago, IL: Irwin, Professional Publishing.

Espahbodi, R. and Hendrickson, H. (1986) 'A cost–benefit analysis of accounting for inflation', *Journal of Accounting and Public Policy* 5 (Spring): 3155.

Espahbodi, R. and Tehranian, H. (1989) 'Stock market reactions to the issuance of FAS 33 and its preceding exposure drafts', *Contemporary Accounting Research* 5 (Spring): 575–91.

Evans III, J.H. (1980) 'Optimal contracts with costly conditional auditing', *Journal of Accounting Research* 18 (Supplement): 108–28.

Falk, H. (1979) 'Current value accounting preferences: the case for Canada', *International Journal of Accounting Education and Research* 14 (2): 29–46.

Falk, H. (1989) 'Contemporary Accounting Research': the first five years', *Contemporary Accounting Research* 5 (Spring): 816–26.

Falk, H. and Frucot, V. (1997) 'Perceived auditor independence', *Asia-Pacific Journal of Accounting* 4 (June): 93–107.

Falk, H. and Gordon, L.A. (1978) 'Assessing industry risk by ratio analysis: validation', *The Accounting Review* 53 (January): 216–27.

Falk, H. and Heintz, J.A. (1978) 'Assessing industry risk by ratio analysis: a reply', *The Accounting Review* 52 (January): 210–15.

Falk, H. and Heintz, J.A. (1982) 'Assessing industry risk by ratio analysis', *The Accounting Review* 50 (October): 758–79.

Felix Jr, W.L. and Kinney Jr, W.R. (1982) 'Research in the auditor's opinion formulation process: state of the art', *The Accounting Review* 57 (April): 245–71.

Feltham, G.A. (1967) *A theoretical framework for evaluating changes in accounting information for managerial decisions*, doctoral dissertation, Berkeley, CA: University of California.

Feltham, G.A. (1968) 'The value of information', *The Accounting Review* 43 (October): 684–96.

Feltham, G.A. (1972) *Information evaluation*, Sarasota, FA: AAA.

Feltham, G.A. (1984) 'Financial accounting research: contributions of information economics and agency theory', in R. Mattessich ed., *Modern accounting research: history, survey and guide*, Vancouver, BC: The Canadian Certified General Accountants Research Foundation: 179–207.

Feltham, G.A. and Demski, J.S. (1970) 'The use of models in information evaluation', *The Accounting Review* 45 (October): 623–40.

Feltham, G.A. and Hughes, J.S. (1988) 'Communication of private information in capital markets: contingent contracts and verified reports', in G.A. Feltham, A.H. Amershi and W.T. Ziemba eds, *Economic analysis of information and contracts: essays in honour of John E. Butterworth*, Boston, MA: Kluwer Academic Publishers: 271–317.

Feltham, G.A. and Xie, J. (1994) 'Performance measure congruity and diversity in multi-task principal/agent relations', *The Accounting Review* 69 (July): 429–53.

Feltham, G.A., Amershi, A.H. and Ziemba, W.T. (eds) (1988) *Economic analysis of information and contracts: essays in honour of John E. Butterworth*, Boston, MA: Kluwer Academic Publishers.

Ferrara, W.L. (1961) 'Overhead costs and income measurement', *The Accounting Research* 36 (January): 63–70.

Ferris, K.R. and Livingstone, J.L. (eds) (1987) 'Management planning and control', Columbus, OH: Century Publishing Co.

Financial Accounting Standards Board (FASB) (1974) *Conceptual framework for accounting and reporting: consideration of the report of the study group on objectives of financial statements*, Stamford, CN: FASB.

Financial Accounting Standards Board (FASB) (1979) 'Financial reporting of changing prices', *Statement of financial accounting standards no. 33*, Stamford, CT: FASB.

Financial Accounting Standards Board (FASB) (1994) 'Discussion of board agenda projects: present-value-based measurements (interest methods)', *FASB status report, no. 254*, Stamford, CT: FASB: 7.

Financial Accounting Standards Board (FASB) (1997) 'Discussion of board agenda projects: present value-based measurements', *Financial accounting standards board status report, no. 287*, Stamford, CT: FASB: 13.

Flamholtz, E.G. (1972) 'Toward a theory of human resource value in formal organizations', *The Accounting Review* 47 (October): 666–78.

Flamholtz, E.G., Das, T.K. and Tsui, A.S. (1985) 'Toward an integrative framework of organizational control', *Accounting, Organizations and Society* 10 (1): 35–50.

Fleischman, R. (ed.) (2005) *Accounting history*, 3 vols, Thousand Oaks, CA: Sage Publishing.

Fleischman, R. and Tyson, T.N. (1993) 'Cost accounting during the industrial revolution: the present state of historical knowledge', *Economic History Review* (August): 503–17.

Flesher, D.L. (1991) *The third-quarter century of the American accounting association, 1966–1991*, Sarasota, FA: AAA.

Fogarty, T.J. (1997) 'Towards progress in gender research in accounting: challenges for studies in three domains', *Asia-Pacific Journal of Accounting* 4 (June): 37–58.

Foster, G. (1980) 'Accounting policy decisions and capital market research', *Journal of Accounting and Economics* 2 (March 1980): 29–62.

Foster, G. (1986) *Financial statement analysis*, 2nd edn, Englewood Cliffs, NJ: Prentice-Hall.

Foster, G. and Horngren, C.T. (1988) 'Flexible manufacturing systems: cost management and cost accounting implications', *Journal of Cost Management* 2 (3): 16–24.

Foster, G. and Svenson, D.W. (1997) 'Measuring the success of activity-based cost management and its determinants', *Journal of Management Accounting Research* 9: 109–41.

Foster, G. and Young, M. (1997) 'Frontiers of management accounting research', *Journal of Management Accounting Research* 9: 63–77.

Francis, J.R. and Reiter, S.A. (1987) 'Determinants of corporate pension funding strategy', *Journal of Accounting and Economics* 9 (March 1987): 35–59.

Frecka, Thomas J. (ed.) (1989) *The state of accounting research as we enter the 1990s*, Urbana, IL: Department of Accountancy, University of Illinois at Urbana-Champaign.

Freeman, R.N. (1983), 'Alternative measures of profit margin: an empirical study of the potential information content of current cost accounting', *Journal of Accounting Research* 21 (Spring): 42–64.

Freeman, R.N. and Senyo Tse, S. (1989) 'Multiperson information content of accounting earnings confirmations and contradictions of previous earnings reports', *Journal of Accounting Research* 27 (Supplement): 49–84.

Frishkoff, P. (1982) *Financial reporting and changing prices: a review of empirical research*, Stamford, CT: FASB.

Frost, C.A. and Pownall, G. (1994) 'Accounting and disclosure practice in the United States and the United Kingdom', *Journal of Accounting Research* 32 (1): 75–102.

Fujita, Y. (1991) *An analysis of the development and nature of accounting principles in Japan*, New York: Garland Publishing, Inc.

Gaa, J.C. (1988) *Methodology foundations of standard setting for corporate financial reporting*, Sarasota, FA: AAA.

Gaa, J.C. (1994) *Auditors and society: the ethical foundations of public accounting*, Vancouver, BC: CGA-Canada Research Foundation.

Gaffikin, M.J.R. (1987) 'The methodology of early accounting theorists', *Abacus* 23 (Spring): 17–30.

Gaffikin, M.J.R. (1988) 'Legacy of the golden age: recent developments in the methodology of accounting', *Abacus* 24 (Spring): 16–36.

Gaffikin, M.J.R. (1994) 'Raymond Chambers (b. 1917)', in J.R. Edwards ed., *Twentieth-century accounting thinkers*, London: Routledge: 1–18.

Gaffikin, M.J.R. and Aitken, M.J. (1982) *The development of accounting theory: significant contributors to accounting thought in the twentieth century*, New York: Garland Publishing, Inc.

Gainen, J. and Locatelli, P. (1995) *Assessment for the new curriculum: a guide for professional accounting programs*, Sarasota, FA: AAA.

Galassi, G. (1978) *Sistemi contabili assiomatici.e. sistemi teorici deduttivi* (Axiomatic accounting systems and theoretical deductive systems), Bologna: Patron Editore.

Galassi, G. (1980) 'Capital-income relations, a critical analysis', *Gino Zappa, founder of concern economics*, Bologna: Academia Italian di Economic Aziendale: 28–49.

Gambling, T.E. (1974) *Societal accounting*, London, UK: George Allen & Unwin.

García García, M. (1972) 'Modernas tendencias metodológicas en contabilidad' (Modern methodological tendencies in accounting), *Revista Española de Financiación y Contabilidad* (January/April): 23–44.

Garner, P. (1954) *Evolution of cost accounting to 1925*, Tuscaloosa, AL: University of Alabama Press.

Gaumnitz, B.R., Nunamaker, T.R., Surdick, J.J. and Thomas, M.F. (1982) 'Auditor consensus in internal control evaluation and audit program planning', *Journal of Accounting Research* 20 (2, Part II): 745–55.

Gibbins, M. (1977) 'Human inference, heuristics and auditors' judgment process', *CICA auditing symposium* (at Laval University, Quebec City), Toronto, ON: Canadian Institute of Chartered Accountants.

Gibbins, M. (ed. and project director) (1994) *Contemporary accounting research: special education issue*, in English and French, Edmonton, AL: Canadian Academic Accounting Association.

Gibbins, M. and Hughes, P. (1982) 'Behavioral research and financial accounting standards', in P.A. Griffin ed., *Usefulness to investors and creditors of information provided by financial reporting: a review of empirical accounting*, 1st edn, Stamford, CT: Financial Accounting Standards Board, Chap. 6: 99–134 (reprinted in R. Mattessich (ed.) (1984) *Modern accounting research: history, survey, and guide*, Vancouver, BC: Canadian Certified General Accountants' Research Foundation: 347–60).

Gibbins, M. and Newton, J.D. (1987) 'Behavioral research, reporting standards, and the usefulness of information', in P.A. Griffin ed., *Usefulness to investors and creditors of information provided by financial reporting*, 2nd edn, Stamford, CT: FASB: 85–114.

Gibbins, M. and Newton, J.D. (1995) 'An empirical exploration of complex accountability in public accounting', *Journal of Accounting Research* 33 (2): 65–186.

Gibbins, M. and Wolf, F.M. (1982) 'Auditors' subjective decision environment: the case of a normal external audit', *The Accounting Review* 57 (January): 105–24.

Givoly, D. and Lakonishok, J. (1979) 'The information content on financial analysts' forecasts of earnings: some evidence on semi-strong inefficiency', *Journal of Accounting and Economics* 1 (3): 165–85.

Gjesdal, F. (1981) 'Accounting for stewardship', *Journal of Accounting Research* 19 (1): 208–31.

Goetz, B.E. (1967) 'Transfer prices: an exercise in relevancy and goal congruence', *The Accounting Review* 42: 435–40.

Goldberg, L. (1965) *An inquiry into the nature of accounting*, Evanston, IL: AAA.

Gonedes, N.J. and Dopuch, N. (1974) 'Capital market equilibrium, information production, and selecting accounting techniques: theoretical framework and review of empirical work', *Journal of Accounting Research* (Special Issue on *Studies in Financial Accounting Objectives*, 12 (Supplement): 48–129.

Gonedes, N.J. and Dopuch, N. (1989) *Analysis of financial statements: financial accounting and the capital market*, Sarasota, FA: AAA.

Gordon, L.A. and Loeb, S.E. (1997a) 'Environmental issues and accounting', *Journal of Accounting and Public Policy* 16 (Summer).

Gordon, L.A. and Loeb, S.E. (1997b) 'The legal liability of independent auditors', *Journal of Accounting and Public Policy* 16 (Winter).

Gordon, M.J. (1960) 'Scope and method of theory and research in the measurement of income and wealth', *The Accounting Review* 35 (October): 603–18.

Gorelik, G. (1994) 'The setting of accounting standards: Canada, the United Kingdom, the United States', *The International Journal of Accounting (Education and Research)* 29 (1): 95–122.

Grady, P. (1965) *Inventory of generally accepted accounting principles for business enterprises*, New York: AICPA.

Graves, O.F. (ed.) (1991) *The costing heritage*, Harrisonburg, VA: Academy of Accounting Historians.

Gray, S.J. (ed.) (1983) *International accounting and transactional decisions*, London: Butterworth.

Gray, S.J. and Vint, H.M. (1995) 'The impact of culture on accounting disclosures: some international evidence', *Asia-Pacific Journal of Accounting* 2 (December): 33–43.

Griffin, P.A. (1982) *Usefulness to investors and creditors of information provided by financial reporting: a review of empirical accounting research*, Stamford, CT: FASB, 1982 (2nd edn, 1987).

Guo, D. (1996) 'China', in M. Chatfield and R. Vangermeersch eds, *The history of accounting: an international encyclopedia*, New York: Garland Publishing, Inc.: 122–3.

Gutiérrez, J.M. (1990) 'An axiomatic approach to inflation accounting', *IMA Journal of Mathematics Applied in Business and Industry* 2: 197–207.

Gutiérrez, J.M. (1992) 'On the gearing adjustment, an axiomatic approach', *Theory and Decision* 33: 207–21.

Gutiérrez, J.M. and Whittington, G. (1997) 'Formal properties of capital maintenance and revaluation systems in financial accounting', *The European Accounting Review* 6 (3): 439–64.

Gynther, R.S. (1966) *Accounting for price-level changes: theory and procedures*, Oxford: Pergamon Press (reprinted 1978).

Gynther, R.S. (1970) 'Capital maintenance, price changes, and profit determination', *The Accounting Review* 45 (October): 712–30.

Hakansson, N.H. (1969) 'Normative accounting theory and the theory of decision', *International Journal of Accounting Education and Research* 4 (Spring): 33–47.

Hakansson, N.H. (1973) 'Empirical research in accounting', in N. Dopuch and L. Revsine eds, *Accounting research 1960–1970: a critical evaluation*, Urbana, IL: Center for International Accounting Education and Research: 33–47.

Hakansson, N.H., Kunkel, J.G. and Ohlson, J.A. (1982) 'Sufficient and necessary conditions for information to have social value in pure exchange', *Journal of Finance* 37 (5): 1169–81.

Hanna, J.R. (1972) 'An application and evaluation of selected alternative accounting income models', *International Journal of Accounting Education and Research* 8 (1): 135–67.

Hansen, P. (1962) *The accounting concept of profit: an analysis and evaluation in the light of the economic theory of income and capital*, Amsterdam: North Holland Publishing.

Harada, F. (1978) *Joho kakei ron* (Accounting in a new informational society), Tokyo: Dobunkan Publishing, Ltd.

Hayes, D.C. (1977) 'The contingency theory of managerial accounting', *The Accounting Review* 52 (January): 22–39.

Hayes, D.C. (1983) 'Accounting for accounting: a story about managerial accounting', *Accounting, Organizations and Society* 8 (2–3): 241–50.

Healy, P. (1985) 'The effect of bonus schemes on accounting decisions', *Journal of Accounting and Economics* 7 (1–3): 85–107.

Heath, L.C. (1987) 'Accounting, communication, and the Pygmalion syndrome', *Accounting Horizons* 1 (March): 1–8.

Heinen, E. (1978) 'Supplemented multi-purpose accounting', *The International Journal of Accounting, Education and Research* 14 (1): 115.

Hempel, G.H. and Simonson, D.G. (1992) 'The case for comprehensive market-value reporting', *Bank Accounting and Finance* 5 (Spring): 23–9.

Henderson, M.S. and Person, G. (1983) *Accounting theory: its nature and development*, Melbourne: Longan Cheshire, Ltd.

Hendriksen, E.S. (1982) *Accounting theory*, 4th edn, Homewood, IL: R.D. Irwin, Inc. (1st edn, 1977; a more recent edition, co-authored with van Breda, 1991) – for later edition and Russian translation, see also Chapter 15.

Herbert, L. (1987) *Auditing the performance of management*, New York: Van Nostrand Reinhold.

Herde, G. (1992) *Präzisierung dreier axiomatischer Theorien des Rechnungswesens in einer formalen Typentheorie* (Generalization of three axiomatic theories of accounting within a formal theory of types), Bamberg: Otto-Friedrich-Universität.

Hernández Esteve, E. (1995) 'A review of recent Spanish publications in accounting and financial history', *Accounting, Business and Financial History* 5 (2): 237–69.

Hicks, D.T. (1999) *Activity-based costing: making it work for small and mid-sized companies*, New York: John Wiley & Sons.

Hill, J.W. and Ingram, R.W. (1989) 'Selection of GAAP or RAP in the savings and loan industry', *The Accounting Review* 64 (October): 667–79.

Hilton, R.W. (1980) 'Integrating normative and descriptive theories of information processing', *Journal of Accounting Research* 18 (2): 477–505.

Hines, R.D. (1988) 'Popper's methodology of falsifications and accounting research', *The Accounting Review* 63 (October): 657–62.

Hoepen, M.A. van, Lambert, I.J. and Moster, F.J. (1989) 'The gearing adjustment in inflation accounting: the financing sequence assumption', *South African Journal of Business* Management 20 (3): 163–7.

Holmström, B. and Milgrom, P. (1991) 'Multitask principal-agent analysis: incentive contracts, asset ownership and job design', *Journal of Law, Economics and Organizations* 7: 24–52.

Holthausen, R.W. and Leftwich, R.W. (1983) 'The economic consequences of accounting choice: implications of costly contracting and monitoring', *Journal of Accounting and Economics* 5 (2): 77–117.

Holthausen, R.W. and Verrecchia, R.E. (1988) 'The effect of sequential information releases on the variance of price changes in an intertemporal multi-asset market', *Journal of Accounting Research* 26 (Spring): 82–106.

Holzer, H.P. (ed.) (1980) *Management accounting 1980: Proceedings of the University of Illinois Management Accounting Symposium*, Urbana-Champaign, IL: University of Illinois.

Holzer, H.P. (ed.) (1984) *International accounting*, New York: Harper & Row.

Holzer, H.P. and Schoenfeld, H.-M. (1963a) 'The German solution to the post-war price level problem', *The Accounting Review* 38 (April): 377–81.

Holzer, H.P. and Schoenfeld, H.-M. (1963b) 'The French approach to the post-war price level problem', *The Accounting Review* 38 (April): 382–8.

Holzer, H.P. and Tremblay, D. (1973) 'Accounting and economic development: the cases of Thailand and Tunisia', *International Journal of Accounting Education and Research* 9 (1): 67–80.

Honko, J. (1959) *Yrityksen vuositulos* (The annual income of an enterprise and its determination – a study from the standpoint of accounting and economics), Helsinki: Oy Weilin & Göös Ab.

Hopper, T.M. and Powell, A. (1985) 'Making sense of research into the organizational and social aspects of management accounting: a review of its underlying assumptions', *Journal of Management Studies* 22 (September): 429–65.

Hopper, T.M., Storey, J. and Willmott, H.C. (1987) 'Accounting for accounting: towards the development of a dialectical view', *Accounting, Organizations and Society* 12 (5): 437–56.

Hopwood, A.G. (1972) 'An empirical study of the role of accounting data in performance evaluation', *Journal of Accounting Research* 10 (Supplement): 156–82.

Hopwood, A.G. (1978) 'Towards an organizational perspective for the study of accounting and information systems', *Accounting, Organizations and Society* 3 (1), 3–14.

Hopwood, A.G. (1987) 'The archaeology of accounting systems', *Accounting, Organizations and Society* 12: 207–34.

Hopwood, A.G. (1988) *Accounting from the outside: the collected papers by Anthony G. Hopwood*, New York: Garland Publishing, Inc.

Hopwood, A.G. and Schreuder, H. (eds) (1984) *European contributions to accounting research – the achievements of the last decade*, Amsterdam: Free University Press.

Hopwood, W.S. and McKeown, J.C. (1985) 'The incremental informational content of interim expenses over interim sales', *Journal of Accounting Research* 23 (Spring): 161–74.

Hopwood, W.S. and Schaefer, T.F. (1989) 'Firm-specific responsiveness to input price changes and the incremental information in current cost income', *The Accounting Review* 64 (April): 313–28.

Hopwood, A.G., Bromwich, M. and Shaw, J. (eds) (1982) *Auditing research: issues and opportunities*, London: Pitman Books.

Horngren, C. (1956) 'The funds statement and its use by analysts', *Journal of Accountancy* (January): 55–9.

Horngren, C. (1962) *Cost accounting: a managerial emphasis*, Englewood Cliffs, NJ (best-selling text with many subsequent editions; see also Horngren, Foster and Datar).

Horngren, C. (1995) 'Management accounting: this century and beyond', *Management Accounting Research* 6 (September): 281–6.

Horngren, C., Foster, G. and Datar, S.M. (1994) *Cost accounting: a managerial emphasis*, 8th edn, Englewood Cliffs, NJ: Prentice-Hall, Inc.

Hoskin, R.E., Hughes, J.S. and Ricks, W.R. (1986) 'Evidence on the incremental information content of additional firm disclosures made concurrently with earnings', *Journal of Accounting Research* 24 (Supplement): 1–32.

Hughes, J.S. (1984) *A contract perspective on accounting valuation*, Sarasota, FA: AAA.

Hughes, J.S. and Ricks, W.E. (1987) 'Associations between forecast errors and excess returns near to earnings announcements', *The Accounting Review* 62 (January): 158–75.

Hughes, P.J. (1986) 'Signaling by direct disclosure under asymmetric information', *Journal of Accounting and Economics* 8 (June): 119–42.

Hughes, P.J. and Schwartz, E.S. (1988) 'The LIFO/FIFO choice: an asymmetric information approach', *Journal of Accounting Research* 26 (Supplement): 41–58.

Hunt III, H.G., (1985) 'Potential determinants of corporate inventory accounting decisions', *Journal of Accounting Research* 23 (Autumn): 448–67.

Hylas, R.E. and Ashton, R.H. (1982) 'Audit detection of financial statement errors', *The Accounting Review* 57 (October): 751–65.

Ijiri, Y. (1965a) 'Axioms and structures of conventional accounting measurement', *The Accounting Review* 40 (January): 36–53.

Ijiri, Y. (1965b) *Goal oriented models for accounting and control*, Amsterdam: North-Holland Publishing Co.

Ijiri, Y. (1967) *The foundations of accounting measures*, Englewood Cliffs, NJ: Prentice-Hall, Inc.

Ijiri, Y. (1975) *Theory of accounting measurement*, Sarasota, FA: AAA.

Ijiri, Y. (1981) *Historical cost accounting and its rationality*, Vancouver, BC: Canadian Certified General Accountants' Research Foundation.

Ijiri, Y. (1983) 'On the accountability-based conceptual framework of accounting', *Journal of Accounting and Public Policy* 2 (2): 75–81.

Ijiri, Y. (1989) *Momentum accounting and triple-entry bookkeeping: exploring the dynamic structure of accounting measurements*, Sarasota, FA: AAA.

Ijiri, Y. (1995) 'Segment statements and informativeness measures: managing capital vs. managing resources', *Accounting Horizon* 9 (September): 55–67.

Ijiri, Y. (1996) 'Academic research in accounting: the last 50 years – commentary', *Asia-Pacific Journal of Accounting* 3 (July): 83–6.

Ijiri, Y. and Kaplan, R.S. (1971) 'A model for integrating sampling objectives in auditing', *Journal of Accounting Research* 9 (1): 73–87.

Institute of Chartered Accountants of England and Wales (1980) *Statement of standard accounting practice no. 16: current cost accounting – provisional statement of standard accounting practice*, London: ICAEW.

Instituto Mexicano de Contadores Público (1975) *Price-level adjustments*, Mexico City: IMdCP.

Itami, H. (1977) *Adaptive behavior: management control and information analysis*, Sarasota, FA: AAA.

Ittner, C.D., Larker, D. and Randall, T. (1997) 'Activity based cost hierarchy', *Journal of Management Accounting Research* 9: 143–62.

Ives, M. (1987) 'Accountability and governmental financial reporting', *Journal of Accountancy* 164 (October): 130–4.

Jaedicke, R.K. (1961) 'Improving break-even analysis by linear programming', *N.A.A. Bulletin*, Section 1 (March).

Jaedicke, R.K. and Robichek, A.A. (1964) 'Cost–volume–profit analysis under conditions of uncertainty', *The Accounting Review* 39 (October): 917–26.

Jeanjean, T. (2005) 'Watts et Zimmerman: les pères fondateurs de la théorie positive de la comptabilité' (Watts and Zimmerman: the founding fathers of the positive theory of accounting), in B. Colasse ed., *Les grands auteurs en comptabilité*, Paris: Éditions EMS: 273–89.

Jelen, B. (2005) *The spreadsheet at 25: the invention that changed the world*, Uniontown, OH: Holy Macro and Independent Publishers Group, 2005.

Jensen, D.L. (1977) 'A class of mutual satisfactory allocations', *The Accounting Review* 52 (4): 842–56.

Jensen, M.C. and Meckling, W.M (1976) 'Theory of the firm: managerial behavior, agency cost, and ownership structure', *Journal of Financial Economics* 3 (October): 305–60.

Jensen, R.E. (1983) *Review of forecasts: scaling and analysis of expert judgments regarding cross-impacts of assumptions on business forecasts and accounting measures*, Sarasota, FA: AAA.

Johansson, S.-E. (1965) 'An appraisal of the Swedish system of investment reserves', *International Journal of Accounting and Education Research* 1: 85–92.

Johnson, H.T. and Kaplan, R.S. (1987) *Relevance lost: the rise and fall of management accounting*, Boston, MA: Harvard Business School Press.

Johnson, J.R., Leitch, R.A. and John Neter, J. (1981) 'Characteristics of errors in accounts receivable and inventory audits', *The Accounting Review* 56 (April): 270–93.

Johnson, W.B. and Dhaliwal, D.S. (1988) 'LIFO abandonment', *Journal of Accounting Research* 26 (2): 326–72.

Jones, R.C. (1956) *Effects of price level changes on business income, capital, and taxes*, AAA.

Joyce, E.J. (1976) 'Expert judgment in audit program planning', *Journal of Accounting Research* 14 (Supplement): 29–60.

Joyce, E.J. and Biddle, G.C. (1981) 'Anchoring and adjustment in probabilistic inference in auditing', *Journal of Accounting Research* 19 (Spring): 120–45.

Joyce, E.J. and Libby, R. (1982) 'Behavioral studies of audit decision making', *Journal of Accounting Literature* 1 (Spring): 103–23.

Jung, W. (1985) *Accounting decisions under asymmetric information*, Los Angeles, CA: University of California (doctoral dissertation).

Kam, V. (1986) *Accounting theory*, New York: John Wiley & Sons (2nd edn, 1989; 3rd edn, 1990).

Kanodia, C.S. (1985) 'Stochastic monitoring and moral hazard', *Journal of Accounting Research* 23 (1): 175–93.

Kao, J. (1994) 'Discussion of industry differences in the production of auditing services', *Auditing: A Journal of Practice and Theory* 13 (Audit Symposium): 146–50.

Kaplan, R.S. (1978) 'The information content of financial accounting numbers: a survey of empirical evidence', in A.R. Abdel-khalik and T.F. Keller eds, *The impact of accounting research on practice and disclosure*, Durham, NC: Duke University Press: 134–73 (reprinted in R. Mattessich(ed.) (1984) *Modern accounting research: history, survey and guide*, Vancouver, BC: Canadian Certified General Accountants Research Foundation: 325–45).

Kaplan, R.S. (1983) 'Measuring manufacturing performance: a new challenge for managerial accounting research', *The Accounting Review* (4, October): 686–705.

Kaplan, R.S. (1984) 'The Evolution of Management Accounting', *The Accounting Review* 59 (July): 390–418.

Kaplan R.S. and Atkinson, A.A. (1989) *Advanced management accounting*, 2nd edn, Englewood Cliffs, NJ: Prentice-Hall Inc.

Kaplan, R.S. and Norton, D.P. (1992) 'The balanced score-card: measures that drive performance', *Harvard Business Review* (January–February): 71–9.

Karen, D.D. and Herbst, A.F. (1990) 'Influence of profitability on a firm's lease-or-borrow decisions', *Advances in Accounting* 8: 25–36.

Kautilya, V.C. (ca. 300 BC) *Arthasástra* (for details, see Bhattacharyya 1988).

Kelly, L. (1983) 'Positive theory research: a review', *Journal of Accounting Literature* (Spring): 111–50.

Kelly, L. (1997) 'Determinants of divisional performance evaluation practices', *Journal of Accounting and Economics* 24 (3): 243–73.

Kemp Jr, R.S. (1987) 'An examination of the relationship of unfunded vested pension liabilities and selected elements of firm value', *Advances in Accounting* 5: 59–72.

Kim, Il.-W. and Song, J. (1990) 'U.S., Korea, and Japan: accounting practices in three countries', *Management Accounting* 72 (2): 26–30.

Kim, J.-B. and Ibrahim, M. (1997) 'An integrated cost-volume-market value analysis under uncertainty and fixed cost effects', *Asia-Pacific Journal of Accounting* 4 (June): 59–71.

King, R.D. and O'Keefe, T.B. (1986) 'Lobbying activities and insider trading', *The Accounting Review* 61 (January): 76–90.

Kinney Jr, W.R. (ed.) (1986) *Fifty years of statistical auditing*, New York: Garland Publishing, Inc.

Kinney Jr, W.R. and Uecker, W.C. (1982) 'Mitigating the consequences of anchoring in auditor judgments', *The Accounting Review* 57 (January): 55–69.

Kirkham, L. and Loft, A. (1993) 'Gender and the construction of the professional accountant', *Accounting, Organizations and Society* 18 (August): 507–58.

Klemstine, C.F. and Maher, M.W. (1983) *Management accounting research: 1926–1983*, Saratoga, FA: AAA – Management Accounting Section.

Koguchi, Y. (1990) 'Towards a regional water management accounting system', *The Annual of the Economic Research Institute of Chuo University* 21 (Tokyo): 121–50.

Kohler, E.L. (1952) 'Accounting concepts and national income', *The Accounting Review* 27 (January): 60–6.

Kohler, E.L. (1966) 'Accounting principles and professional societies', in Morton Backer ed., *Modern accounting theory*, Englewood Cliffs, NJ: Prentice-Hall, Inc.: 48–67.

Kojima, O. (1995) *Accounting history*, Osaka: A.N. Offset Co., Ltd (posthumous English version of *Kaikeisi Nyumon*, Tokyo: Moriama Shoten, 1987).

Kormendi, R.C. and Lipe, R. (1987) 'Earnings innovations, earnings persistence, and stock returns', *Journal of Business* 60 (July): 323–46.

Kosiol, E. (1978) *Pagatoric theory of financial income determination* (Theory of cash flow accounting for financial income determination), Urbana, IL: Center for Education and Research in Accounting.

Kren, L. and Liao, W.M. (1988) 'The role of accounting information in the control of organizations: a review of the evidence', *Journal of Accounting Literature* 7: 280–309.

Kuhn, T.S. (1962) *The structure of scientific revolutions*, Chicago, IL: University of Chicago Press (2nd edn, 1970).

Kunkel, J.G. (1982) 'Sufficient conditions for public information to have social value in a production and exchange economy', *Journal of Finance* 37 (4): 1005–13.

Küpper, H.-U. (1985) 'Investitionstheoretische Fundierung der Kostenrechnung' (Investment theoretical foundations of cost accounting), *Zeitschrift für betriebswirtschaftliche Forschung* 37: 26–46.

Lakonishok, J. and Ofer, A.R. (1985) 'The information content of general price level adjusted earnings: a reply', *The Accounting Review* 60 (October): 711–13.

Landsman, W. (1986) 'An empirical investigation of pension fund property rights', *The Accounting Review* 61 (October): 662–91.

Lapsley, I. (1988) 'Research in public sector accounting: an appraisal', *Accounting, Auditing and Accountability* 1: 21–33.

Larcker, D.F. and Revsine, L. (1983) 'The oil and gas accounting controversy: an analysis of economic consequences', *The Accounting Review* 58 (October): 706–32.

Laughlin, R.C., Lowe, E.A. and Puxty, A.G. (1982) 'Towards a value-neutral positive science of accounting: a comment', *Journal of Business Finance and Accounting* 9 (Winter): 567–72.

Lawson, G.H. (1985) 'The measurement of corporate performance on a cash flow basis: a reply to Mr. Egginton', *Accounting and Business Research* 15 (Spring): 99–108.

Lee, T.A. (1975) *Income and value measurement: theory and practice*, London: Thomas Nelson & Sons Ltd.

Lee, T.A. (1984) 'Cash flows and net realizable values: further evidence of the intuitive concepts', *Abacus* 20 (2): 125–37.

Lee, T.A. (1985) 'Cash flow accounting, profit and performance measurement: a response to a challenge', *Accounting and Business Research* 58 (Spring): 93–8.

Lee, T.A. (ed.) (1988) *The evolution of audit thought and practice*, New York: Garland Publishing, Inc.

Lee, T.A. (ed.) (1990) *The closure of the accounting profession*, 2 vols, New York: Garland Publishing, Inc.

Lee, T.A. and Parker, R.H. (eds) (1994) *The evolution of corporate financial reporting*, New York: Garland Publishing, Inc.

Leftwich, R. (1969) *A critical analysis of some behavioural assumptions underlying R.J. Chambers' Accounting, Evaluation and Economic Behavior*, St Lucia: University of Queensland Press.

Lemke, K.W. (1966) 'Asset valuation and income theory', *The Accounting Review* 41 (January): 33–41.

Lemke, K.W. (1982) 'Financial versus physical capital maintenance', in R.R. Sterling and K.W. Lemke, eds, *Maintenance of capital: financial versus physical*, Houston, TX: Scholars Book Co.: 287–323.

Lev, B. (1969) *Accounting and information theory*, Evanston, IL: AAA.

Lev, B. (1974) *Financial statement analysis: a new approach*, Englewood Cliffs, NJ: Prentice-Hall, Inc.

Lev, B. (1988) 'Toward a theory of equitable and efficient accounting policy', *The Accounting Research* (January): 1–22.

Lev, B. (1989) 'On the usefulness of earnings and earnings research: lessons and directions from two decades of empirical research', *Journal of Accounting Research* 27 (Supplement): 153–201.

Lev, B. and Ohlson, J.A. (1982) 'Market-based empirical research in accounting: review interpretation and extension', *Journal of Accounting Research* 20 (Supplement: *Current research methodologies in accounting: a critical evaluation*): 249–322.

Lewis, B.L. (1980) 'Expert judgment in auditing: an expected utility approach', *Journal of Accounting Research* 18 (Autumn): 594–602.

Libby, R. (1981) *Accounting and human information processing: theory and applications*, Englewood Cliffs, NJ: Prentice-Hall, Inc.

Libby, R. (1989) 'Experimental research and the distinctive features of accounting settings', in T.J. Frecka ed., *The state of accounting research as we enter the 1990s*, Urbana-Champaign, IL: University of Illinois, Department of Accountancy: 126–47.

Libby, R. and Frederick, D.M. (1990) 'Experience and the ability to explain audit findings', *Journal of Accounting Research* 28 (2): 348–67.

Lilien, S. and Pastena, V. (1982) 'Determinants of intra-method choice in the oil and gas industry', *Journal of Accounting and Economics* 4 (December): 145–70.

Lilien, S., Mellman, M. and Pastena, V. (1988) 'Accounting changes: successful versus unsuccessful firms', *The Accounting Review* 63 (October): 642–56.

Lin, J.Z. (1992) 'Chinese double-entry bookkeeping before the nineteenth century', *The Journal of Accounting Historians* 19 (December): 103–22.

Linsmeier, T.L., Lobo, G.J. and Kanaan, G.K. (1995) 'Dispersion in industry price changes and the relative association between alternative income measures and security returns', *Journal of Accounting, Auditing and Finance* 10 (2): 365–82.

Littleton, A.C. (1953) *Structure of accounting theory*, Menasha, WI: American Accounting Association and George Banta Publishing Co.

Littleton, A.C. and Yamey, B.S. (eds) (1956) *Studies in the history of accounting*, Homewood, IL: Richard D. Irwin, Inc.

Littleton, A.C. and Zimmerman, V.K. (1962) *Accounting theory: continuity and change*, Englewood Cliffs, NJ: Prentice-Hall, Inc.

Lobo, G.J. and Song, I.-M. (1989) 'The incremental information in SFAS No. 33, income disclosure over historical cost income and its cash and accrual component', *The Accounting Review* 64 (April): 329–43.

Longman, D. and Schiff, M. (1955) *Distribution cost analysis*, Homewood, IL: Richard D. Irwin.

Lowe, E.A., Puxty, G.A. and Laughlin, R.C. (1983) 'Simple theories for complex processes: accounting policy and the market for myopia', *Journal of Accounting and Public Policy* 2 (Spring): 19–42.

Luft, J.L. (1997) 'Long-term change in management accounting: perspectives from historical research', *Journal of Management Accounting Research* 9: 199–216.

Lukka, K. (1988) 'Budgetary biasing in organizations: theoretical framework and empirical evidence', *Accounting, Organizations and Society* 13 (3): 281–303.

Lukka, K. (1990) 'Ontology and accounting: the concept of profit', *Critical Perspectives of Accounting* 1: 239–62.

Lys, T. (1984) 'Mandated accounting changes and debt covenants: the case of oil and gas accounting', *Journal of Accounting and Economics* 6 (April): 39–65.

McCarthy, W.E. (1979) 'An entity-relationship view of accounting models', *The Accounting Review* 55 (October): 667–86.

McCarthy, W.E. (1982) 'The REA accounting model: a generalized framework for accounting systems in a shared data environment', *The Accounting Review* 57: 554–78.

McHaney, R. (2000) 'Spreadsheets', *Encyclopedia of computers and computer history*, Vol. 2 (M–Z), in R. Rojas ed., Chicago: Fitzroy Dearborn Publishers: 728–9.

Macharzina, K. (1988) 'Recent advances in European accounting: an assessment by use of the accounting culture concept', *Advances in International Accounting* 2: 131–46.

Macharzina, K. and Coenenberg, A.G. (1981) 'Current-cost or current purchasing accounting? An internationally based assessment of FASB Statement No. 33 on financial reporting and changing prices', *International Journal of Accounting* 16 (2): 149–62.

Macintosh, N.B. (2002) *Accounting, accountants and accountability: poststructuralist positions*, London, UK: Routledge.

Macintosh, N.B., Shaerer, N.B., Thornton, D.B. and Welker, M. (2000) 'Accounting as simulacrum and hyperreality: perspectives on income and capital', *Accounting, Organizations and Society* 25: 13–50.

Magee, R.P. (1986) *Advanced managerial accounting*, New York: Harper and Row.

Magee, R.P. (1988) 'Variable cost allocation in a principle/agent setting', *Accounting Research* 63 (January): 42–54.

Magliolo, J. (1986) 'Capital market analysis of reserve recognition accounting', *Journal of Accounting Research* 24 (Supplement): 69–108.

Magnusson, Å. (1974) *Rundgetuppföljining* (Budgetary control: an analysis), in Swedish with English Summary, Stockholm School of Economics, EFI: Stockholm.

Maher, M.W. (1981) 'The impact of regulation on controls: firms' response to the Foreign Corrupt Practices Act', *The Accounting Review* 56 (October): 751–70.

Manes, R.P. and Verrecchia, R.E. (1981–82) 'A new proposal for setting intra-company transfer prices', *Accounting and Business Research* 12 (46): 97–104.

Marker, M. (1995) 'Status report: the use of market value accounting at U.S. banks', *Bank Accounting and Finance* 8 (Summer): 25–30.

Mathews, R. (1960) 'Inflation and company finance', *The Accounting Review* 5 (1): 8–18.

Matsumura, E.M. (1988) 'Sequential choice under moral hazard', in G.A. Feltham, A.H. Amershi and W.T. Ziemba eds, *Economic analysis of information and contracts: essays in honour of John E. Butterworth*, Boston, MA: Kluwer Academic Publishers: 221–45.

Mattessich, R. (1957) 'Towards a general and axiomatic foundation of accountancy: with an introduction to the matrix formulation of accounting systems', *Accounting Research* 8 (October): 328–355 (reprinted in S.A. Zeff ed., *The accounting postulates and principles controversy of the 1960s*, New York: Garland Publishing, Inc., 1982; Spanish translation in *Technica Economica* (April 1958): 106–27).

Mattessich, R. (1961) 'Budget models and system simulation', *The Accounting Review* 36 (July): 384–97 (reprinted in T.H. Williams and C.H. Griffin eds, *Management information: a quantitative accent*, Homewood, IL: Richard D. Irwin, Inc., 1967: 636–54).

Mattessich, R. (1964a) *Accounting and analytical methods: measurement and projection of income and wealth in the micro- and macro-economy*, Homewood, IL: R.D. Irwin, Inc. (reprinted in the 'Accounting Classics Series', Houston, TX: Scholars Book Co., 1977; also in the 'Series of Financial Classics' of Reprints on Demand, Ann Arbor, MI: Microfilms International, 1979, still available; Japanese translation under the direction of Shinzaburo Koshimura, *Kaikei to Bunsekiteki-Hoho Jokan*, 2 vols, Tokyo: Dobunkan, Ltd, Vol. 1: 1972, Vol. 2: 1975; Spanish translation, by Carlos Luis García Casella and Maria del Carmen Ramírez de Rodríguez, Buenos Aires: La Ley, 2002).

Mattessich, R. (1964b) *Simulation of the firm through a budget computer program*, Homewood, IL: Richard D. Irwin, Inc. (reprint edition, 'Reprints on Demand Series', Ann Arbor, MI: Microfilms International, 1979).

Mattessich, R. (1978) *Instrumental reasoning and systems methodology*, Dordrecht, Holland: D. Reidel Publishing Co.

Mattessich, R. (ed.) (1984) *Modern accounting research: history, survey, and guide*, Vancouver, BC: Canadian General Certified Accountants' Research Foundation, 1984 (reprinted in 1989 and 1992, Supplementary volume under the title: *Accounting research in the 1980s and its future relevance*, Vancouver, BC: The Canadian Certified

General Research Foundation, 1991b and its French translation, *La recherche comptable dans les années 80 et sa pertinence future*, Vancouver, BC: CGA-Canada, 1993).

Mattessich, R. (1986) 'Fritz Schmidt (1892–1950) and his pioneering work in current value accounting in comparison to Edwards and Bells theory', *Contemporary Accounting Research* 2 (Spring): 157–78.

Mattessich, R. (1995) *Critique of accounting: examination of the foundations and normative structure of an applied discipline*, Westport, CT: Quorum Books.

Mattessich, R. (1995/2007) *Foundational research in accounting: professional memoirs and beyond*, 1st edn, Tokyo: Chuo University Press, 1995 (previously published serially in Japanese through five instalments in *Chuo Hyoron*, Chuo University Press (April 1992): 154–62; (July 1992): 149–59; (October 1992): 112–20; (January 1993): 124–34; (April 1993): 136–48; 2nd extended English edn, in *De Computis*, scheduled for 2007).

Mattessich, R. (1996a, 1996b) 'Academic research in accounting: the last 50 years'; and 'Accounting research: response to commentators', both *Asia-Pacific Journal of Accounting* 3 (1, June): 3–81, 109–35.

Mattessich, R. (2000) *The beginnings of accounting and accounting thought: accounting praxis in the Middle East (8000 B.C. to 2000 B.C.) and accounting thought in India (300 B.C. and the Middle Ages)*, New York: Garland Publishing, Inc.

Mattessich, R. (2003) 'Accounting representation and the Onion Model of Reality: a comparison with Baudrillard's Orders of Simulacra and his Hyperreality', *Accounting, Organization and Society* 28 (5, July): 443–70 (Spanish translation in the form of a separate Monograph under the title *La Representación contable y el modelo de capascepola de la realidad: una comparación con las 'Ordenes de Simulacro' de Baudrillard y su 'Hiperrealidad'*, Asociación Española de Contabilidad y Administración de Empresas, Madrid: AECA, 2004).

Mattessich, R. and Galassi, G. (2000) 'History of the spreadsheet: From matrix accounting to budget simulation and computerization', in ASEPUC (and E. Hernández Esteve) eds, *Accounting and history: a selection of the papers presented at the 8th World Congress of Accounting*, Madrid: Asociación Española de Contabilidad y Administración de Empresas – Ediciones Gráficas Ortega: 203–32.

Mautz, R.K. (1970) *Financial reporting by diversified companies*, New York: Financial Executives Research Foundation.

Mautz, R.K. and Sharaf, H.A. (1961) *The philosophy of auditing*, Madison, WI: AAA.

May, G.O. (1949) *Business income and price levels: an accounting study*, New York: Study Group on Business Income.

May, R.G. and Sundem, G.L. (1976) 'Research for accounting policy: an overview', *The Accounting Review* (4, October): 747–63.

Melumad, N.D. and Reichelstein, S. (1987) 'Centralization versus delegation and the value of communication', *Journal of Accounting Research* 25 (Supplement): 1–18.

Mepham, M.J. (1980) *Accounting models*, Afferton-Stockton: Polytech Publishers Ltd.

Mévellec, P. (1993) 'Plaidoyer pour une vision française de la méthode ABC' (translated by Michael Adler as 'Activity-based costing: a call for a French approach' in a paper available directly from the author: mevellec@iae.univ.nantes.fr), *Revue Française de Comptabilité* (251): 36–44 (this paper received the 'FMAC Prix de Concours 1994' and resulted from a project funded by a FNEGE–AFC research contract).

Michaelsen, R.H. (1987) 'An expert system for selecting tax shelters', *The Journal of the American Tax Association* (Fall): 7–21.

Michaelsen, R.H. (1988) 'Development of an expert computer system to assist in the classification of estate tax returns', *Accounting Horizons* 2 (December): 63–70.

Milburn, J.A. (1988) *Incorporating the time value of money within financial accounting*, Toronto, ON: Canadian Institute of Chartered Accountants.

Minemura, S. (1980) *Inflation accounting*, Tokyo: Keio Tsushin Co.

Mock, T.J. (1969) 'Comparative values of information structures', *Journal of Accounting Research* 7 (Supplement): 124–59.

Mock, T.J. (1971) 'Concepts of information value and accounting', *The Accounting Review* 46 (October): 765–78.

Mock, T.J. (1976) *Measurement and accounting information*, Sarasota, FA: AAA.

Mock, T.J. and Turner, F. (1981) *Internal accounting control evaluation and auditor judgment*, New York: AICPA.

Mock, T.J. and Vertinsky, I. (1985) *Risk assessment in accounting and auditing: a research report*, Vancouver, BC: The Canadian Certified General Accountants' Research Foundation.

Moonitz, M. (1961) *The basic postulates of accounting*, New York: AICPA.

Moonitz, M. (1973) *Changing prices and financial reporting*, Lancaster: ICRA.

Moonitz, M. (1974) *Obtaining agreement on standards in the accounting profession*, Sarasota, FA: AAA.

Moonitz, M. (1986) *History of accounting at Berkeley*, Berkeley, CA: Professional Accounting Program University of California.

Moonitz, M. and Littleton, A.C. (eds) (1965) *Significant accounting essays*, Englewood Cliffs, NJ: Prentice-Hall.

Moonitz, M. and Stamp, E. (1978) *International auditing standards*, London: Prentice-Hall International.

Morgan, G. (1983) 'Social science and accounting research: a commentary on Tomkins and Groves', *Accounting, Organizations and Society* 8 (4): 385–8.

Morris, D.M. (1992) 'The case against market-value accounting: a pragmatic view', *Bank Accounting and Finance* 5 (Spring): 30–6.

Morse, D. and Richardson, G.D. (1983) 'The LIFO/FIFO decision', *Journal of Accounting Research* 21 (1): 106–27.

Most, K.S. (1982) *Accounting theory*, 2nd edn, Columbus, OH: Grid Publishing, Inc.

Most, K.S. (1984) *International conflict of accounting standards: a research report*, Vancouver, BC: The Canadian Certified General Accountants' Research Foundation.

Mouck, T. (1989) 'The irony of "The Golden Age" of accounting methodology', *The Accounting Historians Journal* 16 (Fall): 85–106.

Mouck, T. (1993) 'The "Revolution" in financial reporting theory: a Kuhnian interpretation', *The Accounting Historians Journal* 20 (June): 33–56.

Moxter, A. (1982) *Betriebswirtschaftliche Gewinnermittlung* (Business economic profit determination), Tübingen: J.C.B. Mohr Verlag.

Moxter, A. (1984) *Bilanzlehre*, Bd. I: *Einführung in die Bilanzlehre* (Financial accounting, Vol. I: Introduction to financial statements), Wiesbaden: Gabler Verlag.

Mozes, H.A. (1992) 'A framework for normative accounting research', *Journal of Accounting Literature* 11: 93–120.

Mueller, G.G. (1963) 'The dimensions of the international accounting problem', *The Accounting Review* 38 (January): 142–5.

Mueller, G.G. and Walker, L.W. (1976) 'The coming of age of financial transnational reporting', *Journal of Accountancy* 142 (1): 67–74.

Murphy, G.J. (1980) 'Some aspects of auditing evolution in Canada', *Accounting Historians Journal* 7 (2): 45–61.

Murphy, G.J. (1987) 'The choice and consequences of generally accepted accounting alternatives', *Issues in Accounting Education* 2 (2): 373–82.

Murphy, G.J. (ed.) (1993) *A history of Canadian accounting thought and practice*, New York: Garland Publishing, Inc.

Namazi, M. (1985) 'Theoretical developments of principal-agent employment contract in accounting: the state of the art', *Journal of Accounting Literature* 4: 113–63.

Needles Jr, B.E. (ed.) (1985) *Comparative international auditing standards*, Sarasota, FA: AAA.

Nehmer, R.A. (1988) 'Accounting information systems as algebras and first order axiomatic models', doctoral dissertation, Urbana-Champaign, IL: Department of Accounting, University of Illinois.

Nelson, C. (1973) 'A priori research in accounting', in N. Dopuch and L. Revsine eds, *Accounting research 1960–1970: a critical evaluation*, Urbana, IL: Center for International Education and Research in Accounting: 3–19.

New Zealand Society of Accountants (1976) *Exposure draft: accounting in terms of current cost and values*, Wellington: NZSA.

New Zealand Society of Accountants (1978) *CCA guidelines*, Wellington: NZSA.

New Zealand Society of Accountants (1982) *Current cost accounting standard no. 1: information reflecting the effects of changing prices*, Wellington: NZSA.

Ng, D.S. and Stoeckenius, J. (1979) 'Auditing: incentives and truthful reporting', *Journal of Accounting Research* 17 (Supplement): 1–24.

Nissen, H.J., Damerow, P. and Englund, R.K. (1993) – see Chapter 3.

Nissen, H.J., Damerow, P. and Englund, R.K. (1993) *Archaic bookkeeping: early writing techniques of economic administration in the ancient Near East* (translated from German by Paul Larsen), Chicago, IL: Chicago University Press.

Nobes, C. and Parker, R.H. (eds) (1981) *Comparative international accounting*, Oxford: Philip Allan Publishers (2nd edn, 1985).

Noreen, E.W. (1988) 'The economics of ethics', *Accounting, Organization and Society* 13 (4): 359–69.

Noreen, E.W. and Burgstahler, D. (1997) 'Full-cost pricing and the illusion of satisficing', *Journal of Managerial Accounting Research* 9: 239–63.

Norman, R. and Ramirez, R. (1993) 'From value chain to value constellation: designing interactive strategy', *Harvard Business Review* 71 (4, July–August): 65–78.

Ohlson, J.A. (1983) 'Price earnings ratio and earnings capitalization under uncertainty', *Journal of Accounting Research* 21 (Spring): 141–54.

Ohlson, J.A. (1987a) *The theory of financial markets and information*, New York: North-Holland Publishing.

Ohlson, J.A. (1987b) 'On the nature of income measurement: the basic results', *Contemporary Accounting Research* (Fall): 1–15.

Ohlson, J.A. (1988) 'The social value of public information in production economies', in G.A. Feltham, A.H. Amershi and W.T. Ziemba eds, *Economic analysis of information and contracts*, Boston, MA: Kluwer Academic Publishers: 95–119.

Ohlson, J.A. (1989) 'Ungarbled earnings and dividends: an analysis and extension of the Beaver, Lambert, and Morse valuation model', *Journal of Accounting and Economics* 11 (July): 109–15.

Ohlson, J.A. (1990) 'A synthesis of security valuation theory and the role of dividends, cash flows, and earnings', *Contemporary Accounting Research* 7 (Spring 2-II): 648–76.

Ohlson, J.A. (1991) 'The theory of value and earnings, and an introduction to the Ball-Brown analysis', *Contemporary Accounting Research* 8 (Fall): 1–19.

Ohlson, J.A. (1995) 'Accounting earnings, book values, and dividends in security valuation', *Contemporary Accounting Research* 12 (Spring): 661–87.

Onida, P. (1970) *I moderni sviluppi della dottrina contabile nord-americana e gli studi economia aziendale*, Milan: A. Giuffrè (English version as a monograph under the title *Modern developments of the North American accounting doctrine and the studies of business economics*, Milan: A. Giuffrè, 1974).

Orbach, K.N. (1978) *Accounting as a mathematical measurement theoretic discipline*, doctoral dissertation, College Station, TX: Texas A & E University, published by Ann Arbor, MI: University Microfilms.

Ou, J.A. and Penman, S.H. (1989a) 'Financial statement analysis and the prediction of stock returns', *Journal of Accounting and Economics* 11 (4): 295–329.

Ou, J.A. and Penman, S.H. (1989b) 'Accounting measurement, price-earnings ratio, and the information content of security prices', *Journal of Accounting Research* 27 (Supplement): 111–52.

Parker, L.D. (1998) 'Accounting for environmental strategy: cost management, control and performance evaluation', *Asia-Pacific Journal of Accounting* 4 (December): 145–73.

Parker, R.H. (1969) *Management accounting: an historical perspective*, London: Macmillan & Co. Ltd.

Parker, R.H. (1984) 'Explaining national differences in consolidation accounting', in T.A. Lee and R.H. Parker eds, *The evolution of corporate financial reporting*, New York: Garland Publishing, Inc.: 124ff.

Patell, J.M. (1976) 'Corporate forecasts of earnings per share and stock price behavior', *Journal of Accounting Research* 14 (2): 246–76.

Peasnell, K.V. (1981) 'On capital budgeting and income measurement', *Abacus* 17 (June): 52–67.

Peasnell, K.V. (1982a) 'Some 'Formal connections' between economic values and yields and accounting numbers', *Journal of Business Finance and Accounting* 9 (August): 361–81.

Peasnell, K.V. (1982b) 'The function of a conceptual framework for corporate financial reporting', *Accounting and Business Research* 12 (48): 243–56.

Peasnell, K.V., Skerratt, L.C.L. and Ward, C.W.R. (1987) 'The share price impact of UK CCA disclosures', *Accounting and Business Research* 18 (69): 3–16.

Peasnell, K.V. and Williams, D.J. (1986) 'Ersatz academics and scholar-saints: the supply of financial accounting research', *Abacus* 22 (September): 121–35.

Pérochon, C. (1971) *Comptabilité national et comptabilité de l'entreprise* (National accounting and business accounting), doctoral thesis, Paris: Université de Paris I.

Pesando, J.E. and Clarke, C.K. (1983) 'Economic models of the labor market and pension accounting: an exploratory analysis', *The Accounting Review* 58 (October): 733–48.

Pfaff, D. (1994) 'Zur Notwendigkeit einer eigenständigen Kostenrechnung-Anmerkungen zur Neuorientierung des internen Rechnungswesens im Hause Siemens' (On the necessity of an independent cost accounting – remarks to the new orientation at the House of Siemens), *Zeitschrift für betriebswirtschaftliche Forschung* 46 (December): 1065–84.

Pincus, K.V. (1990) 'Audit judgment consensus: a model for dichotomous decisions', *Auditing: A Journal of Practice and Theory* 9 (2): 1–20.

Ponemon, L.A. and Gabhart, D.R.L. (1993) *Ethical reasoning in accounting and auditing*, Vancouver, BC: CGA-Canada Research Foundation.

Porter, M. (1996) 'What is strategy?', *Harvard Business Review* 84 (6, November–December): 76–81.

Powelson, J.P. (1955) *Economic accounting*, New York: McGraw-Hill Co.

Prakash, P. and Rappaport, A. (1977) 'Information inductance and its significance for accounting', *Accounting, Organizations and Society* 2 (1): 28–38.

Pree Jr, C.M. de (1989) 'Testing and evaluating a conceptual framework in accounting', *Abacus* 25 (September): 61–73.

Preinreich, G.A.D. (1938) 'Annual survey of economic theory: the theory of depreciation', *Econometrica* 6 (January): 219–41.

Preinreich, G.A.D. (posthumously edited by Richard B. Brief) (1996) *A landmark in accounting theory: the work of Gabriel A.D. Preinreich*, New York: Garland Publishing, Inc.

Previts, G.J. (1980) *A critical evaluation of comparative financial accounting thoughts in America 1900 to 1920*, New York: Arno (originally doctoral dissertation, University of Florida, 1972).

Previts, G.J. and Merino, B. (1979) *A history of accounting in America – a historical interpretation of the cultural significance of accounting*, New York: John Wiley & Sons (later version: *A history of accounting in America – the cultural significance of accounting*, Columbus, OH: Ohio State University Press, 1998).

Puro, M. (1984) 'Auditing firm lobbying before the financial accounting standards board: an empirical study', *Journal of Accounting Research* 22 (2): 624–46.

Puxty A.G., Willmott, H.C., Cooper, D.J. and Lowe, T. (1987) 'Modes of regulation in advanced capitalism: locating accountancy in four countries', *Accounting, Organizations and Society* 12 (3): 273–92.

Rappaport, A. (1964) 'Establishing objectives for published corporate accounting reports', *The Accounting Review* 39 (October): 951–62.

Rappaport, A. (1965) 'Seminar research on uniformity', *The Accounting Review* 40 (3, July): 643–8.

Rappaport, A. (1980) 'The strategic audit', *Journal of Accountancy* 149 (6): 712–31.

Reckers, P.M.J. and Stagliano, A.J. (1977) 'Zero-based budgeting', *Management Accounting* 59 (5): 18–20.

Reichelstein, S. (1992) 'Constructing incentive schemes for government contracts: an application of agency theory', *The Accounting Review* 67 (October): 712–31.

Reider, B. and Saunders, G. (1988) 'Management accounting education: a defense of its criticism', *Accounting Horizons* 2 (December): 58–62.

Requena-Rodriguez, J.U. (1972) 'Teoría de la contabilidad: análisis dimensional', *Revista Española de Financiación y Contabilidad* (January/April): 45–53.

Revsine, L. (1973) *Replacement cost accounting*, Englewood Cliffs, NJ: Prentice-Hall, Inc.

Revsine, L. and Weygandt, J.J. (1974) 'Accounting for inflation: the controversy', *Journal of Accountancy* 138 (4): 72–8.

Richard, C. (2005) 'Anthony G. Hopwood: la comptabilité en action' (Anthony G. Hopwood: accounting in action), in B. Colasse ed., *Les grands auteurs en comptabilité*, Éditions EMS: 255–72.

Richardson, A.J. and Gibbins, M. (with the assistance of John Wilson) (1988) 'Behavioral research on the production and use of financial information', in K.R. Ferris ed., *Accounting research: a critical analysis*, New York: Century VII Publishing Co.: 15–45.

Richardson, G.D. (1989) 'Discussion: timeliness of financial reporting, the firm size effect and stock price reactions to annual earnings announcements', *Contemporary Accounting Research* 5 (Spring): 299–317.

Richardson, G.D., Sefcik, S.E. and Thompson, R. (1988) 'Trading volume reactions to a change in dividend policy: the Canadian evidence', *Contemporary Accounting Research* 5 (Spring): 299–317.

Robbins, B.P. and Swyers, S.O. (1984) 'Accounting for income taxes: predicting timing difference reversals', *Journal of Accountancy* 158 (September): 108–18.

Roberts, J. and Scapens, R. (1985) 'Accounting systems and systems of accountability: understanding accounting practices in their organizational contexts', *Accounting, Organizations and Society* 10 (4): 443–56.

Robinson, C. and Fertuck, L. (1985) *Materiality: an empirical study of actual auditor decisions*, Vancouver, BC: The Canadian Certified General Accountants' Research Foundation.

Roover, R. de (1955) 'New perspectives on the history of accounting', *The Accounting Review* 30 (3): 405–20.

Ronen, J. and Sadan, S. (1981) *Smoothing income numbers: objectives, means and implications*, Bergoston, MA: Addison-Wesley.

Rosen, L.S. (1972) *Current value accounting and price level restatements*, Toronto, ON: Canadian Institute of Chartered Accountants.

Ross, H. (1969), *Financial statements: a crusade for current values*, Toronto, ON: Sir Isaac Pitman & Sons.

Ryan, R.J. (1982) 'Towards a value-neutral positive science of accounting: a comment', *Journal of Business Finance and Accounting* 9 (Winter): 565–6.

Sá, A.L. de (1995) 'Axiomas em contabilidade científica' (Axioms in scientific accounting), *Information Cientifico Cultural* 1 (Setembro de 1995 – Orgâo do Centra de Estudos Superiores de Contabilidade, Belo Horizonte, Minas Gerais, Brasil): 1–5.

Saenger, E. (ed., compiler) (1992) *History and theory of accounting*, Pretoria: University of South Africa.

Sainte Croix, G.E.M. de (1956) 'Greek and Roman accounting', in A.C. Littleton and B.S. Yamey eds, *Studies in the history of accounting*, Homewood, IL: Richard D. Irwin, Inc.

Saito, S. (1972) 'Some considerations on the axiomatic formulation of accounting' (originally in Japanese), *Kaikei* 101: 45–65 (English translation in *The Mushashi University Journal* 20, 1972: 81–99).

Saito, S. (1973) 'Further considerations on the axiomatic formulation of accounting: a reply to Prof. R. Mattessich', *The Mushashi University Journal* 21: 95–107.

Sakurai, M. (1989) 'Target costing and how to use it', *Journal of Cost Management* 5: 39–50.

Sami, H., Curatola, A.P. and Trapnell, J.E. (1989) 'Evidence on the predictive ability of inflation-adjusted earning measures', *Contemporary Accounting Research* 5 (Spring): 556–74.

Samuels, J.M. and Piper, A.G. (1985) *International accounting: a survey*, New York: St Martin's Press.

Samuelson, B.A. and Murdoch, B. (1985) 'The Information content of general price level adjusted earnings: a comment', *The Accounting Review* 60 (October): 706–10.

Samuelson, L.A. (1986) 'Discrepancies between the roles of budgeting', *Accounting, Organizations and Society* 11 (1): 35–46.

Sanders, T.H., Hatfield, H.R. and Moore, U. (1938) *A statement of accounting principles*, New York: American Accounting Association.

Sandilands, F.E.P. (ed.) (Sandilands Committee) (1975) *Inflationary accounting: report of the Inflation Accounting Committee*, London: HMSO.

Schaefer, T.F. (1984) 'The information content of current cost income relative to dividends and historical cost income', *Journal of Accounting Research* 22 (Autumn): 647–56.

Schillinglaw, G. (1961). *Cost accounting: analysis and control*, Homewood, IL: Richard D. Irwin, Inc. (several subsequent editions).

Schipper, K. (1994) 'Academic accounting research and the standard setting process', *Accounting Horizons* 8 (December): 61–73.

Schipper, K. (2003) 'Principles-based accounting standards', *Accounting Horizons* 17 (1): 61–73.

Schipper, K. and Thomson, R. (1985) 'The impact of merger-related regulations using exact distributions of test statistics', *Journal of Accounting Research* 23 (1): 408–15.

Schipper, K. and Weil, R.L. (1982) 'Alternative accounting treatments of pensions', *The Accounting Review* 57 (October): 806–24.

Schmandt-Besserat, D. (1977) 'An archaic recording system and the origin of writing', *Syro-Mesopotamian Studies* 1 (2): 1–32.

Schmandt-Besserat, D. (1978) 'The earliest precursor of writing', *Scientific American* 238 (6): 50–9.

Schmandt-Besserat, D. (1992) *Before writing – Vol. 1: From counting to cuneiform;* Vol. 2: *A catalogue of Near Eastern tokens*, Austin, TX: University of Texas Press.

Schmidt, F. (1921) *Die organische Bilanz im Rahmen der Wirtschaft* (The organic balance sheet in an economic setting), 1st edn, Leipzig: G.A. Gloeckner Verlagsbuchhandlung (2nd edn, 1922, *Die organische Tageswertbilanz*, Leipzig; 3rd edn, 1929; reprint, Wiesbaden: Betriebswirtschaftlicher Verlag Dr T. Gabler, 1953; Japanese translation, *Yukikan taishohyo gakusetsu*, Tokyo: Dobunkan Ltd, 1934).

Schneider, D. (1992) 'Theorien zur Entwicklung des Rechnungswesens' (Theories to the development of accounting), *Zeitschrift für betriebswirtschaftliche Forschung* 44 (1): 3–31.

Schneider, D. (2001) *Betriebswirtschaftslehre*, Vol. 4: *Geschichte und Methoden der Wirtschaftswissenschaften* (History and methods of the economic sciences), Munich: R. Oldenbourg Verlag (previous volumes were Vol. 1: *Grundlagen*, 1993; Vol. 2: *Rechnungswesen*, 1994; Vol. 3: *Theorie der Unternehmung*, 1997).

Schoenfeld, H.-M. (1974) *Cost terminology and cost theory: a study of its development and present state in Central Europe*, Urbana-Champaign, IL: University of Illinois.

Schoenfeld, H.-M. (1992) 'Kapazitätskosten und ihre Behandlung in der Kostenrechnung – ein ungelöstes betriebswirtschaftliches Problem' (Capacity costs and their treatment – an unsolved business problem), in H. Corsten, R. Köhler, H. Müller-Meerbach and H.-H. Schröder eds, *Kapazitätsmessung, Kapazitätsgestaltung, Kapazitätsoptimierung – eine betriebswirtschaftliche Kernfrage, Festschrift für Werner Kern*, Stuttgart: C.E. Poeschel Verlag: 195–207.

Scholes, M. and Wolfson, M. (1992) *Taxes and business strategy: a global planning approach*, Englewood Cliffs, NJ: Prentice-Hall, Inc.

Schrader, W.J. (1962) 'An inductive approach to accounting theory', *The Accounting Review* 37 (October): 645–9.

Schreuder, H. (1984) 'Positively normative (accounting) theories', in A.G. Hopwood and H. Schreuder eds, *European contributions to accounting theory: the achievements of the last decade*, Amsterdam: Free University Press: 213–31.

Schultz Jr, J., (1989) *Reorienting accounting education: reports on the environment, professoriate, and curriculum of accounting*, Sarasota, FA: AAA.

Schultz Jr, J. and Reckers, P.M.J. (1981) 'The impact of group processing on selected audit disclosure decisions', *Journal of Accounting Research* 19 (Autumn 1981), 482–501.

Scott, G.M. and Troberg, P. (1980) *Eighty-eight international accounting problems in rank order of importance: a delphi evaluation*, Sarasota, FA: AAA.

Scott, W.R. (1975) 'Auditor's loss functions implicit in consumption-investment models', *Journal of Accounting Research* 13 (Supplement): 98–117.

Scott, W.R. (1984) 'The state of the art of academic research in auditing', *Journal of Accounting Literature* 3 (Spring): 153–200.

Scott, W.R. (1988) 'Economic effects of a mandated audit in a contingent-claims production economy', *Contemporary Accounting Research* 4 (Spring): 354–88.

Seicht, G. (1970) *Die kapitaltheoretische Bilanz und die Entwicklung der Bilanztheorie* (The capital-theoretic balance sheet and the development of accounting theory), Berlin: Dunker & Humblot.

Shank, J.K. and Govindarajan, V. (1993) *Strategic cost management: the new tool for competitive advantage*, New York: Free Press.

Shapiro, B.P. (1998) 'Toward a normative model of rational argumentation for critical accounting discussions', *Accounting, Organizations and Society* 23 (7): 641–64.

Shaub, M.K. (1988) 'Restructuring the code of professional ethics: a review of the Anderson Committee Report and its implications', *Accounting Horizons* 2 (December), 89–97.

Simon, H. (1990) 'Information technologies and organizations', *The Accounting Review* 65 (July): 658–67.

Simunic, D.A. (1980) 'The pricing of audit services: theory and evidence', *Journal of Accounting Research* 18 (Spring): 161–90.

Simunic, D.A. (1984) 'Auditing, consulting and auditor independence', *Journal of Accounting Research* 22 (Summer): 679–702.

Simunic, D.A. and Stein, M.T. (1987) *Product differentiation in auditing: auditor choice in the market for unseasoned new issues*, Vancouver, BC: The Canadian Certified General Accountants' Research Foundation.

Simunic, D.A. and Stein, M.T. (1996) 'The impact of litigation risk and auditing pricing: a review of the economics and the evidence, *Auditing: A Journal of Practice and Theory* 15: 119–34.

Sinning, K.E. (1986) *Comparative international taxation*, Sarasota, FA: AAA.

Skinner, R.M. (1980) *Pension accounting: the problem of equating payments tomorrow with expenses today*, Toronto, ON: Clarkson Gordon.

Skinner, R.M. (1987) *Accounting standards in evolution*, Toronto, ON: Holt, Rinehardt and Winston.

Smith, C., Whipp, R. and Willmott, H. (1988) 'Case-study research in accounting: methodological breakthrough or ideological weapon?', *Advances in Public Interest Accounting* 2: 95–120.

Solomons, I. (1982) 'Probability assessment by individual auditors and audit teams: an empirical investigation', *Journal of Accounting Research* 20 (Autumn): 689–710.

Solomons, D. (ed.) (1952) *Studies in costing*, London: Sweet & Maxwell.

Solomons, D. (1961) 'Economic and accounting concepts of income', *The Accounting Review* 36 (July): 374–83.

Solomons, D. (1965) *Divisional performance: measurement and control*, New: Financial Executive Research Foundation.

Solomons, D. (1966) 'Economic and accounting concepts of cost and value', in M. Backer ed., *Modern accounting theory*, Englewood Cliffs, NJ: Prentice-Hall, Inc.: 117–40.

Solomons, D. (1987) 'The twilight of income measurement: twenty-five years on', *Accounting Historians Journal* 4 (1): 1–6.

Someya, K. (1996) *Japanese accounting: a historical approach*, New York: Oxford University Press, 1996.

Sommerfeld, R.M. and Easton, J.E. (1987) 'The CPA's tax practice today: and how it got that way', *Journal of Accountancy* 163 (5): 166–79.

Sorter, G. and Ingberman, M. (1987) 'The implicit criteria for the recognition, quantification and reporting of accounting events', *Journal of Accounting, Auditing and Finance* 2 (Spring): 99–114.

Sorter, G.H. (1969) 'An "events" approach to basic accounting theory', *The Accounting Review* 44 (January): 12–19.

Sorter, G.H. and Horngren, C.T. (1962) 'Asset recognition and economic attributes: the relevant costing approach', *The Accounting Review* 37 (July): 391–9.

Spacek, L. (1962) 'Comment, in Robert T. Sprouse and Maurice Moonitz', *A tentative set of broad accounting principles for business enterprises*, New York: AICPA.

Sprouse, R.T. and Moonitz, M. (1962) *A tentative set of broad accounting principles for business enterprises*, New York: AICPA.

Stamp, E. (1980) *Corporate reporting: its future evolution*, Toronto: Canadian Institute of Chartered Accountants.

Stamp, E. (1984) *Selected papers on accounting, auditing and professional problems*, New York: Garland Publishing, Inc.

Stark, A.W. (1987) 'Comment: some thoughts on a cost-benefit analysis of accounting for inflation', *Journal of Accounting and Public Policy* (Fall 1987): 209–18.

Staubus, G.J. (1961) *A theory of accounting to investors*, Berkeley, CA: University of California Press.

Staubus, G.J. (1985) 'An induced theory of accounting measurement', *The Accounting Review* 60 (January): 53–75.

Staubus, G.J. (1987) 'The dark ages of cost accounting: the role of miscues in the literature', *The Accounting Historians Journal* 14 (Fall): 1–18.

Stedry, A.C. (1960) *Budget control and cost behavior*, Englewood Cliffs, NJ: Prentice-Hall, Inc.

Steinbart, P.J. (1987) 'Materiality: a case study using expert systems', *The Accounting Review* 62 (January): 97–116.

Stepp, J.O. (1985) 'Deferred taxes: the discounting controversy', *Journal of Accountancy* 160 (November): 142–50.

Sterling, R.R. (1970) *Theory of the Measurement of Enterprise Income*, Lawrence, KA: University Press of Kansas.

Sterling, R.R. (1979) *Toward a science of accounting*, Houston, TX: Scholars Book Co.

Sterling, R.R. (1990) 'Positive accounting: an assessment', *Abacus* 26 (Fall): 97–135.

Sterling, R.R. and Lemke, K.W. (eds) (1982) *Maintenance of capital: financial versus physical*, Houston, TX: Scholars Book Co.

Stone, M.S. (1982) 'A survey of research on the effects of corporate pension plan sponsorship: implications for accounting', *Journal of Accounting Literature* (Spring): 1–32.

Stone, R. (1986) 'Social accounting: the state of play', *Scandinavian Journal of Economics* 88 (3): 453–72.

Storey, R.K. (1964) *The search for accounting principles*, New York: AICPA.

Sundem, G.L. (1987) 'Overview of four years of submissions to *The Accounting Review*', *The Accounting Review* 62 (January): 191–202.

Sundem, G.L., Williams, D.Z. and Chironna, J.F. (1990) 'The revolution in accounting education', *Management Accounting* 72 (6): 49–53.

Sunder, S. (1975) 'Accounting changes in inventory valuation', *The Accounting Review* 50 (April): 305–15.

Sunder, S. (1976) 'Optimal choice between FIFO and LIFO', *Journal of Accounting Research* 14 (Autumn): 277–300.

Sunder, S. (1996) *The theory of accounting and control*, Cincinnati, OH: South-Western College Publishing.

Swanson, E.P. and Shriver, K.A. (1987) 'The accounting-for-changing prices experiment: a valid test of usefulness?', *Accounting Horizons* 1 (September): 69–78.

Sweeney, J.T. and Roberts, R.W. (1997) 'Cognitive moral development and auditor independence', *Accounting, Organizations and Society* 22 (3/4).

Swieringa, R.J. and Waterhouse, J.H. (1982) 'Organizational views of transfer pricing', *Accounting, Organizations and Society* 7 (2): 149–66.

Swieringa, R.J. and Weick, K.E. (1987) 'Management accounting and action', *Accounting, Organizations and Society* 12 (3): 293–308.

Tanaka, S. (1982) *The structure of accounting language*, Tokyo: Chuo University Press.

Thierauf, R.J. (1990) *Expert systems in finance and accounting*, Westport, CT: Quorum Books.

Thomas, A.L. (1969) *The allocation problem in financial accounting*, Chicago, IL: AAA.

Thomas, A.L. (1974) *The allocation problem: part II*, Sarasota, FA: AAA.

Thornton, D.B. (1983) *The financial reporting of contingencies and uncertainties: theory and practice*, Vancouver, BC: The Canadian Certified General Accountants' Research Foundation.

Thornton, D.B. (1986) 'Current cost disclosures and nondisclosures: Canadian evidence', *Contemporary Accounting Research* 3 (Fall): 1–34.

Thornton, D.B. (1988a) 'Capital value in use vs. replacement costs: theory and Canadian evidence', *Contemporary Accounting Research* 5 (Fall): 343–70.

Thornton, D.B. (1988b) 'Theory and metaphor in accounting', *Accounting Horizons* 2 (December): 1–9.

Thornton, D.B. (1993) *Managerial tax planning: a Canadian perspective*, New York: Wiley & Sons, Inc.

Tiessen, P. and Baker, D.M. (1977) 'Human information processing, decision style theory and accounting information systems: a comment', *The Accounting Review* 52 (October): 984–87.

Tiessen, P. and Waterhouse, J.H. (1983) 'Towards a descriptive theory of management accounting', *Accounting, Organizations and Society* 8 (2/3): 251–67.

Tinker, A.M. (1984) 'Theories of the state and the state of accounting: economic reductionism and political voluntarism in accounting regulation theory', *Journal of Accounting and Public Policy* 3 (Spring): 55–74.

Tinker, A.M. (1985) *Paper prophets: a social critique of accounting*, New York: Praeger Special Studies.

Tinker, A.M., Merino, B.D. and Neimark, M.D. (1982) 'The normative origins of positive theories: ideology and accounting thought', *Accounting, Organizations and Society* 7 (2): 167–200.

Tippett, M. (1978) 'The axioms of accounting measurement', *Accounting and Business Research* 8 (32): 266–78.

Tippett, M. and Whittington, G. (1988) 'General price-level adjustment: some properties of the Edwards and Bell model', *Accounting and Business Research* 19 (Winter): 65–78.

Tomkins, C. and Groves, R. (1983) 'The everyday accountant and researching his reality', *Accounting, Organizations and Society* 8 (4), 361–74.

Tremblay, D. and Cormier, D. (1989), *Théories et models comptables – voies de recherché* (Theories and models of accounting – from a research viewpoint), Quebec City: L'Université du Québec.

Trueblood, R.M. and Cooper, W.W. (1955) 'Research and practice in statistical applications to accounting, auditing, and management control', *The Accounting Review* 30 (2, April): 2219.

Tweedie, D. and Whittington, G. (1984) *The debate of inflation accounting*, Cambridge: Cambridge University Press.

Uecker, W. (1978) 'A behavioural study of information system choice', *Journal of Accounting Research* 16 (1): 169–89.

Underdown, B. and Taylor, P. (1985) *Accounting theory and policy making*, London: Heinemann.

Vance, L.L. (1950) *Scientific methods for auditing*, Berkeley, CA: University of California Press.

Vance, L.L. and Neter, J. (1956) *Statistical sampling for auditors and accountants*, New York: John Wiley & Sons, Inc.

Vangermeersch, R. (1981) 'Let's recognize dissent in standard-making', *Management Accounting* 63 (3): 53–62.

Van Seventer, A. (1975) 'Replacement value theory in modern Dutch accounting', *The International Journal of Accounting* 11: 67–94.

Vasarhelyi, M.A. (ed.) (1989) *Artificial intelligence in accounting and auditing: the use of expert systems*, New York: Markus Wiener Publication, Inc.

Vatter, W.J. (1947) *The fund theory of accounting and its implications for financial reports*, Chicago, IL: University of Chicago Press.

Vatter, W.J. (1950) *Managerial accounting*, Englewood Cliffs, NJ: Prentice-Hall, Inc.

Vatter, W.J. (1966) 'Accounting for leases', *Journal of Accounting Research* (2, Autumn): 133–48.

Verrecchia, R.E. (1982) 'Use of mathematical models in financial accounting', *Journal of Accounting Research* 20 (Supplement): 1–42.

Viganò, E. (1994) 'A comparative view of accounting', *Economia Aziendale* 12 (1): 1–70.

Wagenhofer, A. (1990) 'Voluntary disclosure with a strategic opponent', *Journal of Accounting and Economics* 12 (4): 341–63.

Waller, W.S. and Jiambalvo, J. (1984) 'The use of normative models in human information processing research in accounting', *Journal of Accounting Literature* 3 (Spring): 201–26.

Walton, P. (1995) *European financial reporting: a history*, London: Harcourt Brace & Co.

Wand, Y. and Weber, R. (1989) 'A model of control and audit procedure change in evolving data processing systems', *The Accounting Review* 64 (January): 87–107.

Waterhouse, J.H. and Tiessen, P. (1978) 'A contingency framework for management accounting systems research', *Accounting, Organizations and Society* 3 (1): 65–76.

Watts, R.L. and Zimmerman, J.L. (1978) 'Towards a positive theory of the determination of accounting standards', *The Accounting Review* 53 (January): 112–34 (reprinted in R. Mattessich (ed.) (1984) *Modern accounting research: survey, history, and guide*, Vancouver, BC: Canadian General Certified Accountants' Research Foundation: 81–102).

Watts, R.L. and Zimmerman, J.L. (1979) 'The demand for and the supply of accounting theories: the market for excuses', *The Accounting Review* 54 (April): 273–305 (reprint in R. Mattessich (ed.) (1984) *Modern accounting research: history, survey, and guide*, Vancouver, BC: Canadian General Certified Accountants' Research Foundation: 103–29).

Watts, R.L. and Zimmerman, J.L. (1980) 'On the irrelevance of replacement cost disclosures for security prices', *Journal of Accounting and Economics* 2 (August): 95–106.

Watts, R.L. and Zimmerman, J.L. (1986) *Positive accounting theory*, Englewood Cliffs, NJ: Prentice-Hall, Inc.

Watts, R.L. and Zimmerman, J.L. (1990) 'Positive accounting: a ten year perspective', *The Accounting Review* 65 (January): 131–56.

Weber, C. (Karl) (1966) *Evolution of direct costing*, Champaign, IL: Center for International Education and Accounting Research, University of Illinois.

Weber, R. (1980) 'Some characteristics of the free recall of computer controls by EDP auditors', *Journal of Accounting Research* 18 (1): 214–41.

Wells, M.C. (1971) 'Axioms for historical cost valuation', *Journal of Accounting Research* 9: 171–80.

Wells, M.C. (1976) 'A revolution in accounting thought', *The Accounting Review* 51 (July): 471–82.

Whitley, R. (1988) 'The possibility and utility of positive accounting theory', *Accounting and Business Research* 13: 631–45.

Whittington, G. (1983) *Inflation accounting*, Cambridge: Cambridge University Press.

Whittington, G. (1987) 'Positive accounting theory: a review article', *Accounting and Business Research* 17 (Autumn): 327–36.

Whittington, G. (1989) 'Accounting standard setting in the UK after 20 years: a critique of the Dearing and Solomons Report', *Accounting and Business Research* 19 (75): 195–205.

Willett, R.J. (1985) *Accounting measurement theory*, doctoral dissertation, Weatherby, WY: University of Aberdeen – British Library Documentation Supply Centre.

Willett, R.J. (1987) 'An axiomatic theory of accounting measurement (Part I)', *Accounting and Business Research* 17 (Spring): 155–71.

Willett, R.J. (1988) 'An axiomatic theory of accounting measurement (Part II)', *Accounting and Business Research* 19 (Winter): 79–91.

Williams, J.R., Herring, H., Tiller, M. and Scheiner, J. (1988) *A framework for the development of accounting education research*, Sarasota, FA: AAA (includes user's guide and diskette).

Williams, T.H. and Griffin, C.H. (1964) *The mathematical dimension of accounting*, Cincinnati, OH: South-Western Publishing Co.

Willmott, H.C. (1983) 'Paradigms for accounting research: critical reflections on Tomkins and Groves' "Everyday accountant and researching his reality": further thoughts', *Accounting, Organizations and Society* 8 (4): 389–405.

Wolfson, M.A. (1985) 'Empirical evidence of incentive problems and their mitigation in oil and gas tax shelter programs', in J.W. Pratt and R.J. Zeckhauser eds, *Principals and agents: the structure of business*, Boston, MA: Harvard Business School Press: 101–25.

Wolk, H.I., Francis, J.R. and Tearney, M.G. (1984) *Accounting theory: a conceptual approach*, Cincinnati, OH: South-Western Publishing Co. (2nd edn, 1988; 3rd edn, Boston, MA: Kent Publishing, Inc., 1992).

Wood, W.D. and Campbell, H.F. (1970) *Cost-benefit analysis and the economics of investment and in human resources*, Kingston, ON: Industrial Relations Centre, Queen's University.

Wyatt, A.R. (1988) 'Professionalism in standard setting', *The CPA Journal* 58 (7): 20–33.

Wyatt, A.R. (2004) 'Accounting professionalism – they just don't get it'. *Accounting Horizons* 18 (1, March): 45–53.

Yamey, B.S. (1989) *Art and accounting*, New Haven, CT: Yale University Press.

Yamey, B.S. (1994) 'Benedetto Cotrugli on bookkeeping (1458)', *Accounting, Business and Financial History* 4 (March): 43–50.

Yoshikawa, T., Innes, J. and Falconer, M. (1989) 'Cost management through functional analysis', *Journal of Cost Management* (1, Spring): 14–19.

Young, S.M. (1985) 'Participative budgeting: the effects of risk aversion and asymmetric information on budgetary slack', *Journal of Accounting Research* 23 (Autumn): 817–28.

Yu, L., Richardson, G. and Thornton, D.B. (1997) 'Corporate disclosure of environmental liability information: theory and evidence', *Contemporary Accounting Research* 14 (Fall): 435–74.

Yu, S.C. (1976) *The structure of accounting theory*, Gainsville, FA: University of Florida Press.

Zan, L. (1994) 'Toward a history of accounting histories: perspectives from the Italian tradition', *European Accounting Review* 3 (2): 255–307.

Zannetos, Z.S. (1964) 'Standard costs as a first step to probabilistic control: a theoretical justification, an extension and implications', *The Accounting Review* 39 (April): 296–304.

Zebda, A. (1987) 'The choice of management accounting normative models: a synthesis', *Advances in Accounting* 5: 73–98.

Zeff, S.A. (1963) 'Debating accounting theory', *The Accounting Review* 38 (July): 622–36.

Zeff, S.A. (1972) *Forging accounting principles in five countries: a history and an analysis of trends*, Champaign, IL: Stipes Publishing Co.

Zeff, S.A. (ed.) (1976) *Asset appreciation, business income and price-level accounting: 1918–1935*, New York: Arno Press.

Zeff, S.A. (ed.) (1982a) *The accounting postulates and principles controversy of the 1960s*, New York: Garland Publishing, Inc.

Zeff, S.A. (1982b) 'Truth in accounting: the ordeal of Kenneth MacNeal', *The Accounting Review* 57 (July): 528–53 (reprinted in J.R. Edwards (ed.) (1994) *Twentieth-century accounting thinkers*, London: Routledge: 334–63).

Zeff, S.A. (1991) *The American Accounting Association: its first 50 years 1916–1966*, Sarasota, FA: AAA.

Zéghal, D. (1984) *La comptabilité en périodes de changements de prix* (Accounting in periods of changing prices), Vancouver, BC: The Canadian Certified General Accountants' Research Foundation.

Zéghal, D. (1989) *Le marché de la vérification au Canada* (The auditing market in Canada), Vancouver, BC: The Canadian Certified General Accountants' Research Foundation.

Ziegler, H. (1994) 'Neuorientierung des internen Rechnungswesen für das Unternehmens-Controlling im Hause Siemens' (Re-orientation of cost accounting for business controlling in the House of Siemens), *Zeitschrift für betriebswirtschaftliche Forschung* 46: 175–88.

Zimmerman, V.K. (ed.) (1978) *Written contributions of selected accounting practitioners*, Vol. 2: *Paul Grady*, Urbana-Champaign, IL: University of Illinois.

Zimmerman, V.K. (ed.) (1979) *The impact of inflation accounting: a global view*, Urbana, IL: Center for International Education and Research in Accounting.

13 Accounting research in Finland, the Netherlands and the Scandinavian countries

Aho, T. (1981a) 'Adequacy of depreciation allowances under inflation', *The Finnish Journal of Business Economics* (4): 351–79.

Aho, T. (1981b) 'Analysis of lease financing under inflation', *The Finnish Journal of Business Economics* (3): 239–77.

Åkerblom, M. (1975) *Företag I inflation* (Business firms in inflation), doctoral dissertation in Swedish with English summary, Uppsala: Uppsala University.

Alaluusua, S.J. (1982) *Structural determinants of the budgeting process: an approach with application to Finnish firms*, Helsinki: The Helsinki School of Economics.

Artto, E. (1968) *Yrityksen rahoitus – systematiikka ja mukauttamistavat* (Financing of the firm, conceptual framework for adapting the monetary financial process), doctoral dissertation, Helsinki: Helsinki School of Economics.

Arvidsson, G. (1971) *Internpriser – styrning, motivation resultatbedömning* (Transfer prices – control, motivation, profit evaluation), doctoral dissertation, Stockholm: Stockholm School of Economics.

Arvidsson, G. (1973) *Internal transfer negotiations: eight experiments*, Stockholm.

Ashton, R.K. (1981) *The use and extent of replacement value in the Netherlands*, London: ECAW.

Ask, U. and Ax, C. (1992) *Trends in the development of product costing practices and techniques: a survey of Swedish manufacturing industry*, FE Report No. 333, Department of Business Administration, University of Gothenburg.

Ask, U., Ax, C. and Jonsson, S. (1996) 'Cost management in Sweden: from modern to postmodern', in A. Bhimani ed., *Modern cost management: European perspectives*, Oxford: Oxford University Press: 199–217.

Aukrust, O. (1955) *Nasjonalregnskap – teoretiske prinsipper* (National income accounting – theoretical principles), Oslo: Statistik Sentralbyrå.

Biggs, S., Buijink, W., Maijoor, S., Mock, T., Quadackers, L. and Schilderm S. (1994) 'An assessment of the relevance and respectability of audit research: reflections on reflections of Bindenga', *De Accountant* 100 (6): 387–90.

Bindenga, A.J. (1993) 'Research voor accountants – overpeinzingen na een symposium' (Research for accountants – a symposium), *De Accountant* 100 (1): 15–18.

Bouma, J.L. (1966) *Ondememingsdoel en winst* (Enterprise target as profit), Leiden: Stenfert Kroese.

Bouma, J.L. (1992) 'Management accounting na Limperg: de ontwikkeling in de Praktijk' (Management accounting after Limperg: the development in actual practice), *Limperg Dag 1991*, Limperg Instituut: 7–25.

Bouma, J.L. and Feenstra, D.E. (1975) 'Externe verslaggeving over personeel en personeelsbeheer in een aantal Nederlandse ondememingen over de jaren 1970–1973' (External reporting on personnel management in a number of Dutch firms from 1970–1973), *Maandblad voor Bedriifsadministratie en-Organisatie* 79 (941): 322–8.

Bouma, J.L. and Feenstra, D.W. (1997) 'Accounting and business economics tradition in the Netherlands', *European Accounting Review* 6 (2): 175–98.

Bouma, J.L. and van Helden, G.J. (1994) *Management accounting en economische organisatietheorie* (Management accounting and economic organization theory), Schoonhoven: Academic Service.

Bouma, J.L. and Werkema, H.G. (1965) 'Schattingen en subjectieve interpretaties bij de winstbepaling' (Estimations and subjective interpretations of income determination), *De Economist* 113 (5): 348–69.

Brink, H.L. (1992) 'A history of Philips accounting policies on the basis of its annual reports', *The European Accounting Review* 1 (2): 255–75.

Brommels, H. (1928) *Die eigentliche Abschreibung in der dynamische Bilanz* (The actual depreciation of dynamic accounting), doctoral dissertation, Helsingfors: University of Helsinki.

Brööms, J. and Rundfelt, R. (1979) *Inflationsredovisning – -ett förslag till prisjusterad årsredovisning* (Inflation accounting: an approach to price-adjusted annual reports).

Brunsson, N. (1981) 'Företagsekonomi som forskningsämne – korrumperad oppotunism eller samhällsvetenskapligt ideal', in N. Brunsson ed., *Företagsekonomsanning eller moral?* (Business economics – truth or morality), Lund: Studentlitteratur.

Brunsson, N. (1989) 'The organization of hypocrisy: talk, decision and actionts', *Organizations*, Chichester: Wiley.

Buijink, W.F.J. (1992) *Empirical financial accounting research*, Maastricht: Datawyse.

Burgert, R. (1967) 'Bedrijfseconomisch aanvaardbare grondslagen voor de gepubliceerde jaarrekening' (Applied economic principles for published financial statements), *De Accountant* 74 (4): 153–92.

Burgert, R. (1972) 'Reservations about "replacement value" accounting in the Netherlands', *Abacus* 8 (2): 111–26.

Camfferman, K. (1996a) *Voluntary annual report disclosure by listed Dutch companies 1945–1983*, doctoral dissertation, Amsterdam: Free University of Amsterdam (reprinted New York: Garland Publishing, Inc., 1997).

Camfferman, K. (1996b) 'Netherlands', in M. Chatfield and R. Vangermeersch eds, *The history of accounting: an international encyclopedia*, New York: Garland Publishing, Inc.: 431–3.

Camfferman, K. (1997) 'An overview of recent Dutch-language publications in accounting, business and financial history in the Netherlands', *Accounting, Business and Financial History* 7 (March): 105–37.

Camfferman, K. (1998) 'Deprival value in the Netherlands: history and current status', *Abacus* 34 (1, March): 18–27.

Camfferman, K. (2005) 'Theodore Limperg, Jr: le promoteur de la valeur de remplacement' (Champion of the replacement value, translation by Pierre Labardin), in B. Colasse ed., *Les grands auteurs en comptabilité*, Paris: Éditions EMS, Corlet: 111–23.

Camfferman, K. and Cooke, T.E. (2001) 'Dutch accounting in Japan 1609–1850: isolation or observation?', *Accounting, Business and Financial History* 11 (3, November): 369–83.

Camfferman, K. and Zeff, S.A. (1994) 'The contributions of Theordore Limperg Jr. (1897–1961) to Dutch accounting and auditing', in J.R. Edwards ed., *Twentieth-century accounting thinkers*, London: Routledge: 112–41.

Carlson, S. (1986) 'A century's captains of industry', *Skandinaviska Enskilda Banken Quarterly Review* (2): 52–60.

Cattela, R.S. (1983) 'An introduction to current value accounting and its application within N.V. Philips', in A.J.H. Enthoven ed., *Current value accounting: its aspects and impacts*, Dallas, TX: Center for International Accounting Development.

Christensen, J.A. (1979) *Communication and coordination in agencies: an approach to participative budgeting*, doctoral dissertation, Palo Alto, CA: Stanford Unviversity.

Christensen, J.A. and Demski, J.S. (2003) *Accounting theory: an information content perspective*, New York: McGraw-Hill, Irwin.

Christensen, P.O. and Feltham, G.A. (2003) *Economics of accounting*, Vol. 1: *Information in markets*, Boston, MA: Kluwer Academic Publishers.

Christensen, P.O. and Feltham, G.A. (2005) *Economics of accounting*, Vol. 2: *Performance evaluation* (forthcoming), Boston, MA: Kluwer Academic Publishers.

Clarke, F.L. and Dean, G.W. (1990) *Contributions of Limperg and Schmidt to the replacement cost debate in the 1920s*, New York: Garland Publishing, Inc.

Clarke, F.L. and Dean, G.W. (1992) 'The views of Limperg and Schmidt: discovering patterns and identifying differences from a chaotic literature', *The International Journal of Accounting* 27 (4): 287–309.

Dekker, H.C. (1981) 'Huidige standvan zakenvan de maatschappelijke berichtgeving' (Present position of social accounting), in J.W. Briedé ed., *Sociale rekenschap*, SMO-boek 19, Stichting Maatschappij en Onderneming.

Dijksma, J. (ed.) (1986–1990) *Jaar in, Jaar uit* (Year in and year out), 4 vols, Groningen: Wolters-Noordhoff. Wolters

Edwards, E.O. and Bell, P.W. (1961) *The theory and measurement of business income*, Berkeley, CA: University of California Press.

Eilifsen, A. (1998) 'Auditing regulation and the statutory auditors responsibility in Norway', *European Accounting Review* 7 (4): 709–23.

Engwall, L. (1992) *Mercury meets Minerva*, Oxford: Pergamon Press.

Engwall, L. and Gunnarsson E. (eds) (1994) *Management studies in an academic context*, Acta Universitatis Upsaliensis, *Studia Oeconomiae Negotiorum* 35, Uppsala: Studentlitteratur.

Enthoven, A.J.H. (1976) 'Replacement value accounting: wave of the future?', *Harvard Business – Review* (January–February): 6–8.

Enthoven, A.J.H. (1982) 'Current value accounting: its concepts and practice at N.V. Philips Industries, the Netherlands', *International Accounting Research Study*, No. 3, Dallas, TX: University of Texas.

Enthoven, A.J.H. (ed.) (1983) *Current value accounting: its aspects and impacts*, Dallas, TX: Center for International Accounting Development.

Eriksson, L. (1974) *Koncernredovisningens informationsinnehåll* (On the information in consolidated financial statements), Gothenburg: Gothenburg University.

European Accounting Review (1996) 'Dutch doctoral thesis projects in accountancy', *European Accounting Review* 5 (1): 149–52.

Feenstra, D.W. (1985) *Oordeelsvorming rond de externe berichtgeving* (Standards of external statement presentation), Groningen: Wolters-Noordhoff.

Feltham, G.A. (1967) *A theoretical framework for evaluating changes in accounting information for managerial decisions*, doctoral dissertation, Berkely, CA: University of California.

Flesher, D.L. and Flesher, T.K. (1986) 'Ivar Kreugers contribution to US financial reporting', *The Accounting Review* 31 (July): 421–34.

Flower, J. (ed.) (1994) *The regulation of financial reporting in the Nordic Countries*, Stockholm: Fritzes.

Frenckner, T.P. and Samuelson, L.A. (1984) *Produktkalkyler i Ilidustrin* (Product costing in industry), revised edition Stockholm: Mechanical and Electrical Engineering Industries.

508   *References 13: Finland, the Netherlands, etc.*

Gavatin, P. (1975) *Budgetsimuerling: innebörd, effektivitet och införande* (Budget simulation: meaning, effectiveness and implementation), doctoral dissertation, Stockholm: Stockholm School of Economics.

Gjesdal, F. (1981) 'Accounting for stewardship', *Journal of Accounting Research* 19 (1): 208–31.

Grandell, A. (1944) *Aldre redovisningsformer i Finland, en undersokning av den företagsekonomiska redovisningens utveckling i Finland intill 1800-talets slut*, (Older accounting models in Finland, a study on the development of commercial accounting in Finland until the end of the nineteenth century), Foretagsekonomiska forskningsforeningens skrigtserie: I, doctoral thesis, Helsingfors: University of Helsinki.

Granlund, M. (1994) *The role of management accounting in corporate crisis: theoretical considerations and case-study evidence of the meaning, influence and morality of management accounting and corporate crisis*, Turku: Publications of the Turku School of Economics and Business Administration, Series D: 5.

Gröjer, J.-E. and Stark, A. (1978) *Social redovisning* (Social accounting – with English summary), Doctoral dissertation, Stockholm: Stockholm University.

Grönlund, A. and Jonsson, S. (1990) 'Managing for cost improvement in automated production', in R.S. Kaplan, ed., *Measures for manufacturing excellence*, Boston, MA: Harvard Business School Press.

Gunnarsson, E. (1994) 'Anders Berch – de svenska ekonomiska vetenskapemas anfader' (Anders Berch – the founding father of the Swedish economic sciences), in L. Engwall ed., *Företagsekonomporträtt* (Portraits of Business Economists), Stockholm: SNS.

Hansen, P. (1962) *The accounting concept of profit: an analysis and evaluation in the light of the economic theory of income and capital*, Amsterdam: North Holland Publishing.

Hassink, H. (2000) 'On the role of accounting and auditing in employee contracts: some evidence for the Netherlands', *European Accounting Review* 9 (2): 245–64.

Have, O. ten (1933) *De leervan het boekholding in de Nederlanden tijdens de zeventiende en achtitende eeuw* (The teaching of bookkeeping in the Netherlands during the seventeenth and eighteenth century), Delft: N.p.

Hedberg, B. and Jönsson, S. (1978) 'Designing semi-confusing information systems for organizations in changing environments', *Accounting, Organizations and Society* 3 (1): 47–64.

Helden, G.J. van (1997) 'Cost allocation and product costing in Dutch local government', *European Accounting Review* 6 (1): 131–46.

Honko, J. (1955) *Koneen edullisin pitoaika ja investointilaskelmat – taloudellinen tutkimus* (The economic life time of machinery and the capital investment calculations, a study in business economics), doctoral thesis, Helsinki: Liiketaloustieteellisen tutkimuslaitoksen julkaisuja 19, Helsinki Institute of Business Economics.

Honko, J. (1959) *Yrityksen vuositulos* (The annual income of an enterprise and its determination – a study from the standpoint of accounting and economics), Helsinki: Oy Weilin & Göös Ab.

Honko, J. (1963) *Investointien suunnittelu ja tarkkailu* (Planning and control of investments), Porvoo: WSOY.

Hoogendoorn, M.N. (1993) 'A review of company financial reporting', *The European Accounting Review* 2 (2): 420–25.

Hoogendoorn, M.N. and Bijl, B.L. (eds) (1992) *Financial reporting in the nineties*, Deventer: Kluwer Bedrijfswetenschappen.

Jaaskeläinen, V. (1966) *Optimal financing and tax policy of the corporation*, doctoral dissertation, Helsinki.

Jägerhorn, R. (1965) *Informationsvärdet hos finländska aktiebolags revisionsberättelser* (Information value of audit reports in Finnish companies), doctoral dissertation, Porvoo: Swedish School of Economics and Business Administration.

Jägerhorn, R. (1975) 'Inflaatio, hinnannousu ja tilinpäätös' (Should we adjust our accounts for inflation?), *The Finnish Journal of Business Economics* (1): 28–42.

Jennergren, L.P. (1971) *Studies in the mathematical theory of decentralized resource allocation*, doctoral dissertation, Palo Alto, CA: Stanford University.

Jennergren, L.P. (1980) 'On the design of incentives in business firms: a survey of some research', *Management Science* (26): 180–201.

Johansson, S.-E. (1965) 'An appraisal of the Swedish system of investment reserves', *International Journal of Accounting and Education Research* 1: 85–92.

Jönsson, S. (1982) 'Budgetary behaviour in local government: a case study over three years', *Accounting, Organizations and Society* 7 (3): 287–304.

Jönsson, S. (1988) *Accounting regulation and elite structures*, Oxford: Wiley.

Jönsson, S. (1991) 'Role making for accounting while the state is watching', *Accounting, Organizations and Society* 16 (5/6): 521–46.

Jönsson, S. (1994) 'Changing accounting regulatory structures in the context of a strong state', *Critical Perspectives on Accounting* 5 (4): 341–60.

Jönsson, S. (1996a) *Accounting for improvement*, Oxford: Pergamon Press.

Jönsson, S. (1996b) 'Accounting and business economics tradition in Sweden', *European Accounting Review* 5 (3): 435–48.

Jönsson-Lundmark, B. (1976) *Pensionsavsättningar från resultatmätnings- och finansi- weingssynpunkt* (Pensions from an accounting and financial point of view), Business Administration Studies No. 29, doctoral dissertation, Gothenborg University.

Kaitilia, E. (1940) *Kustannuskäsite liiketaloustieteessä* (The concept of cost in business economics), Helsinki.

Kaitilia, E. (1945) *Kustannusten riippuvaisuus suoritemäärästä* (The relationship of costs and quantity of production), doctoral dissertation, Helsinki: Liiketaloudellinen tutkimus I.

Kaitilia, I.V. (1921a) *Omaisuusvuosibilanssin luonne ja onmaisuusarvostus käytännössä* (Nature and valuation of the balance sheet in actual practice), Lathi.

Kaitilia, I.V. (1921b) *Kirjanpidon ja bilanssiopin oppikirja* (A textbook of bookkeeping and balance sheets), Jyväskylä.

Kaitilia, I.V. (1928) *Teollisuusliikkeen laskentatoimen perusteet, Osa I, Omakustannus- laskenta* (Basic accounting in an industrial firm, Part I: Cost accounting), Jyväskylä.

Kaitilia, I.V. (1940) *Teollisuusliikkeen laskentatoimen perusteet – -kirjanpito* (Basics of industrial accounting – bookkeeping), Liiketaloustieteellisen tutkimuslaitoksen julka- isuja I, Helsinki.

Kasanan, E. and Malmi, T. (1994) 'The structural differences between traditional and activity based costing', *Proceedings of the 17th Annual Congress of the European Accounting Association*, Venice.

Kasanen, E., Lukka, K. and Siitonen, A. (1991) 'Konstruktiivinen tutkimusote liike- taloustieteessä' (A constructive appoach for business studies), *The Finnish Journal of Business Economics* 3: 301–29.

Kedner, G. (1975) *Företagskonkurser: problem, analys, utvärdering, åtgärder* (Bank- ruptcies: problems, analysis, evaluation and measures), doctoral dissertation, Lund: Lund University.

Kettunen, P. (1974) *Yritysten tutkimisesta* (A study of firms), Jyviiskylii.

Kettunen, P. (1980) *Laskentatoimen perusteista* (On the foundations of accounting), Jyväskylä: The University of Jyväskylä.

510   *References 13: Finland, the Netherlands, etc.*

Kettunen, P. (1984) Suomalaisen liiketaloustieteen murrokset ja jännitteet (The origin and development of Finnish business research), *The Finnish Journal of Business Economics* 2: 163–80.

Kettunen, P. (1986) 'Muinaisuuden myyttisistä hahmoista pienten valkoisten kääpiöiden aikaan – teoria ja käytänto suomalaisen liiketaloustieteen historiassa' (From the mythical characters of the past to the time of the white dwarfs theory and practice in the history of Finnish business economics), *Teesi* 2: 7–15.

Kinserdal, A. (1972) *Informasjonen i arsrapportene i norsk industri. Analys og problemdiskusjon* (The information in annual reports in Norwegian industry: an analysis), Bergen.

Klaassen, J. (1975) *De vervangingswaarde: theorie en toepassing in de jaarrekening* (Replacement value: theory and application in financial statements), Alphen aan den Rijn: Samsom.

Klaassen, J. (1991) 'Het institutionele kadervan de jaarverslaggeving in Nederland' (The conceptual framwork of financial statement presentation in the Netherlands), in J.P.C.M. van den Hoeven, A. van de Bos and C.D. Knoops eds, *fMA-Kroniek* Groningen: Wolters-Noordhoff.

Klaassen, J. (1993) 'A review of company financial reporting', *The European Accounting Review* 2 (2): 414–19.

Klaassen, J. and Schreuder, H. (1980) *Het financiële jaarverslagvan ondernemingen: een onderzoek onder gebruikers* (Annual financial reporting of firms: an empirical investigation of users), Leiden: Stenfert Kroese.

Klaassen, J. and Schreuder, H. (1984) 'Accounting research in the Netherlands', in A.G. Hopwood and H. Schreuder eds, *European contributions to accounting research: the achievements of the last decade*, Amsterdam: VU Uitgeverij and Free University of Amsterdam: 113–31.

Kovero, I. (1905) *Suomalainen kauppakirjeenvaihto kauppaoppilaitoksia ja ominpäinopiskelua varten*, Porvoo: W. Söderström.

Kovero, I. (1907–16) *Kirjanpiyo* (Bookkeeping), Porvoo: W. Söderström.

Kovero, I. (1910) *Bilanssioppi kauppaoppilaitoksiaja käytänöä varten* (On balance sheets – a textbook for commercial colleges and for practice), Porvoo: W. Soderstrom Osakeyhtiö.

Kovero, I. (1911a) *Die Bewertung der Vermögensgegenstände in den Jahresbilanzen der privaten Unternehmungen mit besonderer Berücksichtigung der nichtrealisierten Gewinne und Verluste* (Valuation of assets in balance sheets under special consideration of unrealized gains and losses), Berlin: C. Heymann (doctoral dissertation, defended at the Imperial Alexander University in Helsinki – 2nd edn in 1912; reprinted in Osaka: Nihon Shoseki, 1974).

Kovero, I. (1911b) *Kirjanpito I: alkeet ja yleiset muodot kauppaoppilaitoksia ja ominpäinopiskelua varten* (Bookkeeping I: Introduction and common forms for commercial colleges and for self-study), Porvoo: Werner Söderstrom Osakeyhtiö.

Kovero, I. (1926) *Alfabetisk handbok i handelskorrespondens: finisvensk* (Alphabetical handbook of commercial correspondence: Finnish/Swedish).

Kovero, I. (1931) *Progressioperiaatteesta verotuksessa*, Helsinki: Valtioneuvoston kirjapaino.

Kovero, I. (1932) *Ylellisyysverotus*, Helsinki: Valtioneuvoston kirjapaino.

Kovero, I. (1933) *Some views on marginal utility and the theory of taxation*, Helsinki: Helsingin Uusi Kirjapaino Osakeyhtiö.

Kovero, I. (1935) *Tulokäsite ja julkinen talous*, Porvoo: W. Söderström.

Kovero, I. (1938) *Die Prinzipien der Wetproportionalität und der Wertgleichheit in der Besteuerung* (Principles of value proportionality and value equality in taxation), Helsinki: Helsingin Uusi Kirjapaino Osakeyhitö.

Kovero, I. (1959) *Public expenditures and the burden theory*, Helsinki: Suomaleisen tiedeakatemian toimituksia: Series B.

Kraayenhofen, J. (1955) 'The profession in the Netherlands, sixty years of growth and development', *Accountant* (October 1): 382–90.

Laitinen, E.K. (1980) *Financial ratios and the basic economic factors of the firm: a steady state approach*, Jyväskylä: The University of Jyväskylä.

Lehtonen, P. (1976) *On the estimation of statistical cost functions: an empirical study of production and cost functions of Finnish restaurants*, Helsinki: The Helsinki School of Economics.

Lehtovuori, J. (1969) 'Kirjanpidon tehtävät' (Functions of financial accounting) in M. Saario ed., *Yrityksen tulos, rahoitus ja verotus II*, Helsinki: Kauppakorkeakoulun julkaisuja: C: III: 3.

Lehtovuori, J. (1972) *Kirjanpidon perusteet yrityksen tiedotuspolitiikan kannalta* (The foundations of accounting from the viewpoint of the information policy of an enterprise), doctoral dissertation, Helsinki: Acta Academiae Oeconomicae Helsingiensis: Series A: 9.

Lehtovuori, J. (1973) *Liiketaloustieteen metodologista taustaa* (On the methodological background of business economics), Turku: Turun kauppakorkeakoulun julkaisuja, AI-6.

Lilius, A. (1862) *Kiiytännollinen opastus yksinkertaisessa kirjanpidossa varsinkin tehdastelijoille ja ammattilaisille* (A practical guide to single-entry bookkeeping for owners of industrial and commercial firms), Turku: J.W. Lilja jar Kumpp.

Limperg Jr, T. (1917) 'Kostprijsberekening en Kostprijsbeholding' (Current cost accounting and current cost representation), *Accountancy* 15: 42–4, 55–8, 87–9, 104–5.

Limperg Jr, T. (1918) 'Kostprijs' (Current value), *Accountancy*: 2–4.

Limperg Jr, T. (1926) 'The accountants certificate in connection with the accountants responsibility', *Het Internaational Accountants Congres, Amsterdam 1926*, Purmerend: J. Muusses: 85–104.

Limperg Jr, T. (1932–33) 'De functievan den accountant an de leervan her gewekte vertouen', *Maandblat voor Accountancy and Befrjifseconomie* 9: 151–4, 173–7; 10: 193–7 (English translation as: 'The function of the accountant and the theory of inspired confidence', *The social responsibility of the auditor*, Amsterdam: Limperg Institute, 1985).

Limperg Jr, T. (1937) 'De gevolgenvan de depreciatievan de gulden vor de berekeningvan waarde en winst' (Consequences of the depreciation of the Guilder in determining value and profit), *Maandblad voor accountancy en bedrijftshuishoudkunde* 14: 1–8.

Limperg Jr, T. (1964–68), *Bedijfseconomie – Verzamelde werkvan Prof. dr. Th. Limperg Jr*, 7 vols, G.L. Groeneveld, J.F. Harccoû, S. Kleerkoper, E. Limperg and H.A.J.F. Misset (eds) (Business economics – collected works of Limperg), Deventer: Kluwer.

Limperg Jr, T. (1985) *The social responsibility of the auditor: a basic theory on the auditors function* (English translation of essays published 1932–33, including bibliographical references), Amsterdam: Limperg Institute.

Lindström, C.-G. (1972) *Simultan planering av investerings-, produktions- och avsäitningsprocesserna* (Simultaneous planning of investment, production and marketing processes), Turku.

Ljungkvist, M.-O. (1982) 'Prisändringar och den ekonomiska styrningen' (Price changes and management control), research paper, Stockholm: Stockholm School of Economics.

Lukka, K. (1988) 'Budgetary biasing in organizations: theoretical framework and empirical evidence', *Accounting, Organizations and Society* 13 (3): 281–302.

Lukka, K. (1990) 'Ontology and accounting: the concept of profit', *Critical Perspectives of Accounting* 1: 239–62.

Lukka, K. (1991) 'Laskentatoimen tutkimuksen epistemologiset perusteet' (Epistemological foundations of accounting research), *The Finnish Journal of Business Economics* 2: 161–86.

Lukka, K. (1996) 'Cost accounting in Finland: current practices and trends of development', *European Accounting Review* 5 (1): 1–28.

Lukka, K. and Granlund, M. (1996) 'Cost accounting in Finland: current practice and trends in development, *European Accounting Review* 5 (1): 1–28.

Lukka, K., Majala, R., Paasio, A. and Pihlanto, P. (1984) *Accounting research in Finland*, in A.G. Hopwood and H. Schreuder eds, *European contributions to accounting research: the achievements of the last decade*, Amsterdam: Free University Press.

Lumijärvi, O.-P. (ed.) (1993a) *Toimintojohtaminen. Activity based manegementin soumalaisia sovelluksia* (Activity based coating in practice), Jyväskilä: Weilin & Göös.

Lumijärvi, O.-P. (1993b) 'Activity based management perusteet' (The principles of ABM), in O.-P. Lumijärvi ed., *Toimintojohtaminen. Activity based manegementin soumalaisia sovelluksia*, Jyväskilä: Weilin & Göös.

MacDonal, E.B. (1977) 'Postscript to A. Goedeket: an application of replacement value theory', in W.T. Baxter and S. Davidson eds, *Studies in accounting theory*, 3rd edn, London: The Institute of Chartered Accountants in England and Wales: 246–9.

Madsen, V. (1959) *Regnskabsvaesenets opgaver og problemer i ny belysning* (The problems and tasks of accounting in a new perspective), Copenhagen.

Madsen, V. (1970) *Budgettering* (Budgeting), Aarhus.

Madsen, V. and Polesie, T. (1981) *Human factors in budgeting: judgment and evaluation*, London: Pitman.

Magnusson, Å. (1974) 'Rundgetuppföljining' (Budgetary control: an analysis – in Swedish with English summary), Stockholm: Stockholm School of Economics, EFI.

Maijoor, S.J. (1991) *The economics of accounting regulation*, Maastricht: Datawyse.

Majala, R. (1974) Rahanlähtaiden ja käytön järestyksistä' (Concerning the sources and uses of funds), *The Finnish Journal of Business Economics* 2: 197–202.

Majala, R. (1982) *Yrityvksen sosiaalikirjanpito. teoreettisia perusteita ja empiirisäi sovellutuksta* (Corporate social accounting, theoretical foundations and empirical applications), Turku: The Turku School of Economics.

Majala, R. (1987) *Kirjanpitokäytäntöjen vertailevan tutkimuksen käsitteellisen viitekehyksen kehittelyä* (A conceptual frame of reference for comparative studies of international accounting practices), Turku: Turun kauppakorkeakoulun julkaisuja: A: 5.

Majala, R. (1992) 'A conceptual frame of reference for comparative studies of international accounting practices', *The Finnish Journal of Business Economics*, 4: 325–30.

Mäkinen, V. (1976) *Joustavuus pienyrityksen menestymisen edellytyksenä* (Flexibility as a condition for success in small enterprises), Tampere: The University of Tampere.

Mäkinen, V. (1980) *Yritysten toiminnan tutkimisen lähestymistavoista – toimintaanalyyttisen tutkimusstrategian kehittelyä* (Different approaches to study business activities – outlining the effect of the analytical method). Yrityksen taloustieteen ja yksityisoikeuden laitoksen julkaisuja, Tampere: Sarja: A: 2; Tutkielmia ja raportteja 17, Tampereen yliopisto.

Mattessich, R. (2003) 'Accounting research and researchers of the nineteenth century and the beginning of the twentieth century', *Accounting, Business and Financial History* 13 (2, July): 125–79.

May, A. (1966) 'Theodore Limperg and his theory of value and cost', *Abacus* 2 (1): 3–21.

Meer-Kooistra, J. van der (1993) *Coordineren, motiveren en verrekenen: wisselwerking tussen omgeving, onderneming en mensen* (Coodination, motivation and calculation: interdependence between environment, firms and personnel). Groningen: Wolters-Noordhoff.

Meij, J.L. (1948) *Beschouwingen over aard en omvangvan de winst* (Thoughts on the nature and value of profit), Gravenhage: Delwel.

Meij, J.L. (1954) 'De waardetheorieen in de bedrijfshuishouding' (Valuation theories in business economics), *Maandblad voor Accountancy en Bedriifshuishoudkunde* 30: 316–29.

Meij, J.L. (1960) 'Moeilijkheden met de vervangingswaardetheorie' (Difficulties of the replacement value theory), *Maandblad voor Accountancy en Bedriifshuishoudkunde* 36: 428–41.

Meyer, H. (1971) *Kvantitativ analys av skattereformeffekter* (Quantitative analysis of effects of tax reforms), Helsinki: The Swedish School of Economics and Business Administration.

Näsi, J. (1980a) *Liiketaloustiede soveltavana tieteenä, Perusongelmain hahmotus ja analyysi* (Business economics as an applied science. Outlining and analysing the basic problems). Yrityksen taloustieteen ja yksityisoikeuden laitoksen julkaisuja, Tampere: Sarja A: 2: Tutkielmia ja raportteja 8, Tampereen yliopisto.

Näsi, J. (1980b) *Ajatuksia käsiteanalyysista ja sen käytöstä yrityksen taloustieteessä* (Thoughts about conceptual analysis and its use in business economics), Yrityksen taloustieteen ja yksityisoikeuden laitoksen julkaisuja, Tampere: Sarja A: 2: Tutkielmia ja raportteja II, Tampereen yliopisto.

Näsi, J. (1981) *Tutkimusten kokonaiskehysten logiikasta* (On the logic of research frameworks), Yrityksen taloustieteen ja yksityisoikeuden laitoksen julkaisuja, Tampere: Sarja A: 2: Tutkielmia ja raportteja 22, Tampereen yliopisto.

Näsi, J. (1995) 'A Scandinavian approach to stakeholder thinking', in J. Näsi ed., *Understanding stakeholder thinking*, Gummerus Oy, Jyvaskyla.

Näsi, J. and Näsi, S. (1985) *Suomalainen laskentatoimen tutkimus 1940-luvulta nykypäiviin, väitöskirjatuotannon tutkimusstrateginen analyysi* (Accounting research in Finland from the 1940s to the present – an analytical review of the research strategies in doctoral dissertations), Yrityksen taloustieteen ja yksityisoikeuden laitoksen julkaisuja, Tampere: Sarja A: 2: Tutkielmia ja raportteja 39, Tampereen yliopisto.

Näsi, J. and Näsi, S. (1997) 'Accounting and business economics tradition in Finland', *European Accounting Review* 6 (3): 199–229.

Näsi, S. (1990) *Laskenta-ajattelun kehitys viime vuosisadan puolivälisä nykypäiviin, Suomenkieliseen laskentatoimen kirjallisuuteen perustuva historiantutkimus* (The development of accounting thought from the middle of the last century to the present day), doctoral thesis, Tampere: Acta Universitatis Tamperensis, series A, vol. 291.

Näsi, S. (1994) 'Development of cost accounting in Finland from the last century to the 1960s', *European Accounting Review* 3 (3): 489–514.

Näsi, S., Laine, P., Makinen, Y. and Näsi, J. (1993) 'A research strategic analysis of the Finnish doctoral dissertations in accounting', paper presented at the Nordiska Foretagsekonomiska Anmeskonferensen i Lund 18–20 augusti: X.

Nederstigt, W.F. (1952) 'Latente belastingschulden in de jaarrekening in verband met de vervangingswaarde' (Deferred expenses in annual financial statements under replacements value), *Vaga-berichten* (April).

Neilimo, K. (1975) *Kehitysaluepoliittisten toimenpiteiden yritystaloudellinen tehokkuus* (The effectiveness of regional development policy from the point of view of business economics), Tampere: The University of Tampere.

Neilimo, K. (1981) *Laskentatoimenja yhteiskunnallisen laskentatoimen käsitteet* (The concepts of accounting and social accounting), Tampere: The University of Tampere.

Neilimo, K. and Näsi, J. (1980) *Nomoteettinen tutkimusote ja suomalainen yrityksen taloustiede – tutkimus positivismin soveltamisesta* (Nomothetic research method – a study on positivism in business economics in Finland), Yrityksen taloustieteen ja yksityisoikeuden laitoksen julkaisuja, Tampere: Sarja A: 2: Tutkielmia ja raportteja 12, Tampereen yliopisto.

Niskala, M. and Näsi, S. (1995) 'Stakeholder theory as a framework for accounting', in J. Näsi ed., *Understanding stakeholder thinking*, Gummerus Oy, Jyvaskyla.

Nurmilahti, V.P. (1937) *Der formale Aujban der Jahresvermogensbilanz*, doctoral dissertation, Helsinki: Otava and Helsinki School of Economics.

Ohlson, J.A. (1987) *The theory of financial markets and information*, New York: North-Holland Publishing.

Ohlson, J.A. (1988) 'The social value of public information in production economies', in G.A. Feltham, A.H. Amershi and W.T. Ziemba eds, *Economic analysis of information and contracts*, Boston, MA: Kluwer Academic Publishers: 95–119.

Ohlson, J.A. (1995) 'Earnings, book values, and dividends in equity valuation', *Contemporary Accounting Research* 11 (Spring): 661–87.

Ohlsson, I. (1953) 'On national accounting', Stockholm: Konjunktur Institutet.

Oson, O. (1983) *Ansvar och andamal: om utveckling och anviindning av ett kommunalt ekonomisystem* (Responsibility and purpose: on the development and use of a municipal accounting information system), Lund: Doxa.

Östman, L. (1973) *Utveckling av ekonomiska rapporter* (Development of economic reports), doctoral dissertation, Stockholm: Stockholm School of Economics.

Östman, L. (1977) *Styrning med redovisningsmatt* (Control by accounting measures), Stockholm: EFI.

Östman, L. (1980) *Beteendeiriktad redovisning* (Behavioural accounting), Stockholm: EFI.

Östman, L. (1984) 'Some impressions of accounting research in Scandinavian countries', in A.G. Hopwood and H. Schreuder eds, *European contributions to accounting research: the achievements of the last decade*, Amsterdam: Free University Press.

Paasio, A. (1981) *Yrityskybernetiikka ja laskentatoimi* (Managerial cybernetics and accounting), Turku: Turku School of Economics.

Perridon, L. (1956–57) 'Les problèmes économiques du coût et de prix de revient dans la doctrine de lécole d'Amsterdam', *Revue Française de Comptabilité* (1956): 1978–83, 1987–94; (1957): 3–9.

Pihlanto, P. (1978) *Yritys ja rahoittajat. Yrityksen vieraan pääoman rahoituskäyttäytymisen kuvaus* (The firm and its investors: the description of the debt financing behavior of a firm), Turku: The Turku School of Economics.

Pihlanto, P. (1988a) *Laskentajärjestelmii ja toinen ulottuvuus sosiologinen näkökulma laskentatoimeen* (The 'second dimension' in an accounting system: a sociological approach to management accounting), Turku: Turku School of Economics and Business Administration.

Pihlanto, P. (1988b) 'Onko laskentatoimi (kirjanpito) vain rahaprosessin kuvausta?' (Is accounting merely a description of the monetary process of enterprise?), *The Finnish Journal of Business Economics*, 4: 320–75.

Pihlanto, P. (1992) *The action-oriented approach and case study method in management studies*, Turku: Turku School of Economics and Business Administration: Series A: 3.

Pihlanto, P. (1994) *Humanistisen laskentatoimen hahmottelua, tiedeideaali ja ihmiskäsitys* (Outlining social accounting: the approach to science and assumption about human nature), Turku: Turku School of Economics and Business Administration: Series A: 4.

Pihlanto, P. and Lukka, K. (1993) *Martti Saario – suomalaisen laskenta-ajattelun kehittäjä* (Martti Saario – the developer of Finnish accounting thinking), *The Finnish Journal of Business Economics*, 3: 257–77.

Pitkänen, E. (1969) *Tuotostavoitteiden operationaalisuus julkisessa hallinnossa* (Operational output objectives in public administration), doctoral thesis, Helsinki: Helsinki School of Economics: Series A: 3.

Poel, J.H. van de (1986) *Judgment and control*, Groningen: Wolters-Noordhoff.

Polesie, T. (1976a) 'Ändamålsbudgetering: beskrivning och analys av tillämpningar' (Goal-budgeting and direct costing: an empirical study), doctoral dissertation, Gothenburg: Gothenburg University.

Polesie, T. (1976b) *Aildamalsbudgetering* (Budgeting by objectives), Lund: Studentlitteratur.

Prihti, A. (1975) *Konkurssin ennustaminen taseinformaation avulla* (The prediction of bankruptcy with published financial data), Helsinki: The Helsinki School of Economics.

Provstgaard, B. (1972) *Regnskabsvesendet sam led i ledelsens informations-system* (Management accounting as a part of the management information system), Aarhus.

Provstgaard, B. (1976) 'En analyse av erhvervsvirksomheders overskodsopgrelse' (The profit task of accounting), *Revisionsorientering.*

Pruyt, B. (1954) 'Subjectieve schattingen en beleidselementen bij winstbepaling en winstbestemming' (Subjective tendencies in profit definition and profit determination), *De Economist* 102: 737–56.

Quadackers, L., Mock, T. and Maijoor, S. (1996) 'Audit risk and audit programmes: archival evidence from four Dutch audit firms', *European Accounting Review* 5 (5): 217–38.

Rasila, V. (1982) 'Liberalismin aika' (The time of liberalism) in *Suomen taloushistoria 2: Teollistuva Suomi* (The Finnish economic history, 2: The industrialization of Finland), Helsinki: WSOY.

Reponen, T. (1977) *The screening off of investment alternatives in the dynamic planning of expansion programmes for economically interdependent projects*, Turku: The Turku School of Economics.

Riise, A. (1969) *Driftkalkyler for beslutninger og kontroll* (Cost calculations for decisions and control), Oslo.

Riistama, V. (1971) 'Laskentatoimen hyväksikäytöstä' (On the use of accounting measurements), *The Finnish Journal of Business Economics*, 2: 209–23.

Riistama, V. (1978) *Inflaatiovaraus. Tutkimus inflaation vaikutuksista ansaintataloudellisen yrityksen jakokelpoiseen voittoon* (Inflation reserve: an enquiry into the influence of inflation on the distributable profit of a firm), Helsinki: The Helsinki School of Economics.

Riistama, V. and Jirkkiö, E. (1971) *Operatiivinen laskentatoimi* (Management accounting), Jyväskylä: Weilin & Göös (with at least a dozen later editions).

Ruuhela, R. (1972) *Yrityksen kasvu ja kannattavuus* (A capital investment model for growth and profitability of the firm), Helsinki: The Helsinki School of Economics.

Saario, M. (1945) *Realisointiperiaate ja käyttöomaisuuden poistot tuloslaskennassa* (The realization principle and the depreciation of fixed assets in profit calculation), doctoral dissertation Helsinki: Liiketaloustieteellisen tutkimuslaitoksen julkaisuja 6.

Saario, M. (1949) 'Kustannusten etuoikeusjärjestyksestä' (On the theory of priority order of costs), *Huugo Raninen 50 vuotta*, Helsinki: Kauppatieteellisen yhdistyksen vuosikirja.

Saario, M. (1959) *Kirjanpidon meno-tulo-teoria* (The expenditure-revenue theory of accounting), Keuruu: Liiketaloustieteellisen tutkimukslaitoksen julkaisuja 28.

Saario, M. (1965) *Kirjanpidon meno-tulo -teoria* (The theory of expenditure-revenue accounting), Keuruu: Otava.

Salmi, T. (1975) *Joint determination of trade, production, and financial flows in the multinational firm assuming risky currency exchange rates*, Helsinki: The Helsinki School of Economics.

Salmi, T. (1976) 'Puheenvuoro suomalaisista opinnäytetöistä' (A review of Finnish dissertations), *The Finnish Journal of Business Economics*, 1: 84–8.

Salmi, T. (1978) 'Opinnäytetutkimuksen aiheen valinnasta ja kontribuution kätsitteesta liiketaloustieteessä' (On the Finnish concept of scientific contribution and subject selection in doctoral theses in business economics), *The Finnish Journal of Business Economics* 4: 391–401.

Samuelson, L.A. (1973) *Effektiv budgetering* (Effective budgeting), Stockholm: The Economic Research Institute of the Stockhom School of Economics and the Swedish Association of Metalworking Industries.

Samuelson, L.A. (1989) 'The development of models of accounting information systems in Sweden', *Scandinavian Journal of Management* 5 (4): 293–310.

Samuelson, L.A. (1990) *Models of accounting information systems: the Swedish case*, Lund: Studentlitteratur.

Scheffer, C.F. (1962) *Financiële notities*, Eerste deel (Financial notes, Vol. 1, Chapter 17) Gravenhage: Delwel.

Schmidt, F. (1921) *Die organische Bilanz im Rahmen der Wirtschaft* (The organic balance sheet in an economic setting), 1st edn, Leipzig: G.A. Gloeckner Verlagsbuchhandlung (2nd edn, 1922, *Die organische Tageswertbilanz*, Leipzig; 3rd edn, 1929; reprint, Wiesbaden: Betriebswirtschaftlicher Verlag Dr T. Gabler, 1953; Japanese translation, *Yukikan taishohyo gakusetsu*, Tokyo: Dobunkan Ltd, 1934).

Schoonderbeek, J.W. (1987) *Setting accounting standards in the Netherlands*, Amsterdam: Council for Annual Reporting.

Schreuder, H. (1981) 'Employees and the corporate social report: the Dutch case', *The Accounting Review* 56 (4): 294–308.

Schroeff, H.J. van der (1970) *Verleden, hedenen toekomst van de bedrijfseconomie* (Valedictory Lecture, 24 October 1970), Amsterdam: Kosmos.

Schroeff, H.J. van der (1975) *Bedrijfseconomische grondslagenvan de instbepaing* (Foundations of income determination in business economics), Amsterdam: Kosmos.

Seventer, A. van (1969) 'The continuity postulate in the Dutch theory of business income', *The International Journal of Accounting* 4 (2): 1–19.

Seventer, A. van (1975) 'Replacement value theory in modern Dutch accounting', *The International Journal of Accounting* 11 (1): 68–94.

Seventer, A. van (1996) 'Limperg, Theodor, Jr'., in M. Chatfield and R. Vangermeersch eds, *The history of accounting: an international encyclopedia*, New York: Garland Publishing, Inc.: 384–6.

Sillén, O. (1926) *Revisions- und Treuhandwesen* (The auditing profession), Leipzig: G.A. Gloeckner (later edition 1930).

Sillén, O. (1929) 'Zur Geschichte der Bewertungslehre in Schweden' (To the history of valuation theory in Sweden), *Zeitschrift für Handelswissenschaft und Handelspraxis* 22: 118–26.

Skaerbaek, P. (1998) 'The politics of accounting technology in Danish central government', *European Accounting Review* 7 (2): 209–37.

Sloten, P.J. van (1981) 'The Dutch contribution to replacement value accounting theory and practice', ICRA Occasional Paper No. 21, Lancaster: University of Lancaster, International Centre for Research in Accounting.

Solomons, D. (1966) 'Economic and accounting concepts of cost and value', in M. Backer ed., *Modem accounting theory*, Englewood Cliffs, NJ: Prentice-Hall: 117–40.

Straaten, H.C. van (1957) *Inhoud en grenzenvan het winstbegrip* (Content and limits of the income concept), Leiden: Stenfert Kroese.

Tainio, R., Ahlstedt, L. and Pulkkinen, K. (1982) 'Business Economics – administration in Finland: a historical review', *The Finnish Journal of Business Economics*, 1: 18–35.

Tamminen, R. (1976) *A theoretical study in the profitability of the firm*, Vaasa: The Vaasa School of Economics.

Tamminen, R. (1992) 'The development of inquiry approach', the *Finnish Journal of Business Economics*, 1: 42–61.

Tamminen, R. (1993) *Tiedetäi tekemään!* (How to make science!), Jyväskylä: Atena kustannus Oy.

Tornquist, U. (1999) 'An empirical study of accountability: delegation of responsibility and external disclosure in some Swedish companies', *European Accounting Review* 8 (1): 139–57.

Vehmanen. P. (1992) 'Johdon laskentatoimi ja rahoituksen laskentatoimi – ehdotus terminologian tarkistamiseksi' (Management accounting and financial accounting – some terminological considerations), *The Finnish Journal of Business Economics* 1: 77–88.

Vehmanen, P. (1994) 'Toimintolaskenta yrityksen johtamisessa' (Activity-based costing and management), *The Finnish Journal of Business Economics* 3: 329–38.

Vehn, A. ter (1929) *Entwicklung der Bilanzauffassung bis zum AHGB* (Development of accounting theory up to the General Commercial Code), Berlin.

Vehn, A. ter (1936) *Sjiilvkostlzadsberiikningens standardisering* (The standardization of full cost accounting), Stockholm: Norstedts.

Virkkunen, H. (1951) *Teollisuuden kertakustannukset, niiden degressio sekä käsittely ustannuslaskennassa* (Onetime costs of the industry, their digression and handling in cost accounting), doctoral dissertation, Helsinki.

Virkkunen, H. (1954) *Laskentatoimi johdon apuna – systemaattis-teoreettinen tutkmus teollisuusyrityksen laskentatoimen haaroista ja tehtävisäi erityisesti johtotehäivien kannalta* (Accounting as the tool of management – a systematic-theoretical study of the branches and functions of industrial accounting from the viewpoint of management tasks), Helsinki: Liiketaloustieteellisen Tutkimuslaitoksen julkaisuja 18.

Virkkunen, H. (1961) *Teollisen kustannuslaskennan perusteet ja hyväksikäyttö I-II* (The use of industrial cost accounting I–II), Helsinki: Kauppakorkeakoulun julkaisuja: sarja C: l: 9.

Virrankoski, P. (1975) *Suomen taloushistoria kaskikaudesta atomiaikaan* (Finnish economic history from burn-beating to the atomic age), Helsinki.

Virtanen, K. (1979) *Yritysoston suunnittelu prosessina* (Planning of purchase as a process), doctoral dissertation, Helsinki: Helsinki School of Economics: Series A: 31.

Virtanen, K., Malmi, T., Vaivio, J. and Kasanen, E. (1996) 'Drivers of cost accounting in Finland', in A. Bhimani ed., *Modern cost management: European perspective*, Oxord: Oxford University Press: 54–73.

Virtanen, U. (1949) *Suomen teollisuuden kustannusten rakenne v.* 1944 *ja sen kehityksen pääpiirteitä* (The cost structure of the Finnish industry in 1944 and the main features of its development), doctoral dissertation, Helsinki.

Virtanen, U. (1959) *Hyäkauppiastapa ja kirjanpidon periaatteet* (Ethics of business and accounting principles), Porvoo: WSOY.

Waal, P.G.A. de (1927) *De leervan het boekholding in the Nederlanden tijdens de zeventiende en achtitende eeuw* (The teaching of bookkeeping in the Netherlands during the seventeenth and eighteenth century), Rotterdam: Romen.

Wallenius, J. (1975) *Interactive multiple criteria decision methods: an investigation and an approach*, Helsinki: The Helsinki School of Economics.

Wallerstedt, E. (1988) 'Oskar Sillén – professor och praktiker. Nagra drag i företagsekonomiämnets tidiga utveckling vid Handelshögskolan i Stockholm' (Oskar Sillén – professor and practitioner. Some aspects of the early development of business economics at the Stockholm School of Economics), Stockholm: Almqvist & Wiks.

Wallin, J. (1978) *Computer-aided multi-attribute profit planning*, Turku: The Abo Swedish University School of Economics.

Widebäck, G. (1976) *Inflation och budgetering* (Inflation and budgeting), Stockholm.

Zeff, S.A. (1993) 'The regulation of financial reporting: historical development and policy recommendations', *De Accountant* 100 (3): 152–60.

Zeff, S.A., Bujink, W. and Camfferman, K. (1999) ' "True and fair" in the Netherlands: izichtor getrouw beeld?', *European Accounting Review* 8 (3): 523–48.

Zeff, S.A., der Wei, F. and Camfermann, K. (1992) *Company financial reporting: a historical and comparative study of the Dutch regulatory process*, Amsterdam: North Holland (2nd edn, 1999).

14 Accounting publications and research in twentieth-century Japan

Accounting Standards Research Committee (1970) *Kaikei kojun to kaikei kijun* (Accounting postulates and accounting standards), Tokyo: Dobunkan.

Aizaki, K. (1957) *Keizaikaikeigaku josetsu* (Introduction to economic accounting), Tokyo: Moriyama-shoten.

Aizaki, K. (1962a) Bray kyoju no keizaikaikei gainen (On Bray's economic accounting, I), *Kaikei* 81 (4): 69–81.

Aizaki, K. (1962b) Bray kyoju no keizaikaikei gainen (On Bray's economic accounting, II), *Kaikei* 82 (1): 27–37.

Aizaki, K. (1963a) 'Bray kyoju no keizaikaikei gainen' (Bray's economic accounting III), *Kaikei* 83 (4): 14–26.

Aizaki, K. (1963b) 'Bray kyoju no keizaikaikei gainen' (Bray's economic accounting IV), *Kaikei* 83 (6): 37–51.

Aizaki, K. (1966) *Shakaikagaku to shiteno kaikeigaku* (Accounting as a social science), Tokyo: Chuo University Press.

Aizaki, K. (1971) 'Kaikeigaku no shakaikagaku-teki shiko to shakaikaikei' (Accounting as a social science and social accounting), in K. Aizaki and N. Nosse (eds),

Kigyokaikei to shakaikaikei (Business accounting and social accounting), Tokyo: Moriyama-shoten: 257–303.

Aizaki, K. (ed.) (1999) *Kurosawa kaikeigaku kenkyu* (Studies in the accounting thoughts of Kurosawa: Essays in honor of Kiyoshi Kurosawa), Tokyo: Moriyama-shoten.

Aizaki, K. and Nosse, N. (eds) (1971) *Kigyokaikei to shakaikaikei* (Business accounting and social accounting), Tokyo: Moriyama-shoten.

American Accounting Association (AAA) (1936) 'A tentative statement of accounting principles underlying corporate financial statements', *The Accounting Review*, 11 (June): 187–91.

American Accounting Association (AAA) (1966) *A statement of basic accounting theory*, Sarasota, FA: AAA. (Japanese translation by Toshio Iino as: *Kisoteki kaikei riron*, Tokyo: Kunimoto-shobo).

Aoki, S. (ed.) (1976) *Nihon kaikei hattatsu-shi – Wagakuni kaikeigaku no seisei to tenbo* (Accounting evolution in Japan: retrospect and prospect), Tokyo, Doyukan.

Aoyagi, B. (1958) 'Sociological accounting', *Journal of accountancy* (July): 51–5.

Aoyagi, B. (1986) *Amerika kaikeigaku* (Development of accounting in the United States of America), Tokyo: Chuokeizai-sha.

Aoyagi, B. (1991) *Kaikeigaku no Kiso* (Foundations of Accounting), Tokyo: Chuokeizai-sha.

Arai, K. (1969) *Kaikei kojun-ron* (Theory of Accounting postulates), Tokyo: Chuokeizai-sha.

Aukrust, O. (1955/98) 'Forsøk på en aksiomatisk behandling av klassifikasjons – og vurderingsproblemet', *Nasjonalregnskap: teoretiske prinsipper* (National accounting: theoretical principles), Oslo, Statistik Sentralbyrå: Appendix, 77–102. (Japanese translation, Y. Koguchi (1998) 'Kokuminkaikei ni okeru bunrui oyobi hyokamondai ni kansuru koriteki-kenkyu', *Keizaigaku-ronsan* 39 (1/2): 91–112).

Aukrust, O. (1966) 'An axiomatic approach to national accounting: an outline', *The Review of Income and Wealth* 12 (3): 179–90.

Balzer, W. and Mattessich, R. (1991/94) 'An axiomatic basis of accounting: a structuralist reconstruction', *Theory and Decision* 30: 213–43 (Japanese translation, Y. Koguchi (1994) Kaikeigaku no koriteki kiso: kozoshugiteki saikosei, *Keizaigaku Ronsan* 35 (May): 209–32).

Bray, F.S. (1949a) *Social accounts and the business enterprise sector of the national economy*, London: Cambridge University Press.

Bray, F.S. (1949b) *The measurement of profit*, London: Oxford University Press.

Bray, F.S. (1951) *The accounting mission*, Melbourne: Melbourne University Press.

Bray, F.S. (1953) *Four essays in accounting theory*, London: Oxford University Press.

Bray, F.S. (1957) *The interpretation of accounts*, London: Oxford University Press.

Bryant, H.B. and Stratton, H.D. (1871) *Common school bookkeeping* (Japanese translation, Yukichi Fukuzawa, *Choai-no-ho*, 2 vols, Tokyo: Keiogijiuku Shuppankyoku).

Chatfield, M. and Vangermeersch, R. (eds) (1996) *The history of accounting: an international encyclopedia*, New York: Garland Publishing, Inc.

Chiba, J. (1991a) 'Nihon ni okeru kaikei to kaikeigaku no kindaika-katei' (Modernization of accounting and accounting theory in Japan – a socio-historical study of the theories of Kiyoshi Kurosawa), *Kaikei* 139 (1): 31–49.

Chiba, J. (1991b) *Eikoku kindai kaikei seido* (The modern British accounting system), Tokyo: Chuokeizai-sha.

Chiba, J. (1994) 'Kiyoshi Kurosawa (1902–90)', in J.R. Edwards ed., *Twentieth-century accounting thinkers*, London: Routledge: 181–97.

Chiba, J. (1996) 'Japanese experience of corporate accounting control c.1939–c.1945', *Accounting, Business and Financial History* 6 (2): 163–82.

Chiba, J. (1998) *Nihon kindai kaikei seido* (Japan's modern accounting system), Tokyo: Chuokeizai-sha.

Chiba, J. (1999) 'Kigyokaikei no seidoteki-rekishiteki kozo' (Institutional and historical analysis of business accounting), in K. Aizaki ed., *Kurosawa kaikeigaku kenkyu* (Studies in the accounting thoughts of Kurosawa: essays in honour of Kiyoshi Kurosawa), Tokyo: Moriyama-shoten: 81–176.

Choi, D.S. and Hiramatsu, K. (1987) *Accounting and financial reporting in Japan*, Van Nostrand Reinhold Co. Ltd.

Churchman, W. (1961) *Prediction and optimal decision*, Englewood Cliffs, NJ: Prentice-Hall.

Clark, J.M. (1923) *Studies in the economics of overhead costs*, Chicago: University of Chicago Press.

Colasse, B. (2005) *Les grands auteurs en comptabilité* (The great authors of accounting [from the fifteenth century to modern times]), Paris: Éditions EMS.

Cooke, T.E. and Kikuya, M. (1992) *Financial reporting in Japan: regulation, practice and environment*, Oxford: Blackwell.

Cooper, R. (1994) *Nissan Motor Company, Ltd: target costing system*, Boston, MA: Harvard Business School.

Deguchi, H. and Nakano, B. (1986) 'Axiomatic foundations of vector accounting' *Systems Research* 3 (1): 31–9.

Eaves, B.C. (1966) 'Operational axiomatic accounting mechanics', *The Accounting Review* 41 (3, July): 426–42.

Edwards, J.R. (ed.) (1994) *Twentieth-century accounting thinkers*, London: Routledge.

Fisher, I. (1906) *The nature of capital and income*, New York: Macmillan.

Frisch, R. (1943) 'Ökosirk-systemet: Det ökonomiske sirkulasjons system' (The economic circulation system), *Ekonomisk Tidskrift*: 106–21.

Fujita, A. and Garcia, C. (2005) 'Kiyoshi Kurosawa: le premier samuraï de la comptabilité' (Kiyoshi Kurosawa: the first samurai of accounting), in B. Colasse ed., *Les grands auteurs en comptabilité* (The great authors of accounting [from the fifteenth century to modern times]), Paris: Éditions EMS: 163–80.

Fujita, Y. (1968/91) *An analysis of the development and nature of accounting principles in Japan*, University of Illinois (reprinted in New York: Garland Publishing, Inc., 1991).

Fukuzawa, Y. (1873/74) *Choai-no-ho*, 2 vols, Tokyo: Keiogijuku Shuppankyoku.

Gray, R. (1990) *The greening of accountancy: the profession after Pearce*, London: Certified Accountants Publications.

Gray, R., Bebbington, J. and Walters, D. (1993) *Accounting for the environment*, London, Paul Chapman Publishing Ltd.

Harada, F. (1966a) 'Kaikei no shugoron-teki teishikika to sono ippansei' (Set-theoretical formulation of accounting and its generality), *Kaikei* 90 (1): 130–45.

Harada, F. (1966b) 'Kanjo narabi ni torihikigainen no kakudai' (On the extension of the concepts of accounts and transaction), *Kaikei* 90 (4): 171–86.

Harada, F. (1967a) 'Kaikeisokutei no koyusei ni tsuite' (On the essence of accounting measurement, I), *Kaikei* 92 (3): 129–39.

Harada, F. (1967b) 'Kaikeisokutei no koyusei ni tsuite' (On the essence of accounting measurement, II), *Kaikei* 92 (4): 105–16.

Harada, F. (1967c) 'Kaikei ippanriron no tenkai to sono haikei' (The development of a general theory of accounting and its social background), *Keizaigaku-ronsan* 8(2), Chuo University: 49–80.

Harada, F. (1968) 'Kaikei no koriteki kozo to sokuteiron-teki koyusei' (The axiomatic structure of accounting and the essence of accounting measurement), *Kaike* 94 (5): 56–74.

Harada, F. (1974) 'Kaikeiriron no hoho' (Methodological features of the axiomatic approach to accounting), *Kaikei* 105 (4): 18–44.

Harada, F. (1978) *Joho kakei ron* (Accounting in a new informational society), Tokyo: Dobunkan.

Harada, F. (1999) 'Kurosawa kaikeigaku no shiso-teki tenkai' (The evolution of Kurosawa's accounting theory), in K. Aizaki ed., *Kurosawa kaikeigaku kenkyu*, Tokyo: Moriyama-shoten: 3–79.

Hatfield, H.R. (1918/71) *Modern accounting*, New York: Arno Press (first published in 1909; later editions 1916, etc., and in 1976 Japanese translation, Kenkichi Matsuo (1971) *Kindai kaikeigaku*, Tokyo: Yushodo).

Hicks, J.R. (1942/61) *The social framework: an introduction to economics*, Oxford University Press (Japanese translation, Shozaburo Sakai (1961) *Keizai no shakai-teki kozo*, Tokyo: Dobunkan).

Hicks, J.R. and Nosse, N. (1974) *The social framework of the Japanese economy: an introduction to economics*, Oxford: Oxford University Press.

Hirabayashi, Y. (1996) 'Kojima, Osamu (1912–1989)', in M. Chatfield and R. Vangermeersh eds, *The history of accounting: an international encyclopedia*, New York: Garland Publishing, Inc.: 364.

Hirai, Y. (1936) 'Izumo choai no seishitsu' (The nature of *Izumo* bookkeeping), *Kokuminkeiza- zasshi* 61(3): 1–28.

Hiromoto, T. (1989) 'Management accounting in Japan' (in German), *Controlling*: 316–22.

Hiromoto, T. (1991) 'Wie das Management Accounting seine Bedeutung zurückgewinnt' (How management accounting regains its meaning), in IFUA Horvath and Partner, GmbH eds, *Prozesskostenmanagement*, Munich: IFUA.

Hiromoto, T. (1993) *Beikoku kanrikaikei-ron hattatsu-shi* (The development of management accounting in the United States of America), Tokyo: Moriyama-shoten.

Hirose, Y. (1995) *Kaikei kijun-ron* (Theory of accounting standards), Tokyo: Chuokeizai-sha.

Hopwood, A.G. (1988) *Accounting from the outside: the collected papers by Anthony G. Hopwood*, New York: Garland Publishing, Inc.

Ijiri, Y. (1965/70) *Management goals and accounting for control* (based on the author's dissertation: 'Goal oriented models for accounting and control', 1963), Amsterdam: North-Holland Publishing Co. (revised Japanese version as: *Keisu kanri no kiso*, Tokyo: Iwanami-shoten, 1970).

Ijiri, Y. (1967/68) *The foundations of accounting measurement: a mathematical, economic, and behavioral inquiry*, Englewood Cliffs, NJ: Prentice-Hall, Inc. (revised Japanese version, *Kaikei sokutei no kiso*, Tokyo: Toyokeizai-shinposha, 1968).

Ijiri, Y. (1975/76) *Theory of accounting measurement*, Sarasota, FA: American Accounting Association (revised Japanese version, *Kaikei sokutei no riron*, Tokyo: Toyokeizai-shinposha, 1976).

Ijiri, Y. (1979) 'A structure of multisector accounting and its applications to national accounting', in W.W. Cooper, and Y. Ijiri eds, *Erich Louis Kohler: accounting's man of principles*, Englewood Cliffs, NJ: Prentice-Hall, Inc.: 208–23.

Ijiri, Y. (1981) *Historical cost accounting and its rationality*, Vancouver, BC: Canadian Certified General Accountants' Research Foundation.

Ijiri, Y. (1982/84) *Triple-entry bookkeeping and income momentum*, Sarasota, FA: AAA (revised Japanese version, *Sanshiki boki no kenkyu*, Tokyo: Chuokeizai-sha, 1984).

Ijiri, Y. (1989/90) *Momentum accounting and triple-entry bookkeeping: exploring the dynamic structure of accounting measurements*, Sarasota, FA: AAA (revised Japanese version, *Risoku-kaikei nyumon*, Tokyo: Nihonkeizai-shinbunsha, 1990).

Ijiri, Y. (1996) 'Academic research in accounting: the last 50 years – commentary', *Asia-Pacific Journal of Accounting* 3 (July): 83–6.

Inoue, R. (1984) *Kaikei shakaigaku* (Sociological accounting), Tokyo: Chuo University Press.

International Federation of Accountants (1999) *Target costing for effective cost management: product cost planning at Toyota Australia*, New York: IFA.

Ischboldin, B. (1936) 'Die sozialwirtschaftliche Bilanz als eine wichtige Arbeitsidee der nationalökonomischen Forschung' (The socio-economic balance sheet as an important working hypothesis of economic research), *Schmollers Jahrbuch* 60: 537–50.

Ishizaki, A., Ansari, S. and Bell, J. (1995) *Japanese language literature on target costing: an abstract of key ideas*, Arlington, TX: CAM-I.

Ishizuka, H. (ed.) (1987) *Jissho: kaikeijoho to kabuka* (Accounting information and security prices: an empirical study), Tokyo: Dobunkan.

Itami, H. (1977) *Adaptive behavior: management control and information analysis*, Sarasota, FA: AAA.

Ito, K. (1996) *Kaikeiseido no dainamizumu* (Dynamism of accounting system), Tokyo: Iwanami-shoten.

Iwanabe, K. (1996) 'Japan', in M. Chatfield and R. Vangermeersch eds, *The history of accounting: an international encyclopedia*, New York: Garland Publishing, Inc.: 351–3.

Iwata, I. (1954a) *Kaikeishi-kansha* (Auditing by public accountants), Tokyo: Moriyama-shoten.

Iwata, I. (1954b) 'Rijun-keisan no nigenteki-kozo' (The dual structure of income determination), *Sangyo-keiri* 14: 1–6.

Iwata, I. (1955) *Kaikei-gensoku to Kansa-kijun* (Accounting principles and auditing standards), Tokyo: Chuokeizai-sha.

Iwata, I. (1956) *Rijun-keisan-genri* (Principles of income determination), Tokyo: Dobunkan.

Jaedicke, R., Ijiri, Y. and Nielsen, O. (eds) (1966/74/76) *Research in accounting measurement*, Sarasota, FA: AAA. (Japanese translation, Cost Research Project, *Kaikei sokutei no kiso*, 2 vols, Kyoto: Mineruba-shobo, 1974 and 1976).

Japan Accounting Association (ed.) (1978) *Kindai kaikei hyakunen – sono ayumi to bunken mokuroku* (One hundred years of modern accounting in Japan: history and bibliography), Tokyo: Japan Accounting Association.

Kataoka, Y. (1956) *Pacioli bokiron kenkyu* (Studies in Pacioli's bookkeeping), Tokyo: Moriyama-shoten.

Kataoka, Y. (1988) *Itaria bokishi ron* (The history of Italian bookkeeping), Tokyo: Moriyama-shoten.

Kataoka, Y. (ed.) (1998) *Wagakuni Pacioli bokiron no kiseki*, 2 vols (Studies in Pacioli's bookkeeping in Japan), Tokyo: Yushodo.

Kawano, M. (1998) *Seitai kaikeigaku* (Ecological accounting), Tokyo: Moriyama-shoten.

Kawano, M. (1999) 'Keizaikaikeigaku tankyu no kiseki' (Kurosawa in economic accounting), in K. Aizaki ed., *Kurosawa kaikeigaku kenkyu*, Tokyo: Moriyama-shoten: 177–249.

Kim, I.-W. and Song, J. (1990) 'U.S., Korea, and Japan: accounting practices in three countries', *Management Accounting* 72 (2): 26–30.

Kimura, W. (1935) *Ginko boki-ron* (Bank bookkeeping), Tokyo: Yuhikaku (later expanded into his *Ginko boki taiko* (Basic principles of bank bookkeeping), Tokyo: Dobunkan, 1938).

Kimura, W. (1943) *Genkakeisan-ron kenkyu* (Studies in cost accounting), Tokyo: Nihon-hyoronsha.

Kimura, W. (1947) *Genka shokyaku kenkyu* (Studies in depreciation), Osaka: Tanseido-shuppan.

Kimura, W. (1954) *Kaikeigaku-kenya* (Studies in accounting theory), Tokyo: Yuhikaki.

Kimura, W. (1972) *Kagaku to shite no kaikeigaku* (Accounting as a science), 2 vols, Tokyo: Yuhikaku.

Kimura, W. and Kojima, O. (1960) *Kogyo kaikei nyumon* (A primer of industrial accounting), Tokyo: Moriyama-shoten.

Kimizuka, Y. (1991) 'The evolution of Japanese cost accounting to 1945', in F.O. Graves ed., *The costing heritage: studies in honor of S. Paul Garner*, Harrisonburg, VA: The Academy of Accounting Historians (Monograph 6): 74–88.

Kishi, E. (1975) *Kaikei seiseishi: furansu shojiorei kaikeikitei kenkyu* (Accounting evolution in France: study on the accounting rules of the Ordonnance de Commerce), Tokyo: Dobunkan.

Kobe University Accounting Research Project (ed.) (1954) *Schmalenbach kenkyu* (Studies on Schmalenbach), Tokyo: Chuokeizai-sha.

Koga, K. (1999) 'Determinants of effective product cost management during product development: opening the black box of target costing', working paper, Tokyo: Waseda University.

Koguchi, Y. (1990) 'Towards a regional water management accounting system', *The annuals of the Institute of Economic Research* 21, Tokyo: Chuo University: 121–50.

Koguchi, Y. (1997a) 'Ragnar Frish no makurokaikei-ron' (On Ragnar Frish's macro-accounting), *The annuals of the Institute of Economic Research* 27, Tokyo: Chuo University: 191–218.

Koguchi, Y. (1997b) 'Accounting for integrated river basin management', a paper presented at an international symposium organized by Shimane University in Matsue, Japan, from 13 to 15 October 1997 (reproduced in Y. Kurabayashi, K. Koike and N. Yamamoto (eds) (2002) *The progress in environmental and resource accounting approach*, Tottori: Imai-shuppan Co. Ltd: 161–73).

Koguchi, Y. (1999) 'Makuro kaikei-riron no kori-teki tenkai – Aukrust riron no kenkyu' (Studies in Aukrust's axiomatic formulation of macro-accounting), in K. Aizaki ed., *Kurosawa kaikeigaku kenkyu*, Tokyo: Moriyama-shoten: 319–45.

Kojima, O. (1961) *Fukushikiboki hasseishi no kenkyu* (Studies in the origin of double-entry bookkeeping), Tokyo: Moriyama-shoten.

Kojima, O. (1987/95) *Kaikeishi nyumon* (An Introduction to accounting history), Tokyo: Moriama-shoten (posthumous English version, *Accounting History*, Osaka: A.N. Offset Co., Ltd, 1995 – see also Chapter 12).

Kokubu, K. (1998) *Kankyo kaikei* (Environmental accounting), Tokyo: Shinsei-sha (2nd edn, 2000).

Kokubu, K. (1999) *Shakai to kankyo no kaikeigaku* (Accounting for society and the environment), Tokyo: Chuokeizai-sha.

Koshimura, S. (1968) *Gyoretsu boki* (Matrix bookkeeping), Tokyo: Daisan-shuppan.

Koshimura, S. (ed.) (1969) *Gyoretsu kaikeigaku nyumon* (Introduction to matrix accounting – a series of essays by R. Mattessich, A.B. Richards, B.E. Goetz and A.W. Corcoran, translated and compiled by S. Koshimura), Tokyo: Daisan-shuppan.

Kurosawa, K. (1932) 'Taishakutaishohyo ni okeru hyojunka no igi ni tsuite' (On the meaning of standardization of the balance sheet), *Kaikei* 30 (3): 13–39.

Kurosawa, K. (1933) *Kaikeigaku* (Accounting), Tokyo: Chikura-shobo.

Kurosawa, K. (1934) *Boki genri* (Principles of bookkeeping), Tokyo: Toyoshuppan-sha.

Kurosawa, K. (1936) 'Scott no kaikei riron' (The accounting theory of Scott), *Kaikei* 39 (4): 1–11, (6): 75–94.

Kurosawa, K. (1937) 'Keieikeizaiteki taishakutaishohyo to kokuminkeizaiteki taishaku-taishohyo' (Balance sheet in management and national economy), *Shogaku* 24: 105–30.

Kurosawa, K. (1938) *Kogyo kaikei* (Industrial accounting), Tokyo: Chikura-shobo.

Kurosawa, K. (1939) 'Kokumin-keizaigaku, keiei-keizaigaku, keisan-keizaigaku: kaikeigaku' (National economics, managerial economics and quantitative economics: accounting), *Shogaku* 29: 27–36.

Kurosawa, K. (1941a) 'Kokumin-shotoku no sokutei ni okeru kaikeigakuteki hohoron' (Accounting methodology in the measurement of national income), *Kaikei* 48 (1): 1–8, (2): 1–8.

Kurosawa, K. (1941b) *Kakakukeisei to genkakeisan* (Price determination and cost accounting), Tokyo: Moriyama-shoten.

Kurosawa, K. (1951a) *Kindai kaikeigaku* (Modern accounting), Tokyo: Shunju-sha.

Kurosawa, K. (1951b) 'Kigyokaikei to shakaikaikei' (Business accounting and social accounting), *Sangyokeiri* 11 (12): 3–10.

Kurosawa, K. (1952) *Genka kaikei-ron* (Theory of cost accounting), Tokyo: Chikura-shobo.

Kurosawa, K. (1972a) 'Seitai-kaikeigaku no hasso' (Methodology of ecological accounting), *Sangyokeiri* 32 (1): 6–10.

Kurosawa, K. (1972b) 'Kankyo-kaikeigaku no kadai' (Issues in environmental accounting), *Sangyokeiri* 32 (10): 5–10.

Kurosawa, K. (1982) *Nihon kaikeigaku hattenshi josetsu* (The development of accounting in Japan), Tokyo: Yushodo.

Kurosawa, K. (ed.) (1987) *Wagakuni zaimushohyo-seido no ayumi: senzen hen* (The development of the financial statements system in Japan: time before the Second World War), Tokyo: Yushodo.

Kurosawa, K. (1990) *Nihon kaikei-seido hattatsu-shi* (Accounting history in Japan), Tokyo: Zaikeishoho-sha.

Littleton, A.C. (1933/52) *Accounting evolution to 1900*, New York: American Institute of Accountants Publishing Co. (Japanese translation, I. Katano (1952) *Littleton kaikei hattatsu-shi*, Tokyo: Dobunkan).

Matsumura, E.M. (1988) 'Sequential choice under moral hazard', in G.A. Feltham, A.H. Amershi and W.T. Ziemba eds, *Economic analysis of information and contracts: essays in honour of John E. Butterworth*, Boston, MA: Kluwer Academic Publishers: 221–45.

Mattessich, R. (1957) 'Towards a general and axiomatic foundation of accountancy: with an introduction to the matrix formulation of accounting systems', *Accounting Research* 8 (October): 328–355 (reprinted in S.A. Zeff ed., *The accounting postulates and principles controversy of the 1960s*, New York: Garland Publishing, Inc., 1982; Spanish translation in *Technica Economica* (April 1958): 106–27).

Mattessich, R. (1964) *Accounting and analytical methods: measurement and projection of income and wealth in the micro- and macro-economy*, Homewood, IL: R.D. Irwin, Inc. (reprinted in the 'Accounting Classics Series', Houston, TX: Scholars Book Co., 1977; also in the 'Series of Financial Classics' of Reprints on Demand, Ann Arbor, MI: Microfilms International, 1979, still available; Japanese translation under the direction of Shinzaburo Koshimura, *Kaikei to Bunsekiteki-Hoho*, 2 vols, Tokyo: Dobunkan, Ltd, Vol. 1: 1972, Vol. 2: 1975; Spanish translation, by Carlos Luis García Casella and Maria del Carmen Ramírez de Rodríguez, Buenos Aires: La Ley, 2002).

Mattessich, R. (1973a) 'On the axiomatic formulation of accounting: comment on Professor Saito's considerations', *Musashi Daigaku Ronshu* 21 (1/2): 77–94.

Mattessich, R. (1973b) 'On the axiomatic formulation of accounting: comment on Professor Saito's considerations', (Japanese translation, Y. Hatsukade) *Sangyo-keiri* 33 (3): 70–4, (4): 71–5.

Mattessich, R. (1995a) *Critique of accounting: examination of the foundations and normative structure of an applied discipline*, Westport, CT: Quorum Books.

Mattessich, R. (1992–93/1995b/2007) *Foundational research in accounting: professional memoirs and beyond*, Tokyo: Chuo University Press (originally published serially in Japanese as five instalments, *Chuo Hyoron* April 1992: 154–62; July 1992: 149–59; October 1992: 112–20; January 1993: 124–34; April 1993: 136–48; 1st English book edn, 1995; extended 2nd edn, in *De Computis*, scheduled for 2007).

Monden, Y. (1983/85) *Toyota production system: an integrated approach to just-in-time*, Norcross, GA: Industrial Engineering and Management Press, Institute of Industrial Engineers (further editions 1991, 1993, 1998; Japanese version, *Shin Toyota Shisutemu*, Tokyo: Kodansha, 1985).

Monden, Y. (1994/95/97) *Kakaku kyosoryoku wo tsukeru genka kikaku to genka kaizen no giho*, Tokyo: Toyokeizai-shinposha (English translation, *Cost reduction systems: target costing and kaizen costing*, Portland, OR: Productivtiy Press; Spanish translation, *Sistemas de reducción de costes*, Madrid: TGB-Hoshin, 1997).

Monden, Y. (1996) *Japan target-costing system of parts supplier committed to the development phase of the automaker*, Cambridge, MA: Center for International Studies, MIT Japan Program, Massachusetts Institute of Technology.

Monden, Y. (ed.) (2000) *Japanese cost management*, London: Imperial College Press.

Monden, Y. and Sakurai, M. (eds) (1989) *Japanese management accounting: a world class approach to profit management*, Cambridge, MA: Productivity Press.

Morita, T. (1994) 'Iwao Iwata (1905–55)', in J.R. Edwards ed., *Twentieth-century accounting thinkers*, London: Routledge: 166–80.

Nakajima, S. (1979) *Kaisha kaikei kijun josetsu kenkyu* (Study in an introduction to corporate accounting standards), Tokyo: Moriyama-shoten.

Nakanishi, A. (1973) 'Luca Pacioli no seitanchi iseki' (The historic site of Luca Pacioli's birthplace), *Kaikei* 103 (5): 121–9.

Nakanishi, A. (1974) 'Futatabi Luca Pacioli no iseki wo tazunete' (The historic site of Luca Pacioli revisited), *Kaikei* 105 (4): 105–14.

Nakano, T. (1992) *Kaikeiriron seiseishi* (The development of accounting theory), Tokyo: Chuokeizai-sha.

Nishikawa, K. (1956) 'The early history of double entry bookkeeping in Japan', in A.C. Littleton and B.S. Yamey eds, *Studies in the history of accounting*, London: Sweet & Maxwell: 380–7.

Nishikawa, N. (1993) *Mitsui-ke kanjo kanken* (Research in the bookkeeping of the Mitsui family), Tokyo: Hakuto-shobo.

Nosse, N. (1961a) *Shakaikaikei-ron* (Theory of social accounting), Tokyo: Hakuto-shobo.

Nosse, N. (1961b) 'Shakaikaikei to kigyokaikei no dokeisei ni kansuru kosatsu' (On the isomorphism of social accounting and business accounting), *Kaikei* 80 (5): 55–66.

Ogura, E. (1962) *Goshu Nakai-ke choai no ho* (The bookkeeping of Nakai family in Goshu area), Kyoto: Mineruba-shobo.

Ohta, T. (1922) 'Kaikeijo no shisan' (The accounting concept of asset), *Shoji Keikei* (reprinted in his collected papers, *Kaikeigaku kenkyu*, vol. 1, Tokyo: Hakuto-shobo, 1956: 75–84).

Ohta, T. (1968) *Kindaikaikei sokumen-shi* (An aspect of the history of modern accounting in Japan – my academic career of 60 years in accounting), Tokyo: Chuokeizai-sha.

Okamoto, K. (1969) *Beikoku hyojun genkakeisan hattatsu-shi* (The development of standard cost accounting in the United States of America), Tokyo: Hakutou-shobo.

Paton, W.A. and Littleton, A.C. (1940/53) *An introduction to corporate accounting standards*, Sarasota, FA: AAA (Japanese translation, S. Nakajima (1953) *Kaisha kaikei kijun zosetsu*, Tokyo: Moriyama-shoten).

Ricci, D.I. (1940/73/77) *Fra Luca Pacioli – l'uomo e lo scienziato* (Fra Luca Pacioli – the person and the scholar). With an appendix *Testamenti Di Fra Luca Pacioli*, Sansepolcro, *Italy* (Japanese translation, A. Nakanishi and F. Taniguchi (1977) *Pacioli yuigonshu*, Tokyo: Mikuro-keiri, 1973 and *Luca Pacioli no shogai*, Tokyo: Nihon Mikuro Hyobo).

Saito, S. (1972a) 'Kaikei no koriteki teishikika wo meguru jakkan no shomondai', *Kaikei* 101 (4): 45–65.

Saito, S. (1972b) 'Some considerations on the axiomatic formulation of accounting', English translation, *Musashi Daigaku Ronshu* 20: 81–99.

Saito, S. (1973a) 'Futatabi kaikei no koriteki teishikika wo meguru mondai ni tsuite', *Kaikei* 103 (5): 775–88.

Saito, S. (1973b) 'Further considerations on the axiomatic formulation of accounting: a reply to Prof. R. Mattessich', English translation, *Musashi Daigaku Ronshu* 21: 95–107.

Saito, S. (1984) *Shisan saihyoka no kenkyu* (Studies in assets revaluation), Tokyo: University of Tokyo Press.

Sakurai, M. (1989). 'Target costing and how to use it', *Journal of Cost Management* (Summer): 39–50.

Sakurai, M. (1991) *Kaikeiriekijoho no yuyosei* (Usefulness of accounting information on profit), Tokyo: Chikure-shobo.

Sakurai, M. and Huang, P.Y. (1989) 'A Japanese survey of factory automation and its impact on management control systems', in Y. Monden and M. Sakurai eds, *Japanese management accounting: a world class approach to profit management*, Cambridge, MA: Productivity Press: 261–79.

Sanders, T.H., Hatfield, H.R. and Moore, U. (1938) *A statement of accounting principles*, New York: American Institute of Accountants (later, AAA).

Sato, S., Sakate, K., Mueller, G.G. and Radebaugh, L.R. (eds) (1982) *A compendium of research on information and accounting for managerial decision and control in Japan*, Sarasota, FA: International Accounting Section, AAA.

Schluter, W.C., Schuyler, W.M., James, F.C. and Schluter, D.M. (eds) (1933) *Economic cycles and crises: an American plan of control*, New York: Sears Publishing Co.

Schmalenbach, E. (1919/38/50) 'Grundlagen der dynamischen Bilanztheorie (Foundations of dynamic accounting), *Zeitschrift für handelswissenschaftliche Forschung*

13: 1–60, 65–101 (published in book form as *Grundlagen dynamischer Bilanzlehre*, 2 vols, Leipzig: A.G. Gloeckner, 1920; later as *Dynamische Bilanz*, 3rd edn, Leipzig: A.G. Gloeckner, 1925; Japanese translation of the 7th, 1938 edn, Masazo Toki (1950) *Doteki taishaku taishohyoron*, Tokyo: Moriyama-shoten) – see also Chapter 2 (under Schmalenbach 1919).

Schmalenbach, E. (1927/31/38/53) *Der Kontenrahmen* (The master chart of accounts), Leipzig (2nd edn, 1929; Japanese translation, Tokyoshokokaigisho (1931) *Kanjo taikei zuhyo*, Tokyo: Tokyoshokokaigisho; translation of the 4th, 1935 edn, Masazo Toki (1938) *Kaitei hyojun kogyo kaikei zukai*, Tokyo: Dobunkan; and *Kontenrahmen*, Moriyama-shoten, 1953) – see also Chapter 2 (under Schmalenbach 1927).

Scott, D.R. (1925) *Theory of accounts*, New York: Henry Holt & Co.

Scott, D.R. (1931) *The cultural significance of accounts*, New York: Henry Holt & Co.

Shand, A.A. (1873) *Ginko-boki-seiho*, 5 vols (edited translation, K. Yoshikawa of Shand's *Bank bookkeeping*), Tokyo: Ministry of Finance.

Shimme, S. (1937) 'Introduction to double entry bookkeeping in Japan', *The Accounting Review* 22 (September): 290–5.

Shimono, N. (1895/1982) *Boki seiri* (Foundations of bookkeeping); reprinted in the Bookkeeping Classics Series, Tokyo: Yushodo, 1982.

Someya, K. (1989) 'Accounting "revolutions" in Japan', *Accounting Historians Journal* 16 (1): 75–86.

Someya, K. (1996) *Japanese accounting: a historical approach*, New York: Oxford University Press.

Stone, R. (1947) 'Definition and measurement of the national income and related totals', in United Nations ed., *Measurement of national income and the construction of social account*, New York: UN.

Stuvel, G. (1965/67) *Systems of social accounts*, Oxford University Press (Japanese translation, N. Nosse (1967) *Shakai-kaikei no kozo*, Tokyo: Dobunkan).

Stuvel, G. (1986/87) *National accounts analysis*, London: Macmillan (Japanese translation, N. Nosse (1987) *Kokumin keizai keisan*, Tokyo: Dobunkan).

Stuvel, G. (1989/91) *The index number problem and its solution*, London: Macmillan (Japanese translation, N. Nosse and Y. Konishi (1991) *Keizai shisu no riron*, Tokyo: Dobunkan).

Suda, K. (2000) *Zaimukaikei no kino: riron to jissho* (Positive theory of financial accounting), Tokyo: Hakuto-shobo.

Sunder, S. and Yamaji, H. (1999) *The Japanese style of business accounting*, Westport, CT: Quorum Books.

Tanaka, A. (ed.) (1990) *Interview: Nihon ni okeru kaikeigaku-kenkyu no hatten* (Interview: The development of accounting research in Japan), Tokyo: Dobunkan.

Tanaka, S. (1982/86) *The structure of accounting language*, Tokyo: Chuo University Press (revised Japanese version, *Kaikei to kozo*, Tokyo: Zeimukeiri-kyokai, 1986).

Tsuji, A. and Okano, H. (1996) 'Kimura, Wasaburo (1902–1973)', in M. Chatfield and R. Vangermeersh eds, *The history of accounting: an international encyclopedia*, New York: Garland Publishing, Inc.: 361–2.

United Nations (UN) (1993) *Integrated environmental and economic accounting*, Series F, No. 61, New York: UN.

Uno, K. (1995) *Environmental options: accounting for sustainability*, Kluwer Academic Publishers.

Watts, R.L. and Zimmerman, J.L. (1986) *Positive accounting theory*, Englewood Cliffs,

NJ, Prentice-Hall, Inc. (Japanese translation, K. Suda (1991) *Jisshouriron to shiteno Kaikeigaku*, Tokyo, Hakuto-shobo).

Womack, J.P., Daniel, J.T. and Daniel, R. (1990a) *The machine that changed the world*, New York: Rawson Associates.

Womack, J.P., Daniel, J.T. and Daniel, R. (1990b) *Lean seisan-hoshiki ga sekai no jidosha-sangyo wo ko kaeru*, Japanese translation, H. Sawada, Tokyo: Keizaikai.

Yamagami, T. and Kikuya, M. (eds) (1995) *Kankyo kaikei no genjo to kadai* (Present state and issues in environmental accounting), Tokyo: Dobunkan.

Yamagata, Y. (1994) 'Wasaburo Kimura (1902–73)', in J.R. Edwards ed., *Twentieth-century accounting thinker*, London: Routledge: 198–205.

Yamashita, K. (1936) 'Izumo choai ni okeru ryomen kanjo' (Double-sided accounts in Izumo bookkeeping), *Hikone kosho ronshu* 20: 89–136.

Yu, S.C. (1966) 'Microaccounting and macroaccounting', *The Accounting Review* 41 (1): 8–20.

15 Accounting publications and research of twentieth-century Russia

Amodeo, D. (1945) 'La contabilità dei costi nell U.R.S.S.' (Cost accounting in the Soviet Socialist Republics Union), *Economia aziendale* 2.

Androsov, A.M. (1995) *Finansovaya otchetnost v bankakh: practicheskoye rukovodstvo po organisatii buchgalterskogo ucheta i sostavleniyu otchetnosti* (Financial statements in banks: Practical guide for organizing accounting and reporting), Moscow: Menater-Inform.

Anthony, R.N. and Reece, J.R. (1989) *Accounting: text and cases*, 8th edn (translated into Russian), Burr Ridge, IL: Richard D. Irwin, Inc.

Arens, A.A. and Loebecke, J.K. (1991) *Auditing: an integrated approach*, 5th edn (translated into Russian), Englewood Cliffs, NJ: Prentice-Hall.

Arnold, K.I. (1809) *Samouchitel buchgalterii* (Selfinstruction in bookkeeping), Moscow: Tip. F. Liubiia.

Bailey, D.T. (1977) 'The accounting profession in Russia', *Accountancy* [English Journal] (March): 72ff.

Bailey, D.T. (1982) 'Accounting in Russia: the European connection', *International Journal of Accounting Education and Research* (1, Fall): 1–36.

Bailey, D.T. (1990) 'Accounting in the shadow of Stalinism', *Accounting, Organizations, and Society* 15 (6): 513–25.

Bakaev, A.S. (1997) *Zakon o buchgalterskom uchete. Postateinye commentarii* (The Accounting Act: with itemized comments), Moscow: Meshdunarodny centr finansovo-economicheskogo rasvitia.

Basmanov, L.A. (1970) *Teoreticheskie osnovy ucheta i kalkulirovania sebestoimosti pro-muchlennoi productsii* (Theoretical foundations of accounting and industrial product costing), Moscow: Finansy.

Bauer, O. (1911) *Memuary k istorii buchgalterii ...* (Memoirs on the history of book-keeping ...), Moscow: I.G. Aksentova.

Bernstein, L.A. (1993) *Financial statement analysis: theory, application, and interpretation*, 5th edn (translated into Russian), Burr Ridge, IL: Richard D. Irwin, Inc.

Berry, M.H. (1982), 'The accounting function in socialist economies', *International Journal of Accounting Education and Research* 18 (1): 185–98.

Blatov, N.A. (1930) *Balansovedenie* (Balance sheet theory), Leningrad: Economicheskoe obrazovanie.

Blatov, N.A. (1931) *Osnovi obchey buchgalterii* (Fundamentals of general bookkeeping), Moscow: Gostorgizdat.

Bogorodsky, N.V. (1935) *Nisovoii uchet na prompredpriyatii i kalkulatsia* (Basic accounting and cost accounting for industry), Moscow: Isdatelstvo Gosplana.

Bulleten Moscowskogo obschestwa buchgalterov (Bulletin of Moscow's society of accountants), 1909, No. 4: 20.

Bunimovich, V.A. (1971) *Nauchniye osnovy planirovaniya sebestoimosti productsii* (Scientific framework of cost accounting planning), Moscow: Moscowskii Institute Narodnogo Hosyuastva.

Bourmistrov, A.L. and Mellemvik, F. (1999) 'Russian local governmental reforms: autonomy for accounting development?', *European Accounting Review* 8 (4): 675–701.

Bychkova, S.M. (1996a) 'The development and status of auditing in Russia', *The European Accounting Review* 5 (1): 77–91 (similar version presented as 'The development and status of auditing' in 1995 in Bristol, British Accounting Association, National Conference).

Bychkova, S.M. (1996b) 'The regulation of accounting and auditing in Russia', *International Accounting and Finance* (Special Interest Group Newsletter): 3–10.

Bychkova, S.M. and Smirnova, I.A. (1997) 'Comparison of Russian and Western approaches to auditing ethics', Birmingham: Programme of the British Accounting Association, National Conference: 85ff.

Calmes, A. (listed in transliteration as 'Kalmes') (1913) *Buchgalteriya i razschet sebestoimosti produktov na zhelezodelatelnom predpriiatii* (Bookkeeping and the calculation of the output of metalworking enterprises), translated from German under the supervision by V.M. Neledinsky. St Petersburg: Kechedzhi-Shapovalova.

Chambers of Auditors of Russia, Presidium (2003) *Code of professional ethics for auditors in Russia* (in Russian – approved, 3 October), Moscow: Chambers of Auditors of Russia.

Chumachenko, N.G. (1965) *Metody ucheta i kalkulirovaniya sebestoimosti promyshlennoi produktsii* (Methods of industrial accounting and product costing), Moscow: Finansy.

Chumachenko, N.G. and Bedford, N.M. (1968) 'Some distinctive aspects of accounting in the USSR', *International Journal of Accounting Education and Research* 4 (1): 29–40.

Clarkson, J.D. (1961/69) *A history of Russia*, New York: Random House (2nd edn, 1969).

Cooper, W.W. and Ijiri, Y. (1983) *Kohler's dictionary for accountants*, Englewood Cliffs, NJ: Prentice-Hall, Inc.

Degos, J.-G. and Mattessich, R. (2003) 'Accounting research in the French language area: first half of the twentieth century', *Review of Accounting and Finance* 2 (4): 110–28.

Dodonov, A.A. (1973) *Organizatsia ucheta v uslovijakh avtomatizirovannoi sistemy upravlenia* (Accounting organisation under consideration of the management information system), Moscow: Legkaja industria.

Efimova, O.V. (1998) *Finansovy analis* (Financial analysis), Moscow: Buchgaltersky uchet.

Enthoven, A.J. (1999) 'Russia's accounting moves West', *Strategic Finance* 81 (1): 32–7.

Enthoven, A.J., Sokolov, Y.V. and Kovalev, V. V. (1994) *Doing business in Russia and* the other former Soviet Republics: accounting and financial management issues, Montvale, NJ: Institute of Management Accountants.

Enthoven, A., Sokolov, Y.V. and Petrachkov, A.M. (1992) *Doing business in Russia and the other former Soviet Republics: accounting and joint venture issues*, Montvale, NJ: Institute of Management Accountants.

Enthoven, A.J., Sokolov, Y.V., Kovalev, V.V., Bychkova, S.M. and Semenova, M.S. (1998), *Accounting, auditing and taxation in the Russian Federation*, Dallas, TX: Institute of Management Accountants and the University of Texas.

Evzlin, Z. (1909) *Logismografia, G. Cerboni* (Logismography of G. Cerboni), Moscow.

Ezersky, F.V. (1902) *Teorya schetovodstva. Uproschennaya troinaya sistema* (Accounting theory. Simplified triple-entry system), St Petersburg.

Ezersky, F.V. (1915) *Russkaya uproschennaya troinaya sistema ...* (Russian triple-entry system ...), Moscow: Tip. Krestnogo Kalendaria.

Ezersky, F.V. and Shovsky, A.A. (eds) (1906) *Prakticheskaya entsiklopedia, Tom V: Kommercheskie svedeniya ...* (Practical encyclopedia, Vol. 5: Information on commerce ...), Moscow: Knigoizdatelstvo 'Artel Schetovodov'.

Feldhausen, E.E. (1888) *Normalnaia zavodsko-fabrichnaia otchetnostt ...* (Standard factory reporting ...), Moscow.

Gachkel, S. (1946) *Le mécanisme des finances soviétiques – monnaie, prix, crédit, budget* (The mechanism of Soviet finances – money, price, credit, budget), Paris: Payot.

Galagan, A.M. (1912) *Noveishie italianskie formy dvoinoy buchgalterii. logismografiya i statmografiya* (Novel Italian double-entry bookkeeping. logismography and statmography), Moscow.

Galagan, A.M. (1918) *Uchebnik schetovodenia* (Text on bookkeeping), 2nd edn, Moscow.

Galagan, A.M. (1927) *Schetovodstvo v ego istoricheskom razvitii*, Moscow: Gosizdat.

Galagan, A.M. (1928a) *Osnovy obschego schetovedeniya* (Principles of general accounting theory), Moscow: Izdatelstvo Narkomtorga SSSR i RSFSR.

Galagan, A.M. (1928b) *Schetovodstvo/Entsiclopedichesky slovar* (Accounting: encyclopaedia), Vol. 41-V, Moscow: Tovarishestvo Granat.

Galagan, A.M. (1930) *Obschee schetovedenie* (General accountancy), Vol. 1, Moscow.

Galagan, A.M. (1939) *Osnovy buchgalterskogo ucheta* (Principles of bookkeeping), Moscow: L. Gosplanizdat.

Galperin, J. [Ya.] M. (1934) *Kurs balansovogo ucheta* (Course on balance sheets accounting), Moscow: Gosfinizdat.

Gilde, E. K. (1968) *Normativnii uchet i modelirovanie ego organizatsii* ('Normative' accounting and modeling of its organization), Leningrad: Leningradskii oblastnoi sovet nauchno-technicheskih obchestv.

Gomberg, L.I. (1895) *Fabrichnozavodskoye shetovodstvo. Melnichnoe ...* (Factory and works accounting. For milling ...), St Petersburg: Isdatelstvo Journala Schetovodstvo (2nd edn, 1986).

Gomberg, L.I. (1908) *Grundlegung der Verrechnugswissenschaft* (Foundation of the science of accounting), Leipzig: Duncker Homblot (Japanese translation, *Kaikegaku hohoron*, Tokyo: Gansho-do-shoten, 1944).

Gomberg, L.I. (1909) 'Schetovodstvo i ego nauchnaya sistema' (Accounting and its scientific system), *Bulleten Moscowskogo obschestva buhgalterov* 4: 19–26.

Gomberg, L.I. (1912) *L'ecologique (scientifique comptable) et son histoire* (Ecology – scientific accounting and its history), Geneva: Société Général d'Impression.

Gomberg, L.I. (1920) *Histoire critique de la théorie des comptes* (A critical history of accounting theory), Berlin: L. Weiß.

Gorelik, G. (1971) 'Enterprise profit and profitability measurements: Soviet–American convergence', *International Journal of Accounting Education and Research* 6 (2): 1–14.

Gorelik, G. (1973) 'Notes on the development and problems on Soviet uniform accounting', *International Journal of Accounting Education and Research* 9 (1): 135–48.

Gorelik, G. (1974) 'Soviet accounting, planning and control', *International Journal of Accounting Education and Research* 10 (1): 13–25.

Guliaev, A.I. (1905), *Kurs fabrichno-zavodskogo schetovodsta* (Course on factory accounting), Moscow: Tip. V. Gattsuk.

Hendriksen, E.S. and Van Breda, M.F. (1992/97) *Accounting theory*, 5th edn, (translated into Russian), Boston: Richard D. Irwin (Russian translation, Moscow: Finansy i Statistica, 1997) – for previous edition see also Chapter 12.

Horngren, C.T. and Foster, G. (1987) *Cost accounting: a managerial emphasis*, 6th edn, Englewood Cliffs, NJ: Prentice-Hall, Inc. (translated into Russian).

Hügli, F. (1916) 'Dvoinaia kameralnaia buchgalteria' (Double-entry cameral accounting), Petrograd: Kommercheskaia Literatura.

Ijiri, Y. (1989) *Momentum accounting and triple-entry bookkeeping: exploring the dynamic structure of accounting measurements*, Sarasota, FA: AAA.

Ivanov, S.F. (1872) *Obscheponiatnaya dvoinaya buchgalteryia. Dlia rukovodstva zanimaiyuschihsya schetovodstvom ...* (General bookkeeping as a guide for those engaged in accounting ...), Moscow: Isdanie avtora.

Ivashkevich, V.B. (1974) *Problemy ucheta i kalkulirovaniya sebestoimosti produktsi* (Problems of accounting and product costing), Moscow: Finansy.

Kheil, K.P. (1910) *O nekotorych drevneishich obrabottkach traktata Luki Pachiolo po buchgalterii ...* (Some adaptations of Luca Pacioli's tractatus on bookkeeping ...), Mogilev: Tip. Gubernskaia.

Kheil, K.P. (1912) Venedikt Kotrugli iz Raguzy. Ocherk iz istorii buchgalterii (Benedict Cotrugli of Ragusa. An historical essay on bookkeeping), Mogilev: Tip. Gubernskaia.

Kiparisov, N.A. (1940) *Teoria buchgalterskogo ucheta* (Bookkeeping theory), Moscow: Gosplanizdat.

Kolman, E. (1931) 'O vreditelstve v nauke' (About destroying in science), *Bolshevik-Journal* 2: 74ff.

Koshkin, I.A. (1940) *Postroenie buchgalterskikh schetov* (Designing accounts), Leningrad.

Korniliev, M. (1862) *Schetovodsvo po vsem otrasliam promyshlennosti* (Accounting for all branches of industry), Kazan: I.V. Dubrovina.

Kovalev, V.V. (1995) *Finansovy analiz: upravlenie kapitalom. Vybor investitsiy. Analiz otchetnosti* (Financial analysis: capital management, investment choice, analysis of financial statements), Moscow: Finansy i Statistica.

Kovalev, V.V. (1998) *Metodu otsenki investitsionnykh proektov* (Methods of evaluating investment projects), Moscow: Finansy i Statistica.

Kovalev, V.V. and Sokolov, Y. V. (1992) *Upravlenchesky uchet*, St. Petersburg: SPICE.

Küpper, H.-U. and Mattessich, R. (2005) 'Twentieth-century accounting research in the German language area', *Accounting, Business and Financial History* (Special issue on *German Accounting*) 15 (3): 345–410.

Kuter, M.I. (1997) *Buchgaltersky uchet: osnovy teorii. Uchebnoye posobie* (Accounting: theoretical basis, a manual), Moscow: Expertnoye Buro.

Laktionov, S.A. (1924) *Tekhnika ucheta i kontrolya elementov proizvodstva* (Techniques of accounting and the control of production elements), Kharkov: Gosudarstvennoye isdatelstvo Ukrainy.

Laskin, N. (1931) 'The theory of unified Soviet accounting and the artful tricks of Professor A.M. Galagan' (in Russian) *Za sotsialistischeeskii uchet*: 70–80.

Lebow, M.I. and Tondkar, R.H. (1986) 'Accounting in the Soviet Union', *International Journal of Accounting Education and Research* 22 (1): 61–79.

Leontief, W.W. (1951) *The structure of American economy 1919–1939*, 2nd edn, (revised), New York: Oxford University Press (1st edn, 1941).

Leontiev, N.A. (1944) *Osnovy buchgalterskogo ucheta* (Foundations of accounting), Moscow: Gosisdat.

Liberman, L.V. and Eidinov, A.M. (1995) 'The development of accounting in tsarist Russia and the USSR', *European Accounting Review* 4 (4, December): 777–808.

Lokshin, A.J. (1934) *Analiz otcheta* (Report analysis), Vol. II, Moscow.

Lokshin, A.J. (1936) *Novoe pologenie o buchgalterskikh otchetakh i balansakh* (New regulations on accounting reports and financial statements), Kiev: Ukrainskoe otdelenie Gosfinizdata.

Losinsky, A.I. (1938) *Kurs teorii balansovogo ucheta v svyazi s promyshlennym, selskohoziaistvennym i torgovym uchetom* (Course on balance sheet presentation …), Moscow: Soyuztorguchet.

Losinsky, A.I. (1939) *Kurs istorii razvitiya buchgalterskogo ucheta* (Course on the historical development of bookkeeping), Saratov: Saratovskii Universitet.

Lounsky, N.S. (1900) *Kratkii uchebnik kommercheskoi buchgalterii*, (Concise text on commercial bookkeeping), Odessa (3rd edn, Moscow: Tipografiya G. Lissnera i D. Sobko, 1913).

Lounsky, N.S. (1913) *Kratkii uchebnik kommercheskoii buchgalterii* (Short textbook of commerce accounting), 3rd edn, Moscow: tipografiya G. Lissnera i D. Sobko.

Margulis, A.S. (1975) *Buchgalterskii uchet v otraslyah narodnogo hosyaistva* (Accounting in various industrial branches), Moscow: Finansy i statistika.

Masdorov, V.A. (1972) *Istoriya rasvitiya buchgalterskogo ucheta v SSSR: 1917–1972* (History of accounting evolution in the USSR: 1917–1972), Moscow: Finansy.

Masdorov, V.A. (1973) 'Pretvorenie v zhizn Leninskikh idei o sotsialicheskom uchete' (Implementation of Lenin's ideas on socialistic accounting), *Buchgalteristkii uchet* 4: 10–16.

Mattessich, R. (1961) 'Budget models and system simulation', *The Accounting Review* 36 (July): 384–97 (reprinted in T.H. Williams and C.H. Griffin eds, *Management information: a quantitative accent*, Homewood, IL: Richard D. Irwin, Inc., 1967: 636–54).

Mattessich, R. (1964a) *Accounting and analytical methods: measurement and projection of income and wealth in the micro- and macro-economy*, Homewood, IL: R.D. Irwin, Inc. (reprinted in the 'Accounting Classics Series', Houston, TX: Scholars Book Co., 1977; also in the 'Series of Financial Classics' of Reprints on Demand, Ann Arbor, MI: Microfilms International, 1979, still available; Japanese translation under the direction of Shinzaburo Koshimura, *Kaikei to Bunsekiteki-Hoho Jokan*, 2 vols, Tokyo: Dobunkan, Ltd, Vol. 1: 1972, Vol. 2: 1975; Spanish translation, by Carlos Luis García Casella and Maria del Carmen Ramírez de Rodríguez, Buenos Aires: La Ley, 2002).

Mattessich, R. (1964b) *Simulation of the firm through a budget computer program*, Homewood, Illinois: Richard D. Irwin, Inc. (reprint edition, 'Reprints on Demand Series', Ann Arbor, MI: Microfilms International, 1979).

Mautz, R.K. and Sharaf, H.A. (1961) *The philosophy of auditing*, Madison, WI: AAA.

Motyka, W. (1993) *Annotated bibliography of Russian Language publications on accounting 1736–1917*, Vol. 1: *1736–1900;* Vol 2: *1901–1917*, New York: Garland Publishing, Inc.

Mudrov, E.A. (1846) *Schetovodsto dlia vsekh rodov torgovli* (Accounting for all kinds of trade), St Petersburg.

Mueller, G.G., Gernon, H. and Meck, G. (1991) *Accounting: an international perspective*, 2nd edn (translated into Russian), Burr Ridge, IL: Richard D. Irwin, Inc.

Narinsky, N.A. (1976) *Kalkulirovanie sebestoimosti v stroitelstve* (Product costing in the construction industry), Moscow: Finansy.

Needles, B., Anderson, H.R. and Caldwell, S.C. (1991/94) *Principles of accounting*, 4th edn, Boston: MA: Houghton and Mifflin Co. (Russian translation, Moscow: Finansy i Statistica, 1994).

Nikolaev, I.R. (1926) *Problema realnosti balansa* (The problem of balance sheet reliability), Leningrad: Economicheskoye obrasovanie.

Nikolaeva, S. (1993) *Osobennosti ucheta zatrat v usloviyakh rynka: sistema 'direkt-kosting'* (Cost accounting in a market economy – the direct costing system), Moscow: Finansy i Statistica.

Paly, V.F. (1975) *Buchgalterskii uchet v systeme economicheskoi informatsii* (Bookkeeping activity as information system), Moscow: Finansy.

Paly, V.F. and Sokolov, Y.V. (1988) *Teoria buchgalterskogo ucheta* (Theory of bookkeeping), Moscow: Finansy i Statistica.

Pfaff, D. (1994) 'Zur Notwendigkeit einer eigenständigen Kostenrechnung-Anmerkungen zur Neuorientierung des internen Rechnungswesens im Hause Siemens' (On the necessity of an independent cost accounting – remarks to the new orientation at the House of Siemens), *Zeitschrift für betriebswirtschaftliche Forschung* 46 (December): 1065–84.

Pomazkov, N.S. (1929) *Positivnoye napravlenie v chetovodstve: Teoria i practica ucheta*, Vol. 2 (Positive trends in accounting: theory and practice of bookkeeping), Leningrad: Economicheskoe obrasovanie.

Popov, A.Z. (1903) *Kurs po schetnomu iscusstvu* (Course on accounting art), Ekaterinburg: Tip. Vurt.

Popov, N.U. (1910) *Obschie sistemy schetovodstva* (General accounting systems), Krasnoiarsk: M.I. Kokhanovskoi.

Richard, J. (1995) 'The evolution of the Romanian and Russian accounting charts after the collapse of the communist system', *European Accounting Review* 4 (2, July): 305–23.

Rosenkranz, K. (1949) 'Die Organisation der Betriebsbuchführung in der Sowjetunion' (The organization of cost accounting in the Soviet Union), *Zeitschrift für handelswissenschaftliche Forschung* (New Series) 1 (3): 101–25.

Rudanovsky, A.P. (1913) *Prinsipi obchestvennogo schetovedeniya* (Principles of general accounting theory), 1st edn, Moscow: Makis.

Rudanovsky, A.P. (1924) *Rukovodyachie nachala (prinsipy) po schetovodstvy i otchetnosti v gosudarstvennih hosyastvennich obedineniyach*, Moscow: Isdatelstvo Narkomfina RF i SSSR.

Rudanovsky, A.P. (1925) *Prinsipi obchestvennogo schetovedeniya* (Principles of general accounting theory), 2nd edn, Moscow: Makis.

Rudanovsky, A.P. (1924) 'Rukovodyachie nachala (prinsipy) po schetovodstvy i otchetnosti v gosudarstvennih hosyastvennich obedineniyach', Moscow: Isdatelstvo Narkomfina RF i SSSR.

Rudanovsky, A.P. (1925) *Prinsipi obchestvennogo schetovedeniya* (Principles of general accounting theory), 2nd edn, Moscow: Makis.

Satubaldin, S. (1976) 'Methods of analyzing profits of industrial enterprises in the USSR', *International Journal of Accounting Education and Research* 12 (1): 91–9.

Schär, J.F. (1904) *Tecknika bankovogo dela. Chetovodstvo kontokorrentyi ...* (The modus operandi of banking. Accounting, current accounts ...), translated from the German by E.V. Sivers, St. Petersburg: Tip. Obshestv Polza.

Schetovodstvo journal (1889): 227–8.

Schetovodstvo journal (1898): 48–9.

Schetovodstvo journal (1902): 85.

Schetovodstvo journal (1903): 229–32.

Schmidt, F. (1929) 'The valuation of fixed assets in financial statements', presented at the Congress of International Accountants (New York, September 1929; apparently translated into Russian in *Schetovodstvo*, November 1929).

Shchenkov, S.A. (1973) *Sistema schetov i buhgalterskii balans predpriyatiya* (Accounting system and balance sheet of an enterprise), Moscow: Finansy.

Shchenkov, S.A. and Leontiev, N.A. (1938) 'Kratkii kurs buhgalterskogo ucheta' (Short course of bookkeeping), Moscow: Gosisdat.

Sheremet, A.D. and Saifylin, R.S. (1995) *Metodica finansovogo analisa* (Method of financial analysis), Moscow: INFRA.

Sigalas, A. de (1936) *Le statut des entreprises gouvernementales en U.R.S.S* (The status of government enterprises in the USSR), Paris.

Sivers, E.E. (1915) *Obschee schetovodstvo* (General accounting), 4th edn, St Petersburg: Isdanie avtora.

Sivers, E.E. (1917) *Uchebnik schetovodsva dlia torgovych shkol* (Accounting textbook for trade schools), 4th edn, Petrograd (now again St Petersburg).

Smirnova, I.A., Sokolov, Y.V. and Emmanuel, C.R. (1995) 'Accounting education in Russia today', *The European Accounting Review* 4 (4): 833–44.

Sokolov, J.V. (1977) 'Buchgalterskaya periodicheskaya pechat za gody Sovietskoy vlasti' (Accounting periodic for the Soviet power period), *Bughalterslii uchet* 12.

Sokolov, Y.V. (1985) *Istoria rasvitia buchgalterskogo ucheta* (History of bookkeeping development), Moscow: Finansy i Statistika.

Sokolov, Y.V. (1991) *Ocherki po istorii buchgalterskogo ucheta* (Outlines of the history of bookkeeping), Moscow: Finansy i Statistika.

Sokolov, Y.V. (1994) '10 postylatov audita v Rossi' (Ten auditing postulates in Rossi), *Buchgaltersky Uchet*, N11.

Sokolov, Y.V. (1996) *Buchgaltersky uchet: ot istokov do nashikh dney* (Accounting: from the beginning to our days), Moscow: UNITI.

Sokolov, J.V. and Bychkova, S.M. (2004) 'Russian accounting in the twentieth century', in M. Dobija and S. Martin eds, Conference Proceedings: *General accounting theory: towards balancing the society*, Cracow: Leon Komiński Academy of Entrepreneurship and Management: 479–99.

Sokolov, Y.V. and Kovalev, V.V. (1991) *Osnovy upravlencheskogo ucheta* (Basics of management accounting), St Petersburg: SPICE.

Sokolov, J.V. and Kovalev, V.V. (1996a) 'Russia', in M. Chatfield and R. Vangermeersch eds, *The history of accounting: an international encyclopedia,* New York: Garland Publishing, Inc.: 508–9.

Sokolov, J.V. and Kovalev, V.V. (1996b) 'In defense of Russian accounting: a reply to foreign critics', *European Accounting Review* 5 (4): 743–63.

Sopko, V.V. (1976) *Isdersgki proisvodstva i sebestoimost productsii pishevoi promushlennosti* (Production cost and cost calculation in the food industry), Kiev: Technika.

Stotsky, V.I. (1936) *Osnovy kalkulatsii i economicheskogo analysa sebestoimosty* (Basics of costing and its economic analysis), Leningrad: Sotsecgis.

Strumilin, S.G. (1925) *Problemy economiki truda* (Problems of labour economy), Moscow: Gosisdat.

Sucher, P. and Bychkova, S.M. (2001) 'Auditor independence in economies in transition: a study of Russia', *European Accounting Review* 10 (4, December): 817–42.

Sumtsov, A. (1940) *Kurs buchgalterskogo ucheta* (Bookkeeping course), Moscow: Gosfinisdat.

Tugan-Baranovsky, M.I. (1898/1970) *Russkaya fabrika v proshłom i nastoyaschem.* Moscow: (English translation, A. Levin and C.C. Levin (1970) *The Russian factory in the nineteenth century*, Homewood, IL: Richard D. Irwin, Inc.).

Valitsky, I.F. (1877) *Teoriya schetovodstva v primenenii k narodnomu khoziaistvu* (Accounting theory as implemented in the national economy), St Petersburg.

Van der Vil, R. and Paly, V. (1997) *Upravlenchesky uchet* (Management accounting), Moscow: INFRA-M.

Van Horn, J.C. (1989) *Fundamentals of Financial Management* (translated into Russian), Englewood Cliffs, NJ: Prentice-Hall, Inc..

Veitsman, N.R. (1978) *Bughalter – professiya pochetnaya* (Accountant as an honoured profession), Moscow: Finance.

Veitsman, R.Y. (1936) *Kurs schetovodstva* (Accounting course), 16th edn, Moscow (1st edn, Odessa: Obazovanie, 1909; 7th edn, 1917).

Wolf, A. M. (1890/1899) *Dvoinaia buchgalteria v populyarnykh ocherkakh* (Double-entry bookkeeping in popular outlines), St Petersburg: Tip. A.M. Wolfa (3rd edn, 1899).

Zhebrak, M.K. (1950) *Kurs promushlennogo ucheta* (Course of manufacturing accounting), Moscow: Gosplanisdat.

16 Accounting publications and research in Poland and the Ukraine: mainly twentieth century

Arens, A.A. and Loebbecke, J.K. (1991) *Auditing: an integrated approach*, 5th edn, Englewood Cliffs, NJ: Prentice-Hall (Russian translation, Moscow: Finansy i Statistica, 1995).

Aseńsko, J. (1934) *Analiza bilansów* (Balance sheet analysis), Warsaw: Krajowe Towarzystwo Powiernicze S.A.

Bednarek, P. (2003) *Financial reporting system in local governments in Poland and the USA*, in: M. Dobija ed., *General accounting theory in status nascendi*, Cracow: Akademia Ekonomiczna w Krakowie: 549–61.

Berry, M. and Jaruga, A. (1985) 'Industrial accounting in Poland's reorganized economy', *International Journal of Accounting Education and Research* 20 (2): 45–63.

Bilukha, M.T. (1994) *Audyt u biznesi: posibnyk dlia biznesmeniv* (Auditing in business: guide for business people), Dnipropetrovsk: Prescom.

Bilukha, M.T. (1998) *Kurs audytu: pidruchnyk* (Course on auditing: a textbook), Kiev: Znannia.

Bilukha, M.T. (2000) *Audit: Uchebnik* (Auditing: a textbook), Kiev: Znannia.

Borodkin, O.S. (1997) '"Shokova terapiya" dlia buchgalterskogo obliku' ('Shock therapy' for accounting), *Svit buchgalterskogo obliku* 2: 44.

Butynets, F.F. (1998) *Istoriya buchgalterskogo obliku* (Accounting history), Part I, Zhytomyr: Ruta.

Butynets, F.F. (2000) *Teoriya buchgalterskogo obliku: Pidruchnyk* (Accounting theory: a textbook), 2nd edn, Zhytomyr: ZhITI.

536   *References 16: Poland and the Ukraine*

Butynets, F.F. (2001a) *Istoriya buchgalterskogo obliku* (Accounting history), 2nd edn, Part I, Zhytomyr: Ruta.

Butynets, F.F. (2001b) *Istoriya buchgalterskogo obliku* (Accounting history), Part II, Zhytomyr: Ruta.

Butynets, F.F. (ed.) (2002) *Buchgaltersky oblik u silskomu gospodarstvi* (Accounting in agricultural business), Zhitomyr: Ruta.

Butynets, F.F. and Maliuga, N.M. (eds) (2002) *Buchgaltersky oblik v torgivli* (Accounting over trade), 2nd edn, Zhitomyr: Ruta.

Byszewski, W. (1927) *Wykład teoretyczny rachunkowości (buchalterji)* (Theoretical lecture of accounting), Warsaw: Druk. L. Nowak.

Chumachenko, N.G. (1960) *Analiz pribyli promyshlennogo predpriyatia* (Analysis of profitability of the industrial enterprise), Moscow: Gosfinizdat.

Chumachenko, N.G. (1965) *Metody ucheta i kalkulirovaniya sebestoimosti promyshlennoi produktsii* (Methods of industrial accounting and product costing), Moscow: Finansy.

Chumachenko, N.G. (1966) *Normativny uchet proizvodstva v priborostroenii* ('Normative' production accounting in the instrument making industry), Moscow: Mashinostroenie.

Chumachenko, N.G. (1968) *Vnutrizavodskoi ekonomichesky analiz* (Intra-factory economic analysis), Kiev: Tekhnika.

Chumachenko, N.G. (1971) *Uchet i analiz v promyshlennom proizvodstve USA* (Accounting and analysis in the US production industry), Moscow: Finansy.

Chumachenko, N.G. (1997) 'Buchgaltersky uchet: proshloe, nastoyashee … budushee?' (Accounting: past, present and future?), *Svit buchgalterskogo obliku* 4 (April): 2–12; 7 (July): 2–6.

Chumachenko, N.G. (2000) 'Rozvytok upravlinskogo obliku v Ukraini' (Development of management accounting in the Ukraine), *Balans* 23: 27–8.

Chumachenko, N.G. (2003) 'Upravlinsky oblik potrebue pidtrymky' (Management accounting needs help), *Buchgaltersky oblik i audyt* 5: 3–7.

Ciompa, P. (1910) *Grundrisse einer Ökonometrie und die auf der Nationalökonomie aufgebaute natürliche Theorie der Buchhaltung* (Outlines of an 'econometrics' and a natural theory of bookkeeping based on macro-economics), Lemberg: Poeschel Verlag.

Davydov, G.M. (2001) *Audyt* (Auditing), Kiev: Znannia.

Dixon, R. and Jaruga, A. (1994) *The changing face of accountancy in Poland: the new Europe, recent political and economic implications for accountants and accounting*, Urbana-Champaign, IL: University of Illinois, Center for International Education and Research in Accounting: 233–52.

Djoga, R.T. (2001) *Buchgaltersky oblik u budzhetnykh ustanovakh* (Accounting in budgetary organizations), Kiev: KNEU.

Djoga, R.T., Svirko, S.V. and Sinelnyk, L.M. (2003) *Buchgaltersky oblik u budzhetnykh ustanovakh* (Accounting in budgetary organizations), Kiev: KNEU.

Dobija, M. (ed.) (2003) *General accounting theory in status nascendi*, Cracow: Akademia Ekonomiczna w Krakowie.

Dobija, M. and Martin, S. (eds) (2004) *General accounting theory: towards balancing the society*, Cracow: Leon Koźmiński Academy of Entrepreneurship and Management.

Dobija, M. and Martin, S. (eds) (2005) *General accounting theory: towards balanced development*, Cracow: Cracow University of Economics.

Dobija, M. and Napadovska, L. (eds) (2007 – forthcoming) *General accounting theory* (in Ukrainian), Kiev: Kneut.

Dorosh, N.I. (2001) *Audyt: metodologia i organizatsia* (Auditing: methodology and organization), Kiev: Znannia.

Fedak, Z. (1962) *Racunek kosztów produkcji przemysłowej* (Cost accounting for industrial manufacturing), Warsaw: PWE.

Fedak, Z. (1967) *Kierunki rozwoju rachunku kosztów* (Directions of the development of cost accounting), in W. Bień, S. Skrzywan and E. Terebucha eds, *Rachunkowość polska*, Warsaw: PWE: 103–30.

Gmytrasiewicz, M. and Karmańska, A. (eds) (2004) *Polska szkoła rachunkowości* (The Polish school of accounting), Warsaw: Warsaw School of Economics.

Golov, S.F. (2003) *Upravlinsky oblik: Pidruchnyk* (Management accounting: a textbook), Kiev: Libra.

Golov, S.F. and Efimenko, V.I. (1996) *Finansovy ta upravlinsky oblik* (Financial and management accounting), Kiev: Avtointerservis.

Golov, S.F. and Kostiuchenko, V.M. (2001) *Buchgaltersky oblik za mizhnarodnymy standartamy: pryklady ta komentari* (Accounting by international accounting standards: examples and commentaries), Kiev: Libra.

Goncharuk, Y.A. and Rudnytsky, V.S. (2002) *Audyt* (Auditing), Lvóv: Svit.

Góra, W. (1920) *Bilanse: studia ekonomiki prywatnej* (Balance sheets: studies in economics of the firm), Lvóv: Pierwsza Związkowa Drukarnja.

Góra, W. (1938) *Bilanse: studia z dziedziny ekonomiki prywatnej* (Balance sheets: studies in economics of the firm), Warsaw: Pub. Accountants Association in Poland (see also preceding item).

Goritskaya, N.G. (1999) *Novaya finansovaya otchetnost* (The new financial statements), Kiev: Tekhnika.

Grabova, N.N. and Dobrovsky, V.N. (2000) *Buchgaltersky uchet v proizvodstvennykh i torgovykh predpriyatiyakh* (Accounting on industrial and trade enterprises), Kiev: A.S.K.

Grass, V. (1899) *Istoriya razvitiya schetovodstva v Chernigovskom gubernskom zemstve* (History of bookkeeping development in the Chernigov provincial zemstvo), Chernigov.

Gutsailiuk, Z.V., Mekh, Y.V. and Shyrba, M.T. (2002) *Audyt: teoria, metodyka, zbirnyk zavdan* (Auditing: theory, techniques, and cases), Ternopil: Ekonomichna dumka.

Hońko, S. (2003) 'Znaczenie dorobku wybranych polskich teoretyków bilansowych okresu międzywojennego' (Relevance of selected Polish accounting theorists during the interwar period), *Zeszyty Teoretyczne Rachunkowości* 13 (69): 135–47.

Jaruga, A. (1966) *Overhead cost in industrial enterprises*, Warsaw: PWE: 272.

Jaruga, A. (1972) 'Problems of uniform accounting principles in Poland', *International Journal of Accounting Education and Research* 8 (1): 25–41.

Jaruga, A. (1974) 'Recent developments in Polish accounting: an international transaction emphasis', *International Journal of Accounting Education and Research* 10 (1): 1–18.

Jaruga, A. (1976) 'Some developments of the auditing profession in Poland', *International Journal of Accounting Education and Research* 12 (1): 101–9.

Jaruga, A. (1988) 'Accounting in Poland', in D. Bailey ed., *Accounting in Socialist Countries*, London, New York: Routledge.

Jaruga, A. (1991) *Upravlenchesky uchet: opyt ekonomicheski razvitykh stran* (Management accounting: the experience of economically developed countries), Moscow: Finansy i Statistica.

Jaruga, A. (1993a) 'New accounting regulation in Poland, current issues', in R.S.O. Wallace, J.M. Samuels and R.J. Briston (eds), *Research in third world accounting*, Vol. 2, Greenwich, UK: JAI Press Ltd: 85–96.

Jaruga, A. (1993b) 'Changing rules of accounting in Poland', *The European Accounting Review* 2 (1): 115–27.

Jaruga, A. (1995) 'Poland', in D. Alexander and S. Archer eds, *European accounting guide*, London: Harcourt Professional: 1465–84.

Jaruga, A. [in Polish addressed as 'Jarugova'] (1989) *Niektóre kierunki badań naukowych z dziedziny rachunkowości* (Some directions in accounting research), *Accounting*, Lodz: Acta Universitatis Lodziensis, Folia Oeconomica 88: 3–18.

Jaruga, A. and Ho, S.M. (2002) 'Management accounting in transitional economies', *Management Accounting Research* 3: 375–8.

Jaruga, A. and Schroeder, M. (2003) Chapter on 'Poland', in D. Alexander and S. Archer eds, *European accounting guide*, New York: Aspen Publishers.

Jaruga, A. and Skowroński, J. (1986) *Rachunek kosztów w systemie informacyjnym rachunkowości* (*Cost accounting in accounting information system*), revised 3rd edn, Warsaw: PWE.

Jaruga, A. and Szychta, A. (1996) 'Poland', in M. Chatfield and R. Vangermeersch eds, *The history of accounting: an international encyclopedia*, New York and London: Garland Publishing, Inc.: 465–7.

Jaruga, A. and Szychta, A. (1997) 'The origin and evolution of charts of accounts in Poland', *European Accounting Review* 6 (3): 509–26.

Jaruga, A., Fijałkowska, J. and Jaruga-Baranowska, M. (2005) 'Adoption of IAS/IFRS in Poland', in M. Dobija and S. Martin eds, *General accounting theory: towards balanced development*, Cracow: Cracow University of Economics: 179–211.

Jarugowa, A. and Skowroński, J. (1994) 'O wierny obraz rachunku kosztów' (Towards a fair view of cost accounting), *Rachunkowość* 4: 166–72.

Kaneva, T.V. (2004) *Buchgaltersky oblik u budzhetnykh ustanovakh* (Accounting in budgetary organizations), Kiev: KNTEU-Knyga.

Kaplan, R.S. and Norton, D.P. (1996) *The balanced scorecard: translating strategy into action*, Boston, MA: Harvard Business School Press (Russian translation, Moscow: Olimp-Biznes, 2003).

Kaplan, R.S. and Norton, D.P. (2001) *The strategy-focused organization: how balanced scorecard companies thrive in the new business environment*, Boston, MA: Harvard Business School Press (Polish translation in 2000 and 2003; Russian translation in Moscow: Olimp-Biznes, 2004).

Kawa, M. (2002) 'Ewolucja pojęcia majątku jednostek gospodarczych' (Evolution of enterprise assets), *Zeszyty Teoretyczne Rachunkowości* 11 (67): 54–91.

Kindratska, L.M. (1999) *Buchgaltersky oblik v komertsijnykh bankakh Ukrainy* (Accounting in commercial banks of the Ukraine), Kiev: KNEU (2nd edn, 2001).

Kormosh, T. (1895) *Praktychny pidruchnyk dlia tovarystv zadatkovykh* (Practical guide for credit co-operatives), Przemysl.

Kormosh, T. (1912) *Pidruchnyk dlia zarobkovo-gospodarskykh stovaryshen* (Textbook for commercial partnerships), Przemysl.

Krasitski, K. (1851) *Rachunki gospodarski podlug najprosteszyh zasad* (Elementary principles of business accounts), Lwow: Zaklad narodowego Ossolinskich.

Krzywda, D., Bailey, D. and Schroeder, M. (1998) 'The development of the role of statutory audit in the transitional Polish economy', *European Accounting Review* 7 (3): 407–41.

Kuzhelny, M.V. (1985) *Buchgaltersky uchet i ego kontrolnye funktsii* (Accounting and its control functions), Moscow: Finansy i Statistica.

Kuzhelny, M.V. and Linnyk, V.G. (2001) *Teoriya buchgalterskogo obliku* (Accounting theory), Kiev: KNEU.

Kuzminsky, A.M. (1990) *Teoria buchgalterskogo ucheta* (Accounting theory), Kiev: Vysha shkola.

Kuzminsky, A.M. (ed.) (1996) *Audit: prakticheskoe posobie* (Auditing: practical guide), Kiev: Uchetinform.

Kuzminsky, A.M. and Sopko, V.V. (1984) *Organizatsia buchgalterskogo ucheta i ekonomicheskogo analiza v promyshlennosti* (Organization of accounting and economic analysis in the industry), Moscow: Finansy i Statistica.

Lastovetsky, V. (2003) 'Yaky vyd obliku ne e upravlinskym?' (What kind of accounting is not managerial?), *Buchgaltersky oblik i audyt* 4: 40–4.

Lulek, T. (1922) *Teoretyczne podstawy księgowości kupieckiej* (*The theoretical basis of mercantile accounting*), Cracow: J. Czernecki.

Lulek, T. (1922–25) *Metodyczny podręcznik księgowości kupieckiej* (Mercantile accounting methodical textbook), 2 vols, Cracow: J. Czernecki.

Lulek, T. (1925) *Waloryzacja bilansów* (Balance sheets valuation), Cracow: J. Czernecki.

Lulek, T. (1931) *Normalizacja bilansów* (Standardization of balance sheets), Cracow: J. Czernecki.

Lulek, T. (1937) *Zasady rachunkowości kupieckiej* (Mercantile accounting principles), Cracow: 'Nauka'.

Malc, W. (1964) *Publikacje teoretyczne Katedr Rachunkowości w okresie dwudziestolecia PRL* (Theoretical publications by accounting departments in the post-war decades), *Rachunkowość* 7: 209–13.

Malyshev, I.V. (1971) *Teoriya dvoistvennosti otrazheniya khoziaistvennykh faktov v buchgalterskom uchete* (Double-entry theory of accounting), Moscow: Statistica.

Malyshev, I.V. (1981) *Teoriya buchgalterskogo ucheta* (Accounting theory), Moscow: Finansy i Statistica.

Messner, Z. (1967) 'Informacja ekonomiczna w przedsiębiorstwie i jej wykorzystywanie w zarządzaniu, w: Rachunkowość polska' (Economic information in the enterprise and its utilization for management), *Accounting in Poland*, Warsaw: PWE: 143–60.

Ministra Finansów (1983) *Zarządzenie Nr 83 z 7.11.1983r. w sprawie zasad ewidencji, kalkulacji i analizy kosztów produkcji przemysłowej* (Decree No 83 of the Finance Minister of 7.11.1983 on the rules of cost recording, calculation and analysis in industrial manufacturing).

Mnykh, E.V., Shvets, V.E. and Yaremko, L.Y (2000) *Rozvytok obliku v Galychyni: istorychni ta metodologichni aspekty* (Accounting development in Halychyna: historical and methodological aspects), Lvóv: Kameniar.

Murashko, V.M. (1974) *Kontrol i revisiya khoziaistvennoi deyatelnosti torgovykh organizatsij* (Control and revision of business activities over trade organizations), Kiev: Vysha shkola.

Murashko, V.M. (1979) *Khoziaistvenny kontrol i kompleksnaya revisia v torgovle* (The business control and complex revision over trade), Kiev: Vysha shkola.

Napadovska, L.V. (2000) *Upravlinsky oblik*, Dnipropetrovsk: Nauka i osvita.

Nimchynov, P.P. (1976) *Novaya klassifikatsiya schetov buchgalterskogo ucheta* (The new classification of accounts), Kiev: Vysha shkola.

Nimchynov, P.P. (1977) *Obshaya teoria buchgalterskogo ucheta* (General theory of accounting), Kiev: Vysha shkola.

Nowak, E. (2003) 'Rozwój rachunku kosztów w świetle doświadczeń ośrodka wrocławskiego' (Evolution of cost accounting in the light of experience of the Wrocław Centre), *Zeszyty Teoretyczne Rachunkowości* 13 (69): 179–88.

Peche, T. (1959) *Accounting in enterprises and social accounting*, Warsaw: PWG.

Peche, T. (1963) *Zarys ogólnej teorii rachunkowości* (An outline of general accounting theory), Warsaw: PWE.

Petrenko, S.N. (2003) *Kontrolling* (Controlling), Kiev: Nika-Centr, Elga.

Pogodzińska-Mizdrak, E. (2003) 'Rachunkowość polska początku XX wieku na tle epoki (1900–1939)' (Polish accountancy at the beginning of the twentieth century on the epoch overview, 1900–1939), in S. Sojak ed., *Past, present and future of accountancy in Poland*, Toruń: UMK.

Pushkar, M.S. (1991) *Buchgaltersky uchet v sisteme upravlenia* (Accounting and management system), Moscow: Finansy i Statistica.

Pushkar, M.S. (1995) *Upravlinsky oblik* (Management accounting), Ternopil: Poligrafist Ltd.

Pushkar, M.S. (1999) *Tendencii ta zakonomirnosti rozvytku buchgalterskogo obliku v Ukraini: teoretyko-metodologichni aspekty* (Tendencies and laws of accounting development in the Ukraine: theoretical and methodological aspects), Ternopil: Economichna dumka.

Pushkar, M.S., Gavryshko, N.V. and Romaniv, R.V. (2003) *Istoriya obliku i kontrolu gospodarskoi diyalnosti* (The history of accounting and operational control), Ternopil: Cart-blansh.

Redchenko, K.I. (2001) *Audyt strategichnykh upravlinskykh rishen, prognoziv ta proektiv* (Auditing of strategic decisions, management forecasts and budgeting), Lvóv: LAC.

Redchenko, K.I. (2003a) 'Novye aspekty upravlencheskogo kontrolia' (New aspects of management control), *Menedzhment segodnia* 4: 2–10.

Redchenko, K.I. (2003b) *Strategichny analiz u biznesi* (Strategic analysis in business), 2nd edn, Lvóv: Novy Svit-2000.

Red'ko, A. (1995) *Audit: prosto o slozhnom* (Auditing: simple or complicated), Kiev: KNEU.

Robertson, J.C. (1990) *Auditing*, 6th edn, BPI/Irwin (Russian translation, Moscow: KPMG and Kontakt, 1993).

Rudnytsky, V.S. (1998) *Metodologiya i organizaciya audytu* (Methodology and organization of auditing), Ternopil: Economichna dumka.

Ryan, B. (1995) *Strategic accounting for management*, London: The Dryden Press (Russian translation, Moscow: Audit UNITI, 1998).

Scheffs M. (1936) *Bilans kupiecki i podatkowy* (Mercantile and fiscal balance sheets), Warsaw: Accounting Association of Poland.

Scheffs M. (1938) *Oznaczenie wartości przedmiotów bilansowych* (Valuation of balance sheet items), Poznań: Accounting Association of Poland.

Scheffs M. (1939a) *Bilans i rewizja. Zarys przepisów prawnych i zarządzeń* (Balance sheets and audit. Outline of legislation and regulation), Poznań: Biblioteka Związku Księgowych w Polsce.

Scheffs M. (1939b) *Z historii księgowości (Luca Pacioli)* (Accounting history – Luca Pacioli), Poznań: Accounting Association of Poland.

Shank, J.K. and Govindarajan, V. (1993) *Strategic cost management: the new tool for competitive advantage*, New York: Free Press (Russian translation, Moscow: Biznes-Mikro, 1999).

Shkaraban, S.I. (1988) *Osnovy operativnogo ekonomicheskogo analiza* (Foundations of operative economic analysis), Lvóv: Vysha shkola.

Skalski, W. (1928) *Znaczenie księgi głównej w księgowości podwójnej* (The role of the general ledger in double-entry bookkeeping), Poznań: WSH.

Skalski, W. (1934/36) *Zasady inwentaryzowania i bilansowania w przedsiębiorstwach handlowych i przemysłowych*) (Principles of inventory-taking and balancing in commercial and industrial enterprises), Poznań: Księgarnia W. Wilak (2nd edn, 1936).

Skrzywan, S. (1964) Wspomnienia (Memoirs), *Rachunkowość* 7: 204–9.

Skrzywan, S. (1967) 'Rachunkowość w Polsce Ludowej' (Accountancy in Polish People's Republic), *Polish Accountancy*, Warsaw: Biblioteka Stowarzyszenia Księgowych w Polsce: 7–40.

Sokolov, Y.V. (1991) *Ocherki po istorii buchgalterskogo ucheta* (Outlines of the history of bookkeeping), Moscow: Finansy i Statistica.

Sopko, V.V. (1998) *Buchgaltersky oblik* (Accounting), Kiev: KNEU.

Sopko, V.V. *et al.* (1992) *Buchgaltersky oblik v promyslovosti ta inshykh galuziakh narodnogo gospodarstva* (Accounting in industry and other branches of the economy), Kiev: Vysha shkola.

Sterniuk, I. (1926) *Pidruchnyk torgovelno-kooperatyvnogo knygovodstva* (Textbook for commercial and cooperative bookkeeping), Lvóv: Naklad avtora.

Szplit, A. and Hnidan, P. (2005) 'Taxation accounting in Poland', in M. Dobija and S. Martin eds, *General accounting theory: towards balanced development*, Cracow: Cracow University of Economics: 497–503.

Szychta, A. (1989) *Bibliograficzne calendarium rachunkowości w Polsce od XVI do XIX* (Bibliographical calendarium of accounting in Poland (XVI–XIX century)), Warsaw: Public Accounting Association of Poland.

Szychta, A. (1996a) *Bibliographical calendarium of accounting in Poland (XVI–XIX century)*, Warsaw: Foundation for the Development of Accounting in Poland.

Szychta, A. (1996b) *Teoria rachunkowości Richarda Mattessicha w świetle podstawowych kierunków rozwoju nauki rachunkowości – studium metodologiczne* (The accounting theory of Richard Mattessich in the light of major directions of academic accounting development – a methodological study), Warsaw: Foundation for the Development of Accounting in Poland.

Tkachenko, N.M. (2000) 'Buchgaltersky finansovy oblik na pidpryemstvakh Ukrainy' (Financial accounting on the Ukrainian enterprises), Kiev: A.S.K.

Valuev, B.I. (1984) *Problemy razvitiya ucheta v promyshlennosti* (Problems of accounting development in industry), Moscow: Finansy i Statistica.

Vellam, I. (2004) 'The implementation of International Accounting Standards in Poland: can true convergence be achieved in practice?', *Accounting in Europe*, Oxfordshire: Routledge and European Accounting Association: 143–67 (also contained in Dobija, 2003: 157–86).

Voinarenko, M.P. (2002) *Systemy obliku v Ukraini: transformatcia do mizhnarodnoi praktyky* (Accounting systems in Ukraine: re-orientation towards international practice), Kiev: Naukova dumka.

Ward, K. (1992) *Strategic management accounting*, 5th edn, Butterworth-Heinemann (Russian translation, Moscow: Olimp-Biznes, 2002).

Wędzki, D. (2004) 'Bankruptcy predictions in Polish economic conditions', in M. Dobija and S. Martin (eds) (2004) *General accounting theory: towards balancing the society*, Cracow: Leon Koźmiński Academy of Entrepreneurship and Management: 397–414.

Wojciechowoski, E. (1962) *Rachunkowość przedsiebiorstw Polsce powojennej w świetle paktyki i prezpisów normatywnych* (Accounting for enterprises in post-war Poland: regulatory framework and practice), Łódź: Zeszyty Naukowe Uniwersytetu Łudzkiego.

Wojciechowoski, E. (1964) *Zarys rozwoju rachunkowość w Dawnej Polsce* (Accounting in old-time Poland), Warsaw: PWE.

Wójtowicz, P. (2004) 'Effects of shifts in accounting in Poland in connection to IAS', in M. Dobija and S. Martin eds, *General accounting theory: towards balancing the society*, Cracow: Leon Koźmiński Academy of Entrepreneurship and Management: 193–207.

Wójtowicz, P. (2005) 'Objectivity of net income of Polish companies listed: an empirical study', in M. Dobija and S. Martin eds, *General accounting theory: towards balanced development*, Cracow: Cracow University of Economics: 267–81.

Zavgorodny, V.P. (1997) *Buchgaltersky uchet, kontrol i audit v sisteme upravleniya predpriyatiem* (Accounting, controlling and auditing in the management system of enterprise), Kiev: Vakler.

Zavgorodny, V.P. (1999) *Buchgaltersky uchet v Ukraine* (Accounting in the Ukraine), Kiev: A.S.K. (2nd edn, 2001).

Zhebrak, M.X. (1931) *Osnovnye elementy promyshlennogo ucheta v SSSR i za granitsei* (Basic elements of industrial accounting abroad and in the USSR), Moscow-Leningrad: Tekhnika upravlenia.

Zhebrak, M.X. (1934) *Korrespondentsia schetov pri normativnom uchete* (Interrelation of accounts in 'normative' accounting), Moscow: CUNHU Gosplana SSSR.

Zhebrak, M.X. (1948) *Osnovy normativnogo metoda kalkuliatsii* (Foundations of 'normative' costing method), Moscow: Mashgiz.

Zubilevych, S.Y. and Golov, S.F. (1996) *Osnovy audytu* (The foundations of auditing), Kiev: Dilova Ukraina.

17 Accounting books of Argentina: publications, research and institutional background

Note: Many Spanish surnames are double-names.

Alé, M.A. (1983) *Manual de contabilidad pública* (Manual of governmental accounting), Buenos Aires: Macchi.

Alé, M.A. and Gómez, F.M. (1975) *Los contratos con la hacienda pública* (Contracts with the public estate), Buenos Aires: Macchi.

Alfieri, V. (1921) *Ragioneria generale* (Financial accounting), 4th edn, Milan.

Anthony, R.N. (1964) *La contabilidad en la administración de empresas* (Managerial accounting), Mexico: UTEHA (later editions 1968, 1969, 1976 and 1986).

Arévalo, A. (1917a) *Apuntes sobre seguros* (Notes on insurances), Rosario: Emilio Fenner.

Arévalo, A. (1917b) *Explotación agrícola* (Agricultural exploitation), Rosario.

Arévalo, A. (1918) *La partida doble por el método logismográfico* (Double-entry by logismografic method), Buenos Aires: Casant.

Arévalo, A. (1946) *Elementos de contabilidad general* (Elements of financial accounting), Buenos Aires: Selección Contable S.A. (later edition 1973).

Arévalo, A. (1954) *Contabilidad pública* (Governmental accounting), Buenos Aires: Prometeo.

Atchabahian, A. (1996) *Régimen jurídico de la gestión y del control en la hacienda pública.* (Legal aspects regarding managerial decisions and control in governmental organizations), Buenos Aires: Depalma (later edition 1999).

Atchabahian, A. and Massier, G. (1962) *Régimen legal de la contabilidad pública nacional* (Legal aspects of governmental accounting), Buenos Aires: Ergón.

Atchabahian, A. and Massier, G. (1963) *Curso de contabilidad pública* (Course of governmental accounting), Buenos Aires: Aguilar (later edition 1985).

Avilà, H.E., González Bravo, L. and Scarano, E.R. (1988) 'An axiomatic foundation of accounting', working paper, Buenos Aires: Institute of Accounting Research, University of Buenos Aires.

Batardon, L. (1913) *Les caisses de conversion et la réforme monétaire en Argentine et au Brasil* (Monetary reform in Argentina and Brazil), Paris: Giard.

Batardon, L. (1914a) *Comptabilité commerciale* (Financial accounting), Paris: Dunod.

Batardon, L. (1914b) *L'inventaire et le bilan chez le commercant seul dans les societés de personnes et les societés par actions* (Inventory and financial statements of individual firms and companies), Paris: Dunod.

Batardon, L. (1918) *Cours pratique de comptabilité* (Practical accounting course), Paris: Dunod.

Batardon, L. (1920) *La contabilidad al alcance de todos* (Accounting made easy), Barcelona: Labor.

Batardon, L. (1928a) *Contabilidad en empresas* (Business accounting), Barcelona: Labor.

Batardon, L. (1928b) *Elementos de contabilidad* (Elements of accounting), Barcelona: Labor.

Batardon, L. (1929a) *L'inventaire et le bilan* (Inventory and financial statements), Paris: Dunod.

Batardon, L. (1929b) *La contabilidad en hojas movibles* (Loose-leaf accounting), Barcelona: Labor (several later editions from 1932 to 1958).

Batardon, L. (1929c) *Tratado práctico de sociedades mercantiles* (Practical treatise for commercial companies), Barcelona: Labor (several later editions from 1935 to 1970).

Batardon, L. (1932) *La contabilidad por el sistema centralizador* (Accounting in a centralized system), Barcelona: Labor.

Batardon, L. (1933) *Inventarios y balances: estudio jurídico y contable* (Inventories and financial statements: legal and accounting aspects), Buenos Aires: Labor (later editions from 1944 to 1958 – see next item).

Batardon, L. (1944) *La contabilidad por el sistema centralizador* (Accounting in a centralized system), Buenos Aires: Labor.

Batardon, L. (1950) *Cuentas corrientes con intereses* (Current accounts with interests), Barcelona: Labor (is different from Batardon 1950 in Chapter 7).

Bayetto, J. (1928) *Contabilidad pública* (Governmental accounting), Buenos Aires: Revista de Ciencias Económicas.

Bayetto, J. (1931) *Contabilidad pública* (Governmental accounting), Buenos Aires: Baiocco.

Bayetto, J. (1950) *El presupuesto como instrumento fundamental de contabilidad preventiva en la hacienda del estado* (The budget as a fundamental instrument of preventive accounting in public finances), Buenos Aires: Facultad de Ciencias Económicas.

Bértora, H. (1951) *Llave de negocio* (Goodwill), Buenos Aires: R. Calabrese.

Bértora, H. (1975) *Llave de negocio* (Goodwill – for earlier edition see above), Buenos Aires: Macchi.

Besta, F. (1909) *La ragioneria* (Accounting), Milan: (later edition 1912).

Biondi, M. (1969) *Manual de contabilidad* (Manual of accounting), Buenos Aires: Macchi.

Biondi, M. (1973a) *Ensayos sobre teoría contable* (Essays in accounting theory I), Buenos Aires: Macchi.

Biondi, M. (1973b) *Ensayos sobre teoría contable II* (Essays on accounting theory II), Buenos Aires: Macchi.

Biondi, M. (1976) *Enfoques sobre estados contables* (Financial statements), Buenos Aires: Macchi.

Biondi, M. (1984) *Tratado de contabilidad intermedia y superior* (Treatise of intermediate and advanced accounting), Buenos Aires: Macchi.

Biondi, M. (1989) *Interpretación y análisis de estados contables* (Interpretation and analysis of financial statements), Buenos Aires: Macchi.

Biondi, M. (ed.) (2001) *Determinación de las 'bases teóricas' para la armonización de las normas contables en el MERCOSUR* (Determination of the 'theoretical bases' for the harmonization of accounting rules in the MERCOSUR), Buenos Aires: Instituto de Investigaciones Contables de la Universidad de Buenos Aires.

Biondi, M. and Viegas, J.C. (2003) *Bases teóricas para la preparación de la información contable proyectada o prospectiva* (Theoretical bases for the preparation of projected or anticipated accounting information), Research Project UBACYT E017, Buenos Aires: Ediciones Cooperativas.

Bórea, D. (1921) *Contabilidad rural; cuentas culturales y costos de producción* (Rural accounting; production accounts and costs of production), Buenos Aires: Gadola.

Boter Mauri, F. (1929) *De técnica contable* (Accounting technique), Barcelona: Juventud.

Boter Mauri, F. (1935) *Precio de coste industrial* (Industrial costing), Barcelona: Editorial Juventud, S.A.

Boter Mauri, F. (1941) *Tratado de contabilidad general* (Treatise on general accounting), Madrid: Jose Zendrera and Barcelona: Editorial Juventud, S.A.

Boter Mauri, F. (1942) *Teoría general de la contabilidad administrativa* (General theory of managerial accounting), Madrid: Zendrera.

Boter Mauri, F. (1946) *Estudios contables* (Accounting studies), Barcelona: Juventud.

Boter Mauri, F. (1947) *Disolución y liquidación de sociedades mercantiles* (Liquidation of commercial companies), Barcelona: Juventud.

Boter Mauri, F. (1949) *Problemas y ejercicios de contabilidad* (Problems and exercises in accounting), Barcelona: Juventud.

Boter Mauri, F. (1950) *Cuestiones jurídico-contables* (Legal accounting issues), Barcelona: Juventud.

Boter Mauri, F. (1952) *Revisión de contabilidades y balances* (Auditing of accounting and financial statements), Barcelona: Juventud.

Bunge, M. (1983) *Treatise on basic philosophy. Epistemology and methodology II: understanding the world*, Vol. 6, Dordrecht: D. Reidel.

Bunge, M. (1985) *Treatise on basic philosophy. Philosophy of science and technology*, Part 2: *Life science: social science and technology*, Vol. 7, Dordrecht and Boston, MA: D. Reidel.

Bunge, M. (1996) *Finding philosophy in social science*, New Haven, CN and London: Yale University Press.

Carrasco Díaz, D. Hernández Esteve, E. and Mattessich, R. (2004) 'Accounting publications and research in Spain: first half of the twentieth century', *Review of Accounting and Finance* 3 (2): 40–58.

Cascarini, D.C. (1985) *Costeo y evaluación de la producción conjunta* (Cost and evaluation of the joint production), Buenos Aires: El Coloquio.

Cascarini, D.C. (1987) *Técnicas del costeo por procesos* (Process cost methods techniques), Buenos Aires: El Coloquio.

Cassagne Serres, A. (1910) *El estudio de la contabilidad desde la cátedra* (Academic accounting studies), Buenos Aires: Cabaut.

Cassagne Serres, A. (1912) *Orientación y extensión de la enseñanza de la contabilidad comercial* (Orientation and extension of commercial accounting education), Buenos Aires: Cabaut.

Cassagne Serres, A. (1921a) *Contabilidad de seguros* (Accounting in insurance companies), Buenos Aires: Baiocco.

Cassagne Serres, A. (1921b) *Contabilidad bancaria* (Bank accounting), Buenos Aires.

Cassagne Serres, A. (1921c) *Bolsa de comercio; operaciones bursátiles y su contabilidad* (Stock exchange: operations and their registration), Buenos Aires.

Cassagne Serres, A. (1923) *Administración rural y contabilidad agrícola-ganadera* (Rural administration and agricultural accounting), Buenos Aires.

Cassagne Serres, A. (1924) *Bancos hipotecarios; operaciones y contabilidad* (Mortgage banks; operations and their accounting), Buenos Aires: Baiocco.

Castaño Dieguez, F. (1863/1912) *La verdadera contabilidad, o sea curso completo, teórico y práctico de teneduría de libros* (The true accounting – or complete theoretical and practical course of bookkeeping), Madrid: Gómez Fuentenebro (later edition 1946).

Chapman, W.L. (1965) *Procedimientos de auditoría* (Auditing procedures), Buenos Aires: Abeledo Perrot.

Chapman, W.L. (1979) *Responsabilidad del profesional en ciencias económicas* (Responsibility of the professional in the economic sciences), Buenos Aires: Macchi.

Chapman, W.L. (1980) *Ensayos sobre auditoría* (Essays in auditing), Buenos Aires: Macchi.

Chapman, W.L. (1982) *El consumidor como beneficiario social de la actividad empresaria* (The consumer as social beneficiary of economic activity), Vol. XXVII, Buenos Aires: Academia Nacional de Ciencias Económicas.

Chapman, W.L. (1983) *La política laboral de la empresa y su costo-beneficio social* (The firm's labour policy and its social cost-benefit equation), Vol. XXVIII, Buenos Aires: Academia Nacional de Ciencias Económicas.

Chapman, W.L. (1984a) *La responsabilidad de la empresa ante los proveedores, accionistas, gobierno, el contexto ambiental y el contexto humano* (The firm's responsibility to its suppliers, shareholders, government, the environmental context and the human context), Vol. XXIX, Buenos Aires: Academia Nacional de Ciencias Económicas.

Chapman, W.L. (1984b) *Teoría contable* (Accounting theory), Buenos Aires: Macchi.

Chapman, W.L. (1986) *Principio de la fraternidad en la actividad económica* (The principle of the fraternity in the economic activity), Vol. XXXI, Buenos Aires: Academia Nacional de Ciencias Económicas.

Chirom, J. (1985) *La profesión contable* (The accounting profession), Buenos Aires: Editorial Tesis.

Cholvis, F. (1951) *Balances falsos* (Deceptive financial statements), Buenos Aires: Selección Contable.

Cholvis, F. (1954) *Costos standard* (Standard costs), Buenos Aires: Prometeo.

Cholvis, F. (1955) *El balance general* (Financial statements), Buenos Aires: Prometeo.

Cholvis, F. (1962) *Contabilidad: los fraudes del personal* (Accounting: deliberate fraudes), Buenos Aires: Codex.

Coni, E.A. (1917) *Contabilidad y teneduría de libros (agrícola-ganadera) del estanciero* (Accounting and bookkeeping of the rancher – for raising cattle), Buenos Aires: Peuser.

Cortés y Sabater, J. (1932) *Contabilidad general* (General accounting), Barcelona: Montesó.

Corti, C.E. (1918) *Contabilidad de los ferrocarriles del Estado* (Accounting of governmental railroads), Buenos Aires: Boletín del Congreso Sudamericano de Ferrocarriles (later edition 1920).

D'Alvise, P. (1920) *Nozione fondamentali di ragioneria* (Basic concepts of accounting), Padua.

D'Alvise, P. (1934) *Principii.e. precetti di ragioneria* (Accounting principles and rules), 2nd edn, Padua.

Davidson, S. and Weil, R. (1982) *Manual de contabilidad de costos* (Cost accounting manual), Mexico: McGraw-Hill.

Degos, J.-G. and Mattessich, R. (2003) 'Accounting research in the French language area: the first half of the twentieth century', *Review of Accounting and Finance* 2 (4): 110–28.

Delaporte, E.R. (1932) *Organización y contabilidad bancarias* (Organization and accounting of banks), Barcelona: Juventud.

Fernández Casas, J. (1931) *Contabilidad aplicada* (Applied accounting), Barcelona: J. Montesó (later editions in 1941 and 1949).

Fernández Lorenzo, L. and Geba, N. (2000) *Balance social en entidades mutuales* (The social balance in non-profit institutions), La Plata: Editorial Universidad Nacional de La Plata.

Fernández Lorenzo, L., Geba, N. and Montes, V. (1998) *Balance social cooperativo integral. Un modelo argentino basado en la identidad cooperativa* (The integral cooperative social balance. An Argentine model based on the characteristics of these organizations), La Plata: Editorial Universidad Nacional de La Plata.

Fernández Romero, M. (1913) *Finanzas y contabilidad de la Municipalidad del Rosario* (Finances and accounting of the City Hall of Rosario), Buenos Aires: Monkes.

Finney, H.A. (1943) *Curso de contabilidad* (Accounting course), Mexico: UTEHA.

Floriani, H. (1930) *Novísimo tratado de comercio, contabilidad y teneduría de libros* (New treatise of commerce, accounting and bookkeeping), Buenos Aires: El Ateneo.

Floriani, H. (1942) *Primer curso de contabilidad* (First course of accounting), Buenos Aires: El Ateneo.

Floriani, H. (1960). *Contabilidad* (Accounting), Buenos Aires: El Ateneo.

Fortini, H., Lattuca, A., López Santiso, H., Luppi, H., Slosse, C. and Urriza, J. (1980) *Replanteo de la técnica contable* (A redefinition of accounting technique), Buenos Aires: Macchi.

Fowler Newton, E. (1976) *El ajuste de estados contables por inflación* (Inflation adjustment for financial statements), Buenos Aires: Contabilidad Moderna.

Fowler Newton, E. (1977) *Contabilidad básica* (Basic accounting), Buenos Aires: Contabilidad Moderna.

Fowler Newton, E. (1978) *Contabilidad superior* (Advanced accounting), Buenos Aires: Contabilidad Moderna.

Fowler Newton, E. (1980) *Contabilidad con inflación* (Inflation accounting), Buenos Aires: Contabilidad Moderna (later edition La Ley, 2000).

Fowler Newton, E. (1982a) *Cuestiones contables fundamentales* (Fundamental accounting issues), Buenos Aires: Ediciones Contabilidad Moderna.

Fowler Newton, E. (1982b) *Organización de sistemas contables* (The organization of accounting systems), Buenos Aires: Ediciones Contabilidad Moderna.

Fowler Newton, E. (1984) *Análisis de estados contables* (Analysis of financial statements), Buenos Aires: Ediciones Interoceánicas.

Fowler Newton, E. (1989) *Cuestiones fundamentales de auditoria* (Fundamental auditing sigues – for a later edition see below), Buenos Aires: Tesis.

Fowler Newton, E. (1991) *Auditoria aplicada* (Applied auditing), Buenos Aires: Macchi.

Fowler Newton, E. (2001) *Cuestiones contables fundamentales* (Fundamental accounting issues), Buenos Aires: Macchi.

Fowler Newton, E. (2002a) *Contabilidad con inflación* (Inflation accounting), Buenos Aires: La Ley.

Fowler Newton, E. (2002b) *Normas contables profesionales de la FACPCE y del CPCE-CABA* (Professional accounting standards of the FACPCE and the CPCECABA), Buenos Aires: La Ley.

Fowler Newton, E. (2004) *Tratado de auditoria* (Treatise on auditing), Buenos Aires: La Ley.

Fronti de García, L. (1998) 'La doctrina contable y su influencia en la normativa de la contabilidad ambiental' (The accounting doctrine and its influence on the regulation of enviromental accounting), *Revista de Contabilidad y Auditoría* 5.

Fronti de García, L. (1999) *Impacto ambiental* (The environmental impact), Buenos Aires: Economizarte.

Fronti de García, L. and Wainstein, M. (eds) (2000) *Contabilidad y auditoria ambiental* (Accounting and environmental auditing), Buenos Aires: Macchi.

Galante, J. (1907) *Tratado crítico filosófico de contabilidad* (Critical-philosophical treatise of accounting), Buenos Aires: Peuser.

Galassi, G. and Mattessich, R. (2004) 'Italian accounting research in the first half of the twentieth century', presented at the Congress of the European Accounting Association, Seville (abbreviated version published in the *Review of Accounting and Finance* 4 (2): 62–82).

García, N. (2003) *Contabilidad gerencial* (Managerial accounting), Córdoba: Advocatus.

García, S. (1983) *Valores corrientes* (Current values), Buenos Aires: Tesis.

García Casella, C.L. (1997) *Enfoque multiparadigmático de la contabilidad: modelos, sistemas y prácticas deducibles para diversos contextos* (Multi-paradigmatic accounting: models, systems and ensuing practices in diverse contexts), Buenos Aires: CONICET.

García Casella, C.L. (1998) *Aportes a la solución del problema conceptual de la contabilidad* (Contributions to the solution of the conceptual problem of accounting), *Contabilidad y Auditoria* 8: 34–68.

García Casella, C.L. (1999a) *Cuestiones vinculadas a problemas contables* (Issues related to accounting problems), Buenos Aires: Economizarte.

García Casella, C.L. (1999b) *La teoría y los estados contables* (Theory and financial statements), Buenos Aires: Economizarte.

García Casella, C.L. and Rodríguez de Ramírez, M.C. (2000) *Posibles hipótesis y leyes contables* (Possible hypothesis and laws of accounting), Buenos Aires: Economizarte.

García Casella, C.L. and Rodríguez de Ramírez, M.C. (2001) *Elementos para una teoría general de la contabilidad* (Elements of a general theory of accounting), Buenos Aires: La Ley.

García Casella, C.L. and Rodríguez de Ramírez, M.C. (2002) *Hacia un incremento de la modelización contable* (Towards improved accounting modelling), Buenos Aires: Ediciones Cooperativas.

García Casella, C.L. and Rodríguez de Ramírez, M.C. (2004) *Modelos contables con método científico* (Accounting models and the scientific method), Buenos Aires: Ediciones Cooperativas.

Gardó, J. (1925a) *Contabilidad de transportes* (Accounting of the transportation industry), Barcelona: Cultura.

Gardó, J. (1925b) *Contabilidad y cooperativas* (Accounting and cooperatives), Barcelona: Cultura.

Gardó, J. (1926a) *Contabilidad por sistema decimal* (Accounting classification based on the decimal system), Barcelona: Cultura.

Gardó, J. (1926b) *El secreto en la contabilidad* (The secret in accounting), Barcelona: Cultura.

Gardó, J. (1926c) *Manual práctico de contabilidad de talleres* (Practical accounting manual for craftsmen), Barcelona: Cultura.

Gardó, J. (1932) *Contabilidad industrial* (Industrial accounting), 3rd edn, Barcelona: J. Montesó (later edition 1950).

Gillespie, C.M. (1939) *Introducción a la contabilidad de costos* (Introduction to cost accounting), Mexico: UTEHA.

Giménez, C.M. (1979) *Tratado de contabilidad de costos* (Treatise on cost accounting), Buenos Aires: Macchi (reprinted 1987, 1991 and 1992).

Gobbis, F. de (1931) *Ragioneria generale* (General accounting), 19th edn, Roma.

González Bravo, L. (1984) *Conceptos epistemológicos en contabilidad* (Epistemological concepts in accounting), doctoral thesis, Universidad de Buenos Aires.

González Bravo, L. (1990a) 'Axiomatizaciones contables' (Accounting axiomatizations), in L. González Bravo and E. Scarano eds, *Aspectos metodológicos de la contabilidad* (Methodological aspects of accounting), Buenos Aires: Impresos Centro.

González Bravo, L. (1990b) 'La contabilidad desde el punto de vista normativo' (Accounting from the normative point of view), in L. González Bravo and E. Scarano eds, *Aspectos metodológicos de la contabilidad* (Methodological aspects of accounting), Buenos Aires: Impresos Centro.

González Bravo, L. (1996) *La metodología de la investigación* (Research methodology), Buenos Aires: Editorial Belgrano.

Goxens Duch, A. (1948) *Inflación, deflación y tributos en la contabilidad de las empresas* (Inflation, deflation and taxes in entrepreneurial accounting), Madrid: M. Aguilar.

Goxens Duch, A. (1950) *Contabilidad y administración de negocios* (Accounting and business administration), Madrid: Aguado.

Goxens Duch, A. (1961) *Tratado de contabilidad para letrados* (Accounting treatise for lawyers), Madrid: Aguilar.

Goxens Duch, A. (1963) *¿La contabilidad? ¡Pero si es muy fácil!* (Accounting? But it is very easy!), Madrid: Marcombo Boixareu.

Goxens Duch, A. (1979) *Biblioteca práctica de contabilidad* (Practical library of accounting), Barcelona: Océano.

Goxens Duch, A. (1985) *Enciclopedia de la contabilidad* (Accounting encyclopaedia), Barcelona: Océano.

Hatfield, H.R., Sanders, T.H. and Burton, N.L. (1940) *Accounting, principles and practices: an introductory course*, New York: Ginn & Company.

Herrscher, E. (1967) *Contabilidad gerencial* (Managerial accounting), Buenos Aires: Macchi (reprinted 1979).

Himmelblau, D. (1945a) *Fundamentos de contabilidad* (Foundations of accounting) Mexico: UTEHA.

Himmelblau, D. (1945b) *Investigaciones para usos financieros* (Investigations in financial applications), Mexico: Northwestern University.

Holmes, A.W. (1945) *Auditoría* (Auditing), Mexico: UTEHA.

Horngreen, C. (1966) *Contabilidad de costos* (Cost accounting), Mexico: Prentice-Hall.

Horngreen, C. (1973) *Contabilidad y control administrativo* (Managerial accounting and control), Mexico: Diana.

Kester, R.B. (1939) *Contabilidad teórica y práctica* (Practical and theoretical accounting), Barcelona: Labor.

Kieso, D. and Weygandt, J. (1984) *Contabilidad intermedia* (Intermediate accounting), Mexico: Limusa.

Kieso, D. and Weygandt, J. (1987) *Contabilidad moderna* (Modern accounting), Mexico: Ciencia y Técnica. avolpe, A. (1980) *Lineamientos de un sistema de control de costos en la construcción* (Features of a cost control system in the constructions business), Buenos Aires: Macchi.

Lavolpe, A. (2000) *La gestión presupuestaria* (The management of budgets), Buenos Aires: Macchi.

Lavolpe, A., Capasso, C.M., Granda, F.E. and Smolje, A.R. (1993) *Los sistemas de costos, la contabilidad de costos y la contabilidad de gestión* (Cost systems, cost accounting and management accounting), Buenos Aires: UCA.

Lawrence, W.B. (1943) *Contabilidad de costos* (Cost accounting), Mexico: UTEHA.

Lazzati, S.C. (1969/78) *Contabilidad e inflación* (Accounting and inflation), Buenos Aires: Macchi (later edition 1978).

Lazzati, S.C. (1976) *El dictamen del auditor* (The auditor's statement), Buenos Aires: Macchi (previous editions 1972, 1975).

Lazzati, S.C. (1981) *Objetivos y procedimientos de auditoría* (Audit objectives and procedures), Buenos Aires: Macchi.

Lazzati, S.C. (1987) *Contabilidad gerencial e inflación* (Managerial accounting and inflation), Buenos Aires: Macchi.

Lisdero, A. (1970) *El concepto de balance en la doctrina contable* (Financial statements concept in academic accounting), Buenos Aires: Macchi.

Lisdero, A. and Outeiral, L.E. (1973) *Contabilidad e inflación* (Accounting and inflation), Buenos Aires: Macchi.

López Santiso, H. (1969) *Fluctuaciones monetarias y estados contables* (Monetary fluctuations and financial statements), Buenos Aires: Macchi.

López Santiso, H. (1986) *Ajuste impositivo por inflación* (Inflationary tax adjustments), Buenos Aires: Macchi.

López Santiso, H. (2001) *Contabilidad, administración y economía* (Accounting, administration and economics), Buenos Aires: Macchi.

López Santiso, H., Luppi, H.A. and Allemand, A.A. (1988) *Estados contables en moneda constante* (Financial statements for constant purchasing power), Buenos Aires: Macchi.

Ludwig, H. (1930) *Le controle budgetaire dans les entreprises industrielles* (Budgetary control in industrial firms, French translation, J. Marteau), Paris.

Martínez Pérez, E. (1910) *Contabilidad y teneduría de libros* (Accounting and bookkeeping), Madrid: Establecimiento Tipográfico de Madrid.

Mattessich, R. (1995) *Critique of accounting*, Westport, CT: Quorum Books.

Mattessich, R. (1964/2002) *Accounting and analytical methods: measurement and projection of income and wealth in the micro- and macro-economy*, Homewood,

IL: R.D. Irwin, Inc. (reprinted in the 'Accounting Classics Series', Houston, TX: Scholars Book Co., 1977; also in the 'Series of Financial Classics' of Reprints on Demand, Ann Arbor, MI: Microfilms International, 1979, still available; Japanese translation under the direction of Shinzaburo Koshimura, *Kaikei to Bunsekiteki-Hoho Jokan*, 2 vols, Tokyo: Dobunkan, Ltd, Vol. 1: 1972, Vol. 2: 1975; Spanish translation, by Carlos Luis García Casella and Maria del Carmen Ramírez de Rodríguez, Buenos Aires: La Ley, 2002).

Onida, P. (1951a) *Il bilancio di esercizio nelle imprese. Significato economico del bilancio. Problemi di valutazione* (The balance sheet of enterprises ...), Milan: Giuffrè (1st edn, 1945; translated into Spanish as *El bilance de ejercicio en las empresas*, 2 vols, Buenos Aires: El Ateneo).

Onida, P. (1951b) *Il bilancio d'esercizio nelle imprese* (The balance sheet of enterprises), Milan: Giuffrè.

Onida, P. (1970) *I moderni sviluppi della dottrina contabile nord-americana e gli studi economia aziendale*, Milan: A. Giuffrè (English version as a monograph under the title *Modern developments of the North American accounting doctrine and the studies of business economics*, Milan: A. Giuffrè, 1974).

Osorio, O. (1986) *La capacidad de producción y los costos de producción* (Production capacity and production costs), Buenos Aires: Macchi.

Pagano, S.U. (1913) *Clave del tratado teórico-práctico de contabilidad* (Key to the theoretical-practical treatise of accounting), Buenos Aires: Dufour.

Pagano, S.U. (1915) *Tratado teórico práctico de contabilidad de seguros* (Theoretical-practical treatise for the accounting of insurance companies), Buenos Aires: Tailhade y Rosselli.

Pagano, S.U. (1931) *Contabilidad y teneduría de libros* (Accounting and bookkeeping), Buenos Aires.

Pahlen Acuña, R.J. (ed.) (1998) *Los modelos contables y las normas profesionales* (Accounting models and standards), Buenos Aires: Macchi.

Pahlen Acuña, R. (ed.) (2001) *Contabilidad avanzada* (Advanced accounting), Buenos Aires: Cálamo.

Pahlen Acuña, R. and Campo, A.M. (eds) (2000) *Teoría contable aplicada* (Applied accounting theory), Buenos Aires: Macchi.

Paret, L.V. (1942) *Contabilidad de empresas* (Business accounting), Madrid: Dossat.

Paton, W.A. (1943) *Manual del contador* (The accountant's manual), Mexico: UTEHA.

Pérez Alfaro, A.R. (2000) *Control de gestión y tablero de comando* (Management control and balanced score card), Buenos Aires: Depalma.

Prats y Aymerich, J. (1907) *Contabilidad comercial* (Commercial accounting), Barcelona: Soler.

Quijano, D.D. (1937) *La nueva contabilidad: balance general mensual* (The new accounting: the general monthly balance sheet), Buenos Aires: López.

Rodríguez de Ramírez, M.C. (2000) *La contabilidad financiera: un enfoque crítico, el planteo de nuevos rumbos* (Financial accounting: a critical approach, and a proposal of new horizons), Buenos Aires: Economizarte.

Rodríguez de Ramírez, M.C. (2001) *La contabilidad financiera y su relación con otros segmentos contables* (Financial accounting and its relation to other accounting branches), *Revista Contabilidad y Auditoria* 13 (June): 89–111.

Rodríguez de Ramírez, M.C. (2004a) *Contabilidad social y supuestos ontológicos divergentes* (Social accounting and various ontological premises), *Anales del 10ᵐᵒ Encuentro Nacional de Investigadores Universitarios del Area Contable*, 2 July, Paraná: Universidad Nacional de Entre Ríos.

Rodríguez de Ramírez, M.C. (2004b) *Contabilidad y responsabilidad social. En búsqueda de respuestas para una tendencia en vías de consolidación* (Accounting and social responsibility. In search of answers for the trend towards consolidation), *Revista Contabilidad y Auditoria* 20 (December): 33–54.

Ruiz Soler, L. (1923) *Tratado elemental teórico y práctico de contabilidad general* (Elementary theoretical and practical treatise of general accounting), Villafranca de Oria.

Ruiz Soler, L. (1924) *Elementos de administración y contabilidad de empresas* (Elements of administration and business accounting), Irun: Arri.

Sá, A. Lopes de (1956) *La verdadera localización científica de la contabilidad* (The true scientific status of accounting), Buenos Aires: *Revista Selección Contable* 10: 99.

Sá, A. Lopes de (1960a) *Cómo analizar un balance* (How to analyse a financial statement), Buenos Aires: Selección Contable.

Sá, A. Lopes de (1960b) *Cómo hacer un balance* (How to prepare a financial statement), Buenos Aires: Selección Contable.

Sá, A. Lopes de (1962) *Curso de auditoría* (Auditing course), Buenos Aires: Selección Contable.

Sá, A. Lopes de (1963) *Inflação e balance* (Inflation and financial statements), São Paulo: Editôra Atlas.

Sá, A. Lopes de (1964) *Costos* (Costs), Buenos Aires: Selección Contable.

Sá, A. Lopes de (1969) *Auditoría de balances* (Auditing of financial statements), Buenos Aires: Selección Contable.

Sá, A. Lopes de (1990) *Dicionário de contabilidade* (Accounting dictionary), São Paulo: Editôra Atlas.

Sá, A. Lopes de (1992) *Teoria Geral do conhecimento contabli* (General theory of accounting knowledge), Belo Horizonte: IPAT-UNA.

Sá, A. Lopes de (1994) *Autonomía y calidad científica de la contabilidad* (Accounting autonomy and scientific quality), Buenos Aires: Selección Contable.

Sá, A. Lopes de (1998) *Historia geral e das doctrinas da contabilidade* (General history of accounting and its doctrines), 2nd revised edn, Lisboa: Vislis Editores.

Sacristán y Zavala, A. (1925) *Teorías de contabilidad general y de administración privada* (Theories of general accounting and of business administration), Madrid: Rivadeneyra.

Sánchez Brot, L.E. (1995) *Digesto Práctico La Ley: contabilidad y auditoria* (La Ley practical digest: accounting and auditing), Buenos Aires: La Ley (later editions 2000, 2004).

Schneider, E. (1949) *Contabilidad industrial* (Industrial accounting – translated from German), Madrid: Aguilar.

Steiner, R. (1919) 'Die Kernpunkte der Sozialen Frage in den Lebensnotwendigkeiten der Gegenwart und Zukunft' (The core of social issues and present and future needs).

Tua Pereda, J. (2004) Evolución y situación actual del pensamiento contable (Evolution and present situation of accounting thought), *(Revista Internacional Legis de) Contabilidad & Auditoría* 20 (October–December): 43–128.

Vallini, T. (1918) *La contabilidad patrimonial en la hacienda del Estado* (Governmental accounting), Buenos Aires: Cerbán Rivas.

Vázquez, J.C. (1971) *Manual de costos standards* (Manual of standard costing), Buenos Aires: Aguilar.

Vianello, V. (1930) *Istituzioni di ragioneria generale* (General accounting institutions), 6th edn, Milan.

Viegas, J.C., Pahlen Acuña, R.J., Chaves, O.A. and Fronti de García, L. (1996) *Contabilidad: presente y futuro* (Accounting: present and future), Buenos Aires: Macchi.

Vlaemminck, J.H. (1956) *Histoire et doctrines de la comptabilité* (History and doctrines of accounting), Bruxelles: Éditions Dunod et Truremberg, (reprinted Vesoul: Éditions Pragnos, 1979; Spanish translation as *Historia y doctrinas de la contabilidad*, Madrid, 1961).

Wainstein, M. (1974) *Auditoría de compañías de seguro* (Auditing of insurance companies), Buenos Aires: Macchi.

Wainstein, M. (1980) *Manual de ajustes por inflación de los estados contables* (Manual of financial statements for inflation adjustments), Buenos Aires: Cangallo.

Wainstein, M. (1999) *Auditoría: Temas Seleccionados* (Auditing: selected topics), Buenos Aires: Macchi.

Wainstein, M. and Casal, A. (1992) *Informes de auditoría* (Auditing reports), Buenos Aires: Cangallo.

Wainstein, M. and Casal, A. (1996) *La auditoría del medio ambiente en el marco de la auditoría integral y total* (Enviromental auditing in the framework of a totally integrated audit), Buenos Aires: FCE-UBA.

Wirth, M.C. (2001) *Acerca de la ubicación de la contabilidad en el campo del conocimiento* (On the classification of accounting knowldge), Buenos Aires: La Ley.

Wirth, M.C. and Mattessich, R. (2006), 'Accounting books of Argentina: publications, research and institutional background', *De Computis* (4, June): 137–67.

Zappa, G. (1946) *Bilanci di imprese commerciali* (Financial statements of commercial enterprises), Milan: Giuffre.

Zipitria, F.P. (1914). *Apuntes para un curso de contabilidad administrativa* (Notes for a course on managerial accounting), Montevideo: La Razón.

Zipitria, F.P. (1923) *Curso elemental de contabilidad razonada* (Elementary course of accounting), Montevideo.

Zipitria, F.P. (1943) *Curso de contabilidad administrativa* (Course of managerical accounting), Montevideo: Peña.

18 Accounting in other countries: publications and research reports

Abdeen, A.M. (1980) 'The role of accounting in project evaluation and control: the Syrian experience', *International Journal of Accounting Education and Research* 15 (2): 143–58.

Abdeen, A.M. (1984) 'The impact of accounting practices on tax revenue in Syria', *International Journal of Accounting Education and Research* 20 (1) 121–39.

Abdeen, A.M. and Ugur, Y. (1985) 'Current status of accounting education in Saudi Arabia', *International Journal of Accounting Education and Research* 20 (2): 155–73.

Abdel-khalik, A.R. (see Chapter 12).

Abdel-Magid, M.F. (1981) 'The theory of Islamic banking: accounting implications', *International Journal of Accounting Education and Research* 17 (1): 79–101.

Abdolmohammadi, M. (1990) 'The use of corporate financial reports by investors in Saudi Arabia', *Advances in International Accounting* 3: 25–40.

Abu-nassar, M. and Rutherford, B.A. (1996) 'External users of financial reports in less developed countries: the case of Jordan', *The British Accounting Review* 28 (2): 73–87.

Aguirre, A. and Hagigi, M. (1987) 'Accounting, economic, and environmental determinants of financial reporting practice in Guatemala', *International Journal of Accounting Education and Research* 22 (2): 169–91.

Alhashim, D.D. (1977) 'Social accounting in Egypt', *International Journal of Accounting Education and Research* 12 (2): 143–68.

Amorim, J.L. (1929) *Lições de contabilidade general* (Lectures in financial accounting), Vol. I, Oporto: Empresa Industrial Gráfica.

Amorim, J.L. (1969) *Digressão agravés de vetusto mundo da contabilidad* (Discussions of traditional accounting), Oporto: Livraria Avis.

Bait-el-Mal, M.M., Smith, C.H. and Tailor, M.E. (1973) 'The development of accounting in Libya', *International Journal of Accounting Education and Research* 8 (2): 83–101.

Banerjee, B. (1984) *Financial policy and management accounting*, Calcutta: The World Press, Pvt. Ltd.

Banerjee, B. (ed.) (1991) *Contemporary issues in accounting research*, Calcutta: Indian Accounting Association Research Foundation.

Banerjee, B. (1994) *Accounting education in India*, Calcutta: DSA in Commerce, University of Calcutta.

Blake, J. and Gao, S. (eds) (1995) *Perspectives on accounting and finance in China*, London: Routledge.

Briston, R.J. (1978) 'The evolution of accounting in developing countries', *International Journal of Accounting Education and Research* 14 (1): 105–20.

Briston, R.J. and Ahmed El-Ashker, A.A. (1984) 'The Egyptian accounting system: a case study in Western influence', *International Journal of Accounting Education and Research* 19 (2): 129–55.

Bromwich, M. and Bhimani, A. (2002) *Management accounting: pathways to progress*, London: Chartered Institute of Management Accountants (Chinese translation, *Guan li kuai ji: fa zhan de fang xiang*, Beijing: Zhongguo ren min da xue chu ban she, 2002).

Bursal, N.I. (1984) 'The accounting environment and some recent developments in Turkey', *International Journal of Accounting Education and Research* 19 (2): 93–127.

Carmony, L. (1987) 'Accounting in the context of its environment: the Uruguay case', *International Journal of Accounting Education and Research* 22 (2): 41–56.

Carqueja, H.O. (1975) 'Planeamento contabilistico' (Accounting planning), *Revista de Contabilidade e Comércio* Special issue, 41 (163): 307–50.

Carqueja, H.O. (1999) 'O "Método Fácil de Degrange", entre os livros de contabilidad portuguesa até 1900' (Of the 'Easy Method of Degrange' among the Portuguese accounting books until 1900), *Jornal do Técnico de Contas e Empresas* (403): 109–13; (404): 145–50; (405): 176–9; (406): 213–18.

Carqueja, H.O. (2002) 'Do saber da profissão às doutrinas da Academia' (From professional knowledge to an academic subject), *Revista de Contabilidade é Comercio* Special issue, 59 (234/235, Oporto, Potugal).

Center for International Accounting Development (1987) *Accounting and auditing in the People's Republic of China: a review of its practices, systems, education and developments*, Dallas, TX: University of Texas at Dallas jointly with Shanghai cai jing da xue and Coopers & Lybrand (Japanese translation, *Chuka jinmin kyowakoku no kaikei to kansa: sono jitsumu, seido, kyoiku oyobi hatten no kenkyu*, Tokyo: Chuo Keizeisha, 1988).

Cheng, P.C. (1970) 'Accounting in Nationalist China', *International Journal of Accounting Education and Research* 6 (2): 75–88.

Cheng, P.C. and Jain, T.N. (1972) 'Economic prospective and accounting practices in South Korea', *International Journal of Accounting Education and Research* 8 (2): 123–39.

Chu, J.M. (1973) 'Accounting principles and practices in Panama', *International Journal of Accounting Education and Research* 9 (1): 43–52.

Chu, K.-C. (1969) 'Accountancy education in the Republic of China', *International Journal of Accounting Education and Research* 4 (2): 75–91.

Cook, T.E. and Çürük, T. (1996) 'Accounting in Turkey with reference to the particular problem of lease transactions', *European Accounting Review* 5 (2): 339–60.

Costouros, G.J. (1975) 'Accounting education and practice in Greece', *International Journal of Accounting Education and Research* 11 (1): 95–106.

Dhamash, N.H. (1982) 'Public accounting developments in the Arab states: a comparative study', *Journal of Accounting Education and Research* 18 (1): 89–114.

Elliot, E.L. (1972) 'Accounting and economic development in Latin America', *International Journal of Accounting Education and Research* 8 (1): 89–97.

Enthoven, A.J.H. (1973) *Accountancy and economic development policy*, Amsterdam: North-Holland Publishing Co.

Enthoven, A.J.H. (1977) *Accounting systems in third world economies*, Amsterdam: North-Holland Publishing.

Erxing, L. and Farrell, J. (eds) (1985) *Ying han, han ying kuai ji ming ci hui yi* (Accounting terminologies in use in the People's Republic of China and in the United States), Shanghai: Shanghai ren min chu ban.

Everard Martins, R.M. de (1997) 'Ensaio de bibliorafia portugesa de conabilidade' (Essay of Portuguese accounting bibliography), *Revista de Contabilidade e Commercio* 54 (216 – Portugal): 541–64.

Ezzamel, M.A. (2002a) 'Accounting and redistribution: the palace and mortuary cult in the middle kingdom, Ancient Egypt', *Accounting Historians Journal* 29 (1): 61–103.

Ezzamel, M.A. (2002b) 'Accounting working for the state: tax assessment and collection during the New Kingdom, Ancient Egypt', *Accounting and Business Research* 32 (1): 17–39.

Filios, V.P. (1984) 'A transition of systematic accounting from ancient to Byzantine Greece', in Tito Antoni ed., *Fourth International Congress of the History of Accountancy: congress proceedings*, Pisa: ETS Editrice: 171–91.

Firth, M. (1996) 'The diffusion of managerial accounting procedures in the People's Republic of China and the influence of foreign partnered ventures', *Accounting, Organizations and Society* 21 (7/8): 629–54.

Florentino, A.M. (1965) *Fundamentos matemáticos da contabilidade e suas aplicações na didática, programação e análise contábil* (Mathematical foundations of accounting and its educational application to programming and bookkeeping analysis), Rio de Janeiro.

Foroughi, T.K. (1981) 'Accounting in developing countries before and after social crisis: the case of Iran', *International Journal of Accounting Education and Research* 17 (1): 181–223.

Ghartey, A. (1978) 'A new perspective for accounting education in Ghana', *International Journal of Accounting Education and Research* 14 (1): 121–32.

Givoly, D. and Lakonishok, J. (1982) 'Accounting for construction companies, inflation, and market efficiency: analysis of an Israeli case', *Journal of Accounting Education and Research* 17 (1): 121–49.

Gul, F.A. and Yap, T.H. (1984) 'The effects of combined audit and management services on public perception of auditor independence in developing countries', *International Journal of Accounting Education and Research* 20 (1): 95–107.

Guo, D. (1982–89) *Zhongguo kuaiji shigao* (Accounting history of China), 2 vols, Bejing: China Finance and Economic Press.

Guo, D. (1996) 'China', in M. Chatfield and R. Vangermeersch eds, *The history of accounting: an international encyclopedia*, New York: Garland Publishing, Inc.: 122–3.

Holzer, H.P. and Tremblay, D. (1973) 'Accounting and economic development: the cases of Thailand and Tunisia', *International Journal of Accounting Education and Research* 9 (1): 67–80.

Hopper, T. and Hoque, Z. (eds) (2004) *Accounting and accountability in emerging and transition economies*, Amsterdam: Elsevier.

Hsu, T.T. (1981) 'Recent business and accounting developments in China', *International Journal of Accounting Education and Research* 17 (1): 157–60.

Illés, K., Weetman, P., Clarkson, A.H. and Fraser, M. (1996) 'Change and choice in Hungarian accounting practice', *European Accounting Review* 5 (3) 523–44.

Instituto Mexicano de Contadores Público (1975) *Price-level adjustments*, Mexico City: IMdCP.

Jacobsen, L.E. (1964) 'The ancient Inca empire of Peru and the double-entry accounting concept', *Journal of Accounting Research* 2 (2): 221–8.

Jacobsen, L.E. (1983) 'Use of knotted string accounting records in old Hawaii and ancient China', *Accounting Historians Journal* 10 (2): 53–61.

Jagetia, L.C. and Nwadike, E.C. (1983) 'Accounting systems in developing nations: the Nigerian experience', *International Journal of Accounting Education and Research* 18 (2): 69–81.

Jaggi, B. (1970) 'A review of the accounting profession in India', *International Journal of Accounting Education and Research* 6 (1): 35–51.

Jaggi, B. (1973) 'Accounting studies of developing countries', *International Journal of Accounting Education and Research* 9 (1): 159–70.

JAI Press (ed.) (1990–93) *Research in third world accounting* (serial publication), Greenwich, CT: JAY Press.

JAI Press (ed.) (1995–) *Research in accounting in emerging economies* (serial publication), Greenwich, CT: JAY Press.

Ji, X.-D. (2000) 'Evaluation of research on Chinese accounting issues', *Managerial Finance* 26 (5): 41–62.

Jones, G.F. and Kinfu, J. (1971) 'The birth of an accounting profession: the Ethiopian experience', *International Journal of Accounting Education and Research* 7 (1): 89–98.

Kaocharern, S. (1976) 'The development of the security exchange in Thailand', *International Journal of Accounting Education and Research* 12 (1): 19–26.

Kim, I.-W. and Song, J. (1990) 'U.S., Korea, and Japan: accounting practices in three countries', *Management Accounting* 72 (2): 26–30.

Kwang, C.-W. (1966) 'The economic accounting system in state enterprises in mainland China', *International Journal of Accounting Education and Research* 1 (2): 61–99.

Lakis, V. (1996) 'The development of auditing and the problems of its reform in Lithuania', *European Accounting Review* 5 (1): 105–25.

McClure, M.M. (1983) 'An overview of Romanian accounting', *International Journal of Accounting Education and Research* 19 (1): 131–56.

McMahon, T.J. (1972) 'Brazil: a manufacturing capital market seeks accelerated improvements in accounting', *Journal of Accounting Education and Research* 8 (1): 77–87.

Markell, W. (1968) 'Accounting education – its importance in developing countries: Israel – a case study', *International Journal of Accounting Education and Research* 3 (2): 125–33.

Mattessich, R. (2000) 'Hitos de la investigación en contabilidad – segunda mitad del siglo' (Highlights of modern accounting research – the last half century), *Revista de*

Contabilidad 3 (5): 19–66 (reprinted in *Revista Legis del Contador*, April–June: 9–86, Bogotá, Colombia).

Mattessich, R. (2002) 'The oldest writings, and inventory tags of Egypt', *Accounting Historians Journal* 29 (June): 195–208 (reprinted in *Contaduria (de Universidad de Antioquia, Colombia)* 41 (September 2002 – with summaries in Spanish and French): 17–30).

Mattessich, R. and Galassi, G. (2004) 'Historia de la hoja de cálculo' (History of the spreadsheet), *Revista Internacional Legis de Contabilidad & Auditoría* 18 (April–June – Colombia): 41–86 (Spanish translation of: History of the spreadsheet: from matrix accounting to budget simulation and computerization, in E. Hernández Esteve (ed.) (2000) *Accounting and history: a selection of papers presented at the 8th World Congress of Accounting Historians*, Madrid: Asociación Española de Contabilidad y Administración: 203–32) – for the original see Chapter 2 (under Mattessich and Galassi 2000).

Monteiro, M.N. (1965a) *A contabilidade e sea muindo* (Accounting and its world), 2 vols, Lisbon: Portugália Editore.

Monteiro, M.N. (1965b) *Pequena história de contabilidade* (A short history of accounting), Lisbon: APOTEK.

Mora Jr, R.E. (1972) 'The accounting profession in Mexico', *International Journal of Accounting Education and Research* 8 (1): 1–15.

Narayan, F.B. (2000) *Financial management and governance issues in selected developing member countries: a study of Cambodia, China (People's Republic), Mongolia, Pakistan, Papua New Guinea, Uzbekistan, and Viet Nam*, Manila: Asian Development Bank.

Narayan, F.B. (2002) *Diagnostic study of accounting and auditing practices in selected developing member countries: Azabeijan, Fiji Islands, Republic of the Marshall Islands, Phillipines, Sri Lanka*, Manila: Asian Development Bank.

Narayan, F.B. and Reid, B. (2000) *Financial management and governance issues in the People's Republic of China*, Manila: Asian Development Bank.

Naser, K. and Baker, A.N. (1999) 'Empirical evidence on corporate social responsibility reporting and accountability in developing countries: the case of Jordan', *Advances in International Accounting* 12: 193–226.

Ndubizu, G.A. (1984) 'Accounting standards and economic development', *International Journal of Accounting Education and Research* 19 (2): 181–96.

Neves, J.C. das and Fernández, P.P. (1998) 'A reacão do mercado de capitais portugués a publicação de lucros das "blue chips" no paríodo 1991–1995', *Estudios de Gestão* 27 (95): 119–27.

Ninsuvannakul, P. (1966) 'Education for accountancy in Thailand', *International Journal of Accounting Education and Research* 2 (1): 77–114.

Ogan, P. (1978) 'Turkish accountancy: an assessment of its effectiveness and recommendations for improvements', *International Journal of Accounting Education and Research* 14 (1): 133–54.

Ogudele, B. (1969) 'The accountancy profession in Nigeria: an international perspective', *International Journal of Accounting Education and Research* 5 (1): 101–6.

Orellana, E.A. (2005) 'Una contabilidad Precolumbiana: la del imperio Incaico' (A pre-Columbian accounting: from the Inca empire)', *Contabilidad y Auditoría* 11 (22): 57–88.

Osiegbu, P.I. (1987) 'The state of accounting education in Nigeria', *International Journal of Accounting Education and Research* 22 (2): 57–68.

Patton, J. and Zelenka, I. (1997) 'An empirical analysis of the determinants of disclosure in annual reports of joint stock companies in the Czech Republic', *European Accounting Review* 6 (4): 605–27.

Pena, P.A. (1976) 'Special report: a comparison of the accounting professions of Colombia and the United States', *International Journal of Accounting Education and Research* 11 (2): 143–77.

Powelson, J.P. (1967) 'National income estimates in Latin America', *International Journal of Accounting Education and Research* 3 (1): 55–65.

Qureshi, M.A. (1973) 'Private enterprise accounting and economic development in Pakistan', *International Journal of Accounting Education and Research* 9 (2): 125–41.

Radebaugh, L.H. (1975) 'Environmental factors influencing the development of accounting objectives, standards, and practices in Peru', *International Journal of Accounting Education and Research* 11 (1): 39–56.

Rivera, J.M. (1982) 'The financial function of a U.S. multinational company abroad: the Venezuelan experience', *International Journal of Accounting Education and Research* 18 (1): 129–38.

Rodríguez Alvarez, M.-A. (ed.) (2000) *Origen y desarrollo de la contaduría en Mexico 1845–2000* (Origin and development of accounting in Mexico 1845–2000), Mexico City (D.F.): Instituto Politécnico Nacional and Escuela Superior de Comercio y Administración.

Rooz, J. and Stanó, I. (1996) 'The regulation of joint ventures in Hungary', *European Accounting Review* 5 (1): 115–48.

Sá, A.L. de (1960) *Historia da contabilidade*, Brasilia (revised as *Historia geral e das doutrinas de contabilidade*, São Paulo: Atlas, 2000).

Sá, A.L. de (1995) 'Axiomas em contabilidade científica' (Axioms in scientific accounting), *Information Cientifico Cultural* 1 (September – Orgâo do Centra de Estudos Superiores).

Sá, A.L. de (2000a) *Dicionário de contabilidade* (Dictionary of accounting), 9th edn, Belo Horizonte: Atlas.

Sá, A.L. de (2000b) *Perícia contábil* (Expertise in accounting), 6th edn, Belo Horizonte: Atlas.

Sá, A.L. de (2002) *Etica – a revolução necesaria* (Ethics – a necessary revolution), Brasilia: Atlas.

Sá, R. de (1912) *Verificações e examen de escripta* (Auditing), Lisbon: Livraria Ferin-Editora.

Salas, C.A. (1967) 'Accounting education and practice in Spanish Latin America', *International Journal of Accounting Education and Research* 3 (1): 67–85.

Samuels, J.M. and Oliga, J.C. (1982) 'Accounting standards in developing countries', *International Journal of Accounting Education and Research* 18 (1): 69–88.

Santos Feirreira, A. (2002) *Teoria positive da contabilidade* (Positive accounting theory), special issue of *Revista da Contabilidade e Comercio* 59 (234/235, Oporto, Potugal).

Shinawi, A.A. and Krum, W.F. (1971) 'The emergence of professional accounting in Saudi Arabia', *International Journal of Accounting Education and Research* 6 (2): 103–10.

Shuaib, S.A. (1980) 'Accounting information and the development planning process in Kuwait', *International Journal of Accounting Education and Research* 15 (2): 129–41.

Silva, F.V.G. da (1938) *A regulamentação legal de escrituração mercantil* (Legal regulations of accounting), Lisbon: Tipografia de Empresa Nacional de Publicade.

Silva, F.V.G. da (1968) *Contabilidade geral* (Financial accounting), 2 vols, Lisbon: Livraria Sá da Costa Editora.

Silva, F.V.G. da (1970) *Curiosidades, velharias e muidezas contabilísticas* (Subtleties and special details of accounting), Lisbon.

Singh, D.R. and Ahuja, J.M. (1983) 'Corporate social reporting in India', *International Journal of Accounting Education and Research* 18 (2): 151–69.

Sucher, P. and Jindrichovska, I. (2004) 'Implementing IFRS: a case study of the Czech Republic', *Accounting in Europe*, Oxfordshire: Routledge and European Accounting Association: 109–41.

Sucher, P., Seal, W. and Zelenka, I. (1996) 'True and fair in the Czech Republic', *European Accounting Review* 5 (3): 545–58.

Tua Pereda, J. (1988) 'Evolución del concepto de contabilidad a través de sus definiciones' (Evolution of the notion of accounting beyond its limits), in Instituto de Planificación Contable ed., *XXV años de contabilidad universitaria*, Madrid (reprinted in *Revista Contaduría* 13 (September, 1988 – Universidad de Antioquia, Medellín, Colombia)).

Tua Pereda, J. (1992) *La investigación en contabilidad. Una reflexión personal* (Accounting research – a personal view), Bogotá: Fundación para la Investigación y Desarrollo de la Ciencia Contable.

Tua Pereda, J. (1995) *Entorno de la enseñanza de la contabilidad. Una reflexión personal* (On the teaching of accounting – personal view), Bogotá: Asociación de Federaciones de Contadores.

Turk, I. (1976) 'Recent professional statements of accounting principles in Jugoslavia', *International Journal of Accounting Education and Research* 12 (1): 111–20.

Vafeas, N., Trigeorgis, L. and Georgiou, X. (1998) 'The usefulness of earnings in explaining stock returns in an emerging market: the case of Cyprus', *European Accounting Research* 7 (1): 105–25.

Vandendries, R. (1970) 'Social accounting and its application in Peru', *International Journal of Accounting Education and Research* 6 (1): 91–9.

Villalobos de Nucete, M. (1984) 'Evolución histórica en Venezuela', in T. Antoni ed., *Fourth International Congress of the History of Accountancy: congress proceedings*, Pisa: ETS Editrice: 171–91.

Wallace, R.S.O. (ed.) (1995) *Research in accounting in emerging economies*, Vol. 3, Amsterdam: JAI Press.

Wallace, R.S.O. (ed.) (2003) *Research in accounting in emerging economies*, Vol. 5, Amsterdam: JAI Press.

Wallace, R.S.O., Samuel, J.M., Briston, R.J. and Saudagaran, S.M. (eds) (1999) *Accounting and development: a special case for Africa*, Stamford, CT: JAI Press.

Wei, T.Y., Chow, L. and Cooper, B.J. (eds) (1994) *Accounting and finance in China: a review of current practice*, 2nd edn, Hong Kong: Longman.

Wong-Boren, A. and Barnett, A.H. (1984) 'Mexican market efficiency: a study of the information content of accounting numbers', *International Journal of Accounting Education and Research* 20 (1): 45–70.

19 The information economic perspective and the future of accounting

Note: For the many publications of the major pioneers of information perspectives, such as Feltham, Demski and others, we have to refer the reader to the bibliographies provided in the major books discussed in this chapter (i.e. Christensen and Demski 2003; Christensen and Feltham 2003, 2005; Ewert and Wagenhofer 1993/2003; Wagenhofer and Ewert 2003 – the last of which lists nearly six hundred publications).

Ball, R.J. and Brown, P.R. (1968) 'An empirical evaluation of accounting income numbers', *Journal of Accounting Research* 6 (Autumn): 159–78.

Balzer, W. and Mattessich, R. (2000) 'Formalizing the basis of accounting', in W. Balzer, J.D. Sneed and C.U. Moulines eds, *Structuralist knowledge representation: paradigmatic examples*, Amsterdam: Editions Rodopi B.V./Atlanta A.G.: 99–126.

Beaver, W.H. (1968) 'The information content of annual earnings announcements', *Journal of Accounting Research* 6 (Supplement): 67–92.

Beaver, W.H. (2002) 'Review of "John A. Christensen and Joel A. Demski. *Accounting theory: an information content perspective*", Boston, MA: McGraw-Hill, 2003, 480 pp. ISBN: 0–07–229691–7', *The European Accounting Review* 11 (3): 631–3.

Begley, J. and Feltham, G.A. (1999) 'An empirical examination of the relation between debt contracts and management incentives', *Journal of Accounting and Economics* 27: 229–59.

Begley, J. and Feltham, G.A. (2000) 'The relationship between market values, earnings forecasts, and reported earnings', *Contemporary Accounting Research* 19: 1–48.

Bell, D. (1981) 'Models and reality in economic discourse', in D. Bell and I. Kristol eds, *The crisis in economic theory*, New York: Basic Books, Inc.: 46–80.

Benston, G.J., Bromwich, M., Litan, R.E. and Wagenhofer, A. (2003) *Following the money: the Enron failure and the state of corporate disclosure*, Washington, DC: AEI-Brookings Joint Center for Regular Studies.

Bernard, V.L. (1995) 'The Feltham–Ohlson framework: implications for empiricists', *Contemporary Accounting Research* 11 (2): 733–47.

Busse von Colbe, W. and Laßmann, G. (1975) *Betriebswirtschaftstheorie*, Bnd. 1: *Grundlagen, Produktions und Kostentheorie* (Theory of business economics, Vol. 1: Foundations, production and cost theory), Berlin: Springer Verlag.

Chambers, R.J. (1967) 'Continuously contemporary accounting: additivity and action', *The Accounting Review* 42 (4, October): 751–7.

Christensen, J.A. and Demski, J.S. (2003) *Accounting theory: an information content perspective*, New York: McGraw-Hill.

Christensen, P.O. and Feltham, G.A. (2003) *Economics of accounting*, Vol. I: *Information in markets*, Boston, MA: Kluwer Academic Publishers (also New York: Springer).

Christensen, P.O. and Feltham, G.A. (2005) *Economics of accounting*; Vol. II: *Performance evaluation*, Boston, MA: Kluwer Academic Publishers (also New York: Springer).

Clarkson, P. and Simunic, D. (1994) 'The association between audit quality, retained ownership, and firm specific risk in U.S. vs. Canadian Markets', *Journal of Accounting and Economics* 17: 207–28.

Datar, S., Feltham, G.A. and Hughes, J. (1991) 'The role of audit and audit quality in valuing new issues', *Journal of Accounting and Economics* 14: 2–49.

Demski, J.S. and Sappington, D.E.M. (1999) 'Summarization with errors: a perspective on empirical investigations of agency relationships', *Management Accounting Research* 10: 21–37.

Edwards, E.O. and Bell, P.W. (1961) *The theory and measurement of business income*, Berkeley, CA: University of California Press.

Ewert, R. and Wagenhofer, A. (1993/2003) *Interne Unternehmensrechnung* (Managerial accounting), Berlin: Springer Verlag (5th edn, 2003).

Feltham, G.A. and Ohlson, J.A. (1995) 'Valuation and clean surplus accounting for operating and financial activities', *Contemporary Accounting Research* 12 (Spring): 689–731.

Feltham, G.A., Hughes, J. and Simunic, D. (1991) 'Empirical assessment of the impact of auditor quality on the valuation of new issues', *Journal of Accounting and Economics* 14: 375–99.

Fleischman, R.K. (2000) 'The contribution of archival research towards evaluating the theory/practice schism in cost accounting theory', in Asociación Española de Contabilidad y Administración de Empresas and E. Hernández Esteve eds, *Accounting and history: a selection of papers presented at the 8th World Congress of Accounting Historians*, Madrid: AECAE: 23–50.

Gigler, F. and Hemmer. T. (1998) 'On the frequency, quality, and information role of mandatory financial reports', *Journal of Accounting Research* (Supplement): 117–47.

Gigler, F. and Hemmer, T. (2001) 'Conservatism, optimal disclosure policy, and the timeliness of financial reports', *The Accounting Review*: 471–93.

Greene, B. (1999) *The elegant universe: superstrings, hidden dimensions, and the quest for the ultimate theory*, New York: W.W. Norton.

Gutenberg, E. (1957) *Betriebswirtschaftslehre als Wissenschaft* (Business economics as science), Krefeld: Scherpe Verlag.

Ijiri, Y. (1965a) 'Axioms and structures of conventional accounting measurement', *The Accounting Review* 40 (January): 36–53.

Ijiri, Y. (1965b) *Goal oriented models for accounting and control*, Amsterdam: North-Holland Publishing Co.

Ijiri, Y. (1967) *The foundations of accounting measures*, Englewood Cliffs, NJ: Prentice-Hall, Inc.

Lee, C.M.C. (1999) 'Accounting-based valuation: impact on business practices and research', *Accounting Horizons* 13 (4): 413–25.

Liu, J. and Ohlson, J.A. (2000) 'The Feltham–Ohlson (1995) model: empirical implications', *Journal of Accounting, Auditing and Finance* 15(3): 321–30.

Lo, K. and Lys, T. (2000) 'The Ohlson model: contribution to valuation theory, limitations, and empirical applications', *Journal of Accounting, Auditing, and Finance* 15(3): 337–60.

Luce, R.D. and Raiffa, H. (1957) *Games and decisions: introduction and critical survey*, New York: Wiley & Sons.

Mattessich, R. (1964) *Accounting and analytical methods: measurement and projection of income and wealth in the micro- and macro-economy*, Homewood, IL: R.D. Irwin, Inc. (reprinted in the 'Accounting Classics Series', Houston, TX: Scholars Book Co., 1977; also in the 'Series of Financial Classics' of Reprints on Demand, Ann Arbor, MI: Microfilms International, 1979, still available; Japanese translation under the direction of Shinzaburo Koshimura, *Kaikei to Bunsekiteki-Hoho Jokan*, 2 vols, Tokyo: Dobunkan, Ltd, Vol. 1: 1972, Vol. 2: 1975; Spanish translation, by Carlos Luis García Casella and Maria del Carmen Ramírez de Rodríguez, Buenos Aires: La Ley, 2002).

Mattessich, R. (1978) *Instrumental reasoning and systems methodology: an epistemology of the applied and social sciences*, Dortrecht, Holland: D. Reidel Publishing Company (first paperback edition, 1979; second paper back edition, 2003; still available from ProQuest as 'Book on Demand': www.umi.com).

Mattessich, R. (1995) *Critique of accounting: examination of the foundations and normative structure of an applied discipline*, Westport, CT: Quorum Books.

Mattessich, R. (2002) *Contabilidad y métodos analíticos*, Buenos Aires: La Ley (Spanish translation of *Accounting and analytical methods*, Homewood, IL, 1964).

Mattessich, R. (2003) 'Accounting representation and the Onion Model of Reality: A comparison with Baudrillard's Orders of Simulacra and his Hyperreality', *Accounting,*

Organization and Society 28 (5, July): 443–70 (Spanish translation in the form of a separate Monograph under the title *La Representación contable y el modelo de capas-cepola de la realidad: una comparación con las 'Ordenes de Simulacro' de Bau-drillard y su 'Hiperrealidad'*. Asociación Española de Contabilidad y Administración de Empresas, Madrid: AECA, 2004).

Mattessich, R. (2006) 'The information economic perspective of accounting: its coming of age', *Canadian Accounting Perspectives* 5 (2): 209–36.

Ohlson, J.A. (1995) 'Earnings, book values, and dividends in equity valuation', *Contemporary Accounting Research*, 11 (2): 661–87.

Richardson, G. and Tinaikar, S. (2004) 'Accounting based valuation models: what have we learned?', *Accounting and Finance* 44: 223–55.

Savage, L.J. (1954) *The Foundations of Statistics*, New York: Wiley.

Schweitzer, M. and Küpper, H.U. (2003) *Systeme der Kosten- und Erlösrechnung*, 8th edn (Systems of cost and profit accounting), Munich: Verlag Franz Wahlen.

Slaymaker, A.E. (1996) 'Conceptual framework', in M. Chatfield and R. Vangermeersch eds, *The history of accounting: an international encyclopedia*, New York: Garland Publishing, Inc.: 150–4.

Sterling, R.R. (1970) *Theory of the measurement of enterprise income*, Lawrence, KA: University Press of Kansas.

Viganò, E. (1998) 'Accounting and business economics tradition in Italy', *The European Accounting Review* 7 (3): 381–403.

Wagenhofer, A. (2003) 'Internet Review of: Christensen and Demski', *Accounting theory: an information content perspective* in: www.accountingeducation.com/reviews/lev113.htlm

Wagenhofer, A. and Ewert, R. (2003) *Externe Unternehmensrechnung* (Financial accounting), Berlin: Springer Verlag.

Zappa, G. (1927) *Tendenze nuove negli studi di ragioneria* (New trends in accounting research), Milan: Instituto Editoriale Scientifico.

Zeff, S.A. (ed.) (1982) *The accounting postulates and principles controversy of the 1960s*, New York: Garland Publishing, Inc.

Index of names

Subject index

Printed in the USA/Agawam, MA
February 14, 2011